Also by Philip B. Kunhardt III and Peter W. Kunhardt

Lincoln: An Illustrated Biography

Looking for Lincoln

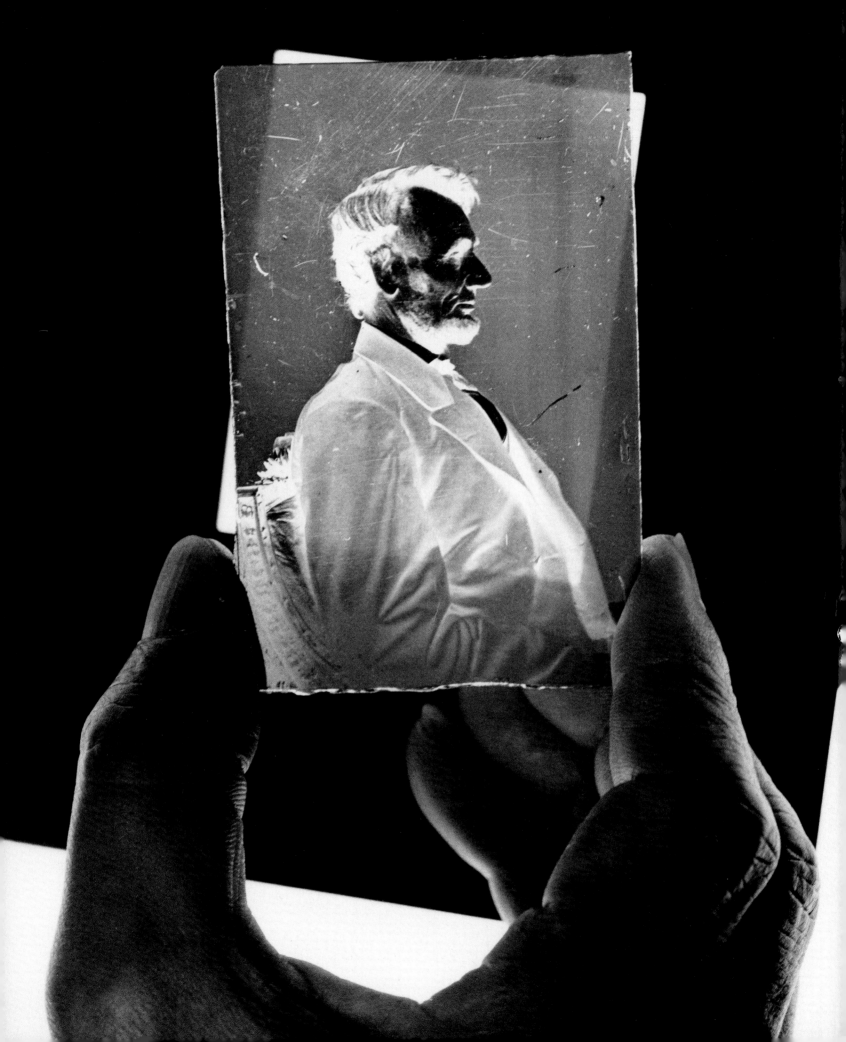

Looking for LINCOLN

The Making of an American Icon

Philip B. Kunhardt III

Peter W. Kunhardt

Peter W. Kunhardt, Jr.

Foreword by David Herbert Donald

Introduction by Doris Kearns Goodwin

Alfred A. Knopf • New York • 2008

THIS IS A BORZOI BOOK
PUBLISHED BY ALFRED A. KNOPF

Copyright © 2008 by Philip B. Kunhardt III,
Peter W. Kunhardt, Peter W. Kunhardt, Jr.
All rights reserved. Published in the United States by
Alfred A. Knopf, a division of Random House, Inc.,
New York, and in Canada by Random House of
Canada Limited, Toronto.

www.aaknopf.com

Knopf, Borzoi Books, and the colophon
are registered trademarks of Random House, Inc.

Library of Congress Cataloging-in-Publication Data
Kunhardt, Philip B., 1951–
Looking for Lincoln: the making of an American
icon / by Philip B. Kunhardt III, Peter W. Kunhardt,
and Peter W. Kunhardt, Jr. — 1st ed.
p. cm.
"A Borzoi book."
ISBN 978-0-307-26713-9
1. Lincoln, Abraham, 1809–1865—Influence.
2. Lincoln, Abraham, 1809–1865—Public opinion.
3. Lincoln, Abraham, 1809–1865—Anecdotes.
4. Lincoln, Abraham, 1809–1865—Anniversaries, etc.
5. Presidents—United States—Biography—
   Miscellanea.
6. Public opinion—United States.
I. Kunhardt, Peter W. II. Kunhardt, Peter W., 1982–
III. Title
E457.2.K86 2008
973.7—dc22
2008014193

Manufactured in the United States of America

First Edition

Contents

Foreword

David Herbert Donald

PRES^T LINCOLN AND FAMILY

The Kunhardt family occupies a unique place in the field of Lincoln studies. For five generations members of this talented family have been writing, editing, designing, and publishing books on aspects of Abraham Lincoln's career that are as beautiful as they are sound.

The tradition began with Frederick Hill Meserve (1865-1962), whose father had fought in the Union Army. Looking for pictures to illustrate his father's wartime recollections, Frederick, then a businessman in New York City, began haunting secondhand bookstores and auctions, buying up old prints and glass negatives discarded by wartime photographers. At that time nobody else seemed much interested in them, so he had little competition. In 1902, visiting a warehouse in New Jersey, he stumbled upon a pile of fifteen thousand glass negatives from Mathew Brady's studio that were about to be destroyed as trash. He bought the whole lot, including, as he discovered, seven photographs of President Lincoln. In 1911, in the first attempt to catalogue and arrange the pictures of Lincoln in chronological order, he published *The Photographs of Abraham Lincoln*, which became a bible for collectors and scholars, especially because he issued supplements from time to time as new photographs turned up. Generously he shared his treasures with other Civil War experts. It is hard to find a book on Lincoln that does not acknowledge the author's indebtedness to Mr. Meserve's collection (now known as the Meserve-Kunhardt Collection).

When Mr. Meserve died, his daughter, Dorothy Meserve Kunhardt, took on the management of the collection. Though occupied with writing and publishing nearly a score of delightful books for children, she somehow found time to expand its holdings, adding thousands of Civil War photographs, books, clippings, and newspapers. In 1958 she acquired the large collection of Lincoln relics owned by Mary Edwards Brown, Mary Lincoln's great-niece, which included Lincoln family scrapbooks and dozens of daguerreotypes of the Lincolns' friends and neighbors in Springfield. Drawing on the Meserve Lincoln Collection, she also published the handsome Time-Life book *Mathew Brady and His World*.

Eventually her son, Philip Kunhardt, Jr., a genial, soft-spoken man who had previously been managing editor at *Life* magazine, became guardian of the collection. Like his mother and his grandfather, he willingly allowed other Lincoln scholars to use it. He also continued the family tradition by writing, with his mother, *Twenty Days*, a superb account, lavishly illustrated, of Lincoln's assassination, and *A New Birth of Freedom*, a fine re-creation of Lincoln's Gettysburg Address.

He moved on in 1992 to his major historical effort, *Lincoln,* a full-length pictorial biography (which accompanied an excellent television series of the same name). To help in this ambitious project, he enlisted his sons, Philip and Peter. The Kunhardts' *Lincoln* is a magnificent book, widely acclaimed and generally recognized as the definitive pictorial record of Abraham Lincoln's life.

After the death of their father in 2006, Philip and Peter Kunhardt continued the family tradition, and they recruited a member of the fifth generation, Peter's son, Peter Kunhardt, Jr., to join their literary team. The result of their collaboration is the present book, *Looking for Lincoln*.

A casual reader who glances at *Looking for Lincoln*, perhaps in a bookstore, may be surprised to find that it begins in 1865, with a moving account of the assassination of the president, followed by an elaborately illustrated narrative of the capture, trial, and execution of the Lincoln conspirators. At this point in a conventional biography the reader might expect a historical flashback to Lincoln's early days and upbringing. Instead the story moves forward from 1865 to 1926, when Robert Todd Lincoln, the president's oldest son, died.

If our reader studies the book more closely, he or she meets other surprises. In addition to tracing an unusual timeline, the Kunhardts offer a special—one might almost say a syncopated—chronology. They follow the dictum of T. S. Eliot (in "Burnt Norton"):

> Time present and time past
> Are both perhaps present in time future,
> And time future contained in time past.

To put the matter less cryptically, they understand that for historians the actual date on which an event occurred is often less significant than when knowledge of that event becomes widely known. For instance, Lincoln's revealing 1837 letters to Mary Owens Vineyard, discussing their on-and-off-again engagement, properly appear here under an 1866 date because that is when they were made public.

In short, our reader will quickly learn that this is not a conventional pictorial biography of Abraham Lincoln but is instead a book of discovery. At the time of Lincoln's death most Americans knew very little about their wartime president, except that he was a frontiersman and a rail-splitter who freed the slaves and preserved the Union, and there was intense public interest in learning more about the martyred president. The postwar generation saw a massive, if uncoordinated, effort to probe Lincoln's ancestry, to reconstruct his boyhood years, to investigate his early political efforts, to learn about his marriage and his family, and to judge his career as a lawyer. Newspapermen and biographers began persistent questioning of those who had known Lincoln well—and of those who pretended to know him well—in search of biographical nuggets.

Looking for Lincoln is a superb reconstruction of these efforts, during the half-century after Lincoln's death, to strip away the veils of mystery and ignorance that cloaked so much of his career in order to find the "real" Lincoln. Here, for example, is a fair-minded appraisal of the efforts of William H. Herndon, Lincoln's law partner for twenty years, to rescue Lincoln's memory from writers like Josiah G. Holland, who portrayed him as a devout—indeed, almost a saintly—leader. Here, too, is the story of the admiring ten-volume life of Lincoln by his former personal secretaries, John G. Nicolay and John Hay, the only biography ever authorized by his overly sensitive son, Robert.

But this is no dry exercise in historiography. Along with the slowly emerging consensus on Lincoln's greatness, the Kunhardts trace—as always with abundant and revealing illustrations—the rival interpretations of the president in sculpture, ranging from the hobbledehoy figure of George Grey Barnard to the reverent statue by Augustus Saint-Gaudens. Nor are these conflicting literary and artistic interpretations of Lincoln presented in isolation. At every stage the Kunhardts take pains to show the background events, such as the formation of the Ku Klux Klan, race riots, and presidential elections, that influenced the changes in how the public viewed Lincoln.

In short, this is a remarkable and highly original book, one that skillfully interweaves text and pictures to tell two closely related stories: the discovery of facts about Abraham Lincoln's life, and the exploration of his place in American memory. It is the Kunhardts' best book, an indispensable guide for readers who want to understand Abraham Lincoln and the world he lived in.

Introduction
Doris Kearns Goodwin

There could be no more fitting way to celebrate Abraham Lincoln's bicentennial than this beautifully illustrated exploration of how Lincoln was remembered and memorialized in the six decades after his life. Through a unique combination of pictures, reminiscences from those who knew him, newspaper stories, and excerpts from biographies, the Kunhardts carry the reader on a fascinating emotional journey.

The story begins by re-creating the happy mood that suffused Lincoln on the last day of his life, when, knowing that the war for the Union was finally won, he "seemed relaxed, as if he were finally attaining his life's purpose." It captures the widespread grief that accompanied his assassination and then reveals, with an uncanny feel for detail, the contradictory images that took hold in the North and the South, between whites and blacks, conservatives and liberals, in the decades that followed. The gradual movement toward a more unified reverence for Lincoln is illustrated through the massive celebrations that accompanied his hundredth birthday, the triumphant opening of the Lincoln Memorial in Washington, attended by representatives of both the Union and Confederate armies, and the decision to make Lincoln "the heart and soul" of the four presidents portrayed at Mount Rushmore.

For Abraham Lincoln, who took comfort all his life in the belief that that the dead live on in the memory of others, there could be no more fitting tribute than this exploration of how his memory attained an ever-deepening hold in the mind and heart of people everywhere—in our country and in the world at large.

His ambition was never simply for office or celebrity. It was the desire to accomplish something worthy enough to stand the test of time. This worthy ambition became his lodestar. It carried him through a significant depression in his early thirties, when three things combined to lay him low. His engagement to Mary Todd had been broken; Joshua Speed, the only friend to whom he had opened his heart, was leaving Springfield; and his political career was on a downward slide. "I am now the most miserable man living," he told a friend. "To remain as I am is impossible; I must die or be better." Worried that he was suicidal, his friends removed all razors and knives from his room.

Speed warned Lincoln, in a conversation both men would remember as long as they lived, that if he did not rally he would certainly die. Lincoln said he was more than willing to die but had done nothing to make any human being remember that he had lived and that to leave the world a better place for his having lived in it was what he desired to live for. Fueled by this ambition, he gradually recovered from his depression. He returned to the state legislature, eventually won a seat in Congress, and then, after losing twice for the Senate, surprised the nation with an upset victory to win the Republican nomination for the presidency over three far better known, far more experienced rivals.

In 1863, when the Emancipation Proclamation was signed, Lincoln invited his old friend Speed to the White House. He reminded Speed of their conversation of two decades earlier. Then, speaking of the proclamation, he declared: "I believe that in this measure . . . my fondest hopes will be realized." As he was about to put his signature on the historic proclamation, however, he found that his arm was numb from shaking a thousand hands at a New Year's reception earlier that day. "If my hand trembles when I sign this," Lincoln said, putting down the pen, "all who examine the document hereafter will say, 'He hesitated.' Yet, I never in my life felt more certain that I was doing right. If my name ever goes into history it will be for this act, and my whole soul is in it." So he waited a moment until he was ready to sign with a bold, clear, and firm hand.

So in the end, the fierce ambition to be remembered that had carried Lincoln through his bleak childhood, his laborious efforts to educate himself, his string of political failures, and the darkest days of the war had been realized in ways he never could have imagined. As this book makes abundantly clear, his story would be told and retold for generations.

Preface

Philip B. Kunhardt III
Peter W. Kunhardt
Peter W. Kunhardt, Jr.

Entered according to Act of Congress, in the year 1861, by D. Appleton & Co. in the Clerk's Office of the United States for the Southern District of New York.

All his life Abraham Lincoln was transfixed by memory. In 1844, at the age of thirty-five, he visited his childhood home in Indiana, the only time he ever returned there. Here his mother lay buried on a windy hilltop alongside his only sibling, his sister, Sarah. Here was the log cabin his father had built, now standing in disarray. The visit opened up waves of feeling in the young man and stirred him to write a poem, one of the few that have come down to us from him. In it he spoke of his sadness at returning, and of the surge of memories that crowded his brain; but also of an intense and curious pleasure that came from remembering. "O Memory! thou midway world/'Twixt earth and paradise,/Where things decayed and loved ones lost/In dreamy shadows rise,/And, freed from all that's earthly vile,/Seem hallowed, pure, and bright,/Like scenes in some enchanted isle/All bathed in liquid light."

Lincoln saw the past as a living reality. Much as Keats spoke of finding true friends in other eras, separated by time yet exerting their influence still, Lincoln turned to the hallowed age of the Founding Fathers, who possessed an almost immortal stature for him. Keeping alive and extending their vision for America became the overarching passion and purpose of his life. Memory had to do with keeping the nation's bonds intact, as Lincoln said forcefully in his First Inaugural Address. "We are not enemies, but friends," he spoke to North and South. "Though passion may have strained, it must not break our bonds of affection." And then he said it was the "mystic chords of memory" that held the country together.

This book is about those chords of memory, which over the past hundred and fifty years have swirled around Abraham Lincoln. For millions of people his memory has served as a touchstone. His democratic leadership, his commitment to human freedom, his public eloquence, and his intensely human presence and refusal to demonize his adversaries have inspired generations, dating back to the years immediately following his assassination.

In 1871 former presidential secretary John Hay wrote, "Lincoln needed no lapse of years to become immortal. In a flash of blinding light he sprang full panoplied into the religion of the people." For millions of people, who had loved Lincoln during his lifetime, he did almost instantly become an object of reverence. Even those more ambivalent to him when he was alive were swept up in the public reverie, deeply affected by this first assassination of an American president. But millions of others, mostly in the South but also in the North, continued to hate Lincoln after his death. As the figure who had presided over the bloodiest war in American history, he was too associated with political partisanship and with massive suffering to attain to any kind of reverence. And yet over the next sixty years that was what happened, as increasingly most of the nation came to venerate him. By the time the Lincoln Memorial was dedicated in 1922 Lincoln had surpassed George Washington in the American pantheon and become a symbol of freedom worldwide.

As early as 1891 Lincoln's friend Carl Schurz warned about the dangers of hero worship. "To the younger generation Abraham Lincoln has already become a half-mythical figure," he wrote, "which, in the haze of historical distance, grows to more and more heroic proportions, but also loses in distinctiveness of outline and feature." In addition to tracing the growth of the Lincoln legend, this book aspires to recapture those long-faded outlines and features of Lincoln's actual life, as revealed by the people who knew him best.

The outpouring of Lincoln memories in the decades after his death produced an accumulation of remembered details from those who knew him. We have selected extracts from newspapers, letters, books, and documents of many kinds to help trace the making of Lincoln's story. While some eyewitness accounts were untrustworthy, written to further personal agendas or just plain wrong, these spurious testimonies, along with the genuine, became part of his unfolding story. And in the end the historical and the mythic Lincoln are often hard to separate, and both are significant.

Lincoln's portrait shifts depending on who is doing the remembering. During the half century after his death, each section of the country remembered Lincoln in its own way. In the East he was recalled very differently than in the West. Political conservatives recalled a markedly different man than the Lincoln progressives remembered. Black and white, Northerner and Southerner, religious and nonreligious, friend and foe all invoked their own visions of Abraham Lincoln. And yet underlying all the versions there was a real historical figure.

Over the course of our research two things became especially clear. One was the role played by African Americans in the safeguarding of Lincoln's legacy. As a tired nation turned away from the progressive goals of the 1860s, African Americans insisted that Lincoln be remembered for his crucial role in emancipation and not only as the savior of the Union. Even when black leaders became more critical of Lincoln they maintained a strong respect for him. "I love him not because he was perfect," wrote W.E.B. Du Bois, "but because he was not and yet triumphed." Second, we came to recognize the significance of Robert Lincoln to his father's story. Robert is the only character to span this entire book. He spent his life as the self-appointed guardian of his father's memory. Some of his influence was excessive and negative, and there is a tragic quality to Robert's life. But he cared tremendously about his father's place in history, and we owe it to him that Lincoln's papers today reside in the Library of Congress.

Five successive generations of our family helped chronicle the photographs and research that went into this book. Our Lincoln connection began with our ancestor William Neal Meserve, who fought in the Civil War, was wounded at Antietam, and met the sixteenth President twice. After the war Meserve asked his son to illustrate his war diary with photographs. Frederick Hill Meserve went on to become the country's preeminent collector and historian of the photographs of Abraham Lincoln. Over a period of sixty years he put together a complex puzzle of images that revealed Lincoln as we know him today. Working alone, then with his daughter, Dorothy Meserve Kunhardt, he gathered mountains of research as the Lincoln story unfolded year after year. Neither could have imagined how pertinent their files, notes, pamphlets, and books would be to us, the fourth and fifth generations of our family who have continued their work into the twenty-first century.

Phil Kunhardt was Meserve's grandson, who wrote extensively about Lincoln. For half a century he preserved what became known as the Meserve-Kunhardt Collection and kept its thousands of prints intact. Father of two of the authors of this book and grandfather of the third, he knew that the bicentennial of Lincoln's birth was the time to present a new look at Lincoln to the public. For six years he championed this book and a companion documentary television series, telling us again and again that it was time for something big. Then, just as we were ready to begin, he was diagnosed with pulmonary fibrosis and given little time by his doctor.

Despite the oxygen tubes that got in his way, he worked to the end, suggesting ideas, conveying his unique knowledge, steering us to little-known resources, and helping us figure out a new Lincoln photograph numbering system that would replace the out-of-date reference created by his grandfather a century earlier. Phil Kunhardt died in 2006 at age seventy-eight. To him this work is lovingly dedicated.

Looking for Lincoln

Just hours before Lincoln's assassination, photographers recorded a flag-raising ceremony at Fort Sumter, and then went on to document these children of former slaves sitting amid the ruins of Charleston, South Carolina.

Part One

April 14 – July 7, 1865

Black Easter

Peace, at Last
April 14, 1865

Lincoln could barely contain his excitement. First had come word of General Ulysses S. Grant's capture of Petersburg, followed almost immediately by news of the fall of Richmond. For the first time in months the President seemed relaxed, as if he were finally attaining his life's purpose. On April 9 came word of Robert E. Lee's surrender at Appomattox, unleashing waves of celebration in Washington. Buildings were decorated, and flags flown, and on April 11 Lincoln appeared at an upstairs window of the White House and addressed the people. He spoke of the future of America, endorsing a plan in Louisiana that included black suffrage. (In the crowd was the actor John Wilkes Booth, who turned to a friend and said, "That means nigger citizenship. Now, by God, I'll put him through!")

On Friday morning, April 14, the President breakfasted with his son Robert. At eleven A.M. he called his cabinet together and described to them a dream he had had that night. "He seemed to be in a singular and indescribable vessel," wrote Navy Secretary Gideon Welles, "moving with great rapidity toward a dark and indescribable shore." Lincoln was certain it portended something important, something to do with the approach of lasting peace. "He was more cheerful and happy than I had ever seen him," recalled Secretary of War Edwin Stanton.

It was from this height of exaltation at war's end that the nation would be plunged into darkness that very evening. Extremes of emotion, coming close together, would cause a maelstrom of grief that, mixing with adulation, would secure Lincoln in the nation's memory for all time. His mystic memory would rise out of war and peace, slavery and emancipation, victory and betrayal—all crowded in upon one another on that fateful day in April.

Victory banners adorned Washington as the city celebrated the approaching end of the Civil War. This group, posing in front of the U.S. Clothing Department on April 14, had no way of knowing their president would be murdered later that day.

Eyewitnesses to Lincoln's Murder

Lincoln's beaver top hat, left behind at Ford's Theatre

Around 10:30 P.M. on April 14, 1865, early in the third act of *Our American Cousin* at Ford's Theatre in Washington, John Wilkes Booth raised a pistol to the back of Abraham Lincoln's head and fired a single bullet into the President's brain. For an instant no one moved. Slowly at first, then picking up fury, a hurricane-like reaction spread across the theater. People shouted and shrieked and then rushed terror-stricken for the exits, creating what witnesses would call a "pandemonium." Charles A. Leale, a young doctor in the audience, made his way to the presidential box, where he found the President slumped unconscious in his chair. He lowered him to the floor, cut away Lincoln's shirt, and tried to treat the fatal wound. Joined in his efforts by two other doctors—Charles Taft (who was lifted up to the box from below) and Africanus F. A. King—the three men decided to remove Lincoln from the theater.

With the help of others they carried him across muddy Tenth Street to the Petersen boardinghouse, where a young man was now beckoning them to bring him. The room inside was small but meticulously kept and contained a spindle bed too short for Lincoln's six-foot-four frame. One of the doctors attempted to break off the end posts, but failing that, they spread the President diagonally across the mattress.

And so began a long night of watching, as the mortally wounded chief executive lay dying. On this night a whole new phase in the Lincoln legend began as eyewitnesses stepped forward to tell their part of the Lincoln story.

Vice President Andrew Johnson should have assumed command, but Lincoln's

Ever since its opening in 1857, on the site of a former Baptist church, Ford's Theatre was one of the most successful playhouses in Washington. The large brick building could hold an audience of 1,700. Lincoln was sitting in this rocking chair when he was shot.

Lincoln's death bed and blood-soaked pillow were photographed by Petersen House boarder Julius Ulke just minutes after the President's body was removed. Not long afterward William Clark, the room's tenant, gathered up Lincoln's boots and hand-darned socks along with towels and snippets of hair, storing them away as sacred relics. "Hundreds daily call at the house," he wrote three days later. "Everybody has a great desire to obtain some memento from my room."

PETERSON HOUSE,
WHERE PRESIDENT A. LINCOLN DIED, APRIL 15, 1865.

Photographs of the Petersen House were mass-produced and in this case labeled with incorrect spelling.

PETERSON HOUSE,
WHERE PRESIDENT A. LINCOLN DIED, APRIL 15, 1865.

Photographs of the Petersen House were mass-produced and in this case labeled with incorrect spelling.

Lincoln's death bed and blood-soaked pillow were photographed by Petersen House boarder Julius Ulke just minutes after the President's body was removed. Not long afterward William Clark, the room's tenant, gathered up Lincoln's boots and hand-darned socks along with towels and snippets of hair, storing them away as sacred relics. "Hundreds daily call at the house," he wrote three days later. "Everybody has a great desire to obtain some memento from my room."

moody, asthmatic Secretary of War Edwin Stanton decided that the attack was of a military nature and that authority over the crisis belonged properly to him. Stanton arrived at the Petersen House by eleven P.M., having already visited Secretary of State William Seward, who had been brutally assaulted in his home an hour earlier. Concerned that the attacks were part of a vast Confederate plot, Stanton was determined to identify the assassins quickly and instigate a dragnet to obtain their capture. Down the hall from where doctors were trying to keep the President alive, he turned a bedroom into his emergency headquarters. There he began issuing orders, composing dispatches, and consulting with army leaders and police. At midnight he put the military on alert and ordered that all routes out of the city be sealed off and that extra security checkpoints be set up on bridges, roads, and waterways heading south. Then he began a preliminary court of inquiry inside the Petersen House, where he summoned eyewitnesses to give testimony essential to the investigation. By luck a young clerk named James Tanner was living in the house next door and announced that he was knowledgeable in shorthand. He had lost both his legs at the Second Battle of Bull Run and now walked into the Petersen House with the aid of artificial limbs, recognizing his chance to serve history.

Corporal James Tanner (below) was called to the Petersen House on April 14 to record the testimony of eyewitnesses. Mary Lincoln was "weeping as though her heart would break," he wrote soon afterward, and in a back room lay the President "breathing hard, and with every breath a groan." Tanner reported to Secretary of War Edwin Stanton (right), who was in overall charge of the investigation. Both of them were present at Lincoln's bedside when he died.

3404. Place where President Lincoln was Assassinated.
[FOR DESCRIPTION OF THIS VIEW SEE THE OTHER SIDE OF THIS CARD.]

Lincoln's rocking chair appears at the right side of this stereoview, turned at an angle so the President could see the stage. At the time of the assassination the stage was set for act three, scene two of *Our American Cousin* (left).

Stanton's First Interview
A. M. S. Crawford

Lieutenant A.M.S. Crawford had been seated close to the presidential box at Ford's Theatre. He carefully described the assassin to Edwin Stanton but was not sure who he was, though "he very strongly resembled the Booths."

I was sitting in the dress circle of Ford's Theatre . . . I suppose about five feet from the door of the box. . . . This murderer came around the middle of the first scene of the 3rd act of the play of *Our American Cousin*. To pass us he had to come around me. . . . I looked up at him four or five times. He attracted my attention. I thought at first he was intoxicated. There was a glare in [his] eye and he was a little over middling [height]. He had a dark slouch hat, a dark coat, jet black hair, dark eyes, a heavy black [mustache], no whiskers, and no beard. It was just at the close of the third scene as all attention was directed to the stage. . . . The next instant the shot was fired. I said at once that it was in the President's box and jumped to the door. I passed through the door and into the box. A gentleman whom I afterwards ascertained to be Major Rathbone . . . asked me not to allow anyone to enter the box and I sent for a surgeon.

Major Henry A. Rathbone

The Killer Identified
Harry Hawk

Harry Hawk

Stanton's second interview was with the actor Harry Hawk, a personal acquaintance of John Wilkes Booth and the sole performer on stage at the moment Lincoln was shot.

I was on the stage at the time of the firing and heard the report of the pistol. My back was toward the President's box at the time. I heard something tear and somebody fell and as I looked toward him he came in the direction in which I was standing and I believe to the best of my knowledge that it was John Wilkes Booth. . . . I only had one glance at him as he was rushing towards me with a dagger and I turned and run and after I ran up a flight of stairs I turned and exclaimed "My God that's John Booth." . . . He had no hat when I saw him on the stage. In my own mind I do not have any doubt but that it was Booth.

The Deed Itself
James P. Ferguson

James P. Ferguson was the owner of a restaurant across the street from Ford's Theatre and was in the audience on the night of the attack. Though Stanton went on to question at least three others, stenographer James Tanner considered this to be the most important of the night's interviews, and Ferguson's testimony was widely published in Monday's newspapers.

After curtain went up for the 3rd act I saw Mr. Booth go to the door leading to the passage of the private box which the president occupied and by the door. In a moment afterwards I was looking with an opera glass to see which the citizen was that was with the President. I then heard the report of the pistol and saw Mrs. Lincoln catch him around the neck. I saw him throw up his right arm and at the same time I saw Booth [put] his hand in his side and pull a knife and move between Mrs. Lincoln and a lady in the same box. He put his hands in the cushion of the box and threw his feet right over. As he jumped over he pulled part of a state flag off and had part of it under his feet when he fell on the stage. The very moment he struck he exclaimed "Sic Semper Tyrannis." As he came across the stage facing me he looked me right in the face and it alarmed me and I pulled the lady who was with me down behind the banister. I looked right down at him and he stopped as he said, "I have done it" and shook the knife.

Booth held this dagger in his left hand when he fired his pistol at Abraham Lincoln. He then used it to fend off and slash the arm of Major Rathbone, before he leaped down onto the stage.

A Doctor Prolongs Lincoln's Life
Charles A. Leale

April 15, 1865

This firsthand account by Dr. Charles Leale was based on detailed notes he made on the day of Lincoln's death.

When I reached the President he was almost dead, his eyes were closed, he was parallel. I placed my finger on his right radial pulse, but could feel no movement of the artery. . . . With the assistance of two gentlemen I immediately placed him in a recumbent position while doing this and holding his head and shoulders my hand came in contact with blood on his left-shoulder, the thought of the dagger then recurred to me, and [I] supposed he might have been stabbed in the [subclavian] artery or some of its branches. I asked a gentleman near by to cut his coat and shirt off that shoulder to enable me if possible to check the supposed hemorrhage, as soon as his arm was bared to a distance below the shoulder, and I saw that there was no wound there, I lifted his eyelids and examined his eyes, the pupil of one of which was dilated.

Dr. Charles A. Leale, military surgeon

I then examined his head and soon discovered a large firm clot of blood situated about one inch below the superior curved line and an inch and a half to the left of the median line of the occipital bone.

The coagnin which was firmly matted with the hair, [I] removed [and] passed the little finger of my left hand directly through the perfectly smooth opening made by the ball, he was then apparently dead.

When I removed my finger which I used as a knife, an oozing of blood followed and he commenced, to show signs of improvement.

The Murderer's Gun
William T. Kent

April 15, 1865

At Metropolitan Police Headquarters on the night of the assassination, seventeen persons were questioned and released. William T. Kent, a government clerk, gave his sworn testimony to the police early that morning.

About half past ten I heard a shot. I thought it was in the play. . . . I immediately left my seat and went around behind the audience and went into the President's box. Some persons had reached the box before me and were placing the President on the floor. The President was insensible. I went out and away from the theater but missing my keys I went back to the theater and went back into the box the President had occupied. In moving about to find my keys, my foot struck against something and staring down I picked up a pistol the same that is shown to me, and in the possession of the Property Clerk of the Metropolitan Police.

Booth used a muzzle-loading derringer to shoot Lincoln. A Currier-Ives print shows how close he was when he fired.

Details of the Dreadful Tragedy
Edwin M. Stanton

April 15, 1865

From his makeshift office down the hall from where Lincoln lay dying, at 1:30 A.M. Secretary of War Stanton released his first official statement. Though he had already determined that John Wilkes Booth was the probable assassin, Stanton withheld the information at this time. His dispatch ran in the morning papers and became the public's first news about the attack on Lincoln.

[Official]
War Department,
Washington, April 15-1:30 A.M.

This evening at about 9:30 P.M., at Ford's Theatre, the President, while sitting in his private box with Mrs. Lincoln, Mrs. Harris, and Major Rathbone, was shot by an assassin, who suddenly entered the box and approached behind the President.

The assassin then leaped upon the stage, brandishing a large dagger or knife, and made his escape in the rear of the theatre.

The pistol ball entered the back of the President's head and penetrated nearly through the head. The wound is mortal. The President has been insensible ever since it was inflicted, and is now dying. . . .

All the members of the Cabinet except Mr. Seward, are now in attendance upon the President. . . .

Edwin M. Stanton
Secretary of War

When the sculptor Augustus Saint-Gaudens saw this cast of Lincoln's face, he swore that it was a death mask. In fact it was made from life by Washington sculptor Clark Mills just nine weeks before the assassination. "[T]he whole expression is of unspeakable sadness and all-sufficing strength," Lincoln's private secretary John Hay later wrote of it. "Yet the peace is not the dreadful peace of death; it is the peace that passeth understanding."

April 15, 1865

The First Lady's Wild Grief

Nobody was affected more by the assassination than was Lincoln's wife, Mary, who had been seated beside him at Ford's Theatre. After her husband's removal she had slowly made her way across manure-strewn Tenth Street, holding on to the badly wounded Henry Rathbone. Inside the Petersen House she rejected proffers of help, crying out "Where is my dear husband? Where is he?" Allowed a quick look at the dying President in bed, she was then escorted to a front parlor, where she would spend most of the night.

That very same afternoon Mary had taken a rare carriage ride with her husband. "I asked him, if any one, should accompany us," she later recalled, and "he immediately replied, 'No—I prefer to ride by ourselves to day.'" For the first time in ages the couple talked about the future—about a family trip to Europe; about one to California. "During the ride he was so gay, that I said to him, laughingly, 'Dear Husband, you almost startle me by your great cheerfulness.'" Lincoln then replied, "[A]nd well I may feel so, Mary, I consider *this day*, the war, has come to a close." And then he added, "We must *both*, be more cheerful in the future—between the war & the loss of our darling Willie—we have both, been very miserable."

Misery had haunted Mary off and on since childhood. Her adored mother had died when she was only six and a half, and when her father remarried just six months later, in many ways she had lost him too. The next decade was a "desolate" time for her, she admitted, in a house with a stepmother who did not love her.

Coming west at age twenty to live with her sister Elizabeth, she had finally blossomed into her natural, outgoing self. She was "quick, lively, gay, frivolous," said her sister, "and loved glitter, show and pomp and power." Among her many suitors was the famous Stephen A. Douglas (whom she later referred to as a "little, little giant"). When she married Abraham Lincoln in 1842, some family members felt he was not good enough for her. But Mary saw things in the prairie lawyer that no one else did, and over the years she became his strongest supporter. With an interest in politics unusual for women of her day, she became an unofficial adviser to Lincoln. "He had great respect for her judgment," recalled her half-sister Emilie Helm. Their children gave them both extraordinary joy, and their parenting style was liberal and progres-

By 1864 Mary Lincoln had recovered from the shock following the death of her son Willie two years earlier and was sketched by Pierre Morand as she walked outside the White House with her husband. Over the next months the Lincolns had more time for each other, and Mary even admitted feeling joyful as she rode with her husband in this carriage on April 14. It was the last happy day of her life.

Mary had once been known for her bright colors
and fashionable dresses, but after Willie's death
she clothed herself in deep mourning. In her widowhood she assumed a permanent shade of black.

Inside this window of a small parlor in the Petersen House sat the grieving First Lady, banished from the bedroom in which her husband lay dying.

sive. It was when four-year-old "Eddy" died in 1850 that Mary had taken her first plunge into deep depression. "Eat Mary for we must live," her desperate husband had begged her, and she had eventually recovered and gone on to have two more children.

Eleven-year-old Willie's death in the White House in early 1862 had pushed Mary over the edge. Her grief was so extreme, and her mental health so precarious, that Lincoln finally had to speak to her firmly. "Try and control your grief, or it will drive you mad," he had warned. But Mary was never quite the same again. Desperately missing Willie, she began to see him at night, as Emilie Helm noted. "He lives, Emilie! He comes to me every night, and stands at the foot of my bed with the same sweet, adorable smile he always had." "If Willie did not come to comfort me, I would still be drowned in tears." Over the next three years, though she wore the black clothes of mourning, little by little Mary pulled herself back into health.

The murder of her husband as she sat beside him at Ford's Theatre catapulted Mary into darkness. Those who saw her that first night described a woman beside herself. Kept outside the death room by the orders of Edwin Stanton, from time to time she was allowed to briefly look in. During her last entrance, early in the morning, she cried out, "Oh, have I given my husband to die?" and then was once again removed from the room. It was her son Robert, after Lincoln's death that morning, who took her back to the White House, driving through a pouring rain as church bells chimed. Brought to a small upstairs bedroom—she could not bear to use any of her old chambers—she began to let out her grief without censure, sending wails and "uncanny shrieks" throughout the silent mansion.

The Panic-Stricken First Lady
Maunsell B. Field

April 17, 1865

One of the earliest eyewitnesses to step forward after the assassination was Maunsell Field, a close political friend of Supreme Court Justice Salmon Chase. Hastening to the Petersen House, he encountered the First Lady there. His account, written that same night, was carried in newspapers two days later and gave the public its first vivid glimpse at the details of Lincoln's death room and at the suffering of Mary Lincoln.

On Friday evening, April 14, 1865, I was reading the evening paper in the reading-room of Willard's Hotel, at about 10½ o'clock, when I was startled by the report that an attempt had been made a few minutes before to assassinate the President at Ford's Theatre.... [I] proceeded to the scene of the alleged assassination ... [and] found not only considerable crowds on the streets leading to the theatre, but a very large one in front of the theatre, and of the house directly opposite, where the President had been carried after the attempt upon his life. With some difficulty I obtained Ingress to the house. I was at once informed by Miss Harris, daughter of Senator Harris, that the President was dying, which statement was confirmed by three or four other persons whom I met in the hall; but I was desired not to communicate his condition to Mrs. Lincoln, who was in the front parlor. I went into this parlor, where I found Mrs. Lincoln.... She at once recognized me, and begged me to run for Dr. Stone, or some other medical man. She was not weeping, but appeared hysterical, and exclaimed in rapid succession, over and over again: "Oh! why didn't he kill me? why didn't he kill me?"'... [B]etween 3 and 4 o'clock ... I again went to the house where ... I obtained Ingress this time without any difficulty.... I proceeded at once to the room in which the President was lying, which was a bedroom in an extension, on the first or parlor floor of the house.... The bed was a double one, and I found the President lying diagonally across it, with his head at the outside. The pillows were saturated with blood, and there was considerable blood upon the floor immediately under him. There was a patchwork coverlet thrown over the President, which was only so far removed, from time to time, as to enable the physicians in attendance to feel the arteries of the neck or the heart, and he appeared to have been divested of all clothing. His eyes were closed and injected with blood, both the lids and the portion surrounding the eyes being as black as if they had been bruised by violence. He was breathing regularly, but with effort, and did not seem to be struggling or suffering.... About fifteen minutes before the decease, Mrs. Lincoln came into the room, and threw herself upon her dying husband's body. She was allowed to remain there only a few minutes, when she was removed in a sobbing condition.

REMAINS OF

ABRAHAM LINCOLN

THE GREATEST MAN OF OUR CENTURY

assassinated April 14th 1865.

President Andrew Johnson

A New President Is Sworn In

A little after 10:15 P.M. on Friday, April 14, Andrew Johnson was awakened by a loud knocking at his door. "Governor Johnson, if you are in this room I must see you," a voice thundered. It was former Wisconsin governor Leonard Farwell, who lived down the hall at the Kirkwood House and who had just witnessed Lincoln's shooting at Ford's Theatre, a few blocks away. While most people at the scene of the crime were focused on the wounded President, Farwell had thought of his friend Johnson and had raced over to check on him and deliver the news. A short while later both men headed over to the Petersen House, where the Vice President joined the vigil gathering inside. But even as he took his place among the other watchers, he was urged by Charles Sumner not to stay too long, lest Mary Lincoln, who was known to dislike him, should find him in the room. Johnson dutifully withdrew. Back at the Kirkwood House he paced the floors and thought of revenge upon the perpetrators.

Senator Johnson of Tennessee had been chosen by the new Union Party in 1864 to replace Hannibal Hamlin of Maine for the second spot on the presidential ticket. Rewarded as the lone senator from a seceded state who had remained loyal to the Union, Johnson would broaden Lincoln's appeal in the border states and among Democrats. But while the public applauded the selection at first, there were soon growing reasons to regret it. At the inauguration in March, Johnson had arrived intoxicated, his speech barely intelligible. There was a medical reason for his condition—the drink he had taken to fortify himself in illness had had an unexpectedly strong effect—but those present were incensed. "The Vice-President elect made a rambling and strange harangue," observed Navy Secretary Gideon Welles in his diary. "I said to Stanton who was on my right, 'Johnson is either drunk or crazy.' Stanton replied, 'There is evidently something wrong.'"

Immediately following Lincoln's death on Saturday morning, his cabinet members—with the exception of William Seward, still fighting for his life after an attack on him simultaneous with that on Lincoln—gathered in the back parlor of the Petersen House and discussed what to do next. As Welles recorded, they "signed a letter which was prepared by Attorney General Speed to the Vice President, informing him of the event, and that the government devolved upon him." Stanton suggested that James Speed be the one to deliver the letter, and Treasury Secretary Hugh McCullough was chosen to accompany him to Johnson's hotel. Then they were to seek out Chief Justice Salmon Chase, whose job it would be to administer the oath.

When Speed arrived at Johnson's, Chase was coincidentally already there, having found the Vice President "calm apparently but very grave." McCullough noted that he was "grief-stricken like the rest" but also "oppressed by the suddenness of the call upon him to become President." When he was asked when he would be ready to be sworn in, Johnson answered that it should take place as quickly as possible, right here at his hotel. A handful of others were quickly assembled, and Speed and McCullough would serve as official witnesses. The ceremony took place a little after ten A.M. in the hotel parlor. After repeating the oath of office, Johnson kissed the Bible and was then pronounced President by Chief Justice Chase, who added, "May God guide, support and bless you in your arduous duties." After being congratulated all

Leonard J. Farwell, the former governor of Wisconsin and a Lincoln appointee at the U.S. Patent Office, was present at Ford's Theatre on the night of the assassination. Determined to protect his friend the Vice President, he ran to the Kirkwood House and pounded on Andrew Johnson's door. "[H]earing no movement I knocked again," he later related, "and called out . . . 'Governor Johnson, if you are in this room I must see you!' In a moment I heard him spring from his bed and exclaim: 'Farwell is that you?'"

around, Johnson made a brief inaugural address.

At noon, the new President presided over a cabinet meeting at the Treasury Department, where Secretary McCullough offered him a reception room as his temporary office. To his department heads he vowed to continue in Lincoln's footsteps—his policy toward the Confederacy would "be the same as that of the late President." And he intended no changes to the presidential cabinet.

The *Chicago Times,* reporting the day's events, wrote, "Upon him devolves the tremendous responsibility of completing the gigantic work left unfinished by Abraham Lincoln. Will he prove equal to the task?"

Chief Justice Salmon Chase swore in Andrew Johnson as the nation's seventeenth President.

On April 16 Andrew Johnson presided over his first cabinet meeting, held in the Treasury Building, which was in the process of being adorned with mourning ribbon (left). He would keep on all of Lincoln's cabinet members.

A Secret Autopsy
Edward Curtis, M.D.

Following Lincoln's death at the Petersen House on April 15, his body was taken on a horse-drawn hearse back to the White House. The second-floor bedroom where Lincoln's son Willie had died three years earlier was transformed into an autopsy chamber and Lincoln's body was placed on a makeshift table. Two pathologists went on to perform a post-mortem on the slain President, as seven other doctors looked on and gave directions. In this letter written to his mother a week after the event, one of the pathologists, Edward Curtis, described the scene.

Dr. Woodward and myself were ordered by the surgeon general to make a post-mortem examination, in his presence, of the body of

Dr. Edward Curtis

the President. Accordingly, at 11 o'clock, we assembled at the White House in the room where the body lay. . . . It contained but little furniture: a large, heavily curtained bed, a sofa or two, bureau, wardrobe, and chairs comprised all there was. Seated around the room were several general officers and some civilians, silent or conversing in whispers, and to one side, stretched upon a rough framework of boards and covered only with sheets and towels, lay—cold and immovable—what but a few hours before was the soul of a great nation. The

Surgeon General was walking up and down the room when I arrived and detailed me the history of the case. He said that the President showed most wonderful tenacity of life, and, had not his wound been necessarily mortal, might have survived an injury to which most men would succumb. Upon the arrival of Doctors Crane, Stone, Woodward and Notson, Dr. Woodward and I proceeded to open the head and remove the brain down to the track of the ball. The latter had entered a little to the left of the median line at the back of the head, had passed almost directly forwards through the center of the brain and lodged. Not finding it readily, we proceeded to remove the entire brain, when, as I was lifting the latter from the cavity of the skull, suddenly the bullet dropped out through my fingers and fell, breaking the solemn silence of the room with its clatter, into an empty basin that was standing beneath. There it lay upon the white china, a little black mass no bigger than the end of my finger—dull, motionless and harmless, yet the cause of such mighty changes in the world's history as we may perhaps never realize.

An Old Friend Is Overcome by Grief
Anson Henry

In a letter to his wife, Eliza, Lincoln's old friend and former physician Anson Henry described his terrible grief upon Lincoln's death. Henry had known the Lincolns for a quarter of a century and had treated Lincoln for depression back in the 1840s. "What a great, big-hearted man he is," Lincoln once wrote. "Henry is one of the best men I have ever known." In Richmond at the time of Lincoln's murder, Henry hurried to Washington to try to be of help and arrived while Lincoln was still in the White House autopsy room. Over the next weeks he would become one of Mary Lincoln's greatest comforters.

Anson G. Henry

I was so stunned by the blow that I could not realize that he was dead untill I saw him lying in the Guests Chamber cold & still in the embrace of Death. Then the terrible truth flashed upon me, & the fountain of tears was broken up and I wept like a child refusing to be comforted, remaining riveted to the spot untill led away by those who came in for the purpose of placing the body

in the coffin. I felt that a mountain load had been suddenly lifted from my heart. I had never before realized the luxury of tears, & I never before wept in the bitterness of heart & soul, & God grant that I may never have cause to so weep again.

After recovering my composure, I sought the presence of poor heart broken Mrs. Lincoln. I found her in bed more composed than I had anticipated, but the moment I came within her reach she threw her arms around my neck & wept most hysterically for several minutes, and this completely unmanned me again, but my sympathy was to her most consoling, and for a half hour she talked very composedly about what had transpired between her and [her] Husband the day & evening of his death, which I will tell you when we meet. She says he was more cheerful and joyous that day and evening than he had been for years.

IMPORTANT.

ASSASSINATION

OF

PRESIDENT LINCOLN

The President Shot at the Theatre Last Evening.

SECRETARY SEWARD

DAGGERED IN HIS BED

BUT

NOT MORTALLY WOUNDED.

The *New York Herald* reported Lincoln's assassination in its Saturday morning paper. Devastated and dazed, brokers gathered outside the New York Stock Exchange.

Word of Lincoln's assassination moved quickly through the nation, with Edwin Stanton's early reports reaching the major cities by three A.M. By eight o'clock on Saturday morning confirmation had been received of Lincoln's death, and news of it began to radiate out into surrounding towns and communities. In New York City business was suspended as dazed citizens came together to share their shock. When an angry mob assembled in front of the Custom House, General James A. Garfield spoke from a balcony to calm them. "Fellow citizens, God reigns and the government at Washington still lives," he was later remembered as saying. In Springfield, Illinois, people gathered silently in the streets, then swarmed over to the statehouse to hear Lincoln's old friend John T. Stuart speak of the dead President.

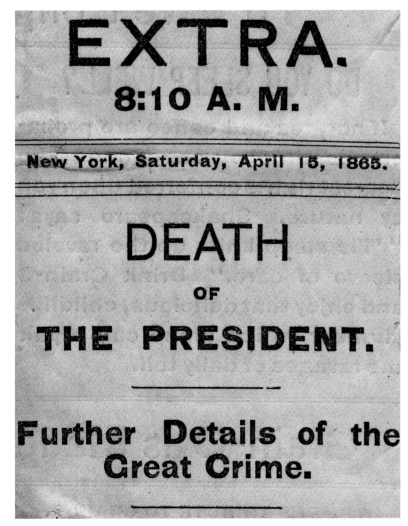

EXTRA.
8:10 A. M.

New York, Saturday, April 15, 1865.

DEATH
OF
THE PRESIDENT.

Further Details of the Great Crime.

Details of the President's death were chronicled in the *New York Herald*.

The following account from Buffalo, New York—typical of many Northern cities— gives a window into how Northerners responded to Lincoln's death.

The direful news of the assassination of the President, and the attempted murder of Secretary Seward, passed from mouth to mouth, until in a space of time incredibly short, it was diffused over the entire city. Workmen on their early way to the forges and shops spoke of the awful calamity with blanched faces; friends met and shook hands in silence or conversed with quivering lips and shocked utterance; bells tolled; the usual sounds peculiar to a busy city on the busiest day of the week were hushed, and it seemed that a pall had been spread over all.

With one accord, as it were, the stores were closed, all the traffic was suspended, and the sable emblems of woe appeared on every hand. From the dwelling of the humblest colored family to the mansion of the most opulent citizen, fluttered the half-mast flag, and there were few localities where some manifestations of sorrow were not apparent. All business was suspended. The streets were crowded, and the telegraph offices were besieged by those eager to obtain the latest tidings; men stood in knots and conversed upon the sad event, and told their hopes and fears for the future, and the usual avocations and pastimes were forgotten in the contemplation of the overwhelming calamity.

ESCAPE OF THE ASSASSINS.

Intense Excitement In Washington.

SCENE AT THE DEATHBED OF MR. LINCOLN.

23

B. M. BRADY,   WASHINGTON, D. C.

William Henry Harrison was the first U. S. President to die in office, just one month after his inauguration.

M. B. BRADY,   WASHINGTON, D. C.

Zachary Taylor's sudden death in office in 1850 set off waves of national grief.

April 16, 1865

The Easter Lincoln

By a quirk of fate the attack on Lincoln had occurred on Good Friday, with his death coming in the early hours the next morning. News of it flashed by telegraph across the North on Saturday, leaving clergy little warning before their Easter services the next day. Orders for Easter flowers had to be canceled, black bunting pulled out to adorn the churches, and carefully prepared sermons completely revised or rewritten.

Rabbis, in the midst of celebrating Passover, were also moved by Lincoln's death, with some reportedly weeping along with their congregants. According to the *Jewish Messenger,* Lincoln became the first non-Jew over whom Kaddish prayers were chanted in the synagogue, and some rabbis compared his death to that of Moses.

Americans had suffered presidential deaths before—William Henry Harrison's in 1841, just a month after his inauguration; Zachary Taylor's one year after his assuming office in 1849. But this was the first time an American president had been assassinated, and the public shock was unprecedented. It was "a crime of pagan Rome . . . or of Revolutionary France," not of America, declared one outraged clergyman.

What is most striking about the Easter sermons is the apotheosis of Lincoln they helped to launch. In what may have been the most highly attended religious services of the century, millions of Americans heard preachers compare Abraham Lincoln to Jesus Christ. Ohio pastor A. D. Mayo spoke of Lincoln's death as an extension of Christ's own. "By the shedding of . . . [Lincoln's] sacred blood, our God and Savior has told us there is remission for all the people's sins," he proclaimed. Nor was this considered blasphemy, insisted Baptist minister C. B. Crane. "As on the first Good Friday peace was established between an apostate race and God, so . . . on that last Good Friday peace was secured between the contending regions of our distracted country."

Forty-nine-year-old Phineas D. Gurley had been the Lincolns' pastor during their four years in Washington. Now on Easter Sunday New York Avenue Presbyterian Church was packed with parishioners and strangers eager for him to help make sense of the national tragedy. Pastor Gurley's message was filled with love for the slain President, but also reflected the pervasive Calvinism of the age. "Above the foul, and cruel, and bloody hand of the assassin—far, far above it—we must see *another hand,*" he said, "—the chastening hand of a wise and faithful God."

Some Northern preachers chose to be openly partisan, using their pulpits to blame the South for the criminal act of John Wilkes Booth. Lincoln's "malice toward none" may have been saintly, they said, but what was needed now was an "iron hand" and a swift justice—"vindication by law [and] by the sword," as one clergyman put it. Even moderates, such as the Rev. James F. Clark of Boston, saw the assassination as a warning never again to trust the South. "As Abraham Lincoln saved us, while living, from the open hostility and deadly blows of the slaveholders and Secessionists, so, in dying, he may have saved us from . . . their poisonous policy."

But if a spirit of vengeance filled some Easter pulpits that morning, the overall effect was glorification. It was on this day that Lincoln's reputation was established as one of the country's greatest secular saints and evermore as the nation's "savior." He was a "Christ-figure" who had died for the sins of his nation, and who would now rise into the hearts of his followers.

"It Is Finished"
The Rev. C. B. Crane

The Rev. C. B. Crane preached his Easter sermon in the South Baptist Church in Hartford, Connecticut.

Oh, friends, on the evening of Good Friday, the memorial day of the crucifixion of our Lord, our good, true-hearted, magnanimous, supremely loyal, great President was smitten down by the hand of the assassin; and yester morn, at twenty-two minutes past seven of the clock, his noble and holy soul went up from its shattered and desecrated tabernacle to its God.

The terrible tragedy is consummated, its heartrending denoument has transpired, there can be no revision of it, it stands the blackest page save one in the history of the world. It is the after-type of the tragedy which was accomplished on the first Good Friday, more than eighteen centuries ago, upon the eminence of Calvary in Judea.

Yes, it was meet that the martyrdom should occur on Good Friday. It is no blasphemy against the Son of God and the Savior of men that we declare the fitness of the slaying of the Second Father of our Republic on the anniversary of the day on which he was slain. Jesus Christ died for the world; Abraham Lincoln died for his country. The consecration of Jesus to humanity began in the antiquity of eternity, and found its culmination when he cried with white, yet triumphant, lips, on the cross, "it is finished." The consecration of Abraham Lincoln to the American people had its phenomenal and most manifest beginning in the summer of 1858, when he entered upon that memorable Senatorial Campaign in which, while he sustained a technical defeat, he gained a substantial victory; it found its culmination on the evening of the fourteenth day of April, 1865, when the sharp pistol report announced with terrible inarticulateness, "it is finished."

A leaf-and-fern-filled bell jar was one of thousands of memorial objects created to honor the slain President. Journalist Noah Brooks summed up the feelings of many when he wrote on April 16, "It is hard to realize that he is gone, that we shall no more see his commanding form, hear his kind voice, or touch his pure and honest hand with its well-remembered earnestness." In a eulogy three days later Ralph Waldo Emerson wrote, "Heaven . . . shall make him serve his country even more by death than by his life."

Fresh Evidence from Booth's Own Hand
John Wilkes Booth

April 17, 1865

On April 17, while the manhunt for John Wilkes Booth continued, his brother-in-law John Clarke turned over an incriminating letter written by Booth the previous November and given to him in a sealed envelope for safekeeping. The letter was filled with an intense hatred for Lincoln's race policies and showed that Booth had long plotted to kidnap the President and put him in Confederate hands. (Only later, after hearing Lincoln's speech in which the President discussed black suffrage, had an enraged Booth changed his plan from kidnapping to murder.)

For four years have I waited, hoped, and prayed for the dark clouds to break, and for a restoration of our former sunshine. To wait longer would be a crime. All hope for peace is dead. My prayers have proved as idle as my hopes. God's will be done. I go to see and share the bitter end. I have ever held that the South were right. The very nomination of Abraham Lincoln, four years ago, spoke plainly war—war upon Southern rights and institutions. . . . This country was formed for the *white*, not for the black man. And, looking upon *African* slavery from the same stand-point held by the noble framers of our Constitution, I, for one, have ever considered it one of the greatest blessings . . . that God ever bestowed upon a favored nation. . . . But there is no time for words, I write in haste. I know how foolish I shall be deemed for undertaking such a step as this. . . . My love . . . is for the South alone. Nor do I deem it a dishonor in attempting to make for her a prisoner of this man, to whom she owes so much of misery. . . . A *Confederate* doing duty *upon his own responsibility*.

J WILKES BOOTH

April 17, 1865

His Northern Critics Silenced

Even those who had disliked Lincoln or disapproved of his policies were swept into the tidal wave of shock and sorrow. In New York, long a city in opposition to Lincoln, enormous crowds took part in the outpouring of grief. "Never was public mourning so spontaneous and general," wrote the diarist and city leader George Templeton Strong on Easter Sunday. "People who could afford to do no more generally have displayed at least a little twenty-five cent flag with a little scrap of crape annexed." The *New York World*, which had been critical of Lincoln throughout his presidency, now honored him in death. "The loss of such a president, at such a conjunction, is an afflicting dispensation which bows a . . . shaken nation in sorrow." The paper referred to the assassination as a "national calamity" that had "caused this whole land to mourn as over the sundering of some dear domestic tie." Former critics among the Republican radicals also changed their public opinions of him. The abolitionist orator Wendell Phillips dropped the anti-Lincoln rhetoric he had long been using, deciding that "Lincoln had won such loving trust among the people that it was impossible to argue anything against it."

In general, people with negative feelings kept them to themselves during the days of mourning, though there are hints of scattered lapses and displays of bad taste. The Rev. C. B. Crane mentioned a Connecticut railroad employee who openly expressed joy at Lincoln's assassination, and a Hartford alderman who cynically referred to Lincoln's "damned black republican bones," which he hoped might now be ground up for use in his garden. And in some cases violence erupted. On the day after Easter, the *Chicago Tribune* ran a story about vigilante action in Washington, D.C. "A rebel resident inquired of a guard in front of the State Department if it were true the President was dead. The soldier replied that it was. The citizen replied, 'I'm damned glad of it.' He had scarcely concluded his utterance when the guard put a ball though his head and he lies now a corpse, execrated by all. The incident fairly illustrates the intensity of popular feeling."

An angry, stunned crowd gathered in Court House Square in Bloomington, Illinois, a town where many had known Lincoln well.

A year earlier, when this photograph was taken, Abraham Lincoln had many critics in the North. Hating him for the long war and for his emancipation policy, one Democrat publicly called for Lincoln's assassination.

"A Deep Hold of Every Class"
Parke Godwin

April 18, 1865

At the Athenaeum Club in New York, on the evening before Lincoln's Washington funeral, members gathered to hold their own remembrances. Club president William T. Blodgett called the assassination "a national calamity . . . which has no parallel in the history of the world in modern times." Later in the evening Parke Godwin, editor of the New York Evening Post, *gave a short address.*

Parke Godwin

Our feelings are now too deep to ask or warrant any attempt at an analysis of the character of the services of the man whose loss we deplore. Standing over his bier, looking down almost into the tomb to which he must shortly be consigned, we are conscious only of our grief. We know that one who was great in himself, as well as by position, has suddenly departed. There is something startling, ghastly, awful in the manner of his going off. But the chief poignancy of our distress is not for greatness fallen, but for the goodness lost. . . . Our hearts still bleed for the companions, friends, brothers that sleep the sleep "that knows no waking," but no loss has been

comparable to his, who was our supremest Leader—our safest Counselor—our wisest Friend—our dear Father. Would you know what Lincoln was, look at this vast metropolis, covered with the habiliments of woe! Never in human history has there been so universal, so spontaneous, so profound an expression of a Nation's bereavement. In all our churches, without distinction of sect; in all our journals, without distinction of party; in all our workshops, in all our counting houses—from the stateliest mansion to the lowliest hovel—you hear but the one utterance, you see but the one emblem of sorrow. Why has the death of Abraham Lincoln taken such deep hold of every class? Partly, no doubt, because he was our Chief Magistrate; but mainly, I think, because through all his public functions there shone the fact that he was a wise and good man; a kindly, honest, noble man; a man in whom the people recognized their own better qualities; whom they, whatever their political convictions, trusted; whom they respected; whom they loved; a man as pure of heart, as patriotic of impulse, as patient, gentle, sweet and lovely of nature, as ever history lifted out of the sphere of the domestic affections to enshrine forever in the affections of the world.

During the days and weeks after Lincoln's murder millions of Americans wore badges like this one, and collected mourning cards like the one below, pasting them into family scrapbooks.

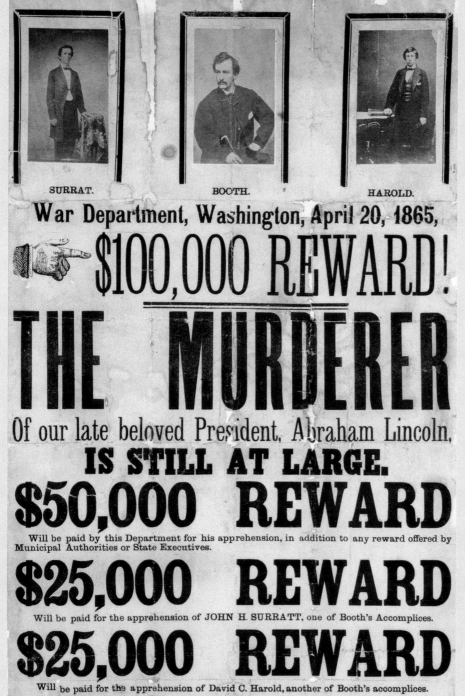

SURRAT.   BOOTH.   HAROLD.

War Department, Washington, April 20, 1865,

$100,000 REWARD!

THE MURDERER

Of our late beloved President, Abraham Lincoln,

IS STILL AT LARGE.

$50,000 REWARD

Will be paid by this Department for his apprehension, in addition to any reward offered by Municipal Authorities or State Executives.

$25,000 REWARD

Will be paid for the apprehension of JOHN H. SURRATT, one of Booth's Accomplices.

$25,000 REWARD

Will be paid for the apprehension of David C. Harold, another of Booth's accomplices.

LIBERAL REWARDS will be paid for any information that shall conduce to the arrest of either of the above-named criminals, or their accomplices.

All persons harboring or secreting the said persons, or either of them, or aiding or assisting their concealment or escape, will be treated as accomplices in the murder of the President and the attempted assassination of the Secretary of State, and shall be subject to trial before a Military Commission and the punishment of DEATH.

Let the stain of innocent blood be removed from the land by the arrest and punishment of the murderers.

All good citizens are exhorted to aid public justice on this occasion. Every man should consider his own conscience charged with this solemn duty, and rest neither night nor day until it be accomplished.

EDWIN M. STANTON, Secretary of War.

DESCRIPTIONS.—BOOTH is Five Feet 7 or 8 inches high, slender build, high forehead, black hair, black eyes, and wears a heavy black moustache.

JOHN H. SURRAT is about 5 feet, 9 inches. Hair rather thin and dark; eyes rather light; no beard. Would weigh 145 or 150 pounds. Complexion rather pale and clear, with color in his cheeks. Wore light clothes of fine quality. Shoulders square; cheek bones rather prominent; chin narrow; ears projecting at the top; forehead rather low and square, but broad. Parts his hair on the right side; neck rather long. His lips are firmly set. A slim man.

DAVID C. HAROLD is five feet six inches high, hair dark, eyes dark, eyebrows rather heavy, full face, nose short, hand short and fleshy, feet small, instep high, round bodied, naturally quick and active, slightly closes his eyes when looking at a person.

NOTICE.—In addition to the above, State and other authorities have offered rewards amounting to almost one hundred thousand dollars, making an aggregate of about TWO HUNDRED THOUSAND DOLLARS.

A broadside, published at the request of Secretary of War Edwin Stanton, offered rewards for the apprehension of John Wilkes Booth and his accomplices and threatened death to anyone aiding and abetting the fugitives.

J. Wilkes Booth

Booth was such a popular actor in his prime that many Americans owned his carte-de-visite portrait. During the manhunt one irate citizen wrote on the back of his copy "Do recognize him some where, & kill him."

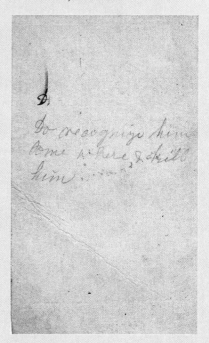

April 19, 1865

The Grief of African Americans

No group was more affected by the death of Abraham Lincoln than were African Americans across the country. For them Lincoln was "the Great Emancipator"—the beloved President who had issued the Emancipation Proclamation and then labored to secure passage of the Thirteenth Amendment. When he had entered Richmond in triumph just two weeks before he died, he found that black people had flooded onto the streets to welcome him. "The colored population was wild with enthusiasm," reported T. Morris Chester in the *Philadelphia Press*. African Americans recognized Lincoln's basic respect for them. When an old man approached the President and solemnly bowed, Lincoln stopped and bowed to the man in return. Witnessed by a reporter from the *Atlantic Monthly*, "it was a bow which upset forms, laws, customs, and ceremonies of centuries."

On the morning of April 15, as church bells tolled, Secretary of the Navy Gideon Welles saw in front of the White House a crowd of "several hundred colored people, mostly women and children, weeping and wailing their loss." They remained there all day in the rain and cold, observed Welles. "They seemed not to know what was to be their fate since their great benefactor was dead, and their helpless grief affected me more than almost anything else. . . . There were no truer mourners, when all were sad."

"We mourn for the loss of our great and good President," wrote a black soldier from New York, Edgar Dinsmore, to his fiancée. "Humanity has lost a firm advocate, our race its Patron Saint, and the good of all the world a fitting object to emulate. The name of Abraham Lincoln will ever be cherished in our hearts and none will more delight to lisp his name in reverence than the future generations of our people."

When Lincoln entered Richmond just two weeks before he died, "the colored population was wild with enthusiasm," reported T. Morris Chester in the *Philadelphia Press*. "Old men thanked God in a very boisterous manner and old women shouted upon the pavement as high as they had ever done at a religious revival. . . . One enthusiastic old negro woman exclaimed, 'I know that I am free, for I have seen Father Abraham and felt him.'" Accompanying Lincoln on April 4 was his young son Tad, whose twelfth birthday was that same day.

All over the country it was the same. In Vicksburg, Mississippi, a large crowd of former slaves gathered to honor Lincoln's memory, assembling in front of a store window that displayed a large photograph of Abraham Lincoln. A black correspondent wrote, "The grandeur was beyond description. The colored citizens turned out in full force and were well-received. . . . We can only look on in breathless silence and think of a great change."

In New Orleans ten thousand blacks held a mass meeting on April 22, marching through the city to a central gathering point where they pledged to wear mourning bands for the next thirty days in honor of Abraham Lincoln. "In giving us our liberty, he lost his life," summed up the city's African American newspaper the *Black Republican*.

On Hilton Head, South Carolina, a group of former slaves, freed in 1861 by the Union Army, gathered to honor the memory of Abraham Lincoln. And just weeks after his death a national movement took shape among leading blacks to raise up a memorial in Lincoln's name—the first effort by any group in America.

The Mourning of the Former Slaves

April 19, 1865

Four days after the assassination, the New York Times *reported on the impact Lincoln's death was having on African Americans.*

On this day of national mourning, when . . . a whole people is bowed in affliction, there will be no deeper mourning for the beloved and honored head of the Republic than in the cabins of the slaves. In lonely huts, where the news of the great crime has penetrated, in the villages of the emancipated from Virginia and the Carolinas, in the crowded haunts of the poor negroes within the great cities, there will be grief to-day, such as needs no funeral orations, or badges of gloom and mourning. The tears of the forgotten and outcast and oppressed slave, now redeemed to his manhood, will be the sincerest tears that fall on the grave of the President. From the cottages of the poor and the downtrodden will come his truest requiem. And hundreds of thousands of honest hearts, whom the world knows not of, will mourn this day the loss of their best friend and their emancipator. It has long been known to those dealing with the freedmen of the South, that in the eyes of that simple people, Mr. Lincoln was a kind of a prophet and divine leader. His Proclamation of Emancipation has echoed in every slave settlement of the rebel States. He was known to be their great friend, and was looked forward to as their deliverer. . . .

It is most fitting that for such a statesman the poor and the bondmen should most of all mourn, and that with the tears of the nation he led to a higher justice and unity, should fall also the tears of the subject race for whom he effected so much while living, and for whom, in part, he died.

A camp hand for General Grant's officers at City Point, Virginia, was among the former slaves stunned by the assassination.

In a scene replicated in many cities across the South, a group of former slaves gathered outside the First African Church in Richmond, Virginia.

31

Actress Ione Burke, in a role symbolizing the South

Little Mourning in the South

In Virginia, upon hearing the news of Lincoln's death, Robert E. Lee called Booth's act "deplorable." And General Joseph E. Johnston exclaimed it "the greatest possible calamity to the South." But many other Southerners rejoiced. As the war had deepened, Lincoln had been widely perceived as the dispenser of death, responsible for the murder of tens of thousands of Southern men. "We have seen his face over the coffins of our brothers and relatives and family," wrote Virginian John S. Wise shortly after the assassination—"in the flames of Richmond, in the disaster of Appomattox. . . . To us Lincoln was an inhuman monster." One clergyman, forced to give a service for Lincoln, simply announced the fact of the Northern President's death and then bade his people stand and sing the doxology—"Praise God from Whom all blessings flow."

In many places in the South, John Wilkes Booth was celebrated as "Our Brutus," the bold and patriotic slayer of the American Tyrant. A brisk trade began in Booth's photograph, and many homes erected shrines to the Lost Cause. Virginia's Edmund Ruffin, the proud secessionist who had fired one of the first shots at Fort Sumter, wrote admiringly in his diary one week after Lincoln's murder: "These remarkable & daring acts took place on the night of Good Friday & the anniversary of the first surrender of Fort Sumter." Ruffin had read the texts of some of the Easter sermons on Lincoln and was "utterly disgusted by the servile sycophancy, the man-worship, of the low-bred & vulgar & illiterate buffoon & the near approach to blasphemy of these holy flatterers." In Mississippi, Elizabeth Avery Meriwether had a similar reaction. "Is it insanity or pure mendacity to liken a man of this nature to the gentle and loving Nazarene?" she asked. "Did he once during the four years of the cruel war, utter or write one kind word to the people on whom he had brought such unspeakable misery?" Kate Stone of Texas, on hearing news of the assassination and of the simultaneous attack on William Seward, wrote in her diary, "All honor to J. Wilkes Booth, who has rid the world of a tyrant. . . . What torrents of blood Lincoln has caused to flow, and how Seward has aided him in his bloody work. I cannot be sorry for their fate. They deserve it. They have reaped their just reward."

In an anti-Lincoln cartoon, the President is portrayed as the beast-like tool of William Seward, tromping on American liberties in order to offer emancipation to Southern blacks. To South Carolina's Paul Hamilton Hayne, writing long after the assassination, Lincoln was a "gaudy, coarse, not overly clean" man whose idealization by "Yankee fancy . . . would be ludicrous, were it not disgusting."

"Weltering in His Own Life Blood"
Galveston News

April 28, 1865

In areas of the South under Union occupation, newspapers were expected to take part in the Lincoln reverie or else be subject to the replacement of their editors. But in places where there was little or no Union presence, local newspapers expressed their opinions openly. In late April the Galveston News *revealed the powerful hatred of Lincoln that was widespread in much of the South.*

Our country was bleeding and suffering from the war that [Lincoln's] party waged against it, and with deliberate malice, he gloated over our sufferings and visited them on our own heads. We were the "wicked man" and he, forsooth, was the instrument designed by providence for our punishment. On the 14th of April Abraham Lincoln was weltering in his own life blood, and the words sic semper tyrannis were ringing his death knell. In the plenitude of his power and arrogance he was struck down, and his soul ushered into eternity, with innumerable crimes to answer for. . . . It does look to us . . . as if an avenging Nemesis had brought swift and inevitable retribution upon a man stained with so many bloody crimes.

A dead Confederate soldier lies in the trenches at Petersburg in the weeks just before Lincoln's assassination.

"Righteous Retribution"
Caroline S. Jones

April 20, 1865

On April 20, 1865, Caroline Jones, whose husband had once been mayor of Savannah, wrote of her strong anti-Lincoln feelings in a letter to her mother-in-law, Mary Jones.

We are almost paralyzed here by the rapid succession of strange and melancholy incidents that have marked the last few weeks—the sudden collapse of our tried and trusted General Lee and his army, about which, sad as it is, I feel no mortification, for I know he did all that mortal man could do; then the rumors of peace, so different from the rapturous delight of a conquered peace we all looked forward to; then the righteous retribution upon Lincoln. One sweet drop among so much that is painful is that he at least cannot raise his howl of diabolical triumph over us.

At the end of the war Robert E. Lee sat for a portrait, taken in the basement of his house in Richmond.

Washington Says Goodbye

The day of Lincoln's Washington funeral, April 19, was a day of mourning. At the White House the darkened East Room was transformed into a great chapel, its chandeliers removed or wrapped in black cloth and its huge mirrors dressed in white. On an ornate platform sat the mahogany coffin, open at the top and strewn with roses and lilies. Inside lay the President dressed in the suit he had worn at his first inauguration, when he had pleaded with the nation not to go to war. The previous day members of the public had been allowed to pay their respects, the eerie silence of the house broken only by the sounds of sobbing. But with thousands more unable to get in, it had been decided that a second viewing would take place at the U.S. Capitol following the funeral.

Shortly after eleven that Wednesday morning the funeral ceremony began. Clergymen processed in first and took their places beside the catafalque, followed by government officials and special guests. Governors marched in, then assistant secretaries, Supreme Court members, and foreign dignitaries. On and on the procession continued, taking almost an hour until all were assembled. Relatives and friends of the slain President and his wife were seated in front of the delegations from Illinois and Kentucky. Tad, the young son of the Lincolns, had to be taken off, crying "as if his heart would break," noted one eyewitness. Mary Lincoln was nowhere to be seen. Deeply distressed, still reliving the assassination in her mind, she remained upstairs in a corner bedroom. Robert Lincoln, the oldest son, now represented the family—"a worthy son of a worthy father," observed presidential aide Edward Neil. At noon President Andrew Johnson was escorted in and the service began. Four clergymen presided—Dr. Hall of the Episcopal Church, Bishop Simpson of the Methodist, Dr. Gurley, the President's Presbyterian pastor, and Dr. Gray, chaplain of the United States Senate. The service lasted for two hours.

Black bunting seemed to be everywhere on the day of Lincoln's funeral. At the White House service, Edwin Stanton, who rarely ever spoke publicly, offered a brief eulogy. "There lies the most powerful ruler of men the world has ever seen," he said. "Why . . . ? Because he was the perfect ruler of himself."

At the U.S. Treasury mourners arrived early to claim seats on the portico and rooftop from which to view the funeral procession later that day.

At the end of the liturgy the coffin was prepared for a grand procession to Capitol Hill, where just six weeks earlier Lincoln had been sworn in for a second term and delivered his extraordinary address pledging "malice toward none." As the thousands of marchers took their places outside in carefully orchestrated ranks, a late-arriving regiment of African Americans unintentionally ended up heading the entire procession.

As the coffin made its way through the city, bells were tolled and guns fired. At the Capitol, where thousands had gathered on the grass and on the steps, Lincoln's coffin was carried up to the Great Rotunda, its walls draped in black and all its statues covered—except that of George Washington. Here it would remain for the next thirty-six hours, as tens of thousands of Americans came to pay their last respects.

Rank upon rank, the funeral procession moved up Pennsylvania Avenue toward Capitol Hill, pausing for special ceremonies along the way.

A derrick (left) was still in place next to the newly completed Senate building at the time of Lincoln's funeral. Washington D. C.'s hearse (above) looked very much like a decorated wagon. But with its side curtains lowered, and hitched up to six white horses, it was transformed into an ornate funeral car.

A Second Small Coffin

On the morning of April 21 a group of workmen drove out to Oak Ridge Cemetery in Georgetown and disinterred a body from its temporary vault. It belonged to William Wallace Lincoln, the son of Abraham and Mary, who had died three years earlier at the age of eleven.

The Lincolns' middle child had been named for his uncle William Wallace, the husband of Mary's much loved sister Frances. Conceived shortly after the death of the Lincolns' four-year-old Eddy in 1850, Willie had brought joy back into his parents' lives. "He was a very beautiful boy," bragged his mother in one of her letters, "with great amiability and cheerfulness of character." He was also the most "spiritual" of Mary's sons, she thought—"a most peculiarly religious child." Willie was also smart; by eight he was writing letters and regularly attending the theater with his parents. With Robert away at school and Tad still young, Willie shined in the eyes of adult observers. He had a "fearless and kindly frankness," noted journalist Nathaniel P. Willis, and his own unique "single heartedness."

Willie and his brother Tad were inseparable. In the White House they played games in the huge, mysterious attic, once creating a "snowstorm" out of a collection of historic calling cards they found there. They befriended Civil War Officer Elmer Ellsworth, attended rallies for his Zouave troops, and later were present at his funeral. They put on a circus production for the White House servants, broke in on cabinet meetings to barrage their father with questions, and at the end of a long day offered the busy President precious moments of relaxation and fun. And when Lincoln presented Willie with his own pony, the delighted boy rode it every day, even in winter. "Willie . . . was always the idolized child, of the household," Mary wrote. "So gentle, so meek. . . . We were having *so much bliss.*"

Then in February 1862 Willie became seriously ill. Diagnosed with "bilious fever," he probably had contracted typhoid from polluted drinking water. By mid-month his condition was extremely dangerous, and at five P.M. on February 20, with his family beside him, eleven-year-old Willie died. Mary was devastated, and refused ever again to enter the boy's room, seeing his death as a punishment for her own "worldliness." Lincoln, who came to interpret the death as part of his share in the sufferings of the Civil War, spent part of every Thursday in the boy's room, communing with his lost son. Sometimes he asked to be taken down to Georgetown Cemetery to stand in proximity to his son's remains. Twice he had the boy disinterred so he could gaze on him. And though his immense responsibilities made it impossible for him to overindulge his sadness, the loss of Willie was never far from his mind. On February 10, 1864, when a fire broke out in the White House stables, the President raced outdoors to the burning barn to try to make his way through the flames to save Willie's pony. Eventually he had had to be pulled away.

Now on April 21, 1865, with the train bearing Lincoln's coffin about to pull away from Washington station, nearby sat Willie's much smaller casket. The two Lincolns would once again be together—reunited in death for the long journey home to Illinois.

William Wallace Lincoln, as he looked two years before he died at the White House

In Georgetown, Willie's coffin was held for three years in the Carroll family tomb. At least twice Lincoln requested that the crypt be opened so he could gaze upon his little son. In April Willie's coffin was placed next to Lincoln's to be taken to Illinois for burial.

The Journey Home

The funeral train set out April 21 on a twelve-day journey to Springfield—following almost the reverse route of Lincoln's inaugural trip to Washington four years earlier, except with two cities eliminated and Chicago added. The entire affair was under Edwin Stanton's authority and operated under military discipline. A corps of officers and an Honor Guard amounting to thirty-five men had been assigned to accompany the coffin all the way to Springfield. In addition, a large group of civilians representing the various states and territories had been invited to take part in the funeral company. A special embalmer and an undertaker were also included in order to attend to any problems that might arise. And in each state special dignitaries would join the official party and ride for a portion of the journey.

In all, major stops had been planned for ten American cities to allow for local observances and public viewing. In Philadelphia these ceremonies took place at Independence Hall, where Lincoln's coffin was placed beside the Liberty Bell, which had been draped in black ribbon and adorned with flowers. Lincoln had come to this city in 1861 to pay homage to the great document that was at the heart of his and the nation's creed. "It was something in the Declaration of Independence," he had said, "giving liberty, not only to the people of this country, but hope to the world for all future time . . . that all should have an equal chance." If the nation could not be saved except by giving up this idea, Lincoln had said, then he "would rather be assassinated on this spot."

J. F. Drigg

Driggs

John Fletcher Driggs, a Michigan member of the House of Representatives, was part of the congressional committee charged with accompanying the Lincoln train.

The funeral train was met by crowds as it arrived in Philadelphia (right). Different engines were used to pull the train westward, some adorned with flags, others with Lincoln's photograph.

Each city provided an elaborate hearse. In Philadelphia it slowly made its way along a crowded Broad Street.

Services in the City of Brotherly Love
John Carroll Power

April 21, 1865

John Carroll Power rode the funeral train and later became custodian of Lincoln's tomb.

It was eight o'clock when the funeral car arrived at the southern entrance to Independence Square, on Walnut Street. The Union League Association was stationed in the square, and when the procession arrived at the entrance, the Association took charge of the sacred dust, and conveyed it into Independence Hall, marching with uncovered heads to the sound of a dirge performed by a band—stationed in the observatory over the Hall—the booming of cannon in the distance, and the tolling of bells throughout the city. The body was laid on a platform in the centre of the Hall, with feet to the north, bringing the head very close to the pedestal on which the old Independence bell stands....

Honor guards took turns sitting beside Lincoln's coffin during the trip west.

Evergreens and flowers of rare fragrance and beauty were placed around the coffin. At the head were boquets, and at the feet burning tapers....

An old colored woman managed to find her way into the Hall, and approached the Committee of Arrangements with a rudely constructed wreath in her hand, and with tears in her eyes requested that it might be placed on the coffin. When her request was granted, her countenance beamed with an expression of satisfaction. The wreath bore the inscription: "The nation mourns his loss. He still lives in the hearts of the people."

A Poignant Stop in New York City

On April 24 Lincoln's funeral car was brought by ferry to New York City, where nearly three quarters of a million people witnessed the mighty procession. As the casket was pulled down Broadway to City Hall, among the witnesses was six-and-a-half-year-old Theodore Roosevelt, leaning out of a window to see the event that would affect him for the rest of his life. At City Hall, Lincoln's casket was opened to public view, and over the next day 120,000 people gazed into Lincoln's face. When a photographer took pictures of Lincoln lying in state, an irate Edwin Stanton ordered the negatives destroyed—but not before keeping a single small print that later came into the possession of John G. Nicolay's papers, where it remained unknown to the public for generations. It was the only time Lincoln was photographed in death.

Theodore Roosevelt was just six and a half when he gazed out his window to watch Lincoln's funeral procession in New York.

The New York procession made its way to City Hall (left), where Lincoln's body lay in state for public viewing. David R. Locke said that the President's face "had the expression of absolute content, of relief, of throwing off a burden such as few men have been called upon to bear." On the following afternoon 85,000 people joined the procession (above) as it headed back up Broadway.

When Edwin Stanton learned that New York cameraman Jeremiah Gurney had photographed Abraham Lincoln lying in his coffin at City Hall, he was furious. Standing guard in the picture are Admiral Charles H. Davis and General Edward D. Townsend, representing the U.S. Navy and Army.

In his weekly sermon on April 23, the nation's preeminent preacher, Henry Ward Beecher, spoke of the majestic spirit of Lincoln's epic journey home.

And now the martyr is moving in triumphal march, mightier than when alive. The nation rises up at his coming. Cities and States are his pall-bearers, and cannon beat the hours with solemn procession. Dead ! dead ! dead ! he yet speaketh ! Is Washington dead? . . . Is David dead? Now, disenthralled of flesh, and risen to the unobstructed sphere where passion never comes, he begins his illimitable work. His life is grafted upon the Infinite, and will be fruitful now as no earthly life can be.

Four years ago, O Illinois, we took him from your midst, an untried man from among the people. Behold, we return him a mighty conqueror. Not thine, but the nation's; not ours, but the world's! Give him place, ye prairies! In the midst of this great continent, his dust shall rest a sacred treasure to millions who shall pilgrim to that shrine, to kindle anew their zeal and patriotism. Ye winds that move over the mighty spaces of the West, chant his requiem! Ye people, behold a martyr, whose blood as articulate words, pleads for fidelity, for law, for liberty!

And so the solemn march continued, with Americans rising up in city after city to pay homage to their great martyr—in Baltimore, Harrisburg, Philadelphia, New York, Albany, Buffalo, Cleveland, Columbus, Indianapolis, and Chicago. Echoing ancient rites for kings and pharaohs, it was one of the grandest funeral spectacles in recorded history. In between the major cities mourners and the just-plain-curious lined the tracks in great numbers to view the train as it lumbered by almost in slow motion—traveling at just five miles an hour. There was something about the slow speed of the train that added to its dreamlike dignity and that was calming to the frayed nerves of the nation. In small town after small town great crowds assembled as bells tolled, salutes were fired, and ordinary persons stood by with hats in hand and tears streaming.

Local citizens posed with the engine that pulled Lincoln through Ohio (above), and with the hearse that awaited him in Cleveland.

The Capture of John Wilkes Booth

In the midst of the funeral journey to Illinois came dramatic news that Lincoln's assassin had been apprehended. Following his attack on the President on April 14, John Wilkes Booth had exited Ford's Theatre onto a rear alley, where a family friend, Edman Spangler, had placed a horse at the waiting. He then escaped from Washington across the Navy Yard Bridge, where an unsuspecting guard let him pass despite the curfew. Close behind, also on horseback, rode his co-conspirator Davie Herold, who, after giving his name as Smith, was also permitted to cross. Reunited, the two made their way to the boardinghouse of a friend, Mary Surratt, where they picked up a rifle, ammunition, and some whiskey. By this point Booth's left ankle, broken during his leap from the presidential box at Ford's Theatre, was in severe pain, and the pair headed straight to the house of Dr. Samuel Mudd for medical attention. Mudd would later claim not to have recognized the fugitive, despite the fact that he had met with him at least three times since November, and despite the fact that the words "J. Wilkes" were printed clearly inside the boot he now removed. Mudd splinted the fracture and allowed the fugitive to recuperate at his place for most of a day. Then Booth and Herold began a harrowing attempt to evade capture. For six days and nights they hid out in a Maryland woods with the help of Confederate sympathizers Samuel Cox and Thomas Jones. At one point, in order to quiet the horses, Davie Herold led them deep into a bog, shot them, and let them sink out of sight.

On the night of April 22, using a boat and compass provided by Jones, the conspirators crossed the Potomac River into Virginia. Four days later, on the day of Lincoln's New York City funeral, they were asleep in a tobacco barn at Garrett's farm in Bowling Green when agents with the U.S. Cavalry finally caught up with them. At his mentor's insistence, Herold surrendered immediately; Booth declared he would resist until the end. One of the officers then set fire to the barn and, with the dark night illumined by the roaring flames, Sergeant Boston Corbett was able to get a bead on his target through a slat in the barn wall. According to Corbett, he then without warning shot Booth through the neck. Lincoln's assassin died three hours later. The manhunt had lasted eleven days.

An artist added a pistol and dagger to a photograph of Booth and depicted a devil whispering in his ear as he stood outside the presidential box at Ford's Theatre.

"Baptist Alley" behind Ford's Theatre, along which Booth made his escape

Mary Surratt's boardinghouse in Washington (left) was where the conspirators often met before the assassination. It was in Dr. Mudd's house (center) that Booth's broken ankle was treated. And the Garrett farm (one of its buildings shown at right) was where Booth died. Below is an artist's rendition of the capture and shooting of John Wilkes Booth inside a burning tobacco barn near Port Royal, Virginia.

Booth's Last Hours
George Alfred Townsend

April 28, 1865

After he was shot through the neck, Booth lingered on for a few hours. As he lay dying, the soldiers who had captured him tried to make him comfortable. George Townsend's article appeared two days later in the New York World *and was the first detailed report of the scene. It was based on an extensive interview with Lafayette C. Baker, chief of the Secret Service, and showed Townsend's tendency to romanticize John Wilkes Booth.*

A mattress was brought down, on which they placed him and propped his head, and gave him water and brandy. The women of the household . . . were nervous, but prompt to do the dying man all kindnesses, although waived sternly back by the detectives. They dipped a rag in brandy and water, and this being put between Booth's teeth he sucked it greedily. When he was able to articulate again, he muttered to Mr. [Luther B.] Baker the same words, with an addenda. "Tell mother I died for my country. I thought I did for the best." Baker repeated this, saying at the same time "Booth, do I repeat it correctly." Booth nodded his head. Twice he was heard to say, "kill me, kill me." His lips often moved but could complete no appreciable sound. . . .

Now and then, his heart would cease to throb, and his pulses would be as cold as a dead man's. Directly life would begin anew, the face would flush up effulgently, the eyes open and brighten, and soon relapsing, stillness re-asserted, would again be dispossessed by the same magnificent triumph of man over mortality. Finally the fussy little doctor arrived, in time to be useless. He probed the wound to see if the ball were not in it, and shook his head sagely, and talked learnedly. Just at his coming Booth had asked to have his hands raised and shown him. They were so paralyzed that he did not know their location. When they were displayed he muttered, with a sad lethargy, "Useless, useless." These were the last words he ever uttered.

The Murderer's Burial

The USS *Montauk* was tied up alongside the USS *Miantonomah* in Washington.

In the days leading up to Booth's capture, eight suspected co-conspirators had been rounded up and imprisoned: on April 17, Edman Spangler, the Ford's Theatre employee thought to have helped in Booth's escape; later that same day Michael O'Laughlin and Samuel Arnold, both part of Booth's earlier kidnapping plot; and on that same night the boardinghouse owner Mary Surratt, along with Lewis Powell (alias Payne), who had attacked William Seward. George Atzerodt, a former ferry man for Confederate spies, was captured on April 20, and Dr. Samuel Mudd was picked up on the 24th. Most of the men were taken aboard the ironclad *Saugus*, which at Stanton's request had been anchored in the Anacostia River off the Navy Yard, in an effort to isolate the prisoners from a prying public.

On April 26, at Garrett's farm, Booth's body was sewn up in a saddle blanket and taken by horse and wagon to Belle Plain, Virginia, where the steamship *Ide* was hailed and then took them to Washington. That evening Herold and Booth were turned over to the safekeeping of Lafayette C. Baker, whom Stanton had placed in overall charge, warning him to let no unauthorized person see or touch the assassin, as "every hair of his head would be a valued relic to the sympathizers of the South." In the middle of the night Davie Herold and the remains of John Wilkes Booth were transferred to the ironside *Montauk*, anchored not far from the *Saugus*.

On the morning of the 27th, on the open deck of the *Montauk*, Booth's body was laid out on a carpenter's bench and subjected to identification and autopsy. Seven witnesses who had known the actor, including his former doctor, John Frederick May, attested that the body belonged to John Wilkes Booth. The photographer Alexander Gardner, who had been requested to come on board, along with his assistant Timothy O'Sullivan, now took a single exposure of the Booth autopsy. (A print was later given to Lafayette Baker, but it has never surfaced.) Gardner stayed on for the rest of the day and photographed all the prisoners on both ships. His photographs were soon published as engravings in the weekly news magazines.

Booth's body was carefully guarded the rest of the day. Once, however, after Baker had left the deck for a time, he returned to find a group of strangers standing around the corpse, with a woman "of secession proclivities" in the process of cutting a lock of hair from its head. Baker seized the illegal relic and banished the group, but clearly there was mounting interest in what was going on aboard the *Montauk*.

At midnight, in an effort to fool the public, Baker rowed the assassin's body off into the foggy river, to give the impression of a secret burial at sea. Instead, he circled back and took his cargo to shore, where Booth was then buried in an unmarked grave on the grounds of the Washington Arsenal outside the Old Penitentiary Building.

Boston Corbett (right) was given credit for shooting Booth inside the burning barn. On board the *Montauk* Booth's autopsy was photographed. Although the picture was used to make an illustration in *Harper's Weekly* (left), the photograph then disappeared, probably destroyed at the order of Edwin Stanton.

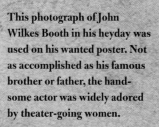

This photograph of John Wilkes Booth in his heyday was used on his wanted poster. Not as accomplished as his famous brother or father, the handsome actor was widely adored by theater-going women.

The Unknown Grave
George Alfred Townsend

April 28, 1865

The intense secrecy surrounding the autopsy and burial of John Wilkes Booth was carried out at least in part to try to foil any attempt to turn the assassin into a hero. George Townsend and the New York World, either through ignorance or complicity, misled the public in its reporting about Booth's burial.

Yesterday the Secretary of War, without instructions of any kind, committed to Colonel Lafayette C. Baker, of the secret service, the stark corpse of J. Wilkes Booth. The secret service never fulfilled its volition more secretively. "What have you done with the body?" said I to Baker. "That is known" he answered, "to only one man living besides myself. It is gone. I will not tell you where. The only man who knows is sworn to silence. Never till the great trumpeter comes shall the grave of Booth be discovered." And this is true. Last night, the 27th of April, a small row boat received the carcass of the murderer; two men were in it; they carried the body off into the darkness, and out of that darkness it will never return.

The military supplied the press with this deliberately misleading sketch illustrating how Booth's body had supposedly been disposed.

A Son Mourns His Father

At the White House Robert Lincoln was relieved when he received the news of Booth's capture. He had not accompanied his father's funeral train, staying in Washington to help his grieving mother, writing the many letters she could not write and coping with the daily problems that invariably arose. It was he who implored President Andrew Johnson to allow his mother more time before she had to vacate the White House. "In our day of sorrow and adversity," Mary later wrote, Robert proved himself "a youth of great nobleness."

Privately Robert was wracked with remorse. His father had asked him to come to the theater with them, but Robert had opted to stay at home with his friend John Hay. What if he had chosen differently? he now asked himself. Would he have been able to thwart the assassination—to fight off the assailant and prevent the murder of his father?

Robert's relationship with his larger-than-life father had been complex since the beginning. Lincoln once described his first-born son as "'short and low' and I expect always will be." "I sometimes fear he is one of the little rare-ripe sort, that are smarter at five than ever after." With Lincoln often absent during Robert's childhood, the boy grew up distant and reserved. Neither of his parents ever seemed quite pleased enough with him. He was never "great" in his father's estimate, only "very well, considering"; never "excellent" in his mother's eyes, only "much improved." This parental ambivalence haunted Robert and helped make him the most aloof of the Lincoln children.

During Lincoln's presidency Robert yearned for his father's attention, yet received "scarcely even . . . ten minutes [of] quiet talk" with him. The little advice he got from him was usually negative. When Robert told his father of his decision to enter law school, his response was "If you do, you should learn more than I ever did but you will never have so good a time." "Any great intimacy between us was impossible," Robert later wrote.

In part to win his father's admiration, in February 1865 Robert ignored his mother's fierce objections and with Lincoln's assistance entered the army under Ulysses S. Grant with the rank of captain. Appearing in uniform at the White House, Robert was introduced by his father to a colleague, the President's arm around his son's shoulders. An eyewitness that day said he could never forget "the look of fatherly pride Mr. Lincoln gave his son."

Now in late April, as he attended to his duties, Robert was consumed by thoughts of what might have been different. "In all my plans for the future," he wrote one of his Harvard professors thirteen days after the assassination, "the chief object I had in view was the approbation of my father. And now that he is gone, and in such a way, I feel utterly without spirit or courage. I know that such a feeling is wrong, and that it is my duty to overcome it. I trust for the sake of my Mother and little brother that I will be able to do so."

Robert Lincoln had always wanted to be closer to his famous father. "During my childhood and early youth he was almost constantly away from home," he wrote. And during his presidency "I scarcely even had ten minutes . . . quiet talk with him."

April 27, 1865

Sealing Lincoln's Papers

Supreme Court Justice David Davis as he looked in 1865

One of Robert Lincoln's first acts after the assassination had been to telegraph his father's old friend David Davis, asking him to come immediately to Washington from Chicago, where he was on circuit duty. Judge Davis, now a justice on the Supreme Court, had long thought well of Lincoln's oldest son, who was now reaching out to him "as to a second father."

He arrived in Washington in time for Lincoln's funeral and stayed on to take charge of the family's affairs. It was soon clear that his top priority was Lincoln's papers and making sure they were gathered up for immediate removal from the White House. Robert had become convinced that these papers contained items that could be "damaging to men now living" and that it was essential they be gotten under lock and key. Looters had already started breaking into the President-less mansion and walking off with souvenirs. And on top of this Judge Davis suspected unnamed individuals of wanting to walk off with papers. "My object in having the papers removed," Davis later wrote, "was principally to get them fr[om] Washington. . . . I did not want some persons to get hold of them."

Abraham Lincoln had always been rather casual about his papers. During his Springfield days he kept his correspondence and incoming letters in desk drawers at his home, or scattered about his law office—even in the lining of a favorite hat. One pile of papers on his office floor had his handwritten note on it: "If you can't find it anywhere else, look here." On his trip east in 1861 to assume the presidency, Lincoln had packed his important papers—including his draft of the inaugural address—in a "gripsack" that he asked his oldest son to carry. When Robert misplaced it along the way, handing it over, he thought, to "a waiter—or somebody," his father had one of his rare fits of temper. But the bag containing what Lincoln called his "certificate of moral character" was recovered, much to Robert's relief.

In the White House, letters poured in from the general public, and Lincoln's correspondence ballooned. While his private secretaries, John G. Nicolay and John Hay, tended to the routine letter opening and answering, Lincoln wrote numerous letters each day. He kept in regular written touch with his cabinet members and generals; wrote out his own speeches; answered letters; crafted state documents; jotted down thoughts; and worked out complex political problems on paper. All in all, his papers multiplied into the tens of thousands, stored mostly in his office and private quarters.

In Lincoln's day presidential papers belonged to the occupant of the office. Past presidents had taken their public papers with them, and there were as yet no formal presidential libraries. So after the assassination Robert laid claim to them. Here was an essential ingredient for understanding the real Lincoln, and Robert wanted to control that record. At the order of David Davis, Nicolay and Hay were soon at work gathering up and boxing the voluminous materials. The cartons were sealed under the authority of Edwin Stanton and by April 27 had been shipped off to Davis's home in Illinois. "These boxes were sent . . . under guard . . . to my residence," Davis later explained to a government official. "They are sealed & when they will be opened and examined has not yet been determined."

Security at the White House was lax after Lincoln's funeral and looting became a serious problem.

As a young lawyer Lincoln had visited Judge David Davis's house in Bloomington, Illinois. In late April 1865 his presidential papers were sent here.

A Journalist on Lincoln's Papers
Noah Brooks

May 17, 1865

Noah Brooks was the Washington correspondent for the Sacramento Daily Union *and Mary Lincoln's favorite reporter. In an article written during this period, he described the President's system for organizing his letters.*

The private papers of the late President have been sealed up by Robert Lincoln, the oldest son of the President, and he intends to publish them after a considerable lapse of time shall have passed—not before three or four years. Then he will merely spread before the world the letters of his father, arranged in some order, with brief annotations, leaving the material to future historians or biographers to arrange at their own convenience. The correspondence which the President kept in his own hands was not large, comparatively speaking, the whole accumulation of four years being in a set of pigeonholes and locked up in his room in a case about three-by-five feet in dimension. The pigeonholes were lettered in his own hand, alphabetically, different compartments being allotted to a few such prominent men as McClellan, Grant, "Father Blair," Horace Greeley, and Halleck. One pigeonhole was lettered "Weed and Wood," being for Thurlow and Fernando of that name. Lincoln's name will never suffer from the publication of these letters and answers filed away together. But the friends of a few men who now fill a large space in public esteem will have occasion to blush when they know some things concerning their favorites.

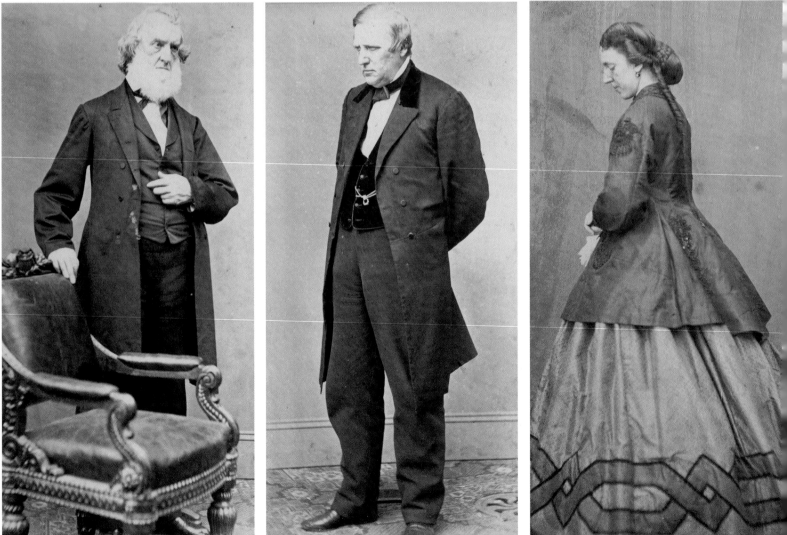

Willing to Pose in Their Grief

Hardly had the funeral train left Washington than a flurry of activity commenced in town around an ambitious new project—an illustrated depiction of Lincoln's last hours that eventually would involve most of the President's official family. On April 15 the Boston-based printer John Bachelder had rushed to Washington "determined to collect such materials as should be necessary for an historical picture commemorating that sad scene." He knew from the papers that over the course of the night almost four dozen people had been allowed into the room where Lincoln lay dying. Though the actual room was tiny and never held more than a dozen or so people at a time, Bachelder wanted to show forty-six persons gathered simultaneously around the President's bed. Though he planned to use a leading artist to paint the scene, he himself designed the sketch for it. Then he began to contact or visit all those known to have been in the room and to convince them to pose for photographs for the artist. Astonishingly, many said yes, some right away, and others a bit later. They included Gideon Welles, Joseph Barnes, John P. Usher, President Johnson, Clara Harris, Edwin Stanton, and, amazingly, Robert Lincoln. Each was brought to the studio of Mathew B. Brady and photographed in the posture that Bachelder had planned in his original sketch. Though the poses were artificial, the emotions were very real. Here before Brady's camera stood Gideon Welles, who just days earlier "could not restrain tears" following Lincoln's murder. Here stood Clara Harris, who had sat behind the President with her fiancé at Ford's Theatre, and whose face, hands, and dress had been drenched with blood. "That terrible Friday night . . . [was] like some dreadful vision," she recalled. Most moving of all, here was Robert Lincoln. With head bowed, still in shock, and clutching a handkerchief to his chest, he seemed to ponder a future without his father.

Artist Alonzo Chappel used posed photographs as models for his large canvas of the death bed scene (above, left). John Bachelder planned to sell engravings of the painting, and Robert Lincoln was among those who signed up for a $100 "artist's proof." To the left, striking their poses, are Gideon Welles, John P. Usher, and Clara Harris.

Robert Lincoln posed for Mathew Brady's cameraman just weeks after the assassination, attempting to recapture how he had stood by his father's deathbed.

Mary Lincoln's veto of an in-town burial site—what was known as the Mather property—was not received well in Springfield. As is evident in this letter from Illinois lawyer Henry Bromwell, who visited Springfield just five days before Lincoln's funeral, the controversy over the burial had become the talk of the town.

Henry P. H. Bromwell

I got here on Thursday night and have been very well. The people are all very busy making preparations for the funeral on Thursday the 4th.

They are draping the State House inside and out, and the big columns are covered with evergreens from bottom to top. They sent to Michigan for pines, and they have wagon loads of black goods. The coffin will be placed on a Catafalque in the Rep. Hall, with a canopy of Broadcloth supported on six pillars 12 feet high covered with crape and white rosettes.

The people have bought the Mather grounds in the heart of the city six acres for a burial place. It is a beautiful grove of native trees. They got it for $5300.00 and have a vault nearly finished, but last night Mrs. Lincoln telegraphed that she would not let him be buried there. The people are in a rage about it and all the hard stories that ever were told about her are told over again. She has no friends here.

Many in the East wanted Lincoln to be buried in Washington, in the large crypt beneath the Capitol Rotunda originally designed for George Washington but never occupied. But shortly before his death Lincoln had told his wife, "When I die lay me in some quiet place," and Mary was determined to carry out his wishes. She was also adamant that she and her children would one day be buried alongside him. Her preference was for a lakeside burial in Chicago, and if not that, then in the new Oak Ridge Cemetery in Springfield, Illinois.

In Springfield, however, friends and associates had their own ideas. Meeting at the state capitol on the very day of Lincoln's death, the City Council had resolved that Lincoln's body must reside in his hometown. But there was one significant difference between their wishes and those of Mary: she wanted her husband to rest in a quiet place; they wanted him in the center of their city.

The city fathers were already inclined to discount the First Lady's wishes. In Springfield she had been well known for her ferocious temper and had become dreaded by certain local merchants. She was remembered for returning open perfume bottles, accusing icemen of cheating her, being too tough on domestic servants, and alienating friends. In 1860 David Davis had written home, "The people of Springfield do not love Lincoln's wife, as they do him."

With Mary beset with grief and seemingly out of the picture, the town fathers moved ahead with their plan, purchasing a large property in the city center and erecting a temporary vault there at city expense. When word of this reached Mary at the White House, with the funeral train still en route, Robert fired off a telegram to Illinois governor Richard Oglesby warning the committee not to oppose his mother's wishes. "Both the temporary and final interment must take place in Oakridge Cemetery," he insisted. In response, the committee made the requested arrangements but continued to work on the city site, hoping for an eventual in-town burial. It became a struggle over Lincoln's mythic image and who controlled it— would he be remembered alone, in glorious splendor, or more humbly, in a quiet cemetery lying beside his wife and children? As it turned out, Mary Lincoln would have much to say about this matter.

Mary Lincoln considered having her husband buried here in the crypt beneath the Capitol Rotunda originally meant for George Washington.

May 4, 1865

Illinois Welcomes Lincoln Home

On May 1 the funeral train reached Illinois, where Lincoln received a special welcome. Tens of thousands had gathered for an outdoor ceremony at Park Place in Chicago, where a gigantic funeral arch had been erected. At the ceremonies here thirty-six high school girls in white dresses each deposited a garland on the coffin as they walked by it. Then a crowd of 150,000 accompanied the coffin to the Court House rotunda, where a great banner read "Illinois clasps to her bosom her slain but glorified son." Over the next two days half a million people paid tribute; Republicans and Democrats put aside political differences in honor of their martyred fellow citizen. And then the final leg of the journey began. As Lincoln's funeral train headed southwest toward Springfield, people gathered along the railroad line to participate in any way they could. Flags and handmade signs were everywhere. "He saved our country and freed a race," said one; another read simply, "Come Home." For mile after mile as the train moved through the night, its tracks were lighted by a pathway of hand-held torches. In the town of Joliet a great archway had been built over the tracks; in the town of Lincoln, named after the one-term congressman well before he had become nationally famous, a local choir of women sang out a requiem as the train passed.

Thirty-six high school girls dressed in white stood next to Lincoln's coffin at the Chicago funeral procession.

Citizens streamed out of Chicago's courthouse after viewing Lincoln's body.

Lincoln's favorite horse, Old Bob, attended by longtime servant and friend Henry Brown, posed in front of the Lincolns' Springfield home at Eighth and Jackson Streets. Old Bob went on to lead the funeral procession to the cemetery.

The funeral train pulled into Springfield on Wednesday, May 3, at nine A.M. Altogether it had covered 1,662 miles, and kept to a near perfect schedule. After following a published timetable for nearly two weeks, it arrived in Lincoln's hometown just one hour late. The casket was now taken by hearse from the railroad depot to the statehouse where it was laid out in House of Representatives Hall, where Lincoln had delivered his pivotal "House Divided" speech. Over the next twenty-four hours the public was permitted entrance—allowed to climb the stairs to the second floor, file quietly in front of the open coffin, and then make their way downstairs and out the back. All day and night long visitors continued to come, paying their silent respects to the man many remembered personally.

At ten in the morning on Thursday, May 4, Lincoln's coffin was closed. Robert Lincoln had now arrived—at the last minute he had hurried west to represent the family at the funeral. In the procession old friends of the President, including Stephen T. Logan, Jesse K. Dubois, and John Todd Stuart, served as honorary pallbearers alongside the hearse. Directly behind, Henry Brown, a black clergyman who had once worked for the Lincolns, led Lincoln's horse Old Bob. Mourners followed in a great loop from the State House, past Lincoln's home, and out the two miles to Oak Ridge Cemetery. Here, following another long ceremony, Lincoln's body, along with Willie's, was placed in the public receiving vault. Mary intended to come out later and choose the best spot for the family tomb.

During the lead-up to Lincoln's funeral, visitors arrived at the Lincoln home at the rate of 200 every five minutes. Mrs. Tilton, the house's tenant, allowed many of them to enter and walk through the rooms where Lincoln had spent his happiest days. This delegation included Lincoln's friend Schulyer Colfax, the Speaker of the House, who posed in front of the right-hand window. The wooden ladder on the ground had been used for putting up decorations.

Every building in Springfield was decorated in honor of Lincoln, including his now famous law office (right). At the Lincoln house (above) a carpenter, Edmond Beall, had been employed to put up the bunting. "I was let down the roof with a rope," he later recalled. "I . . . put the droopers on the eaves of the house and . . . rosettes about eight feet apart."

May 2, 1865

President Andrew Johnson

PRESIDENTIAL PROCLAMATION:

Whereas, It appears, from the evidence in the Bureau of Military Justice, that the atrocious murder of the late President, Abraham Lincoln, and the attempted assassination of the Hon. W. H. Seward, Secretary of State, were incited, concerted, and procured by and between Jefferson Davis, late of Richmond, Va., . . . and other rebels and traitors against the Government of the United States, harbored in Canada;

Now, therefore, to the end that justice may be done, I, Andrew Johnson, President of the United States, do offer and promise for the arrest of said persons or either of them, within the limits of the United States, so that they can be brought to trial, the following rewards: One hundred thousand dollars for the arrest of Jefferson Davis. . . . The provost marshal general of the United States is directed to cause the descriptions of said persons, with notice of the above rewards, to be published.

May 10, 1865

The Capture of Jefferson Davis

Even though her husband's funeral was now over, Mary Lincoln remained in the White House. President Johnson had allowed her extra time in the mansion, but had never written her a note of condolence, or contacted her in any way. And though she was cordial in her communications to the new President, asking for favors such as the keeping on of White House doorkeeper Thomas Pendel and for patronage involving other friends, secretly she despised him. She had been mortified by his drunkenness at the inaugural ceremonies in March and considered him a dangerous "demagogue." And she had recently learned a disturbing fact from Edwin Stanton—that on the very day of the assassination John Wilkes Booth had left a calling card for Johnson at the Kirkwood House, saying, "Don't want to disturb you. Are you at home?" Susceptible to seeing conspiracy plots around her, she suspected that Johnson might have been involved in the assassination.

Along with others, including Stanton, Mary believed that the assassination was part of a vast Confederate conspiracy, spearheaded by President Jefferson Davis, who was still at large. To avoid capture, Davis and the remnants of his government had been on the move for a month, ever since the fall of Richmond, traveling on horseback, often covering twelve miles a day. But Davis was no part of the Booth conspiracy, although his government may have encouraged Booth's original plan to kidnap Lincoln and ransom him for Confederate prisoners of war. When Davis heard news of the assassination he had been genuinely dismayed. "Certainly I have no special regard for Mr. Lincoln," he had said. "But there are a great many men of whose end I would rather hear than his. I fear it will be disastrous for our people and I regret it." (When his wife Varina heard the news, she had burst into tears, in part out of

Jefferson Davis, the former President of the Confederacy

Thomas Nast's mocking cartoon depicted Davis disguised in women's clothing.

"sorrow for the family of Mr. Lincoln.") Davis had other reasons for regret as well. He had been devastated on April 9 when Robert E. Lee had surrendered to Ulysses S. Grant at Appomattox Courthouse. And he was enraged when General Joseph Johnston surrendered to William Tecumseh Sherman on April 17. That left intact just the western portion of his army, and unwilling to give up the Confederate cause, Davis saw them as his last hope. There were rumors in the North that he was planning to flee to Texas to try to reestablish the Confederacy there.

On May 2, upon pressure from Stanton, President Johnson issued a proclamation charging Jefferson Davis with complicity in the assassination and offering a $100,000 reward for his capture. A manhunt led to Irwinsville, Georgia. There, in the early hours of May 10, Davis made his last stand. He donned a raincoat, wrapped one of his wife's shawls around his head and shoulders, and tried to escape into a thick woods, along with his wife and children and some loyal others. He was captured by the Fourth Michigan Cavalry and mocked for having been caught in "women's clothing." News of Davis's apprehension was greeted with enthusiasm in Washington, where an exultant Andrew Johnson declared the war now "virtually at an end." For Mary Lincoln it came as a personal blessing, as she wrote to her friend Charles Sumner. "The news of the capture of Davis, almost overpowers me!—In my crushing sorrow I have found myself almost doubting the goodness of the Almighty." It was the first break of light in Mary's month of darkness.

Just three days after his capture, Jefferson Davis and his family were driven through Macon, Georgia, inside a heavily guarded ambulance.

"Who Killed My Father?"

Mary was not the only family member to be groping through darkness in these early days of May; her son Tad was also deeply affected by his father's murder. On April 15 he had approached Secretary of the Navy Gideon Welles and cried out, "Oh, Mr. Welles, who killed my father?" The man Lincoln used to refer to as "Old Neptune" was not able to hold back his own tears, "nor give the poor boy a satisfactory answer."

Named Thomas Lincoln after his paternal grandfather and nicknamed "Tadpole" by his father, Tad grew up with adoring parents and little discipline. To Lincoln's law partner William Herndon, he and his brother Willie were "little devils." Dropped off at the office while Mary was in church, they "would take down the

Tad Lincoln was "the favorite of every man, woman and child in the White House," recalled doorkeeper and bodyguard Tom Pendel, who comforted the terrified twelve-year-old on the night of the murder. "The little fellow . . . put his little arms around my neck, and sobbed . . . 'O, Tom Pendel, they've killed my papa-day.'"

books, empty ash buckets, coal ashes, inkstand, papers, gold pens, etc. etc. in a pile and then dance on the pile. Lincoln would say nothing so abstracted was he and so blinded to his children's faults. Had they [shat] in his hat and rubbed it on his boots he would have laughed and thought it smart." In the White House John Hay remembered Tad as "a tricky little sprite . . . so full of life and vigor, so bubbling over with health and high spirits, that he kept the house alive with his pranks and his fantastic enterprise." To ease the pain after Willie's death in 1862, Tad had moved into his father's bedroom, and the President and he became constant companions. Tad traveled to the front lines, visited soldiers in the hospitals, and went on shopping expeditions with his father, becoming a familiar sight in Washington. "When the President laid down his weary pen toward midnight," wrote John Hay, "he generally found his infant goblin asleep under the table or roasting his curly head by the open fireplace; and the tall chief would pick up the child and trudge off to bed with the drowsy little burden on his shoulder."

If Lincoln was notorious for overlooking his children's flaws, Tad had many. Like his mother he was prone to temper tantrums, and often the only one who could calm him down was Lincoln. Plagued with learning disabilities and a bad lisp, he refused to study, becoming the bane of the many tutors engaged to try to teach him.

The assassination of his father sent Tad into a tailspin. On the day after the murder, Mary's seamstress saw him crouched at the foot of his mother's bed "with a world of agony in his young face." His mother's out-of-control wailing frightened the twelve-year-old boy. "Don't cry so, Mama," Tad was heard to say, "or you will make me cry, too!" Over the next weeks Tad tried hard to comfort his mother, even as he held on to his strong belief that his father was now in heaven.

Lincoln was never photographed with his wife, Mary, or his son Robert, but on two occasions he sat for pictures with his youngest son, Tad. This second portrait of the two together was taken just ten weeks before the assassination.

Matthew Wilson's portrait of Lincoln was based on a photograph taken by Alexander Gardner on February 5, 1865.

Lincoln's Last Portrait

Early in 1865 the English-born artist Matthew Wilson had been approached by his friend Gideon Welles to paint a portrait of the President. At a meeting at the White House on February 4, Lincoln had agreed to sit not only for the artist but for a series of photographs to help guide his painting. A date was set for the next day at Alexander Gardner's studio at 350 Pennsylvania Avenue. On Sunday afternoon, accompanied by Tad, President Lincoln sat for a series of five photographs. His expression that day was more relaxed than usual, and in one print he looked almost jubilant—with his head cocked back slightly, his eyes sparkling, and a slight but definite smile on his lips. Selecting a reversed version of this image as his model, over the next two weeks Wilson worked furiously, coming to the White House on at least two occasions to work from life. On February 20, in what Lincoln thought would be his last session with the artist, he posed as Wilson made his final touches.

Two days later the artist Francis Carpenter was in Lincoln's office and saw Wilson's new painting hanging "temporarily upon the wall of the room." Its owner, Gideon Welles, was also there, celebrating the recent capture of Fort Anderson. "Turning to the picture," Carpenter narrated, "Mr. Welles remarked he thought it a successful likeness. 'Yes,' remarked the President, hesitatingly; and then came a story of a western friend whose wife pronounced her husband's portrait, painted secretly for a birthday present, 'horribly like'; 'and that,' said he, 'seems to be a just criticism of this!'"

Matthew Wilson at work on a painting

Others soon recognized that the painting captured the mixture of strength and inner peace that characterized Lincoln in the final months of the war. Lincoln's friend Joshua Speed, visiting the White House in early April, was so impressed he asked Wilson to paint him a copy. And so in the last days of Lincoln's life Wilson returned to the White House and was granted a final session with the President. Lincoln's "last portrait" was still a work in progress when he died on April 15. Wilson, who had also painted his own master version of the portrait, immediately painted two copies of it—one for the Navy Department and one for the lithographer Louis Prang. In May 1865 Prang published the striking new image of Lincoln that for many Americans became the way they would always remember him. In the days ahead Matthew Wilson would accept orders for more and more copies of his popular portrait, until he finally wearied of the "interminable, everlasting Lincoln."

**The smiling portrait of Lincoln
upon which Wilson based his painting**

Lewis Powell, wearing head bag and shackles, was sketched by a correspondent for *Frank Leslie's Illustrated Newspaper.*

The seven-week trial took place on the third floor of the Old Penitentiary Building in Washington. At the White House, Mary Lincoln followed the prosecution and on May 18 allowed Tad to attend. He was anxious to get a glimpse of the people who had plotted his father's death and Mary hadn't the heart to say no.

The Trial of the Century

On the night that John Wilkes Booth was secretly buried in Washington, his co-conspirators were transferred to the Old Penitentiary Building at the Washington Arsenal where they would remain in captivity for the next six weeks. In their cells they were fitted with canvas head bags— eyeless, hot, and padded with cotton to prevent suicide by banging heads against the stone walls.

It had been determined to try the prisoners by a special military tribunal in which the government could keep full control over the proceedings. "Let the stain of innocent blood be removed from the land," Edwin Stanton had proclaimed in an official bulletin, revealing some measure of the vindictiveness of the government's motives. The trial began on May 10 inside a third-story chamber in the Old Penitentiary Building, near the cells where the prisoners were being kept in solitary confinement. With General Joseph Holt, the judge advocate of the army, serving as the government's chief prosecutor, a nine-member commission would hear the cases and pronounce sentence. Unlike in civilian courts, conviction here would require a simple majority of five, and the death penalty a two-thirds majority of six. Though qualified counsel was assigned to the eight defendants, no appeal to a higher court was permitted, only to the President of the United States.

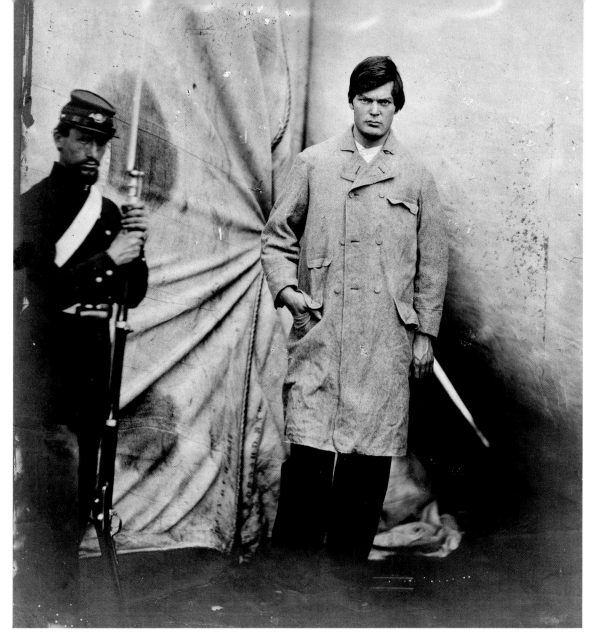

Lewis Powell (alias Payne) had attacked Secretary of State William Seward on the night of Lincoln's assassination. At the trial his attorney, William E. Doster, did not argue for his innocence. When he had asked Powell why he did it, he had said, "I believed it was my duty."

The three commissioners in the Lincoln conspiracy trial were John A. Bingham, Joseph Holt, and Henry L. Burnett.

Judge Holt had wanted complete secrecy for the proceedings, but under pressure from the press Stanton overruled him and permitted limited access. A reporters' stand was set up to accommodate journalists, whose pro-Union credentials were first carefully scrutinized. Under the supervision of Benjamin Pittman, a group of six court reporters made official transcripts of the proceedings, with Pittman providing copies of each day's testimony to two leading newspapers. A total of 366 witnesses would give testimony during the trial.

It was clear from the start that Davie Herold, the nineteen-year-old backcountry guide who had been Booth's right-hand man, was doomed; so was Lewis Powell, the Confederate deserter who had slashed the throat of Secretary of State William Seward; and George Atzerodt, the Confederate boatman who had been assigned to kill the Vice President that same night. Arnold and O'Laughlin, who had been involved in an earlier abduction plot but not in the assassination, were nevertheless treated as full members of the conspiracy, as was Mary Surratt, at whose house the conspirators had met. Edman Spangler and Samuel Mudd—of different degrees of involvement—were also swept up into the fury of the government prosecution. Speaking for the defense, Senator Reverdy Johnson of Maryland claimed the military trial was an illegal usurpation of executive power, but few listened. A year later the Supreme Court would make military trials of civilians illegal.

At the far end of the courtroom was a raised prisoners' dock, with its own exit directly to the prisoners' cells. A long table near the windows was for the nine military judges, and beyond it was the witness stand and tables for the prosecution and defense. The wide table in the center accommodated designated members of the press. And the chairs at the left were for ticketed observers.

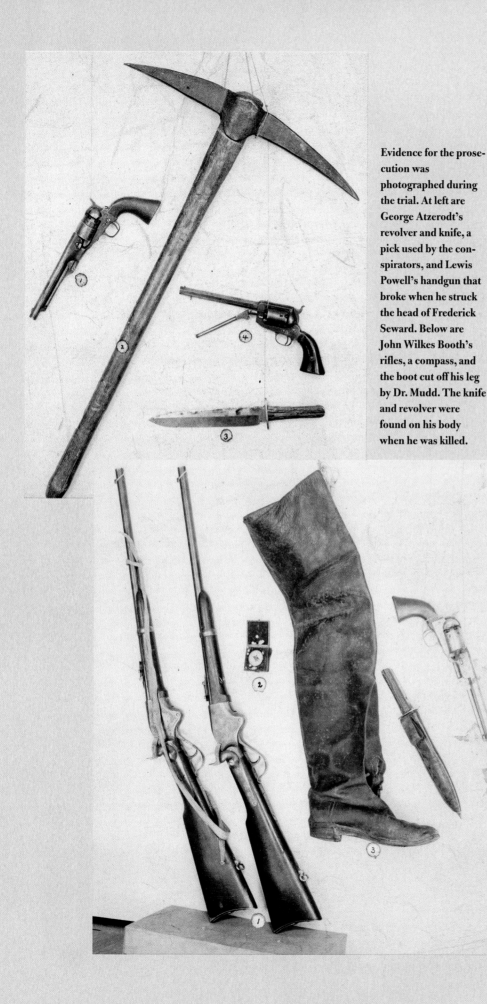

Evidence for the prosecution was photographed during the trial. At left are George Atzerodt's revolver and knife, a pick used by the conspirators, and Lewis Powell's handgun that broke when he struck the head of Frederick Seward. Below are John Wilkes Booth's rifles, a compass, and the boot cut off his leg by Dr. Mudd. The knife and revolver were found on his body when he was killed.

"A Proper Person to Pass"
Silas T. Cobb

May 16, 1865

In dramatic testimony given at the trial of the conspirators, Silas T. Cobb told how on the night of April 14 he had inadvertently allowed first Booth, then another man, probably Herold, to escape Washington over the Navy Yard Bridge. Booth's arrival at the checkpoint came an hour or so before Edwin Stanton's imposition of martial law and the sealing off of the city.

On the night of the 14th of April, I was on duty at the Navy Yard bridge. At about half-past 10 or 11 o'clock, a man approached rapidly on horseback. The sentry challenged him, and I advanced to see if he was a proper person to pass.

I asked him, "Who are you, sir?" He said, "My name is Booth." I asked him where he was from. He made answer, "From the city." "Where are you going?" I said; and he replied, "I am going home." I asked him where his home was. He said . . . "I live close to Beantown; but do not live in the town." I asked him why he was out so late; if he did not know the rule that persons were not allowed to pass after 9 o'clock. He said it was new to him; that he had had somewhere to go in the city, and it was a dark night, and he thought he would have the moon to ride home by. The moon rose that night about that time. I thought he was a proper person to pass, and I passed him.

The Navy Yard Bridge over which Booth escaped into Virginia

A Glimpse at the Conspirators
Noah Brooks

May 22, 1865

In the reporters' stand on May 22 sat a close friend of the Lincolns, Noah Brooks, covering the trial for the Sacramento Daily Union *and sharing the general prejudice against the eight accused.*

One of the most interesting places of resort in Washington at this time is the courtroom of the eight conspirators arraigned for being concerned in the plot against the lives of the heads of government. . . . For the sake of looking at the proceedings and describing the villains on trial, I went down to the court the other day and found my way past

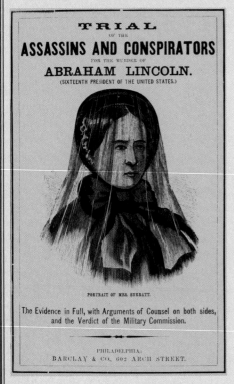

Mary Surratt on the cover of a trial pamphlet

sentries posted all along the street leading from the main avenue of the city to the penitentiary where the trial is held. . . . Each man has his feet chained by manacles connected by a chain about a foot long, and his hands are in similar iron cuffs kept apart by a stiff iron bar about ten inches long. . . .

Inside the railing on the left sits Mrs.

David E. Herold

Surratt, deeply veiled, with her face to the wall, slowly fanning herself and never raising her head except when commanded to show her face for the purpose of identification. . . . She is accused of being privy to the whole plot, assisting Booth before and after the assassination. Herold is a small, dark man about twenty years of age, with a low forehead, scanty black hair on his face, stooping figure, and a sottish expression generally, only his small, deep-set black eyes serving to light up his vulgar face. . . . Herold was Booth's man Friday in all his movements, leaving him only when he was burnt out, like a rat, from the barn.

Next is Payne, the assassin detailed for the murder of Secretary Seward. He sits bolt upright against the wall, looming up like a young giant above the others. Payne has a face in which good and bad are mixed. Determination and courage are evident, and if his coarse, black hair were well brushed off his broad, low forehead, he might pass for a good-looking young man. . . . The low, cunning man who sits

George A. Atzerodt

next is Atzerodt, detailed to murder the Vice President, but whose heart failed him when the time came to strike. This fellow has the meanest face of the whole crowd. . . .

O'Laughlin, supposed to have been set apart for the murder of Stanton or Grant, sits next. He wears all the aspect of the traditional stage villain made up for the occasion. . . .

Michael O'Laughlin

Lewis Powell (alias Payne)

A man about forty years old, heavy-built, sandy, slovenly in appearance, looking like a mechanic, but cunning hidden in his mask-like face, sits next; this is Spangler, the stage carpenter and scene shifter. This man Spangler fixed the scenes at the theater

Edman Spangler

so that Booth had an easy exit when his work was done. He held the assassin's horse, kept the way from the rear of the theater clear, and was a sort of lackey to his superior ruffian at all times. . . .

Samuel A. Mudd

The only intellectual face in this gang of big ruffians is that of Dr. Mudd, who sits next to the stage carpenter, the customary guard being between. . . . Mudd was a companion and associate of Booth . . . , received the fleeing assassins into his house on the night of the murder, and set Booth's fractured limb, though he afterward swore that he did not know the man for whom he performed the operation. . . .

Last in the row, looking out of the window upon the pleasant scene without,

lounging about, leaning his head on the rail, inattentive wholly to all that passes, and as uneasy as a caged whelp, is Arnold. . . . He backed out of the conspiracy and was caught at Fortress Monroe where he had gone to get out of the way until suspicion was well over. It now appears that he figured only in the original plan of abducting the President and was to have caught him on the stage when the rest of the villains had thrown him over from the box.

Samuel Arnold

Nine military judges presided over the trial. From left are Generals David R. Clendenin, Charles H. Hopkins, Thomas M. Harris, Alvin P. Howe, James A. Ekin, Lew Wallace, David Hunter, August V. Kautz, and Robert Foster. Next to them, on the far right, are the three commissioners, Bingham, Burnett, and Holt.

The Grand Review
Noah Brooks

May 23, 1865

On May 23 the city of Washington's attention was fixed on the Grand Review of the Union Armies. It was the country's chance to give thanks for the soldiers, and the soldiers' chance to give thanks for Lincoln. Noah Brooks reported for the Sacramento Daily Union.

This has been a great day, a day of days in Washington, for today the grand armies of the republic, their labors done and their victories complete, have commenced their grand farewell march through the national capital, to be welcomed and applauded in the national metropolis, and many of them will see for the first time that city for whose defenses they have fought so bravely and so well and for which so many noble lives have been laid down upon the field of battle. The sight and the occasion are forever memorable, and it will always be a proud thing to say that we were among those who saw the victorious hosts, and a prouder boast will it be for those who can say that they were among those who fought bravely and returned in triumph to march through the capital of the nation. . . . On every pennon, banner, banneret, guidon, and corps flag floats a streamer of mourning for Abraham Lincoln, beloved by the soldiers with a passionate devotion. He who loved the soldier and longed to see this day sleeps in his grave far away, but he, like the gallant men who now march by for their last review, has done his work well.

Major General John A. Logan led the Army of the Tennessee during the Grand Review of the Armies in Washington. Despite the celebration of the victorious soldiers, the Capitol flag still flew at half mast, in memory of their fallen commander in chief.

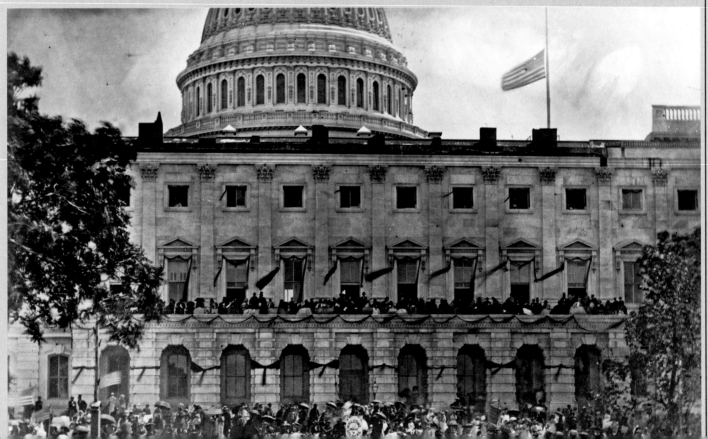

The First Lady Moves On

It took Mary more than five weeks before she was ready to leave the White House. She seemed to Noah Brooks to be "more dead than alive, shattered and broken by the horrors of that dreadful night as well as worn down by bodily sickness." She later told a friend she had no memory at all of these terrible weeks. She was also not ready to depart from the place where her life, and that of her husband, had reached its pinnacle.

Mary's life as First Lady had started out successfully, but over time her old habit of making enemies had asserted itself. Kindly, considerate, and generous one day, she could be irritable, despondent, and grasping the next, and prone to seeing the worst in other people. She often took out her frustrations on the two presidential secretaries, Nicolay and Hay, who among other things routinely kept her away from her husband. Hay soon dubbed her the "Hell-Cat" and Nicolay referred to her as "Her Satanic Majesty." Emotionally needy, Mary turned to material things to help fill the void. She overspent her White House decorating allowance, spent too much money on fancy clothes, and accepted gifts from fawning strangers. "She is accessible to the influence of flattery," wrote diplomat William Henry Russell, "and has permitted her society to be infected by men who would not be received in any respectable private hotel in New York."

As she stayed on upstairs in the weeks after the assassination, widespread looting took place on the ground floor, as greedy servants and unauthorized visitors made away with the contents of the house. Mary would later be accused of having stolen White House property, whereas in fact the dozens of boxes and trunks that she eventually packed were largely filled with clothes and bonnets.

On May 23, on the same day as the Grand Review of the Union Armies when no one would notice her slipping away, Mary Lincoln left Washington, planning never to return. But she did not head for Springfield. It would have been too painful for her to return, as both Robert and David Davis had urged her to do. "To place me in the home deprived of his presence and the darling boy we lost in Washington," Mary wrote, "it would not require a day, for me to lose my entire reason." Instead she settled in the city of Chicago, where she had spent happy times with her husband.

MRS. LINCOLN.

Entered according to Act of Congress in the year 1861, by M.B. Brady, in the Clerk's office of the District Court of the U.S. for the So. District of New-York

Mary Lincoln, as she looked when she arrived in Washington in 1861 with high hopes

John Todd Stuart was deeply sensitive to Mary Lincoln's wishes. Without his advocacy there might never have been a Lincoln Tomb in Springfield.

The Mather lot in Springfield was where local citizens tried unsuccessfully to have Lincoln buried. It later became the site of the new state capitol building.

In Springfield the National Lincoln Monument Association had become a legal entity that May—its stated purpose to create a fitting monument to Lincoln inside the city of Springfield. If Lincoln's widow would not allow the President's body to reside there, they had decided, they would proceed with their elaborate memorial without it. But in June, Mary once again intervened, warning them in a letter that she would remove her husband's body from the state of Illinois if they did not comply with her wishes and drop all plans for the in-town monument. The one memorial she wanted was to be at the site of her husband's future tomb, to be built, she insisted, within the confines of Oak Ridge Cemetery. The association was furious with Mary's latest message, and many of its members voted to ignore her and move ahead with their plans. Fortunately, Mary's cousin John Todd Stuart was a member of the Monument Association Board and chairman of its executive committee. He argued on behalf of Mary's feelings and to her rights and prerogatives as Lincoln's widow. The final vote to move the memorial to Oak Ridge Cemetery passed in Mary's favor by a majority of just one.

"My Oft Expressed Wishes"
Mary Lincoln

June 10, 1865

Members of the committee soon arrived in Chicago to try to change Mary's mind about the Springfield memorial. But she refused to see them. Instead in a letter to Illinois governor Richard Oglesby, she threatened the committee for the final time. It worked.

Dear Sir:

I perceive by the paper of to day, that notwithstanding, the note, I recently addressed you, yourself & Mr Hatch are en route to Chicago, to *consult,* with me, on the subject. My determination is unalterable, and if you will allow me again to add, that without I receive the 15th of this month a formal & written agreement that *the* Monument shall be placed over the remains of my Beloved Husband, in *Oak Ridge* Cemetery, with the *written* promise that no other bodies, save the President, his Wife, his Sons & Sons families, shall ever be deposited within the enclosure; in the event of my *not* receiving a *written* declaration to that effect, I shall rigidly comply with my resolution. If I had anticipated, so much trouble, in having my wishes carried out, I should have readily yielded to the . . . request of the *many* & had *his* precious remains, in the *first instance* placed in the vault of the National Capitol—A tomb prepared for Washington the Father of his Country & a fit resting place for the immortal Savior & Martyr for Freedom—Lest you do not accede to my wishes, it is best that I should be apprised of your intended action, so that changes, *if come, they must,* shall be made . . . immediately.

Very Respectfully,
Mary Lincoln

A dirt road up a wooded hillside led to block number 7, the location in Oak Ridge Cemetery for the Lincoln Tomb. "The beauty & retirement of the spot," wrote Isaac Arnold years later in Mary's defense, "would certainly have been her husband's choice."

The New President at Bull Run
June 11, 1865

Even as Mary Lincoln was fighting over her husband's memorial in Illinois, an impressive monument was being dedicated at Bull Run, the site of the first great battle of the Civil War. Present for the ceremony on June 11 was President Johnson, shown here standing in profile wearing a soldier's cap. A number of Union generals were in attendance, including Samuel P. Heintzelman (with grizzled beard to the left of Johnson in this picture) who had fought at Bull Run and was one of the day's speakers. The dedication was the beginning of a massive effort, in both the North and South, to memorialize the war.

An African American Lincoln Memorial
William Howard Day

July 4, 1865

On July 4, 1865, a large ceremony was held on the White House lawns—the first ever by African Americans. Led by Henry Highland Garnet and the newly formed Colored People's National Lincoln Monument Association, the goal was to create a new institution of learning in Lincoln's honor. A young black printer and orator from New York, William Howard Day, gave the opening address.

William Howard Day

All the heroes of all the ages, bond and free, have labored to secure for us the right we rejoice in to-day. . . . And now, in their presence, living and dead, as over the prostrate form of our leader, Abraham Lincoln—by the edge of blood-red waves, still surging, we pledge our resistance to tyranny . . . whether in the iron manacles of the slave, or in the unjust written manacles of the free. . . .

This Lincoln Monumental Institute is a fitting memorial. It will be an additional monument of the colored people's gratitude, of the colored man's industry, of the colored man's executive ability, of the col-ored man's brains, of the colored man's fitness for every duty and every privilege.

Let it rise as our wing of the new temple of freedom. At its altar let genius minister. There let benisons be pronounced from the heart of a rising race. There let the riches of learning be brought, ready to be laid on the knee and in the lap of every colored child in the land. Let solid floors echo the patterings of a thousand feet, all going up, up, up through the dawn to a brighter morning. Let the niches in your gallery here be filled with the white figures of Lincoln, and Stanton, and Wendell Phillips, and Garrison, and Gerrit Smith, and John Brown, and Chase, and Seward, and many, many others; but let them also glisten with those of "God's image cut in ebony." I repeat, let the Institute rise on our wing of the new temple of freedom.

Henry Highland Garnet

A Letter of Support
Frederick Douglass

July 1, 1865

Frederick Douglass

Though Douglass could not attend the commemoration at the White House, he sent along a letter of endorsement.

Gentlemen: Accept my best thanks for your note of 28th June, inviting me to be present at your proposed celebration of the 4th, in Washington. Had your note come a few days earlier, I might have been able to mingle my voice with those who shall participate in the commemoration of the birthday of freedom at the Capital. As the matter now stands, I can only send you the assurance that I shall be with you in spirit and purpose.

The one thought to be emphasized and deeply underscored on that occasion is this: The immediate, complete, and universal enfranchisement of the colored people of the whole country. This is demanded both by justice and national honor. Besides, it is the only policy which can give permanent peace and prosperity to the country. The great want of the country is to be rid of the negro question, and it can never be rid of that question until justice, right, and sound policy are complied with. I hope the able men who will speak on the occasion of your celebration will show that the prophecy of 1776 will not be fulfilled till all men in America shall stand equal before the laws.

Yours, very truly,
FRED'K DOUGLASS.

The Execution of the Conspirators

MRS. SURRATT IN HER CELL, ATTENDED BY HER SPIRITUAL ADVISERS.

The seven-week trial of the Booth conspirators culminated on June 29 when the prosecution made its final summation, to which the defense was not allowed to respond. The courtroom was then cleared for deliberation. For the next two days, behind closed doors, the commissioners discussed the evidence, and late on Friday they issued their decision. All eight defendants were found guilty. Three were sentenced to life imprisonment, one to six years, and four, including Mary Surratt, were given the death penalty. Despite a petition to lighten Surratt's sentence, on July 5 Andrew Johnson approved the sentencing, and execution day was set for Friday, July 7. The fifty-year-old Surratt would be the first woman ever executed by the federal government.

All day long on Thursday came the sounds of saws and hammers as a wooden gallows was erected in the prison courtyard. That night Washington hotels were filled to overflowing as visitors streamed into the city hoping to gain entrance to the historic event. On Friday morning thousands gathered outside the prison only to learn that attendance would be strictly limited to invited guests of the military.

Only Powell and Herold were able to sleep that night. Mrs. Surratt had to be given opiates to calm her. Her daughter remained with her through the night, trying unsuccessfully to quiet the despairing woman.

Artists for *Frank Leslie's Illustrated Newspaper* depicted a variety of scenes on the day of the execution, including this one of Mary Surratt, inconsolable despite the efforts of her spiritual adviser, a Roman Catholic priest.

Witnesses of the execution stand in front of the gallows. This photograph was taken just after the trap doors fell open.

The Strange Scene on the Plaza
George Alfred Townsend

One eyewitness to the execution was the ubiquitous George Alfred Townsend, still serving as a special correspondent for the New York World.

I entered a large, grassy yard, surrounded by an exceedingly high wall. On the top of this wall soldiers, with muskets in their hands, were thickly planted. The stage was . . . filled with people; the crisis of the occasion had come; the chairs were all withdrawn, and the condemned stood upon their feet, and the process of tying the limbs began. It was with a shudder, almost a blush, that I saw an officer gather the ropes tightly three times about the robes of Mrs. Surratt, and bind her ankles with cords. She half fainted, and sank backward upon the attendants, her limbs yielding to the extremity of her terror, but uttering no cry. Payne, with his feet firmly laced together, stood straight as one of the scaffold beams, and braced himself up so stoutly that this in part prevented the breaking of his neck. Herold stood well beneath the drop, still whimpering at the lips. Atzerodt, in his groveling attitude, while they tied him, began to indulge in his old vice of gabbing. Again, when the white death-cap was drawn over his face, he continued to cry out under it, saying: "Good-by, shentlemens who is before me now," and again, "May we meet in the other world; God help me." Herold protested against the knot, it being as huge as one's double fist. Mrs. Surratt asked to be supported, that she might not fall. When the death-caps were all drawn over the faces of the prisoners, and they stood in line in the awful suspense between absolute life and immediate death, an officer signaled the executioners, and the great beams were darted against the props simultaneously. The two traps fell with a slam, the four bodies dropped like a single thing. The bodies were allowed to hang about twenty minutes, when Surgeon Otis, U. S. V., and Assistant Surgeons Woodward and Porter, U.S.A., examined them and pronounced all dead.

Sometime before noon on Friday the four condemned prisoners were brought down from their third-floor cells to await the final procession. The day was unbearably hot, and tensions were high as the death march commenced at 1:15 P.M. Mrs. Surratt was in the lead, with her priests and attendants; Atzerodt was second, with his two chaplains; Herold walked third, accompanied by an Episcopal priest; and lastly came Payne, accompanied by two Baptist ministers. Out they marched into the Penitentiary Yard, not far from where John Wilkes Booth lay buried. The wooden scaffold stood adjacent to four freshly dug graves, beside which waited four rough-hewn pine coffins. Inside the yard, and lining the top of the thirty-foot-high prison wall, were some 3,000 spectators, mostly soldiers as well as some members of the press.

The executioner, Christian Rath, had spent the previous night hand-knotting each noose and making new head-bags for each conspirator so that their suffering faces would not be seen as they died. Now in front of all the witnesses and two official photographers, the canvas bags were put in place and the victims' hands and legs bound with strips of white cloth. At precisely 1:26 P.M. the four condemned criminals were dropped to their deaths—in punishment of what was now being called "the great crime of the century."

Just to the side of the gallows were freshly dug holes and four wooden coffins.

The four doomed conspirators were prepared for execution. Christian Rath, in white jacket, placed the noose on David Herold.

Mary Surratt

Lewis Powell

David Herold

George Atzerodt

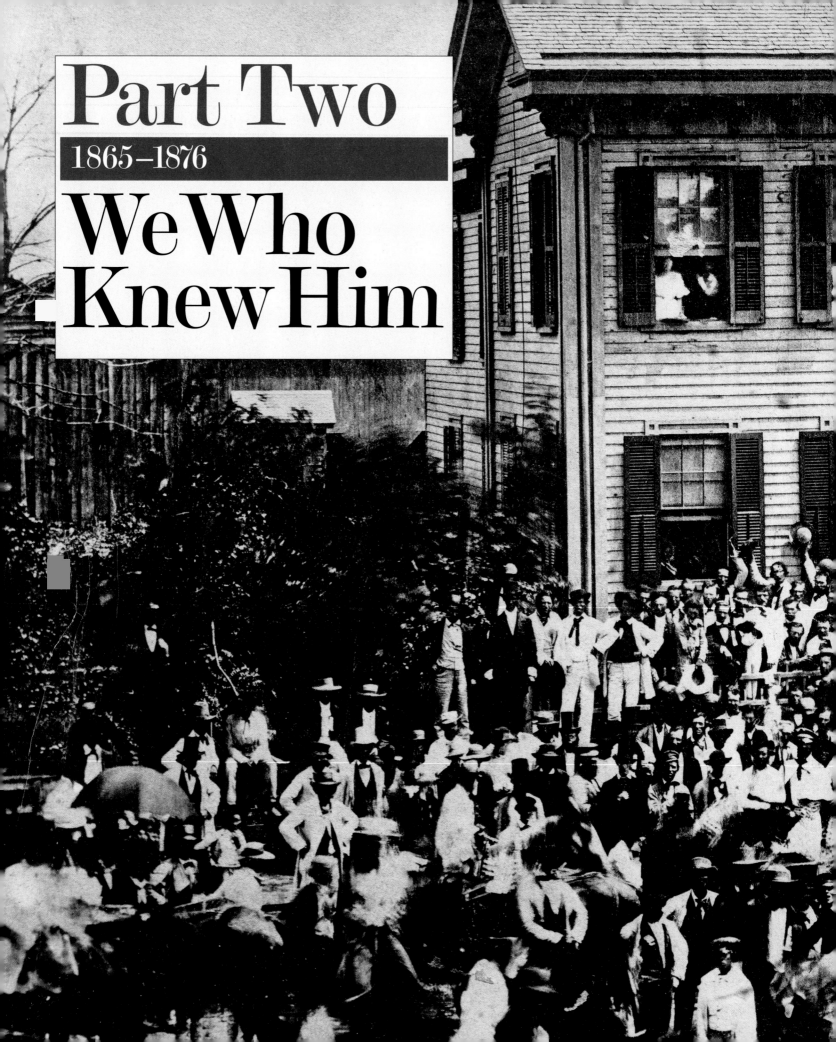

Part Two

1865–1876

We Who Knew Him

On August 8, 1860, after a huge Republican rally at the state fairgrounds in Springfield, crowds followed Lincoln to his house, where he was coaxed to join them for a photograph. Standing to the right of the front door in his white summer suit, the six-foot-four presidential candidate loomed above others.

Trying to Hold On to Him
1865–1876

Abraham Lincoln's impact was worldwide, but from the beginning he belonged in a special way to those who had known him. Over his lifetime he touched thousands of individuals, leaving a lasting impression on almost everyone who encountered him. Special status belonged to his inner circle—his family, his law partner, the members of his cabinet, his private secretaries. Then in widening sweeps there were hundreds of others—old friends from New Salem; close associates from the days in Springfield; political allies, and adversaries, in Washington. There were people like Joshua Speed who were longtime friends, and others, like Frederick Douglass, who saw him infrequently. There were Civil War generals, leading figures in Congress, newspaper editors, and religious leaders. It was an era when feelings were raw, memories fresh, and competing views of Lincoln clashed in the public square. Northerners and Southerners, blacks and whites, easterners and westerners all had different perspectives on him. And there were people who during Lincoln's life had not been known by the public at large, but who had unique access to him day to day—his barber, his coachman, artists who painted him, his wife's seamstress.

Lincoln reminiscence began as a slow trickle, became a stronger current by the 1870s, and eventually widened out into a torrent. With it came some new problems. The memories of some were self-serving, and the public was offered both valuable and distorted recollections. But as the first cadre of Lincoln biographers stepped forward, they gathered the key building blocks for all future understanding of the man.

The period from 1865 to 1876 was an era in which Lincoln's political legacy was tested—in which the new birth of freedom he had helped usher in for the nation was put into practice and then gradually snuffed out in the South. But during these years interest in Lincoln continued to strengthen. For many of his generation he was a father figure—more so than any President since George Washington.

Shortly after the assassination, people began what would become an American tradition—they traveled to the places where Lincoln had lived to pose for a photograph. This group of teachers gathered in front of the old Lincoln cabin in Indiana.

The First Reminiscences

During the first weeks after Lincoln's assassination, newspapers focused primarily on his martyrdom. But in late April personal reminiscences of him began to appear in print. There had been published recollections during Lincoln's lifetime, but these new ones were different. Now that he was gone, it seemed more important than ever to those who had known him to put their memories down, to shed light on the man who had meant so much to the nation.

One of the earliest came from Thomas Drummond, a federal judge in Chicago who had known Lincoln in the 1850s. Writing on the prairie lawyer's treatment of his law clients, Drummond brought to life Lincoln's human touch. Another description was penned by the artist Francis B. Carpenter, writing from New York City just two weeks after the assassination. Carpenter, who would later publish a book of recollections, recalled a conversation with the President in 1864 about his unwillingness to change his daily habits after receiving threats to his life. To a public still reeling from the first murder of an American President, it helped explain why Lincoln had attended the theater on April 14.

Few men had known Lincoln as well as Judge David Davis, who had traveled with him on the law circuit, sometimes sharing the same bedroom. In mid-May, shortly after helping Robert pack up his father's papers, Davis spoke out. He addressed the Indiana Bar Association about the man who "from the humblest poverty, without education, or means of obtaining it; unaided by wealth or influential family connections," rose "to the highest position in the world" and died "the greatest man of the generation in which he lived." He went on to reminisce about their days together on the circuit.

Late in the month came another recollection, this time from the Democratic journalist Charles Halpine. Right after the assassination Halpine had written a eulogy for the *New York Herald* in which he called Lincoln "as indigenous to our soil as a cranberry crop, and as American in his fibre as the granite foundations of the Appalachian range." Now in May Halpine wrote of an incident from 1862, when he was a member of General Henry Halleck's staff and had been frequently at the White House. It was a revealing portrait of Lincoln during his public visiting hours, when at his own insistence anyone could come to the White House without an appointment, wait their turn, and speak with the President.

Judge David Davis knew Lincoln for nearly thirty years and in the 1840s called him "the best Stump speaker in the State." Davis was dedicated and honest and revered Lincoln's memory, but Mary Lincoln found him cold and controlling.

Lincoln as he looked in November 1863

"This Simple Life He Loved"
David Davis

May 19, 1865

David Davis delivered this address before the Indianapolis Bar Association.

I do not propose to deliver a eulogy on the life and character of Mr. Lincoln.... To you, gentlemen, it has seemed more appropriate I speak of Mr. Lincoln as a lawyer.... I enjoyed for over a quarter of a century the personal friendship of Mr. Lincoln. We were admitted to the bar about the same time, and traveled for many years, what is known in Illinois as the Eighth Judicial Circuit. In 1848, when I first went on the bench, the circuit embraced fourteen counties, and Mr. Lincoln went with the court to every county.

Railroads were not then in use, and our mode of travel was either on horseback or in buggies. This simple life he loved, preferring it to the practice of the law in a city, where, although the remuneration would be greater, the opportunity would be less for mixing with the great body of the people, who loved him, and whom he loved.... In all the elements that constitute the great lawyer, he had few equals.... His mind was logical and direct, and he did not indulge in extraneous discussion. Generalities and platitudes had no charms for him. An unfailing vein of humor never deserted him, and he was always able to chain the attention of court and jury, when the cause was the most uninteresting by the appropriateness of his anecdotes....

He hated wrong and oppression everywhere, and many a man, whose fraudulent conduct was undergoing review in a court of justice, has writhed under his terrific indignation and rebukes.... The people where he practiced law were not rich, and his charges were always small.

A Man Accustomed to Death Threats
Francis B. Carpenter

April 28, 1865

A late number of the *Tribune* ... contained a full account of an elaborate conspiracy, matured in Richmond, either to assassinate or abduct the person of the President. Five hundred or a thousand men were said to be sworn to accomplish the deed. Several days subsequent to its publication, I asked Mr. Lincoln if he had seen the statement. He said he had not, nor even heard of it.

I then, at his request, gave him the details. We were walking together at the time, and I remember distinctly the conversation. After I had concluded he smiled incredulously, and said: "Well even if true, I do not see what the rebels would gain by either killing or getting possession of me. I am but a single individual, and it would not help their cause or make the least difference in the progress of the war. Every thing would go right on just the same. Soon after I was nominated at Chicago," he continued, "I began to receive letters threatening my life. The first one or two made me a little uncomfortable, but I came at length to look for a regular instalment of this kind of correspondence in every week's mail, and up to inauguration day I was in constant receipt of such letters, and it is no uncommon thing even to receive them now—but they have ceased to give me any apprehension." I expressed some surprise at this, but he replied in his peculiar way: "There is nothing like getting used to things!" Alas, that the nation should to-day be sitting under the shadow of the great crime—the consummation of those very threats—which he had come to regard so lightly.

A "Sincerity and Earnestness of Manner"
Thomas Drummond

April 20, 1865

Nature gave him ... much sagacity in judging of the motives and springs of human conduct.... With a voice by no means pleasant, and, indeed, when excited, in its shrill tones, sometimes almost disagreeable; without any of the personal graces of the orator; without much in the outward man indicating superiority of intellect; without great quickness of perception—still his mind was so vigorous, his comprehension so exact and clear, and his judgment so sure, that he easily mastered the intricacies of his profession, and became one of the ablest reasoners and most impressive speakers at our bar. With a probity of character known to all, with an intuitive insight into the human heart, with a clearness of statement which was itself an argument, with uncommon power and felicity of illustration—often, it is true, of a plain and homely kind—and with that sincerity and earnestness of manner which carried conviction, he was, perhaps, one of the most successful jury lawyers we have ever had in the State. He always tried a case fairly and honestly. He never intentionally misrepresented the evidence of a witness or the argument of an opponent. He met both squarely, and, if he could not explain the one or answer the other, substantially admitted it. He never misstated the law according to his own intelligent view of it....

Lincoln in 1858

The White House during Lincoln's administration was open to the public. A statue of Thomas Jefferson greeted visitors.

His "Public-Opinion Baths"

Charles G. Halpine

May 31, 1865

G.D.FREDRICKS & CO N.Y.

General C. G. Halpine

Once—on what was called "a public day," when Mr. Lincoln received all applicants in their turn—the writer was struck by observing, as he passed through the corridor, the heterogeneous crowd of men and women, representing all ranks and classes, who were gathered in the large waiting-room outside the Presidential suit[e] of offices. Being ushered into the President's chamber by Major Hay, the first thing he saw was Mr. Lincoln, bowing an elderly lady out of the door—the President's remarks to her being, as she still lingered and appeared reluctant to go: "I am really very sorry, madame; very sorry. But your own good sense must tell you that I am not here to collect small debts. You must appeal to the courts in regular order." When she was gone, Mr. Lincoln crossed his legs, locked his hands over his knees, and commenced to laugh— this being his favorite attitude when much amused. "What odd kinds of people come in to see me," he said, "and what odd ideas they have about my office! Would you believe, Major, that the old woman who has just left, came in here to get from me an order stopping the pay of a treasury clerk, who owes her a board bill of about $70?" And the President rocked himself backward and forward, and appeared intensely amused. . . .

"For myself, I feel though the tax on my time is heavy—that no hours of my day are better employed than those which thus bring me again within the direct contact and atmosphere of the average of our people. Men moving only in an official circle are apt to become merely official—not to say arbitrary—in their ideas, and are more apt, with each passing day, to forget that they only hold power in a representative capacity. Now this is all wrong. I go into these promiscuous receptions of all who claim to have business with me twice each week, and every applicant for audience has to take his turn as if waiting to be shaved in a barber's shop. . . . I call these receptions my public-opinion baths—for I have but little time to read the papers and gather public opinion that way; and though they may not be pleasant in all their particulars, the effect, as a whole, is renovating and invigorating to my perceptions of responsibility and duty. It would never do for a President to have guards with drawn sabers at his door, as if he fancied he were, or were trying to be, or were assuming to be, an Emperor."

"I Might Run Away"
Henry C. Deming

June 8, 1865

Another early reminiscence came from Congressman Henry C. Deming of Connecticut, whose Lincoln lecture, delivered in Hartford in early June, included memories of conversations in the White House.

I once myself ventured to ask the President if he had ever despaired of the country? and he told me, that "when the Peninsular Campaign terminated suddenly at Harrison's Landing, I was as nearly inconsolable as I could be and live." In the same connection I inquired, if there had ever been a period in which he thought that better management, upon the part of his Commanding General, might have terminated the War? and he answered that there were three[:] that the first was at Malvern Hill where McClellan failed to command an immediate advance upon Richmond, that the second was at Chancellorville, where Hooker failed to reinforce Sedgwick, after hearing his cannon upon the extreme right, and that the third was after Lee's retreat from Gettysburg, when Meade failed to attack him in the bend of the Potomac. After this commentary I waited for an outburst of denunciation, for a criticism at least upon the delinquent officers, but I waited in vain; so far from a word of censure escaping his lips, he soon added, that his first remark might not appear uncharitable, "I do not know that I could have given different orders had I been with them myself; I have not fully made up my mind how I should behave, when minnie balls were whistling and these great oblong shells shrieking in my ear. I might run away."

A Premonition of Death
Noah Brooks

July 1865

Even as Noah Brooks continued his duties as a newspaper reporter, he began composing his recollections of Lincoln. Brooks had met Lincoln in Illinois in 1856. He had moved to California in 1859 to work as a newspaperman, but the sudden death of his wife in childbirth had propelled him east in search of change. Serving as a Washington correspondent for the Sacramento Daily Union, *in 1862 he renewed his friendship with the Lincolns. Feeling sorry for the young widower, they took him under their wing and soon found what a loyal and likable friend he was. He was given unprecedented access to the White House—he was often there several times a week—and became the first journalist to report "behind the scenes" of a presidential administration. Lincoln took him to political meetings and to battlefields and often invited him to dinner or to spend the night. Part White House correspondent, part war reporter, part Washington gossip columnist, by 1865 he had been approached by Lincoln to become his next private secretary. Just three months after the assassination Brooks's "Recollections" were published in* Harper's Monthly Magazine, *containing an account of Lincoln's premonition of his own death.*

Shortly after the presidential election, in 1864, he related an incident which I will try to put upon paper here, as nearly as possible in his own words: "It was just after my election in 1860, when the news had been coming in thick and fast all day, and there had been a great 'Hurrah, boys!' so that I was well tired out, and went home to rest, throwing myself down on a lounge in my chamber. Opposite where I lay was a bureau, with a swinging-glass upon it"—(and here he got up and placed furniture to illustrate the position)—"and, looking in that glass, I saw myself reflected, nearly at full length; but my face, I noticed, had *two* separate and distinct images, the tip of the

It was in this bedroom mirror that Lincoln saw what he considered an ominous double image of himself.

nose of one being about three inches from the tip of the other. I was a little bothered, perhaps startled, and got up and looked in the glass, but the illusion vanished. On lying down again I saw it a second time plainer, if possible, than before; and then I noticed that one of the faces was a little paler, say five shades, than the other. I got up and the thing melted away, and I went off and, in the excitement of the hour, forgot all about it—nearly, but not quite, for the thing would once in a while come up, and give me a little pang, as though something uncomfortable had happened. When I went home I told my wife about it, and a few days after I tried the experiment again, when [with a laugh], sure enough, the thing came again; but I never succeeded in bringing the ghost back after that, though I once tried very industriously to show it to my wife, who was worried about it somewhat. She thought it was 'a sign' that I was to be elected to a second term of office, and that the paleness of one of the faces was an omen that I should not see life through the last term."

May 1865

Abraham Lincoln's Successor

In mid-May 1865 President Andrew Johnson took control of Reconstruction. A month earlier, when he had vowed to carry on the struggle against the Southern rebellion, he had been seen in many circles as even more forceful than Lincoln, something welcomed by the radical Republicans. "It may be that President Lincoln was unfitted by his natural gentleness & humanity . . . to execute . . . stern justice," wrote one observer. Perhaps he had been "removed to make way for Andrew Johnson, who . . . will be more ready to act the bloody part." Johnson's proclamation for the arrest of Jefferson Davis, and his refusal of clemency for Mary Surratt, seemed to underscore the new rigor he was bringing to the office.

But it was not long before the former senator from Tennessee was making a complete reversal in policy—advocating the speedy restoration of the Confederacy to the Union. As Johnson pointed out, Lincoln himself had opposed radical plans for restructuring the South. He had rejected the Reconstruction Bill of 1864 and was in favor of letting Southern states return to the Union by simply swearing allegiance and by recognizing the end of slavery. But Johnson disagreed with many of his predecessor's positions. Lincoln had favored federal control over conquered territories and had been adamant that black freedoms in the South be safeguarded. And while Johnson dutifully supported the Thirteenth Amendment, he had no sense of obligation to the former slaves. Stubborn, cantankerous, a firm believer in states' rights, he hated slavery not out of sympathy for the slaves but out of disdain for the elite planters. And if he had none of Lincoln's commitment to black rights, he utterly lacked his predecessor's political skill and pragmatism.

With Congress out of session until December, in mid-May Johnson acted unilaterally, by proclamation. He set up new state governments in Virginia and North Carolina and began parallel processes in six other Southern states. While they would be expected to ratify the Thirteenth Amendment, there would be virtually no other requirements; nor would the North oversee their reconstruction. It would be an honor system, with the state governments in charge. Simultaneously Johnson ordered the restoration of Confederate property and issued a wide-sweeping amnesty proclamation and a broad array of special pardons. It was the start of a massive political reversal, and Lincoln's friends were incensed.

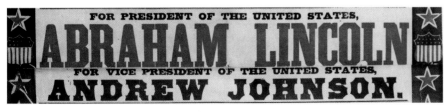

Andrew Johnson replaced Hannibal Hamlin on the Union ticket and was elected as Lincoln's Vice President in 1864.

Dr. Anson G. Henry

Mary, Robert, and Tad Lincoln moved into the newly opened Hyde Park Hotel, seven miles outside Chicago.

Mary Lincoln's Best Friend

In Chicago, Mary Lincoln was deeply unhappy. With store debts amounting to $10,000, she had been placed on a strict allowance by her husband's executor, David Davis. The series of hotels she was forced to live in she disparagingly referred to as her "boarding houses." By July she had settled in the Hyde Park Hotel, south of the city, where she and her sons squeezed into three small rooms. After their life in the executive mansion, and in their spacious house in Springfield, it was a difficult adjustment. ("I would almost as soon be dead as be compelled to remain three months in this dreary house," said Robert.) Here Mary remained closeted away from the world—seeing almost no one, avoiding contact with anything that might remind her of her former life. "Day by day, I miss my beloved husband, more and more," she wrote a friend in July. "I have become almost blind, with weeping." She carried on a correspondence with a few select friends, including her husband's former doctor and longtime family friend Anson Henry, who had been so kind to her after the assassination. To Dr. Henry she revealed her mounting resentment toward Davis, who had insisted that she rent rooms rather than purchase a house. Mary longed for her own home again, she told Henry, where she could bury herself away in her sorrows. But when Judge Davis told her in July how pleased he was with her living arrangements, she had blurted out she would "board no longer than next Spring," after which she would rather be "a vagrant" anywhere else in the nation than in a state that owed her husband such "a deep debt of gratitude" and yet would not provide for his bereaved wife. "What I would not give, to have one of our old chats together again," Mary told Dr. Henry. "I cannot express how lonely & desolate we are." But that same month, on a voyage to Washington Territory where he served as surveyor-general, Anson Henry's ship was lost at sea. News of the disaster would come as another terrible shock to Mary Lincoln. He had been her "best & dearest friend," she wrote lovingly to his widow.

An Old Friend in the White House

August 4, 1865

In August Mary received a letter from Charles Forbes, her husband's former foot-man and White House messenger. Forbes had accompanied the Lincolns to Ford's Theatre on April 14 and had been invited inside to watch the play. Ironically it was he, not a bodyguard, who had stopped John Wilkes Booth outside the presidential box, only to let him enter after Booth displayed a card that seemed to authorize his presence. (Forbes would forever be haunted by this mistake.) In his letter to Mary, Forbes said he was thinking of moving to Chicago and asked if she considered this a good idea. Her reply on August 5—before she had heard the news of Dr. Henry's death—showed her loyalty to an old friend.

Near Chicago, Aug. 5th, 65

My friend Charles:

Your letter was received some two weeks since. I have been unable to reply to it sooner, in consequence of quite severe illness. We would, all of us, be much pleased to have you come to Chicago to reside. It is destined to be a great city in time—great wealth here, very elegant residences & some very delightful people. Yet to me, Charles, the world, henceforth, is as nothing. I do not desire to live long under no circumstances whatever without my husband. I miss his extreme devotion to myself and sons every moment. When my life closes it will be to me a most pleasant exchange, for I am willing to go any hour our Maker calls me hence.

Dear little Taddie is well & makes friends wherever he goes. Robert is reading law, and is still as thoughtful & as attentive as ever. God has blessed me certainly in my sons, if by the removal of my husband, He, has made me the most miserable of women. Life is to me a torment, instead of a blessing, yet for the sake of those who are left, I must submit to remain. The years will not be many ere I am reunited to my idolized husband. . . .

Write soon.
Your friend as ever,

Mary T. Lincoln.

Charles Forbes, a White House servant, remained devoted to the Lincolns.

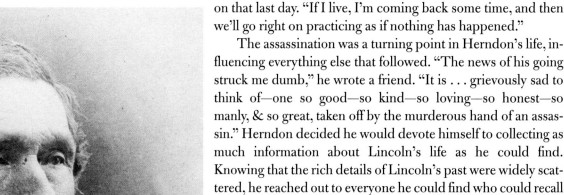

June 1865

Herndon's Oral History Project

No one had known Lincoln as well as William H. Herndon—or so he believed. For sixteen and a half years they had worked together side by side, sharing a law office in downtown Springfield. There the cool, self-taught Lincoln and the fiery, better-educated Herndon had developed a trust and an effective working partnership, together handling nearly 3,500 cases. Their relationship—that of a mentor to an energetic associate—became one of the most important ingredients of Herndon's life. When Lincoln left for Washington in 1861, he had urged his partner to leave up their sign "Lincoln and Herndon." "Let it hang there undisturbed," he had said to "Billy" on that last day. "If I live, I'm coming back some time, and then we'll go right on practicing as if nothing has happened."

The assassination was a turning point in Herndon's life, influencing everything else that followed. "The news of his going struck me dumb," he wrote a friend. "It is . . . grievously sad to think of—one so good—so kind—so loving—so honest—so manly, & so great, taken off by the murderous hand of an assassin." Herndon decided he would devote himself to collecting as much information about Lincoln's life as he could find. Knowing that the rich details of Lincoln's past were widely scattered, he reached out to everyone he could find who could recall pieces of his story. In Petersburg, Illinois, dozens of former residents of the little town of New Salem, where Lincoln had lived as a young man, were willing to share their memories. Herndon spent days with the old-timers, soaking up their reminiscences of the young Lincoln. "I have been with the People," he wrote excitedly; "ate with them—slept with them, & thought with them—cried with them too." His conversations were followed by lengthy exchanges of letters, as Herndon transcribed the firsthand accounts of the people who remembered Lincoln most vividly.

The letters and interviews presented an array of detail: Lincoln's fondness for cats; his need for periods of time by himself; his ability to inspire confidence in others. All agreed he had been devoted to reading and had an extraordinary memory. Many noted his kindness and personal honesty.

In June 1865 Herndon turned his attention to a distant cousin of Lincoln's named Dennis Hanks, who was in Chicago exhibiting what he claimed to be an authentic Lincoln log cabin. Hanks was the illegitimate son of one of Lincoln's great-aunts and had known "Abe" ever since he had come into the world as a tiny, screaming baby. Herndon traveled to Chicago and sat him down for a long interview. Though he quickly realized Hanks could be self-serving, as when he claimed it was he who had taught Lincoln to read and write, it was clear he was also an important source of firsthand recollection.

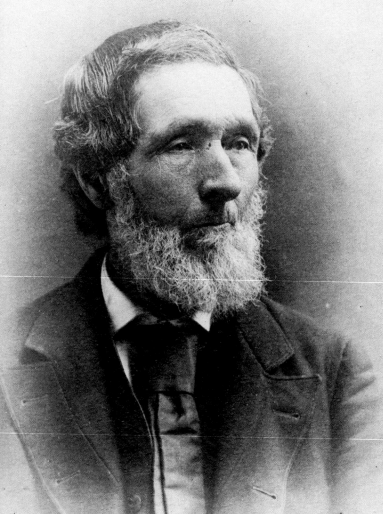

Lincoln described his longtime law partner William Herndon as "far better equipped on almost all subjects than I have ever been." In 1860 Herndon bragged, "I know Lincoln better than he knows himself."

An Affectionate Boy
Dennis Hanks

June 13, 1865

Few people knew Lincoln better during his formative years than his older cousin Dennis Hanks, who lived just two miles away from the farm where Abraham Lincoln was born in February 1809. Hanks had followed the Lincoln family to Indiana and moved in with them from 1818 to 1821. He had married Lincoln's stepsister, Sarah Johnston, and later sent his daughter Harriet to live with the Lincolns in Springfield. In a reminiscence given to Herndon in June 1865, he recalled the death of Lincoln's mother in 1818.

Abe was a good boy—an affectionate one—a boy who loved his father & mother dearly & well always minding them well—Sometimes Abe was a little rude. When strangers would ride along & up to his fathers fence Abe always, through pride & to tease his father, would be sure to ask the stranger the first question, for which his father would sometimes knock him a rod. Abe was then a rude and forward boy[.] Abe when whipped by his father never bawled but dropt a kind of silent unwelcome tear, as evidence of his sensations—or other feelings. . . .

We had no trouble with the Indians in Indiana, they soon left and westward. In the fall & winter of 1819 & 20 we Commenced to cut the trees—clear out the brush and underwoods & forest for our new grand old log cabin, which we Erected that winter: it was one Story—18 by 20 feet—no passage—on[e] window—no glass in it. The lights were made from the leaf Coming off from the hog's fat. This was good mellow light & lasted well. The house was sufficiently high to make a kind of bedroom over head—a loft. This was approached by a kind of ladder made by boring holes in the logs . . . peg over peg we Climed aloft, the pegs creaking & screching as we went. Here were the beds—the floor of the loft was clap boards & the beds lay on this.

Lincoln's garrulous older cousin Dennis Hanks

Here I and Abe slept and I was married there to Abes stepsister—Miss Elizabeth Johnston—not Johnson. During this fall Mrs Lincoln was taken sick, with what is known with the Milk sick: she struggled on day by day—a good Christian woman and died on the 7th day after she was taken sick. . . . She knew she was going to die & Called up the Children to her dying side and told them to be good & kind to their father—to one an other and to the world, Expressing a hope that they might live as they had been taught by her to love men—love—reverence and worship God. Here in this rude house, of the Milk Sick, died one of the very best women in the whole race, known for kindness—tenderness—charity & love to the world.

An early illustration of Lincoln at his mother's grave

THE ORIGINAL
LINCOLN LOG CABIN!

Now on exhibition at the

One of the most popular exhibits at the Great Northwestern Sanitary Fair in Chicago (above) was the log cabin supposedly built by Lincoln and his father in 1830. Cousin John Hanks proclaimed he had helped split the logs. Dennis Hanks (left, in top hat) told stories about the young Lincoln.

by J. L. CAMPBELL, in the Clerk's Office of the District Court of the Northern District of Illinois.

Dennis and John Hanks posed in front of the Lincoln cabin at the Sanitary Fair in Chicago. Later it traveled east to Boston and New York, appearing inside P. T. Barnum's American Museum in September.

Lincoln's Stepmother

In September William Herndon set out to meet Lincoln's aging stepmother, Sarah Bush Lincoln, who still lived on the family farm where her husband had died fourteen years earlier, about eight miles south of Charleston, Illinois. Herndon knew that his partner had adored this kindly woman who had come into his life shortly after the death of his mother and showered him and his sister Sarah with the love they so yearned for. Over the years Lincoln had visited her at this farm, including just days before leaving Illinois to assume the presidency. More than anyone else, it was she who had helped him become the person he wanted to become.

Riding out to the farm in early September, Herndon introduced himself to Sarah as a close friend of her son's. "I found Lincoln's step-mother very old—far gone into second childhood," he recounted. "[T]he step-mother's talk was prattle; intelligence and memory both buried in dotage. At last I got down on my knees before her, and, like a child myself, by simple questions drawing her on from her birth-place, finally by sympathy made her comprehend." Her suspicions melting, Sarah proceeded to grant Herndon the richest interview of any he ever received. She recalled young Abe's dislike of physical labor—how he "went to bed early—got up Early & then read," and how he wrote and ciphered "on boards" because he usually had no paper. She told how from a young age he was "diligent for knowledge—wished to Know"; how whenever older guests came to the house, he would sit silently soaking up their comments, then afterward "must understand Everything—even to the smallest thing—Minutely & Exactly." Only "when it was fixed in his mind to suit him" would he become "Easy and he never lost that fact or his mastery of it."

When the visit was over, and Herndon was ready to leave, the old lady arose. "She . . . took me by the hand—wept—and bade me goodbye—Saying I shall never see you again." And then she asked Herndon to deliver a message to Mary Lincoln and to her grandchildren: "Tell them I send them my best & tenderest love." Herndon then went off in search of the grave of Thomas Lincoln.

"Abe was a good boy," Sarah Bush Lincoln said to William Herndon in 1865. "His mind & mine . . . seemed to run together."

Memories in Indiana

Herndon's next destination was Gentryville, Indiana, where the Lincolns had lived for fourteen years after moving from Kentucky in 1816. Here he discovered Nat Grigsby, whose brother had been married to Lincoln's sister, Sally, and who agreed to serve as Herndon's Indiana guide. Their first objective was to visit the site of the old Lincoln farm on Pigeon Creek. The two men rode out together and found the abandoned homestead—the log cabins gone or in disarray, the wells "all caved in," five or six old apple trees indicating a yard that was grown over. Here was the homestead where Lincoln's mother had died not long after arriving, and where Sarah Bush Johnston had arrived in 1819 to find nine-year-old Abe and his eleven-year-old sister living in an unfurnished, dirt-floored cabin. It took awhile for Herndon and Grigsby to find the grave of Nancy Lincoln, deep in the woods high atop a knoll. The grave was unmarked, just a sunken hollow, and the men paused to pay their respects. "After . . . contemplating in silence the mutations of things—death—immortality—God, I left, I hope . . . a better man," Herndon wrote.

Nathaniel Grigsby was one of Lincoln's closest friends in Indiana.

A Good-natured Friend
Joseph C. Richardson

September 14(?), 1865

Joseph Richardson grew up with Lincoln in Indiana and recalled his friend as intellectually gifted and exceptionally strong. (He once "saw him carry a chicken house made of poles . . . that weighed at least 600 pounds if not much more.")

Onc[e] Lincoln & Squire Hall raised some water melons—Some of us boys lit into the melon patch accidentally. We got the melons—went through the Corn to the fence—got over—All at onc[e] to our Surprise and mortification Lincoln Came among us—on us—good naturedly said boys "now I've got you["]—sat down with us—cracked jokes, told stories & helped to eat the melons.

A Helping Hand for Others
David Turnham

September 15, 1865

David Turnham had been a close neighbor and friend of Lincoln's in Indiana.

One night when Lincoln & I were returning home from Gentryville we were passing along the road in the night. We saw something laying near or in a mud hole and Saw that it was a man: we rolled him over and over—waked up the man—he was dead drunk—night was cold—nearly frozen—we took him up—rather Abe did—Carried him to Dennis Hanks—built up a fire and got him warm—I left—Abe staid all night—we had been threshing wheat …—had passed Lincolns house—Lincoln stopt & took Care of the poor fellow—Smith—This was in the year 1825 There was one Store in Gentryville. Don't publish the mans name: he was an honorable man having now near us Excellent, dear & near relatives

"Didn't Love Work"
John Romine

September 14, 1865

In September Herndon interviewed sixty-year-old John Romine, a former neighbor of Lincoln's in Indiana who remembered the young man who used to labor on his farm.

He worked for me in 1829 pulling fodder. I Say Abe was awful lazy: he would laugh & talk and crack jokes & tell stories all the time, didn't love work but did dearly love his pay. He worked for me frequently—a few days only at a time. His breeches didn't & socks didn't meet by 12 inches—Shin bones Sharp—blue & narrow Lincoln said to me one day that his father taught him to work but never learned him to love it.

Lincoln's Springfield Neighbors

William Herndon also documented informants in the city of Springfield, where Lincoln had made his home for twenty-four years. Here were Mary Lincoln's sisters Elizabeth and Frances, and Elizabeth's husband, the prominent merchant Ninian Edwards. Here was Richard Oglesby, the governor of Illinois, who lived not far from the State Capitol building. And James Matheny, groomsman at Lincoln's wedding, who recalled sitting with Lincoln day after day in his old office above the courtroom. Here was William Jayne, the Lincoln family doctor, still serving as a physician. And here was a host of others—John T. Stuart, Lincoln's mentor and first law partner; Stephen Logan, an acknowledged leader of the Springfield bar and Lincoln's second law partner; and Charles Zane, who had served in the office of Lincoln and Herndon and then succeeded Lincoln as Herndon's partner. Here was Bunbry Lloyd, a local dentist; and James Gourley, a close neighbor of the Lincolns who had known both husband and wife well over many years.

Over the course of 1865 and 1866 Herndon interviewed at least thirty Springfield residents and had informal conversations with many others. Some of the local opinion about the Lincolns was not pleasant. John Todd Stuart referred to Lincoln as "a kind of vegetable" who excreted odors out of his pores; Ninian Edwards recalled his brother-in-law as "not a warm-hearted man"; and James Matheny spoke poorly of Mary Lincoln who, he said, "often gave L[incoln] Hell." But most of the interviews were extremely positive, and a composite picture began to emerge of Lincoln as a widely respected figure in town.

Herndon himself had some of the most vivid recollections of his friend. "Mr. Lincoln sometimes walked our streets cheerily—good humoredly—it may be joyously," he wrote, "and then it was on meeting a friend—he cried 'Howdy'—clasping one of his friends hands in both of his, giving a good hearty-soul welcome. Sometimes he might be seen wending his way to his office—to the court rooms or to platforms with his toga on, looking like a rail in broad cloth. Of a winter's morning he might be seen stalking and stilting it toward the market house basket on his arm, his old gray shawl . . . wrapped around his neck." Children in particular were attracted to this strange man, whom they could tell looked kindly upon them.

Herndon hated depictions of Lincoln that made him out to be a monolithically sad man, saying those who wrote such things didn't know the real Lincoln. Though melancholy at times "dripped from him," Herndon admitted, he was a vibrant, outgoing man during his Springfield years, "the favorite of everybody, man, woman and child, where he was loved and was known, and he richly deserved it."

The east side of State Square in Springfield, across the street from Lincoln's law office

"I Knew Him Well"
James Gourley

1865–1866

One of Herndon's favorite interviews was with James Gourley, a boot- and shoemaker who served as deputy sheriff of Sangamon County, and who was brimful of Lincoln memories.

I lived next door neighbor to Lincoln 19 years: Knew him & his Family relations well: he used to Come to our house with Slippers on—one Suspender & an old pair of pants—Come for milk—our room was low & he Said Jim—you have to lift your loft a little higher: I Can't stand in it well. He used to say to my wife that little people had Some advantages: it did not take quite So much wood & wool to make their house & Clothes.

Lincoln never planted . . . any trees—he did plant Some rose bushes once in front of his house: he planted no apple trees, cherry trees—pear trees, grape vines Shade trees and Such like things—he did not it seems Care for Such things.

He once—for a year or So had a garden & worked in it: he Kept his own horse—fed & curried it—fed & milked his own Cow: he Sawed his own wood generally when at home. He loved his Horse well. . . .

Lincoln would take his Children and would walk out on the rail way out in the Country—would talk to them—Explain things Carefully—particularly. He was Kind—tender and affectionate to his children—very—very—. . . . Bob & my boy used to harness up my dog & they would take him & go into the woods and get nuts.

Lincoln's horse Old Bob

Clockwise from the top, Lincoln's Springfield neighbors included his close friends Henry and Mary Remann and their daughter Josephine, who grew up to marry Mary Lincoln's nephew Albert Edwards; R. Francis Ruth, a nephew of Lincoln's druggist Roland Diller and a close friend of Tad Lincoln's; Alexander Black, Mary Remann's brother; and Dr. John Todd, Mary's uncle, who was one of the earliest settlers of Springfield.

William Herndon took possession of Lincoln's law office books, refusing to comply with Robert Lincoln's repeated requests for them.

"A Domestic Man"
Frances Todd Wallace

1865–1866

Frances Todd Wallace, one of Mary Lincoln's two older sisters, had been a devoted, lifelong friend of Abraham Lincoln.

Mr L before he was married used to Come to our house—was attatched to my eldest girl—very much so—. He was not attatched to Children generally as I think—was to his own—was to my oldest girl—one year older than Bob Lincoln—Don't think Mr L. was much attatched to Cats & dogs—one reason was that Bob once had a little dog—he bit Bob—Lincoln took him off to the Mad Stone in Terrehaute or other place in Indiana I think. . . . L's—back yard was used as a woodpile he used to Saw wood for Exercise—: he really loved to do it: he was the very best and Kindest father I ever saw: he was a domestic man I think by nature. I used to go over and see my sister and L was always at home if in town: he would read generally aloud. . . .

    Mr nor Mrs Lincoln loved the beautiful—I have planted flowers in their front yard myself to hide nakedness—ugliness &c. &c. have done it often—and often—Mrs L never planted trees—Roses—never made a garden, at least not more than once or twice—

Chopped His Own Wood
John B. Weber

November 1, 1866

John B. Weber was a Springfield cabinet-maker who knew Lincoln during his days on the law circuit.

He was frequently away from home for a week or so at a time attending Court & on political discussions. One night he Came home late at night. I heard an axe: it rang out at Lincoln's—got up—Saw Mr Lincoln in his Shirt Sleeves Cutting wood—I suppose to cook his supper with: it was a cold night—the moon was up—and I looked at my clock—it was between 12 & 1 o'cl. This I remember well—used to tell it on the stump.

A Lover of Dirty Stories
Henry Enoch Dummer

1865–1866

The Hon. Henry Dummer was John T. Stuart's law partner in Springfield before Lincoln had taken the position in 1841.

Lincoln used to come to our office in Spfgd and borrow books—don't Know whether he walked or rode: he was an uncouth looking lad—did not say much—what he did say he said it strongly—Sharply.

    In 1859 I was in the Supm Court room in the State house: Lincoln was or had been telling his yarns. A man—a Kind of lick spittle—a farmer Said—["]Lincoln why do you not write out your stories & put them in a book" Lincoln, drew himself up—fixed his face, as if a thousand dead carcusses—and a million of privies were Shooting all their Stench into his nostrils, and Said "Such a book would Stink like a thousand privies."

    Lincoln had 2 characters—one of *purity*—& the other as it were an insane love in telling dirty and Smutty Stories—A good story of that Kind has a point with a sting to it.

The backyard of Lincoln's house had a wooden walkway that ran to the barn and outhouse. Lincoln prided himself in keeping his wood box full.

December 1865

Lincoln's First Biographers

Books and pamphlets about Abraham Lincoln had been published during his lifetime—including at least twenty campaign biographies from 1860 and 1864. But in the tremendous outpouring of grief following the President's assassination, it became clear that a full biography was needed, and an array of authors stepped forward to try to provide it. The earliest was a small book by Phebe Ann Hanaford, a Massachusetts teacher on her way to becoming the Universalist Church's first woman minister. Entitled *Abraham Lincoln: His Life and Public Services*, it was described by its author as a "record of his stainless life and martyr's death."

Before long, four much larger biographies appeared, each laden with reprints of Lincoln's published writings—by L. P. Brockett, Frank Crosby, Joseph H. Barrett, and Henry Raymond. Mary Lincoln borrowed this last one from a friend in November and found it "the most correct history" of her husband that had been written. Tad, overhearing her say this to Robert, piped, "Mother, I am going to save all the little money you give me and get a copy."

But by far the most influential Lincoln biography of this first year after the assassination was one written by a former doctor and schoolteacher turned newspaper editor—Josiah Holland of the *Springfield Republican*. A devout Christian whose mother always thought he should have been a preacher, Holland saw journalism and public speaking as his "lay pulpit." In April 1865 he delivered a eulogy in Springfield, Massachusetts, in which he portrayed Lincoln as a humble man from the backwoods whose Christian faith undergirded everything he did. A savvy publisher contacted him and asked for a full biography, and the eastern journalist dropped everything to pursue it.

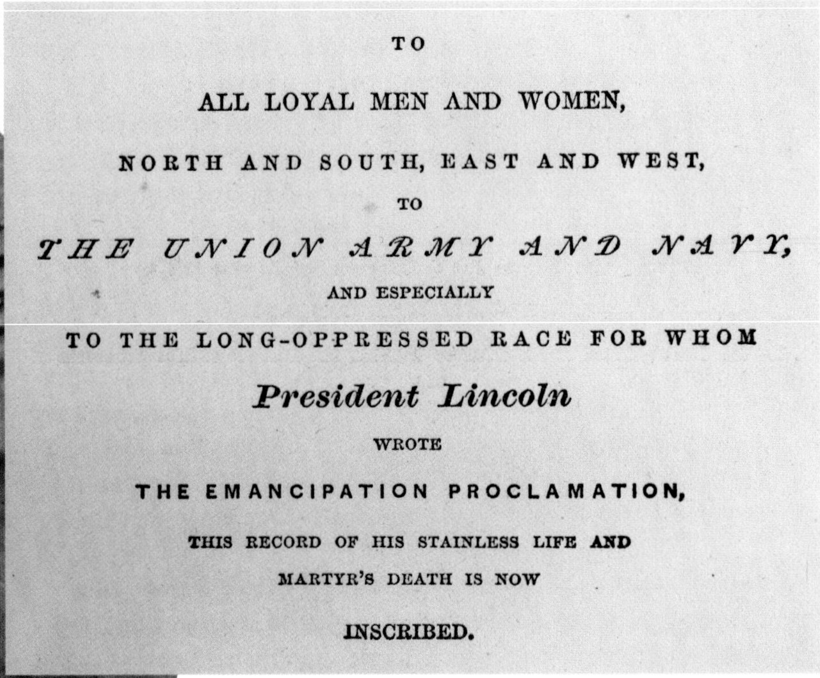

TO

ALL LOYAL MEN AND WOMEN,

NORTH AND SOUTH, EAST AND WEST,

TO

THE UNION ARMY AND NAVY,

AND ESPECIALLY

TO THE LONG-OPPRESSED RACE FOR WHOM

President Lincoln

WROTE

THE EMANCIPATION PROCLAMATION,

THIS RECORD OF HIS STAINLESS LIFE AND

MARTYR'S DEATH IS NOW

INSCRIBED.

Phebe Ann Hanaford was a cousin of abolitionist Lucretia Mott. She admired Lincoln most of all for his Emancipation Proclamation.

Holland had not known Lincoln, but he reached out to those who had. In May he traveled to Springfield and met with a dozen or more people, including William Herndon, Lincoln's longtime law partner, and Newton Bateman, an Illinois educator whose office had been near Lincoln's during the summer and fall before his election. After their visit in Springfield, Bateman mailed Holland an eight-page letter in which he described a conversation with Lincoln that had supposedly taken place in late October 1860. As the presidential candidate had paced the floor of Bateman's office in the state capitol, he claimed he suddenly stopped, burst into tears, and began to speak. "I know there is a God and that He hates injustice and slavery," Lincoln said, according to Bateman. "I see the storm coming and I know that His hand is in it. If He has a plan and work for me—and I think He has—I believe I am ready. . . . I know I am right because I know that liberty is right, for Christ teaches it, and Christ is God."

When Holland received this testimony, he was elated, finding in it the "golden link in the chain of Lincoln's history." It "illuminates every page of his subsequent record," he wrote. And so Lincoln's Christianity became the central thesis of this first widely popular Lincoln biography, which sold more than 100,000 copies.

William Herndon, who had given Holland considerable help, was furious when he read the book. He believed that the Bateman conversation, as related by Holland, simply could not have occurred. Herndon knew that for most of his life Lincoln had been an "open infidel"—"sometimes bordering on atheism"—and had "always denied that Jesus was the Son of God." Furthermore, why would Lincoln, on the verge of his election as president, have confided such things to a man he hardly knew? Either Holland had exaggerated, or Bateman had lied. Herndon said that when Holland had come to Springfield in May, he had been determined to find proof of Lincoln's religious faith. When he kept running into evidence to the contrary, Holland had decided to manufacture it. "He then asked me—'What about Mr. Lincoln's religion,' to which I replied 'the less said the better!' He then made this expression—'O never mind, I'll fix that' with a sort of a wink and a nod." Realizing that Holland's biography was in some ways defective, old friends of Lincoln urged Herndon to write the true story.

Even Mary Lincoln, who read a copy of Holland's biography in late 1865 and found it to her "great satisfaction," felt that he had embellished on the religious theme. She wrote him in December saying that she believed he had quoted from unreliable sources, including an unnamed nurse in Washington, D.C., who claimed to have had a religious conversation with Lincoln. "With all the President's deep feeling, he was *not* a demonstrative man," Mary wrote. "It was not *his* nature to commit his griefs and religious feelings so fully to words."

Josiah Gilbert Holland

"Eminently a Christian President"
Josiah Holland

1865

Lincoln's religious faith deepened over the course of his presidency, but Holland's emphasis on this theme was exaggerated.

He was a religious man. The fact may be noted without any reservation—with only an explanation. He believed in God, and in his personal supervision of the affairs of men. He believed himself to be under his control and guidance. He believed in the power and ultimate triumph of the right, through his belief in God. This unwavering faith in a Divine Providence began at his mother's knee, and ran like a thread of gold through all the inner experiences of his life. . . .

He believed in his inmost soul that he was an instrument in the hands of God for the accomplishment of a great purpose. The power was above him. In him, Providence, the people and the purpose of both met; and as a poor, weak, imperfect man, he felt humbled by the august presence, and crushed by the importance with which he had been endowed. . . .

He grew more religious with every passing year of his official life. The tender piety that breathed in some of his later state papers is unexampled in any of the utterances of his predecessors. In all the great emergencies of his closing years, his reliance upon divine guidance and assistance was often extremely touching. "I have been driven many times to my knees," he once remarked, "by the overwhelming conviction that I had no where else to go." . . .

Moderate, frank, truthful, gentle, forgiving, loving, just, Mr. Lincoln will always be remembered as eminently a Christian President; and the almost immeasurably great results which he had the privilege of achieving, were due to the fact that he was a Christian President.

"I Saw Him Mostly Alone"

Not long after the assassination, the orator and abolitionist Frederick Douglass received a package from Mary Lincoln containing her husband's favorite walking staff. "I know of no one who would appreciate this more than Fred. Douglass," she wrote. Douglass, who was devastated by the President's murder, wrote back that he would treasure the cane as an "object of sacred interest"—and a reminder of Lincoln's "human interest in the welfare of my whole race."

Douglass was not an unqualified Lincoln supporter. During the early years of the Civil War the former slave had been an outspoken critic, attacking the President on his slowness in declaring emancipation and for his advocacy of racial separation. In August 1862, following Lincoln's public letter to Horace Greeley, he called him an "itinerant colonization lecturer" who exemplified America's widespread "prejudice and Negro hatred." But after Lincoln issued the Emancipation Proclamation, Douglass changed his opinion. On August 10, 1863, he was invited to meet Lincoln in person and was deeply impressed by his directness and humanity. Over the next two years the two men drew even closer, meeting on several occasions. Though Douglass reserved the right to criticize, as when Lincoln failed to retaliate after the 1864 Confederate slaughter of black troops, in March 1865 he was warmly welcomed after the second inaugural—the first time in history that a U.S. President openly socialized with a black colleague. This cemented Douglass's loyalty to the frontier President. In a speech in June, following the assassination, Douglass called Lincoln "emphatically the black man's president: the first to show any respect to their rights as men." And now in the final days of December, in a special Lincoln address, he praised his famous friend as "one of the best men that ever presided over the destinies of this or any country."

Lincoln's antler-headed cane was Mary's gift to Frederick Douglass. Over the years she built a lasting bond with Douglass, who recognized her as a person remarkably free from racial prejudice.

"He Was a Progressive Man"
Frederick Douglass

From the first moment of my interview with him I seemed to myself to have been acquainted with him for years. For while he was among the most solid men I ever met he was among the most transparent. What Mr. Lincoln was in company with white men, of course I cannot tell. I saw him mostly alone; but this much I can say of him, he was one of the very few Americans who could entertain a negro and converse with him without in anywise reminding him of the unpopularity of his color. . . .

On one occasion, I remember while conversing with him, his messenger twice announced as in an adjoining room and as wishing to see him Governor Buckingham of Connecticut. Tell the Governor to wait, said President Lincoln. I wish to have a long talk with my friend Douglass. I remained a full hour after this, while the Governor of Connecticut waited without for an interview. . . .

The last days of Mr. Lincoln were his best days. . . . Had Mr. Lincoln lived, we might have looked for still greater progress. Learning wisdom by war, he would have learned more from Peace. Already he had expressed himself in favor of extending the right of suffrage to two classes of colored men; first to the brave colored soldiers who had fought under our flag, and second to the very intelligent part of the colored population [of the] South. This declaration on his part though it seemed to mean but little meant a great deal. It was like Abraham Lincoln. He never shocked prejudices unnecessarily. Having learned statesmanship while splitting rails, he always used the edge of the wedge first—and the fact that he used this at all meant that he would if need be, use the thick as well as the thin. He saw the absurdity of asking men to fight for a Government which should degrade them, and the meanness of enfranchising enemies and disfranchising friends. He was a progressive man, a human man, an honorable man, and at heart an antislavery man. He had exhausted the resources of conciliation upon the rebels and the slaveholders and now looked to the principles of Liberty and justice, for the peace, security, happiness, and prosperity of his country. I assume therefore, had Abraham Lincoln been spared to see this day, the negro of the South would have more than a hope of enfranchisement and no rebels would hold the reins of Government in any one of the late rebellious states. Whosoever else have cause to mourn the loss of Abraham Lincoln, to the colored people of the country his death is an unspeakable calamity.

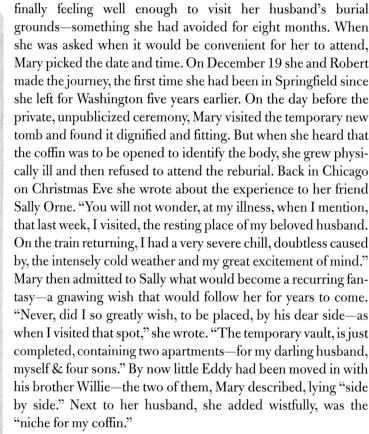

December 21, 1865

A Temporary Tomb

For Mary Lincoln, the shock and amnesia she experienced at the time of the assassination gradually gave way to the dull ache of sorrow. In her hotel in Chicago she pored over the letters Lincoln had written her over the decades—"his dear, loving letters to me, many of them . . . quite yellow with age." She sought consolation in her belief that, along with Willie and Eddy, her husband awaited her "in their blessed home" in the afterlife, where he loved her even more than ever. For Mary, Lincoln was becoming "the worshipped one"—the idolized man who not only had been her husband but the nation's savior. It was Mary who helped pioneer the cult of the mythic Lincoln—the godlike figure that was fast replacing the flesh-and-blood man from Illinois.

In December Mary received word from Springfield that they were ready to move Lincoln's body from the receiving vault at Oak Ridge Cemetery to a new temporary tomb built on the six-acre plot. The simple brick structure was built to hold all members of the Lincoln family until a formal memorial could be created nearby. Mary was finally feeling well enough to visit her husband's burial grounds—something she had avoided for eight months. When she was asked when it would be convenient for her to attend, Mary picked the date and time. On December 19 she and Robert made the journey, the first time she had been in Springfield since she left for Washington five years earlier. On the day before the private, unpublicized ceremony, Mary visited the temporary new tomb and found it dignified and fitting. But when she heard that the coffin was to be opened to identify the body, she grew physically ill and then refused to attend the reburial. Back in Chicago on Christmas Eve she wrote about the experience to her friend Sally Orne. "You will not wonder, at my illness, when I mention, that last week, I visited, the resting place of my beloved husband. On the train returning, I had a very severe chill, doubtless caused by, the intensely cold weather and my great excitement of mind." Mary then admitted to Sally what would become a recurring fantasy—a gnawing wish that would follow her for years to come. "Never, did I so greatly wish, to be placed, by his dear side—as when I visited that spot," she wrote. "The temporary vault, is just completed, containing two apartments—for my darling husband, myself & four sons." By now little Eddy had been moved in with his brother Willie—the two of them, Mary described, lying "side by side." Next to her husband, she added wistfully, was the "niche for my coffin."

MRS LINCOLN

A temporary tomb at Oak Ridge Cemetery housed Lincoln's remains until the completion of the Lincoln Monument. Though Mary declined to take part in any ceremony here, Robert wrote, "My mother & myself were at Springfield yesterday & were present at the transfer of my father's remains from the old vault to the new."

The following selections from George Bancroft's forty-eight-page lecture on Abraham Lincoln reveal his style of back-handed praise.

ON LINCOLN'S SLOWNESS TO ACT

The habits of his mind were those of meditation and inward thought, rather than of action. . . . He excelled in logical statement more than in executive ability. He reasoned clearly, his reflective judgment was good, and his purposes were fixed; but, like the Hamlet of his only poet, his will was tardy in action, and, for this reason, and not from humility or tenderness of feeling, he sometimes deplored that the duty which devolved on him had not fallen to the lot of another.

ON HIS LACK OF IMAGINATION

Like Jefferson and Lafayette, he had faith in the intuitions of the people, and read those intuitions with rare sagacity. He knew how to bide time, and was less apt to run ahead of public thought than to lag behind. . . . Yet his sensibilities were not acute; he had no vividness of imagination to picture to his mind the horrors of the battle-field or the sufferings in hospitals, his conscience was more tender than his feelings.

ON HIS INABILITY TO JUDGE CHARACTER

Lincoln was one of the most unassuming of men. . . . He was no respecter of persons, and neither rank, nor reputation, nor services overawed him. In judging of character he failed in discrimination, and his appointments were sometimes bad; but he readily deferred to public opinion, and in appointing the head of the armies he followed the manifest preference of Congress.

February 12, 1866

A Strange Keynote on the Nation's First "Lincoln Day"

In December 1865, following an eight-month recess, Congress reconvened. While it had been out of session, President Johnson had rescinded the privileges of free blacks on the southern coastline and ordered that their lands, given to them by General Sherman and others, be restored to their former white owners. In state after state the secessionists were rising back to power.

One of Congress's first acts, after adopting the Thirteenth Amendment, was to vote to host a Lincoln commemoration at the Capitol, on what would have been the slain President's fifty-seventh birthday. By selecting that day, rather than the anniversary of his death, Congress established a precedent—that annual Lincoln Day celebrations would focus on his life and accomplishments and not on his martyrdom.

The committee's first choice for speaker was Edwin Stanton, Lincoln's loyal secretary of war who continued to serve under Andrew Johnson. But when Stanton declined, an invitation was sent to the historian George Bancroft, who had given the congressional eulogy for Andrew Jackson decades earlier. To many it was not clear why an aging Democrat from Massachusetts who had met Lincoln only once, and who had been critical of his policies, had been chosen to speak at the first Lincoln Day celebration.

On February 12, 1866, the Capitol was closed except to those with tickets. House of Representatives Hall was decorated for the occasion, its Speakers Desk

The first Lincoln Day celebration in Washington took place inside the House of Representatives, seen here in the distance.

draped in black mourning swag. At noon a grand procession of virtually the entire government of the United States, as well as friends and foreign dignitaries, entered the chamber for the solemn ceremony. After the Marine Band played a dirge, the chaplain of the House offered an opening prayer, and then Lafayette Foster, the Senate's president pro tempore, gave the introduction of the keynote speaker.

But if those gathered had expected words of unvarnished praise for the inspired leadership and self-sacrifice of the fallen President, Bancroft offered up instead what was to many a mind-numbing history lesson. He spoke of ancient Greece and India, of Europe and the early American Republic. He didn't even mention Lincoln until he was fifty minutes into his oration. And then after he began his short biography of the "impoverished" westerner, he drifted off from his subject again for another twenty-five minutes to discuss Britain's disdain for the Union during the Civil War (in the process insulting the British minister who was present).

When Bancroft finally began his assessment of Lincoln, many in the audience were dumbfounded. For the portrait Bancroft painted was of a well-meaning but ineffective leader, cursed by indecision and sluggishness of imagination—a man whose administration of the war had been at times nothing short of callous.

Those who had known Lincoln best were outraged. David Davis, who had come in from Chicago specifically for the address, was furious, not only with Bancroft but with the committee that had chosen him. And John Hay, in a letter written to William Herndon, called the two-and-a-half-hour-long address "a disgraceful exhibition of ignorance and prejudice" from a fussy academic who had never understood Lincoln. "Miss Nancy Bancroft and the rest of that patent leather kid glove set know no more of him than an owl does of a comet, blazing into his blinking eyes."

While some reviewers appreciated the nuanced, critical approach of George Bancroft's Lincoln address, even they had to admit it was in many ways a disappointment. The *New York Times*, which said that the historian "did his subject justice," added, "He inspired no enthusiasm. . . . He drew a picture cold in outline."

"As Cold as an Icicle"
David Davis

February 22, 1866

There were some who were highly pleased by Bancroft's effort, including Washington officeholder Benjamin French, who called it "very eloquent" and said that "the latter part of it" was "applauded constantly." But in a candid letter to William Herndon, David Davis expressed contempt for both the address and the speaker.

Dear Herndon,

Mr. Bancroft totally misconceived Mr. Lincoln's character, in applying "unsteadiness" & confusion to it—Mr Lincoln grew more steady & resolute, & his ideas were never confused—If there were any changes in him after he got here, they were for the better—I thought him always the master of his subject—He was a much more self possessed man than I thought—He thought for himself, which is a rare quality nowadays. How could Bancroft know anything about Lincoln, except as he judged of him as the public do—He never Saw him, & is himself as cold as an icicle—I should never have selected an old Democratic politician, & one from Mass &c to deliver an eulogy on Lincoln— . . .

Yr Frd D. Davis

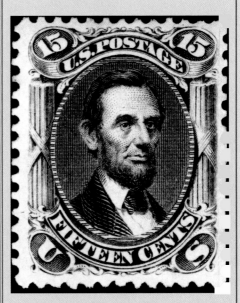

In 1866 the Post Office Department issued the nation's first commemorative stamp.

Birth of the Ku Klux Klan

In early 1866 a secret organization was founded in Pulaski, Tennessee, dedicated to the restoration of white supremacy. Called the Ku Klux Klan, after the Greek word for "circle," it was soon headed up by former officers of the Confederate Army. Its first Grand Wizard was General Nathan Bedford Forrest, responsible for the massacre of black soldiers during the Civil War. According to supporters, the Klan was a chivalrous organization set up to protect whites from potential uprisings in an era where in many places former slaves now greatly outnumbered whites. But in fact the Klan was in open defiance of Lincoln's policies of emancipation and increased black rights. Targeting former slaves and their white supporters, and especially blacks who tried to vote or to take part in politics, the Klan used violence and intimidation to defy state and federal law. Just "name the right of the negro to vote," said Frederick Douglass, "and Ku-Klux Klans . . . commence to hunt and slay the unoffending black." Wearing hoods and claiming to be the ghosts of slain Confederate soldiers, over the years they would murder hundreds of innocent men and women, in an attempt to unmake the world that Lincoln had helped bequeath.

Ku Klux Klan members regularly terrorized former slaves and their supporters.

Blasting the President
Frederick Douglass

February 28, 1866

In early February 1866 Frederick Douglass led a delegation of freedmen to plead the cause of black suffrage to the President. Johnson was blatantly rude to the group and insisted that each state must decide the suffrage question for itself. At one point he leaned over and whispered to Douglass that if whites and blacks were "thrown together at the ballot box," a full-blown race war would be the result. After they left, the President turned to his private secretary Philip Ripley and said, "Those damned sons of bitches thought they had me in a trap. I know that damned Douglass; he is just like any nigger and he would sooner cut a white man's throat than not."

On February 19 Johnson vetoed the Freedmen's Bureau Bill, which would have set up federal jurisdiction in the South and protected the rights of the former slaves. In response, on February 28 Douglass spoke before a large and sympathetic crowd in Chicago.

It is said that Andrew Johnson is following in the footsteps of Abraham Lincoln. It is a foul and black slander on the dead[.] It was my privilege to know Mr. Lincoln, and I have to say, were he living now, he would stand today with the men who go farthest in asserting equal rights to all people. He was preeminently a progressive man.... The fact that Lincoln would invite a black man to the White House was an indication of the character of the man—an indication that he possessed the courage to contradict a popular prejudice, and go athwart a popular custom.... One of the lessons of the assassination was to teach us that we may not bind the chain around our neighbor without having one end around our own neck.... Jeff Davis was a great traitor, but he was at least a consistent traitor. He was a wolf, but not a wolf in sheep's clothing.... He did not put himself at the head of the rebel cause to betray it, as Andrew Johnson has done to the loyal cause.

The plight of former slaves was of little concern to Andrew Johnson's administration.

Memories "Burned In" with a "Branding Iron"

Benjamin French

April 15, 1866

Benjamin Brown French was Commissioner of Public Buildings in Washington and had regular contact with President Lincoln. In 1865 he helped oversee preparations for his funeral. "I was with the President's remains most of the time," he wrote in a letter, "and felt responsible for many of the arrangements." On the first anniversary of Lincoln's death, French recorded his memories of that terrible day.

One year ago this morning, Abraham Lincoln, the good President, and the best man I ever knew, died. How my memory goes back to that awful morning, and all the little circumstances connected with it that fell under my observation. How I stood by the bed of death—how my hand was wrung by Mrs. Lincoln as she sat on the sofa in an adjoining room—the overwhelming distress of Capt. Robert Lincoln, who sat in the room with his mother—how, at the request of the family, I got into the President's carriage and rode to Secy. Welles's after Mrs. Welles—how I waited there until she could rise from her sickbed, dress, and take a little refreshment—how we rode to the White House, where I remained to take charge of it & see that it was placed in proper care, while the carriage bore Mrs. Welles to Mr. Peterson's in 10th St. where the President lay—how I returned to my house & breakfasted—how, just as I had finished, the bells commenced tolling—how I returned to the President's house in time to accompany the remains in & to the guestchamber where they were deposited —how I saw them taken from the box in which they were enclosed, all limp and warm, and laid upon the floor, and then stretched upon the cooling board. All this and a hundred things more that occurred that day, are indelibly impressed upon my memory, and death alone will erase them. Indeed, all of the events of the ensuing terrible week are there burned in, as it were, with a heated branding iron!

By 1866 a national trend had emerged as Lincoln's name and likeness were increasingly used to sell commercial products. A maker of stomach medicine tried to capitalize on Lincoln's honesty, and a lead manufacturer associated its product with his "purity and excellence."

May 23, 1866

Lincoln's Struggles with Love

As William Herndon continued his biographical research, he harbored a fascination with Lincoln's early love life and with his rocky path to his marriage to Mary Todd. In the fall of 1865 while in Petersburg he heard of a woman named Mary Owens whom Lincoln had supposedly once tried to marry. He tracked her down to Missouri, where she was married to a man named Vineyard. Finally, after many inquiries from Herndon, she answered. In a letter sent on May 23, 1866, she enclosed correspondence from Lincoln from 1837 proving that as a young man he had offered to marry her. It was an astonishing discovery, completely unknown to the wider world.

Mary was a native of Kentucky who had moved to New Salem in 1836 and soon afterward became involved with Lincoln. In the fall of the next year, despite serious misgivings, Lincoln made a halfhearted proposal of marriage to her. But by this point Mary was having second thoughts about him. In contrast to the genteel men she had known back in Kentucky, he seemed crude and at times thoughtless. Once, while riding with friends, he had failed to help her cross a creek on horseback, demonstrating a heedlessness, she thought, that didn't bode well for the future. "When I rode up beside him, I remarked you are a nice fellow; I suppose you did not care whether my neck was broken or not." He laughingly replied, (I suppose as a way of complement) that he knew I was plenty smart to take care of myself." When Lincoln made his proffer of marriage official, she promptly turned him down, by letter. Though relieved, Lincoln was shocked by the refusal. "I have now come to the conclusion never again to think of marrying," he wrote to a friend. "I can never be satisfied with anyone who would be block-head enough to have me."

By the time Lincoln wrote these words, he was living in Springfield. There he was soon introduced to Mary Todd, the vivacious younger sister of Mrs. Ninian Edwards. Before long the gangly young lawyer was breaking his own rule and courting the young belle in earnest. But once again the path of romance was a rocky one. Following an engagement and a set wedding date, their relationship began to crumble and then abruptly ended in what Lincoln afterward called "that fatal first of Jan[uar]y."

Few incidents in Lincoln's life have been as disputed as this one, as Herndon found out when he began interviewing people about it. Some said Mary had called off the engagement after Lincoln had forgotten to show up for a date. Others said Lincoln had ended it in a fit of jealousy after watching Mary flirt with another man. Ninian Edwards claimed that Lincoln had fallen in love with his cousin, Matilda Edwards, and that this had caused the breakup. But Ninian's wife, Elizabeth, with the insight of a married woman, said that Lincoln had had an attack of self-doubt in which he had questioned his ability to make a woman happy. (Later the Edwardses' son Albert complicated things further, claiming the marriage was called off due to the opposition of his parents.)

When this photograph was taken in 1858, Lincoln was practicing law in Springfield with William Herndon and preparing for a Senate race against Stephen A. Douglas. Herndon was fascinated with his partner's personal life but was rarely if ever invited inside Lincoln's home.

"Deficient" in What Makes Up a "Woman's Happiness"
Mary Owens

May 23, 1866

Mary Owens Vineyard not only corresponded with William Herndon, she sent him Lincoln's letters to her revealing his complicated feelings when as a young man he had been torn between feelings for her, a strong sense of duty, and an even stronger desire to get out of the relationship. She might easily have accepted his odd proposal, she wrote, but "I suppose my feelings were not sufficiently enlisted to have the matter consummated." Her final reason for rejecting him was that she "thought Mr. Lincoln was deficient, in those little links which make up the great chain of woman's happiness."

Springfield Aug. 16th 1837
Friend Mary.

. . . I want in all cases to do right, and most particularly so, in all cases with women. I want, at this particular time, more than any thing else, to do right with you, and if I knew it would be doing right, as I rather suspect it would, to let you alone, I would do it. And for the purpose of making the matter as plain as possible, I now say, that you can now drop the subject, dismiss your thoughts (if you ever had any) from me forever, and leave this letter unanswered, without calling forth one accusing murmer from me. And I will even go further, and say, that if it will add any thing to your comfort, or peace of mind, to do so, it is my sincere wish that you should. Do not understand by this, that I wish to cut your acquaintance. I mean no such thing. What I do wish is, that our further acquaintance shall depend upon yourself. If such further acquaintance would contribute nothing to your happiness, I am sure it would not to mine. If you feel yourself in any degree bound to me, I am now willing to release you, provided you wish it; while, on the other hand, I am willing, and even anxious to bind you faster, if I can be convinced that it will, in any considerable degree, add to your happiness. This, indeed, is the whole question with me. Nothing would make me more miserable than to believe you miserable—nothing more happy, than to know you were so. . . .

Your friend
LINCOLN.

Mary Owens was photographed a few years after her ill-fated relationship with Lincoln. In a letter to a friend written after the breakup, Lincoln mocked her, writing that "her skin was too full of fat."

"A Cold Man"
Elizabeth Todd Edwards

1865–1866

One of Herndon's Springfield informants was Elizabeth Todd Edwards, an older sister of Mary Lincoln's.

I Knew Mr L well—he was a cold Man—had no affection—was not Social—was abstracted—thoughtful. . . . Could not hold a lengthy Conversation with a lady—was not sufficiently Educated & intelligent in the female line to do so—He was charmed with Mary's wit and fascinated with her quick sagacity—her will—her nature—and Culture—I have happened in the room where they were sitting often & often and Mary led the Conversation—Lincoln would listen & gaze on her as if drawn by some Superior power, irresistably So; he listened—never Scarcely Said a word. I did not in a little time think that Mr L. & Mary were Suitable to Each other & so Said to Mary. Mary was quick, lively, gay—frivalous it may be, Social and loved glitter Show & pomp & power. She was an Extremely Ambitious woman and in Ky often & often Contended that She was destined to be the wife of some future President—Said it in Earnest. Mr Lincoln loved Mary—he went Crazy in my own opinion—not because he loved Miss Edwards as Said, but because he wanted to marry and doubted his ability & Capacity to please and support a wife.

Elizabeth Todd Edwards

Whatever the cause of the breakup, it threw Lincoln into the worst mental crisis of his life. Numerous witnesses told Herndon that he had gone "crazy" at this time. His roommate Joshua Speed said that in December 1840 he had to "remove razors from his room—take away all knives and all other dangerous things" lest he commit suicide. Lincoln himself said after January 1 that he was "the most miserable man living," writing a friend, "If what I feel were equally distributed to the whole human family, there would not be one cheerful face on the earth."

Joshua Speed nursed Lincoln through these days, and in an astonishing letter in July 1842 Lincoln revealed much about the nature of his crisis: "I must regain my confidence in my own ability to keep my resolves once they are made. In that ability, you know, I once prided myself as the only, or at least the chief, gem of my character; that gem I lost—how, and where, you too well know. I have not yet regained it; and until I do, I cannot trust myself in any matter of much importance." Lincoln had loved Mary when he had proposed to her in 1840. But when an attack of doubt led him to back out (perhaps influenced by the Edwardses' opposition to the marriage or by his lack of luck with Matilda Edwards), it had left him as a man who could no longer trust himself.

It was Dr. Anson Henry who helped bring the couple back together. Henry had been treating Lincoln for his "hypochondriasm" and had come to greatly admire the young man. He took it upon himself to explain to Mary how depressed Lincoln was and how he still cared for her. Mary and Lincoln began meeting again, this time in secret, and gradually allowed their old feelings to blossom again. Their relationship was stronger now, and less vulnerable to the views of others. And finally Lincoln once again proposed and was accepted. On a rainy night in November 1842, with only the meagerest of planning, Abraham Lincoln and Mary Todd were married inside the Edwards home. Lincoln placed a gold ring upon her finger on which were engraved the words "Love is Eternal." One week later he wrote a friend cheerfully, "Nothing new here, except my marrying, which to me, is a matter of profound wonder."

The earliest known photograph of Mary Lincoln, along with a matching portrait of her husband, was taken just four years into their marriage.

113

In his description of the signing of the Emancipation Proclamation on January 1, 1863, Arnold included his memory of Lincoln's spoken account of the incident.

A friend on one occasion, reminded [Lincoln] that he had given the pen with which the proclamation was signed, to Senator Sumner. "Yes," said the President, "I had promised Sumner the pen. On New Year's day . . . the final proclamation was all ready to be signed and sent to the press. . . . I went down to the parlor and held a very crowded reception. During the time I was receiving calls, the information which would enable me to fill up these blanks was furnished me, and I left the drawing

The gold pen that Lincoln used to sign the Emancipation Proclamation

room and hastened up stairs to sign and send to the associated press, the proclamation. As I took up a pen to sign the paper, my hand and arm trembled and shook so violently, that I could not write. I could not for a moment, control my arm. I paused, and a superstitious feeling came over me which made me hesitate. . . . In a moment I remembered that I had been shaking hands for hours, with several hundred people, and hence a very simple explanation of the trembling and shaking of my arm. With a laugh at my superstitious thought, I signed and sent off the paper. Sumner soon after calling for the pen, out of half a dozen on my table, I gave him the one I had most probably used."

1866
Two New Lincoln Books

Less than a year after Lincoln's death, and not long after the appearance of Josiah Holland's biography, two new books were published by men who had each known Lincoln well. The first, by Isaac Arnold, was a seven-hundred-page work entitled *History of Abraham Lincoln and the Overthrow of Slavery*. A Chicago lawyer and politician, Arnold had been a close friend of Lincoln's for more than twenty years. In April 1865 the President had asked him to prepare a record of his administration concentrating in particular on the overthrow of slavery. He had promised to help Arnold with the task, but then came the assassination. When Andrew Johnson made the commission formal, Arnold went to work. In his book he called the Emancipation Proclamation "the most important historical event of the nineteenth century" and praised Lincoln as "the greatest . . . and best man our country has produced." One of the most important of the early biographies, it helped solidify Lincoln's reputation as "The Great Emancipator."

The second Lincoln book to come out in 1866 was by the artist Francis B. Carpenter. It was a small collection of reminiscences entitled *Six Months at the White House with Abraham Lincoln*, quickly republished as *The Inner Life of Abraham Lincoln*. "Aspiring in no sense to the dignity of a biography," the author wrote, it was a brief "sketch" that he hoped might afford "glimpses" into "the character of the man." Two years earlier Carpenter had painted the historic scene of Lincoln presenting the Emancipation Proclamation to his cabinet. He had been invited to work inside Lincoln's White House and to sketch the President as he went about his business. "My access to the official chamber was made nearly as free as that of the personal secretaries," Carpenter wrote. If anyone objected to his presence in the room, the President would say, "Oh, you need not mind him, he is just a painter."

Carpenter made the most of his extraordinary access, creating not only a historic painting but a little book that went on to become a huge best seller.

When Mary Lincoln read it, however, she was not pleased. "This man Carpenter, never had a dozen interviews with the late President," she fired off to a friend. "To think of this stranger, silly adventurer, daring to write a work entitled 'The Inner Life of Abraham Lincoln.' Each scribbling writer, almost strangers to Mr. L., subscribe themselves . . . [as] his most intimate friend!"

Abraham Lincoln on May 16, 1861

Francis B. Carpenter, a few years before getting his commission to paint Lincoln

An early illustration showed Francis Carpenter at work in the White House.

Isaac Arnold was Lincoln's friend and an early biographer, and some found in him a Lincolnesque quality. "He is a tall, lithe, sinewy sort of man," wrote one observer of Arnold, "with a brownish complexion . . . [and] a quick penetrating eye."

Lincoln Laughing
Francis B. Carpenter

1866

Carpenter had not known Lincoln well, but his stories brought the President alive in a vivid new way.

I had been engaged in the official chamber until quite late one evening, upon some pencil studies of accessories, necessary to introduce in my picture. The President, Mrs. Lincoln, and the Private Secretaries had gone to the opera, and for the time being I had undisturbed possession. Towards twelve o'clock I heard some persons enter the sleeping apartment occupied by Mr. Nicolay and Major Hay, which was directly opposite the room where I was sitting; and shortly afterward the hearty laugh of Mr. Lincoln broke the stillness, proceeding from the same quarter. Throwing aside my work, I went across the hall to see what had occasioned this outbreak of merriment. The Secretaries had come in and Hay had retired; Mr. Nicolay sat by the table with his boots off, and the President was leaning over the "footboard" of the bed, laughing and talking with the hilarity of a schoolboy. It seemed that Hay, or "John," as the President called him, had met with a singular adventure, which was the subject of the amusement. Glancing through the half-open door, Mr. Lincoln caught sight of me, and the story had to be repeated for my benefit. The incident was trifling in itself, but the President's enjoyment of it was very exhilarating. I never saw him in so frolicsome a mood as on this occasion. . . . Mr. Lincoln's "laugh" stood by itself. The "neigh" of a wild horse on his native prairie is not more undisguised and hearty. . . . Mr. [Isaac] Arnold [once] remarked . . . "That laugh has been the President's life-preserver!"

In a corner of his desk he kept a copy of the latest humorous work; and it was his habit when greatly fatigued, annoyed, or depressed, to take this up and read a chapter, frequently with great relief.

August 1866

Lincoln's Third Secretary

In the late summer of 1866 William O. Stoddard, formerly of Lincoln's staff, began to publish his White House reminiscences in a series of articles for the *New York Citizen*. While the public had heard of John Nicolay and John Hay, few knew anything about their low-profile colleague.

As a young Illinois journalist Stoddard had been one of the first to endorse Lincoln for President, and then had pestered him for a job in his new administration. In order to bring him on, Lincoln granted him a clerkship in the Interior Department, with the task of signing land patents. Before long he was transferred to the White House, where for the next three years he served as Lincoln's third secretary. Stoddard moved into Hay's office in the northeast corner of the executive mansion, where he occupied a "green-covered desk" and busied himself with "exceedingly hard work." One of his jobs was to create a daily synopsis of the public journals, since Lincoln now had little time to read the newspapers. It was also his responsibility to cull through the President's incoming mail and remove crank letters and death threats before they ever reached Lincoln's desk.

Over time John Hay became annoyed by his young assistant, describing him as lazy, self-serving, and often absent from the job. "Stod is more & more worthless," he dashed off to Nicolay in 1863; "I can scarcely rely on him for anything." But Nicolay called Stoddard "a man of considerable talent," and he won the trust of both the President and the First Lady. Stoddard was placed in charge of Mary Lincoln's correspondence and became known unofficially as her personal secretary. (Unlike Nicolay or Hay, Stoddard was devoted to Mary, whom he described as a "kind-hearted lady.")

In late 1864, at Stoddard's request, Lincoln appointed him U.S. Marshal of Arkansas. He was working there in his new capacity when word of the President's assassination arrived. "I feel for the first time how much I loved and venerated Abraham Lincoln," he wrote to John Hay on April 22. "I only wish to say that something of personal sympathy for you and Nicolay mingles tonight with my sorrow for the man who had done more for me than all my other friends."

Stoddard's thirteen essays for the *Citizen* covered different aspects of Lincoln's presidency, which he would later weave into his memoir *Inside the White House in War Times*.

William O. Stoddard assisted Nicolay and Hay in the White House and had a close relationship with Mary Lincoln. "What'll we do with the Madam after Stod goes?" Nicolay wrote Hay in 1864. "You and I can't manage her."

Nicolay and Hay Close Up
William O. Stoddard

August 25, 1866

This insider's description of Lincoln's secretaries, Nicolay and Hay, came from their younger colleague William O. Stoddard. It was published in the New York Citizen.

Mr. Nicolay, the Private Secretary, and the only attache of the President who had any claim to that specific title, was a man of somewhat over thirty, a native of Baden Baden in Germany, but from early youth a resident of Illinois. A fair French and German scholar, with some ability as a Writer and much natural acuteness, he nevertheless—thanks to a dyspeptic tendency—had developed an artificial manner the reverse of "popular," and could say "no" about as disagreeably as any man I ever knew. That, however, for which we all respected him, which was his chief qualification for the very important post he occupied, was his devotion to the President and his incorruptible honesty Lincoln-ward. He measured all things and all men by their relations to the President, and was of incalculable service in fending off much that would have been unnecessary labor and exhaustion to his overworked patron. For this, and more, he deserves the thanks of all who loved Mr. Lincoln, even if at times they had reason to grumble at "the bulldog in the ante-room." Mr. Hay was, by courtesy, "Assistant Private Secretary"; but, as the law recognized no such office, he was first made a clerk in the Pension Office, and afterward an officer in the army and ordered to the White House for special duty. He is quite young, and looks younger than he is; of a fresh and almost boyish complexion; quite a favorite among the ladies, and with a gift for epigram and repartee.

John G. Nicolay

John Milton Hay

Lincoln's breech-loading Spencer carbine

Shooting with the President
William O. Stoddard

September 1865

William Stoddard was once described as "a crack shot with both hands" who could "plug a visiting card right and left at twelve paces." During his White House years he sometimes accompanied the President out to the wetlands behind the White House to test newly designed rifles for use by the military.

On the grounds near the Potomac, south of the White House, was a huge pile of old lumber, not to be damaged by balls, and a good many mornings I have been out there with the President, by previous appointment, to try such rifles as were sent in. There was no danger of hitting any one, and the President, who was a very good shot, enjoyed the relaxation very much. One morning early we were having a good time—he with his favorite "Spencer," and I with a villainous kicking nondescript, with a sort of patent backaction breech, that left my shoulder black and blue—when a squad from some regiment which had just been put on guard in that locality pounced on us for what seemed to them a manifest disobedience of all "regulations." I heard the shout of the officer in command and saw them coming, but as the President was busy drawing a very particular bead—for I had been beating him a little—I said nothing until down they came. In response to a decidedly unceremonious hail, the President, in some astonishment, drew back from his stooping posture, and turned upon them the full length six feet four of their beloved "Commander-in-Chief." They stood and looked one moment, and then fairly ran away, leaving his Excellency laughing heartily at their needless discomfiture. He only remarked: "Well, they might have stayed and seen the shooting."

Johnson and Lincoln Compared

September 9, 1866

In September the Chicago Tribune *wrote an editorial castigating Andrew Johnson and contrasting him sharply with Abraham Lincoln.*

Andrew Johnson has visited the grave of Abraham Lincoln. Under other circumstances, the scene would have been in the highest degree impressive, and worthy of preservation in the most enduring colors of art. Twelve months ago, it was within the power of Andrew Johnson to write his name in history, side by side with the immortal name of Lincoln. It was in his power to gather in the rich harvest of unity and freedom, so faithfully sown by his predecessor, and to receive as his reward the blessings and the love of a grateful and happy country. Had he been faithful to the principles he professed, and to the great trust confided to him, the heart of the nation would have been touched with profound sympathy and reverence to see the living champion of liberty weep by the tomb of its greatest martyr. As it is, the country feels that the malice of its sainted dead have been desecrated by the presence of an unworthy successor of its murdered President, whose heart is filled with envy for his greatness, and with bitterness for his friends. . . .

There could be no stronger contrast than that presented by the private character and public career of the dead President and of the living successor who stood by his grave. The one had been the faithful servant of the Republic; the other is threatening to subvert its liberties and plunge it into civil war. The one was a statesman; the other is a demagogue. The one was loyal; the other is a traitor at heart. The one toiled to crush rebellion; the other seeks to revive its smoldering fires. In the one, the loyal men of the South found a friend and protector; in the other they find a malignant enemy, an oppressor, and a slanderer. The one sought to elevate and enlighten the poor and weak; the other tramples them under his feet.

September 9, 1866
A Presidential Pilgrimage to Lincoln's Tomb

Back in March, determined to take charge of Reconstruction, Congress had passed the Civil Rights Act, declaring citizenship to all persons born in the United States regardless of race, color, or previous condition. As expected, Andrew Johnson vetoed it. But this time, unlike after the Freedmen's Bill in February, Congress overrode his veto. The balance of power was shifting in Washington. In May, much to Johnson's dismay, Congress proposed the Fourteenth Amendment. And when it was ratified, even in his home state of Tennessee, Johnson became known as "the dead dog of the White House."

In late August he headed out on a cross-country tour to take his case directly to the American people, and to try to influence the upcoming midterm elections. In city after city Johnson gave impassioned speeches in which he tried to explain his plan to restore Southern states to the Union and his offer to pardon the former Confederates. But he was greeted almost everywhere by scornful audiences. In Cleveland, Ohio, he declared that Lincoln was lucky not to be alive during these vengeful times, that had he lived "the vials of wrath would have been poured on him." Referring to Lincoln's death as an act of "Providence," he claimed his own ascension to the presidency to be a blessing to the American people. More than once he compared himself to Jesus Christ.

When Johnson headed for Springfield to visit Lincoln's tomb, his disingenuousness was reported in the press. In an editorial the *Chicago Tribune* wrote, "It was not for respect to the memory of the man whose death he described as an act of God's justice. It was to make political capital for Andrew Johnson and his policy. There is not within him the love or fidelity to truth, that could alone render him capable of appreciation of the character of his illustrious predecessor. At the very shrine of the nation's martyr he was plotting . . . in what manner most effectually to wreak vengeance . . . upon the friends of Abraham Lincoln."

In Chicago, Mary Lincoln read about Johnson's pilgrimage and was disgusted. "The party desecrated my beloved husband's resting place by their presence," she wrote to her friend Charles Sumner. "Our country is in a fearful state & another civil war appears inevitable."

General Ulysses S. Grant, Secretary of the Navy Gideon Welles, and President Andrew Johnson posed in New York State during the 1866 presidential tour. Not long afterward Grant wrote his wife that Johnson's speeches were "a national disgrace."

118

President Johnson sits flanked by Welles and Grant at a political picnic during their cross-country tour.

"What Promise Have You Kept?"
Isaac N. Arnold

September 30, 1866

In late September 1866 Isaac Arnold, Lincoln's friend and biographer, resigned from his position at the United States Post Department. He did so in a frank letter to President Johnson, who he said was now doing everything he could to subvert black rights in the South.

You have betrayed the great Union party which elected Abraham Lincoln.... You have deserted its principles, and are today, in open cordial communion with those who sought the overthrow of the Republic; of those who for four long years made war on our flag, and who crowned their long catalogue of crimes by the murder which placed you in the Executive Chair....

Mr. President, the American people in their hour of bitterest anguish, when almost stupefied with grief over the murder of the noblest grandest character which has adorned our history, heard your voice uttering bold, indignant, loyal patriotic words. They took you to their hearts and gave you their confidence. Where are you today? Who are your associates and advisers? What promise made over the dead body of Lincoln have you kept? What pledge there uttered have you not broken? ...

To the loyal black man, and the loyal white man of the South, Mr. Lincoln prom-ised protection and security. He kept his promise.... How can you, Mr. President, occupy the the Executive Mansion as the successor to Lincoln[?] ... Do you remember that Mr. Lincoln said "Negroes like other people act upon motives. If they stake their lives for us, they must be prompted by the strongest motive—even the promise of freedom; *and the promise being made must be kept.*"

The nation promised the negro liberty and protection, for helping put down the rebellion. You have turned him over to his exasperated master, whom he helped to subdue....

Believing you are to-day exerting your vast power in the interest of traitors, and that your policy should be overthrown ... I retire from office that I may more freely and effectively aid in that overthrow.

Lincoln in 1857

During his years of research Herndon received hundreds of letters describing Lincoln. This one came in response to a newspaper ad he had placed requesting Lincoln letters.

Herndon Continues

Throughout 1866 and early 1867, William Herndon continued his Lincoln research. His greatest omission was his failure to visit Kentucky; somehow his plans to get there kept falling through. But in Indiana and Illinois he was tireless. In a probing and comprehensive effort, he asked questions of his informers, challenged inconsistencies, provoked memories, and uncovered long-lost secrets. Determined to avoid false reverence, he aimed for "truth" no matter what emerged in the process. He investigated controversial matters such as Lincoln's early atheism, the possible illegitimacy of his mother, and even his rumored sexual affairs. "Sacred lies will not protect us," he wrote to one of his sources; he was after "the real man," foibles and all. In all, he collected eyewitness testimonials from 250 different individuals. And he carried on a vigorous correspondence with many of them. Their statements, though at times controversial and contradictory, added up to the most vivid portrait of Lincoln ever assembled. Thousands of facts about the pre-presidential Lincoln might have disappeared forever had they not been gathered up and written down by this tireless researcher, who planned now to become Lincoln's definitive biographer.

LAND DEPARTMENT

Illinois Central Rail Road Co.

Chicago, Oct. 12 1866

Hon. W. H. Herndon.

Springfield,

Dr Sir! —

I saw your advertisement a few weeks since, in the evening Journal requesting all who had received letters from Mr Lincoln, whether important

"The Most Secretive Man I Ever Saw"
David Davis

September 20, 1866

In September 1866, over a period of two days, Herndon interviewed David Davis in his hometown of Bloomington. Davis spoke freely as Herndon took dictation, carefully keeping his notes for future reference. Even though Davis had been chosen to serve as Lincoln's executor, the old judge revealed to Herndon that in some ways he hadn't really known his friend.

Mr Lincoln was not a social man by any means: his Stories—jokes &c. which were done to whistle off sadness are no evidences of sociality: he loved the struggling masses—all uprising toward a higher Civilization had his assent & his prayer. His was a peculiar nature

Lincoln had no spontaneity—nor Emotional Nature—no Strong Emotional feelings for any person—Mankind or thing. He never thanked me for any thing I did—never as I before said asked my advice about anything—never took my advice, Except as to the dollar: he asked no man advice—took no mans advice—listened patiently to all that had an idea—

. . . I don't Know anything about Lincoln's Religion—don't think anybody Knew. The idea that Lincoln talked to a stranger about his religion or religious views—or made such speeches, remarks &c about it as published is absurd to me. I Know the man so well: he was the most reticent—Secretive man I Ever Saw—or Expect to See. . . .

After he had returned from Congress and had lost his practice, Goodrich of Chicago proposed to him to open a law office in Chicago & go into partnership with him. Goodrich had an Extensive—a good practice there. Lincoln refused to accept—gave as a reason that he tended to Consumption—That if he went to Chicago that he would have to sit down and Study hard—That it would Kill him—That he would rather go around the Circuit—the 8 Judicial one than to sit down & die in Chicago.

A Prodigious Memory
Joshua F. Speed

December 6, 1866

No friendship was closer in Lincoln's young adult life than that with his roommate Joshua Speed, who wrote to Herndon in December.

I once remarked to him that his mind was a wonder to me—That impressions were easily made upon his mind and never effaced—"No said he you are mistaken—I am slow to learn and slow to forget that which I have learned—My mind is like a piece of steel, very hard to scratch any thing on it and almost impossible after you get it there to rub it out."

Lincoln's best friend, Joshua F. Speed

Journalists interviewed the presidential candidate in his sitting room in Springfield.

Springfield's Famous Citizen
John S. Bliss

January 29, 1867

Among the hundreds of letters that Herndon received during his period of research was one from John Bliss, a Wisconsin journalist who had been assigned to interview Lincoln on July 18, 1860, two months after his nomination for the presidency.

One beautiful July morning eighteen hundred and Sixty—I awoke in the city of Springfield Illinois. . . . [A] favorable opportunity offered itself for a morning walk, and it was but a brief time before I presented myself to the door of our nominee, for the highest office in the gift of a great nation. . . . I was ushered into the sitting room—by the young man who answered the bell, and from that place, I Sent my verbal card to Mr Lincoln—I was prepared with no letter of introduction—but as unarmed as I was, I waited for Mr. Lincoln I was sitting opposite the door and partly in sight of the Stairs. After a short time, Mr L. came tripping down the Stairs, as lively as a young man of sixteen years of age—sliding his right hand on the bannister—He approached me and after shaking hands—we were soon immersed in a lively conversation on various topics. . . . While sitting there, the Chimney Swallows came down behind the fireboards, and absolutely twittered, fluttered and Sung as to nearly drown our voices. I remarked that the birds rarely decend so low, but Mr. L. replied, "that they usually came down once a day."

A French Tribute to Lincoln

Mary Lincoln received more sympathy and compassion from foreigners than from her fellow Americans. While President Johnson never even communicated with her after the assassination, she received thoughtful and tender letters from Queen Victoria and the Empress Eugenie—the first described herself as a "deeply bereaved wife" and the second wrote that she herself was "a stranger to sorrow."

The French in particular were full of sympathy for a woman whose husband represented the ideals of liberty, democracy, and human rights. Shortly after the assassination the Frenchman Charles Louis Chasson had started a public subscription for a medal in Lincoln's honor to be presented to his grieving widow. A committee had been set up to take charge of the contributions and soon included the illustrious author Victor Hugo. The plan was to present the medal to Mary Lincoln on the first anniversary of her husband's death. But the anniversary came and went with no sign of the French medal. Mary heard news that it was still in the works and would be sent to Secretary of State William Seward, who would make arrangements for its presentation. But then more months went by, and Mary became suspicious. She had never liked Seward, or her husband's secretaries, Nicolay and Hay, who were both now in France and possibly meddling with her prize, she thought. In a letter to Alexander Williamson, Tad's former tutor, she put out a feeler. "I have a great curiosity to find out what has become of the medal," she wrote, asking him to make discreet inquiries about it. "—if Seward[,] Hay or Nicolay could stop its reaching me," she added, "they would do so—They are a great set of scamps—"

On December 4, 1866, the medal was officially turned over to the U.S. minister in Paris, John Bigelow. "Tell Mrs. Lincoln that this little box is the heart of France," Bigelow was instructed.

A month later the ambassador arrived in Chicago and went directly to see Mary and make the presentation. Lincoln's widow was overwhelmed. On the large medal was a bold profile of her husband, and on its back was an image of his gravesite flanked by two former slaves. Printed in French were the words "Lincoln the Honest Man / Abolished Slavery Reestablished the Union / Saved the Republic . . ."

The next day Mary wrote her thanks to the Committee of the French Democracy for this signal act of recognition and respect. "I cannot express to you the emotions, with which I receive this manifestation of the feelings of so many thousands of your fellow countrymen," she wrote. "So grand a testimonial to the memory of my husband, given in honor of his services in the cause of liberty . . . is deeply affecting."

The gold medal was issued to Mary Lincoln by the Committee of the French Democracy despite opposition from Napoleon III's dictatorship. It was paid for by 40,000 French citizens in honor of Lincoln's contributions to "the cause of human liberty." In a letter signed by Victor Hugo and nineteen others, Mary was told, "If France had the freedom enjoyed by Republican America, not thousands, but millions among us would have been counted as admirers."

Booth's Hidden Diary

By 1867 the battle between Congress and President Johnson had reached a new level of intensity. In an effort to curtail the president's powers of removal, Congress enacted the Tenure of Office Act over Johnson's veto, mandating the Senate's consent before any removal from office. It was designed in part to protect Secretary of War Edwin Stanton, whom Johnson planned to remove.

In February Congress passed the Reconstruction Bill, which provided for a military government in the South. Johnson cursed the bill in the presence of Charles Nordhoff, managing editor of the *New York Evening Post*. "[He] expressed the most bitter hatred of the measure in all its parts, declaring that . . . the people of the South, poor, quiet, unoffending, harmless, were to be trodden under foot 'to protect niggers.'" The President was "a pig-headed man with only one idea," wrote Nordhoff, "a bitter opposition to universal suffrage & a determination to secure the political ascendancy of the old Southern leaders."

Within weeks prominent members of Congress were contemplating impeachment, and the Judiciary Committee was assigned to assemble evidence. Stanton was called in for questioning and was forced to turn over John Wilkes Booth's diary, which had been in his secret possession since the capture of the assassin. The diary showed how Booth's kidnapping and murder plots were two separate efforts—information that might well have exonerated Mary Surratt. And with eighteen pages mysteriously missing, it was rumored that Stanton had cut them out to protect unnamed individuals. The diary also cast doubts upon Jefferson Davis's complicity in the assassination and helped lead to having all charges against him dropped.

The diary of John Wilkes Booth was missing eighteen pages when it was submitted as evidence.

"Hunted Like a Dog"
John Wilkes Booth

Booth's small diary, seized by the War Department in 1865, had never been entered into evidence in the trial of the conspirators. His words shed new light on the assassin's final days.

Until to day nothing was ever *thought* of sacrificing to our country's wrongs. For six months we had worked to capture. But our cause being almost lost, something decisive & great must be done. But its failure was owing to others, who did not strike for their country with a heart. I struck boldly and not as the papers say. I walked with a firm step through a thousand of his friends, was stopped but pushed on. A colonel was at his side. I shouted Sic semper *before* I fired. In jumping broke my leg. I passed all his pickets, rode sixty miles that night with the bone of my leg tearing the flesh at every jump. I can never repent it, though we hated to kill. Our country owed all her trouble to him, and God simply made me the instrument of his punishment. . . .

After being hunted like a dog, through swamps, woods, and last night being chased by gun-boats till I was forced to return wet cold and starving, with every man's hand against me, I am here in despair. And why? For doing what Brutus was honored for.

A building on Garrett's farm in Bowling Green, Virginia, where Booth was caught and killed

Herndon Becomes the "Dirty Dog"

William Herndon grew disgusted with Lincoln biographers, calling them "blind-bat-eyed hero worshippers, timid-souled creatures, orthodox theologians, and other rigid souled men." He vowed that he would reveal the real man.

After nearly a year and a half, William Herndon had completed most of his Lincoln research. In the process, however, he had neglected his law practice and his personal finances were in disarray. Though he wanted nothing more than to work full-time on his biography, his "pecuniary position" would not allow it. He had a wife and family to support, and clients depending on him. "Duty holds me to my profession," he lamented.

He did find time to undertake a series of public lectures in which he presented his emerging portrait of Lincoln. The first two addresses were analyses of Lincoln's character, and the third focused on his statesmanship. Though Herndon had loved Lincoln and "revered him now that he was dead and gone," he felt obligated to counteract the stream of eulogies that kept portraying the man as a flawless saint. The real Lincoln, he told overflowing crowds, had been "exceedingly ambitious," had possessed a "greed for office," and had not always been totally honest, often telling people only what he wanted them to know. But he had also possessed "great powers of Reason," a strong sense of "Right & Equity," and an "intense love and worship of what was true and good."

The lectures were greeted with immediate acclaim and picked up by newspapers across the country, making Herndon famous. Many of Lincoln's closest professional friends found his remarks eminently fair and just—a compelling portrait of Lincoln "as he really was."

But Herndon's fourth lecture utterly changed his public standing. Herndon had been the first researcher to discover Lincoln's early relationship with a woman named Ann Rutledge, and how he had descended into a terrible despair after her death. He had amassed considerable evidence about this early love affair and through his visits to the area could vividly imagine it. To prepare for his fourth lecture he had traveled to New Salem in the late autumn and spent a day wandering among the tangled ruins. A single log cabin was all that remained of the once bustling village, but as Herndon sat gazing, the town came to life before his eyes. "In my imagination, the little village perched on the hill is astir with the hum of busy men, and the sharp quick buzz of women." Here Lincoln had come to manhood and independence, and here he had loved and lost Ann Rutledge.

In September 1866 Mary Lincoln had agreed to sit for an interview with Herndon and told him that Lincoln was "the kindest—most tender and loving husband & father in the world." But Herndon did not believe her descriptions of marital happiness. He had never liked Mary; as early as 1861 he had called her an "excentric—wicked woman" and had described her husband as "domestically . . . desolate." He had long been of the opinion that the marriage was "loveless." And shortly after sitting with Mary Lincoln, he went public with his theories.

Herndon's lecture on November 16 amounted to a thinly veiled attack upon Lincoln's marriage. He delivered his speech, entitled "A. Lincoln—Miss Ann Rutledge, New Salem—Pioneering, and the Poem called Immortality," to an overflowing crowd. Herndon speculated that a part of Lincoln had died with Ann Rutledge—that "his heart, sad and broken," lay buried with her in her grave. After Ann's death, he said, Lincoln had become incapable of tenderness and had gradually turned into an "abstracted" man. "He never addressed another woman, in my opinion, 'yours affectionately'" and thereafter abstained from using the word "love." His marriage, Herndon implied, had been for political purposes—with Lincoln needing "a whip and a spur to rouse him to deeds of fame."

When Mary Lincoln read the printed version of Herndon's fourth lecture in March 1867, she was horrified, then furious. She had never heard of Ann Rutledge— never once had her husband mentioned such a name. As she had written a friend, "It was always music in my ears, both before and after our marriage, when my husband, told me, I was the only one, he had ever thought of, or cared for." How dare William Herndon suggest that her husband had harbored a lifelong flame for another woman, and a dead one at that?

In Springfield, the community was outraged. Grant Goodrich of Chicago, who had known Lincoln during their practice in the federal courts, wrote of the "injury and injustice you did to the memory" of Lincoln, and the "mortification you caused his friends, especially his widow and children." Commenting on the long-buried relationship of Lincoln and Ann Rutledge, he wrote, "I should have as soon thought of exposing his dead body, un coffined, to the vulgar gaze of the public's eye. . . . [This] should never have been dug up." Mrs. Lincoln's former pastor, the Rev. James Smith, wrote that Herndon was in some ways worse than John Wilkes Booth, whose bullet, after all, had catapulted Lincoln into glorious martyrdom. His "false friend's" attack, in contrast, had "attempted to bring him down to posterity with infamy branded on his forehead." Herndon's lecture, he said, was a "poisoned chalice."

Lincoln's former partner was outwardly stoical but inwardly devastated. He dropped his series of lectures, lost focus on his biography, increasingly came to despise his law career, and in late 1867 made a total change of life. Herndon took over the sprawling farm north of town that he had inherited from his father and attempted to become a gentleman farmer.

Herndon's farmhouse, which he called Fairview, stood on the edge of Chinkapin Hill, looking out over a broad Illinois valley.

"His Ugly Features Sprang to Beauty"
William Herndon

December 12, 1865

In his first lecture, entitled "Analysis of the Character of Abraham Lincoln," Herndon gave an extraordinary physical description of his longtime colleague and friend.

Abraham Lincoln was about six feet four inches high, and when he left this city was 51 years old, having good health and no gray hairs—or but few in his head. He was thin—tall—wirey—sinewy, grisly—raw boned man, thin through the breast to the back—and narrow across the shoulders, standing he leaned forward—was what may be called stoop shouldered, inclining to the consumptive by build. His usual weight was about 160 pounds. . . . His structure—his build was loose and leathery. His body was shrunk and shrivelled—having dark skin—dark hair—looking woe struck. The whole man— body & mind worked slowly —creekingly, as if it wanted oiling . . . . When Mr. Lincoln walked he moved cautiously, but firmly, his long arms—his hands on them hanging like giants hands, swung down by his side. . . . He was not a pretty man by any means—nor was he an ugly one: he was a homely looking man. . . . [B]ut when that eye and face and every feature were lit up by the inward soul or fire of emotion, then it was that all these apparently ugly features sprang to organs of beauty. . . . Sometimes it appeared to me that Lincoln's soul was fresh, just from the presence of its God.

Most of Lincoln's height was in his legs, as can be seen in this full-length portrait taken in 1860 for the use of the sculptor Henry Kirke Brown.

Lincoln's Supposed One True Love
William Herndon

In his fourth lecture, Herndon launched the story that Ann Rutledge had been the true love of Lincoln's life. He even suggested that the two were now together in Paradise.

Abraham Lincoln loved Ann Rutledge with all his soul, mind and strength. She loved him as dearly, tenderly and affectionately. They seemed made in heaven for each other....

—she was taken sick. She struggled, regretted, grieved, became nervous. She ate not, slept not, was taken sick of brain fever, became emaciated, and was fast sinking in the grave. Lincoln wished to see her. She silently prayed to see him.... Mr. Lincoln did go to see her about the 10th day of August, A.D. 1835. The meeting was quite as much as either could bear, and more than Lincoln, with all his coolness and philosophy, could endure. The voice, the face, the features of her; the love, sympathy and interview fastened themselves on his heart and soul forever. Heaven only knows what was said by the two. God only knows what was thought.... Miss Rutledge died on the 25th of August, A.D. 1835, and was buried in the Concord cemetery, six miles north, bearing a little west, of New Salem. ... Mr. Lincoln has stated that his heart, sad and broken, was buried there....

He never addressed another woman, in my opinion, "yours affectionately"; and generally and characteristically abstained from the use of the word "love." ... He sorrowed and grieved, rambled over the hills and through the forests, day and night. ... He slept not, he ate not, joyed not. This he did until his body became emaciated and weak, and gave way. His mind wandered from its throne....

Lincoln was a boarder at Bowling Green's house in New Salem, which was later abandoned. Here the young surveyor courted Ann Rutledge.

"Ann Rutledge Is a Myth"
Mary Lincoln

Mary Lincoln was disgusted by William Herndon, and when she wrote to family lawyer David Davis, she hinted at the possibility of a future lawsuit.

My dear Sir:

Permit me to point your attention to another sentence, in a lecture of the *distinguished* W[illiam] H[erndon] which is of great significance and indicates more clearly if possible, the malignity of *his* remarks, than any thing else. *He* pointedly says, "for the last *twenty three* years, Mr Lincoln has known no joy,"—it was evidently framed, for the *amiable* latitude he was breathing and was intended to convey a false impression. ... This is the return for all my husband's kindness to this miserable man! Out of pity he took him into his office, when he was almost a hopeless inebriate and although he was only a drudge, in the place, he is very forgetful of his position and assumes, a confidential capacity towards—Mr Lincoln—

As you justly remark, each & every one has had, a little romance in their early days—but as my husband was *truth itself,* and as he always assured me, he had cared for no one but myself, the false W. H. (au contraire) I shall assuredly remain firm in my conviction—that *Ann Rutledge,* is a myth—for in all his confidential communications, such a romantic name, was never breathed, and concealment could have been no object, as Mr H's vivid imagination, supposed this pathetic tragedy to occur when Mr L was eighteen & I did not know him, until he was thirty years old! Nor did his life or his joyous laugh, lead one to suppose his heart, was in any unfortunate woman's grave—but in the proper place with his loved wife & children—I assure you, it will not be *well with him*—if he makes the *least* disagreeable or false allusion in the future. *He* will be closely watched....

Mary Lincoln

As First Lady, Mary Lincoln became known for her fancy dresses, something Lincoln sometimes criticized but also admired. As President he once said, "My wife is as handsome as when she was a girl, and I, a poor nobody, fell in love with her." Two years after her husband's death, Mary attempted to sell her White House wardrobe (right).

October 1867

The "Old Clothes" Fiasco

Mary Lincoln's chief concern in 1867 was money. With the settlement of her husband's estate, she would inherit a large amount, but there was in the meantime the $10,000 debt incurred through her buying sprees during the White House years. Still living on the small allowance granted by David Davis, in her rented rooms Mary felt destitute. In May 1866 she used most of her husband's final salary payment to buy a home, at 375 West Washington Street in Chicago. But it soon became clear that she couldn't afford the house's upkeep. Desperate, she donned disguises and hawked jewelry at local pawnshops, but it wasn't enough, and before long she was forced to let go of her dream. "It is so painful to me . . . to be compelled to give up a home," Mary wrote to Davis in the spring of 1867. But she simply was "without sufficient to live upon." She and Tad moved into rooms at the Clifton House, while an angered Robert went his own way and took up residence at a neighboring hotel. "I am done with wasting time in urging you to beware . . . [my] advice," Robert wrote his mother.

That summer, assured by unscrupulous promoters that she could raise $100,000 by selling her White House wardrobe, Mary agreed to a sale in New York City. Traveling under the name of Mrs. Clarke to avoid recognition, she arrived there in September. But instead of the windfall that Mary hoped for, it turned into a public debacle. Her identity was discovered, and few buyers showed up for what the press scathingly called her "old clothes" sale. The *Springfield* (Massachusetts) *Republican* branded her a "dreadful woman" who "persists in forcing her repugnant individuality before the world." The *Cincinnati Commercial* dredged up rumors of her supposed disloyalty during the Civil War. The *Columbus* (Georgia) *Sun* called her "a mercenary prostitute." And the *Chicago Journal*, attempting to be sympathetic, blamed her "strange course" of behavior on the fact that "she is insane." "R[obert] came up last evening like a maniac, and almost threatening his life, looking like death, because the letters of the World were published in yesterday's [Chicago] paper," wrote Mary Lincoln to a friend in October. Mortified by the bad publicity, Robert wrote to his fiancée, Mary Harlan, "[I]t is very hard to deal with someone who is sane on all subjects but one"—money.

"My Dear Lizzie"

In April 1868, six months after the "old clothes" affair, Mary's friend Elizabeth Keckly published a memoir entitled *Behind the Scenes*. It contained intimate details of the Lincoln White House drawn from Keckly's four years as the First Lady's seamstress and confidante. And it came as a complete surprise to Mary Lincoln.

Keckly was a former slave who had bought her freedom in 1855. Through ambition and persistence she had become a successful Washington seamstress, sewing clothes for the families of Jefferson Davis and President Buchanan, and at one point having twenty young women in her employ. When Mary Lincoln arrived in Washington in February 1861, she had been directed to Elizabeth to make her inaugural gown, and the two women had begun a remarkable relationship. By the fall of 1861 she had become Mary's official seamstress, with the previous one, Mary Ann Cuthbert, shifted to housekeeping duty. Keckly was soon playing a central role in Mary's life. She was present during the final illness of the Lincolns' eleven-year-old son, Willie, and she cared for Mary during her nervous breakdown following his death. About her increasingly frequent headaches and gynecological problems, Mary wrote, "If it had not been for Lizzie Keckley, I do not know what I should have done."

Keckly encouraged Mary to become a full-fledged abolitionist, involving her in a charity she had created, the Contraband Relief Organization of Washington. She became close to the President and often brushed his bristly hair; was in the White House during the tense election of 1864; and was present on the family trip to Virginia five months later, entering Richmond along with the presidential party. And on the night of Lincoln's murder, it was Lizzie Keckly for whom Mary Lincoln cried out in her despair: "I want her just as soon as she can be brought to me."

In the months ahead, Keckly had continued on in Mary's service, remaining a close supporter during the terrible first years of her widowhood. And when the two were not together they exchanged letters; during one six-week period in 1867 Mary wrote to Keckly sixteen times. She called her "my dear Lizzie" and in October 1867 wrote, "I consider you my best living friend."

But then came the publication of *Behind the Scenes*, written, Keckly later claimed, to help raise money for her friend and endeavoring to show the world her life's "good side as well as its bad." On the bad side it included private information on Mary's out-of-control spending habits, her lack of self-restraint during periods of grief, and her hatreds for specific individuals in government, which she had expressed privately to Lizzie. It also contained transcripts of personal letters from Mary.

Elizabeth Keckly

Furious that her confidante had broken their sacred trust, Mary severed all ties. She ordered her son Robert to purchase hundreds of copies of Keckly's book in an effort to lessen its impact. In a letter she coldly referred to her former friend as "the Colored historian." And when Elizabeth came to her home to try to apologize, an angry Robert met her at the door and brusquely ordered her to leave and never come back.

To the end of her life Elizabeth Keckly refused to be bitter. Though her attempt to help Mary had backfired, she continued to remember her former friend fondly. Above her dresser she kept a photograph of Mary Lincoln, next to a gift from the former First Lady—a comb and brush that had once belonged to Abraham Lincoln.

BEHIND THE SCENES.

BY

ELIZABETH KECKLEY,

FORMERLY A SLAVE, BUT MORE RECENTLY MODISTE, AND FRIEND TO MRS. ABRAHAM LINCOLN.

OR,

THIRTY YEARS A SLAVE, AND FOUR YEARS IN THE WHITE HOUSE.

NEW YORK:

G. W. Carleton & Co., Publishers.

M DCCC LXVIII.

Though publishers spelled her name "Keckley," Elizabeth used only one *e*. Her tell-all book (above) included a vivid description of the death of Willie Lincoln, seen here with his mother and his younger brother Tad in 1860. The public betrayal alienated Mary Lincoln from her White House dressmaker, who in the years since the assassination had become her closest friend.

"The Moses of My People"
Elizabeth Keckly

April 1868

In her book Keckly described being summoned to the White House on the morning of April 15, 1865, after Lincoln's death.

I hastily put on my shawl and bonnet, and was driven at a rapid rate to the White House. Everything about the building was sad and solemn. I was quickly shown to Mrs. Lincoln's room, and on entering, saw Mrs. L. tossing uneasily about upon a bed. The room was darkened, and the only person in it besides the widow of the President was Mrs. Secretary Welles, who had spent the night with her. Bowing to Mrs. Welles, I went to the bedside.

"Why did you not come to me last night, Elizabeth—I sent for you?" Mrs. Lincoln asked in a low whisper.

"I did try to come to you, but I could not find you," I answered, as I laid my hand upon her hot brow. . . .

She was nearly exhausted with grief, and when she became a little quiet, I asked and received permission to go into the Guests' Room, where the body of the President lay in state. . . . Never did I enter the solemn chamber of death with such palpitating heart and trembling footsteps as I entered it that day. No common mortal had died. The Moses of my people had fallen in the hour of his triumph. . . . They made room for me, and approaching the body, I lifted the white cloth from the white face of the man that I had worshipped as an idol—looked upon as a demi-god. . . .

Returning to Mrs. Lincoln's room, I found her in a new paroxysm of grief. Robert was bending over his mother with tender affection, and little Tad was crouched at the foot of the bed with a world of agony in his young face. I shall never forget the scene—the wails of a broken heart, the unearthly shrieks, the terrible convulsions, the wild, tempestuous outbursts of grief from the soul. I bathed Mrs. Lincoln's head with cold water, and soothed the terrible tornado as best I could.

Eyewitness to Willie's Death
Elizabeth Keckly

April 1868

The death of Willie Lincoln, and Mary's emotional breakdown that followed, had been an intensely private matter. And yet Keckly included these and other stories in her tell-all book. In her account she recalled the night of the Lincolns' White House reception when Willie lay sick upstairs.

[I] was not in the room when Willie died, but was immediately sent for. I assisted in washing him and dressing him, and then laid him on the bed, when Mr. Lincoln came in. I never saw a man so bowed down with grief. He came to the bed, lifted the cover from the face of his child, gazed at it long and earnestly, murmuring, "My poor boy, he was too good for this earth. God has called him home. I know that he is much better off in heaven, but then we loved him so. It is hard, hard to have him die!" Great sobs choked his utterance. He buried his head in his hands, and his tall frame was convulsed with emotion. I stood at the foot of the bed, my eyes full of tears, looking at the man in silent, awe-stricken wonder. . . .

Mrs. Lincoln's grief was inconsolable. The pale face of her dead boy threw her into convulsions. . . . In one of her paroxysms of grief the President kindly bent over his wife, took her by the arm, and gently led her to the window. With a stately, solemn gesture, he pointed to the lunatic asylum.

"Mother, do you see that large white building on the hill yonder? Try and control your grief, or it will drive you mad, and we may have to send you there."

Threats of Assassination
Elizabeth Keckly

April 1868

In a memorable passage Keckly described Lincoln's refusal to be intimidated by threats.

Frequent letters were received warning Mr. Lincoln of assassination, but he never gave a second thought to the mysterious warnings. The letters, however, sorely troubled his wife. She seemed to read impending danger in every rustling leaf, in every whisper of the wind. "Where are you going now, father?" she would say to him, as she observed him putting on his overshoes and shawl. "I am going over to the War Department, mother, to try and learn some news." "But, father, you should not go out alone. You know you are surrounded with danger." "All imagination. What does any one want to harm me for? Don't worry about me, mother, as if I were a little child, for no one is going to molest me;" and with a confident, unsuspecting air he would close the door behind him, descend the stairs, and pass out to his lonely walk.

The War Department in the 1860s was located adjacent to the White House. "[Y]ou will remember the footpath, lined and embowered with trees, leading from the back door," once said Speaker of the House Schuyler Colfax. Lincoln "walked through unseen dangers" along this path, without "the dread of death."

December 27, 1863

In December 1863, after hearing the President was ill, Florville wrote to his old friend. He was the only black person from Lincoln's past ever to write him in the White House.

Dear Sir— I, having for you, an irrisisteble feeling of gratitude for the kind regards Shown, and the manifest good wishis exhibited towards me, . . . have for the above reasons and our long acquaintance, thought it might not be improper for one so humbler in life and occupation, to address the President of the United States—

Yet, I do so, feeling that if it is received by you (and you have time for I know you are heavily Tax) it will be read with pleasure as a communication from Billy the Barber. this I express and feel. for the truly great Man regards with corresponding favor the poor, and down troden of the Nation, to those more favored in Color, position, and Franchise rights. And this you have Shown, and I and my people feel greatful to you for it. . . . I was Surprised at the announcement of the death of your Son Willy. I thought him a Smart boy for his age, So Considerate, So Manly: his Knowledge and good Sence, far exceeding most boys more advanced in years. yet the time Comes to all, all must die.

I should like verry much, to See you, and your family. but the priviledge of enjoying an interview, may not soon, if ever come.

My family are all well. My son William is Married and in buisness for himself. I am occupying the Same place in Which I was at the time you left. Tell Taddy that his (and Willys) Dog is a live and Kicking doing well he stays Mostly at John E Rolls with his Boys Who are about the Size now that Tad & Willy Ware When they left for Washington

Your Residence here is Kept in good order. Mr Tilton has no children to ruin things. . . .

. . . Sincere feelings of your obt Servant

William Florville the Barber

April 13, 1868

An Old Friend Dies

William Florville, known to many as "Billy the Barber," had known Lincoln longer than any other man in Springfield. Lincoln had had numerous black acquaintances in his hometown, some of whom he had hired to work for him. There was the boot maker William Donnegan and his brother Tom; "Aunt" Maria Vance, for ten years a cook and laundress in the Lincoln home; Ruth Stanton, who worked for Mary Lincoln; and Henry Brown, a Methodist minister who at various times served as Lincoln's stable hand and carriage driver, and who had led Old Bob in the funeral procession. At least twenty-one African Americans lived within three blocks of Lincoln's home, and according to tradition many had sought Lincoln out for legal counsel.

Lincoln had met William Florville in 1831, when the Haitian-born barber arrived in New Salem seeking work. At Lincoln's advice he settled in the larger town of Springfield, where he set up the city's first barbershop. Soon "Billy the Barber's" became a favorite gathering place and in the 1840s and 1850s came to be described as Lincoln's "second home." Here the much-loved proprietor described himself as "the barber king" and his clients as his "trusty subjects." (When business was slow, he wrote playfully in the local paper, "His Majesty would suggest the propriety of his subjects . . . to pay into the treasury all demands that may be found against them, as the pecuniary affairs of the government at this time is not in a very flourishing condition.")

Florville was also interested in real estate, sometimes trading an agreement to shave a client for life in return for the gift of a building or piece of land. He asked Lincoln to help him manage these investments, and in the 1850s the prairie lawyer was handling the taxes on four of Florville's lots in Bloomington. Over the years the industrious barber amassed fifteen businesses and apartment houses in Springfield as well as an eighty-acre farm in Rochester, Illinois.

In February 1861, before Lincoln went east for the inauguration, Florville cut his hair for the last time. Then, from a distance, he followed the news of his friend's presidency, rejoicing with other black Americans at the Emancipation Proclamation and with the slow but steady progress of the war.

According to his family, Florville was devastated by the assassination and was never the same afterward. At Lincoln's funeral in Springfield he was offered a place of honor in the procession but instead chose to walk in the rear with the other black citizens of the city. Now, at his own death three years later, the *Illinois State Journal* gave the old citizen high honor. In an editorial noting his demise it stated, "Only two men in Springfield understood Lincoln, his law partner, William H. Herndon, and his barber, William de Fleurville."

Lincoln's barber William Florville

Lincoln the Aggressor

Southerners continued to see Lincoln as their mortal enemy and to recall their own struggle with the North in heroic terms. In 1866 a Virginia journalist named Edward A. Pollard wrote a book titled *The Lost Cause*. Pollard, who had earlier advocated reopening the slave trade, used the book in part as an attack on Abraham Lincoln. He described Lincoln as "destitute of the highest order of sensibilities," a man who had brought to the presidency "the buffoonery and habits of a demagogue of the back-woods." An "ill-educated man," unequipped for the national crisis, he had pretended to care only about restoring the Union, but had secretly been under the influence of the "Abolition party." And after the battle of Antietam he had dropped his "mask" and proclaimed his war upon slavery—a war upon slaveowners and their property.

In the years ahead, Southern authors routinely blamed Lincoln for having started the war. And in 1868 Alexander Stephens published his own belief that Lincoln had caused the war by his actions. It didn't matter who had fired the first shot, he wrote. "The *aggressor* in a war is not the *first* who *uses force*, but the first who renders force *necessary*."

Confederate graves were a grim reminder of the South's hatred of Abraham Lincoln. "Human lives are nothing to him," wrote Southern nurse Kate Cumming. Though Alexander Stephens (above) admired Lincoln as a human being, he deplored his prosecution of the war as "despotic" and "cruel."

General Lorenzo Thomas

The Impeachment of Andrew Johnson

The first attempt to gather evidence with which to impeach Andrew Johnson took place in the summer of 1867. In secret proceedings before the Judiciary Committee, investigators sought a link between Johnson and Lincoln's assassination. It was at this time that Edwin Stanton was called as a witness and was forced to turn over Booth's missing diary. Stanton had long been a thorn in Johnson's flesh. Now, in addition to the diary, Johnson learned that his secretary of war had withheld a petition on behalf of Mary Surratt that might have convinced him to pardon her instead of signing her death sentence. Enraged, that same day Johnson asked for Stanton's resignation. When Stanton refused, the President suspended him. Refusing to surrender his office, Stanton locked himself in the War Department, resulting in a standoff that lasted for the next six months.

In February 1868 Johnson decided to act. Declaring Stanton's position null and void, he appointed a new secretary of war, Lorenzo Thomas, without asking for a confirmation from the Senate. On Monday, February 24, an aroused Congress voted to impeach. The complaints against Johnson included violation of the Constitution, which mandates the Senate's confirmation of presidential appointments; violation of the Tenure of Office Act; abuse of the presidential pardon power; abuse of the veto; aiding and abetting of Southern racists, including a de facto license given to the Ku Klux Klan; and in general an open defiance of Congress.

The ensuing trial became a national sensation. During the debates on the Senate floor the name of Lincoln was often invoked as both sides tried to enlist him to their cause. At times the rhetoric was highly inflammatory, as when Benjamin Butler, in favor of removal, said, "By murder most foul he succeeded to the Presidency, and is the elect of an assassin to that high office, and not of the people." Finally, on May 16, it came to a vote. Thirty-five senators declared Johnson guilty; nineteen voted to acquit. The result was exactly one vote short of the two-thirds majority needed to convict. Andrew Johnson had escaped removal by the narrowest of margins.

After President Johnson was handed a summons, his impeachment trial became a Washington attraction. The seven House managers in charge of the proceedings were James F. Wilson, George S. Boutwell, John A. Logan (standing), Benjamin F. Butler, Thaddeus Stevens, Thomas Williams, and John A. Bingham (seated).

Opposing Opinions on Johnson's Impeachment

April 1868

On May 16 the vote on impeachment was cast.

Charles Sumner of Massachusetts was one of sixteen Republican senators strongly committed to convicting the President. Garrett Davis of Kentucky was one of a group of Democrats who supported Johnson throughout the trial. Joseph Fowler of Tennessee was a neutral Republican who voted for conviction. In the end the impeachers lacked just one vote.

Senator Charles Sumner of Massachusetts:

Andrew Johnson is the impersonation of the tyrannical slave power. In him it lives again. He is the lineal successor of John C. Calhoun and Jefferson Davis; and he gathers about him the same supporters. Original partisans of slavery north and south; habitual compromisers of great principles; maligners of the Declaration of Independence; politicians without heart; lawyers, for whom a technicality is everything, and a promiscuous company who at every stage of the battle have set their faces against equal rights; these are his allies. . . . With the President at their head, they are now entrenched in the Executive Mansion. . . . He once declared himself the Moses of the colored race. Behold him now the Pharaoh. . . . If Andrew Johnson is not

guilty, then never was a political offender guilty before; and, if his acquittal is taken as a precedent, never can a political offender be found guilty again. The proofs are mountainous.

Senator Garrett Davis of Kentucky:

Mr. Johnson became President by having been elected Vice-President, and by the operation of the Constitution, upon the death of the President, Mr. Lincoln. He is as much the President as if he had been elected to that office instead of to the vice-presidency. His presidential term commenced when he was inaugurated into the office, and is to continue to last, for the residue of the term for which Mr. Lincoln was elected President and he Vice-President. . . . The presidency, while Mr. Johnson has been filling it and performing its duties under the Constitution, is as much his office as it was Mr. Lincoln's when he held the same relation to it; and the proposition that this time of Mr. Johnson in the office is not his term but a continuation of Mr. Lincoln's term, is not sustained by the Constitution, fact, or reason.

Senator Joseph Fowler of Tennessee:

Suppose that the tenure-of-civil-office act had been in force during the administration of Abraham Lincoln, and that distinguished patriot had under the law, from some personal pique, suspended Edwin M. Stanton, a man who has organized more victories for freedom than any living civilian; suppose Mr. Lincoln to have submitted his reasons for such suspension to the Senate, and that body, after due deliberation, to have determined against the sufficiency of the alleged cause of suspension, and (as authorized by the law) to have ordered that Mr. Stanton resume the functions of his office; and that then Mr. Lincoln . . . should have issued an order for the absolute and unqualified removal of Mr. Stanton. . . . [W]ould Abraham Lincoln have been entitled to an acquittal? No. If all the tenderness of feeling which now clusters around the memory of our martyred President had belonged to him while living, and the issue had been thus conspicuously forced upon us . . . duty would have impelled an adjudication for his removal. . . . That justice which would have been executed against Abraham Lincoln must be impartial when applied to Andrew Johnson, and I shall vote for conviction.

President James Buchanan

The Death of James Buchanan

Ever since his retirement in 1861 James Buchanan had been living quietly at his Pennsylvania estate, Wheatland. Hugely unpopular when he left office, he had been called a "sick man" by the *Chicago Tribune*—a "weak," "indecisive," and "traitorous" chief executive who had opposed Southern secession while insisting he was constitutionally incapable of preventing it. In his final Message to Congress he had sided with the South, blaming the mounting crisis on Northerners and advocating constitutional changes to protect slavery.

It was a sorry end for the "Old Public Functionary." Buchanan had been one of the outstanding statesmen of the country—serving in the U.S. Congress, as secretary of state, and as minister to Great Britain before finally reaching the presidency in 1857. But his dislike of controversy and basic timidity did not serve him well in the turbulent second half of the 1850s. At the White House on March 4, the day of Lincoln's inauguration, he spoke openly of his relief to be turning over the job: "If you are as happy, my dear sir, on entering this house as I am in leaving it and returning home, you are the happiest man in the country."

Buchanan may have been weak, but he was not a traitor. Throughout the Civil War he supported Lincoln and the Union, and though he disagreed with the new policy of emancipation he stood up to those who accused the President of having provoked the war. "Mr. Lincoln had no alternative but to defend the country against dismemberment," Buchanan wrote. "I certainly should have done the same thing had they begun the war in my time." But his respect for Lincoln did not change most Northerners' negative opinion of him. In 1867 the *Chicago Tribune* proclaimed, "Let him die in such peace as his sins will give him, and let him go directly to his own place."

A year later Buchanan died at seventy-seven. In a sign that even failed presidents still meant much to the American people, five thousand showed up to say goodbye.

President Buchanan escorting President-elect Abraham Lincoln on the day of his inauguration

Just two weeks after Buchanan's death, the radical Congressman Thaddeus Stevens, who had always been impatient with Lincoln's political moderation, also died. When his coffin lay in state inside the Great Rotunda of the Capitol (left), it was placed with unintended irony beneath Lincoln's statue. "Thad will be all right when he's dug up a few hundred years hence," Lincoln once said about him. "I must look out for these four years, and as much further as I can see."

Thomas ("Tad") Lincoln

Robert Todd Lincoln

Mary Harlan Lincoln

Mary Lincoln Leaves the Country

By the summer of 1868 Mary Lincoln had had more than she could take. Herndon's story of her husband's "loveless marriage" and his life-long adoration of Ann Rutledge had deeply wounded her. Her ridicule in the press for trying to sell her White House clothes had added to a growing sense of paranoia. And her break with Lizzie Keckly—whom she had considered her closest friend—had left her alone and vulnerable. Although she had finally inherited $36,000 from her husband's estate, she had been unsuccessful in raising money either from the public or from Congress. Desperate to escape an "ungrateful Republic"—and to raise Tad in a more benign and affordable environment—Mary decided to leave for Europe.

During the past three years she and Tad had been inseparable. For a time Mary refused to send him to school. Her son slept with her in her bedroom and accompanied her everywhere. "Only my darling Taddie prevents me from taking my life," she wrote in 1867. "It is my intent . . . not to be separated from Taddie, for a day." But years of coddling were taking their toll. Unable to tie his shoes at age twelve, Tad still could not write at fourteen, and his lisp made him the brunt of teasing when he finally did begin school—his nickname became "Stuttering Tad."

Coming east in July, Mary booked passage on the *Baltimore* for later that summer. Then in mid-August Robert announced his plans to be married in September to his longtime girlfriend Mary Harlan, the daughter of Senator James and Ann Harlan of Iowa. Mary was genuinely delighted. She had "known & loved the young lady since her childhood," she wrote, and considered her a perfect match for her son. This was "the only sunbeam in my sad future," she wrote. But there was one big problem—the marriage was to take place at the bride's home in Washington, which meant Mary would have to return to the city of her nightmares. In a letter to a friend she confessed, "The terror of having to proceed to Washington to witness it, almost overpowers me."

Mary briefly considered not attending, but Tad wouldn't hear of it. So she re-booked their passage for October 1 and dutifully arrived for the nuptials in late September. It was a small ceremony with only thirty or so in attendance. Among the guests were Ellen Stanton and her son Edwin, and Gideon and Mary Jane Welles and their son Edgar, the young men being two of Robert's closest friends. Mary attended in full mourning attire and marveled at the array of brilliant gifts laid out for the couple. "If they had had a large wedding," she later wrote, "they would have had an immense assortment." Upon returning to Baltimore later that day, Mary was so emotionally drained that during dinner she fainted.

By now she was having serious troubles with Tad, who declared he didn't want to go to Europe after all but wanted to stay close to Robert and his new sister-in-law. But Mary was determined to press forward with her plans, and on October 1—just one week after the wedding—she and Tad set sail for Bremen, Germany. With Robert and Mary already on their honeymoon in New York, no one showed up at the pier to wave goodbye to them.

As a widow Mary Lincoln wore black at all times—even to Robert's wedding. By now she had the sense that her husband's murder had been inevitable. Even "if he had remained in the W[hite] H[ouse] on that night of darkness," she wrote in a letter, "he would have been horribly *cut to pieces*—Those fiends had too long contemplated, this inhuman murder to have allowed, *him,* to escape."

BRADY.   WASHINGTON, D. C.

As President, Ulysses S.
Grant retired his uniform.

November 3, 1868

President-Elect Grant

E ven though Andrew Johnson was the official successor in office, it was Ulysses S. Grant who inherited Abraham Lincoln's mantle. Wherever he went after the Civil War, the General in Chief of the Union Armies was serenaded by enthusiastic crowds and often presented with tokens of the North's appreciation. At least fourteen horses were among the gifts he received; New York City offered a cash present of $100,000; and his hometown of Galena, Illinois, presented a fully furnished mansion, as did Washington and Philadelphia.

The poor son of a leather tanner, Grant had failed at almost everything he tried before he rejoined the army in 1861. He rose quickly in the ranks and in February 1862 gave the Union its first major victory, at Fort Donelson. In 1863 he was placed in charge of the assault on Vicksburg and ran a campaign that Lincoln said was "one of the most brilliant in the world." Though the President had not yet formally met his taciturn general, he considered him to be of "inestimable" value. Here was a commander unlike any other Lincoln had; "He doesn't worry and bother me. He isn't shrieking for reinforcements all the time." He "is the most extraordinary man in command that I know."

In 1864 Grant was named lieutenant general, a rank previously held by only Winfield Scott and George Washington. Appearing at a White House reception on the day before his presentation, Grant was introduced to Lincoln. "The President," wrote John G. Nicolay that same evening, "knew from the buzz and movement of the crowd that it must be him; and when a man of modest mien and unimposing exterior presented himself, the President said, 'This is General Grant, is it?' The general replied 'Yes.' and the two greeted each other more cordially, but still with that modest deference . . . so appropriate to both—the one the honored Ruler, the other the honored Victor of the nation and the time."

Lincoln stood by his top general for the remainder of the war, praising him as "vigilant and self-reliant." And though that summer and the following winter saw horrendous Union casualties, leading Mary Lincoln to call Grant "a butcher," it was clear that under his command Lincoln would win the war.

Had Grant accompanied the Lincolns to Ford's Theatre as originally planned and advertised, it is very possible that he would have been killed along with the President. During the next three years he sided politically with his fellow Republicans. He refused to back Andrew Johnson in his firing of Edwin Stanton and in 1868 supported the President's impeachment. It was during Johnson's trial that Grant was nominated as the Republican candidate for President. And on November 3 he went on to win the election by a strong electoral margin.

F. GUTEKUNST.   PHOTOG'R.

Lincoln's general

An Exchange of Letters Between Lincoln and Grant

April 30 & May 1, 1864

From the President
Washington, April 30, 1864

Not expecting to see you again before the Spring campaign opens, I wish to express, in this way, my entire satisfaction with what you have done up to this time, so far as I understand it. The particulars of your plans I neither know, or seek to know. You are vigilant and self-reliant; and, pleased with this, I wish not to obtrude any constraints or restraints upon you. While I am very anxious that any great disaster, or the capture of our men in great numbers, shall be avoided, I know these points are less likely to escape your attention than they would be mine. If there is anything wanting which is within my power to give, do not fail to let me know it. And now with a brave Army, and a just cause, may God sustain you.

From the General
Culpepper C. H. Va. May 1st 1864

Your very kind letter of yesterday is just received. The confidence you express for the future, and satisfaction with the past, in my Military administration is acknowledged with pride. It will be my earnest endeavor that you, and the country, shall not be disappointed.

From my first entrance into the Volunteer service of the Country, to the present day, I have never had cause of complaint, have never expressed or implied a complaint, against the Administration, or the Sec. of War, for throwing any embarassment in the way of my vigerously prosse-cuting what appeared to me my duty. Indeed since the promotion which placed me in command of all the Armies, and in view of the great responsibility, and importance of success, I have been astonished at the readiness with which every thing asked for has been yielded without even an explainatin being asked. Should my success be less than I desire, and expect, the least I can say is, the fault is not with you.

Andrew Johnson's Midnight Pardons

March 3, 1869

Before leaving office in 1869, prior to Ulysses S. Grant's inauguration, Andrew Johnson, who had earlier proclaimed a general amnesty for all former Confederates, pardoned the three still-living prisoners of the Lincoln murder conspiracy who had been held ever since their conviction in the Dry Tortugas. Michael O'Laughlin had died in captivity in 1867. But Dr. Samuel Mudd, Edman Spangler, and Samuel Arnold were all now given their freedom. And on the eve of Grant's inauguration, Johnson granted the family of John Wilkes Booth the right to claim his body.

Samuel A. Mudd

Samuel Arnold

Edman Spangler

Four years after the assassination of his commander, war hero Ulysses S. Grant was sworn into office as President.

April 12, 1869

A Sad Day at Goosenest Prairie

Four years after Lincoln's assassination, his eighty-year-old stepmother still lived in the double cabin at Goosenest Prairie south of Charleston, Illinois, where she and Lincoln's father had resided until his death in 1851. There had been something remarkable between mother and son. According to Augustus Chapman, son-in-law of Dennis Hanks, "she had been his best Friend in this world & and . . . no Son could love a Mother more than he loved her." And when Abraham and she parted after his last visit in 1861, she had embraced him and said she felt his enemies would assassinate him. "No, no Mama," he had reportedly said to her in return, "they will not do that . . . we

From 1851 until 1869 the log cabin at Goosenest Prairie was known locally as "Old Mrs. Lincoln's Farm." The house was built by Thomas Lincoln in 1831.

will See each other—again."

Sarah was inside the cabin at Goosenest Prairie when she received the news of her son's death. According to her grandson, John Hall, she buried her head in her apron and cried out that she had known they would kill him. "She never had no heart after that to be chirp and peart like she used to be," Hall recalled.

When she died four years later, her funeral took place at the Lincoln cabin, with the family seated inside near her coffin. Outside there was a gathering of neighbors, with the minister standing in the doorway to be able to speak to both groups. It was said that more people attended her service than any funeral that ever took place in those parts. John Hall described the old woman as being buried in the simple black wool dress that her stepson had given to her on their last visit together.

Spring/Summer 1869

"The Rebellion Seems Not to Be Dead Yet"

By the end of the 1860s it was clear there was still a deep division in America. In the North Lincoln was fast becoming an icon, while in many places in the South the sixteenth President was still despised. In 1869 the Massachusetts journalist Russell H. Conwell made a journey through the South, filing twenty-five stories for the Boston *Daily Evening Transcript*. Traveling through ten of the eleven former Confederate states, he visited battlefields, cemeteries, and historic sites of the Civil War and spoke with Southerners, white and black, wherever he went. In Virginia he drove out to the former estate of Robert E. Lee—Arlington House—which had been seized by the Federals during the Civil War and transformed into what would become Arlington National Cemetery. "The grand old mansion with its barns and Negro quarters is occupied by the keeper of the cemetery," Conwell wrote; "from its very doorway, stretching far down the hillside, are the graves of Union soldiers."

As he moved through the old Confederacy, Conwell found ruined cities, wrecked economies, and former aristocrats reduced to manual labor. Near Malvern Hill he came upon a young woman from one of Virginia's best families driving a two-wheeled mule cart. She had "dirty hands, poor teeth, dozy eyes, towseled red hair," and wore a "ragged dress," Conwell noted. At Cold Harbor he saw black men with large sacks "collecting the bones of dead horses" to sell to bone-grinders. Union cemeteries in this region were in utter disrepair, either dug up or "exposed through the action of the rain," with "skulls, ribs, legs, and arm-bones . . . scattered about in fearful array."

Conwell discovered that Southern resentments toward the North were also not well buried. In Alabama he shared a railroad car with a Presbyterian minister who shocked him by his refusal to see any good coming out of the war, especially not from Lincoln's act of emancipation. Insisting that blacks had been better off as slaves, he declared that "the devil" had conducted the late war, "aided by his satellites, the Yankees."

But it was in Alexandria, Virginia, that Conwell found the clearest signs of ongoing regional hatred. "Its inhabitants are as bitter enemies of the nation as they ever were," he wrote. "Portraits of Jeff Davis and Lee hang in all their parlors, decorated with Confederate flags. Photographs of Wilkes Booth, with the last words of great martyrs printed upon its border; effigies of Abraham Lincoln hanging by the neck with a darkey hung at each heel, together with Confederate songs, mottoes, and keepsakes, adorn their drawing-rooms. . . . They keep the graves in the Confederate cemetery decorated with flowers, and by word and look expel every Northerner that they know to be within its gates. . . . This same Alexandria, which was the first to raise the Confederate flag in Virginia, is also the last to lay it aside. . . . [T]he rebellion . . . seems not to be dead yet."

In 1869 journalist Russell Conwell (above) visited the site of Robert E. Lee's former estate in Virginia, captured by the Union Army during the Civil War. "Had any one said that his lands should be taken, the grounds of his house used as a graveyard, his barns taken as a storage for Yankee coffins, and his . . . slaves . . . hired to decorate the graves of the enemies, he would have considered it impossible."

Children of freed slaves in the South after the Civil War

A Lincoln Portrait for the White House

Until Lincoln lived and died there, the White House never had a strong sense of its own history. Hanging in the East Room was the famous Gilbert Stuart painting of George Washington—rescued just before the White House was burned to the ground by the British during the War of 1812. And during his presidency Lincoln kept a portrait of Andrew Jackson in his office. But otherwise there were few pictures of his predecessors. This historical neglect changed after Lincoln's death. In 1868 Andrew Johnson's daughter Martha Patterson was rooting around in the mansion's attic when she discovered six unframed paintings by the artist George Healy. Commissioned by Congress before the Civil War and then forgotten, they included portraits of John Quincy Adams, Martin Van Buren, John Tyler, James K. Polk, Millard Fillmore, and Franklin Pierce. With money obtained from Congress, the six portraits were framed and hung in the front hall of the state floor, where they became the first White House Portrait Gallery. The gallery was immensely popular with the public, and it quickly became clear that it needed to add a portrait of Lincoln.

On March 3, on the eve of Ulysses S. Grant's inauguration, Congress set aside funds for a new Lincoln portrait, then put out a public call for submissions. The winner would be chosen by a blue-ribbon panel that would include President Grant, General Sherman, General Sheridan, and Elihu Washburne, Grant's secretary of state and later ambassador to France. The cash award would be $3,000.

George Healy heard about the contest in Rome and decided to submit a painting he had made shortly after the assassination—a seated Lincoln, head in hand, in a uniquely contemplative pose. But if Healy, the official painter of presidents, thought he had a lock on the contest, he was mistaken. Twelve other paintings were submitted from across the country, among them one from a young Chicago artist named William Cogswell. Unlike the others, Cogswell had sketched the President from life, claiming he had obtained a private sitting with him in 1864. In the years since he had labored over his painting and was still working on it when word came of the public competition. Cogswell sent in his finished canvas sometime that spring or early summer of 1869. It depicted a majestic Lincoln standing on the porch of the White House, with the Capitol dome in the distance, grasping in his hand the Emancipation Proclamation.

By August the contest had come down to two finalists—Healy and Cogswell. Sherman was strongly inclined to support Healy (a friend), as was Robert Lincoln, who quietly advised from the sidelines. But Grant preferred Cogswell, as did Sheridan, and when it was announced that the standing Lincoln was the winner, critics agreed with the selection. The *New York Times* wrote, "Cogswell's portrait, besides being full-length, was so much the superior in facial lines and in the expression almost always worn by the late President, that it easily carried off the prize."

In Chicago, Robert Lincoln was not pleased. "It turned out that there was really no competition," he told a friend, "and Healy's work never had the slightest chance of acceptance." Robert was so irritated by the results, and so enamored of Healy's portrait, that he eventually bought it from the artist, and it became one of his prized possessions.

George P. A. Healy

148

Healy's portrait was purchased by Robert Lincoln and many years later bequeathed to the White House.

William Cogswell's painting won the competition.

A Midnight Encounter
Lawrence Gobright

1869

In his 1869 book, Recollections of Men and Things at Washington, *journalist Lawrence A. Gobright described an encounter with a half-dressed Lincoln five years earlier.*

A despatch was received at Philadelphia, and telegraphed to Washington, that our fleet had captured the city of Charleston. The two gentlemen who received the "good news," proceeded to the White House to communicate it to President Lincoln. It was about eleven o'clock at night, and Mr.

Lincoln had gone to bed. The doorkeeper said the gentlemen could not, therefore, see him. Insisting upon an interview, and being satisfied, from the nature of their errand, that the President would excuse the interruption, they prevailed upon the doorkeeper to disturb him. He soon returned, saying they would see the President in a style of costume in which no other visitors had ever seen him, and this was true. Entering the room, there was Mr. Lincoln, with no clothing on excepting his shirt! He invited his guests to be seated, and he himself took a chair. He inquired as to the date of their news; and on being informed, said he had three days later intelligence, and that "the bombardment was then going on."

The visitors began to apologize for disturbing his slumbers. The President said it made no difference, and good-humoredly bade them good night, with a profound bow.

Lawrence Gobright was the first Washington correspondent for the Associated Press.

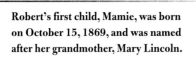

Robert's first child, Mamie, was born on October 15, 1869, and was named after her grandmother, Mary Lincoln.

December 24, 1869

Edwin Stanton's End

In late 1869 came word that Edwin Stanton was seriously ill. It had been a fateful year for Lincoln's former cabinet. In March, Attorney General Edward Bates had died in St. Louis; and in September, Secretary of the Treasury William Pitt Fessenden, in Portland, Maine. Now the fifty-five-year-old former war secretary, whom Lincoln once said reminded him of a Methodist preacher, had been reduced to sitting in a chair coughing and wheezing, the victim of a long-concealed struggle with asthma.

Few men had known Lincoln better than Stanton. Tough, pragmatic, a man of action, he had struck some, such as Gideon Welles, as being "ungracious and rough"—a man whose "bearish manner would terrify or humiliate those who were subject . . . to him." But he was exactly what the gentler-tempered Lincoln had needed at his side, and the two of them had practically run the war together. After replacing Simon Cameron in early 1862, Stanton spent more time in Lincoln's presence than any other cabinet member. And in thoughtful, carefully reasoned letters, he advised the President on all aspects of the war—speaking out against unwise acts of clemency, urging Lincoln to move forward on the organization of black troops, and arguing in favor of bounties for enlisting soldiers. And it was he who worried most about Lincoln's safety. On July 9, 1864, he wrote Lincoln that he had received a report from his department's watchman that "your carriage was followed by a horseman not of your escort and dressed in a uniform unlike that used by our troops." Stanton advised the President to have his guard "on the alert tonight."

Although Stanton came under criticism for his supposed mishandling of the government's response to the assassination, and was even accused by some of having been disloyal to the President, John Hay, among others, knew better. In a speech he called Stanton "among the few" who had stood by Lincoln throughout the war "and never faltered."

Despite news of Stanton's worsening condition, on December 20, 1869, President Grant nominated him for a position on the Supreme Court. It was a grand gesture, and Congress confirmed him on the same day. Four days later, on Christmas Eve, Edwin Stanton died.

Mary Lincoln received the news in Germany. "I, too, dearly loved Mr Stanton," she wrote a friend, and "greatly appreciated the services he rendered his country, our loved, bleeding, land, during the trying rebellion." Following the assassination, Stanton had visited in the White House each day, often sitting quietly with Robert to share the young man's grief. Just two days after his death, his son Edwin Jr. received a note from Robert. "I know it is useless to say anything," Robert wrote, "and yet when I recall the kindness of your father to me, when my father was lying dead and I felt utterly desperate, hardly able to realize the truth, I am as little able to keep my eyes from filling with tears as he was then."

Edwin Stanton was criticized in later years, and even considered disloyal to President Lincoln, but John Hay's opinion of him never wavered. "Not everyone knows as I do," he wrote Stanton after the war, "how close you stood to our lost leader, how he loved you and trusted you, and how vain all the efforts to shake that trust and confidence not lightly given and never withdrawn."

March 30, 1870

A Dream Fulfilled

In his last public address Abraham Lincoln had advocated black suffrage—or at least a gradually increasing form of it. "I would myself prefer that it were now conferred on the very intelligent, and on those who serve in our cause as soldiers," he had said. How rapidly Lincoln would have supported universal suffrage is not known, but almost immediately after his death he was adopted to that cause. Clergymen praised his egalitarianism, and radicals like Frederick Douglass claimed him as part of their movement. Hadn't he said at Gettysburg that all men are created equal? Mustn't he at heart have believed in universal suffrage? It took five years to fulfill the dream. Finally in February 1869 the Republican-led Congress passed the Fifteenth Amendment, granting the right to vote to all citizens regardless of "race, color, or previous condition of servitude," and granting Congress the power to enforce the new right. It was an astonishing step forward, as newspapers noted. "How much we have gained since Lincoln spoke at Gettysburg," wrote the *Washington Chronicle* that spring. "In November of 1863 we had a theory of liberty, a hope of equality, a dream of justice to all men. In May of 1869 that theory is fact, that hope is fulfilled, that dream is a reality." Lincoln had been the all-important precursor—his successors had brought his great dream to fruition. Following its adoption in Georgia the next year, the Fifteenth Amendment became law on March 30, 1870, leading to widespread rejoicing in the North. "The black man is free," boomed out Lincoln's friend Frederick Douglass. "Never was revolution more complete."

Frederick Douglass, around the time of the passage of the Fifteenth Amendment

A lithograph highlighted new freedoms ushered in by the Fifteenth Amendment. Land ownership, legal marriage, religious liberty, and citizenship were all made possible because of Lincoln's Emancipation Proclamation.

Six thousand people showed up in Baltimore on May 20, 1870, to celebrate the passage of the Fifteenth Amendment. Soon after this photograph was taken, the crowded speakers' stand collapsed. Undeterred, Frederick Douglass climbed onto the rubble and addressed the crowd.

Full citizenship, the long-held dream of the former slaves, seemed finally to have arrived.

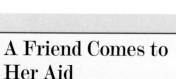

Mary Lincoln, in traveling attire

July 14, 1870
Mary's Exile

Mary Lincoln remained in Frankfurt, Germany, where she and Tad had come in search of a new life. Her husband had promised to take her to Europe after his presidency, and in a sad way Mary was trying to catch a glimmer of what that might have been for them. She had also come seeking a cure for constant ailments but found the deep chill of the German winters little help. And while it was a relief to get away from the constant disparagements of the American press, she felt lonely in "this distant land"—"this land of strangers"—as she called it.

Mary had placed Tad in a German boarding school for English-speaking students, and after two years of academic troubles he had finally begun to settle down. She resided nearby in a single room, living for Tad's days off and vacations. "Taddie, is like some *old woman*, with respect to his care of me," she wrote during their second winter in Frankfurt. "When I was so very sick—his dark loving eyes—watching over me, reminded me so much of his dearly beloved father's—so filled with *his* deep love." Though her son made progress in his studies, learning to speak German fluently and to draw and dance, neither his nor his mother's health was good. Both were prone to lung infections, compounded by their poorly heated living quarters. At one point Mary left Tad in school and traveled to the Mediterranean coast of France in an attempt to find sun and happiness. But her nerves and her nightmares followed her there, and she returned to find Tad sickly and thin.

In the summer of 1869 she took him on a seven-week holiday in Scotland, where the two spent their happiest time since the assassination. To avoid recognition, they traveled under assumed names, and they made a pilgrimage to the birthplace of Robert Burns, Lincoln and Mary's favorite poet. They also visited James Smith, their former pastor from Springfield, whom Lincoln had appointed American consul at

A Friend Comes to Her Aid
Sarah Orne

September 12, 1869

When Mary Lincoln's friend Sarah Orne arrived in Germany, she was shocked by what she found and wrote about it to Charles Sumner.

In a small cheerless desolate looking room with but one window—two chairs and a wooden table with a solitary candle—I found *the wife the petted indulged wife* of my *noble* hearted just good *murdered*

President Abraham Lincoln. . . . My very blood boiled within my veins and I almost *cried out—shame on my countrymen—*Mrs Lincoln was completely overwhelmed with grief—her sobs and tears wrung my own heart and I thought at the moment if her *tormentors* and *slanderers* could see her—they surely *might be satisfied.*

Mary and Tad Lincoln settled in Frankfurt, Germany, where raising her son became her overriding mission. "[T]he young life of my Taddie," she wrote to a friend, "is all that makes life endurable for me."

Dundee. Wherever they went, they found people who revered Lincoln. "I know the manner of his death made all persons his friends," Mary said.

As a new decade began, Mary's friends took up the matter of her pension. Tens of thousands of Civil War widows were by then receiving government annuities, and Mary believed she deserved to be included among them. Her husband, after all, had been Commander in Chief of the Union forces, outranking all the generals and admirals whose wives were now well taken care of. On May 2 the House of Representatives passed her bill. But the Senate then stalled it, on the grounds that Lincoln was a civilian, not a military officer, and that his widow didn't need the money. Claiming she had a net worth of $60,000, they mocked her for wanting to live in the manner of European royalty. When news of their rebuff reached Mary in Germany, she collapsed in shock. "I cannot believe that those who revere even the name of the late beloved President, whose precious life was sacrificed for his country, will longer delay action in this case." "When I hear, from cruel—wicked, reckless assertions—how rich I am . . . I sigh . . . to be at rest by my darling husband's side."

Two months later Charles Sumner convinced the Senate to reconsider the bill. In the debate that ensued on the Senate floor Illinois's Democratic senator Richard Yates spoke for the opposition. He condemned the former First Lady for sympathizing with the South during the Civil War (a groundless rumor) and hinted that she had been unfaithful to Lincoln. ("A woman should be true to her husband. . . . I will not go into details. . . . My tongue is sealed.") On moral grounds alone, he implied, she was not fit for a government pension. And he believed that, "could Mr. Lincoln speak from the abodes of heaven, he would say as I do."

But Lincoln's former friends argued forcefully. Lyman Trumbull, Henry Wilson, Simon Cameron, and others rose and called for the immediate passage of the bill. No matter what people thought of Mary, they said, she was the widow of Abraham Lincoln and as such deserved to be highly honored by Congress.

On July 14, 1870, Mary Lincoln's pension bill finally passed. Signed into law by President Grant the next day, it guaranteed her financial stability for the rest of her life.

The eccentric millionaire Benjamin Richardson was enraptured by all things Lincoln.

On November 7, 1870, Mary Lincoln wrote from England to Captain Benjamin Richardson, a millionaire friend in Brooklyn, New York. Two years earlier, to help him launch a museum of relics of famous Americans, she had given him the gloves Lincoln had worn on his last night alive. Tad had hand-carried them over to his house, along with a photograph of Lincoln. Richardson's plans included buying the Lincoln house in Springfield, enclosing it in a huge glass bubble, and allowing pilgrims to the site to look in free of charge. None of these plans ever materialized, but Richardson became one of the few people to correspond with Mary in Europe during this obscure time in her life.

My Dear Sir—Strange to say, your letter of July last has only been recently received by me. It is very pleasant in this land of strangers to receive tidings and kind remembrances from friends in our beloved land who can never be forgotten either by my young son or myself. Taddie in Germany became quite proficient in the language, but in the meantime his own mother tongue was [so] much neglected that it has become necessary to place him with an English tutor, with whom, I am happy to say, he is studying very hard.

Taddie speaks of you very frequently, and it is very pleasant to me to remember that you took so great an interest in him. Be assured he will never pass through New York without calling on you to pay his respects. He is growing very much like his dear father and possesses his amiability of character and nobleness of nature. He will return home before long. He loves his country very dearly, and we can but hope that when he grows up he will become one of its best citizens. Go where we will, we see no such nation as ours and the noblest and kindest-hearted people on the face of the earth.

155

In a letter written in 1868 Lee gave his own account of Lincoln's offer of the command of the United States Army, and his decision to turn it down and to throw in his lot with the Confederacy.

I never intimated to any one that I desired the command of the United States Army; nor did I ever have a conversation with but one gentleman, Mr. Francis Preston Blair, on the subject, which was at his invitation, and, as I understood, at the instance of President Lincoln. After listening to his remarks, I declined the offer he made me, to take command of the army that was to be brought into the field; stating, as candidly and as courteously as I could, that, though opposed to secession and deprecating war, I could take no part in an invasion of the Southern States. I went directly from the interview with Mr. Blair to the office of General Scott; told him of the proposition that had been made to me, and my decision. Upon reflection after returning to my home, I concluded that I ought no longer to retain the commission I held in the United States Army, and on the second morning thereafter I forwarded my resignation to General Scott.

October 12, 1870

The Death of Robert E. Lee

During the five years since the end of the Civil War, Robert E. Lee had come to be for much of the South what Lincoln had become for the North—its great ethical, almost mythical hero. Officially pardoned after the war by Andrew Johnson, he had gone on to become president of Washington University in Lexington, Virginia. Although still distrusted by many Northerners—considered a traitor who should have been hung instead of pardoned—Lee did have some Yankee support. Admiring Northerners recalled how Lincoln had turned to him to take command of the Union armies, how he had "wept tears of blood over this terrible war," but how a sense of duty had not permitted him to "lift my hand against my own state and people." Lincoln too had been an admirer and became one again when the war was over. According to Elizabeth Keckly, on the morning of April 14, 1865, Robert Lincoln had visited him in the White House, carrying a portrait of Robert E. Lee in his hand. "The President took the picture," Keckly recalled, "laid it on a table before him, scanned the face thoroughly, and said 'it is a good face; it is the face of a noble, noble brave man. I am glad that the war is over at last.'" Lee, too, was magnanimous at war's end. Unlike others in the South, he refused to celebrate Lincoln's assassination, declaring it "a crime previously unknown to this country, and one that must be deprecated by every American."

Lee's death came as a shock to the old Confederacy, where he was mourned as the South's "incomparable man," and "the most glorious illustration" of its nationality. "Lee was ours," tolled the *Atlanta Constitution*. "This can never be torn from us." He was "part of our history, and his character redeems our defeat."

Robert E. Lee's funeral procession carried the war hero through his hometown of Lexington, Virginia, on October 12, 1870.

Lee's funeral was held at Washington College, where he had served as president since 1865. The college was renamed Washington and Lee University.

In life Robert E. Lee was revered, dedicating his final years, he said, to "the restoration of peace and harmony." His tomb was inside the newly renamed Lee Memorial Chapel at the university.

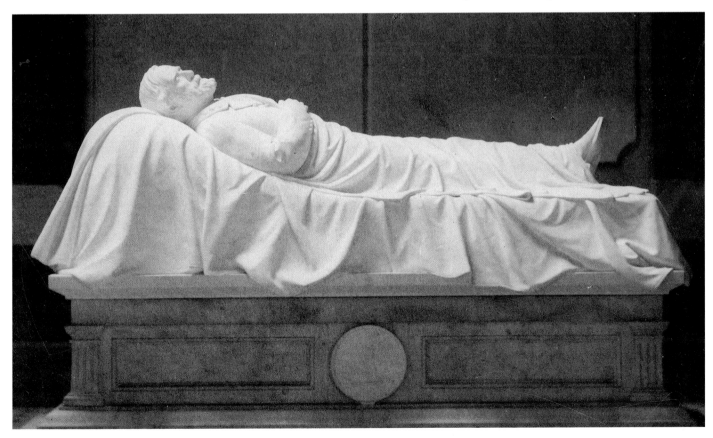

In 1871, just about everyone was talking about Vinnie Ream, a young woman who had created a major sculpture of Abraham Lincoln. She had come to Washington with her parents during the Civil War and begun work in the Post Office Department and as a hospital volunteer. In 1864 she met the sculptor Clark Mills, who recognized her natural talent and became her teacher. After she molded a lifelike bust of Abraham Lincoln, friends helped her gain an audience with the wartime president, at which she asked permission to sculpt him. Lincoln liked her and invited her back for a series of sittings. "He seemed to find a strange sort of companionship in being with me, although we talked but little," Ream later recalled. "I made him think of Willie. He often said so and as often wept." She decided to try to capture the sadness of Lincoln—a man, she later wrote, "of unfathomable sorrow."

Two years later Congress announced a national competition for a life-size sculpture of the martyred President, to be prominently displayed inside the U.S. Capitol. Ream, now eighteen, was the only woman to apply and seemed destined to lose out to one of the eighteen male competitors. Her chances worsened when two senators publicly challenged her qualifications. Charles Sumner called her "not competent to produce the work," and Jacob Howard said he expected "a complete failure." The Washington journalist Jane Grey Swisshelm accused Ream of trying to use her "feminine wiles" to win over the congressional judges. But when a number of western senators rose to her defense, in August 1866 Ream won the contract. In addition to the award of $10,000, Ream was given space in the Capitol basement, and here in a makeshift studio she began work on a large clay model.

Determined to render the real man, Ream approached White House doorkeeper Alphonso Dunn, who had been given the black suit and square-toed boots Lincoln had worn on his last night alive. The artist requested that Dunn lend them to her so that she could depict Lincoln as he actually looked. When Mary Lincoln heard about the request, she urged Dunn not to cooperate. Ream was an "unknown person," she said, "who by much forwardness & unladylike persistence, obtained from Congress, permission to execute a statue of my husband. . . . From her inexperience I judge she will be unable to do this." Two weeks later, reconsidering her ungenerous remarks, Mary wrote again, saying Dunn was of course free to do whatever he wanted to with the clothing.

In 1868 the Library of Congress bought a bust of Lincoln by Boston artist Sarah Fisher Ames, making it the first national Lincoln sculpture. Vinnie Ream remained hard at work on her standing Lincoln. In 1869 she took a cast of her completed model and sailed for Italy to find the marble and stonecutters to finish her work. By the end of the next year it was finally completed, and an unveiling was scheduled for

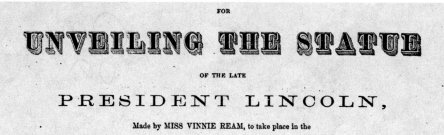

FOR

UNVEILING THE STATUE

OF THE LATE

PRESIDENT LINCOLN,

Made by MISS VINNIE REAM, to take place in the

The dedication of Vinnie Ream's statue took place on Wednesday evening, January 25, inside the Capitol Rotunda. Supreme Court Justice David Davis presided over the unveiling.

the Capitol Rotunda. On January 25 a distinguished group assembled—President Grant, Vice President Colfax, members of Congress and the Supreme Court, and a special delegation of Lincoln's Illinois friends. Standing nearby, Ream seemed younger than her twenty-four years, "pale and anxious, and . . . childlike in her appearance." As the Marine Band played, Lincoln's old friend David Davis pulled back a large flag, and the life-size statue was revealed. "There was a momentary hush," reported the *Evening Star.* "And then everybody turned to where the little sculptor stood, a little in the rear with glad tears in her eyes, and congratulations were poured upon her." For Judge Davis the statue was a stunning success: "There stood the man as [I] . . . had so long known and loved him." For the Democratic congressman James Brooks, it was the dawning of a new era. "Here in this Rotunda we now see the equal rights of woman, if not with the ballot, with the chisel." Although the *New York Tribune* attacked the sculpture as a "frightful abortion . . . lifeless and soulless, void of thought and meaning," for most it was a success—"one of the very best literal representations" of Lincoln yet made. Created by the first woman ever to receive a federal commission, it took up permanent residence in the Capitol's Statuary Hall.

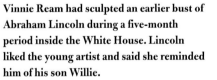
Vinnie Ream had sculpted an earlier bust of Abraham Lincoln during a five-month period inside the White House. Lincoln liked the young artist and said she reminded him of his son Willie.

July 15, 1871

Tad Lincoln's Sad End

In the fall of 1869 Mary Lincoln was greeted by welcome news. Robert's wife had given birth to a first child—named Mary after her grandmother. Tad, now an uncle, was overjoyed, and the news made him desperately homesick. A year later he was "almost wild to see Bob, you and the baby," Mary wrote to her daughter-in-law in January 1871. But the journey home from Europe would have to wait until Tad finished up work with a private tutor in England.

The ocean crossing that spring was traumatic, with high swells and raging winds lasting for days. "Rough was no word for it," Mary later described. "We certainly thought we were doomed to destruction every moment during the tremendous gale." They arrived in New York City on May 11 and were greeted there by their old friend John Hay, who had been out of the country much of the time since the assassination.

Hay noted how much Tad had changed since he last saw him—he was taller, spoke more clearly (though with a bit of a German accent), and all in all seemed "greatly improved"—though there was something stiff and sad about the former sprite who had so endeared himself to all in the White House. When mother and son reached Chicago a few days later, a reporter commented on Tad's rosy "red cheeks," taking them as evidence of "perfect health." In fact, the boy was sick with a new ailment, probably the beginning of tuberculosis.

By June 8 his lungs were so filled with fluid, he had to sleep upright in a chair. For Robert it was agony to see his brother so ill—this "good boy," so "firm in his friendships," he later described him, "so manly and self-reliant." When Tad's legal guardian, David Davis, visited on July 8, he remarked afterward "if he recovers it will be almost a miracle."

Mary prayed for divine intervention. But it was not to be. The boy briefly improved the following week and on Friday was shown a photograph of his new niece, Mary. "Tad was delighted with it," Robert wrote to his wife the next day, "and it was really the last pleasure he had on earth."

On Saturday morning, July 15, 1871, eighteen-year-old Thomas Lincoln slipped away, leaving Mary, who had suffered so much tragedy, utterly bereft. "As grievous as the other bereavements have been," she later wrote, "not one great sorrow, ever approached the agony of this.... My idolized & devoted son, torn from me, when he had bloomed into such a noble promising youth." Without "my inseparable companion . . . the world is complete darkness."

Once again, as at her husband's death, Mary was too distraught to attend the funeral, and it was twenty-seven-year-old Robert who made all the arrangements. Tad's body was taken by night train to Springfield, where it was laid out at the house of Mary's sister Elizabeth Edwards—the same house where Robert's parents had been married twenty-nine years earlier. The funeral took place on July 17 at the Lincolns' former parish. And then, on a blistering hot day, 105 degrees in the shade, Tad was taken out to Oak Ridge Cemetery, where he was placed in the temporary Lincoln family tomb, beside his father and his brothers Eddy and Willie.

Thomas Lincoln

Tad Lincoln, near the end of his short life. Five years earlier his father had said to a journalist, "When this war is over . . . I tell my boy Tad that we will go back to the farm, where I was happier as a boy . . . than I am now; I tell him I will buy him a mule and a pony and he shall have a little cart and . . . a little garden . . . all his own."

Remembering Tad
John Hay

July 17, 1871

Few people outside the Lincoln family knew Tad better than had the President's personal secretary John Hay. Just days after Tad's death Hay wrote about the boy in the pages of the New York Tribune.

Most of those who read the dispatch announcing the death of Thomas Todd Lincoln will never think of the well-grown gentleman who died on Saturday at Chicago. The name of "Tad" . . . recalls the tricksy little sprite who gave to that sad and

Mansion. He was idolized by both his father and mother, petted and indulged by his teachers, and fawned upon and caressed by that noisome horde of office-seekers which infested the ante-rooms of the White House. He had a very bad opinion of books and no opinion of discipline, and thought very little of any tutor who would not assist him in yoking his kids to a chair or in driving his dogs tandem over the South Lawn. He was as shrewd as he was lawless, and always knew whether he could make a tutor serviceable or not. If he found one with obstinate ideas of the superiority of grammar to kite-flying as an intellectual employment, he soon found means of getting rid of him. He had so much to do that he felt he

kindly and unlettered natures. "Let him run," the easy-going President would say; "he has time enough left to learn his letters and get pokey."

Although still a mere child at the death of his father, this terrible shock greatly sobered and steadied him. His brother Robert at once took charge of his education, and he made rapid progress up to the time of his sailing for Europe with his mother. He has ever since remained with her, displaying a thoughtful devotion and tenderness beyond his years, and strangely at variance with the mischievous thoughtlessness of his childhood. He came back a short while ago, greatly improved by his residence abroad, but always the same

The irrepressible Tad Lincoln

Tad, in full dress uniform

He was his father's comic relief.

solemn White House of the great war the only comic relief it knew. . . .

He was so full of life and vigor—so bubbling over with health and high spirits, that he kept the house alive with his pranks and his fantastic enterprises. He was always a "chartered libertine," and after the death of his brother Willie, a prematurely serious and studious child, and the departure of Robert for college, he installed himself as the absolute tyrant of the Executive

could not waste time in learning to spell. . . .

The President took infinite comfort in the child's rude health, fresh fun, and uncontrollable boisterousness. He was pleased to see him growing up in ignorance of books, but with singularly accurate ideas of practical matters. He was a fearless rider, while yet so small that his legs stuck out horizontally from the saddle. He had that power of taming and attaching animals to himself, which seems the especial gift of

cordial, frank, warm-hearted boy. In his loss the already fearfully bereaved family will suffer a new and deep affliction, and the world, which never did and never will know him, will not withhold a tribute of regret for the child whose gayety and affection cheered more than anything else the worn and weary heart of the great President through the toilsome years of the war.

Fire destroyed downtown Chicago. As the city burned, panicked residents seized their belongings, many heading for the safety of Lincoln Park on Lake Michigan.

Robert Lincoln's house at 653 Wabash Avenue was spared, but just blocks away the homes of his friends succumbed to the flames.

October 8, 1871
The Great Chicago Fire

In the autumn of 1871, following the death of Tad that summer, Mary Lincoln left the Clifton House in downtown Chicago and moved in with Robert and his family at 653 Wabash Avenue. "I am suffering greatly with violent palpitation of the heart," she wrote a friend on October 4. "I am ordered perfect quiet." Three days later the worst fire in Chicago history erupted in a cowshed and began spreading to the north and east. With most buildings and all the sidewalks made of wood, the tinder-dry city was soon ablaze, with fire visible for miles in every direction. Gale-force winds blew all Sunday night, and the flames leaped rapidly northward, consuming the center city. "Who can describe the awful scene at the hour of midnight?" wrote an eyewitness; "—the surging multitudes, the walls falling all around, the wind howling with rage."

One by one the great old buildings of Chicago were destroyed. Up in flames went Tremont House, where Lincoln had once spoken in rebuttal to Stephen A. Douglas and where later he was introduced to his vice-presidential running mate, Hannibal Hamlin. Up too went the *Chicago Tribune* building—the paper that had so long supported Lincoln. Chicago's most impressive building was the great courthouse and city hall, where Lincoln had often appeared as a lawyer and where in 1865 his body had lain in state. The stone building was considered to be inviolable, and all through the night its bell tolled, ringing out the disaster. As the heat intensified, wrote one Chicago paper, "marble buildings were burned to quicklime and crumbled." When the flames began to threaten the courthouse, it was decided to release all the prisoners there and abandon the building. Finally its huge dome caught on fire and its mighty bell crashed down as an inferno engulfed the entire building.

Robert's house was extremely close to the fire. His street, Wabash Avenue—known as the avenue of churches—was burning from several blocks north of him all the way to its end. By coincidence, John Hay was visiting from New York, and early on Monday morning the two men ran out to see if they could salvage anything from Robert's law office. When they entered the building, it was already in flames. Robert "opened the vault," Hay reported, "and piled up in a table cloth the most valuable papers, then slung the pack over his shoulder, and escaped amid a shower of falling firebrands."

Robert then hurried home and told his mother it was time to evacuate. Miraculously, the fire never reached Robert's house. It was left standing, untouched, close to the very edge of the burned-out city.

The Chicago fire was devastating to Abraham Lincoln's memory. Burned up were the records of his legal practice here—all the bankruptcy proceedings and trials before the Illinois court. Gone was the major part of his Springfield furniture, sold in 1860 to a Chicago businessman whose house was devoured in the flames. Mary Lincoln's hotel, the Clifton House, where Tad had died, was among the 18,000 buildings destroyed, as was Tad's last school, the Chicago Academy. Allen Pinkerton, the detective, lost the only complete records of the Secret Service of the Army of the Potomac, with their irreplaceable information about Lincoln's presidency. And Isaac Arnold's grand house north of the Chicago River was destroyed, along with his library and huge collection of Lincoln books and pamphlets, including ten volumes of collected letters from Lincoln and others. Ever since Lincoln's death he had been gathering materials for a Lincoln biography, and he had already written several chapters. "These, along with many rare and curious relics, prints, and engravings, have all perished," reported a local writer.

But the most devastating loss of all was at the Chicago Historical Society, whose prized possession was the original draft of the final Emancipation Proclamation. Lincoln had considered the Proclamation the most important accomplishment of his presidency; he once said it was "the one thing that would make people remember I ever lived." He had written it out by hand before January 1, 1863, and planned to keep it as a remembrance of his days in the White House. But when he was approached by the Northwest Sanitary Fair to donate the manuscript on behalf of Union soldiers, he acquiesced. "I had some desire to retain the paper," Lincoln wrote, "but if it shall contribute to the relief or comfort of the soldiers that will be better." When those in charge of the fair thanked him, they promised that the "treasure shall be carefully guarded & skillfully managed." And they were true to their word; the document fetched $3,000 at the fair—the highest price paid for any item. The purchaser then donated it to the Chicago Soldiers home, which in due time turned it over to the Chicago Historical Society.

As the fire raged through the city on October 8, the society's impressive building was considered a safe spot for people to seek refuge, and at least twenty gathered in the basement to wait it out. But as a wall of fire consumed the building, all of them died, and the Emancipation Proclamation went up in smoke.

The east side of the Chicago River was hit hardest. Here men examine what is left of the corner of Washington and LaSalle.

A Lincoln Autobiography Comes to Light

Before 1872 few knew of the short autobiography Lincoln had written thirteen years earlier.

I was born Feb. 12. 1809, in Hardin county, Kentucky. My parents were both born in Virginia, of undistinguished families—second families, perhaps I should say. My mother, who died in my tenth year, was of a family of the name of Hanks, some of whom now reside in Adams, and others in Macon counties, Illinois— My paternal grandfather, Abraham Lincoln, emigrated from Rockingham county, Virginia, to Kentucky, about 1781 or 2, where, a year or two later, he was killed by indians, not in battle, but by stealth, when he

"No Other Marks or Brands Recollected"
Abraham Lincoln

March 1872

Five months after the Chicago fire, the nation learned of the existence of a short autobiography written in Abraham Lincoln's hand. It had been composed in December 1859 at the request of Jesse Fell, an Illinois attorney active in Lincoln's presidential campaign. "There is not much of it," Lincoln had written Fell at the time, "for the reason, I suppose, that there is not much of me." Promising to make only "modest use" of the material, Fell had sent it to a friend in Pennsylvania, Joseph Lewis, who used it to help compose a short campaign biography, instrumental in getting Lincoln better known in that key state.

Jesse W. Fell

Lewis held on to the manuscript for the next twelve years, until Jesse Fell finally convinced him to return it. In March 1872 Fell had the three-page Lincoln manuscript framed and placed on exhibition in Bloomington, Illinois. He also provided the text to newspapers and had it published as a poster along with a portrait of Lincoln. And soon almost everyone was agreeing: this brief document in Lincoln's hand, written without thought of publication, was one of "the most valuable souvenirs of Mr. Lincoln in existence."

I was born Feb. 12, 1809, in Hardin County, Kentucky. My parents were both born in Virginia, of undistinguished families—second families, perhaps I should say. My mother, who died in my tenth year, was of a family of the name of Hanks, some of whom now reside in Adams, and others in Macon counties, Illinois. My paternal grandfather, Abraham Lincoln, emigrated from Rockingham County, Virginia, to Kentucky, about 1781 or 2, where, a year or two later, he was killed by indians, not in battle, but by stealth, when [where?] he was laboring to open a farm in the forest. His ancestors, who were quakers, went to Virginia from Berks County, Pennsylvania. An effort to identify them with the New-England family of the same name ended in nothing more definite, than a similarity of Christian names in both families, such as Enoch, Levi, Mordecai, Solomon, Abraham, and the like.

My father, at the death of his father, was but six years of age; and he grew up, litterally without education. He removed from Kentucky to what is now Spencer county, Indiana, in my eighth year. We reached our new home about the time the State came into the Union. It was a wild region, with many bears and other wild animals still in the woods. There I grew up. There were some schools, so called; but no qualification was ever required of a teacher, beyond "readin, writin, and cipherin," to the Rule of Three. If a straggler supposed to understand latin, happened to so-journ in the neighborhood, he was looked upon as a wizzard. There was absolutely nothing to excite ambition for education. Of course when I came of age I did not know much. Still somehow, I could read, write, and cipher to the Rule of Three; but that was all. I have not been to school since. The

little advance I now have upon this store of education, I have picked up from time to time under the pressure of necessity.

I was raised to farm work, which I continued till I was twenty two. At twenty one I came to Illinois, and passed the first year in Macon county. Then I got to New-Salem (at that time in Sangamon, now in Menard county), where I remained a year as a sort of Clerk in a store. Then came the Black-Hawk war; and I was elected a Captain of Volunteers—a success which gave me more pleasure than any I have had since. I went the campaign, was elated, ran for the Legislature the same year (1832) and was beaten—the only time I ever have been beaten by the people. The next, and three succeeding biennial elections, I was elected to the Legislature. I was not a candidate afterwards. During this Legislative period I had studied law, and removed to Springfield to practice it. In 1846 I was once elected to the lower House of Congress. Was not a candidate for re-election. From 1849 to 1854, both inclusive, practiced law more assiduously than ever before. Always a whig in politics, and generally on the whig electoral tickets, making active canvasses. I was losing interest in politics, when the repeal of the Missouri Compromise aroused me again. What I have done since then is pretty well known.

If any personal description of me is thought desirable, it may be said, I am, in height, six feet, four inches, nearly; lean in flesh, weighing, on an average, one hundred and eighty pounds; dark complexion, with coarse black hair, and grey eyes—no other marks or brands recollected.

Lincoln recalled his years in Indiana, where he and his family lived in this small cabin until he was seven.

With his love of fine clothing and penchant for liquor, Ward Hill Lamon was in many ways Lincoln's opposite, but the two became fast friends.

Ward Hill Lamon

In the spring of 1872 Ward Hill Lamon, a Washington lawyer and longtime associate of Abraham Lincoln's, prepared to bring out a new biography of his famous friend. A big-fisted strongman of a lawyer, Lamon had met Lincoln in the late 1840s when they began to ride the circuit together. He wore fine clothes, which amused the indifferently dressed Lincoln, and sang songs, which delighted his prairie companion. From 1852 to 1857 he served as Lincoln's legal associate, first at Danville and then at Bloomington. He worked for both of Lincoln's Senate campaigns and was present at many of the debates with Stephen A. Douglas. When Lincoln ran for the presidency, he was there to help. And when the President-elect left for Washington in February 1861, he asked Lamon to come along, in part to offer protection, for the burly, well-armed sidekick was doggedly loyal.

In Washington "Hill" Lamon was appointed chief marshal, which placed him in charge of a local prison as well as a variety of public ceremonies. It was he who ran the ceremonial procession at Gettysburg in 1863 and had the honor of introducing Lincoln on the platform that day. By the following year he was increasingly worried about the President's safety. When he lost confidence in Lincoln's formal bodyguards, he began sleeping outside his White House bedroom. John Hay saw him one November night "rolling himself up in his cloak . . . at the President's door; passing the night in that attitude of touching and dumb fidelity with a small arsenal of pistols and bowie knives around him." Once when he discovered a prowler outside the

White House, the barrel-chested Lamon reportedly beat him to death with his fists.

Lincoln's assassination profoundly affected Lamon—he never forgave himself for being out of town on April 14. In the years that followed he made a halfhearted attempt to obtain the governorship of Idaho Territory but chose instead to return to the practice of law. It was then that he decided to write a Lincoln biography.

Lamon was many things, but he knew he was not a writer. And so he turned to a friend—the anti-Republican, antiabolitionist Chauncey Black—to serve as the primary author of what would become known as "Lamon's Life of Lincoln." The truth behind the authorship, they agreed, would be kept a secret, for if it came out that a Democrat had written the book, it would ruin its chances for financial success.

In early 1869 Lamon visited William H. Herndon in Illinois, knowing that he was an essential source for information on the young Lincoln. He was so impressed by Herndon's research that he offered to buy his materials outright. Herndon was shocked. He would rather cut off "a foot," he said, than part with his research. But he also needed money. In the terrible economic climate of the late 1860s he had been forced to sell land and farm machinery and was heading toward financial ruin.

Not mentioning to Lamon that he had had a complete copy of his Lincoln research made, Herndon agreed to sell the collection of papers for $4,000—half up front and half later. And he agreed to a noncompete clause—he would not write his own Lincoln book for at least ten years. After arranging for financing, Lamon agreed to the terms. By 1870 he had received the papers—not the originals as expected but the copies. He and Black were now ready to begin working on their book, part one of a planned two-part life of Lincoln.

As marshal of Washington, D.C., and Lincoln's self-appointed bodyguard, six-foot-three Lamon accompanied him to Antietam in October 1862. Wearing a top hat, he chose to remain seated for a group portrait, in order that he not distract attention from the President.

"An Authentic Biography of Mr. Lincoln"
Ward H. Lamon

1872

In Lamon's preface to his 1872 book he acknowledged the contributions of William Herndon, who had provided him with his richest source material. Herndon at first liked the new book, which was the opposite of the stiff, pietistic work of Josiah Holland. "The Life is true," he wrote to Chauncey Black that summer; "true to the letter and spirit of your Hero." But within months, as the bad publicity mounted, he denied having had any hand in the writing and was very pleased he had kept his original research for his own future attempt to write Lincoln's biography.

At the time of Mr. Lincoln's death, I determined to write his history, as I had in my possession much valuable material for such a purpose. I did not then imagine that any person could have better or more extensive materials than I possessed. I soon learned, however, that Mr. William H. Herndon of Springfield, Ill., was similarly engaged. There could be no rivalry between us; for the supreme object of both was to make the real history and character of Mr. Lincoln as well known to the public as they were to us. He deplored, as I did, the many publications pretending to be biographies which came teeming from the press, so long as the public interest about Mr. Lincoln excited the hope of gain. Out of the mass of works which appeared, of one only—Dr. Holland's—is it possible to speak with any degree of respect. Early in 1869, Mr. Herndon placed at my disposal his remarkable collection of materials—the richest, rarest, and fullest collection it was possible to conceive. Along with them came an offer of hearty co-operation, of which I have availed myself so extensively, that no art of mine would serve to conceal it. Added to my own collections, these acquisitions have enabled me to do what could not have been done before—prepare an authentic biography of Mr. Lincoln.

August 1872

Lamon's Lincoln

Over the course of 1871 "Lamon's Lincoln" took shape. As a literary technique, in order to vividly demonstrate how far Lincoln had risen, Chauncey Black decided to exaggerate his impoverished and unhappy upbringing. The Lincoln home on Nolin Creek was described as "a miserable cabin"—sitting on "dull and unsightly plains"; Lincoln's father, Thomas, was "idle, thriftless, poor, and a rover"—"satisfied with indifferent shelter, and a diet of 'corn-bread and milk'"; Lincoln's parents were said to have been never formally married, owing their common-law status to mere "cohabitation." And Lincoln himself was branded as illegitimate—his real father, Black claimed, was a man named Abraham Enloe. This last assertion was part of a block of erroneous passages that was deleted from the book before publication, after a secret payment was made by Judge David Davis to suppress the most outrageous assertions.

Black's idea was to make Lincoln stand out against his background like a "diamond on a dunghill." But though he succeeded with the dunghill, he was less successful with the diamond. By massing together the most negative of the eyewitness opinions and neglecting many of the more positive ones, Black built up a strange and unfamiliar portrait. His Lincoln was "morbid, moody, meditative"— "unsocial, cold, impassive." His engagement to Mary Todd was "one of the great misfortunes of his life." He was a user of people, "had no heart," and "seldom . . . praised anybody." He was a "shrewd" and "by no means unselfish politician," a man of "overweening ambition" for high office, who had "not a particle of sympathy" for former friends once he had attained his goals. And knowing that the public admired honesty in its leaders, "he made simplicity and candor the mask of deep feelings carefully concealed."

According to Chauncey Black, Lincoln only pretended to care about the rights of black people and had made his true feelings known on several occasions. Additionally, Black's Lincoln was a religious "infidel"—the opposite of what Holland had depicted six years earlier. And instead of presenting this as a strength, as Herndon later would, Black called it "the fatal misfortune of his life," a bad habit picked up on the rude frontier and connected to Lincoln's lifelong struggle with depression. "When the black fit was on him, he suffered . . . much mental misery. . . . But the unfortunate conviction . . . that there was no truth in the Bible, made all consolation impossible, and penitence useless."

The book was published in May 1872 and met with disdain. The reading public didn't want a flawed Lincoln and was disgusted by many of the details in Lamon's book. Critics recognized that it contained vast amounts of new information and was the fullest treatment of Lincoln's early life to date. But they disliked its overall effect. Literary giant James Russell Lowell castigated its author as "a vulgar man" who had "vulgarized a noble subject." The *New York Times* called the book "repulsive" and summed it up as "an abomination." Perhaps not unexpectedly the book's best reviews were in the South, where Lamon's book affirmed what had been long suspected—that the "true" Lincoln was nothing more than an ambitious and false politico—"the low, ignorant, and vulgar railsplitter of Illinois."

Lincoln's friends, of course, were deeply unhappy with the book. Isaac Arnold said he could not recognize in it the Lincoln he had known, who was the exact opposite of a cold and wily politician. Orville Browning despised the book's sensationalism and said so one day at breakfast with David Davis. Davis told him how much worse the original draft had been and how he had paid for the suppression of numerous stories in it. "He said . . . that Chauncey Black . . . was the real author of the book, and that it had the appearance of having been written by an enemy."

By August the *New York Sun* had figured out the secret authorship and was criticizing the contradictory and "patchwork manner" of the book. "The parts of the work which exalt Mr. Lincoln's character belong to Mr. Herndon, who was a warm admirer of Mr. Lincoln; and those parts which tend to decry Mr. Lincoln, and to make him a cunning politician rather than a conscientious statesman, belong to Black. . . . The real life of Abraham Lincoln has yet to be written."

Mary Lincoln was mortified by the book and considered it another frontal attack upon herself. In a letter she spoke of its terrible "slanders," and of "the vile, unprincipled and *debased* character of the author." "This man, Lamon, thrust himself, upon my too good natured husband," she wrote. "Now, when this good man is gone, he would draw the life blood, from his loved & deeply afflicted widow . . . [to] enrich his coffers—Severe retribution will yet visit this wretch."

Lincoln was just an inch taller than the much burlier Ward Hill Lamon, shown here standing side by side just as they would have in life.

A Book Full of Falsehoods
Robert Lincoln

December 4, 1872

Robert Lincoln was so disgusted by what he heard about Lamon's book that he refused to read it. In December he asked his cousin Dennis Hanks to help him identify the book's factual errors.

My dear Sir:

On my return from Europe I find your letter of Oct 1st. I have not seen Lamon['s] book and I do not intend to read it. I am told by several persons that it is full of falsehoods invented by Herndon, who sold them to Lamon.

There is one point to which my attention has been called and which you know something about. Herndon makes the astonishing statement that he believes my father's father and mother were never married. I understand his reasons for it are that [there was on file] no record of the marriage in the County where my father was born. I do not propose to as[k] for the question as to its being proper to draw such a conclusion from such a fact, even if it may be a fact.

Yesterday a gentleman showed to me a leaf, slightly torn, apparently from a Bible, which purports to be a record of the marriage of Thomas Lincoln and Nancy Hanks (giving the age of each) and to the birth of Sarah Lincoln and of Abraham Lincoln. . . . I wish you could tell me how and when and where you put the paper and if you know where the rest of the Bible is from which it was taken. . . .

You also say that you have seen statements from Lamon's book which are false. I will today send you two copies of the book one for you to keep for yourself and I will be obliged if you will take a pen and in reading the other one, when you come to a lie that you know to be a lie write your opinion on the margin of the book and also anything else you may think proper.

Herndon has acted like a scoundrel & your notes may be of great use.

Please do not communicate this letter to anyone.

Yours very truly
Robert T. Lincoln

Lincoln and His Father

Ward Hill Lamon's biography of Lincoln, though harsh when it came to depicting his childhood, succeeded in getting some things right—including that Lincoln and his father had not been close.

Thomas Lincoln was barely literate and dirt poor—an honest, hardworking man who was never able to understand his brilliant son. Though the two shared traits—including a love of wrestling and of storytelling—from early on there was a profound distance between them. "I Never could tell whether Abe Loved his farther Very Well or Not," wrote Dennis Hanks. "I Don't think he Did." According to Hanks, young Lincoln could sometimes be overly talkative with guests "for which his father would sometimes knock him a rod." When whipped, Abraham usually kept his feelings inside, but gradually built up resentment for his rough-mannered father. Within the reminiscences there are odd stories indicating that not all was well between father and son. Thomas is recalled as killing a pet pig of Abe's. Perhaps in revenge, Lincoln is said to have dressed up one of his father's dogs in a raccoon skin and let it loose to be torn up by the neighborhood pack. In retaliation, Thomas is said to have killed one of his son's dogs. It was his father's lack of interest in education that especially galled the studious Lincoln. In a brief autobiography written in 1860 he dismissed his father as a man "litterally without education" who "never did more in the way of writing than to bunglingly sign his own name." For years Thomas mocked his son for "fooling hisself with eddication. I tried to stop it, but he got that fool idea in his head, and it can't be got out."

When Lincoln left home at the age of twenty-two, he never looked back. When he and Mary married a decade later, neither his father nor stepmother was invited to the wedding. Neither parent ever laid eyes on Mary or any of the children. William Herndon once said

Though in many ways Lincoln was the opposite of his rough-hewn father (left), in fact they had several similarities. Both were extremely strong and were standout wrestlers, and both were excellent storytellers. "[H]e was a social man—loved Company—peeple and their Sports very much," wrote Thomas Johnston of his stepgrandfather. "He read his bible—told Indian stories—that thrilled my young nature."

that if Thomas and Sarah Lincoln had ever appeared at their door in Springfield "I doubt whether Mrs. Lincoln would have admitted them." Lincoln did help his father financially from time to time, paying him for forty acres of farmland in 1841 and then allowing his parents to live there for the rest of their lives. But when his law business took him to Coles County, Lincoln rarely stayed with his father, choosing to lodge instead with Dennis Hanks or at a nearby hotel.

In 1849 Lincoln received a letter from Hanks's son-in-law begging him to come and visit his severely ill father. "He is very anxious to see you before he dies & I am told that His cries for you for the last few days are truly Heart Rendering." The next day a second letter arrived from his stepbrother John Johnston, reiterating the plea. "[H]e wants you to Come—if ar able to git hur; for you are his only Child that is of his own flush & blood. . . . He says he has almost Despaired of see ing you. . . . He wants me to tell your wife that he Loves hure." Lincoln made the trip to Coles County on May 29 and spent two days with his father. But they were not happy ones.

Sixteen months later, when his father was once again close to death, again came the letters from family members. At first Lincoln didn't answer. Finally, in a response to a plea from his niece Harriet Chapman, he explained to Johnston why he had not written earlier: "because it appeared to me I could write nothing which could do any good." Professing that his wife was sick and that he was too busy to travel, he asked his stepbrother to give Thomas a final message. "Say to him that if we could meet now, it is doubtful whether it would not be more painful than pleasant."

Lincoln did not attend his father's funeral or make any effort to mark his grave. For the next ten years it was utterly neglected. Then, less than two weeks before his departure for Washington in 1861, he made a trip out to Coles County to say good-bye to his stepmother. Seventy-three-year-old Sarah was now living with her daughter Matilda, and she and her stepson had a long and heartfelt visit, after which Lincoln visited his father's grave. While standing there, he asked a companion to help arrange for a suitable tombstone, saying he would provide the money. But Lincoln never sent it as he had promised, and his father's headstone was never erected during his lifetime.

Abraham Lincoln in 1860, nine years after his father's death

"Tell Him to Call on Our Great, and Good, and Merciful Maker"
Abraham Lincoln

January 12, 1851

Lincoln refused to visit his father on his deathbed, asking his stepbrother John D. Johnston to deliver a message to him instead.

Dear Brother:

On the day before yesterday I received a letter from Harriett, written at Greenup. She says she has just returned from your house; and that Father [is very] low, and will hardly recover. She also s[ays] you have written me two letters; and that [although] you do not expect me to come now, yo[u wonder] that I do not write. I received both your [letters, and] although I have not answered them, it is no[t because] I have forgotten them, or been uninterested about them—but because it appeared to me I could write nothing which could do any good. You already know I desire that neither Father or Mother shall be in want of any comfort either in health or sickness while they live; and I feel sure you have not failed to use my name, if necessary, to procure a doctor, or any thing else for Father in his present sickness. My business is such that I could hardly leave home now, if it were not, as it is, that my own wife is sick-abed. (It is a case of baby-sickness, and I suppose is not dangerous.) I sincerely hope Father may yet recover his health; but at all events tell him to remember to call upon, and confide in, our great, and good, and merciful Maker; who will not turn away from him in any extremity. He notes the fall of a sparrow, and numbers the hairs of our heads; and He will not forget the dying man, who puts his trust in Him. Say to him that if we could meet now, it is doubtful whether it would not be more painful than pleasant; but that if it be his lot to go now, he will soon have a joyous [meeting] with many loved ones gone before; and where [the rest] of us, through the help of God, hope ere-long [to join] them.

Write me again when you receive this. Affectionately

A. LINCOLN

The Death of William Seward

By all odds William Seward should have been elected president back in 1860 instead of his younger Republican rival Abraham Lincoln. For years he had been one of the most prominent leaders in the nation, called second in stature only to John Quincy Adams. As a New York state senator, governor of New York, then U.S. senator, he was a political moderate who opposed the extension of slavery and who had proved his intellectual brilliance and moral courage on numerous occasions. But in the West he was perceived as too radical a candidate, and when he abandoned his New York ally

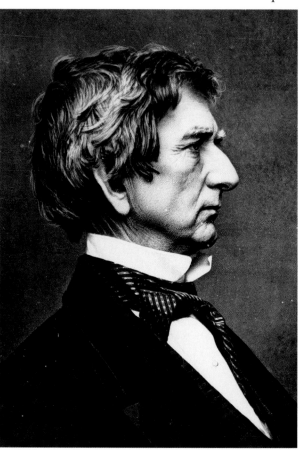

William Seward had been the favored Republican candidate in 1860. Though Lincoln had "snatched away . . . the prize of a laborious life-time," wrote John Hay, he had gone on to reward Seward with the first position in his cabinet. And gradually the President and his secretary of state became close friends.

Horace Greeley, Seward lost the nomination to the far less experienced Lincoln. Though outwardly gracious, Seward was mortified. He later erupted at a congressman who didn't want to be "disappointed" over an act of patronage: "Disappointment! You speak to me of disappointment. To me, who was justly entitled to the Republican nomination for the presidency, and also had to stand aside and see it given to a little Illinois lawyer! You speak to me of disappointment!"

Despite his hurt pride, Seward campaigned for his party's candidate. Lincoln not only thanked him for his help, but once elected he turned to him to serve in his cabinet, along with three others of his leading rivals, Salmon P. Chase, Simon Cameron, and Edward Bates. After a period of coy reluctance Seward accepted the post of secretary of state, secretly hoping he might become the power behind the administration.

From the beginning he had problems with Lincoln's leadership. He felt he was too harsh in his attitudes toward the South and convinced him to change the wording in his inaugural address in order to assuage the secessionists and help prevent war. He opposed Lincoln's policy of holding on to Federal forts in the South, and at times worked behind his back to countermand presidential orders. On April 1, 1861, he wrote a strident memorandum attacking Lincoln's lack of coherent policies and offering, obliquely, to assume full responsibility for foreign affairs. In reply Lincoln wrote out his own memo, which he may never have sent, then confronted Seward in person and made it clear who was in charge.

After the Civil War broke out, Seward became loyal and useful to Lincoln for the next four years. In 1862 the President agreed to his request to delay the Emancipation Proclamation until after a Union victory, which finally came at Antietam. Gradually the two men became close friends, and Seward let go of the jealousy he had carried with him. Of all the cabinet members, only he was given access to Lincoln on Sundays; and on many evenings Lincoln would wander across Lafayette Square to Seward's house, where the two relaxed by the fireplace and talked.

One by one the other original cabinet members fell by the wayside: Simon Cameron was discharged for incompetence and replaced by Edwin Stanton; Caleb Smith, Edward Bates, Montgomery Blair, and Salmon Chase—all wrote resignations that were asked for or accepted. Only William Seward and Gideon Welles remained all the way through. At one point in the middle of Lincoln's presidency, Seward admitted to fellow New Yorker George Templeton Strong that Lincoln was "the best and wisest man I have ever known."

On the night of the assassination, Seward was also attacked—by Booth's accomplice Lewis Payne. The assailant pushed past his son Frederick, cracking his skull with a pistol, and entered the secretary's bedroom, where he lay recuperating from a carriage accident. Payne slashed at his face with his long knife and would have killed Seward had not a servant pulled him off and frightened him away. The secretary's wounds were so severe that Stanton, who saw him that night, predicted he could not survive.

To spare him the shock, doctors withheld news of Lincoln's death, forbidding him access to newspapers. But on Easter morning Seward asked for his bed to be moved over to his window so he could look out onto the spring morning. Suddenly he saw the American flag atop the War Department building flying at half-mast. "The President is dead," he said to his attendant. "If he had been alive he would have been the first to call on me, but he has not been here, nor has he sent to know how I am, and there's the flag at halfmast." As Noah Brooks narrated it, Seward then fell back onto his bed in silence, "the great tears coursing down his gashed cheeks, and the dreadful truth sinking into his mind."

Seward remained on to be part of Andrew Johnson's government and ended up disappointing old friends when he supported the President's pro-Southern policies. His most visionary act during these final years of public service was his purchase of Alaska from Russia in 1867. Three years later he visited Alaska in retirement, to see for himself what he had bought for the nation. Then he crossed the Pacific to Japan and China, where he was greeted with great enthusiasm and ceremony, recognized as Abraham Lincoln's right-hand man.

He returned home to Auburn, New York, to write about his journey, and here he grew sick over the next year. John Hay publicly praised him in 1871 when he spoke of his tremendous closeness with Abraham Lincoln: "The history of governments affords few instances of an official connection hallowed by a friendship so absolute and sincere as that which existed between these two magnanimous spirits." On October 10, 1872, with Seward's wife, Francis, and their daughter Fannie gathered round, this central pillar of Abraham Lincoln's cabinet fell.

After his face was slashed in a near fatal attack on the night of Lincoln's murder, William Seward was rarely photographed except in profile. "Perhaps, when his wounds have healed," wrote Gideon Welles, "and the fractured jaw is restored, he may recover . . . his former looks, but I apprehend not." Above, Seward poses head-on in the sole known portrait that reveals the scars he carried for the rest of his life. To the left, he relaxes on the family porch in Washington. He talks with his son Frederick, whose skull injuries from the night of April 14, 1865, caused him to wear a fez for the remainder of his days.

Charles Francis Adams

Setting the Record Straight

Following the death of William Seward, Charles Francis Adams, the son of former president John Quincy Adams, gave a memorial lecture in Albany, New York. In his eulogy he stated that Seward, not Lincoln, had been the driving force of the administration and that the President had in many ways been "inattentive and indifferent." While few could doubt Seward's influence, especially in foreign policy, the attacks on Lincoln led to a national protest. The published lecture forced former secretary of the navy Gideon Welles to respond. Recognizing that what was at stake was the historical memory of Lincoln, Welles—who had long disliked Seward—wrote a series of articles for *Galaxy Magazine,* followed by a book published the next year entitled *Lincoln and Seward.* In it Welles insisted that Lincoln had been the "master mind" of his government, and that in crisis after crisis he had proven to have extraordinary sagacity and skill; Seward, while gifted, had been at best a secondary character. The controversy revealed how much Lincoln was still revered nine years after his death. "How strong is his hold on the American people," *Harper's Weekly* noted. "Everybody feels that he understands him and has property in him. . . . The wisest and the simplest found him a companion and friend."

A "Keen and Shrewd Sagacity"
Gideon Welles

1873

Welles's piece on Lincoln and Seward ran in Galaxy Magazine.

To those who knew Abraham Lincoln, or who were at all intimate with his Administration, the representation that he was subordinate to any member of his Cabinet, or that he was deficient in executive or administrative ability, is absurd. Mr. Lincoln was modest, kind, and unobtrusive, but he had nevertheless sturdy intellectual independence, wonderful self-reliance, and, in his unpretending way, great individuality. . . . He could have dispensed with any one of his cabinet and the administration not been impaired, but it would have been difficult if not impossible to have selected any one who could have filled the office of chief magistrate as successfully as Mr.

Lincoln in that troublesome period. . . .

Mr. Lincoln was in many respects a remarkable, though I do not mean to say an infallible man. No true delineation or photograph of his intellectual capacity and attributes has ever been given, nor shall I attempt it. His vigorous and rugged, but comprehensive mind, his keen and shrewd sagacity, his intellectual strength and mental power, his genial, kindly temperament—with charity for all and malice towards none—his sincerity, unquestioned honesty and homely suavity, made him popular as well as great.

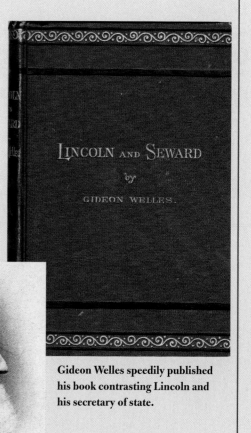

Gideon Welles speedily published his book contrasting Lincoln and his secretary of state.

In this souvenir montage of Lincoln's cabinet, issued by Mathew Brady in the summer of 1864, Salmon Chase
had already been replaced by William P. Fessenden as secretary of the treasury. Hannibal Hamlin still remained
as Lincoln's Vice President, a role he would keep until March 1865. And Montgomery Blair, who would resign
in September, was still shown, as was Edward Bates, who would last until November.

May 7, 1873

Salmon P. Chase's Demise

Salmon P. Chase of Ohio had been the most vigorous and radical member of Lincoln's cabinet, but by 1873 his health was failing. As a lawyer in the 1830s and 1840s he had been known for his principled and courageous stands, including his defense of fugitive slaves and of unpopular abolitionists. But unlike other radicals such as William Lloyd Garrison, Chase believed in working through the legal and political system, and in 1850 he won a seat in the U.S. Senate. Five years later he was elected governor of Ohio, and from that position he made a run for the presidential nomination in 1860.

Like Seward, Chase was considered a much stronger candidate than Lincoln. But, overconfident, Chase neglected to appoint a competent set of managers to run his campaign. And when his own state of Ohio was unable to unite around his candidacy, it too collapsed. The delegates all turned to their second choice—Abraham Lincoln—and on May 18 he was named the Republican Party's nominee.

Once elected, Lincoln did for Chase what he had done for Seward, offering him a place within his cabinet. Though he felt he deserved better than the position he was offered, Chase accepted. As secretary of the treasury he faced the difficult task of figuring out how a nearly bankrupt nation could fight what turned out to be a long and expensive war. Chase came up with controversial but creative ideas—the imposition of a federal income tax, the first ever; the significant increase of federal borrowing; and major tightenings of the regular budget. He proposed slashing government wages by 10 percent, revoking the congressional privilege of free postage, and scrutinizing every line of the federal budget. Eventually, by issuing government bonds and new paper money, he was successful in financing the war.

Despite his hard work in the treasury, Chase's cabinet experience was not a happy one. He found Lincoln too cautious in his antislavery views, and he thought his Emancipation Proclamation didn't go far enough. Unlike Seward, he maintained his presidential ambitions and even courted a draft-Chase movement in 1864. "He is a man of unbounded ambition," observed Lincoln, "and has been

Salmon P. Chase, as secretary of the treasury, and (above) in January 1865 as Chief Justice of the Supreme Court. It was Chase who administered Lincoln's inaugural oath, later sending Mary Lincoln the Bible her husband had kissed, writing, "I hope the Sacred Book will be to you an acceptable souvenir of a memorable day."

working all his life to become President. That he can never be." In October 1864 Lincoln finally demanded Chase's resignation, explaining in a letter that their relations had "reached a point of mutual embarrassment." Angered, and oblivious to his insubordination, Chase wrote in his diary, "I had found a good deal of embarrassment from him but what he had found from me I could not imagine. . . . He had never given me the active and earnest support I was entitled to."

But just two months later Lincoln surprised Chase once again, nominating him as Chief Justice of the Supreme Court. John G. Nicolay was appalled and awed by the decision. "Probably no other man than Lincoln," he wrote, "would have had . . . the degree of magnanimity to thus forgive and exalt a rival who had so deeply . . . intrigued against him." When Chase received the news on the night of December 6, he drafted Lincoln a grateful and chastened reply. "I cannot sleep before I thank [you] for this mark of your confidence. . . . Be assured that I prize your confidence and good will more than nomination or office."

He held the new position for the next nine years, presiding over, among other things, Andrew Johnson's impeachment. Though he continued to have presidential ambitions, the Supreme Court suited him admirably. As his health declined in 1873, he made plans for a summer visit to Colorado where he hoped the clear, dry air would benefit him. On his last day in Washington he was visited by Charles Sumner, also ailing, and the two men talked over old times. Then on May 7, at the home of his daughter Nettie, Salmon P. Chase, the lifelong proponent of black freedom and civil rights, became the sixth of Lincoln's thirteen cabinet members to join him in death.

Salmon Chase, late in life

His Personal Diary
Salmon Chase

1874

Salmon Chase kept one of the most important diaries in the Lincoln administration, ranking alongside those of Gideon Welles and John Hay. It was first published in 1874, the year after his death. One of the most important passages in it had to do with the lead-up to Lincoln's Preliminary Emancipation Proclamation. The entry, made for September 22, 1862, gives a detailed look into the President's thought processes and method of working with his cabinet members. Lincoln had already agreed to delay the proclamation until after a Union victory. Now he felt the time had come.

Went to the White House.

All the members of the Cabinet were in attendance. There was some general talk; and the President mentioned that Artemus Ward had sent him his book. Proposed to read a chapter which he thought very funny. Read it, and seemed to enjoy it very much. . . .

The President then took a graver tone, and said:—"Gentlemen, I have, as you are aware, thought a great deal about the relation of this war to Slavery. . . . When the rebel army was at Frederick, I determined, as soon as it should be driven out of Maryland, to issue a Proclamation of Emancipation such as I thought most likely to be useful. I said nothing to any one; but I made a promise to myself, and (hesitating a little)—to my Maker. The rebel army is now driven out, and I am going to fulfill that promise. I have got you together to hear what I have written down. I do not wish your advice about the main matter for that I have determined for myself. This I say without intending any thing but respect for any one of you. But I already know the views of each on this question. They have been heretofore expressed, and I have considered them as thoroughly and carefully as I can. What I have written is that which my reflections have determined me to say. If there is anything in the expressions I use or in any minor matter, which any one of you thinks had best be changed, I shall be glad to receive your suggestions. One other observation I will make. I know very well that many others might, in this matter as in others, do better than I can; and if I was satisfied that the public confidence was more fully possessed by any one of them than by me, and knew of any constitutional way in which he could be put in my place, he should have it. I would gladly yield it to him. But though I believe that I have not so much of the confidence of the people as I had some time since, I do not know that, all things considered, any other person has more; and, however this may be, there is no way in which I can have any other man put where I am. I am here. I must do the best I can, and bear the responsibility of taking the course which I feel I ought to take."

The President then proceeded to read his Emancipation Proclamation, making remarks on the several parts as he went on, and showing that he had fully considered the subject, in all the lights under which it had been presented to him.

A Correspondent's Encounters with Lincoln
James M. Winchell

July 1873

In the July 1873 issue of the Galaxy, *former Washington correspondent for the* New York Times *James M. Winchell wrote an article entitled "Three Interviews with President Lincoln." Though Lincoln's place in history was still "too early to determine," Winchell wrote, there was an increasing public recognition of his "remarkable powers," and a growing appetite for authentic witnesses to his life and career. Two of the stories Winchell related had to do with visits he made to the White House, one in early 1863 and another in 1864.*

A SELF-TAUGHT MILITARY EXPERT

With surprising readiness, he entered on a description of the situation, giving the numbers of the contending armies, their movements previous to the beginning of the battle, and the general strategical purposes which should govern them both. Taking from the wall a large map of the United States, and laying it on the table, he pointed out with his long finger the geographical features of the vicinity, clearly describing the various movements so far as known, reasoning rigidly from step to step, and creating a chain of probabilities too strong for serious dispute. His apparent knowledge of military science, and his familiarity with the special features of the present campaign, were surprising in a man who had been all his life a civilian, engrossed with politics and the practice of the law, and whose attention must necessarily be so much occupied with the perplexing detail of duties incident to his position. The fact once comprehended that he had profoundly studied the war in its military aspect, the less astonishing though not less admirable was the logic in which he involved his facts.

A DESIRE TO DO THE RIGHT THING

He was not quite sure whether he desired a renomination. Such had been the responsibility of the office—so oppressive had he found its cares, so terrible its perplexities—that he felt as though the moment when he could relinquish the burden and retire to private life would be the sweetest he could possibly experience. But, he said, he would not deny that a reelection would also have its gratification to his feelings. He did not seek it, nor would he do so; he did not desire it for any ambitious or selfish purpose; but, after the crisis the country was passing through under his Presidency, and the efforts he had made conscientiously to discharge the duties imposed upon him, it would be a very sweet satisfaction to him to know that he had secured the approval of his fellow citizens and earned the highest testimonial of confidence they could bestow.

The White House during the Lincolns' day

The Piano

Once America's leading lady of the stage, by 1873 Laura Keene had shut herself away from the public, living alone with her most valuable possession, a Chickering piano. Eighteen years earlier she had brought it with her to Ford's Theatre for her one-thousandth performance of *Our American Cousin*, where Abraham Lincoln would be in the audience. In honor of the President—and of General Grant, who was expected to be with him—a special program of patriotic songs had been planned for after the play. Laura would sing solo, accompanied by her piano. But then came John Wilkes Booth's bullet.

During the mass hysteria that broke out after the shooting, Keene played a pivotal role she hadn't anticipated. Sensing the need for leadership, she walked boldly onto the stage and urged the audience to remain calm. Then she found a pitcher of water and made her way to the second floor and into the state box where Lincoln lay. "While we were waiting for Mr. Lincoln to regain strength," Dr. Leale wrote, "Laura Keene appealed to me to allow her to hold the President's head. I granted the request, and she sat on the floor of the box and held his head in her lap."

Keene was never the same after this night. Her career derailed; she lost her luster with the public; for a time, to make money, she agreed to display her bloodstained dress. And then she got sick. By 1873 the fifty-three-year-old former beauty was living in a cottage in New Jersey with her piano. Haunted by the night at Ford's Theatre, she never played it again after Lincoln's death. It sat unused like a silent witness until her own death in November.

Laura Keene was America's leading lady. The English-born performer was a singer, a wonderful mimic, and a comic actress—worthy, one critic wrote, of "a poem of epic proportions." To the left is her Chickering piano, on which she was to play for Lincoln on the night of his murder. After Keene's death it went to her two "nieces," who were actually her daughters, a fact that she kept secret.

The Rev. Dr. Noyes Miner was a neighbor of the Lincolns' and a close friend of Mary's. His statement on Lincoln's religion was solicited by the University of Chicago in 1871 for inclusion in their Lincoln archives. It was published in newspapers in 1872 during the national discussions involving Lincoln's religion.

I first became acquainted with Mr. Lincoln in the Spring of 1855. Living on the same street with him, my residence being on the opposite corner, I saw him almost daily. I was a frequent visitor at his house, and knew him intimately, sympathizing with him in his political views, and admiring his honesty and moral integrity. . . .

At this period I do not think Mr. Lincoln was what is termed an experimental Christian. I used to see him sometimes at the funerals of his old neighbors, and sometimes at church on the Sabbath; but he was not a constant attendant on the means of grace. But during my long and intimate acquaintance with him, and the many conversations I had with him from time to time on numerous subjects, I never heard a word fall from his lips that gave me the remotest idea that his mind was even tinctured with infidel sentiments. . . .

After the election of Mr. Lincoln to the Presidency, he seemed to have fully comprehended the vast responsibility of his high office and, the dangers and difficulties he would have to encounter in the discharge of his duties. This led him to serious reflection; and feeling that he was inadequate to meet and discharge those duties in his own wisdom and thought, he asked Christians to pray for him, that he might have help from on High. . . . He was doing his duty manfully, and looking up to God for help in time of need.

December 12, 1873

A Christian, an Atheist . . . or Something in Between

As a young man Lincoln had shown little interest in religion, despite the wishes of his devout stepmother Sarah Bush. "Abe . . . didn't think of that question at the time, if he ever did," she told Herndon in 1865. Sometimes he would attend religious services, she recalled, and listen carefully to the words of the preacher. Then he would "come home—take the children out—get on a stump or log and almost repeat it word for word." But this was all out of fun, not because of any natural piety. "Abe read the Bible some, though not as much as said: he sought more congenial books—suitable for his age." Elizabeth Crawford of Indiana remembered the young Lincoln as "well behaved" in church when he happened to come, but possessing "no pretensions of religion." His faith seemed to be about wanting to do good to others; in Crawford's words, he was "a well wisher."

As he grew older, Lincoln was attracted to religious skepticism. At age twenty-five he went so far as to write "a little book" on the subject, critiquing such ideas as biblical inerrancy and belief in an afterlife. A friend, Samuel Hill, foresaw political trouble from such a book and one day seized it. "It was in the winter time," recalled Hill's son, "while there was a fire in the stove, & . . . there it was burned."

By 1843 Lincoln's lack of religion had become a political handicap, as he himself realized. "It was every where contended that no ch[r]istian ought to go for me, because I belonged to no church, [and] was suspected of being a deist," Lincoln wrote to a friend after a failed try for the Whig nomination to Congress. And so he learned to be far more discreet on the subject. According to Herndon, he permitted himself to be "misunderstood" by Christians and thus capable of winning their vote. (Critics in 1872 said this practice made Lincoln into a hypocrite. Herndon replied, on the contrary, it made him a sensitive man who hated to offend others.)

During the 1840s and 1850s Mary's pastor, Dr. Smith, tried hard to convert Lincoln to Christianity, giving him a copy of his book *The Christian Defense*. But, as Herndon noted, Lincoln threw it into his desk and never opened it. When Smith later asked him for a response to the book, Lincoln told him that his argument was "unanswerable."

In late 1872 the Rev. James A. Reed of the Presbyterian church in Springfield delivered a public lecture on the subject of Lincoln's religion. Even though he had never known Lincoln personally, he had spoken with many of Herndon's informants, and in the newly charged atmosphere following Lamon's controversial publication, one by one they had changed their earlier stories. John T. Stuart had told Herndon in the 1860s that Lincoln was "an avowed and open infidel, sometimes bordering on atheism." He had denied the divinity of Christ, Stuart said, as well as all Christian hope in an afterlife. Now, to James Reed, Stuart said that he had never spoken such words and claimed to know that after Edward Lincoln's death in 1850, Lincoln had been brought by his pastor Dr. James Smith "into the fold of Christian belief." Springfield neighbor and close friend James Matheny had once told Herndon about Lincoln's outspoken irreverence. "Lincoln, when all were idle and nothing to do, would talk about Religion—pick up a Bible—read a passage—and then Comment on it—show its falsity—and its follies on the grounds of Reason." He said that Lincoln "bordered on absolute Atheism: he went far that way & often shocked me." Now in

1873 Matheny also backpedaled. He said his remarks to Herndon applied only to Lincoln's early life and that over the years he had watched Lincoln grow into "a firm believer in the Christian religion." Even Mary Lincoln had by now changed her tone. In her interview with Herndon in 1866 she had said, "Mr. Lincoln had no faith and no hope in the usual acceptation of those words." But by the 1870s she was calling her husband a "true Christian gentleman," a man "who never failed to look on God's promises & looked up to him for protection."

James Reed's lecture, claiming Lincoln for Christianity, was published in *Scribner's Monthly* and gained a wide national audience. On his farm, still in debt, Herndon heard about it from Chauncey Black, who urged him to prepare a strong rebuttal. It was an opportunity that Lincoln's former partner could not resist. He knew that despite a spiritual deepening after Eddy's death, Lincoln had remained highly skeptical of Christian doctrine. An enthusiastic supporter of Darwin's theory of evolution, Lincoln was Christian only in the broadest sense of the word, Herndon believed. When he used the word "God" he didn't mean what others meant, and he had absolutely no belief in the efficacy of prayer.

On December 12 Herndon appeared before a large crowd at the Springfield courthouse to address the issue of Lincoln's religion. Though it was the most hastily written of his five Lincoln lectures, it contained some telling and essential points. Herndon denied that James Smith had converted Lincoln to Christianity. He blasted Stuart and Matheny for their nervous recantings. And he reiterated the statement made by Mary Lincoln in 1866 that her husband had lacked both faith and hope. Herndon closed his lecture by stating that Lincoln "died an unbeliever."

For this lecture Herndon was widely vilified and branded a "Judas in Springfield." But to some it was clear that he was largely correct in his views. John G. Nicolay soon weighed in on the subject of Lincoln's supposed conversion to orthodoxy, claimed by some to have taken place during his presidency. "I am very sure he gave no outward indication of his mind having undergone any change in that regard while here," Nicolay insisted. And in late December Lincoln's old friend William Jayne added his explanation for the controversy: "The orthodox world is determined to claim Abraham & and are not willingly going to give up one of their idols."

Robert Lincoln once said his father "did not have any interest in Church matters," but when he died the churches claimed him as one of their own. Never able to accept complicated Christian doctrine, shortly before his death Lincoln had said, "When any church will inscribe over its altar, as its sole qualification for membership the Savior's condensed statement . . . 'Thou shalt love the Lord thy God with all thy heart, and with all thy soul, and with all thy mind, and thy neighbor as thyself,' that church will I join with all my heart and all my soul."

Though Charles Sumner was at first frustrated by Lincoln's slowness as president, he soon warmed to him and came to appreciate his sincerity. After the assassination he said that Lincoln "had made speeches that nobody else could have made—& early dedicated himself to the support of Human Rights."

In a eulogy for Sumner (shown here in a memorial souvenir), the nation's foremost preacher, Henry Ward Beecher, wrote that no one, not even Lincoln, was "a greater martyr for liberty."

The Death of Charles Sumner

On March 11, 1874, another towering contemporary of Lincoln's succumbed to death, the victim in part of injuries received seventeen years earlier when he had been nearly beaten to death on the Senate floor by a Southern congressman avenging an insult. He was Charles Sumner, the most courageous and uncompromising antislavery politician in the United States.

For twenty-three years a member of the Senate, Sumner had clashed with Lincoln on numerous occasions. Impatient with those who didn't agree with his views, he found the President too cautious and slow on the slavery issue. In July 1861 he visited Lincoln in the White House and urged him to adopt a policy of emancipation. The President said he could not agree and that it was necessary to continue a policy of "forbearance." Afterward he told historian C. Edwards Lester, "I think Sumner . . . would upset our apple-cart altogether." Better to keep the "bombshell" of emancipation for a later time, when he could force the Confederates "to touch it off themselves."

But if it was Lincoln's job to proceed cautiously, it was Sumner's to push the moral issue. His public speaking during the early years of the war helped prepare the North for abolition, and his continued pressure on President Lincoln helped lead to the Emancipation Proclamation. Lincoln once told Sumner he was just "a month or six weeks" behind him on the issue, and slowly the abolitionist had warmed up to the President.

The bachelor senator sought out a friendship with Mary Lincoln, paying special visits to her at the White House. "[W]e would have such frequent & delightful conversations," Mary wrote, and "often late in the evening—My darling husband would

SKELETON LEAVES.

Charles Sumner.

Charles Sumner.

JOHN P. SOULE, 199 WASHINGTON ST. BOSTON.
Entered according to Act of Congress, in the year 1874, by L. L. Rogers, in the Office of the Librarian of Congress, at Washington, D. C.

join us & they would laugh together, like *two* school boys." Sumner and Lincoln became "great chums," Mary wrote.

On the night of the assassination the senator rushed to the Petersen House and was soon "seated on the right of the President's couch, near the head," said an eye-witness, "with his head bowed down almost on the pillow of the bed on which the President was lying." Robert Lincoln stood nearby, as Gideon Welles recorded. The President's son "bore himself well, but on two occasions gave way to overpowering grief and sobbed aloud, turning his head and leaning on the shoulder of Senator Sumner."

Over the next decade Sumner continued on as a voice of conscience, becoming the Senate's leading voice for African American rights. In the 1870s as the nation wearied of the civil rights struggle and many Republicans began to turn their backs on the issue, Sumner labored on. He dared "to march ahead of his followers when they were afraid to follow," said Carl Schurz in his eulogy. Sumner's funeral in March touched off a wave of sorrow in the North second only to that for Lincoln nine years earlier. A funeral train took the senator's body from Washington to Boston, stopping off along the way at Philadelphia, New York, New Haven, and other cities, where grieving admirers showed up in great numbers. In Boston a horse-drawn hearse escorted the casket through the city to the statehouse, where a catafalque had been erected in Doric Hall, and where 35,000 people visited over the next day. On top of Sumner's casket, spelled out in violets against white carnations, was a final passionate message from the senator: "Don't let the Civil Rights Bill Fail."

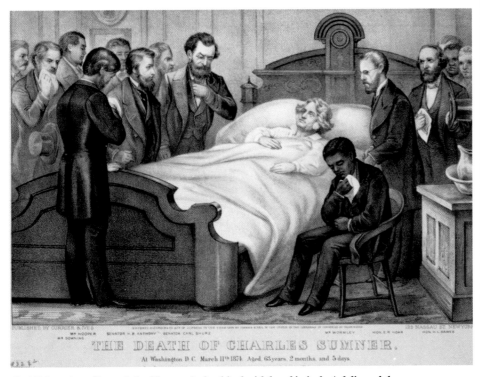

THE DEATH OF CHARLES SUMNER.

At Washington D.C. March 11th 1874. Aged 63 years, 2 months, and 5 days.

Carl Schurz (standing at left of Sumner's deathbed with hand in jacket) delivered the eulogy at the senator's funeral and compared him to Abraham Lincoln. Though they differed, he declared, in their methods and means, "no two men could be more alike as to their moral impulses and ultimate aims."

"A True Friendship"
August Laugel

August 19, 1874

Following Sumner's death came a stream of tributes from around the world, including an article by August Laugel in the Revue des Deux Mondes. *The Frenchman had visited him at his home in Boston, and then in Washington, D.C., where he was introduced to Lincoln, Seward, and others.*

Shall I be allowed to speak of the most happy hours spent with Sumner in the company of the poet Longfellow, his most intimate friend, of Emerson, of Oliver Wendell Holmes, of James Lowell, of Agassiz, and some others of the Literary Club of Boston? I found in this select circle something of the enthusiasm of our late poetical pleiades, friends without jealousy, the most lively curiosity with regard to Europe, ... the greatest calm among the overturnings of civil war, nevertheless the warmest patriotism. ... All these men were conscious of being engaged in a great work; they were moulding the mind of a young nation. ... Sumner was the object of great respect in this circle. ...

A few weeks after, I found Mr. Sumner in Washington. He was kind enough to conduct me to the White House. ... I remained long enough to become convinced that the President entertained the feelings of a great deference for the Senator from Massachusetts. He did not indulge before him in those sallies which he used generally with other men, mostly, however, to close the mouths of his indiscreet and importunate visitors. He showed rather sadness, which was the natural bent of his character. His common sense, somewhat uncultivated, asked for instruction as well as it gave advice. Sumner—is it necessary to say?—had numerous and bitter enemies. Mr. Lincoln was very careful not to weaken one of the greatest supporters of his cause. His goodness succeeded in dispelling the first fears of Sumner. Their cast of mind was very different, but their alliance, founded on mutual respect, became finally true friendship.

During Lincoln's funeral, plans for his tomb began to take shape. Visitors to his black-draped parlor (above) were asked to contribute to a "monument fund" (below).

Early on, a huge monument in honor of Abraham Lincoln (right) was proposed for the middle of Springfield. Later, the Lincoln Monument and the Lincoln Tomb were merged into a single memorial at Oak Ridge Cemetery.

The Lincoln Tomb

It had been decided in the 1860s that the Lincoln Tomb complex at Oak Ridge Cemetery would be larger than any ever created for an American President. A national contest had been launched to choose a designer, and in September 1868 the winner was announced—a Vermont sculptor named Larkin Mead who lived and worked in Florence, Italy. Mead decided he would supply drawings of the tomb for others to build, while he would sculpt the major statues, including the huge bronze centerpiece of Lincoln.

The sum of $250,000 had to be raised, largely through private subscription, and pleas for help went out through the states and across the nation. Sixty thousand schoolchildren contributed to the fund, and money came from thousands of former slaves in the South.

By 1874, five years after the work was commissioned, the tomb was finished. The large stone building was crowned by a ninety-eight-foot-tall obelisk, and Mead's two-ton sculpture of Lincoln had been lifted in place. On October 15 fifty thousand people gathered for the dedication, including Generals Sherman, Custer, McDowell, and Pope, Vice President Colfax, and the guest of honor, President Grant. An ailing Mary Lincoln decided not to come, and so Robert, once again, represented the family.

Nine years after Lincoln's funeral, the city of Springfield was again decorated. But now, instead of black crepe and mourning bands, there were flowers everywhere and colored banners. The ceremony began at one P.M. with a festive band playing opening music and a choir singing a song based on Lincoln's words "With malice toward none." Lincoln's old friend Jesse Dubois gave a short history of the Monument Foundation, and then a long poem was read connecting the tomb to the quest for human freedom. Finally the main speaker stepped forward amid cheers. It was Senator Richard Oglesby, the former governor of Illinois. Standing before the draped figure of Mead's Lincoln, he spoke of slavery as the great "stain" upon the American Republic and said that Lincoln's most important accomplishment had been to preside over slavery's end. His message was stirring and was designed to immediately precede the unveiling. And so at his closing words—"Behold the image of the man"—two nuns let drop the red-white-and-blue silk cloth that covered the statue. An eyewitness described how the "vast multitude stood for a moment in breathless silence" and then erupted into applause.

Unlike romanticized images, Mead's sculpture seemed to capture the real man—with the slight stoop of the shoulders, the wrinkled face and brow, and the prominent nose that William Howard Russell once said "[stood] out from the face with an inquiring, anxious air, as though it were sniffing for some good thing in the wind." In the long fingers of the left hand was the Emancipation Proclamation; in the right hand was the pen used to sign the historic order. And on the pedestal of the figure, in bas relief, was the American eagle, with Lincoln's olive branch of peace held out in the First Inaugural thrown down upon the ground and in its beak, instead, the broken chains of slavery. President Grant then rose and gave a few brief remarks, one of the only times that this taciturn man ever spoke personally about Lincoln.

Inside the tomb lay the mortal remains of Abraham Lincoln. It seemed essential that the sacred bones be part of this monument, just as ancient cathedrals were built around the relics of saints. Beside Lincoln lay three of his sons—Eddy and Willie to-

Larkin G. Mead was the architect who designed the Lincoln Tomb.

Mead's two-ton statue of Abraham Lincoln stood amid dramatic bronze sculptures that depicted scenes from the Civil War.

Grant Speaks at Lincoln's Tomb
Ulysses S. Grant

October 15, 1874

The presence of President Grant at the Springfield dedication was the highlight of that extraordinary day. His mention of Lincoln as a true "friend" of the South was a message that would be amplified in years ahead.

It was not my fortune to make the personal acquaintance of Mr. Lincoln till the beginning of the last year of the great struggle for national existence. During those years of doubt and despondency, among the many patriotic men of the country, Abraham Lincoln never for a moment doubted but the final result would be in favor of peace, union, and freedom to every race in this broad land. . . . Amidst obloquy, personal abuse, and hate undisguised, and which was given vent to without restraint through the press, upon the stump, and in private circles, he remained the same sta[u]nch, unyielding servant of the people, never exhibiting revengeful feelings toward his traducers. He rather pitied them and hoped for their own sake and the good name of their posterity that they might desist. . . .

From March, 1864, to the day when the hand of an assassin opened a grave for Mr. Lincoln, then President of the United States, my personal relations with him were as close, as intimate, as the nature of our respective duties would permit. To know him personally was to love and respect him for his great qualities of head and heart, and for his patience and patriotism. With all his disappointments from failures on the part of those to whom he intrusted command, and treachery on the part of those who had gained his confidence but to betray it, I never heard him utter a complaint, or cast censure for bad conduct or bad faith. It was his nature to find excuses for his adversaries. In his death the nation lost its greatest head. In his death the South lost its most just friend.

gether in one coffin, and Tad beside them. On the other side were two empty marble sarcophagi—the one next to Lincoln for his wife, Mary, and the other, should he want it, for their oldest son, Robert.

From a distance, Mary followed news of the event and was pleased. Her cousin John Stuart had fulfilled all his promises to her made back in 1865; the arrangements were just what she had hoped for.

With the memorial still under construction in 1874, the monument's obelisk was in place at the time of President Grant's dedication.

The Ten-Year Anniversary

The tenth anniversary of Lincoln's death was eclipsed by efforts across the country to get ready for the nation's centennial the following year. And when a group of citizens petitioned Congress to make Lincoln's birthday a federal holiday, the move was opposed in the South and went nowhere.

What celebration there was took place in Illinois, where the *Chicago Tribune*, recognizing that there would be higher promontories to come, called the ten-year mark "a little hilltop of history." The highlight event in Illinois would involve former Vice President Schuyler Colfax, Speaker of the House in the 1860s, who planned to present a new Lincoln lecture in honor of the tenth anniversary.

Colfax was a political radical who had worried Lincoln during his administration, but who had ended up in his good graces. His speech, which he would repeat many times throughout 1875, took place first in mid-January in Chicago before a packed crowd. Colfax began by blaming Lincoln's murder on the Confederacy. Then, after painting a brief portrait of Lincoln's life and career, he drew upon his own memories, which included a visit with the President on his last day alive. Not only had he seen and talked with Lincoln on that morning of April 14, he had returned that evening just as the President was leaving for Ford's Theatre. Declining an invitation to join the presidential party, he became the last person to say goodbye to Abraham Lincoln. As he detailed those final hours for the first time, the audience was transfixed, and the speech was soon considered the "lecture-sensation of the season."

On April 14, the tenth anniversary of the assassination itself, Illinois newspapers acknowledged the milestone. "The event seems distant," the *Chicago Tribune* editorialized, "and yet how vivid the recollection of that strange and appalling catastrophe! How tremulous with emotion is the national heart on every recurring anniversary of that great affliction! What other memory in our annals moves men so quickly to tears?"

The *Tribune* went on to describe the final week of Lincoln's life, a week that was now becoming legendary: how his return from Virginia to Washington on April 9 had coincided with Robert E. Lee's surrender to Ulysses S. Grant and had unleashed a surge of rejoicing in the North; how Lincoln himself had never been happier during these days—everyone noticing his relaxed countenance and good humor; how on April 11 he had given his last public address on the upcoming work of reconstruction; and how on that Thursday evening there had occurred a grand illumination of Washington, with all the government buildings "ablaze with light"; how a magnificent display of fireworks had been set off that night in front of the White House, from the upstairs windows of which Lincoln and his family had watched for hours. It was from such a height of gladness at the war's end that Lincoln's murder the following night had plunged the nation into darkness.

Lincoln's boots, left behind in the Petersen House when he died

Schuyler Colfax, whom Lincoln called "the Smiler," was Speaker of the House in the 1860s and Vice President under Grant. In 1875 he made a career out of Lincoln reminiscence.

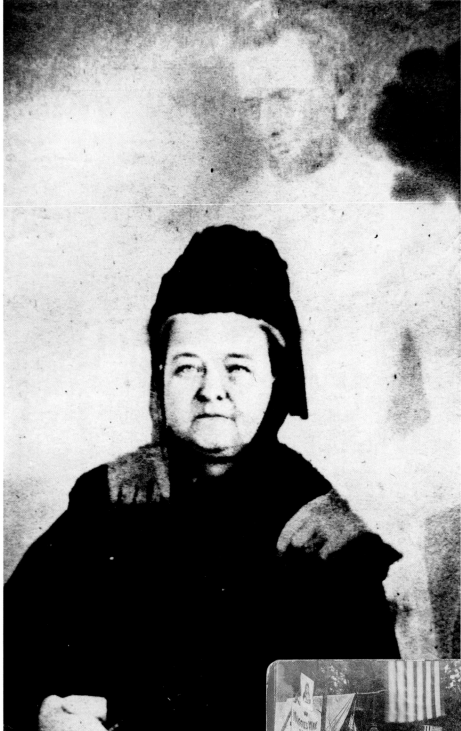

County Court of Cook County.

Mary Lincoln

INSANE.

VERDICT OF JURY.

Filed May 19th A. D. 1875

CLERK.

Mary Lincoln's sadness and eccentricity increased with every year, and after Tad's death she attended spiritualist gatherings like the one below. In 1872 she visited spirit photographer William Mumler, who captured a ghostly image of Lincoln appearing behind her (left). And as the document above shows, in May 1875 her son Robert had her arrested and tried for insanity in an Illinois court.

May 18, 1875

Mary Lincoln's Great Crisis

After Tad's death in 1871 Mary Lincoln largely disappeared from public sight, dividing her time between health spas and spiritualists, often traveling incognito. For reasons she could not understand, she had become one of the most despised women in America. Thanks to William Herndon and Ward Hill Lamon, she was beginning to be seen as the unworthy successor to Ann Rutledge. No one seemed to care that she had lost almost everyone dear to her, that one by one her family members had been taken from her, leaving Mary convinced that her life was cursed.

People who saw her during the early 1870s described a "heart-sick" woman in almost constant tears. Once again, as she had after Willie's death, she turned to spiritualism for succor, traveling across the country to mediums who promised to help her make contact with her husband and children. In Boston she sought out the services of William Mumler, a "spirit photographer" who claimed to be able to capture the image of a lost loved one. After a solemn session in his studio, Mumler proudly produced what Mary so desperately wanted—a photograph of her, and, behind, a ghostly Lincoln with his hands resting tenderly on her shoulders. It was the last portrait ever taken of Mary.

During this period of his mother's wanderings, Robert Lincoln became increasingly worried about her. He believed her delusions were becoming abnormal. She thought her money was not safe in any bank and so had begun carrying $57,000 in securities on her person. And she believed that unnamed people were trying to poison her food. Part of her paranoia may have been justified—Robert had hired a private detective to follow her about, and she was subliminally aware of his presence. In Florida on the tenth anniversary of her husband's murder, Mary took sedatives and had a bad reaction. She became convinced that Robert was deathly ill. But as she raced back to Chicago, she experienced a wave of paranoia and came to believe he was actually trying to murder her. Robert finally had enough. With the help of David Davis and Leonard Swett he had his fifty-six-year-old mother arrested and brought to trial for insanity.

It was a bitter moment for Mary Lincoln, who faced seventeen witnesses appearing for the prosecution. And without her knowledge, her attorney, Isaac Arnold, had secretly agreed to cooperate with Robert. With no chance for Mary to speak in her own defense, on May 18 an all-male jury found her insane. She was ordered confined to a mental hospital. When her son approached her at the end of the trial, Mary recoiled: "O Robert, to think that my son would ever have done this."

Mary never forgave Robert for his betrayal. Months later, after she had hired her own attorney—a woman—and proved herself sane in another court of law, Mary broke all ties with her "monster of mankind son." Writing to him she demanded the return of all her belongings, saying, "You have tried your game of robbery long enough." Condemning his "wickedness against me and High Heaven," she brusquely signed her letter "Mrs. A. Lincoln."

Robert Lincoln never apologized for having his mother confined to an asylum. Years later he wrote, "I could not hold her back from doing many things that distressed me beyond any power of description. . . . It all nearly wore my life out." After Mary proved her sanity in another court, she severed all ties with her only surviving son.

William T. Sherman Remembers

In May 1875 General William T. Sherman published his long-awaited *Memoirs of the Civil War*. Following the appearance one year earlier of Confederate General Joseph E. Johnston's *Narrative*, it was the first book of its kind by an important Union officer. And it shed new light on the figure of Lincoln.

Sherman had met the new President in March 1861 and been unimpressed by his seeming inaction and calm. Having recently lived down South in Louisiana, he knew "the country was sleeping on a volcano that might burst forth any minute," but Lincoln seemed to have no plan to counter it. Vowing to stay out of politics, in May, Sherman joined the army. He was present at the Union defeat at Bull Run and not long afterward met Lincoln again, in the field. This time he was favorably impressed, as was Lincoln by him. In the months and years ahead he rose steadily in rank.

Sherman's capture of Atlanta in August 1864 helped ensure Lincoln's re-election and was followed by his infamous "march to the sea." Slashing and burning his way across the Confederate landscape, making his name forever hated throughout the South, Sherman and his army arrived at the coast in late December. In a telegram to the President on the twenty-second he wrote, "I beg to present you as a Christmas-gift the city of Savannah, with one hundred and fifty heavy guns and plenty of ammunition, also about twenty thousand bales of cotton." The message reached Lincoln on Christmas Eve and was widely printed in Northern newspapers on Christmas Day.

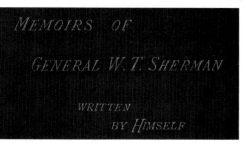

In March 1865 Sherman met with Lincoln in Virginia, aboard the presidential ship the *River Queen*, finding him alone in one of the ship's cabins. "He remembered me perfectly and at once engaged in a most interesting conversation. He was full of curiosity about the many incidents of our great march."

Robert E. Lee surrendered on April 9, and Sherman was on the verge of negotiating a surrender with General Johnston when he received word that the President had been assassinated. Suppressing the news lest it cause dissension in the ranks and derail his negotiations, he revealed it in private to General Johnston. "The perspiration came out in large drops on his forehead, and he did not attempt to conceal his distress," Sherman wrote. "He denounced the act as a disgrace to the age, and hoped I did not charge it to the Confederate Government."

After the war Sherman succeeded Grant as Commanding General of the U. S. Army, and oversaw the Indian wars in the West. But, out of favor with the government, he took time off to travel and write and by 1875 his two-part memoir was finished. The *Chicago Tribune*, which ran excerpts detailing Sherman's encounters with Lincoln, called the books "two of the most striking, eloquent, and original works the literature of the war has produced."

An Encouraging Visit from the President

William T. Sherman

1875

In this passage from Sherman's memoirs he describes a July 23, 1861, meeting with Lincoln.

I was near the river-bank, looking at a block-house which had been built for the defense of the aqueduct, when I saw a carriage coming by the road that crossed the Potomac River at Georgetown by a ferry. I thought I recognized in the carriage the person of President Lincoln. I hurried across a bend, so as to stand by the road-side as the carriage passed. I was in uniform, with a sword on, and was recognized by Mr. Lincoln and Mr. Seward, who rode side by side in an open hack. I inquired if they were going to my camps, and Mr. Lincoln said: "Yes; we heard that you had got over the big scare, and we thought we would come over and see the 'boys.'" . . . As we slowly ascended the hill, I discovered that Mr. Lincoln was full of feeling, and wanted to encourage our men. I asked if he intended to speak to them, and he said he would like to. I asked him then to please discourage all cheering, noise, or any sort of confusion; that we had had enough of it before Bull Run to ruin any set of men, and that what we needed were cool, thoughtful, hard-fighting soldiers—no more hurrahing, no more humbug. He took my remarks in the most perfect good-nature. Before we had reached the first camp, I heard the drum beating the "assembly," saw the men running for their tents, and in a few minutes the regiment was in line, arms presented, and then brought to an order and "parade rest!"

Mr. Lincoln stood up in the carriage, and made one of the neatest, best, and most feeling addresses I ever listened to, referring to our late disaster at Bull Run, the high duties that still devolved on us, and the brighter days yet to come. At one or two points the soldiers began to cheer, but he promptly checked them, saying: "Don't cheer, boys. I confess I rather like it myself, but Colonel Sherman here says it is not military; and I guess we had better defer to his opinion."

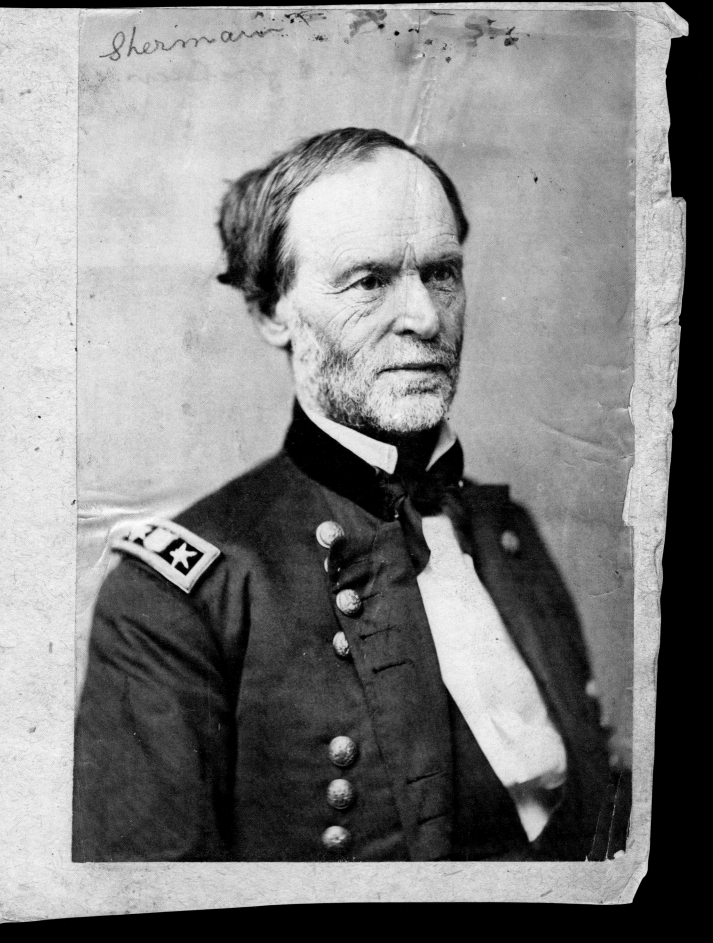

Sherman

William T. Sherman, who served as Commanding General of the United States Army for fourteen years, grew old in his uniform.

Horatio Seymour - Democratic Candidate for President.   Frank P. Blair

Frank P. Blair.   Geo. H. Pendleton.   Sen. T. Q. Hendricks.

Siamese Twins.

O. W. Holmes.   Com. Nutt.   Gladstone.   Palmerston.

Lincoln's Photographer Sells His Collection

Back on February 27, 1860, just a few hours before delivering his Cooper Union Address, Abraham Lincoln had sought out the New York studio of Mathew B. Brady. The world-famous photographer had agreed to a sitting with the up-and-coming young politician from Illinois. Observing Lincoln's thin neck poking up out of his rumpled suit, Brady asked if he might arrange his collar. "Ah," said Mr. Lincoln, "I see you want to shorten my neck," which was exactly what Brady intended. The resulting photograph, retouched and softened by Brady's artists, showed a handsome, beardless Lincoln on the verge of political ascendancy. Widely circulated in newspapers and issued as a carte de visite for public sale, it brought Lincoln's face into homes across America and, as he himself said, helped him win the November election.

Prior to this point Lincoln had been photographed about seventeen or so times. But once he fully recognized the power of photography to broaden his political appeal, he relied on it often, sitting for more than one hundred portraits during the next five years.

His first photographs in Washington were taken at Brady's studio, where Alexander Gardner served as manager and chief camera operator. Brady himself showed up for Lincoln's second visit in April, overseeing pictures that captured the new President's steely resolve and intellectual shrewdness. Over the course of the next four years, Brady and his operators were responsible for dozens more portraits.

Early on in the Civil War, Mathew Brady risked his fortune on a massive effort to chronicle the national conflict. His pictures of battlefields and slain soldiers were widely published, and in October 1861 *Humphrey's Journal* wrote, "The public are indebted to Brady of Broadway for numerous excellent views of 'grim-visaged war.'"

Though this project made him famous worldwide, it also overstretched his capacities. By 1864 he was in serious financial trouble and was forced to sell a half interest in his Washington gallery. But things got worse. A near deal to sell his collection to the New-York Historical Society fell through in the late 1860s and left him on the brink of bankruptcy. To avoid his creditors he secretly moved his entire collection into storage, then returned to Washington, where he tried to sell his negatives and prints to the U.S. government. "I have spent a life-time collecting the works I now offer," he wrote. "In my exertion to save the collection entire, I have impoverished myself." It was a frustratingly slow process that took five years to complete, but finally in 1875 Congress paid Brady $25,000 for seven thousand of his glass negatives, which finally now resided in the War Department.

Mathew B. Brady (above) and one of the pages from his studio order books from the 1860s (far left)

The highlight of Brady's life was when he documented the Civil War. Here he appears leaning against a tree with General Edward Potter and staff. In his hand may be the trigger switch for his remote camera.

Nicolay's Research

John Nicolay worked hard to maintain exclusive access to the Lincoln papers, which by the 1870s were being sought out by several other writers. Gideon Welles in particular wanted a number of essential Lincoln memos for a book he was writing about Lincoln and Seward. "[Y]our design to let Mr. Welles use the papers in question is the most rash and inconsiderate step . . . yourself and Judge Davis could possibly devise," Nicolay wrote Robert Lincoln in July 1874. "I protest against the injustice you would do myself and Col. Hay in the course you propose."

John G. Nicolay's job as marshal of the Supreme Court gave him time each summer during the court's recess to work on his and John Hay's new book. Their first task, he decided, was to obtain Lincoln's papers, still under lock and key in Bloomington, Illinois, where David Davis had taken them eight years earlier. In a letter to Robert Lincoln in May 1873 Nicolay urged him to release the papers into his custody, which he and Hay would "need in writing the history we propose." But Robert would not easily part with them. He had considered writing his own book based on the papers, and as the self-appointed guardian of his father's reputation, he wanted to make sure he knew exactly what was in those boxes. The following spring Robert moved them to Chicago, where he began to examine their contents. Nicolay became concerned that he might do harm to the papers and in an urgent letter begged Robert to wait until he could come out and join him. "I am . . . especially anxious—and I press this point particularly—that not a scrap of paper of any kind be destroyed. The merest memorandum, mark, signature or figure, may have a future historical value, which we cannot now arbitrarily determine, and the only good rule is to save everything."

Robert finally agreed to let the papers go, and that summer the boxes arrived at Nicolay's house near the Capitol and were carried up to his second-floor study. This was Nicolay's inner sanctum. Here on a wall, above a wide bookcase, hung a large photograph of Lincoln flanked by his two loyal secretaries, taken at the time Lincoln wrote the Gettysburg Address. Here was also the giant desk Nicolay had used in the White House that he had been able to buy from the government. Over the next four years, in this room often flooded with sunlight, Nicolay labored to place the complex manuscripts in order.

In the late spring of 1875 Nicolay traveled to Springfield to begin a series of interviews to supplement his research. On June 17 at the Leland Hotel he conducted his first—a two-hour-long conversation with Lincoln's old friend Orville Browning in which he took extensive notes in shorthand. Browning noted the conversation that night in his diary. "He told me that he and John Hay were engaged in a biography of Mr Lincoln, and that they wanted all the aid I could give them." A week later Nicolay interviewed John Todd Stuart, and over the next weeks there followed sessions with Clark Smith, William Butler, Jesse K. Dubois, Milton Hay, Stephen Logan, and others. In addition, Nicolay wanted to include, as Herndon hadn't, the men of Lincoln's administration. "Many of these are growing old," he wrote to Robert, and "will not reappear here many winters."

In Washington he conducted a second series of interviews with a wide range of men who had been close to Lincoln. (He did not interview any women.) And although he fell short of his goal to interview everyone in Washington who had known Lincoln, over a two-year period he amassed a trove of information.

Alexander Gardner's portrait of Lincoln and his two secretaries was among Nicolay's most prized possessions. "Nico and I immortalized ourselves," wrote John Hay in his diary back in November 1863, "by having ourselves done in a group with the Prest."

"Everybody Liked Him"
John T. Stuart

June 23, 1875

Nicolay's second interview in Springfield was with John Todd Stuart, Mary Lincoln's cousin and now president of the Springfield City Railroad Company. Early on Stuart had taken Lincoln under his professional wing. He loaned him books, promoted his political career, and gave him his first job in town—as his law partner.

I first knew Lincoln in the Black Hawk War. I was in the foot Regt. Thos. Moffett was captain of the Horse Company. Lincoln was captain of the foot company which went from New Salem. . . . I knew him very well in this expedition. He was then noted

John T. Stuart

mainly for his great strength, and skill in wrestling and athletic sports—in fact he had the reputation of being the best wrestler in the army—he could generally throw down anybody he came across. He was also noted for being a kind genial and companionable man, a great lover of jokes and teller of stories. Everybody liked him—he told good anecdotes and was always very entertaining and amusing—he became very popular in the army. We had a first rate time on this campaign—we were well provided— the whole thing was a sort of frolic— Lincoln had no military qualities whatever except that he was a good clever fellow and kept the esteem and respect of his men. He made a very good Captain. He had the wildest company in the world—it was mainly composed of the Clary Grove boys.

"Never Anything Mean About Him"
Jesse K. Dubois

July 4, 1875

Jesse Kilgore Dubois had been a fellow legislator with Lincoln and later helped him win the presidential nomination. Though he was sorely disappointed when he received no political reward, he remained loyal to the friend to whom he had once written, "I am for you against the world." Sixty-four years old when Nicolay interviewed him in Springfield, Dubois died the following year.

Lincoln and I first met at Vandalia in 1834, though there are people . . . in my county who saw him when he drove an ox team through Lawrenceville when they moved to this country. He was then of course dressed

Jesse K. DuBois

very badly—his pantaloons didn't meet the tops of his shoes by a good deal. He was then, generally, a long awkward gawky looking boy. But when he came to the Legislature in 1834, he was a very decent looking young fellow. He was then dressed in a very respectable looking suit of jeans. . . .

Lincoln didn't take much prominence in the first session of the legislature in 1834. Stuart at that time quite overshadowed him. . . . But the next session Lincoln was very prominent. He had by that time become the acknowledged leader of the Whigs in the House. . . . Mr. Lincoln was always a good man. There was never anything mean about him. He never played any tricks on anybody.

196

A Valuable Mentor
Stephen Trigg Logan

July 6, 1875

Stephen T. Logan was the acknowledged leader of the Illinois bar. As Lincoln's second law partner he had served for a while as the young man's mentor. William Herndon called him a "cold, avaricious," and "mean" man, and Logan had largely refused to cooperate with him. But on July 6, 1875, the seventy-six-year-old Springfield luminary granted John G. Nicolay an extensive interview.

My partnership with him in the practice of law was formed in 1841. . . . Lincoln's knowledge of law was very small when I took him in. . . . I think he began reading

Stephen T. Logan

perhaps a couple of years before he came up here. . . . While he was down there at New Salem I think his time was mainly given to fun and social enjoyment and in the amusements of the people he came daily in contact with. After he came here to Springfield however he got rid to a great degree of this disposition. Both he and Baker were exceedingly useful to me in getting the good will of juries. Lincoln seemed to put himself at once on an equality with everybody—never of course while they were outrageous, never while they were drunk or noisy or anything of the kind. I never in my life saw Lincoln taste liquor. In going around the circuit with him I sometimes myself got and took a little after having got wet in a storm, or swam a creek, or something of the sort; but he didn't even take it then.

"A Good Surveyor"
Peter Van Bergen

July 7, 1875

Peter Van Bergen was a Springfield real estate investor and moneylender who early on employed Lincoln as a surveyor. But when Lincoln and Berry's New Salem store failed in 1835, the note they signed to borrow money ended up in Van Bergen's hands. Unable to collect, he sued Lincoln, and then in lieu of payment took possession of his surveying instruments and horse. It was a terrible blow to a man who was dependent on his tools. (His friends paid off the debt and bought back his equipment, and Lincoln worked for years to pay them back in full.) For Van Bergen it was a matter of business as usual, and in his interview with Nicolay he spoke fondly of his former employee.

Mr. Lincoln was a good surveyor I employed him to go with me and lay out a town on the Mississippi River. . . . We traveled over there on horseback—found stopping places on the road—stayed there about a week, and Lincoln surveyed and laid out the town site—he did it all himself, without help from anybody except chainmen &c. and also made a plat of it. . . . [T]here was a man living on the land and a little settlement about there—The place is opposite the mouth of the Iowa river

We started from here when they had the cholera—I had some good brandy with me and used to take it as a preventative of cholera—but Lincoln always refused to take any even for that purpose. People sometimes refused to let us stay all night when they found we were from Sp[ringfield] where the cholera was. At New Salem L[incoln] used to be amongst very rough people—among drinking people, though he never drank himself

The Berry-Lincoln store in New Salem

His "Leg Cases"
Joseph Holt

October 29, 1875

In Washington Nicolay interviewed Judge Advocate General Joseph Holt, who had served as chief prosecutor in the trial of the Lincoln assassins. During the Civil War, he had worked closely with Lincoln, prosecuting cases of disloyalty and treason, and advising Lincoln on the matter of pardons.

You of course remember the class of cases the President used to call his "leg cases"— i.e. sentences of death for desertion, or misbehavior in face of the enemy &c &c. He was always very loth to act on these, and sometimes kept them a long while before disposing of them, which was generally by commuting the sentence to imprisonment at hard labor &c. I used to try and argue the necessity of confirming and executing these sentences. I said to him, if you punish desertion and misbehavior by death, these men will feel that they are placed between two dangers and of the two they will choose the least. They will say to themselves, there is the battle in front where they may be killed, it is true, but from which they also have a good chance to escape alive; while they will know that if they fly to the rear their cowardice will be punished by certain death. To all which the President would reply: Yes, your reasons are all very good, but I don't think I can do it. I don't believe it will make a man any better to shoot him, while if we keep him alive, we may at least get some work out of him. You have no doubt, continued he, heard the story of the soldier who was caught and asked why he had deserted. "Well, Captain," said the man, "it was not my fault. I have got just as brave a heart as Julius Cesar but these legs of mine will always run away with me when the battle begins." I have no doubt that is true of many a man who honestly meant to do his duty but who was overcome by a physical fear greater than his will. These came to be familiarly known between us as his "leg cases."

"He Wouldn't Budge an Inch"
Norman B. Judd

February 28, 1876

Norman B. Judd recalled for Nicolay how he had been present at the second Lincoln-Douglas debate at Freeport, Illinois, in 1858.

When Lincoln was going up to make his Freeport speech, Lincoln telegraphed to Peck and myself to meet him at Freeport.... We got . . . [to Mendota] about two oclock at night, and we had Lincoln waked right up. We went up into his bed room, and had our talk with him there. He looked very comical sitting there on one side of his bed in his short night shirt, &c &c. He then read to us his answers to Douglas' Ottawa

Norman B. Judd

questions. You remember they were concerning the Fugitive Slave law, and the abolition of Slavery in the District of Columbia &c. As we were up there in northern Illinois where the Anti-Slavery sentiment was very strong I insisted upon a slight change of the phraseology—not to make any material difference of the sense, but to make his declarations a little more palatable to the Republicans of that section. But I couldnt stir him. He listened very patiently to both Peck and myself, but he wouldn't budge an inch from his well studied formulas. "Now" said he "gentlemen, that is all. I wouldn't tomorrow mislead any gentleman in that audience to be made President of the U.S."

197

Andrew Johnson's End

After Andrew Johnson's impeachment he had become a lame duck president. Furious at the Republicans, among his last acts in office was a Christmas Day pardon of all those in the South who had taken part in the rebellion. Embittered, he returned to his native Tennessee, where he set his sights on a political comeback. Twice he ran for and failed to win election to the U.S. Congress. Then in 1875 he became the only former president ever to be elected to the U.S. Senate. "I'd rather have this information," he said upon receiving the news, "than to learn that I had been elected President of the United States. Thank God for the vindication." But just a few months later, at the home of his daughter in Elizabethtown, Tennessee, Lincoln's successor succumbed to a stroke and died. To the end he had insisted that his political beliefs and practices were the same as those of Abraham Lincoln. Others saw him as Lincoln's opposite; but none could doubt his ferocious loyalty to the Union. At his request, his body was wrapped in an American flag and buried on top of a copy of the United States Constitution.

For Johnson's funeral in Greenville, Tennessee, special trains brought in dignitaries from across the South. Five thousand people—as many as had mourned Buchanan—joined the procession to his burial site, high up on Signal Hill outside the city.

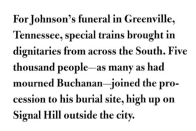

In the 1870s a Lincoln monument was proposed to be built in London, as a tribute to Abraham Lincoln and the cause of freedom. During the Civil War the British government, though officially neutral, had openly sympathized with the Confederacy. But following the Emancipation Proclamation in 1863 Lincoln had been widely embraced by the English people and by war's end was universally admired. By November 1875 a two-hundred-foot-tall stone tower was completed, visible from Westminster Bridge and from the Houses of Parliament. It was the first monument to a foreign leader ever built on English soil, and it demonstrated the growing reach of Lincoln's influence around the world. Robert Lincoln, still struggling with the issue of his mother's sanity, would later take part in the official opening.

Lincoln Tower in London

1875

African Americans in Politics

In 1875 Blanche K. Bruce was elected to the Senate from Mississippi, taking the former seat of Jefferson Davis. The years 1870 to 1876 represented a high point for blacks in American politics. With the Fifteenth Amendment granting black men the vote, sixteen African Americans were elected to the U.S Congress, beginning with Hiram Revels of Mississippi, elected to the Senate in 1870, and Joseph Hayne Rainey to the House of Representatives in the same year. Soon there were many others in the House, including Benjamin Sterling Turner from Alabama and John Roy Lynch from Mississippi. At the state level there were dozens of other elected blacks—including a governor (of Louisiana), six lieutenant governors, and seven secretaries of state. White Southerners were largely opposed to these great changes, and there was mounting opposition to what was called "nigger rule." To counter it, Congress passed the Civil Rights Act of 1875, outlawing racial discrimination in hotels, railroads, and theaters and strengthening the federal government's ability to enforce the laws. But it was the last effort of the nation's first civil rights movement. The following year, 1876, for all intents and purposes, Reconstruction ended.

Blanche K. Bruce

Hiram Revels

Joseph H. Rainey

Robert Smalls

John R. Lynch

Alonzo J. Ransier

199

April 14, 1876

Freedom's Memorial

Back in 1865 an idea had spread among American blacks to build a monument to the emancipator Abraham Lincoln. In Ohio a newly freed slave named Charlotte Mott sent five dollars of her wages to the Sanitary Commission in St. Louis, specifying it should go to a Lincoln memorial. It was the start of what would become known as the Freedmen's Memorial Fund, and soon all across the country former slaves were sending in money. By the end of 1865 more than $16,000 had been collected.

Three years later the Unitarian minister William Greenleaf Eliot was visiting the studios of Massachusetts sculptor Thomas Ball in Florence, Italy. There he spotted a small marble sculpture of Lincoln emancipating a slave. Ball said he had carved it shortly after the assassination and wanted nothing more than to see it erected on a grand scale. When he offered to create a large new version of the statue and donate it to the Sanitary Commission for the relatively modest cost of casting it in bronze, a deal was made.

But there would have to be one change. In carving the freed slave, Ball had used an image of himself as a guide, and it was the one aspect of the sculpture that Eliot didn't like. He asked Ball to use a real black man for a model and recommended an employee of his named Archer Alexander, a former slave and the last person in Missouri captured under the Fugitive Slave Act. Back home Eliot asked him if he would pose for a series of photographs, and Alexander agreed.

The bronze statue was completed in 1874, and Congress provided funds for a granite base and pedestal. It was erected in the new Lincoln Square on Capitol Hill and dedicated on April 14, 1876.

The day of the unveiling was a legal holiday in Washington, and 25,000 people showed up for the ceremonies. Among the crowds were colored troops from the Civil War, as well as both black and white schoolchildren. On the speakers' stand were President Grant, his cabinet members, the Chief Justice and other members of the Supreme Court, senators and representatives, and foreign dignitaries. Nothing like this had ever occurred before in America—an interracial ceremony involving the highest levels of government.

Following a reading of Lincoln's Emancipation Proclamation, the time for the unveiling arrived. President Grant, a man of few words, did the official uncovering; in one observer's words he "hopped up . . . pulled a cord—and sat down again, without having moved a muscle of his thin lips." A hushed silence fell upon the crowd, followed by a wave of applause. In glistening bronze the great figure of Lincoln stood tall, with Emancipation Proclamation in hand. Beneath him, half kneeling, was a strong young freedman, rising from chains he has helped to break, his eyes filled with hope. Few knew that the stirring figure was based on an actual ex-slave.

Shortly before the dedication of the Lincoln sculpture in Washington, Virginians unveiled in Richmond a statue of Stonewall Jackson.

Thomas Ball (above) sculpted the Freedmen's Statue in Florence, and had it cast in bronze at a foundry in Munich. To the left is a model of the statue with Alexander's face unmistakable.

Archer Alexander, the last fugitive slave captured in Missouri, served as the model for the slave in the finished sculpture of the Freedmen's Memorial. When he was shown a photograph of the finished statue, he said he "laughed all over."

The Keynote Speaker

The keynote speaker at the unveiling of the Freedmen's Memorial was Frederick Douglass. He had not spoken out publicly about Lincoln since the 1860s, spending his time working for the passage of the Fifteenth Amendment and for the groundbreaking Civil Rights Act of 1875. Never before had a black man been invited to address such a crowd—one that included the President of the United States and most of the leaders of government. "We stand today at the nation's center," he began, "to perform something like a national act—an act which is to go into history. . . . We are here to express, as best we may . . . our grateful sense of the vast, high, and premier service rendered to ourselves, to our race, to our country, and to the world by Abraham Lincoln."

But Douglass knew that to come together for a pleasant ceremony remembering the past would not be enough. Progress on black freedom was faltering; in the South many rights had already been stripped away, and in the North there was decreasing energy to maintain Reconstruction. Something had to be said that would pierce through the sentimentality and demonstrate how much more had to be done before blacks could be equal citizens. Nor was it proper to simply idolize Lincoln or to make him into something he wasn't. Douglass's words that day were full of anger and moral outrage. And at the end, when he finally praised Lincoln, he left many in the audience moved to tears.

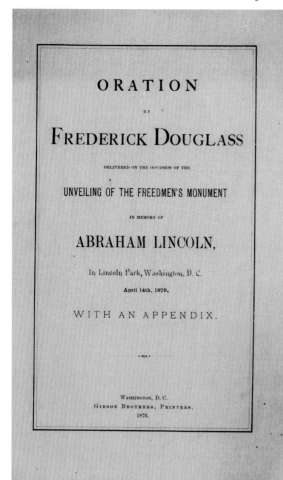

ORATION

BY

FREDERICK DOUGLASS

DELIVERED ON THE OCCASION OF THE

UNVEILING OF THE FREEDMEN'S MONUMENT

IN MEMORY OF

ABRAHAM LINCOLN,

In Lincoln Park, Washington, D. C.

April 14th, 1876,

WITH AN APPENDIX.

WASHINGTON, D. C.
GIBSON BROTHERS, PRINTERS.
1876.

Frederick Douglass's oration at the unveiling of the Freedmen's Monument was published as a pamphlet that same year. Douglass included the speech as an appendix to his 1881 autobiography. To the right is his handwritten manuscript for the keynote address.

> Friends and Fellow-citizens:
>
> I warmly congratulate you upon the highly interesting object which has caused you us to assemble in such numbers and spirit as you have to-day This occasion is in some respects remarkable. Wise and thoughtful men of our race, who shall come after us, and study the lesson of our history in the United States; who shall survey the long and dreary spaces over which we have travelled, who shall count the links in the great chain of events by which we have reached our present position; will make a note of this occasion—they will think of it, and speak of it, with a sense of manly pride and complacency.
>
> I congratulate you also upon the very favorable

"At Best Only His Step-children"
Frederick Douglass

April 14, 1876

The Unveiling of the Freedmen's Monument, Washington, D.C.

[T]ruth compels me to admit, even here in the presence of the monument we have erected to his memory, Abraham Lincoln was not, in the fullest sense of the word, either our man or our model. In his interests, in his associations, in his habits of thought, and in his prejudices, he was a white man.

He was preëminently the white man's President, entirely devoted to the welfare of white men. He was ready and willing at any time during the first years of his administration to deny, postpone, and sacrifice the rights of humanity in the colored people to promote the welfare of the white people of this country. In all his education and feeling he was an American of the Americans. He came into the Presidential chair upon one principle alone, namely, opposition to the extension of slavery. His arguments in furtherance of this policy had their motive and mainspring in his patriotic devotion to the interests of his own race. . . . You are the children of Abraham Lincoln. We are at best only his step-children; children by adoption, children by force of circumstances and necessity. To you it especially belongs to sound his praises, to preserve and perpetuate his memory, to multiply his statues, to hang his pictures high upon your walls, and commend his example, for to you he was a great and glorious friend and benefactor. . . . But while in the abundance of your wealth, and in the fullness of your just and patriotic devotion, you do all this, we entreat you to despise not the humble offering we this day unveil to view; for while Abraham Lincoln saved for you a country, he delivered us from a bondage. . . .

Abraham Lincoln . . . knew the American people better than they knew themselves, and his truth was based upon this knowledge.

Privately Frederick Douglass criticized the Freedmen's statue, saying that it "showed the Negro on his knees when a more manly attitude would have been indicative of Freedom."

September 1876
Shocked by His Likeness

In September 1876 Mary Lincoln decided to leave the country for good. "I cannot endure to meet my former friends," she told her sister Elizabeth. "They will never cease to regard me as a lunatic." She could also not abide to be near Robert any longer. "I was cruelly persecuted, by a bad son," she later wrote, "on whom I had bestowed, the greater part of . . . my heart." Elizabeth tried to dissuade Mary from going, but she said it was necessary—who knows when she might be forcibly incarcerated again? And so, swearing her to secrecy lest Robert try to interfere, in mid-September Mary slipped out of town.

During her months at her sister's house, she had grown close to her grand-nephew Edward "Lewis" Baker. Devoted to Mary, he reminded her of Tad, and when she asked him to accompany her to the East Coast, Lewis cheerfully agreed. They traveled together from Illinois to Kentucky, where they spent several days visiting Mary's childhood home and paying respects at the family graveyard. Then it was off to Philadelphia, before the final destination of New York.

In 1876 Philadelphia seemed to be everyone's destination—host city of America's Centennial Exhibition, located on 285 acres overlooking the beautiful Schuylkill River. It was the country's first world's fair, and thirty-seven nations had sent exhibits that were displayed at 250 different pavilions. Though dedicated to the theme of industrial progress, the exhibition also included art and history. Much of this was centered in an imposing white stone building known as Memorial Hall—the most beautiful edifice on the grounds. Inside were paintings and sculptures from around the world, including a very special canvas that had been sent from Frankfurt, Germany.

Mary Lincoln

Opening day of the 1876 Centennial was crowded in Philadelphia. Inside the grand Memorial Hall, shown here, Mary saw the oil painting of her husband.

It was a full-length portrait of the sixteenth President, painted from life in the fall of 1864 by the German artist William Travers. Travers had come from Germany to enlist in the Union Army and, when he was rejected on medical grounds, had decided instead to paint President Lincoln. He waited for his opportunity, then one day approached Lincoln on the streets in Washington and asked him outright for the privilege of painting him. Lincoln was so impressed by the man's earnestness and good will that he agreed to a series of sittings.

When the drawings were complete, Travers took them to Germany, where he finished the portrait shortly after the assassination. Four years later he sold it to the U.S. consul in Frankfurt, William P. Withers, who hung it on his office wall and treasured it. In 1876 Withers had a brainstorm—he would send the painting to America to the Centennial Exhibition, to be included in the art galleries in Memorial Hall.

The portrait was immensely popular with the American public. Ward Hill Lamon, visiting that summer, declared it the most lifelike painting of Lincoln he had ever seen. Mary knew nothing about it. Here she was about to leave the country forever, alienated from her only living offspring, branded as a lunatic, and still bereft at the loss of her husband and best friend. When she stepped in front of the painting, she was suddenly overwhelmed by emotion. According to a newspaper report at the time, Mary fainted on the spot and had to be carried from the hall.

Memorial Hall housed the Centennial art exhibition of more than 3,000 paintings from twenty nations, including William Travers's life portrait of Lincoln.

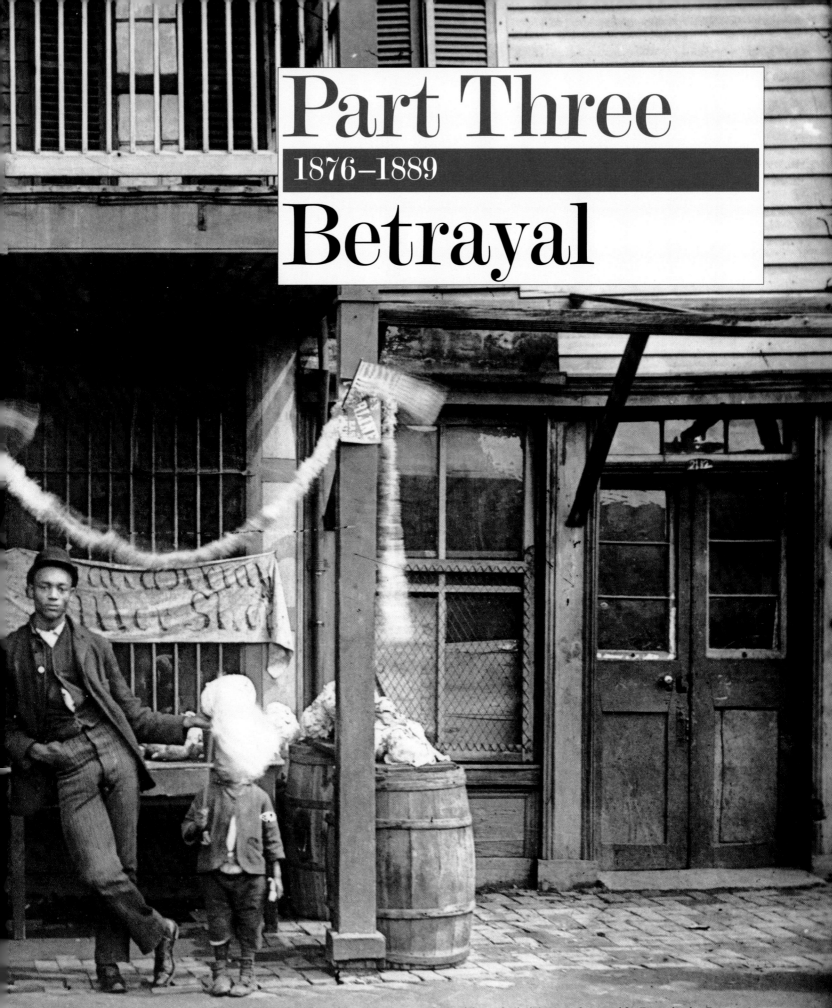

Part Three

1876–1889

Betrayal

African Americans gather outside a Richmond, Virginia, store decorated for Emancipation Day, 1888.

A Bold Era Slips Away
1876–1889

With the collapse of Reconstruction in 1877, the South returned to home rule, and the nation's first civil rights movement ground to a halt. Though freed by proclamation and by the Thirteenth Amendment, and made equal citizens by the Fourteenth and Fifteenth Amendments, blacks in the South soon found themselves in a position akin to slavery—"worse off, in many respects," said Frederick Douglass. Deprived of the right to vote, forced to work as sharecroppers, and often terrorized by vigilantes, blacks entered one of the bleakest periods in their history. Once again Douglass attempted to awaken the national conscience, calling the situation a betrayal of everything Lincoln had stood for and denouncing emancipation as "a stupendous fraud," adding, "It was not meant so by Abraham Lincoln." He criticized the failure of the federal government to provide justice and equality among its citizens, and he accused Americans of caring more for the reunion of North and South than for the plight of millions of suffering black people.

The memory of Lincoln during these years continued to expand. Friends and acquaintances wrote reminiscences; interesting controversies arose; and important new biographies were published, helping preserve the record of Lincoln the man and the leader. At the same time Lincoln tourism expanded; Lincoln statuary continued to be erected; and Lincoln collections were built up and sometimes opened to the public. But increasingly it was an era of nostalgia and sentimentality. And there was the sense that a bold period of progress and expanding freedoms was now receding into the past.

By the end of the nineteenth century, Lincoln's house in Springfield was a gathering place for rallies and celebrations. Here members of the Illinois Association of Ex-Prisoners of War listened to speakers at a ceremony in Lincoln's backyard.

The Attempt to Steal Lincoln's Body

In the autumn of 1876, the nation's Centennial year, a plot was hatched among a group of Chicago counterfeiters to steal the body of Abraham Lincoln. The idea was to break into the unguarded Springfield tomb at Oak Ridge Cemetery, remove the casket bearing the remains of the President, and hide it until a large ransom could be obtained as well as the release from prison of master counterfeiter Benjamin Boyd. Three men besides Boyd were involved in the scheme: "Big Jim" Kenealy, the plot's ringleader; Terence Mullen, a Chicago saloon-keeper; and Jack Hughes, a small-time bill "shover." A fourth man, Lewis Swegles, a convicted horse thief, was also enlisted to help. Unbeknownst to the gang he was a federal informer, and through him the U. S. Secret Service became aware of the plot.

The break-in was set for Tuesday, November 7, the night of the presidential elections—a chaotic time when it was hoped the thieves' movements would go unnoticed. The plot was an audacious one: after breaking into the tomb and removing the casket, Mullen, Hughes, and Swegles would take Lincoln's body by wagon to the nearby Sangamon River, dump it from a bridge, and let it settle to the sandy bottom. Kenealy would remain in Chicago to ensure an alibi.

On the afternoon of November 7 federal agents positioned themselves inside the Lincoln Monument and awaited the arrival of the body-snatchers. On Swegles's signal they planned to enter the tomb and catch the men red-handed.

It was dark when the criminals arrived and took their places at the rear door of the Lincoln Monument. After sawing and filing their way through a large iron padlock, they entered into the catacomb. There in front of them, visible in the glow of their lamps, lay the marble sarcophagus of Abraham Lincoln, inscribed with the words "With Malice Toward None." They proceeded quickly now, prying open the heavy lid and exposing the wooden coffin inside, then managing to pull it partway out. But when they realized it weighed close to five hundred pounds, they dispatched Swegles to get help. That was when he gave his signal, causing federal agents to stream out the front doorway and around the monument to the back. But, to their surprise, the officers who entered the catacomb found it empty. Something had spooked Mullen and Hughes, who had withdrawn to a safe distance.

The next day the press reacted to news of the break-in with disgust. The *Chicago Tribune* called it an attempt to "perpetrate one of the most infamous outrages which the mind of man can conceive—that of stealing the bones and ashes of Abraham Lincoln. . . . Unfortunately the perpetrators escaped . . . [and] the clues are next to nothing."

The body-snatchers might have gotten away entirely, had not Swegles led the authorities to them ten days later. The two men were arrested, tried, convicted, and sent to prison—to serve one-year sentences, the longest that could be given under Illinois law.

Terence Mullen was one of the accomplices in the plot to steal Lincoln's body.

Eyewitness to the Tomb Raid
John Carroll Power

November 7, 1876

John Carroll Power was the first custodian of the Lincoln Tomb, serving from 1873 until his death twenty-one years later. "Cheerful, kind and of a good nature," as he was described, he loved to regale visitors with colorful stories about Lincoln. He was present inside the tomb at the time of the November break-in and often spoke of that dramatic night.

[T]he first intimation we inside had of the presence of the conspirators, was a very brilliant light from a bull's eye or dark lantern, being thrust in between the rods of the outer door to Memorial Hall. It almost touched the glass of the inner door, and was turned about quickly, as though finding all locked, satisfied the parties with the lantern that the Hall was unoccupied. The light soon disappeared, and footsteps as of more than one person were heard, retreating towards the catacomb at the north end of the Monument. It was Swegles and Hughes. [Agent] Tyrrell then directed [me] . . . to unlock the doors, but leave them closed, which . . . [I] did, and had barely time to resume [my] . . . position when the lantern appeared again, this time carried by Swegles alone who gave Tyrrell the password adopted for that night, "Wash," and informed Tyrrell that Hughes and Mullens had commenced sawing the lock at the rod door of the catacomb. . . .

For fifteen or twenty minutes after that not a man moved out of the Hall, and yet there were hurried movements and whisperings going on inside. . . . [I] had never seen a single one of those men until within a few hours of that time. Thoughts ran thick and fast through . . . [my] mind. . . . Then came a slight movement at the door. More whisperings were heard and a hurried exit, followed by a few moments of deathlike stillness, and [I] . . . began to realize that . . . [I] was alone in the blackness of darkness. A man soon entered and called . . . [my] name. It was the voice of

Lincoln's sarcophagus was photographed not long after the attempted tomb robbery.

Tyrrell. He directed . . . [me] to bring the lamps from the interior of the Monument which was quickly done. Tyrrell had gone out without his boots that his footsteps might not be heard. He put them on hurriedly and departed again. He had been out but a few moments, when—

Hark! What is that? Crack! crack!! crack!!! A succession of pistol shots rang out on the night air. As the men filed in to the light, hurried words were spoken. "The villains are gone." "Oh, Lord! What a narrow escape," one exclaimed. All were pale and quivering with emotion. With the lights we proceeded to the Catacomb.

HORRIBLE.

Dastardly Attempt to Despoil the Lincoln Monument.

Thieves Trying to Steal the Bones of the Martyr President.

Warning Given, and Steps Taken to Arrest Them.

Elmer Washburn and His Assistants Waiting in the Dark.

The Robbers Interrupted by Accident, and Contrive to Escape.

Special Dispatch to The Tribune.
SPRINGFIELD, Ill., Nov. 7.—An attempt was

The *Chicago Tribune* reported the crime the next day.

CURLEY.

GENERAL CUSTER'S SCOUT AND ONLY SURVIVOR OF THAT HORRIBLE MASSACRE OF 1876.

Eleven years after Lincoln's death, his flamboyant general George Armstrong Custer was killed while fighting Indians. His Crow scout Ashishishi, known to General Custer as Curley, was the only member of his company to survive the Battle of Little Bighorn.

Lincoln and Indians

In late 1876, the year of Custer's Last Stand, an American diplomat named Albert Rhodes published a reminiscence about a visit to Lincoln's White House by a delegation of western Indians. The article revealed how little progress had been made in white attitudes toward Indians since Lincoln's time.

As a man of the frontier, Lincoln had been aware of Indians all his life. He had grown up hearing tales about his grandfather Abraham, who had come west from Virginia along the Boone trail, arriving in Kentucky during a period of intense Indian upheavals. In May 1784, while out clearing a field with his sons, this Abraham had been attacked and killed by Indians. His six-year-old son, Thomas, Lincoln's future father, sat down in shock near his father's body, then was grabbed by one of the Indians. But Thomas's older brother Mordecai had meanwhile run into the family cabin to find a rifle. Taking aim at a silver half-moon trinket around the Indian's neck, he shot him dead. Both boys grew up with a hatred of Native Americans.

Born twenty-four years later, Abraham Lincoln did not share this hatred. But as an adult, like most men on the western frontier, he participated in communal vigilance against Indians. In 1832, at the age of twenty-three, he signed up to fight in the Black Hawk War. Though, as he described, there were "Indians all about us, constantly watching our movements," his company saw no action. They did discover a white encampment that had been attacked, leaving five men scalped, a vivid memory for Lincoln. And there was the time an old Indian wandered into camp and was almost killed by the men. Lincoln intervened, pointing to the letter the old man carried from Lewis Cass denoting his trustworthiness. In so doing he gained a reputation for being soft on Indians.

As President, Lincoln largely ignored Indian affairs, overlooking the tremendous corruption that existed within the department that had led to widespread poverty and starvation among Native Americans. In August 1862, however, he was forced to take notice when an uprising in Minnesota among the Sioux resulted in the killing of 350 whites. John G. Nicolay was coincidentally visiting Minnesota at the time and wrote to Lincoln that "the massacre of innocent white settlers has been fearful." Lincoln sent General John Pope to the area and he quickly assumed a hard-line attitude. "It is my purpose utterly to exterminate the Sioux," he wrote. "They are to be

Hole-in-the-Day, an Ojibwa chief, met with Lincoln at the White House on February 20, 1863.

Following the Sioux uprising of 1862, a prison camp was set up at Fort Snelling in Minnesota.

treated as maniacs or wild beasts." A military commission was set up under General Henry H. Sibley, and within weeks it had sentenced 303 Sioux warriors to death. In a letter to Lincoln, Sibley explained that only a massive public execution would "satisfy the longings of the most blood-thirsty" whites. Horrified at what looked like a rush to judgment, Lincoln put a hold on the hangings and ordered his War Department lawyers to study the trial records and determine who among the large group actually deserved death. It became clear to Lincoln that a travesty of justice had been committed—some trials had lasted just ten minutes; evidence had been based on hearsay; and many Indians had been denied due process and counsel. Lincoln became convinced that the majority of the sentenced had not participated in the massacre, and on December 12 he commuted 264 of the sentences. He then wrote out precise instructions about who was to be spared, spelling out their names phonetically so there could be no mistake. In the end, 38 Sioux Indians were hanged on the day after Christmas in Mankato, Minnesota, in the largest mass execution in U.S. history.

When Albert Rhodes's article appeared in the November 1876 issue of *St. Nicholas Magazine*, it came at a time of widespread new anti-Indian sentiment. The massacre of Custer and his men at Little Bighorn that summer had left the American public once again clamoring for vengeance. The meeting Rhodes described between Lincoln and the western chiefs took place just four months after the mass hanging in Mankato.

Chief Little Crow was leader of the Sioux revolt of 1862.

Sioux captives huddled outside a Minnesota jail. To the left, Lincoln specified by phonetic spelling which Indians were to be executed. Though 303 had been sentenced to death, in the end 38 were hanged.

A Reminiscence of Abraham Lincoln
Albert Rhodes

The event that Albert Rhodes recalled took place on March 27, 1863. Lincoln's response to the western chiefs was filled with common stereotypes of the day. And his suggestion that the Indians embrace agriculture included a cruel irony—for by then most Native Americans had been relegated to lands that white people didn't want, and much of it was unsuitable for farming.

There was an interesting though unimportant scene in the life of Abraham Lincoln, of which I was an eye-witness. It was on the occasion of the visit of about twenty Indian chiefs to the Executive Mansion, delegated by their respective tribes to treat personally with the Great Father in the adjustment of their affairs. They were habited in their attire of feathers and paint, and each one was impressed with the greatness of the occasion, the most eventful, probably, of their lives. Their interpreter placed them in the form of a crescent in the spacious East room, on the floor, as they would have been ill at ease on chairs. Thus they sat on the carpet in decorous silence and waited the arrival of the Chief Magistrate. . . .

At length Abraham Lincoln came into the room and stood before the dusky crescent. . . . "My red brethren," said Lincoln, "are anxious to be prosperous and have horses and carriages like the pale faces. I propose to tell them how they may get them."

At this the dusky men were all attention, and manifested their satisfaction by the usual Indian guttural sounds.

"The plan is a simple one," said the President, as the interpreter turned his words into the tongue of the red men. Their curiosity was fully aroused. Even the spectators looked inquiringly at Lincoln, to know how he was going to provide horses and carriages for those who thus bluntly asked for them.

"You all have land," said Lincoln. "We will furnish you with agricultural implements, with which you will turn up the soil, by hand if you have not the means to buy an ox, but I think with the aid which you receive from the Government, you might at least purchase one ox to do the plowing for several. You will plant corn, wheat, and potatoes, and with the money for which you will sell these you will be able each to buy an ox for himself at the end of the first year. At the end of the second year, you will each be able to buy perhaps two oxen and some sheep and pigs. At the end of the third, you will probably be in a condition to buy a horse, and in the course of a few years you will thus be the possessor of horses and carriages like ourselves."

This plan for becoming proprietor of

In March 1863 eight Native American delegates met with Lincoln at the White House. They were then taken on a tour of the mansion, including its conservancy, where they were photographed. Sitting in front, from the left, were Standing in the Water, War Bonnet, Lean Bear, and Yellow Wolf. Standing in the center of the back row was John G. Nicolay, and at the far right was the First Lady, Mary Lincoln.

horses and carriages was not relished, for it meant work, and the faces of the Indians bore a disappointed expression as the President unfolded it.

"I do not know any other way to get these things," added Lincoln. "It is the plan we have pursued—at least those of us who have them. You cannot pick them off the trees, and they do not fall from the clouds."

Father Neptune Fades Away

Thomas Nast portrayed Secretary of the Navy Gideon Welles as Father Neptune.

He was the last of the originals from the Lincoln cabinet. A lifelong Democrat, who considered himself part of the loyal opposition, Gideon Welles was also the least well known. "On the avenues, on a fine day," wrote the *New York Times*, "he might be seen, pacing sedately along, recognized by a few people, distinguished by his dignified carriage, the luxuriant and snowy curls of his wig, and his colorless, but placid face." But if he was outshined by the likes of Seward, Stanton, and Chase, the aging secretary of the navy was both efficient and effective. Though "slightly fossiliferous," thought Noah Brooks, he was well liked by Lincoln, who dubbed him "Father Neptune." Welles could be irreverent about Lincoln—he once quoted Chase that arguing with the President was as useless as "throwing water on a duck's back." But he recognized Lincoln's greatness. In the midst of the war, when Lincoln was struggling with his officials and with his national popularity, Welles wrote, "The President has well maintained his position, and under trying circumstances acquitted himself in a manner that will be better appreciated in the future than now."

After Lincoln's assassination, Welles continued to serve as Andrew Johnson's secretary of the navy. He believed that Johnson was a worthy successor to the office and wrote that his Reconstruction policy "had commenced with Mr. Lincoln, and I believed it correct." When he joined the opposition to congressional Reconstruction, he became widely disliked among Republicans. And in the pages of his private diary—one of the most detailed of the entire period—he continued to make trenchant comments about the political scene.

In the 1870s Welles returned to his hometown of Hartford, Connecticut, and settled into a quiet retirement. He continued to speak out against radical Republicans, disliked President Grant, and vigorously opposed a third term for him. In late 1877 a malignant growth appeared on the back of Welles's head and grew rapidly over the next months. By February it was clear that his condition was fatal, and on the eleventh Father Neptune died. In his honor, the Navy Department closed its doors, and the entire War Department was draped in mourning.

Under the command of Welles (right), a naval attack on Fort Fisher, North Carolina, in January 1865 was waged by the largest American fleet that had ever been assembled.

An Uneasy Commemoration

February 1878 marked the dedication in Washington of a giant painting, fifteen feet wide and nine feet tall, portraying Lincoln with his entire cabinet. Painted by Francis Carpenter inside the White House in 1864, it depicted Lincoln's first reading of the Emancipation Proclamation in August 1862. That historic moment was "an act unparalleled for moral grandeur," Carpenter had decided soon after hearing about it. It was second, he felt, only to the signing of the Declaration of Independence, the famous painting of which by John Trumbull had hung for years in the Capitol Rotunda. "I wish to paint this picture now," Carpenter wrote to a friend in early 1864, and he got his wish.

Francis Carpenter had been given unparalleled access to his subject. Determined to represent the scene "as it actually transpired; room, furniture, accessories, all," Carpenter sketched out a master plan for the painting and submitted it to Lincoln for his critical feedback. Later, with Lincoln's approval, he made changes, rearranging the cabinet members' positions around the table to emphasize their symbolic roles. To help him accurately depict the various faces, he arranged for each man to be photographed at Mathew Brady's studio and twice accompanied Lincoln there for pictures. Dissatisfied with the results, he arranged for a photo session inside the White House and obtained candid pictures of Lincoln in his office.

The work on the mural-like painting took all winter and spring. Carpenter was given permission to move into the State Dining Room, where he could paint by the light of the great chandeliers and where he often worked straight through the night until dawn. At one point, as John Hay recorded in his diary, William Seward came in and protested the very subject of the painting. "[T]he anti-slavery acts of this administration are merely incidental," he insisted. The "great work is the preservation of the Union." But Lincoln himself considered the Emancipation Proclamation the "central act" of his administration and the "one thing that will make people remember I ever lived." And Carpenter painted on.

On July 22, after six months of work, the artist held a private viewing for the President and members of the cabinet, followed by a public exhibit in the East Room. Before the painting was taken down, Lincoln asked if he might take a last look, and sat before it, along with Carpenter, for many minutes in silence. After suggesting a few small changes, Lincoln gave his final assessment. "Carpenter—I believe I am about as glad over the success of this work as you are."

During the next decade the painting was exhibited across the country, while Carpenter looked for a permanent home for it in Washington. In 1873 the government came close to acquiring it, but balked at his asking price of $25,000. Finally in 1877 New York philanthropist Elizabeth Thompson purchased the huge canvas and donated it to Congress and the American people.

The official dedication was planned for February 12, 1878—the sixty-ninth an-

Artist Francis Carpenter worked on his portrait of Lincoln in the White House State Dining Room, shown here as it looked in the 1870s.

"Let The Reunited Nation Cherish It Forever"
James Garfield
February 12, 1878

In the name of political "balance," two keynoters spoke at the dedication of Carpenter's painting—James Garfield and Alexander Stephens. Critics said the arrangement distorted the memory of Lincoln's achievement.

[Lincoln] was a character so unique that he stood alone, without a model in history or a parallel among men. . . . Gifted with an insight and a foresight which the ancients would have called divination, he saw, in the midst of darkness and obscurity, the logic of events, and forecast the result. From the first, in his own quaint, original way, without ostentation or offence to his associates, he was pilot and commander of his administration. He was one of the few great rulers whose wisdom increased with his power, and whose spirit grew gentler and tenderer as his triumphs were multiplied.

This was the man, and these his associates, who look down upon us from the canvas. . . .

The severely plain chamber, not now used for Cabinet councils; the plain marble mantel, with the portrait of a hero President above it; the council table at which Jackson and his successor had presided; the old-fashioned chairs; the books and maps; the captured sword, with its pathetic history; — all are there, as they were in fact fifteen years ago. But what is of more consequence, the portraits are true to the life. Mr. Seward said of the painting, "It is a vivid representation of the scene, with portraits of rare fidelity"; and so said all his associates.

Without this painting, the scene could not even now be reproduced. The room has been remodelled; its furniture is gone; and Death has been sitting in that council, calling the roll of its members in quick succession. Yesterday he added another name to his fatal list; and to-day he has left upon the earth but a single witness of the signing of the Proclamation of Emancipation.

James A. Garfield

Alexander H. Stephens

"Slavery Was Not Without Its Compensations"
Alexander Stephens
February 12, 1878

I knew Mr. Lincoln well. We were together during one congress. I was as intimate with him as with any other man. . . . He was warm-hearted. He was generous. He was, as he afterwards said, possessed of a heart which has "malice to none and charity to all.". . . Every fountain of his heart was ever overflowing with the milk of human kindness. . . .

Now, as to the great historical event which this picture commemorates, and which we here today commemorate. . . . The people of this day and generation are not exactly in the condition to weigh rightly and judge correctly. . . . Emancipation was not the chief object of Mr. Lincoln. . . . That proclamation . . . originated more from the necessities of war than from any purely humanitarian views. Let this be noted in our history. . . . The proclamation itself did not make free or declare free all the colored race. It was only to operate in those parts which were in resistance to the government. Had resistance ceased that would have been all.

If emancipation of the colored race be a boon to that race, and Providence has yet to determine that, it depends much on themselves. If it is, I, representing the southern states here, may claim in their behalf that freedom was never fully consummated till the southern states sanctioned the thirteenth amendment, which they did, every one of them, and by their own constituencies. . . .

Indulge me for a moment on the subject of so-called slavery. It was not an unmitigated evil. It was not without its compensations. . . . It is past with us. . . . Let sectional strife be done away with and then there is a higher and grander future for us.

219

Francis Bicknell Carpenter

niversary of Lincoln's birth. Only once before had a joint session of Congress met to receive a national gift—the 1848 presentation of George Washington's sword and Benjamin Franklin's staff. This time the event was organized around the theme of national reunion, and it would be the first major Lincoln commemoration in which both Northerners and Southerners took part.

The late 1870s was a very different world from the 1860s, and the scene depicted in Carpenter's painting was already receding into the past. By now everyone in the portrait, except Montgomery Blair, was dead—Gideon Welles had died just one day earlier.

The elaborate ceremony took place in the House of Representatives Hall where the painting was set up behind the Speaker's Chair and draped in a large American flag. The chambers were crowded to overflowing, and African Americans were concentrated in their own separate gallery. Following the seating of special guests, the picture was unveiled so all could gaze on it. Two speakers had been chosen for the occasion. The first, representing the North, was Congressman James Garfield of Ohio, whose address was entitled "Lincoln and Emancipation." It contained one of the most sublime appreciations of Lincoln ever delivered, but it also carefully avoided the partisanship of earlier days and honored Lincoln primarily as the savior of the Union. "The speech was entirely free from any allusion that could give offense to any section or party," reported the *Atlanta Constitution*.

The second speaker, representing the South, was Alexander Stephens, the former Vice President of the Confederacy, now politically resurrected and serving as a congressman from Georgia. Like other Southern leaders, he had accepted the reality of the end of slavery, but during the past decade he had strongly resisted Reconstruction, opposing the Fourteenth and Fifteenth Amendments, and fighting hard against the Civil Rights Act of 1875. In his speech—delivered from a wheelchair

One of Carpenter's original sketches

and his last as a congressman—he spoke warmly of Abraham Lincoln but rejected the importance of the Emancipation Proclamation, and questioned whether it had done any good at all. And then, following Stephens's speech, the ceremony was over.

It was an odd commemoration, and Minnesota's *Freeborn County Standard* saw through the forced politeness of the occasion. "The 'bloody chasm' across which Garfield and Stephens, as representatives of the 'Blue' and the 'Grey' . . . so cordially shook hands last Thursday, manifests a pensive dislike to being bridged over, or to having its ragged, serrated edges in close apposition."

In part to make up for it, a second ceremony was soon held at Howard University, to which Carpenter donated a large engraving of his famous painting. President Rutherford B. Hayes was in attendance, as was Frederick Douglass, who spoke, and Robert Lincoln's wife, Mary. This time emancipation was the dominant theme. "The wisdom, the righteousness, and the grandeur of Abraham Lincoln's act of emancipation, no man will deny," proclaimed Hayes. But then, reflecting the new tenor of the times, he went on to challenge his mostly black audience, saying that it was now up to them to make freedom meaningful. At ceremony's end, as a black couple sang out "The Freedmen's Song," all clasped hands, and many shed tears together.

At Carpenter's request, Lincoln was photographed in his office on April 26, 1864. The seated image served as a guide for the artist's fifteen-foot-wide painting of Lincoln's first reading of his Emancipation Proclamation to his cabinet (below). Visible (above, left) is Lincoln's high-top desk, pushed in front of a door that led out to a hallway down which the President could make secret escapes. Behind Lincoln (above, right) can be seen the fireplace that he often lit in the evening. The legs to the side of him belong to John G. Nicolay.

Frederick Douglass (front row, fifth from right) on one of his many speaking engagements, at a reunion of the 1st Maine Cavalry

1877
Reunion

HEAD QUARTERS OF THE FIRST ME. CAVALRY.

Frederick Douglass's Plea

By 1878 Frederick Douglass, now marshal of Washington, D.C., was growing more and more discouraged with his country. Over the past year he had watched Reconstruction end in the South as Southern blacks were once again thrown on the mercy of their former masters. It was a betrayal of everything Abraham Lincoln had stood for, he believed, and of the great freedom revolution that he had helped inaugurate. And so when Douglass was invited by the Abraham Lincoln Post of the Grand Army of the Republic to speak on Decoration Day in New York in front of a Lincoln statue, he quickly agreed. It was an ideal location for him to try to reinvigorate the American conscience.

Decoration Day was a new American tradition—observed in both North and South in late May and later known as Memorial Day. It was an occasion on which to visit the graves of fallen soldiers and to give honor and thanks to their memory. In rural communities the day often became a family event with picnics out in the cemeteries and visits to family graves. In major cities large parades became associated with the holiday, and presidents and famous orators were often invited to address large crowds, which always included veterans.

May 30 was rainy and windy in New York, but thousands showed up for the outdoor ceremony, crowding around Henry Kirke Brown's bronze Lincoln statue in Union Square Park, erected in 1870 and on this day garlanded with flowers. Following an invocation at nine A.M. by the black clergyman John P. Newman, and then the reading of a poem, it was Frederick Douglass's turn to speak. "A hush fell on the crowd," reported the *New York Times*. "Raising his right hand and pointing significantly to the statue of Lincoln, while the crowd broke into enthusiastic shouts," the great orator began. He thanked the G.A.R. for inviting him to give its keynote address, noting its "moral courage" and "soldierly independence" for being willing to have a black speaker. "Abraham Lincoln was the first President of the United States," he said, "brave enough to invite a colored gentleman to sit at table with him, and the post that bears his honored name is the first in this great City to invite any colored man to deliver an address on national memorial day." Douglass praised the gathered veterans for their sacrifices in the Civil War and then turned his attention to the political situation at hand—the withdrawal of federal troops from the South and the subsequent breakdown of black rights there.

Douglass recognized that the nation increasingly wanted to "forget and forgive"—"to strew flowers alike and lovingly, on rebel and on loyal graves." He could appreciate this genuine longing for peace, this great desire for sectional reunion—but not at the price of national amnesia. "Let us have peace," he said, "but let us have liberty, law, and justice first. Let us have the Constitution, with its thirteenth, fourteenth, and fifteenth amendments, fairly interpreted, faithfully executed, and cheerfully obeyed." This day needed to be about remembering, and about staying true to the ideals of those who gave their lives. "There was a right side and a wrong side in the late war," Douglass thundered, "which no sentiment ought to cause us to forget."

Union Square, New York

Peace with Justice
Frederick Douglass

Douglass delivered this speech in New York City to a large crowd of veterans.

Fellow-citizens, I am not here to fan the flame of sectional animosity, to revive old issues, or to stir up strife between races; but no candid man, looking at the political situation of the hour, can fail to see that we are still afflicted by the painful sequences both of slavery and of the late rebellion. In the spirit of the noble man whose image now looks down upon us we should have "charity toward all, and malice toward none.". . . [But when] the supreme law of the land is systematically set at naught; when humanity is insulted and the rights of the weak are trampled in the dust by a lawless power; when society is divided into two classes, as oppressed and oppressor, there is no power, and there can be no power, while the instincts of manhood remain as they are, which can provide solid peace. I do not affirm that friendly feeling cannot be established between the people of the North and South. I do not say that between the white and colored people of the South, the former slaves and the former masters, friendly relations may not be established. I do not say that Hon. Rutherford B. Hayes, the lawful and rightful President of the United States, was not justified in stepping to the verge of his constitutional powers to conciliate and pacify the old master class at the South; but I do say that some steps by way of conciliation should come from the other side. The prodigal son should at least turn his back upon the field of swine, and his face toward home, before we make haste to fall upon his neck, and for him kill the fatted calf. He must not glory in his shame, and boast his non-repentance.

"Little Miss" Tells Her Tale
Grace Bedell Billings

October 2, 1878

In the fall of 1878 John C. Power, the super-intendent of the Lincoln Tomb in Springfield and an ardent collector of Lincolniana, heard of the existence of a young woman in Delphos, Kansas, who as a girl of eleven had convinced Lincoln to grow a beard. William Herndon had corresponded with her some years earlier and may have been the one to put Power on her trail. On October 2 came Grace's reply to Power's letter, explaining how she and the President-elect had met eighteen years earlier.

We were at that time residing at Westfield, New York. My father, who was a staunch Republican, brought one day to me . . . a picture of Lincoln and Hamlin, one of those coarse, exaggerated, so-called like-nesses, which it seems to be the fate of our long-suffering people to have thrust, upon them in such contests. . . .

As I regarded the picture, I said to my mother: "He would look better if he wore whiskers, and I mean to write and tell him so." She laughingly assented, and I proceeded to give him my name, age, place of residence, my views as to his fitness for the Presidency, opinion of his personal appearance, and that I thought it would be much improved if he would cultivate whiskers, adding as an inducement, that if he would, I would try and coax my two Democratic brothers to cast their votes for him. In my heart of hearts I feared that this rather free criticism might give offense, and so tried to soften the blow . . . by assuring him that I thought the rail-fence around his picture looked real pretty, and ended by asking him if he had not time to answer my letter, to allow his little girl to reply for him. . . .

[A]fter his election, he inquired of Hon. G. W. Patterson, who accompanied him on his trip from Springfield to Washington, and whose residence was also at Westfield, if he knew a family bearing the name of Bedell. Mr. Patterson replying in the affirmative, Mr. Lincoln said that, he had received a letter from a little girl, "advising me to wear whiskers, as she thought it would improve my looks, and you see I have followed her suggestion." When the train reached Westfield, Mr. Lincoln made a short speech from the platform of the car, saying that he had a little correspondent at Westfield, called Grace Bedell, and if she were present he would like to see her. I was present, but the crowd was so great that I had neither seen nor heard the speaker, but a friend helped me forward, and Mr. Lincoln stepped down to the platform where I stood, shook hands with and kissed me, saying as he touched his beard, "You see I let these whiskers grow for you, Grace," shook my hand again cordially and re-entered the car; and that was the first and last I ever saw of this hero and martyr.

Grace Bedell Billings, and the letter Lincoln wrote to her when she was eleven

Springfield, Ills Oct 19. 1860

Miss Grace Bedell

My dear little Miss.

Your very agreeable letter of the 15th is received —

I regret the necessity of saying I have no daughter — I have three sons — one seventeen, one nine, and one seven, years of age — They, with their mother, constitute my whole family —

As to the whiskers, having never worn any, do you not think people would call it a piece of silly affectation if I were to begin it now?

Your very sincere well-wisher

A. Lincoln

Her Letter to Him

October 15, 1860

Westfield Chatauque Co N Y
Oct 15. 1860

Hon A B Lincoln

Dear Sir

My father has just [gotten] home from the fair and brought home your picture and Mr. Hamlin's. I am a little girl only eleven years old, but want you should be President of the United States very much so I hope you wont think me very bold to write to such a great man as you are. Have you any little girls about as large as I am if so give them my love and tell her to write to me if you cannot answer this letter. I have got 4 brother's and part of them will vote for you any way and if you will let your whiskers grow I will try and get the rest of them to vote for you   you would look a great deal better for your face is so thin. All the ladies like whiskers and they would tease their husband's to vote for you and then you would be President. My father is a going to vote for you and if I was a man I would vote for you to   but I will try and get every one to vote for you that I can. I think that rail fence around your picture makes it look very pretty I have got a little baby sister she is nine weeks old and is just as cunning as can be. When you direct your letter dire[c]t to   Grace Bedell Westfield Chatauque County New York

I must not write any more   answer this letter right off   Good bye

Grace Bedell

His Letter to Her

October 19, 1860

Springfield, Ills. Oct 19. 1860
Miss Grace Bedell

My dear little Miss

Your very agreeable letter of the 15th is received—

I regret the necessity of saying I have no daughters. I have three sons—one seventeen, one nine, and one seven, years of age. They, with their mother, constitute my whole family.

As to the whiskers, having never worn any, do you not think people would call it a piece of silly affect[at]ion if I were to begin it now?

Your very sincere well-wisher

A. LINCOLN.

Below is the last beardless portrait ever taken of Lincoln, and, above it, the first one showing his whiskers, just sprouting.

225

Mythmaker

After a flood of Lincoln literature in the 1860s, the 1870s represented a kind of drought. It was as if the country needed to pause and take stock of the overwhelming events of Lincoln's death and its aftermath. But in the final year of the decade came a popular new book that signaled the beginning of a new era in Lincoln publishing. A Presbyterian clergyman and author from Chicago named J. B. McClure had decided to collect the best Lincoln stories he could find. He had earlier completed books on Thomas Edison, Dwight L. Moody, and others and was an acknowledged expert on "entertaining anecdotes"— bringing to life such iconic figures as Daniel Webster and Henry Ward Beecher through warmhearted and popular storytelling. Now he would do the same for Abraham Lincoln. The book came out in July 1879 and was titled *Anecdotes of Abraham Lincoln and Lincoln Stories*. It contained 150 entries in five categories—Early Life, Professional Life, White House Incidents, War Stories, and Miscellaneous. McClure's chief source was newspapers, from which he clipped most of his accounts, with little concern for authenticity. (In the flyleaf of his personal copy of the book, Isaac Arnold wrote he thought half the stories inside didn't come from Lincoln at all.) And yet many of them had a distinctively Lincolnian "feel"—in some cases affording glimpses of Lincoln unavailable elsewhere. Here, just fourteen years after Lincoln's death, was a mixture of the historical and the mythic Lincoln—a fun-loving, larger-than-life western hero who was already becoming part of American mythology.

Washington receiving Lincoln.

George Washington was "the mightiest name on earth," Abraham Lincoln once proclaimed. By pairing the Union's "Father" and its "Savior," mythmakers helped elevate Lincoln's reputation into the stratosphere.

J. B. McClure's book included these anecdotes:

Giving a Bully a Thrashing

While showing goods to two or three women in Offutt's store one day, a bully came in and began to talk in an offensive manner, using much profanity, and evidently wishing to provoke a quarrel. Lincoln leaned over the counter, and begged him, as ladies were present, not to indulge in such talk. The bully retorted that the opportunity had come for which he had long sought, and he would like to see the man who could hinder him from saying anything he might choose to say. Lincoln, still cool, told him that if he would wait until the ladies retired, he would hear what he had to say, and give him any satisfaction he desired.

As soon as the women were gone, the man became furious. Lincoln heard his boasts and his abuse for a time, and finding that he was not to be put off without a fight, said—"Well, if you must be whipped, I suppose I may as well whip you as any other man." This was just what the bully had been seeking, he said, so out of doors they went, and Lincoln made short work with him. He threw him upon the ground, held him there as if he had been a child, and gathering some "smart-weed" which grew upon the spot, rubbed it into his face and eyes, until the fellow bellowed with pain. Lincoln did all this without a particle of anger, and when the job was finished, went immediately for water, washed his victim's face, and did everything he could to alleviate his distress. The upshot of the matter was that the man became his fast and life-long friend, and was a better man from that day. It was impossible then, and it always remained impossible, for Lincoln to cherish resentment or revenge.

Lincoln and His New Hat

Mr. G. B. Lincoln tells of an amusing circumstance which took place at Springfield soon after Mr. Lincoln's nomination in

1860. A hatter in Brooklyn secretly obtained the size of the future President's head, and made for him a very elegant hat, which he sent by his townsman . . . to Springfield. About the time it was presented, various other testimonials of a similar character had come in from different sections. Mr. Lincoln took the hat, and after admiring its texture and workmanship, put it on his head and walked up to a looking-glass. Glancing from the reflection to Mrs. Lincoln, he said, with his peculiar twinkle of the eye, "Well, wife, there is one thing likely to come out of this scrape, any how. We are going to have some *new clothes!*"

His Philosophy of Canes

A gentleman calling at the White House one evening carried a cane, which, in the course of conversation, attracted the President's attention. Taking it in his hand, he said "I always used a cane when I was a boy. It was a freak of mine. My favorite one was a knotted beech stick, and I carved the head myself. There's a mighty amount of character in sticks. Don't you think so? You have seen these fishing-poles that fit into a cane? Well, that was an old idea of mine. Dogwood clubs were favorite ones with the boys. I suppose they use them yet. Hickory is too heavy, unless you get it from a young sapling. Have you ever noticed how a stick in one's hand will change his appearance? Old women and witches wouldn't look so without sticks."

A Joke on Lincoln's Big Feet

He had walked his hundred miles to Vandalia, in 1836, as he did in 1834, and when the session closed he walked home again. A gentleman in Menard County remembers meeting him and a detachment of "The Long Nine" on their way home. They were all mounted except Lincoln, who had thus far kept up with them on foot. If he had money he was hoarding it for more important purposes than that of saving leg-weariness and leather. The weather was raw, and Lincoln's clothing were none of the warmest. Complaining of being cold to one of his companions, this irreverent member of "The Long Nine" told his future President that it was no wonder he was cold—"there was so much of him on the ground." None of the party appreciated this homely joke at the expense of his feet (they were doubtless able to bear it) more thoroughly than Lincoln himself. We can imagine the cross-fires of wit and humor by which the way was enlivened during this cold and tedious journey. The scene was certainly a rude one, and seems more like a dream than a reality, when we remember that it occurred not very many years ago, in a state which now contains hardly less than three millions of people and seven thousand six hundred miles of railway.

Rocking a Cradle with His Foot

One gentleman who met him during this period, says that the first time he saw him he was lying on a trundle-bed, covered with books and papers, and *rocking a cradle with his foot.* The whole scene, however, was entirely characteristic—Lincoln reading and studying, and at the same time helping his landlady by quieting her child.

Jeff Davis

One of the latest of Mr. Lincoln's stories, was told to a party of gentlemen, who, among the tumbling ruins of the Confederacy, anxiously asked "what he would do with Jeff. Davis?" "There was a boy in Springfield," replied Mr. Lincoln, "who saved up his money and bought a 'coon,' which, after the novelty wore off, became a great nuisance. He was one day leading him through the streets, and had his hands full to keep clear of the little vixen, who had torn his clothes half off of him. At length he sat down on the curb-stone, completely fagged out. A man passing was stopped by the lad's disconsolate appearance, and asked the matter. 'Oh,' was the only reply, 'this coon is such a trouble to me.'

"'Why don't you get rid of him, then?' said the gentleman.

"'*Hush!*' said the boy; 'don't you see he is gnawing his rope off ? I am going to let him do it, and then I will go home and tell the folks *that he got away from me!*'"

How He Ate When Alone

A party of gentlemen, among whom was a doctor of divinity of much dignity of manner, calling at the White House one day, was informed by the porter that the President was at dinner, but that he would present their cards. The doctor demurred at this, saying they would call again. "Edward" assured them that he thought it would make no difference, and went in with the cards. In a few minutes the President walked into the room, with a kindly salutation, and a request that the friends would take seats. The doctor expressed his regret that their visit was so ill-timed, and that his Excellency was disturbed while at dinner. "Oh! No consequence at all," said Mr. Lincoln, good-naturedly. "Mrs. Lincoln is absent at present, and when she is away, I generally '*browse*' around."

Lincoln While in Bed Pardons a Soldier

The Hon. Mr. Kellogg, representative from Essex County, New York, received a dispatch one evening from the army, to the effect that a young townsman . . . had, for a serious misdemeanor, been convicted by a court-martial, and was to be shot the next day. Greatly agitated, Mr. Kellogg went to the Secretary of War, and urged, in the strongest manner, a reprieve. Stanton was inexorable. "Too many cases of the kind had been let off," he said, "and it was time an example was made.". . . Mr. Kellogg said, "Well, Mr. Secretary, the boy is not going to be *shot*—of that I give you fair warning!" Leaving the War Department, he went directly to the White House, although the hour was late. The sentinel on duty told him that special orders had been issued to admit no one whatever that night. . . . The President had retired, but . . . Judge Kellogg pressed his way through all obstacles to his sleeping apartment. . . . "This man must not be shot, Mr. President," said he. . . . "I can't allow him to be shot." Mr. Lincoln had remained in bed, quietly listening to the vehement protestations of his old friend (they were in Congress together). He at length said: "Well, I don't believe *shooting* him will do him any good. Give me that pen." And, so saying, "red tape" was unceremoniously cut, and another poor fellow's lease on life was indefinitely extended.

Gettysburg Address Controversy

November 14, 1879

In 1879 a minor controversy erupted that shed light on the significance of Lincoln's Gettysburg Address. Ward Hill Lamon, who had served as marshal of the day's proceedings, stated publicly that Lincoln's address had been a failure, an embarrassment to people who heard it and to Lincoln himself. When his statement was published, it elicited instant response from several individuals, including the Cincinnati journalist Murat Halstead, who had also been at the ceremony. His reply to Lamon was carried in the Cincinnati Chronicle *and picked up by newspapers across the country.*

Lamon's Statement

I was present on that memorable occasion, and heard Mr. Lincoln's speech. I was never more disappointed in my life. I felt not only that Mr. Lincoln had failed to do himself justice, but had lost a great opportunity. Mr. Seward concurred in that opinion, and told me that he had hoped for something better from Mr. Lincoln. Edward Everett, the orator of the day, whom I asked what he thought of the President's speech, observed that it was not what he had anticipated, and that Mr. Lincoln had signally failed to come up to his expectations. The opinion of everyone who heard the speech was that Mr. Lincoln had not been equal to the occasion, and had, in fact, acquitted himself poorly. The real worth of the immortal words uttered by Mr. Lincoln was not discovered until after the assassination.

Halstead's Reply

This is a remarkable statement to say the least. The writer was also present on that memorable occasion. He remembers how patiently the great crowd stood about the platform, in the presence of the new-made trenches and graves of the patriot-soldiers, while Mr. Everett delivered his elaborate and highly-polished oration. Nothing could have been more in striking contrast than the appearance of the two men. Everett, ever handsomer in his silver-white hair curling about his head then in middle life, faultlessly dressed, with a modulated voice and graceful action, delivering the well-balanced periods; and the President, tall, ungainly, but with every line of his face expressive of care and grief, delivering his short and epigrammatic sentences in a shrill, piping voice. There was as much difference in the manner as in the matter of the two speakers. . . . As he pronounced those now immortal words, a visible sensation ran through the crowd, and tears fell from eyes not easily moved to weeping. The oration of Mr. Everett, abounding in classical references and faultless in rhetoric, did not move the hearts of the people as did the plain, sententious speech of Mr. Lincoln. That we know, for the effect was to be seen. It was an occasion, however, when all hearts were subdued, and when whatever men felt was only seen in the quivering lip and silent tear. . . . There was also a story current, for which we cannot vouch, that when Mr. Everett was asked his opinion of the speech, he replied he would willingly give all he had written and spoken that day to be the author of it.

One of the five known handwritten texts of Lincoln's Gettysburg Address

ing place of those who here gave their lives, that that nation might live. It is altogether fitting and proper that we should do this.

But in a larger sense we can not dedicate— we can not consecrate— we can not hallow this ground. The brave men, living and dead, who struggled here, have consecrated it far above our poor power to add or detract. The world will little note, nor long remember, what we say here, but can never forget what they did here. It is for us, the living, rather to be dedicated here to the unfinished work, which they have, thus far, so nobly carried on. It is rather for us to be here dedicated to the great task remaining before us— that from these honored dead we take increased devotion to that cause for which they here gave the last full measure of devotion— that we here highly resolve that these dead shall not have died in vain; that this nation shall have a new birth of freedom; and that this government of the people, by the people, for the people, shall not perish from the earth.

John C. Power was custodian of the National Lincoln Monument in Springfield and served as the first secretary of the Lincoln Guard of Honor.

The nine original members of the Lincoln Honor Guard were B. B. Wiggins, E. S. Johnson, C. C. Conkling, and H. C. Chapin (standing), J. F. McNeill, J. C. Power, G. S. Dana, J. N. Reece, and J. P. Lindley (seated).

April 15, 1880

The Lincoln Guard of Honor

The attempted theft of Lincoln's body in 1876 led to the creation of a new voluntary organization, incorporated on Lincoln's birthday in 1880: the Lincoln Guard of Honor. John C. Power, the custodian of the Lincoln Tomb and Monument, was named secretary of the new organization, which included eight other prominent Springfield men. With its primary purpose "to guard the precious dust of Abraham Lincoln from vandal hands," the organization pledged to hold regular memorial services at the tomb site and to keep alive the memory of Abraham Lincoln. Its concerns included safeguarding the Lincoln home in Springfield and collecting and preserving "mementos" of Lincoln's life and death.

Over the years the Lincoln Tomb had become a place of pilgrimage, with thousands showing up each year to pay their respects. A register book inside its Memorial Hall allowed visitors to sign their names, and postcards and books were sold here to supplement the custodian's meager income. Power gave guided tours of the site and told stories about Lincoln, including that of the infamous break-in of 1876. A publication put out a call for gifts of Lincoln materials for the "archives" and promised to "take care of any relics entrusted to them."

The Honor Guard's first public ceremony took place on April 15, 1880, the fifteenth anniversary of Lincoln's death. An English clergyman at the service, William Affleck, was struck by how emotional the people were that day—"citizens, admiring friends, and many strangers whose cheeks are also moistened with tears." Why, after fifteen years, he asked, was there still such grief? Was it because Americans had never received such a trauma as Lincoln's murder, and that therefore emotions would reverberate for years to come? Was it because Lincoln had "had love too ardent, sympathies too deep, a soul too benign, a heart too tender" ever to be forgotten, especially here? Affleck called the job of the Guard of Honor "a sacred trust," for a nation which he described as "freedom's hope and home."

<table>
</table>

1880

Lincoln's Closest Friend

During the decade and a half since the assassination, the world had heard from most of Lincoln's closest friends and associates. A few, like Robert Lincoln and his father's closest friend, Joshua Speed, remained notoriously quiet. But in 1880 Speed decided to break his public silence and speak about his relationship with Lincoln.

It had begun in 1837 when, fresh from New Salem, Lincoln had moved into the upstairs of Speed's store in Springfield and shared a bed with the younger man. It was an age when beds were scarce and men didn't mind sharing them, and before long the two were close friends. "No two men were ever more intimate," Speed said. They discussed everything from politics to poetry to town affairs to women. During their successive courtships—to Mary Todd and to Fanny Henning—they compared notes, gave each other advice, and offered badly needed moral support (though Lincoln complained that Speed could have been more helpful, earlier). They agonized together, shared their deepest joys, and

Joshua Fry Speed

often saw each other's lives more clearly than they saw their own. Following Lincoln's broken engagement with Mary in 1841, which left him almost suicidally depressed, Speed nursed his "much loved friend" back to life. Only after both married did their intense closeness begin to fade.

By the 1850s it had become clear that the two disagreed on some fundamental political questions. As Lincoln became ever more vocal on the slavery issue, Speed became less so, now living in Kentucky, having inherited a number of slaves from his father. In a letter to him in 1855, Lincoln wrote, "How can anyone who abhors the oppression of negroes, be in favor of degrading classes of white people?. . . As a nation, we began by declaring that '*all men are created equal.*' We now practically read it 'all men are created equal, *except negroes.*'"

After Lincoln was elected President, he met with Speed in Chicago and asked him if he was interested in a position in the new government. His old friend declined but over the next years became an informal adviser to the President, offering indispensable assistance in the border state of Kentucky. In a meeting with Lincoln in the White House one day he participated in a frank discussion about the President's still-secret Emancipation Proclamation. As Lincoln spoke of it privately to Speed, he brought up the subject of his breakdown in 1841—what he called his "great depression." He said one of the things that had prevented him from taking his own life at that time was a realization that he "had done nothing to make any human being remember that he had lived." And that to connect himself with something truly important for "his fellow man was what he desired to live for." And then Lincoln added, "with earnest emphasis" Speed recalled, "I believe that in this measure (meaning his proclamation) my fondest hopes will be realized."

In his 1880 lecture, later published as a book, Speed treated the public to a long series of reminiscences about his and his friend's extraordinary relationship. Less than two years later, Speed was dead at age sixty-eight, eulogized as "the bedfellow of Abraham Lincoln."

"Well, Speed, I Am Moved"
Joshua Fry Speed

1880

In his 1880 lecture Joshua Speed recalled the day Lincoln became his roommate.

It was in the spring of 1837, and on the very day that he obtained his license, that our intimate acquaintance began. He had ridden into town on a borrowed horse, with no earthly property save a pair of saddle-bags containing a few clothes. I was a merchant at Springfield, and kept a large country store, embracing dry goods, groceries, hardware, books, medicines, bed-clothes, mattresses, in fact every thing that the country needed. Lincoln came into the store with his saddle-bags on his arm. He said he wanted to buy the furniture for a single bed. The mattresses, blankets, sheets, coverlid, and pillow, according to the figures made by me, would cost seventeen dollars. He said that was perhaps cheap enough; but, small as the sum was, he was unable to pay it. But if I would credit him till Christmas, and his experiment as a lawyer was a success, he would pay then, saying, in the saddest tone: "If I fail in this I do not know that I can ever pay you." As I looked up at him I thought then, and think now, that I never saw a sadder face.

I said to him: "You seem to be so much pained at contracting so small a debt, I think I can suggest a plan by which you can avoid the debt and at the same time attain your end. I have a large room with a double bed up-stairs, which you are very welcome to share with me."

"Where is your room?" said he.

"Up-stairs," said I, pointing to a pair of winding stairs, which led from the store to my room.

He took his saddle-bags on his arm, went upstairs, set them down on the floor, and came down with the most changed countenance. Beaming with pleasure he exclaimed: "Well, Speed, I am moved!"

Mary Lincoln's Second Exile

For four years Mary Lincoln made her home in Pau, France, a health resort in the Pyrenees known for its mineral baths and high society. She had chosen France out of gratitude for its gift of the Lincoln medal, and she was delighted to finally be in a place that appreciated her. Before long, however, she was finding the French "superficial" and was keeping increasingly to herself. During these years she kept in close touch with two Americans—her financial manager, Jacob Bunn, an old friend of Lincoln's in Springfield, and her grandnephew Lewis Baker, to whom she regularly opened her heart. To Lewis she wrote of her undying hatred for her son Robert whom she described as "that wretched young man, but old in sin." She described Robert's childhood in the bitterest of terms—calling him an unhappy and controlling member of the family, insolent to her when his father was not looking, "so different from our other sons." Lincoln himself, she told Lewis, had even remarked on this to her: "always said he never knew, from whence, such a mean nature came." They had been happy to send Robert off to school in the East, she claimed, and said their household had been much more peaceful after he was gone. (Mary's letters from the 1850s and 1860s, however, contain no such resentful feelings.)

In the spring of 1878, in search of warmth and a bit of happiness, Mary took a trip to Italy, where she had spent a holiday eight years earlier. But unlike her last visit, now she could "take no interest whatever." One of the only things to excite her dur-

"My mother is somewhere in Europe," wrote Robert during this period. "[S]he has for unfortunate reasons ceased to communicate with me + I do not know her proper address." Mary Lincoln's home in France was the resort town of Pau, where she soon became alienated from the local inhabitants. "With the exception of a *very few*," she wrote, "I detest them all."

ing this period was stumbling upon a newspaper article in 1879 mentioning Robert as a possible presidential candidate. Despite her alienation from him, she found herself strangely "elated." The thought of her son in the White House, and his little children running through its halls, brought back waves of happy memories. And yet in a letter she could not help contrasting him with his father—Robert who had "so cruelly & unmercifully wronged" his mother, and her husband who had been "kind even to his stepmother."

During these years of exile Mary was consumed by a fear of poverty. She wrote often to Jacob Bunn, asking for her latest disbursements and showing a remarkable degree of knowledge about her investments. She held her husband's lifetime savings in bonds. Considering them her "sacred deposits," she was unwilling to spend any of the principal. Though she was a relatively well-to-do woman by this point, she constantly feared sudden reversals.

In December 1879 Mary fell from a rickety chair she was using as a stepladder. When it collapsed beneath her, she was thrown backward, hitting the corner of a table and seriously injuring her spinal cord. Six months later she fell again, down a flight of stairs. It was obvious she could no longer live alone. Not wanting to die among strangers, as a niece later put it, Mary made plans to return to the United States. In October she boarded the French steamer *L'Amerique* and set sail for New York City. During a storm at sea Mary was descending a staircase and during a lurch of the ship was almost thrown to her death. She was saved by the actress Sarah Bernhardt, who happened to be nearby and grabbed her. When she told Mary that she might easily have died that day, Mary wistfully replied, "It was not God's will."

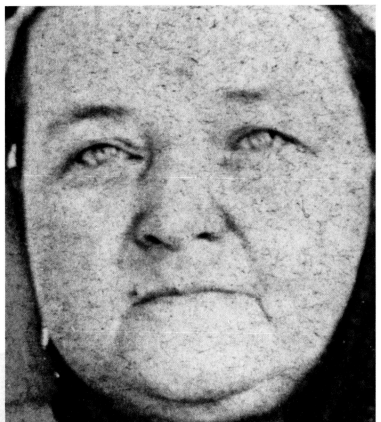

Mary Lincoln sailed home to the United States aboard the French steamer *L'Amerique*. The actress Sarah Bernhardt, who was also aboard, described her as "dressed in black, with a sad, resigned face."

May 1881

Mary, Robert, and Grandchildren

On Mary's arrival in New York City in late October, reporters described her as she came off the ship as a "white-haired, feeble," bent old lady, "almost shabbily clad" and attracting no attention from the crowds. She was whisked away to the Clarendon Hotel by her nephew Lewis Baker. There she laid plans to see the distinguished New York surgeon Dr. Lewis Sayre, who had known Mary since she was a girl in Lexington, Kentucky. Sayre was troubled by what he found. Not only was her spine damaged, but she had developed kidney problems as well. He prescribed bed rest among loved ones and recommended moving in with her sister in Springfield. He had heard the rumors that Mary was insane, but he found her anything but. "The poor woman has had trouble enough to drive many a strong man crazy," he later said, castigating those who would criticize her.

The social climate had changed during Mary's absence. The constant flurry of negative press about her had quieted in her absence, and there was a new tenor of sympathy for her in many quarters. On November 17 the *Washington Post*, once an ardent critic, urged that "a check for $10,000 be forwarded at once" to Mary Lincoln, out of funds being raised on behalf of Ulysses S. Grant. There is no one "who more deserves to be tenderly cared for by the country," the *Post* wrote.

707 BROADWAY, N. Y.

Mary Lincoln's New York doctor, Lewis Albert Sayre, was the country's leading orthopedic surgeon.

Mary moved into the Springfield home of her sister Elizabeth Edwards, where she lived for the final year of her life. Here she retreated from the world, "immersing herself in a perfectly dark room and for a light using a small candle," wrote an old friend. "No urging could induce her to go out into the fresh air."

"Considering the illustrious service of her husband the pension she receives from the Government is but a niggardly pittance. . . . In the name . . . of common self-respect—in the name of common patriotism and gratitude—let the lady suffer no more."

Mary settled in with her sister and brother-in-law, Elizabeth and Ninian Edwards, in the house where she had been married thirty-eight years earlier. In a sign that she was not entirely welcome, her brother-in-law insisted on charging her rent for her bedroom and an extra storage room. But though there were tensions between the sisters, it was a good place for Mary to be and allowed her to keep her distance from Robert in Chicago.

Robert's usefulness to the Republican Party was becoming increasingly evident. In 1880 he campaigned for a third term for Ulysses S. Grant, then cast one of Illinois's electoral votes for James A. Garfield. Rumors circulated that Garfield would offer Robert a cabinet position. He in fact did not want one. "I like my present way of life," he wrote a friend, "and think I would not like a political career." But his wife, Mary, was eager to get back to Washington, and when the offer of secretary of war came on February 28, Robert accepted. He would be James Garfield's Edwin Stanton.

In May 1881, before heading east with his family of five, Robert paid a visit to his mother—their first contact since their break five years earlier. To ease the tension, he brought along his eleven-year-old daughter, Mamie—Mary's first grandchild and namesake. Mary might have refused to see him out of principle. But she was tired of hating Robert and was genuinely proud of his new appointment. And Mamie melted her heart.

Robert Lincoln remained unsympathetic to his mother's worsening condition. "The reports you have heard about her are exaggerated very much," he wrote to her friend Sally Orne in June. "She is undoubtedly far from well and has not been out of her room for six months and at times she thinks she is very ill." It was Robert's children (below), Jack, Mamie, and Jessie, who helped lead to a reconciliation between mother and son.

Lincoln's Battlefield Angel

Clara Barton was a former schoolteacher and Patent Office worker who discovered her life's calling during the Civil War. Using a quartermaster's pass, she took a team of nurses into the field and was present at Bull Run and then Cedar Mountain—where, a week after the battle, three thousand men still lay in agony upon the ground. She became known as "the Angel of the Battlefield," kneeling by the side of wounded soldiers, receiving their dying words, binding up their wounds, and giving them hope—she called it all her "sacred work." But as the newly formed Sanitary Commission expanded its mission in 1862, she and her teams were displaced and forced to stop their activities. Undaunted, she came up with a new plan—to help locate tens of thousands of missing Union soldiers—either imprisoned men or those whose bodies had not yet been discovered or identified.

On March 11, 1865, Barton met with President Lincoln, who agreed to support her plan. Lincoln greatly admired Barton and reportedly wrote out a letter on her behalf: "To the friends of missing persons; Miss Clara Barton [has] kindly offered to search for the missing prisoners of war. Please address her at Annapolis, Maryland, giving name, regiment, and company of any missing prisoner."

The day before that meeting, Clara's brother Stephen had died and was to be buried soon in Massachusetts. She told Lincoln about her loss and how she "could not commence yet" the work of her agency. Lincoln listened to her story and then said softly, "Go bury your dead, and then care for others." "How kind he was!" Clara later recalled.

Lincoln didn't live to see Barton's new office in Maryland, where letters soon came in to her at the rate of a hundred a day. But it was his endorsement that ensured her success. "The undertaking . . . received a cordial and written sanction of our late, beloved President," she wrote that summer.

In the years ahead, Barton became friends with Susan B. Anthony and Elizabeth Cady Stanton and supported the cause of women's suffrage. But her life's passion continued to center on humanitarian aid and increasingly on the Red Cross movement, which began in Europe in 1870. She spent a decade advocating an American chapter of the organization, enlisting the support of President Garfield and his war secretary, Robert Lincoln. Meeting with Robert in March 1881, she spoke to him of her great appreciation of his father, and of his kindness to her back in 1865. Robert "was much affected and very grateful" for her words, according to Barton's nephew who accompanied her, and he offered to help her in any way he could. On March 21, 1881, Clara Barton's dream finally came true—the American Red Cross was born.

In later years Clara Barton wrote of her nursing work during the Civil War, "All night long we made compresses and slings and bound up and wet wounds when we could get water."

The Decoration Day Secret

In Springfield, Illinois, Decoration Day 1881 was an emotional occasion. The Illinois chapter of the Grand Army of the Potomac—made up of Union veterans of the Civil War—gathered at the tomb of Abraham Lincoln, now overseen by the dedicated members of the Lincoln Honor Guard. The old soldiers wanted to gaze on the marble sarcophagus of their fallen chief and recall his service to the nation.

After the near theft of Lincoln's body back in 1876, officials had worried about the safety of the tomb. In November of that year a small group of them met at midnight and removed Lincoln's casket from its sarcophagus, carrying it to an inner room at the base of the obelisk. Here it was set upon two large timbers. John C. Power, the custodian, was asked to dig a hole, but he found the work so difficult that he decided it could stay where it was—in a dusty corner behind an old barrel.

For the next three years here it remained, in secret. But following the highly publicized theft in New York of the body of millionaire entrepreneur A. T. Stewart, it was decided something more secure had to be done. In November 1879 Power buried the coffin under the monument basement. Here it would stay, officials decided, until they could plan a far more secure burial inside the catacomb.

On Decoration Day 1881 it was Power and the others of the Lincoln Honor Guard who welcomed the Grand Army of the Republic to Lincoln's tomb. In preparation they had had the catacomb lavishly decorated, and during the ceremony veterans were invited to enter and place flowers on Lincoln's sarcophagus. What none of the moist-eyed veterans suspected was that their fallen chief was in fact not inside his marble coffin but lay secretly buried below the monument.

The rear entrance to Lincoln's tomb on Decoration Day 1881

For years newspapers questioned whether Lincoln was really inside his coffin.

On Decoration Day 1881 few knew that Lincoln's sarcophagus was empty.

For three years Lincoln's casket was hidden in the back corner of a small room deep inside the monument's foundation.

Garfield's Assassination

The transition to life in Washington was not easy for Robert Lincoln. In Chicago he had forged his own highly successful career as a corporate lawyer and was an up-and-coming trustee of the Illinois Central Railroad. But in Washington he was once again in the shadow of his larger-than-life father, with rumors circulating that he had gotten the cabinet position only because of his famous name. Ulysses S. Grant had in fact strongly opposed the appointment, writing, "To give him a position which he could not sustain himself well in, would be an injustice to Robert himself." And the *Daily Constitution*, commenting on whether he was qualified for the job, revealed how little in fact was known of him. "If Mr. Lincoln has the good sense and capacity which he is credited with, he would not take a cabinet place as a tribute to his father unless he felt he had the capacity to assume all its duties."

One of Robert's first responsibilities as a member of the cabinet was to accompany President Garfield on a railroad trip to New England to attend commencement exercises at Williams College. On Saturday, July 2, he had just arrived at the railroad station at Sixth and B Streets in Washington, when a crazed gunman, Charles J. Guiteau, stepped forward and fired two bullets into Garfield's back. Robert was the first to reach the wounded President and called out to his driver to go quickly find a doctor. He himself was badly shaken. For Robert, this second presidential assassination in the country's history was like the return of a nightmare. "How many hours of sorrow have I passed in this town," he was heard to say.

Garfield lived on for eleven weeks, during which time Lincoln was often turned to by the press for public statements. When the President died in September, Robert, who would stay on in Chester Arthur's cabinet, took part in the funeral ceremonies that echoed those of his father sixteen years earlier.

As the second U.S. president to be assassinated, it was inevitable that James Garfield would be remembered alongside Abraham Lincoln. Once again the White House was draped in mourning (top right), and a grand public funeral took place that spellbound the nation (bottom right). Robert Lincoln, who had been near Garfield at the shooting, predicted that his successor would also be killed "by some crazy person or by a fanatic."

Lincoln's Sculptor Tells His Story
Leonard Volk

December 1881

Century Magazine was launched in November 1881 and from the beginning was closely associated with Abraham Lincoln. The magazine's founding editor—who died suddenly in October—was Josiah Holland, author of the first biography of Lincoln. His successor, Richard Watson Gilder, in the second issue of the magazine, published a story by the Chicago sculptor Leonard Volk, who in the spring of 1860 had made a plaster cast of Lincoln's face, then traveled to Springfield to cast his hands. Since Volk had made these objects as a guide for his own sculpting, no one had ever seen them before, and readers were astonished by the story and the photograph of the plaster face.

My studio was in the fifth story, and . . . I soon learned to distinguish his steps on the stairs, and am sure he frequently came up two, if not three, steps at a stride. . . . He sat naturally in the chair when I made the cast, and saw every move I made in a mirror opposite, as I put the plaster on without interference with his eyesight or his free breathing through the nostrils. It was about an hour before the mold was ready to be removed, and being all in one piece, with both ears perfectly taken, it clung pretty hard, as the cheek-bones were higher than the jaws at the lobe of the ear. He bent his head low and took hold of the mold, and gradually worked it off without breaking or injury; it hurt a little, as a few hairs of the tender temples pulled out with the plaster and made his eyes water. . . .

By previous appointment, I was to cast Mr. Lincoln's hands on the Sunday . . . at nine A.M. I found him ready, but he looked more grave and serious than he had appeared on the previous days. I wished him to hold something in his right hand, and he looked for a piece of pasteboard, but could find none. I told him a round stick would do as well as anything. Thereupon he went to the wood-shed, and I heard the saw go, and he soon returned to the dining-room (where I did the work), whittling off the end of a piece of broom-handle. I remarked to him that he need not whittle off the edges.

"Oh well," said he, "I thought I would like to have it nice."

When I had successfully cast the mold of the right hand, I began the left, pausing a few moments to hear Mr. Lincoln tell me about a scar on the thumb.

"You have heard that they call me a rail-splitter, and you saw them carrying rails in the procession Saturday evening; well, it is true that I did split rails, and one day, while I was sharpening a wedge on a log, the axe glanced and nearly took my thumb off, and there is the scar, you see."

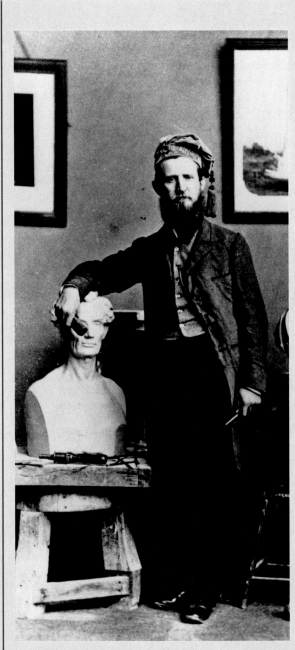

Leonard Volk in his Chicago studio

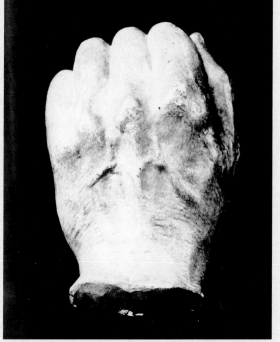

Volk made plaster casts of Lincoln's head and hands in 1860. Lincoln's hands (below) were those of a man who hewed the axe as well as the pen.

Mary's grandniece, Mary Edwards

Mary's sister Elizabeth Edwards and, below, a close-up of her house, showing where Mary lived

Mary Lincoln's End

At her sister's house in Springfield, Mary Lincoln was becoming increasingly reclusive. On her first Christmas there she shut herself in her room and refused to take part in the family festivities. An article in the *Chicago Tribune* described her as covering her shuttered windows with heavy quilts to block out sunlight and keeping her room pitch dark except for the light of a tallow candle. On the floor of her room were sixty-four large trunks, mostly filled with old clothing and swaths of material bought in Europe. Commenting that she was rarely seen in public, the paper called her a "veritable silk-worm in its self-woven cocoon." Mary was frequently visited during this period by Elizabeth's granddaughter Mary Edwards, who later described her eccentric great-aunt. The old lady wore a money belt day and night, she observed, and obsessed about her belongings. "Every day she got up and went through those trunks for hours," she recalled. Elizabeth noted caustically that though her sister complained frequently of being deathly ill, she seemed to have plenty of energy to bend over those trunks all day.

Following the death of Garfield in September, Congress awarded his widow a generous pension of $5,000 a year. Soon public voices were raised urging that Mary's pension be raised to the same level. On February 2, 1882, President Chester Arthur signed the bill that granted her an additional pension—an increase of $2,000 a year. Before long a second bill was passed and signed awarding her an additional sum of $15,000, representing the unpaid salary of her husband's second term. It was what she had been seeking for seventeen years, and it made Mary into a wealthy woman.

But she was not a healthy one. By summer, following a trip to New York City to see her doctor, Mary was back in Springfield now bedridden at Lizzie's house. In July painful boils erupted on her back and sides. Her system was shutting down. When her fingers began to swell, Mary took off her wedding ring.

Then, on the anniversary of Tad's death—July 15, 1882—Mary collapsed and fell into a coma. On the next evening, those present at the moment of death saw her face undergo a profound change, releasing all its pain and adopting a faint smile. Mary Lincoln was sixty-three years old.

A newspaper ran a story about her wedding ring. "It is of Etruscan gold and is now quite thin from wear. It is inscribed with 'A.L. to Mary, Nov. 4, 1842. Love is Eternal.' The ring will be put on and probably buried with her."

The mayor of Springfield declared the day of her funeral a holiday, and the First Presbyterian Church was filled to overflowing. In his sermon the Rev. James Reed spoke poetically about Mary and her husband, comparing them to two stately pine trees killed by the same strike of lightning.

Robert Lincoln had come west from Washington for the services. Now he led the procession out to Oak Ridge Cemetery. There, where three of her beloved sons were already buried, Mary's casket was placed alongside that of her husband.

Years earlier, speaking of her immense sorrow, Mary had written ,"Time, does not soften it, nor can I ever be reconciled to my loss, until the grave closes over the remembrance, and I am again reunited with him—the worshipped one." Now finally, after so much waiting, Mary Lincoln got her wish.

Robert Lincoln at the time of his mother's death, and, below left, Mary's Springfield funeral service

MRS. LINCOLN'S FUNERAL.

SPRINGFIELD, Ill., July 17.—The funeral of the late Mrs. Abraham Lincoln will take place on Wednesday at 10 in the morning from the First Presbyterian Church, unless otherwise ordered by Mr. Lincoln on his arrival. The body will be deposited in the vault under the Lincoln Monument with those of other members of the family. The crypt in the monument was opened to-day and prepared for the reception of the body. It was stated that Mrs. Lincoln's estate, not rekoning apparel, and personal effects, amounts to $74,000, all in United States bonds. Her wedding ring, found to-day, will be placed on her finger. It is of Etruscan gold and inscribed, " A. L. to Mary, Nov. 4, 1842. Love is eternal." The arrangements for the funeral are very elaborate, and business in the city will probably be entirely suspended during the hours of the services.

Springfield's William Jayne had known Mary Lincoln all his life, and over the years he had watched her change from a "bright, lively . . . attractive" woman, to a "fleshy + stout" matron, and finally to a bent and suffering old woman. "When I last looked upon her upturned face when she was laid out in her coffin," he later wrote, "I thought she looked . . . much as she did when I knew her so well in her girlhood days."

243

Collected Memories

By now hundreds of testimonials and eyewitness accounts of Lincoln had appeared in newspapers, magazines, published lectures, and biographies, yet no one had published a collection of reminiscences. The first person to do so was an Ohio-born Lincoln enthusiast named Osborn Oldroyd.

A captain in the Civil War, Oldroyd was with his fellow Union soldiers in Washington when he first heard the news of Lincoln's assassination. Already an avid Lincoln collector, he swore then and there that he would devote the rest of his life to searching out "everything in the land" that had to do with Lincoln. Almost nothing lay outside Oldroyd's interest. Lincoln letters, documents, books, photographs, statuary, medallions, newspaper articles, clothing, and furniture all found their way into his fast-growing treasure trove. He obtained the top hat that Lincoln wore on the night of his assassination; the wooden cradle in which Tad and Willie Lincoln were rocked; the cook stove from the Lincoln house in Springfield; and eventually the horsehair rocker in which Lincoln was shot. Encouraged by William Herndon, from whom he acquired pieces of furniture from Lincoln's law office, Oldroyd also made trips to visit with eyewitnesses, seeking out "old friends" of Lincoln's boyhood and listening to their "unvarnished stories."

On the fifteenth anniversary of Lincoln's death, Oldroyd was attending ceremonies at the Lincoln Tomb when a flash of insight came upon him. He would build a grand Memorial Hall in Springfield to house his collection and help preserve Lincoln's memory. Enthused by this goal, he redoubled his efforts to amass

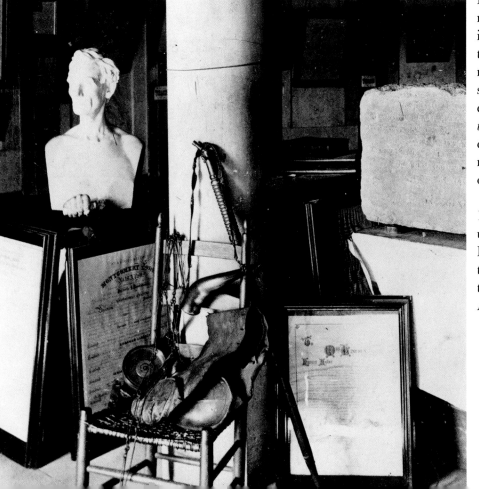

Lincolniana. To increase the size of his document collection, in 1882 he wrote letters to leading figures who had known Lincoln asking for their reminiscences. His request brought in more than two hundred written replies. That summer he published them in a 571-page book entitled *Lincoln Memorial Album of Immortelles*. The essays were of varying length and quality—some were just brief sentences of admiration. But the book set a standard that many others would follow.

In his preface, written in Springfield in July 1882, Oldroyd announced that he intended to use the profits from sales of the book to build a Lincoln Memorial Hall where he could "display to the public, free of charge, my life work in the collection of memorials and sources of Abraham Lincoln."

Oldroyd's book included an important new

In the 1880s Lincoln's tomb housed a small exhibit in its "memorial hall." It inspired Osborn Oldroyd to open a Lincoln museum in Springfield.

His Sense of Wonder
Adeline Judd

Among those Oldroyd sought out was Adeline Judd, the widow of Lincoln's old friend Norman Judd, who had helped to organize the Lincoln-Douglas debates and been instrumental in Lincoln's election to the presidency. Mrs. Judd sent in a story about a visit by Lincoln in 1856 to their lakeside house in Chicago.

Adeline and Norman Judd

Mr. Judd had invited Mr. Lincoln to spend the evening at our pleasant home on the shore of Lake Michigan. After tea, and until quite late, we sat on the broad piazza, looking out upon as lovely a scene as that which has made the Bay of Naples so celebrated. . . . Whilst we sat there the great white moon appeared on the rim of the Eastern horizon, and slowly crept above the water, throwing a perfect flood of silver light upon the dancing waves. The stars shone with the soft light of a midsummer night, and the breaking of the low waves upon the shore . . . added the charm of pleasant sound to the beauty of the night.

Mr. Lincoln, whose home was far inland from the great lakes, seemed greatly impressed with the wondrous beauty of the scene, and carried by its impressiveness away from all thought of the jars and turmoil of earth. In that mild, pleasant voice, attuned to harmony with his surroundings, as was his wont when his soul was stirred by aught that was lovely or beautiful, Mr. Lincoln began to speak of the mystery which for ages enshrouded and shut out those distant worlds above us from our own, of the poetry and beauty which was seen and felt by seers of old when they contemplated Orion and Arcturus as they wheeled, seemingly around the earth, in their nightly course; of the discoveries since the invention of the telescope, which had thrown a flood of light and knowledge on what before was incomprehensible and mysterious; of the wonderful computations of scientists who had measured the miles of seemingly endless space which separated the planets in our solar system from our central sun, and our sun from other suns. . . . He speculated on the possibilities of knowledge which an increased power of the lens would give in the years to come. . . . When the night air became too chilling to remain longer on the piazza, we went into the parlor.

"His Evident Weariness"
Jane Grey Swisshelm

Oldroyd found the once famous journalist Jane Grey Swisshelm at her home outside Pittsburgh, now in the last years of her life. In Lincoln's day she had been an outspoken antislavery activist and she had volunteered her free time as a nurse during the Civil War.

I stood for some time watching him receive his guests and getting back my own breath and circulation; not realizing the full measure of the effect his presence had on me, but fully impressed by a conviction, of his honesty. His simplicity and self-forgetfulness . . . were evident at a glance. To himself he was no greater as Commander-in-chief than he would have been as corporal or private. His aims were all his country's. . . . His evident weariness, and the patience with which he stood shaking hands, as one might pump on a sinking ship, made me angry with the senseless custom. . . . So when he took my hand I said: "May the Lord have mercy on you, poor man; for the people have none!"

He threw up his head and laughed pleasantly, and those around him joined the laugh.

"I Cheerfully Give This Tribute to His Memory"
Alexander H. Stephens

Osborne Oldroyd reached out to Southerners and well as Northerners, including the former Vice President of the Confederacy, Alexander Stephens, in the last year of his life. Stephens, who had known Lincoln ever since he was a freshman in Congress, speculated that if he had lived, he would never have permitted radical Reconstruction.

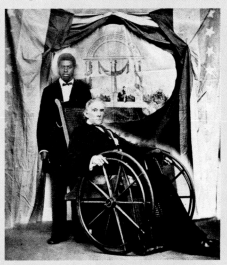

Alexander Stephens with his valet

Mr. Lincoln was careful as to his manners, awkward in his speech, but was possessed of a very strong, clear and vigorous mind. He always attracted the riveted attention of the House when he spoke; his manner of speech as well as thought was original. He had no model. He was a man of strong convictions, and was what Carlyle would have called an earnest man. He abounded in anecdotes; he illustrated everything that he was talking or speaking about by an anecdote; his anecdotes were always exceedingly apt and pointed, and socially he always kept his company in a roar of laughter. In my last interview with him at the celebrated Hampton Roads Conference in 1865, this trait of his character seemed to be as prominent and striking as ever. He was a man of strong attachments, and his nature overflowed with the milk of human kindness.

account by former congressman James S. Rollins of Missouri, revealing how Lincoln had enlisted him to help procure votes for the passage of the Thirteenth Amendment.

Lincoln considered the Emancipation Proclamation the greatest act of his presidency, but he knew that it had serious limitations. As a war measure it would probably lapse at the end of the conflict; and it had deliberately not extended freedom to the slaves of the border states. What was needed, Lincoln realized, was a constitutional amendment—what he came to call a "King's cure" for the epidemic of slavery, abolishing it permanently throughout the United States. A similar amendment had been introduced in Congress in late 1863 but had failed in the House the following year. In the 1864 elections Lincoln insisted that the amendment be a central part of his party's platform. "It is a fitting, and necessary conclusion to the final success of the Union cause," he told his renomination committee in June. Upon his victory in November he proclaimed a presidential mandate. "It is the voice of the people now, for the first time heard upon the question," he said in his annual message in December. "[I]t is the will of the majority" to pass this amendment.

But passage would not be easy in the thirty-eighth Congress, where a two-thirds majority would be needed. And so Lincoln focused his political skill into an effort to obtain the needed votes. In January he met with Democrats to try to convince them to support the amendment. In some cases he made deals, trading patronage for votes.

On January 31 the resolution came to a vote. When the Speaker of the House Schuyler Colfax announced the results, the resolution had passed by just three votes, leading to wild cheers in the halls. The *New York Times* declared it "the most important step ever taken by Congress." When the resolution reached Lincoln's desk on February 1, 1865, he did one more thing to show his complete identification with it. Though the Supreme Court had ruled that presidential signatures were unnecessary on such resolutions, Lincoln signed the document anyway. That evening, outside the White House, he addressed a crowd of well-wishers and said that his own state of Illinois had that day ratified the amendment, the first state to do so, which made him very proud. He said he hoped that all "would witness that he had never shrunk from doing all that he could to eradicate Slavery by issuing an emancipation proclamation." He had come to realize that it was not strong enough medicine. "But this amendment is a . . . cure for all the evils," he said. "It winds up the whole thing." He then congratulated all present, including himself, as well as "the country, and the whole world upon this great moral victory."

On January 31, 1865, Congress passed the Thirteenth Amendment ending slavery. According to Henry Highland Garnet, the upper galleries of the House of Representatives were packed with white and black visitors—"a salt and pepper mixture," he enthusiastically reported. Abolitionist William Lloyd Garrison told a Boston audience, "And to whom is the country more immediately indebted? . . . [T]o the humble rail splitter of Illinois—to the Presidential chainbreaker for millions of the oppressed—to Abraham Lincoln!"

An Amendment "to Clinch the Whole Subject"
James S. Rollins

1882

Perhaps Oldroyd's most important account came from the former Missouri congressman James S. Rollins. Though he had been one of the largest slaveholders in Missouri, he had agreed to support Lincoln in his effort to procure the Thirteenth Amendment and to lobby other slaveholding congressmen for their votes. And his account gave detailed witness to Lincoln's determination to end slavery forever.

James S. Rollins

On February 5, just days after signing the Thirteenth Amendment resolution, a triumphant Lincoln was photographed by Alexander Gardner.

Mr. Lincoln often spoke to me about the Emancipation Proclamation. He had no great faith in its efficacy. I heard him say a number of times it only affected those who were free, i.e., those behind the Federal lines, and of course it would not reach the vast number of slaves who remained within the lines of the Southern army. This made him exceedingly anxious in reference to the passage of the 13th amendment to the Constitution of the United States, abolishing African Slavery in our country. . . . The President had several times in my presence expressed his deep anxiety in favor of the passage of this great measure. He and others had repeatedly counted votes in order to ascertain as far as they could the strength of the measure upon a second trial in the House. He was doubtful about its passage, and some ten days or two weeks before it came up for consideration in the House, I received a note from him, written in pencil on a card, while sitting at my desk in the House, stating he wished to see me, and asking that I call on him at the White House. I responded that I would be there the next morning at nine o'clock. I was prompt in calling upon him, and found him alone in his office. He received me in the most cordial manner and said in his usual familiar way: "Rollins, I have been wanting to talk to you for some time about the 13th amendment proposed to the Constitution of the United States, which will have to be voted on now before a great while." I said: "Well, I am here and ready to talk upon that subject." He said . . . "It is going to be very close; a few votes one way or the other will decide it." . . . He said: "I would like you to talk to all the Border State men whom you can approach properly, and tell them of my anxiety to have the measure pass; and let me know the prospect of the Border State vote," which I promised to do. He again said: "The passage of this amendment will clinch the whole subject; it will bring the war, I have no doubt, rapidly to a close." . . . Several days after the passage of this amendment through Congress, I called upon President Lincoln, and I never saw him evince greater joy at the news of any victory won upon the field of battle, than he did over the passage of this amendment.

The Last Photograph
Alexander Starbuck

October 1882

In October 1882 Alexander Starbuck sent in to the Century *this story about how his friend, the photographer H. F. Warren, had captured the last photograph of Lincoln taken in life. Though Starbuck didn't know it, in fact Warren had taken two.*

Alexander Starbuck

About the last of February, 1865, Mr. H. F. Warren, a photographer of Waltham, Mass., left home, intending, if practicable, to visit the army in front of Richmond and Petersburg. Arriving in Washington on the morning of the 4th of March, and finding it necessary to procure passes to carry out the end he had in view, he concluded to remain there until the inauguration ceremonies were over, and, having carried with him all the apparatus necessary for taking negatives, he decided to try to secure a sitting from the President. At that time rumors of plots and dangers had caused the friends of President Lincoln to urge upon him the necessity of guard, and, as he had finally permitted the presence of such a body, an audience with him was somewhat difficult. On the afternoon of the 6th of March, Mr. Warren sought a presentation to Mr. Lincoln, but found, after consulting with the guard, that an interview could be had on that day in only a somewhat irregular manner. After some conversation with the officer in charge, who became convinced of his loyalty, Mr. Warren was admitted within the lines, and, at the same time, was given to understand that the surest way to obtain an audience with the President was through the intercession of his little son "Tad." The latter was a great pet with the soldiers, and was constantly at their barracks, and soon made his appearance, mounted upon his pony. He and the pony were soon placed in position and photographed, after which Mr. Warren asked "Tad" to tell his father that a man had come all the way from Boston, and was particularly anxious to see him and obtain a sitting from him. "Tad" went to see his father, and word was soon returned that Mr. Lincoln would comply. In the mean time Mr. Warren had improvised a kind of studio upon the south balcony of the White House. Mr. Lincoln soon came out, and, saying but a very few words, took his seat as indicated. After a single negative was taken, he inquired, "Is that all, sir?" Unwilling to detain him longer than was absolutely necessary, Mr. Warren replied, "Yes, sir," and the President immediately withdrew. At the time he appeared upon the balcony the wind was blowing freshly, as his disarranged hair indicates, and, as sunset was rapidly approaching, it was difficult to obtain a sharp picture. Six weeks later President Lincoln was dead, and it is doubtless true that this is the last photograph ever made of him.

Tad Lincoln on his horse Little Jeff

Lincoln was on the South Porch of the White House (shown below) when he posed for what would be his final photograph.

H. F. WARREN, PHO:,   WALTHAM, MASS.

PRESIDENT LINCOLN.   M-93

Pho. on the Balcony at the White House, March 6, 1865.

The last photograph of Lincoln in life

Alexander Gardner's best remembered portrait became known as the "cracked" Lincoln. When the large glass negative broke across the top, Gardner pieced it together to make a single Imperial print, then discarded the glass.

Lincoln's Other Photographer

In December 1882 came news that Alexander Gardner had died in Washington, D.C., at the age of sixty-one. Except for Mathew Brady, no photographer was more associated with Abraham Lincoln.

Born in Scotland, Gardner had worked as a newspaper publisher before coming to America in the 1850s and finding a job with Mathew Brady in New York City. In 1858 Brady sent him to Washington to oversee his prestigious gallery there. During the Civil War he served as an official photographer to the Army of the Potomac, and his pictures of battlefield dead established him as one of the foremost chroniclers of the Civil War. In 1862 he photographed Lincoln at Antietam when he met with General George McClellan in the field.

Late that same year Gardner resigned from Brady's employ and six months later opened his own studio in Washington. Here he would take numerous new portraits of President Lincoln, including a series in February 1865 that would go down in history. Among these was a large Imperial negative that was damaged during processing, broken in two across the top of Lincoln's head. Gardner pieced the glass together and made a single print of it, then discarded the negative. Gardner also photographed the Second Inaugural on March 4, taking a series of eight pictures showing Lincoln seated and then reading his historic address.

That same year Gardner published his *Photographic Sketch Book of the War*, which included one hundred images of battlefields, camps, and war scenes. "Verbal representations of such places . . . may or may not have the merit of accuracy," he wrote; "but photographic presentations of them will be accepted by posterity with an undoubting faith."

Gardner went on to become an important photographer of the West, taking extraordinary portraits of Sioux and Cheyenne Indians. At his death he was eulogized as "one of photography's staunchest friends" but was given no notice for his portraiture of Abraham Lincoln. Although his former employer Mathew Brady overshadowed him, Gardner had taken more photographs of Lincoln than anyone else. His thirty-seven portraits, made over a period of four years, represent almost a third of those ever taken of Lincoln.

After leaving the employ of Mathew B. Brady, Gardner opened his own Washington studio in May 1863. Lincoln was first photographed there that summer.

"The Best That I Have Yet Seen"
Abraham Lincoln

On Sunday, August 9, 1863, Lincoln walked over to the new studio of Alexander Gardner for the first time. John Hay, who accompanied him, described the President that day as being "in very good spirits." In all, seven exposures were taken, and not long afterward Gardner sent prints to the White House for the President to see. When Lincoln thanked him by letter, he offered high praise for one of the portraits in particular.

Executive Mansion,
Washington, August 18, 1863.

My Dear Sir

Allow me to return my sincere thanks for the cards and pictures which you have kindly sent me. I think they are generally very successful. The imperial photograph in which the head leans upon the hand I regard as the best that I have yet seen.

I am very truly
Your Obt Servt
A. Lincoln

The Gardner photograph that Lincoln liked best

"And Ain't I a Woman?"

Sojourner Truth—born Isabella Baumfree around 1799—burst onto the national scene in 1850 with the publication of her autobiography, *The Narrative of Sojourner Truth*. Suddenly this fiery former slave who wore Quaker dress and turban seemed to be everywhere. To a feminist convention that tried to prevent her from speaking, she uttered her soon famous words, "And ain't I a woman?" A sought-after speaker at anti-slavery meetings, she combined evangelical fervor and moral passion with a total absence of timidity. Once, accused of being a man, she publicly bared her breasts. At a Boston meeting she chastised Frederick Douglass, urging him to trust in God instead of in human revolution. (She "seemed to feel it her duty to trip me up," said

Claiming to be 107, Sojourner Truth was hailed as the oldest living orator in America. (In fact she was eighty-four when she died.) Frederick Douglass called her a "strange compound of wit and wisdom, of wild enthusiasm, and flint-like common sense."

Douglass.) She once arrived unannounced at the home of Harriet Beecher Stowe and sat waiting downstairs until the famous author would see her. (Stowe was so impressed she wrote a long article for *The Atlantic Monthly* that propelled the aging orator even more into the national consciousness.) And in 1864, deeply impressed by Abraham Lincoln, Sojourner traveled from Michigan to Washington, D.C., to introduce herself to the President. Unable to gain entrance, she got help from fellow activist Lucy Colman, who worked through inside channels to arrange for an introduction. It took place on October 29, 1864. "Upon entering his reception room we found about a dozen persons in waiting," narrated Sojourner, who remained illiterate all her life. "The President was seated at his desk. . . . He then arose, gave me his hand, made a bow, and said 'I am pleased to see you.'" She congratulated Lincoln on his Emancipation Proclamation and called him "the best president who has ever taken the seat." Lincoln replied that George Washington and others would have done just as he had if they had lived in this time period. And then he added, "If the people over the river (pointing across the Potomac) had behaved themselves, I could not have done what I have." Lincoln showed his visitor a Bible that had been presented to him by the "colored people of Baltimore." And then he signed a card for her autograph book, writing "For Aunty Sojourner Truth." Years later Lucy Colman criticized Lincoln for calling her friend Aunty, "as he would his washerwoman." But in Sojourner's account, dictated just weeks after the visit, there was nothing but elation. "I never was treated by any one with more kindness and cordiality," she said, "than was shown me by that great and good man, Abraham Lincoln." The story of their meeting added to Sojourner Truth's mythic stature and to Lincoln's reputation as sympathetic to black people. And when she died in 1883, she was remembered as Lincoln's friend.

A painting of Sojourner Truth with Abraham Lincoln was made after her death by Michigan artist Franklin C. Courter. Her image was based on a photograph from the 1860s that she once sold to help support herself. To the right is the card Lincoln signed for Truth's autograph book.

For Aunty
Sojourner Truth

A. Lincoln

Oct. 29. 1864

Other Victims of Booth's Bullet

It was said at the funeral of Mary Lincoln that there were two victims of John Wilkes Booth's bullet—Abraham Lincoln, who had died right away, and Mary, who lingered on for seventeen long years. Something similar can be said for the two other persons who shared Lincoln's box at Ford's Theatre that night—thirty-one-year-old Clara Harris and twenty-eight-year-old Henry Rathbone.

Actually the couple was there as a last resort. The Lincolns had invited more than a dozen other people, all of whom for various reasons had declined. Finally they got an acceptance from the daughter of New York senator Ira Harris and from her stepbrother and fiancé, Major Rathbone. The couple was seated on a sofa just eight feet away from President Lincoln when they heard the explosion of Booth's pistol. "I instantly sprang toward him and seized him," Rathbone later testified. "He wrested himself from my grasp, and made a violent thrust at my breast with a large knife."

On the night of Lincoln's assassination Major Henry R. Rathbone was sitting beside his stepsister and fiancée Clara Harris in the presidential box at Ford's Theatre. The tragedy that night led to their undoing.

Raising his left arm to try to block the blow, Rathbone was cut deeply between the shoulder and the elbow. After Booth's escape over the balcony, not long afterward Henry assisted Mary Lincoln in her exit from the theater, with Clara Harris following behind. By now he was staggering. "The wound which I had received had been bleeding very profusely," he recalled, "and on reaching the house, feeling very faint from the loss of blood, I seated myself in the hall and, soon after fainted away."

Clara was in a state of shock, her dress covered in her fiancé's blood. At the Petersen House she bound his wound and sent him home in a carriage. She remained for the rest of the night with Mary Lincoln trying to comfort the distraught First Lady. "Poor Mrs. Lincoln all through that dreadful night would look at me with horror and scream Oh! My husband's blood, my dear husband's blood."

Clara and Henry were married in 1867, but it turned out to be a deeply troubled union. Unhinged by the events of the assassination, he suffered from attacks of anxiety, debilitating headaches, and jealous rages. He became furious if his wife even spoke to another man. His temperament grew worse after he was appointed consul to Hamburg, Germany, where he brought his family in 1882. On Christmas Eve 1883, he became convinced that his wife planned to abandon him. In a fit of rage he turned on her and the children. Pulling out a knife, he stabbed her in the chest, and then shot her repeatedly. His wife's sister, Louise, who was visiting, escaped with the three children before Rathbone could harm them. He then turned his gun on himself. Though he survived, he was committed to a German asylum, where he lived out the remainder of his days. "I don't think he ever recovered from the shock of his night in President Lincoln's box," observed a friend, Colonel James Berret. "The scene always haunted his mind."

After murdering his wife, Henry Rathbone spent the rest of his life in an asylum.

1883

The Lincoln House

In 1883, following his successful Lincoln publication, Osborn Oldroyd decided to make Springfield his home and was looking for a place to build his Memorial Hall. Word reached him that the old Lincoln home on Eighth and Jackson Streets might be available for rent.

The Lincolns had bought the house in 1844 from the Episcopal minister who married them, Charles Dresser. Originally a simple cottage, they had added a second story in the 1850s so that each of their boys could have his own bedroom. Here Lincoln lived the happiest days of his life, and here, in the downstairs dining room, he received official word of his nomination to the presidency.

Prior to leaving for Washington in 1861, they had arranged to rent the house, Lincoln himself sprucing it up, painting walls, and hanging wallpaper. It was the only home they had ever owned, and he was not sure if he would ever see it again.

In the years since, the house had passed through a series of tenants, some of them (in the words of a later custodian) "unscrupulous in caring for the premises." The building had been used as a dentist's office and as a boarding-house and for periods had sat unoccupied. In 1870 George Harlow, the assistant secretary of state for Illinois, lived there with his wife and young children. During his residency, a group of reformers attending a women's rights convention decided to visit the home. Unable to find their way, they asked an old black man pushing a wheelbarrow if he knew which was the Lincoln house. Beaming brightly he said he'd "know that" even if he knew "nothing else." The women found the house and rang the bell, and a young black servant answered and bid them enter. "I like to show people through his house," she told them, speaking of "strong men" who came here "and wept." One recent visitor, she said, was a bishop of the African Methodist Episcopal Church, who put his hand over his heart and said, "I never come here but what I feel a rising here." After their tour, when the women turned to depart, "a sudden awe and hush fell over our spirits, as if we were overshadowed by greatness." That was the effect of the house upon visitors—Lincoln's spirit seemed to inhere to its very walls.

But nine years later, when President Hayes visited the home, he found it "neglected" and proclaimed that it "may as well be taken down as left so." It was soon afterward that Osborn Oldroyd approached the house's new owner, Robert Lincoln, whose mother had just died, and obtained a lease to rent the home. He and his wife, a Springfield native, moved into the upstairs rooms and cleared out the ground floor to serve as a Lincoln museum. Here Oldroyd would display his large and growing collection of Lincolniana.

RELICS OF LINCOLN.

Priceless Treasures in the Springfield Homestead.

ALL OF THEM AUTHENTIC.

Mr. Oldroyd's Collection and How It Was Gathered.

HIS WORK A LABOR OF LOVE.

Captain Osborn Oldroyd contacted Robert Lincoln's agent, Clinton Conkling, and secured rental of the most famous house in Springfield for twenty-five dollars a month. He then turned it into a museum to display his Lincoln relics.

Copyrighted by O. H. Oldroyd, 1885.

Oldroyd converted Lincoln's parlors into public exhibition spaces, filling them with artifacts, photographs, flags, pieces of furniture, and books. Robert Lincoln was furious when he heard about the commercialization of his family home, and that a photograph of John Wilkes Booth was said to be displayed on the mantelpiece. Below, Oldroyd poses outside the house he renamed the Lincoln Homestead.

A Recollection of His Father
Robert Todd Lincoln

January 5, 1885

In January 1885, in his last months as head of the War Department, Robert Lincoln broke a long silence about his father and wrote to John G. Nicolay, who was deep at work on his Lincoln research and writing.

In July 1863, while I was in Washington during the vacation of Harvard College, and after the battle of Gettysburgh, I went into my father's office room at the time in the afternoon at which he was accustomed to leave his office to go to the Soldiers Home, and found him in [much] distress, his head leaning upon the desk in front of him, and when he raised his head there were evidences of tears upon his face. Upon my asking the cause of his distress he told me that he had just received the information that Gen. Lee had succeeded in escaping across the Potomac river at Williamsport without serious molestation by Gen. Meade's army. He then told me that after the battle of Gettysburg and after Lee reached the Potomac River and after our army had closed in upon him at that point, he felt sure that the final blow could be struck, and he summoned Gen. Haupt, in whom he had great confidence as a bridge builder, and asked him how long in view of the materials which might be supposed to be available under Lee, would it take him to devise the means and get his army across the river. That Gen. Haupt after reflection replied that if he were Gen. Lee's chief engineer, he could devise the means and put him across the river with the materials at hand within twenty four hours, and he had no doubt that Gen. Lee had just as good engineers for that purpose as he was. My father then said that he at once sent an order to Gen. Meade . . . directing him to attack Lee's army with all his force immediately, and that if he was successful in the attack he might destroy the order, but if he was unsuccessful he might preserve it for his vindication. My father then told me that instead of attacking upon the receipt of the order, a council of war had been held, as he understood, with the result that no attack was made, and Lee got across the river without serious molestation.

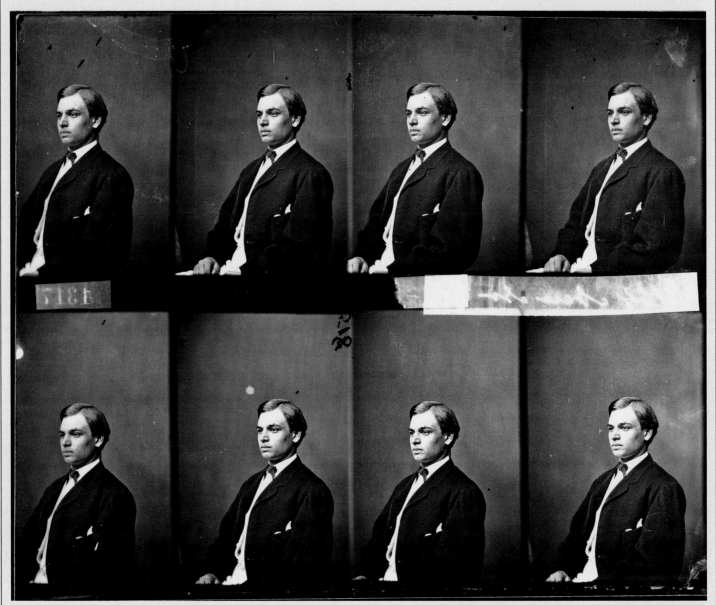

An eight-lens camera captured Robert at the time he was heading off to Harvard.

"Solely Upon His Own Merits"

Robert Lincoln's life was burdened by constant comparisons with his famous father. On one hand he was immensely proud of his heritage and carried a sense of responsibility for his memory as a glorious burden. On the other hand he wanted to avoid even the slightest perception that he was willing to profit by his association with his father. Early on he made a policy never to speak at Lincoln events. Writing to Schuyler Colfax, he explained he "always declined invitations to lecture," especially when he felt he had been asked "for no known merits of my own." This intense need to become his own person was a driving dynamic all of Robert's life. The problem was, it was difficult to sort out his own achievements, obtained without the influence of his name.

As secretary of war Robert worked hard to make his mark, and over the course of his term he became widely respected. In 1883 he briefly considered running for senator from Illinois, to take the seat being vacated by David Davis. And by that fall he was being talked about as a potential candidate for president. Possessing a "force of character" and "respectable talents," he was seen as a potential unifier of a badly divided Republican Party. But then came the words he must have hated to read—his greatest qualification was his "mighty name." Robert's hometown newspaper, the *Chicago Tribune*, didn't see him as presidential timber. It called him a "negative" man who lacked the personal qualities necessary for the presidency. In Illinois he was known to be standoffish and timid, unable to sway a jury or give a rousing political speech. The people's fondness for him, the paper insisted, was due to their love for his father and not for him or his achievements.

In the summer of 1883 Robert accompanied Chester Arthur on a fishing and hunting expedition out West, visiting a high spot in the Rockies recently named the Robert Lincoln Pass. That fall he announced his support for Arthur in the coming election. The following year Grover Cleveland became the first Democrat since James Buchanan to win the presidency, ending Robert's period of influence.

Secretly he was glad it was all about to be over. By nature reclusive, he hated politics and yearned to return to private life. When he left the War Department, this man of few words said he was "satisfied to have got out of it without more grief." And then, in what must have been most gratifying to him, the *Chicago Tribune* finally recognized his accomplishments. "Secretary Lincoln undoubtedly received his appointment through his family position," the paper wrote, "but the appointment has proven one of the best that could have been made. Mr. Lincoln stands today solely upon his own merits."

Robert Lincoln, as secretary of war

Robert sits (second from right) next to President Chester Arthur in a group portrait taken in Yellowstone Park in 1883.

259

Isaac Newton Arnold

Isaac Newton Arnold

When he was once speaking of Isaac Newton Arnold, Abraham Lincoln said he "loved him as a brother" and "revered him as one of the greatest and best of men." A Republican congressman from Illinois during Lincoln's presidency, Arnold was a former schoolteacher and attorney, and one of the most idealistic of Lincoln's friends. A committed foe of slavery, he stood by Lincoln during the dismal days of 1864 when, as Lincoln wrote in a memorandum to himself, he did not expect to be reelected. Republican A. K. McClure recalled Lincoln saying that he had lost confidence in everyone in Congress except for Isaac Arnold.

In 1866, after resigning in protest from Andrew Johnson's government, Arnold returned to the practice of law. He served as Mary Lincoln's non-too-helpful counsel during her insanity trial, then came to regret his role in the affair and stood by Mary when others turned on her. His first book, *Lincoln and the Overthrow of Slavery*, was followed by numerous others, and he became known for his powerful public speaking. In May 1881, at the age of sixty-five, Arnold traveled to London to deliver an address on Abraham Lincoln before the Royal Historical Society. It was an important moment in the internationalization of Lincoln and showed how his reputation was continuing to expand overseas.

Arnold returned home that summer to work on a new Lincoln biography, and like most others he reached out to William Herndon. Herndon agreed to answer his many questions, and in the fall of 1882 they began a rich exchange of letters. "I do not think Mr. Lincoln was fond of horses—dogs—cats—rats—or any other such animal, unless they could be of service to him," Herndon wrote. "I do not think that he was very fond of men, unless he could utilize them somehow & for some purpose." In reply Arnold wrote, "I rather agree with You—about Lincoln's affection for men—if you mean personal attachments. He had warm friends though."

During this period Arnold traveled to Herndon's farm outside Springfield and was the first person in years to lay eyes on his vast oral history collection, which had been stored in boxes for many years now. Herndon generously allowed him to make copies of Lincoln writings and shared his wide-ranging knowledge freely.

Arnold also plumbed his own rich memory, and over the course of the next year his book slowly took shape. He finished it in April 1884, just before descending into a fatal illness. In an introduction, written after Arnold's death on the twenty-fourth, Lincoln friend Elihu Washburne praised the author, saying that "few had known Mr. Lincoln better than had Mr. Arnold, and no man was more familiar with his life, or had studied more profoundly his personal and political character."

The book was hailed as the best biography of Lincoln ever written. "Twenty years have passed since the strong and kindly giant . . . fell by the hand of a madman," wrote the *Chicago Tribune*, "and not until now have an American people possessed a fitting record of a life which in all essentials touched the high-water mark of virtuous human endeavor."

In this passage from the closing pages of Arnold's biography he discussed how much Lincoln aged over the course of his presidency.

[H]is greatest relief was when he was visited by his old Illinois friends, and for a while, by anecdotes and reminiscences of the past, his mind was beguiled from the constant strain upon it. These old friends were sometimes shocked with the change in his appearance. They had known him at his home, and at the courts in Illinois, with a frame of iron and nerves of steel; as a man who hardly knew what illness was, ever genial and sparkling with frolic and fun, nearly always cheery and bright. Now, as the months of the war went slowly on, they saw the wrinkles on his face and forehead deepen into furrows, the laugh of old days was less frequent, and it did not seem to come from the heart. Anxiety, responsibility, care, thought, disasters, defeats, the injustice of friends, wore upon his giant frame, and his nerves of steel became at times irritable. He said one day, with a pathos which language cannot describe: "I feel as though I shall never be glad any more."

Abraham Lincoln as Arnold remembered him

"Every Dead-Beat" Claims to Have Known "Lincoln's Inmost Secrets"

By the mid-1880s, the outflow of Lincoln reminiscences had become a torrent. Many contained firsthand accounts that were valuable additions to the public record. But the further and further removed their authors were from the events they narrated, the more untrustworthy became their recollections. On top of this people increasingly tended to exaggerate their own importance to the Lincoln story, leading John Hay to exclaim in the 1880s, "Every dead-beat politician in this country is coming forward to protest that he was the depository of Lincoln's inmost secrets." And some of the reminiscences were almost certainly fabrications. Confederate General George Pickett's wife, LaSalle, claimed that Lincoln had come to her door to comfort her late in the war. Ben Butler said that in 1865 Lincoln agreed with his suggestion to ship black soldiers out of the country after the war to prevent them from arming themselves and turning against white Americans. Most notorious of all was the 1885 account of Charles P. T. Chiniquy, a former Roman Catholic priest who claimed to have met with Lincoln three times in the White House. According to this virulently anti-Catholic writer, Lincoln had privately agreed with him in 1861 that attempts on his life had been orchestrated by Catholics, and that the Civil War itself was a Roman Catholic plot.

Gurney & Son, 5 Fifth Ave, N. Y.

Though John Hay was quick to criticize self-serving reminiscences, he realized the importance of primary sources and eyewitness accounts. "Real history is not to be found in books," he later wrote, "but in the personal anecdotes and private letters of those who make history."

The former Roman Catholic priest Charles P. T. Chiniquy had been represented by Lincoln in a slander case in the 1850s. In his 1885 autobiography he told of an improbable visit to the White House and put virulently anti-Catholic words into the President's mouth.

At the end of August [1861], having known from a Roman Catholic priest, whom, by the mercy of God, I had persuaded to leave the errors of Popery, that there was a plot among them to assassinate the President, I thought it was my duty to go and tell him what I knew. . . . Knowing that I was among those who were waiting in the antechamber, he sent immediately for me, and received me with greater cordiality and marks of kindness than I could expect. . . . I was exceedingly moved, my voice was as choked, and I could hardly retain my tears. But the President was perfectly calm. When I had finished speaking, he . . . said: ". . . I will be for ever grateful for the warning words you have addressed to me about the dangers ahead of my life, from Rome. I know that they are not imaginary dangers. If I were fighting against a Protestant South, as a nation, there would be no danger of assassination. . . . Unfortunately, I feel more and more, every day, that it is not against the Americans of the South, alone, I am fighting, it is more against the Pope of Rome, his perfidious Jesuits and their blind and blood-thirsty slaves, than against the real American Protestants, that we have to defend ourselves, Here is the real danger of our position. So long as they will hope to conquer the North, they will spare me; but the day we will rout their armies (and that day will surely come, with the help of God), take their cities, and force them to submit; then, it is my impression that the Jesuits, who are the principal rulers of the South, will do what they have almost invariably done in the past. The dagger, or the pistol of one of their adepts, will do what the strong hands of the warriors could not achieve."

Lincoln's General

In the spring of 1884, Ulysses S. Grant threw himself into a vast new project—the writing of his highly anticipated memoirs. He had long determined not to write such a book—in fact never to write "anything for publication." But a serious financial reversal had nearly wiped out his savings and forced him to come up with a way to make money. He started by providing articles for *Century Magazine* and soon discovered that he enjoyed writing and that people responded to it. Ensconcing himself inside his home in New York City, he began to relive the most important days of his life. He worked at a large table on the second floor of his townhouse, writing all morning and afternoon, with his son Fred doing copy work and fact-checking, and an assistant, Civil War authority Adam Badeau, helping with historical questions.

He wrote of his boyhood and early days in the army, and of his struggles and lack of direction in his thirties. How in 1861 he was working in his family's Illinois leather business, unhappy and lacking a sense of direction, when a telegram arrived announcing President Lincoln's call for volunteers. Instantly Grant knew what he would do. "I am going to Springfield as soon as I can get there," he said, "and report to headquarters for duty." Everything changed for him after this moment of decision, and within a few years Grant became Lincoln's indispensable man.

The bulk of his book relived the Civil War years—battle by battle, memory by painful memory. Strangely he wrote nothing about his presidency, though he had been the first president to complete two terms since Andrew Jackson. But though Grant himself was impeccably honest, his presidency had been riddled with corruption. Over the years Grant had gained the reputation of being uncommunicative—"Grant the Silent," people had called him. It was not even known if he was capable of writing a book. And yet apart from Lincoln, and from Robert E. Lee, he

During the war, when Winslow Homer worked as a sketch artist for *Harper's Weekly*, he made this charcoal drawing of Lincoln and Grant. The little boy holding Lincoln's hand is Tad.

General Grant in 1862 after his promotion to major general

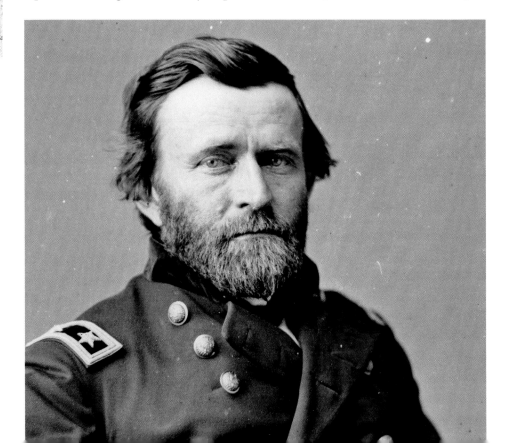

had been the key figure of the Civil War, and no one could take that away from him.

In the midst of his writing, in the fall of 1884, Grant was diagnosed with throat cancer. Knowing that he did not have long to live, he redoubled his efforts, working at an almost fevered pitch. Grant wrote without a contract, but that winter he finally sold his book to the new publishing company of Samuel Clemens. Mark Twain planned to sell the book door to door, with the hope of moving 300,000 boxed sets. By now Grant had finished volume one of the series and had begun work on the second. But in February his throat pain, which had grown steadily worse, became "very serious." In March he was near death and asked Badeau to be prepared to finish the book without him. But then—following a fit of coughing and spitting blood—he rallied. When rumors circulated that it was Badeau who was doing the actual writing (an idea that Badeau did nothing to squelch), Grant terminated their relationship and vowed to finish the book alone.

In the late spring he removed to his summer house in Saratoga Springs, taking his large and attentive family with him. Not expecting ever to return home, he put his affairs in order. By now his throat was so bad he could not speak, and he scrawled out his writing using a thick pencil so that Fred could transcribe it. By July the book was finished, and so was he. He died on the morning of the twenty-third.

In death all his earlier popularity flooded back, and once again, as in the 1860s, Grant was America's greatest hero. "He fought as if fate were behind him," wrote one eulogist—"as though he were merely the projectile of destiny. He was irresistible because he believed in his irresistibility." That December the *Memoirs* were published to great fanfare. Julia Grant was sent a check for $200,000 —the largest royalty ever paid in the United States to that time.

Gravely ill in the summer of 1885, Ulysses S. Grant sat on his porch at Mount McGregor near the Adirondacks. Determined to leave his wife financially secure, he worked furiously on his manuscript until his death in late July. Toward the end of his memoir he proclaimed: "I feel we are on the eve of a new era, where there is to be great harmony between Federal and Confederate. I cannot stay to be a living witness to the correctness of this prophecy; but I feel it within me that this is to be so."

Memories of Lincoln
Ulysses S. Grant

1865

Grant's 1885 book contained these remembrances of Abraham Lincoln.

With Lincoln at Hampton Roads
February 2, 1865

[A]bout the 2d of February, I received a dispatch from Washington, directing me to send the commissioners to Hampton Roads to meet the President. . . . He spoke of his having met the commissioners, and said he had told them that there would be no use in entering into any negotiations unless they would recognize, first: that the Union as a whole must be forever preserved, and second: that slavery must be abolished. If they were willing to concede these two points, then he was ready to enter into negotiations and was almost willing to hand them a blank sheet of paper with his signature attached for them to fill in the terms upon which they were willing to live with us in the Union and be one people. He always showed a generous and kindly spirit toward the Southern people, and I never heard him abuse an enemy. Some of the cruel things said about President Lincoln, particularly in the North, used to pierce him to the heart; but never in my presence did he evince a revengeful disposition—and I saw a great deal of him at City Point, for he seemed glad to get away from the cares and anxieties of the capital.

After the Fall of Petersburg
April 2, 1865

The . . . morning after the capture of Petersburg, I telegraphed Mr. Lincoln asking him to ride out there and see me, while I would await his arrival. . . . [T]here was not a soul to be seen, not even an animal in the streets. . . . About the first thing that Mr. Lincoln said to me, after warm congratulations for the victory, and thanks both to myself and to the army which had accomplished it, was: "Do you know, general, that I have had a sort of a sneaking idea for some days that you intended to do something like this."

Comparing Lincoln and Stanton
Spring 1865

It may not be out of place to again allude to President Lincoln and the Secretary of War, Mr. Stanton, who were the great conspicuous figures in the executive branch of the government. . . . They were the very opposite of each other in almost every particular, except that each possessed great ability. Mr. Lincoln gained influence over men by making them feel that it was a pleasure to serve him. He preferred yielding his own wish to gratify others, rather than to insist upon having his own way. It distressed him to disappoint others. In matters of public duty, however, he had what he wished, but in the least offensive way. Mr. Stanton never questioned his own authority to command, unless resisted. He cared nothing for the feeling of others. . . . It was generally supposed that these two officials formed the complement of each other. The Secretary was required to prevent the President's being imposed upon. The President was required in the more responsible place of seeing that injustice was not done to others. . . . It is not a correct view, however, in my estimation. Mr. Lincoln did not require a guardian to aid him in the fulfilment of a public trust.

Hearing of Lincoln's Murder
April 14, 1865

Mrs. Grant was with me in Washington at the time, and we were invited by President and Mrs. Lincoln to accompany them to the theatre on the evening of that day. I replied to the President's verbal invitation to the

Grant's coachman, Albert Hawkins, drove the hearse in the funeral procession.

effect, that if we were in the city we would take great pleasure in accompanying them; but that I was very anxious to get away and visit my children, and if I could get through my work during the day I should do so. I did get through and started by the evening train on the 14th, sending Mr. Lincoln word, of course, that I would not be at the theatre.

At that time the railroad to New York entered Philadelphia on Broad Street; passengers were conveyed in ambulances to the Delaware River, and then ferried to Camden, at which point they took the cars again. When I reached the ferry, on the east side of the City of Philadelphia, I found people awaiting my arrival there; and also dispatches informing me of the assassination of the President and Mr. Seward, and of the probable assassination of the Vice President, Mr. Johnson, and requesting my immediate return.

It would be impossible for me to describe the feeling that overcame me at the news of these assassinations, more especially the assassination of the President. I knew his goodness of heart, his generosity, his yielding disposition, his desire to have everybody happy, and above all his desire to see all the people of the United States enter again upon the full privileges of citizenship with equality among all.

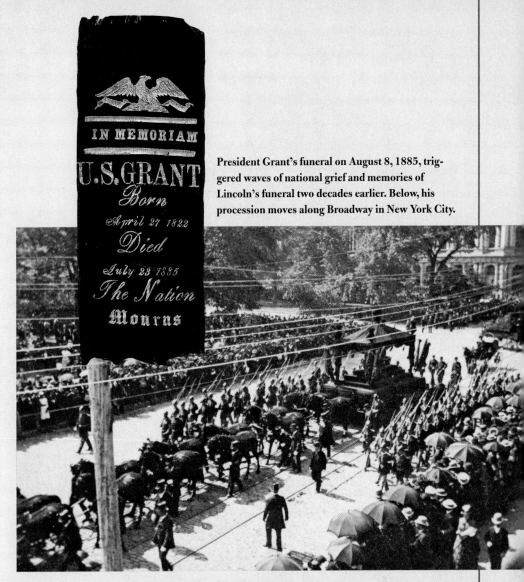

President Grant's funeral on August 8, 1885, triggered waves of national grief and memories of Lincoln's funeral two decades earlier. Below, his procession moves along Broadway in New York City.

Grant's unadorned coffin was placed in a temporary burial chamber. Over the next twelve years a public funding effort raised $600,000 to construct a mighty tomb overlooking the Hudson River.

265

In George B. McClellan's 1886 memoir, he wrote about meeting with President Lincoln in 1862 on the Antietam battlefield.

1886

McClellan's Story

Ｎone of Lincoln's generals had been more controversial than George B. McClellan. Appointed by Lincoln in July 1861 to organize what would become the Army of the Potomac, he had soon begun to show the fatal arrogance that would infect much of his career. "By some strange operation of magic," he wrote, "I seem to have become the power of the land. The people call on me to save the country. . . . I must save it, and cannot respect anything that is in the way." He was so insubordinate to General in Chief Winfield Scott that the old general recommended strongly that Lincoln relieve him of duty. Writing home to his wife, McClellan commented, "the Presid't is an idiot, the old general is in his dotage—they cannot or will not see the true state of affairs." Though he was widely acknowledged to be a superb military organizer, it was soon clear that McClellan preferred drilling his soldiers to taking them into battle. Month after month he refused to engage the enemy. When Lincoln tried to pressure him to move south, McClellan began to refer to him as a "baboon" and a "gorilla." But Lincoln continued to put his faith in "Little Mac." In November he elevated him to general in chief. But he soon had reason to question his decision. In late January Lincoln commanded McClellan to move his army. But his campaign that spring was plagued by further procrastination, and in March Lincoln temporarily removed him as general in chief, himself assuming direct command of the Union armies. When Robert E. Lee attacked McClellan's army and then plagued it again during its retreat, the young general sent a seething letter to Edwin Stanton (censored by an army telegrapher): "You have done your best to sacrifice this army."

In September McClellan faced Robert E. Lee's army near the little town of

Antietam, Maryland. The ferocious battle that ensued—the bloodiest day of the Civil War—ended in a long-awaited Union victory. "Those in whose judgments I rely," McClellan wrote, "tell me that I fought the battle splendidly and that it was a masterpiece of art." In the aftermath of the battle Lincoln visited him in the field and according to McClellan expressed complete satisfaction in his leadership. But Lincoln was deeply frustrated that he was failing to pursue Lee's army. And when McClellan ignored a direct order to engage the enemy, on November 7 Lincoln removed him from duty. He never again held a military position.

McClellan went on to oppose Lincoln politically, running on the Democratic ticket for president in 1864. In campaign speeches he said he opposed "forcible abolition" and would allow slavery to be reinstated if the war could be ended.

In his final decades Little Mac traveled to Europe, resumed his former engineering trade, and served a single term as New Jersey's governor. But he could not shake off his bad reputation. Widely considered a failure for his Civil War record, he finally decided to tell his own story. A first draft of his memoirs was destroyed in a fire in the late 1870s, but by 1881 he had written them over again, though he said they weren't to be published until after his death. "I never sought rank nor command," he wrote in his preface. "I have, therefore, been able to maintain a calm front under abuse, and . . . have remained satisfied with the conviction that, after my death at least, my countrymen will recognize the fact that I loyally served my country in its darkest hour."

The memoirs appeared in 1886, just months after McClellan's death. But if their author had thought they would help to resurrect his reputation, he was mistaken. The books, filled with examples of conceit and self-delusion, only added to the nation's low esteem of his war service.

One month after meeting with McClellan at Antietam, Lincoln fired him.

"A Very Ugly Matter"
George B. McClellan

1886

General George B. McClellan's growing tensions with his commander in chief are visible in his account of a confrontation on March 8, 1862.

[The President] appeared much concerned about something, and soon said that he wished to talk with me about "a very ugly matter.". . . He said that it had been represented to him . . . that my plan of campaign . . . was conceived with the traitorous intent of removing its defenders from Washington, and thus giving over to the enemy the capital and the government, thus left defenceless.

It is difficult to understand that a man of Mr. Lincoln's intelligence could give ear to such abominable nonsense. I was seated when he said this, concluding with the remark that it did look to him much like treason. Upon this I arose, and, in a manner perhaps not altogether decorous towards the chief magistrate, desired that he should retract the expression, telling him that I could permit no one to couple the word treason with my name. He was much agitated, and at once disclaimed any idea of considering me a traitor, and said that he merely repeated what others had said, and that he did not believe a word of it.

In 1864 McClellan ran against Lincoln for the presidency. Although a political cartoon implied that Lincoln saw his opponent as a "little joke," he was in fact deeply concerned about McClellan's candidacy and at one point prepared for a possible defeat.

June 1886
Herndon and Weik

During the 1870s William Herndon had lived the life of a subsistence farmer, wrestling with his old demon alcohol. He lost most of his old friends, suffered the jeers of a negative press, and gave up coming into town except to sell vegetables from a wooden cart. Though he still had his six-hundred-acre farm, Chinkapin, and was able to provide food for his large family, financial setbacks forced him to sell his beloved library. By 1881 newspapers were listing him as a "pauper," noting that "Whiskey" was the cause.

But this same year was a turning point in Herndon's life. President Garfield's assassination shocked him into awakeness, flooding him with memories of Lincoln's murder. "Lincoln and Garfield," he wrote, were the "twin stars" of the modern world—"Oh, how each suffered in his own way and for the Eternal Right!" He wrote these words to a young college graduate from Indiana who six years earlier had written him asking for an autograph of Lincoln. His name was Jesse Weik and over the next decade he would become Herndon's close associate, helping him finally bring to fruition his long-postponed Lincoln project.

In 1882 Weik's employer at the Department of the Interior assigned him to work in Springfield. There in November the young man first met the legendary law partner of Abraham Lincoln. The two instantly hit it off. Herndon showed him his boxes of Lincoln letters and memorabilia; gave him a tour of their old law office; and took him to see the little room above a store in town where Lincoln had composed his First Inaugural address. He introduced Weik to numerous people who had known

Jesse Weik as a young man

Covered wagons lined the streets of Springfield in Lincoln's days. Decades later William Herndon gave Jesse Weik a complete tour of Lincoln's hometown.

Lincoln and encouraged him to conduct his own interviews with them. Eventually Weik met with "almost every person then living in that region who had known or talked to Lincoln." That included Dennis Hanks, now in his eighties, and Elizabeth Edwards, in whose home Mary Lincoln had died that same year. Much as Herndon had done twenty years earlier, Weik traveled to the ruined site of the old village of New Salem, looking for ghosts of Lincoln.

In 1885 Jesse Weik moved back to Greencastle, Indiana, and soon began corresponding with Herndon about collaborating on a Lincoln biography. Herndon was overjoyed. His ten-year noncompete agreement with Ward Lamon was drawing to a close; he still possessed almost all of his original interviews and letters from the 1860s; and he had a wealth of Lincoln memories he was burning to share.

And so the collaboration began. Between October 1885 and June 1886 Herndon sent Weik thirty-five long letters, brimful with Lincoln information that unfolded in a sometimes bewildering stream of consciousness. "I'll give you the facts," he wrote to Jesse. "You must write." These letters would continue, intermittently, for the next five years. And writing them would bring Herndon back to life.

After his single term in Congress, Lincoln issued a card announcing his return to his law practice. Many years later Herndon brought Weik to his former law office (below) to show him where Lincoln and he had worked.

Memories of a Law Partner
William Herndon

1885–1887

Herndon's letters to Jesse Weik contained valuable reminiscences of Lincoln.

Mr. Lincoln's habits . . . were to come into the office, pick up book, newspaper, etc., and to sprawl himself out on the sofa, chairs, etc., and read aloud, much to my annoyance. I have asked him often why he did so and his invariable reply was: "I catch the idea by two senses, for when I read aloud I hear what is read and I see it; and hence two senses get it and I remember it better, if I do not understand it better." Sometimes in reading he would have his body on the sofa, one foot on one chair and one foot on the table. He spilt himself out easily over one-quarter of the room. I have had to quit the office frequently because of this reading aloud. . . .

Of a Sunday, Lincoln might be seen, if in summer in his shirtsleeves, hauling his babies in a little wagon up and down the pavement north and south on Eighth Street. Sometimes Lincoln would become so abstracted that the young one would fall out and squall, Lincoln moving on the while. . . . It happened that sometimes Lincoln would come down to our office of a Sunday with one or two of his little children, hauling them in the same little wagon, and in our office, then and there, write declarations, pleas, and other legal papers. The children—spoilt ones to be sure—would tear up the office, scatter the books, smash up pens, spill the ink, and p[is]s all over the floor. I have felt many and many a time that I wanted to wring their little necks, and yet out of respect for Lincoln I kept my mouth shut. . . .

In our disputes on law points—on principles in any line—Lincoln was never to me insulting nor domineering; he was cool and patient, kind and tender. We used to discuss philosophy, which I have written to you so much about. Lincoln never read much law, and never did I see him read a law book through, and no one else ever did. Politics were Lincoln's life and newspapers his food.

Remembering Lincoln

In 1886, encouraged by the successes of Osborn Oldroyd and of *Century Magazine*, the editor of the *North American Review*, Allen Thorndike Rice, brought out a large new collection of Lincoln reminiscences.

Rice had a curious background. Born in 1851, two years before Tad Lincoln, he was the son of a wealthy New York merchant, Henry Rice, and of the heir to a Boston shipping fortune, Elizabeth Thorndike. His parents divorced when he was eight, and when a court awarded custody to his father, Elizabeth kidnapped her son. In the fall of 1859 a carriage pulled up to the boy's schoolyard in Nahant, where he was playing with his classmate Henry Cabot Lodge. Beckoned to get in, he was whisked off and taken to Germany.

After an extended education in England he returned to the United States, where he used his large inheritance to purchase a moribund journal—the *North American Review*. Rice decided it should become the "mouthpiece of both sides of every question" and sought out leading figures in the arts, the sciences, politics, and the military. He was soon recognized as a brilliant editor and entrepreneur, and the *Review* began to outdistance all its competitors. Among its distinguished writers were Charles Darwin, Oliver Wendell Holmes, Walt Whitman, Thomas Edison, Andrew Carnegie, and James Garfield.

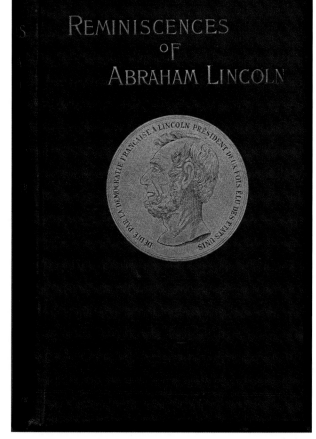

Thorndike Rice used his skills as a journalist to collect and edit a wide range of Lincoln recollections.

Using these and other contacts, in 1885 Rice launched his Lincoln project. His goal was to pull together "a mass of trustworthy evidence concerning the personal traits . . . of Abraham Lincoln," leaving out no "eminent associate of Lincoln" still living. "For the time is fast coming," Rice warned, "when we shall seek in vain for survivors of the dark days that fashioned the career of Abraham Lincoln. Already, within the brief period of one year, death has stricken many names from the list—among them the historic ones of Grant, McClellan, Hancock, and McDowell. Yet a little while, and few witnesses will remain to tell the tale."

Rice's final collection featured thirty-three contributors, including some of the most illustrious names in America. Curiously, many of Lincoln's old friends, such as Henry Whitney and William Herndon, were left out. (In a letter to Herndon, Whitney complained that Rice had turned to "codfish" like "Ben Perley Poore, Dan Voorhes, [and] Walt Whitman" instead of to authentic friends of Lincoln's like "you, John T. Stuart & Jim Matheny." It all proved "how humbug rules the world.")

Most reviewers, however, applauded the book. The *Washington Post* called it "the most valuable collection of American historical [reminiscence] . . . that has ever been made," and praised its editor as an "industrious genius." The book was also popular with the reading public and went through eight printings in three years. But by then its famous editor was dead. At the age of thirty-seven, Rice contracted acute tonsillitis and choked to death in his bed in New York.

"He Seemed to Dislike Clothing"
David R. Locke

1886

David Locke, better known in his time as "Petroleum V. Nasby," was Lincoln's favorite humorist. In this passage from Rice's anthology Locke described meeting Lincoln in October 1858 in Quincy, Illinois.

David R. Locke

I found Mr. Lincoln in a room of a hotel, surrounded by admirers, who had made the discovery that one who had previously been considered merely a curious compound of genius and simplicity was a really great man. . . . I succeeded in obtaining an interview with him after the crowd had departed, and I esteem it something to be proud of that he seemed to take a liking to me. He talked to me without reserve. . . . He sat in the room with his boots off, to relieve his very large feet from the pain occasioned by continuous standing; or, to put it in his own words: "I like to give my feet a chance to breathe." He had removed his coat and vest, dropped one suspender from his shoulder, taken off his necktie and collar, and thus comfortably attired, or rather unattired, he sat tilted back in one chair with his feet upon another in perfect ease. He seemed to dislike clothing, and in privacy wore as little of it as he could. I remember the picture as though I saw it but yesterday.

"Is That All?"
James B. Fry

1886

General James B. Fry of Illinois served in the Union Army and witnessed Lincoln's response to military telegrams after the Battle of Gettysburg.

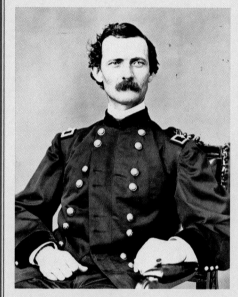

General James B. Fry

Lincoln watched the operations of the armies in the field with the deepest interest, the keenest insight, and the widest comprehension. The congratulatory order which General Meade published to his troops after the battle of Gettysburg was telegraphed to the War Department. During those days and nights of anxiety, Lincoln clung to the War Office, and devoured every scrap of news as it came over the telegraph wires. He hoped for and expected substantial fruits from our dearly bought victory at Gettysburg. I saw him read General Meade's congratulatory order. When he came to the sentence about "driving the invaders from our soil," an expression of disappointment settled upon his face, his hands dropped upon his knees, and in tones of anguish he exclaimed, *"Drive the invaders from our soil! My God! Is that all?"*

A Rare Outburst of Anger
John B. Alley

1886

John B. Alley was a congressman from Massachusetts who was close to Charles Sumner, and who saw Lincoln throughout the war years.

John B. Alley

He was an exceedingly patient and even-tempered man. I have often seen him placed in the most provoking and trying positions, and never but once knew him to lose his temper. That was the day after he had received very bad news from the army. A couple of office-seekers who knew him well, intercepted him, on his way from the White House to the War Department, and teased him for an office which he told them he could not give. They persisted in their importunity until it was unbearable. The President, evidently worn out by care and anxiety, turned upon them, and such an angry and terrific tirade, against those two incorrigible bores, I never before heard from the lips of mortal man.

"The Homeliest Man I Ever Saw"
Donn Piatt

1886

An Ohio journalist, once described as an incurable liar, Donn Piatt's recollections were often filled with inaccuracies. But his description of meeting Lincoln for the first time at his home in Springfield in 1860 has a ring of authenticity.

Donn Piatt

Mr. Lincoln was the homeliest man I ever saw. His body seemed to me a huge skeleton in clothes. Tall as he was, his hands and feet looked out of proportion, so long and clumsy were they. Every movement was awkward in the extreme. He sat with one leg thrown over the other, and the pendent foot swung almost to the floor. And all the while two little boys, his sons, clambered over those legs, patted his cheeks, pulled his nose, and poked their fingers in his eyes, without reprimand. He had a face that defied artistic skill to soften or idealize. It was capable of few expressions, but those were extremely striking. When in repose, his face was dull, heavy, and repellent. It brightened like a lit lantern when animated. His dull eyes would fairly sparkle with fun, or express as kindly a look as I ever saw, when moved by some matter of human interest.

A Greeting for General Sherman
Absalom Markland

1886

In charge of the mails under the command of Ulysses S. Grant, Colonel Markland was a strong supporter of Abraham Lincoln.

My last interview with Mr. Lincoln had a touch of pathos I can never forget, and I cannot properly describe. I remember his words well, but the expression of his countenance and the modulation of his voice is far beyond any description I could give. When General Grant directed me to proceed to a point where I might possibly hear something of General Sherman's approach to the sea, he directed me also to call on Mr. Lincoln in Washington, and take any message Mr. Lincoln might have for General Sherman. When I called, Mr. Lincoln was engaged with some gentlemen in his office. My card was sent to him, and immediately I was admitted. As I entered the door he arose and met me in the center of the room. Extending his hand to me, he said:

"Well, Colonel, I got word from General Grant that you were going to find Sherman, and that you would take him any message I might have. I know you will find him, because we always get good news from you. Say to General Sherman, for me, whenever and wherever you see him, 'God bless him and God bless his army.' That is as much as I can say, and more than I can write."

He held my hand during the delivery of this message, and our eyes looked into each other's. The tear-drops gathered in his eyes, his lips trembled, and his voice faltered. He gave evidence of being greatly affected. He shook my hand, bade me good-by, and I proceeded toward the door, when he called to me. When I looked back he was standing like a statue where I had left him. "Now, remember what I say," and then he repeated the message. I passed out the door and never saw Mr. Lincoln again, but the language and picture of that meeting will never be forgotten.

On the Afternoon Before His Murder
Charles A. Dana

1886

The former managing editor of the New York Tribune, *Charles Dana served as assistant secretary of war under Edwin Stanton and occasionally as a messenger between Stanton and President Lincoln.*

Charles A. Dana

The last time I saw Mr. Lincoln to speak with him was in the afternoon of the day of his murder. The same Jacob Thompson was the subject of our conversation. I had received a report from the Provost Marshal of Portland, Maine, saying that Mr. Thompson was to be in that town that night for the purpose of taking the steamer for Liverpool; and what orders had the Department to give? I carried the telegram to Mr. Stanton. He said promptly, "Arrest him"; but as I was leaving his room, he called me back, adding, "You had better take it over to the President." It was now between four and five o'clock in the afternoon, and business at the White House was completed for the day. I found Mr. Lincoln with his coat off in a closet attached to his office washing his hands. "Halloo, Dana," said he, as I opened the door, "what is it now?" "Well, sir," I said, "here is the Provost Marshal of Portland, who reports that Jacob Thompson is to be in that town tonight, and inquires what orders we have to give." "What does Stanton say?" he asked. "Arrest him," I replied. "Well," he continued, drawling his words, "I rather guess not. When you have an elephant on hand, and he wants to run away, better let him run."

"His Entire Freedom from Popular Prejudice"
Frederick Douglass

1886

Over the years Douglass spoke often about his visits with Abraham Lincoln, sometimes changing his emphasis or adding detail. In his submission to Rice's book he gave the definitive account of his presence at Lincoln's second inaugural.

For the first time in my life, and I suppose the first time in any colored man's life, I attended the reception of President Lincoln on the evening of the inauguration. As I approached the door I was seized by two policemen and forbidden to enter. I said to them that they were mistaken entirely in what they were doing, that if Mr. Lincoln knew that I was at the door he would order my admission, and I bolted in by them. On the inside I was taken charge of by two other policemen, to be conducted as I supposed to the President, but instead of that they were conducting me out the window on a plank.

"Oh," said I, "this will not do, gentlemen," and as a gentleman was passing in I said to him, "Just say to Mr. Lincoln that Fred. Douglass is at the door."

He rushed in to President Lincoln, and almost in less than a half a minute I was invited into the East Room of the White House. A perfect sea of beauty and elegance, too, it was. The ladies were in very fine attire, and Mrs. Lincoln was standing there. I could not have been more than ten feet from him when Mr. Lincoln saw me; his countenance lighted up, and he said in a voice which was heard all around: "Here comes my friend Douglass." As I approached him he reached out his hand, gave me a cordial shake, and said: "Douglass, I saw you in the crowd today listening to my inaugural address. There is no man's opinion that I value more than yours: what do you think of it?" I said: "Mr. Lincoln, I cannot stop here to talk with you, as there are thousands waiting to shake you by the hand;" but he said again: "What did you think of it?" I said: "Mr. Lincoln, it was a sacred effort," and then I walked off. "I am glad you liked it," he said. That was the last time I saw him to speak with him.

In all my interviews with Mr. Lincoln I was impressed with his entire freedom from popular prejudice against the colored race. He was the first great man that I talked with in the United States freely, who in no single instance reminded me of the difference between himself and myself, of the difference of color.

Frederick Douglass was present at Lincoln's Second Inaugural ceremony and called his address "a sacred effort." Above, left of center, Lincoln was seated next to incoming Vice President Andrew Johnson. Next to him sat outgoing Vice President Hannibal Hamlin, hat in hand.

The Everyday Life of Abraham Lincoln

In the 1880s the Chicago literary editor Francis F. Browne, impressed by the scattered recollections of Lincoln, began collecting "books, pamphlets, magazines and newspapers"—anything that contained firsthand accounts of his hero. He traveled to the sites of historical collections, seeking out scraps of unpublished recollection. And in addition to mining the public record, he entered into correspondence with still-living Lincoln eyewitnesses, looking for "experiences, incidents, anecdotes, and reminiscences" that might shed light on Lincoln's personality. Eventually more than five hundred friends and contemporaries of Lincoln submitted material to him.

Browne was the first to admit he was no historian, and he made no attempt to analyze the quality of his sources. Instead he pieced them together in chronological order, ending up with something that had the look of a sprawling biography. In the fall of 1886 he published *The Everyday Life of Abraham Lincoln.* Though it had an exciting, modern, journalistic feel, critics saw it as a hodgepodge of a book, filled with genuine but also dubious accounts, united around an intention to portray Lincoln as a near-perfect man. It was a vast stitching together of recollections, "prepared and arranged" by the book's "compiler."

Francis Fisher Browne

Browne's book possessed a massive subtitle that sounded like a P. T. Barnum circus bulletin: *A biography of the great American President from an entirely new standpoint, with fresh and invaluable material. Lincoln's Life and Character portrayed by those who knew him. A series of pen-pictures by friends, neighbors, and daily associates, during his whole career. Estimates and impressions of distinguished men, with reminiscences, incidents, and tributes from universal sources. A complete Personal Description and Biography of him who was the humblest and greatest of American citizens, the truest and most loyal of men, and a central figure in the world's history. With nearly 100 original illustrations.*

Like Barnum's autobiography, and Grant's too, the book was sold by subscription, with agents, working on commission, going door to door. It became extremely popular with the reading public and added luster to Lincoln's growing mythic stature.

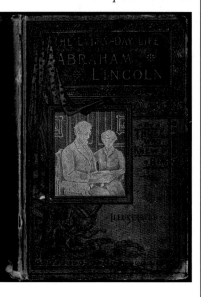

To appeal to a popular audience, Browne chose an engraving of Lincoln and Tad for the cover of his book.

A Familiar Sight in Town
Page Eaton

Page Eaton was an old resident of Springfield when Browne sought him out as an informant. Eaton had been a carpenter back in the 1840s and 1850s and once said he thought Lincoln would never make a good lawyer because he was too honest.

Mr. Lincoln always did his own marketing, even after he was elected President, and before he went to Washington. I used to see him at the butcher's or baker's every morning, with his basket on his arm. He was kind and sociable, and would always speak to every one. He was so kind, so childlike, that I don't believe there was one in the city who didn't love him as a father or brother.

An early children's book illustration showed Lincoln in Springfield pulling his youngest son behind him in a wagon. The artist mistakenly put a beard on Lincoln but captured the feel of his informality.

A Favorite Among the Young Lawyers
Gibson W. Harris

1886

One of Browne's chief informants for Lincoln's Springfield days was G. W. Harris, a clerk in Lincoln's law office who had first encountered Lincoln when he was a boy. The tall lawyer had come into Harris's log-cabin schoolhouse in 1840 to borrow a copy of Byron's works from the schoolmaster. When he received the copy, Harris later recalled, he smiled "a smile such as I have never seen on any other man's face." Here he recalls Lincoln in the 1850s.

Gibson W. Harris

Mr. Lincoln was fond of playing chess and checkers, and usually acted cautiously upon the defensive until the game had reached a stage where aggressive movements were clearly justified. He was also somewhat fond of ten-pins, and occasionally indulged in a game. Whatever may have been his tastes in his younger days, at this period of his life he took no interest in fishing-rod or gun. He was indifferent to dress, careless almost to a fault of his personal appearance. The same indifference extended to money. So long as his wants were supplied—and they were few and simple—he seemed to have no further use for money, except in the giving or the lending of it, with no expectation or desire for its return, to those whom he thought needed it more than he. Debt he abhorred, and under no circumstances would he incur it. He was abstemious in every respect. I have heard him say that he did not know the taste of liquor. At the table he preferred plain food, and a very little satisfied him.

Under no circumstances would he, as an attorney, take a case he knew to be wrong. Every possible means was used to get at the truth before he would undertake a case. More cases, by his advice, were settled without trial than he carried into the courts; and that, too, without charge. When on one occasion I suggested that he ought to make a charge in such cases, he laughingly answered, "They wouldn't want to pay me; they don't think I have earned a fee unless I take the case into court and make a speech or two." When trivial cases were brought to him, such as would most probably be carried no farther than a magistrate's office, and he could not induce a settlement without trial, he would generally refer them to some young attorney, for whom he would speak a good word at the same time. He was ever kind and courteous to these young beginners when he was the opposing counsel. He had a happy knack of setting them at their ease and encouraging them. In consequence he was the favorite of all who came in contact with him. When his heart was in a case he was a powerful advocate. I have heard more than one attorney say that it was little use to expect a favorable verdict in any case where Lincoln was opposing counsel, as his simple statements of the facts had more weight with the jury than those of the witnesses.

An Earlier Attack on His Life
John W. Nichols

1886

John W. Nichols was the retired president of the Omaha Fire Department when Browne learned about his special recollection. As part of Company K of the Pennsylvania 150th Volunteers, Nichols had been one of President Lincoln's bodyguards, serving from mid-1862 to 1865. In the summer before Lincoln's reelection he witnessed a nearly successful attack on the President's life. His account of it was the first time Americans had ever heard of it.

John W. Nichols

One night, about the middle of August, 1864 I was doing sentinel duty at the large gate through which entrance was had to the grounds of the Soldiers' Home, near Washington, where Mr. Lincoln spent much time in summer. About eleven o'-clock I heard a rifle-shot in the direction of the city, and shortly afterwards I heard approaching hoof-beats. In two or three minutes a horse came dashing up, and I recognized the belated President. The horse he rode was a very spirited one, and was Mr. Lincoln's favorite saddle-horse. As horse and rider approached the gate, I noticed that the President was bareheaded. As soon as I had assisted him in checking his steed, the President said to me: "He came pretty near getting away with me, didn't he? He got the bit in his teeth before I could draw the rein." I then asked him where his hat was; and he replied that somebody had fired a gun off down at the foot of the hill, and that his horse had become scared and had jerked his hat off. I led the animal to the Executive Cottage, and the President dismounted and entered. Thinking the affair rather strange, a corporal and myself started off to investigate. When we reached the place whence the sound of the shot had come—a point where the driveway intersects, with the main road—we found the President's hat. It was a plain silk hat, and upon examination we discovered a bullet-hole through the crown. We searched the locality thoroughly, but without avail. Next day I gave Mr. Lincoln his hat, and called his attention to the bullet-hole. He made some humorous remark, to the effect that it was made by some foolish marksman and was not intended for him; but added that he wished nothing said about the matter. We all felt confident it was an attempt to kill the President, and after that he never rode alone.

John G. Nicolay

John M. Hay

November 1886

Nicolay and Hay

"This is the hour for the biographer," trumpeted *Century Magazine* in October 1886. Twenty-one years after Lincoln's death, it was considered an appropriate time to tell his full story. Earlier efforts had had to contend with the intense emotion surrounding his murder; later attempts would not benefit from the firsthand knowledge that was still accessible. "With Lincoln . . . [the] moment of clearest visibility is now." *Century* wrote these words as it announced the upcoming serialization of a massive new Lincoln work that would overshadow all others—Nicolay and Hay's *Abraham Lincoln: A History*.

Over the course of the 1870s John G. Nicolay and John Hay had both had demanding careers—Nicolay as marshal of the Supreme Court and Hay as a journalist and then assistant secretary of state. And so work on their book had proceeded slowly. In 1881 Hay resigned from public service to devote himself entirely to the work, and both men grew increasingly devoted to the project. No one was better suited for it, they believed. "We knew Mr. Lincoln intimately before his election," they wrote. "We came from Illinois to Washington with him, and remained at his side and in his service—separately and together—until the day of his death. We were the daily and nightly witnesses of the incidents, the anxieties, the fears, and the hopes which pervaded the Executive Mansion and the National Capital."

Determined that their book be a definitive treatment, they assembled an authoritative collection of primary sources, cross-checked contemporaneous written evidence, and consulted their own diaries and notes made in the 1860s. They had at their disposal the official papers of Abraham Lincoln—Robert had given them exclusive access. And they had documents that Lincoln himself had put into their hands specifically to help them write this book. Disgusted by many of the recollections that had poured forth since 1865, they vowed not to rely upon "any memory of the events narrated," saying they had "seen too often the danger of such reliance in the reminiscences of others."

The work was grueling, and over time both men developed eye problems. Hay's headaches became so severe he had to resort to writing by dictation. But they continued their work for almost sixteen years, aging considerably in the process. When Robert once tried to force them to release key documents before they were ready, Nicolay balked, writing, "I beg you to no longer think of us as boys."

In November 1886 portions of the book began running in serialized form and would continue to do so every month for the next three years. Unlike the personal and partial efforts of Ward Hill Lamon and Francis Carpenter, this was a serious treatment of Lincoln's whole life, with emphasis upon the presidency. Based on the otherwise unknown Lincoln Papers, the articles contained some startling revelations: Lincoln's 1861 rebuke of his ambitious Secretary of State William Seward; his full awareness of Salmon Chase's duplicity; an incident when George B. McClellan rudely walked right past Lincoln, who had been waiting for nearly an hour in his parlor; and the terrible anxiety Lincoln felt in 1864 when he believed he might lose the upcoming presidential election. The *Century* compared the articles to a "gigantic statue set up in an open square but still partly veiled from the public eye." People's reading, month by month, of this "minute and illuminating history" would be the gradual unveiling of the statue.

Lincoln, as Nicolay and Hay remembered him in 1861 as President-elect, and, to the right, pages from the *Century Magazine* serialization of their massive Lincoln history

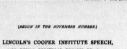

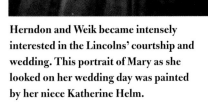

Herndon and Weik became intensely interested in the Lincolns' courtship and wedding. This portrait of Mary as she looked on her wedding day was painted by her niece Katherine Helm.

August 1887

Little Things That Made Lincoln What He Is

By February 1886 Herndon's letters to Weik had begun to slow down, allowing his partner time to digest their rich content. Soon he knew what he needed next from Herndon—his precious collection of oral history transcripts and notes from the 1860s. In a sign of how much he now trusted his new friend, in the fall Herndon shipped the entire collection to Greencastle, where Weik began the intensive work of sorting and arranging. That autumn Weik headed out on a series of interviews around Illinois to take testimony on many subjects, including Ann Rutledge.

Back home it soon became clear to Weik that there was a major gap in the Herndon materials: they contained almost nothing about Lincoln's early years in Kentucky. Although Herndon had always planned to go there and conduct interviews, he had never made it. Now he wanted Weik to investigate rumors there that Abraham Lincoln was illegitimate. So in March 1887 Weik made the journey to Kentucky, seeking out the few old souls who still had any memory of the young Lincoln. The results were meager, but Weik got a feel for Lincoln's childhood home and for the countryside where he had grown up. While he was away, he received a letter from the son of Mary Owens, Lincoln's first fiancée back before he met Mary Todd, along with a photograph of his mother taken when Lincoln had courted her.

By now Herndon and Weik had a new incentive. Nicolay and Hay's Lincoln articles had begun appearing in *Century Magazine*. While impressed by their scholarship, Herndon saw a fatal flaw in their work: it was too long, too impersonal, and too official ever to be truly popular. "N. and H. have introduced too much collateral and unimportant matter that does not touch any part of Lincoln's life," he wrote Weik. "[T]hey have wearied the people, tired them out. In writing our book let us avoid this step." Herndon knew exactly what was missing. "Let us write directly of Lincoln and Lincoln alone," he advised. What the public wants are "all those little and big things, thought & done, while Lincoln was growing up . . . little things that made Lincoln what he is." In others words an extremely personal and human story that Herndon felt only he and Weik could deliver.

Herndon was determined that they depict Lincoln's courtship and marriage in the most accurate detail. To supplement his earlier research, he conducted numerous new interviews in the late 1880s with people who knew different parts of the story. On July 27, 1887, he met with Elizabeth Edwards, Mary's sister, to discuss why Lincoln and Mary had broken their engagement in 1841. Then he corresponded with William Jayne about the hasty preparations for the wedding in November 1842. (Jayne was the younger brother of Mary Lincoln's bridesmaid Julia and in the 1850s served as the Lincolns' family doctor.) Finally Herndon sought out his old friend James Matheny, Lincoln's groomsman, and asked him for details about the marriage ceremony itself.

Before long it was time for the two authors to collaborate in earnest, which meant working together under the same roof. On August 1, 1887, an excited William Herndon left his family in Illinois and traveled to Greencastle to join his partner for an intensive writing session.

The Broken Engagement

Elizabeth Edwards

July 27, 1887

Mary Lincoln's sister Elizabeth spoke to Herndon about the Lincoln wedding.

Mrs. Lincoln was an ambitious woman—the most ambitious woman I ever saw—spurred up Mr. Lincoln, pushed him along and upward—made him struggle and seize his opportunities. Lincoln's & Mary's engagement &c were broken off by her flirtations with Douglas—Mr Edwards & myself told Lincoln & Mary not to marry—said so more or less directly: they were raised differently and had no [congruity?]—no feelings &c—alike. We never opposed Lincoln's marriage with Mary. It is said that Miss Edwards had something to do in breaking Mary's engagement with Lincoln—its not true. Miss Edwards told me that Lincoln never condescended to pay her even a poor compliment: it was the flirtation with Douglas that did the business. Mr. Lincoln and Mr Speed were frequently at our house—seemed to enjoy themselves in their conversation beneath the dense shade of our forest trees. After the match was broken off between Mary and Lincoln Mrs Francis shrewdly got them together. Doct. Henry who admired and loved Mr. Lincoln had much to do in getting Mary and Lincoln together again.

Stephen A. Douglas, Mary Todd's suitor

Short Notice for a Wedding

William Jayne

August 17, 1887

William Jayne

Dr. William Jayne was the brother of Mary Lincoln's bridesmaid, Julia Jayne.

Mr and Mrs Edwards, knew nothing of the wedding until the morning of the day of the wedding. Only meager preparations could be made on so-short notice & only a few friends were present—the company present was quite limited in numbers. Mrs Lincoln at the time of her marriage was a bright, lively, plump little woman—a good talker, & capable of making herself quite attractive to young gentlemen . . .—decided in her friendships & intense in her dislikes—my own acquantance with her was pleasant & is kindly impressed on my memory[.]

The sperm-oil, astral lamps that sat on the Edwardses' mantel and provided light for the wedding ceremony

Chuckles During the Ceremony

James H. Matheny

August 21, 1888

James Matheny had been Lincoln's groomsman.

The Wedding incident, refered to was one of the funiest things to have witnessed imaginable—No description on paper can possibly do it justice. . . . Old Judge Brown was a rough "old timer" and always said just what he thought without regard to place or surroundings—There was of course a perfect hush in the room as the ceremony progressed. Old Parson Dresser in clerical robes—Brown standing just behind Lincoln—the Parson handed Lincoln the ring, and as he put it on the brides finger, went through the church formula. "With this ring I thee endow with all my goods and chattles, lands and tenements"—Brown who had never witnessed Such a proceeding, was Struck with its utter absurdity and spoke out So everybody could hear, in an expression, used by him on all occasions by way emphasis, "Lord Jesus Christ, God Almighty, Lincoln, the Statute fixes all that"—This was too much for the Old Parson—he broke down under it—an almost irresistable desire to laugh out, checked his proceeding for a minute or so—but finally recovered and pronounced them Husband & wife.

James H. Matheny, Lincoln's groomsman

The Standing Lincoln

In 1883 Augustus Saint-Gaudens, the son of a shoemaker and by now America's greatest sculptor, secured a new commission—to create a large Lincoln statue for downtown Chicago. It was "the greatest work" that he had ever been asked to create, he said, and it filled him with "a sense of great responsibility."

Saint-Gaudens had actually seen Lincoln twice—once as a thirteen-year-old boy, as Lincoln rode by at a distance; and then again four years later at his New York funeral. So moved was Augustus by the sight of the martyred President, he had twice stood in the long viewing line.

As a sculptor Saint-Gaudens was a perfectionist and a mystic. He said he wanted to find the "inner" Lincoln—to capture the "character, the life, the emotions, and the very soul of the man." He read everything he could get his hands on about Lincoln, and gathered together all the photographs he could find. To help him model the figure, he hired a nearby Vermonter who resembled Lincoln to pose for him. And to assist him with the face he obtained the life mask of Lincoln made by Leonard Volk in 1860. By the fall of 1887 the sculpture was finished and ready for the Chicago dedication.

October 22 was a raw, rainy day, but ten thousand people showed up for the official unveiling, including Saint-Gaudens along with his wife and son. The keynote speaker was Lincoln's old friend Leonard Swett. He gave a moving tribute to a man he had known well, though Swett cut his remarks short due to the cold, windy weather. "In all time hereafter," he said, ending his address, "wherever the slave shall groan under the lash, or the poor shall sigh for something better than they have now, there his name will be honored and his example imitated." And then Robert Lincoln's fifteen-year-old son, Abraham, pulled the cord that held the statue's coverings. Saint-Gaudens's Lincoln stood in front of his chair as if having risen for a special purpose. The head tilted downward, as if in deep thought, pondering some grave matter before beginning to speak. His right hand was held behind his back; the left grasped his lapel in a gesture of readiness. Visitors noted he looked "lonely." All felt Lincoln's presence in the looming bronze figure, which has ever since been considered one of the definitive likenesses.

Augustus Saint-Gaudens used an 1864 Mathew Brady photograph (left) to help model his *Standing Lincoln*. To the right, the sculptor stands behind his triumphant statue, which was soon to be moved to Lincoln Park in Chicago.

A Sacred Remembrance

In 1878 Frederick Douglass and Anna, his wife of forty years, purchased Cedar Hill, a fifteen-acre estate outside Washington with views all the way to the U. S. Capitol. In its entrance hall he hung a portrait of Abraham Lincoln, who symbolized for him the nation's unfinished commitment to racial justice. Here, in his book-lined library, he wrote his third and final autobiography, *Life and Times of Frederick Douglass*. And here in 1882, the year after President Garfield appointed him recorder of deeds for the District of Columbia, Anna died.

Over this decade Douglass spoke often of Lincoln's role in emancipation. Once

President Rutherford B. Hayes appointed Frederick Douglass United States marshal for the District of Columbia, and he now made his home in Washington, D.C.

he called him, astonishingly, one of the great "leaders of the colored people, far greater than I, an humble citizen, can ever hope to be." Radical critics began to say he had been co-opted by the Republican Party, and for a time his speeches seemed to lack his old fire. When he married his former secretary, a white woman named Helen Pitts, a rain of criticism fell upon him from both whites and blacks. But Douglass boldly rejected all racial stereotyping. "If I have advocated the cause of the colored people," he insisted, "it is not because I am a negro, but because I am a man."

In 1886 he and Helen left the country on an extended tour of England and the Continent. When they returned two years later, he was appalled by what he found. Douglass declared that blacks in the South were "worse off, in many respects," than when they were slaves.

On Lincoln's birthday in 1888 seventy-year-old Douglass was invited to speak. Twelve years earlier, at the dedication of the Freedmen's Memorial, he had tried to shock the nation into caring about black rights. In doing so he had been critical of Abraham Lincoln. But over the decade since, his understanding of Lincoln had deepened. He now saw the sixteenth President as the great exemplar of national leadership, and the key person on whom to peg the future equality of his race. Douglass realized that blacks needed to keep Lincoln's emancipationist legacy alive, even if many white Americans wanted to forget it.

On February 12, 1888, he appeared at the meeting of the Republican League in Washington. In the audience were prominent senators and congressmen; the atmosphere was charged. Once again Douglass told the story of his and Lincoln's friendship and of Lincoln's extraordinary importance to the African American community. And then for the first time he also spoke about Mary Lincoln, who he said had been in full sympathy with her husband's antislavery views and whom, he said, he "loved." As he spoke, he held in front of him the cane Mary had given him twenty-three years earlier—Mr. Lincoln's favorite walking stick. "I am the owner of this cane you may depend on that," Douglass exclaimed; "and I mean to hold it and keep it in sacred remembrance of Abraham Lincoln who once leaned upon it."

Douglass at his writing desk at Cedar Hill

Lincoln's Aging Cousin

Ever since the 1860s, when Dennis Hanks had begun displaying one of Lincoln's log cabins, he had been associated with the name of Abraham Lincoln. A first cousin once removed, he represented the clan from which Lincoln had arisen—rough-hewn, semiliterate, sparkling with fun, an American original. Hanks was certain of his centrality to Lincoln's legend, writing to Herndon, "if you Don't have my name Very frecantly in you[r] Book it wont gaw [go] of it at all."

Ten years older than Lincoln, he had come into and out of the life of his brilliant cousin many times over the decades. He had even visited Lincoln in the White House in 1864 where, as he described it, an emotional "Abe gathered me in his arms." After a long talk, Lincoln had given him a parting gift— a silver watch. Dennis was overwhelmed and in the years ahead kept the trophy always with him, hiding it carefully away in a secret pocket of his vest.

Dennis was amassing a small Lincoln collection of his own. After the assassination he remembered that back in 1851 Lincoln had recorded information inside the big family Bible. So he hurried to Sarah Lincoln and asked for the book, then tore out the page as a souvenir. In the mid-1880s Jesse Weik sought out Dennis and obtained a short interview from him. Herndon had warned him not to take Dennis's word as literal truth, and Weik had heard the same admonition from others too. James Rardin, a young neighbor of Hanks in Coles County, wrote that "Dennis is not only old but he is also noted for years as being a pretty big liar even in his pristine days." But in their book Weik and Herndon paid him high honor, calling him "the irrepressible and cheerful waif, Dennis Hanks."

By the mid-1880s Hanks was a minor celebrity. When Robert McIntyre interviewed him for the *Chicago Tribune* he found him "hale and erect" and still overflowing with Lincoln stories. McIntyre observed that in profile his face was "strikingly Lincoln-like." The old man, who often wore a top hat like his famous cousin, was still claiming to have taught Lincoln to read and write.

In January 1889 Hanks was interviewed for the *Tribune*, this time by Eleanor Atkinson, writing under the pseudonym Nora Marks. Now ninety years old, he was living with his daughter Sarah Dowling in her snug brick home in Charleston, Illinois. Atkinson found the old man sitting in a split-bottomed chair, holding a knotted thorn stick in his bony hands. At the end of the interview he began hollering, then seemed relieved and began to pull something out of his pocket. "If you don't tell nobody I'll show you something!" he said. It was his silver watch that Lincoln had given him twenty-five years earlier. "Abe gimme that," he said proudly, showing Atkinson his prize. Then he added, "Thar's a fellow up in Chicago, that's plumb crazy over Abe, an' he offered me five hundred dollars for it, but no money can buy it. There ain't many people even gits to see it, I can tell you."

Dennis Hanks at age ninety posed with five generations of his family, including his daughter Sarah, and her daughter, granddaughter, and great-granddaughter Hazel. By 1889 Hanks boasted of almost seventy offspring. In contrast, there were now only four Abraham Lincoln descendants.

Vivid Memories of His Early Life
Dennis Hanks

January 1889

Hanks recalled well the log cabin in which Lincoln was born.

Eleanor Atkinson's interview with Dennis Hanks in 1889 was considered "one of the most notable contributions which have yet been made to the literature of Abraham Lincoln's early life." She later added to her account and published it in the American Magazine.

You bet I was tickled to death. Babies wasn't as plenty as blackberries in the woods o' Kaintucky. Mother come over an' washed him an' put a yaller flannen petticoat an' a linsey shirt on him, an' cooked some dried berries with wild honey fur Nancy, an' slicked things up an' went home. An' that's all the nuss'n either of 'em got. Lordy! women nowadays don't know what their grandmothers went through an' lived—some of 'em. A good many of 'em died arly. Abe's said many a time that Nancy'd lived to be old if she'd had any kind o' keer, an' I reckon she must 'a' ben strong to 'a' stood what she did.

"What you goin' to name him, Nancy?" I asked her.

Daniel Boone, a distant relative, had led Lincoln's grandfather into Kentucky.

"Abraham," she says, "after his gran'-father that come out to Kaintucky with Dan'l Boone. He was mighty smart an' wasn't afeered o' nothin', an' that's what a man has to be out here to make anything out o' hisself."

I rolled up in a b'ar skin an' slep' by the fire-place that night, so I could see the little feller when he cried, and Tom had to git up an' 'tend to him. Nancy let me hold him purty soon. Folks are always askin' me if Abe was a good-lookin' baby. Well, now, he looked jist like any other baby, at fust; like red cherry-pulp squeezed dry, in wrinkles. An' he didn't improve none as he growed older. Abe never was much fur looks. I ricollect how Tom joked about Abe's long legs when he was toddlin' round the cabin. He growed out o' his clothes faster'n Nancy could make 'em.

But he was mighty good comp'ny, solemn as a papoose, but inter*est*ed in everything. An' he always did have fits o' cuttin' up. I've seen him when he was a little feller, settin' on a stool, starin' at a visitor. All of a sudden he'd bust out laughin' fit to kill. If he told us what he was laughin' at, half the time we couldn't see no joke. . . .

Abe never give Nancy no trouble after he could walk except to keep him in clothes. Most o' the time we went b'ar-foot. Ever wear a wet buckskin glove? Them moccasins wasn't no putection ag'inst the wet. Birch bark, with hickory bark soles, stropped on over yarn socks, beat buckskin all holler, fur snow. Me 'n' Abe got purty handy contrivin' things thataway. An' Abe was right out in the woods, about as soon

he was weaned, fishin' in the crick, settin' traps fur rabbits an' muskrats, goin' on coon-hunts with Tom an' me an' the dogs; follerin' up bees to find bee-trees, an' drappin' corn fur his pappy. Mighty inter*est*in' life fur a boy, but thar was a good many chances he wouldn't live to grow up. . . .

[T]he Sparrows both died o' milk-sickness an' I went to Tom's to live. Then Nancy died o' the same disease. The cow et pizen weeds, I reckon. O Lord, O Lord, I'll never furgit the mizry in that little green-log cabin in the woods when Nancy died!

Me 'n' Abe helped Tom make the coffin. He tuk a log left over from buildin' the cabin, an' I helped him whipsaw it into planks an' plane 'em. Me 'n' Abe held the planks while Tom bored holes an' put 'em together, with pegs Abe'd whittled. . . . We laid Nancy close to the deer-run in the woods. Deer was the only wild critters the women wasn't afeerd of. Abe was some'er's 'round nine years old, but he never got over the mizable way his mother died. . . .

Abe had a powerful good mem'ry. He'd go to church an' come home an' say over the sermon as good as the preacher. He'd often do it fur Aunt Sairy, when she couldn't go, an' she said it was jist as good as goin' herself. He'd say over everything from beloved brethren to Amen without crackin' a smile, pass a pewter plate fur a collection an' then we'd all jine him singin' the Doxology. Aunt Sairy thought a heap o' Abe, an' he did o' her, an' I reckon they'd a done most anything fur one another.

Robert Lincoln Returns to the White House
March 30, 1889

In March 1889 Benjamin Harrison assumed the presidency, moving into a White House previously occupied by Grover Cleveland. One of his first acts was to name Robert Lincoln minister to London. Robert arrived at the Executive Mansion on March 30 to accept the appointment. During his visit he saw President Harrison and also members of the White House staff who remembered him fondly.

A New Home in the West for Lincoln Relics

In 1888 a group of Chicago businessmen intent on transforming their city into a world-class destination decided to capitalize on the public's fascination with Lincoln and the Civil War. Their plan was to buy the old Libby Prison in Richmond, Virginia, and transport it to Chicago. Here it was to be reconstituted as the nation's first Civil War museum—and a proper stage for the exhibition of the greatest Lincoln collection in the country.

Libby Prison was infamous during the Civil War, but in the years since it had been used as a warehouse for fertilizer, its old wood floors now covered with stinking animal carcasses and fish. And yet no site in all of Richmond drew northern tourists like this building, where fifty thousand Union soldiers had been held in captivity. When word of the Chicago purchase was announced in the press, there was an outcry from local Virginians who feared a loss of tourism, and from former soldiers in the North, who protested what they called a "nefarious project." It was feared that it would be turned into a "ghastly circus exhibition," and that unprincipled speculators were committing a "violation of the sanctity of the soldiers' sufferings." But with $24,000 already invested in the move, in December 1888 the dismantling of the building began. By spring, hundreds of thousands of stones, beams, and boards were on their way to Chicago.

That summer the old prison was reassembled on its new site, with a huge new Gothic-style castle wall surrounding it. In charge of the project was Chicago candy manufacturer Charles F. Gunther, a self-made millionaire who had emigrated as a boy from Germany. Gunther had briefly fought during the Civil War on the

Charles F. Gunther

During the Civil War spectators could see Union captives peering out behind the barred windows of Libby Prison. Known for its poor treatment of prisoners of war, the institution was despised in the North. During 1888–89 it was dismantled and moved from Richmond to Chicago.

Confederate side, then spent the last twenty years collecting Lincoln relics and Civil War memorabilia, much of it displayed in his candy store. The Libby Prison War Museum would be the new venue for his collection.

The museum catered to a growing public appetite for authentic relics from the past. It included the table on which Robert E. Lee had signed his surrender at Appomattox; Jefferson Davis's saddle; a huge cannon raised from Charleston Harbor especially for the museum. It featured prisoner-of-war diaries; a re-creation of the tunnel used by escaping prisoners in 1861; and a water battery taken from the Potomac River embedded with cannon balls. Civil War veterans served as visitor guides and shared their experiences with tourists young and old; former prisoners who visited the museum were encouraged to register in an official log and to place a bronze plaque on the very spot on the floor where they had once slept. A quarter of a million visitors came to the museum in its first year, from North and South, and it became a national center for Civil War veterans. Gunther called it "a shrine for patriotic memories," and at its center was a major Lincoln exhibit displayed in the former hospital room of the prison.

Over the course of the 1880s, Gunther had acquired most of the furniture from the Lincoln death room, many relics from Ford's Theatre, and the autopsy table on which Lincoln was examined. He bought the large carriage the Lincolns had used in Washington; a signed copy of the Emancipation Proclamation; leaves from the old Lincoln family Bible, which had been sold off piecemeal by William Herndon; original photographs of Lincoln's father and of his log cabin; and one of Volk's life casts of Lincoln's head and hands. All of these and much more were put on display at the Libby Prison War Museum's Lincoln exhibit.

The Libby Prison War Museum was popular for more than a decade. Later, Charles Gunther would transfer much of his collection to the Chicago Historical Society.

The "Prisoners' Reception Room" at Libby Museum became a meeting place for Union and Confederate veterans.

The cashier at the Libby Museum collected fifty cents from adults and a quarter from children.

289

Lincoln in 1854, when his law partner was William Herndon

Herndon as he looked around 1870

Preserving Lincoln

William Herndon arrived at Jesse Weik's hometown in early August 1887. It was the first time in years he had had the luxury of working full time on Lincoln, and he seemed twenty years younger. The two men worked side by side in a sweltering, second-floor room over the Weik family bakery, its tin roof offering little protection from the Indiana heat. Although Weik was to be the book's principal writer, both men scribbled copiously. By September Herndon was exhausted; he had done everything he could and bade his friend farewell. "I . . . am worn out," he wrote a colleague, and "must take rest and recover." Weik continued writing on his own and in October began sending finished chapters for Herndon's approval. When he saw that they were written out in longhand, Herndon wrote back, "Go to any necessary expense in getting a typewriter."

Both men wanted their book to be a financial success and they reviewed why other Lincoln books had failed. Lamon and Black's biography had been overly dark and iconoclastic. Nicolay and Hay's was often boring, a cardinal sin in publishing. And Herndon himself, in his published lectures on Lincoln's religion, had brought upon himself waves of public disapproval. They must suppress Herndon's suspicion of Lincoln's illegitimacy, as well as the stories he had collected of Lincoln's supposed visits to prostitutes or his rumored bout with syphilis. "We need not, nor must we, lie," Herndon wrote Weik from Illinois, "but by all means let us . . . [m]ake things straight & rosy. Success is what we want. We want no failures."

As chapters came in from Weik, they triggered new ideas about how to enrich them, which Herndon outlined in a new series of letters to his partner. He also sent Weik his Lincoln lectures from the 1860s. At times his partner felt overwhelmed by all the material, but by July 1888 the final manuscript was ready. Because of Herndon's association with Lamon, he had a questionable reputation in the publishing world. On top of this many houses thought that Nicolay and Hay's massive book, about to be published in full, would saturate the Lincoln market. But finally a third-rate publisher, Belford, Clarke, agreed to bring their book out. In September the authors added their finishing touches and shipped the bulky manuscript to New York.

By this point Herndon and Weik were having problems. Desperately poor, Herndon had repeatedly borrowed cash from his partner, eventually totaling $650. In return, Weik wanted Herndon to gift him his oral history collection. But Herndon balked, wanting more money. And now Weik wanted joint credit as author, something Herndon had never promised him. But since Weik had control over the final draft of the book, he made sure that when it was published it would carry a title page listing the authors as William H. Herndon and Jesse William Weik.

When Herndon received his pre-publication copy in June, he was horrified to see the title page. Jesse had violated their agreement which stipulated that he would be named as the book's editor and that the only other mention of his name would be in the book's preface. And yet "I find your name scattered around—as author—aide—assistant &c. &c." Herndon also saw that his many corrections to the proofs had never been incorporated.

When the three-volume work appeared in July, it was met with widespread critical acclaim. Many recognized it as an essential contribution to the field, a work that would influence all Lincoln biographers to come. Those who had feared another

Lamon-like book were relieved, including many of Lincoln's old friends in Springfield. Writing in the *Nation* of "Mr. Herndon's personal recollections of Lincoln," General Jacob D. Cox said, "The sincerity and honesty of the biographer appears on every page."

There were also bad reviews, many of them in Herndon's home state. The *Chicago Evening Journal* said it "vily distorts . . . the image of an ideal statesman, patriot and martyr." The *Decatur Republican* called it "a filthy book upon a grand subject."

In September Herndon's publisher went into bankruptcy, and all distribution of the book ceased. And rumors began circulating that Robert Lincoln, by then serving as minister to England, was buying up as many copies of the book as he could in order to suppress its impact. In a letter to his partner Herndon called Robert "a damned fool," saying he was a "Todd and not a Lincoln"—"a little bitter fellow of the pig-headed kind, silly and cold and selfish." Their book would "be read when he is dead and forgotten," Herndon crowed. "Can he stop the sun from shining?"

Herndon never made a penny off his Lincoln biography. The royalties due him all went to pay off his debt to Weik. And in March 1891, when William Herndon died, Jesse Weik retained possession of all his Lincoln papers.

Newspapers were kind to Herndon in their eulogies. The *New York Post* called his biography of Lincoln "a labor of love, but at the same time a labor of the strictest veracity." Comparing the work to Boswell's *Life of Johnson*, they said no one else had succeeded as Herndon had.

No biography of Lincoln did more to shape how Americans came to see him. Compared to the drier historical writing of Nicolay and Hay, Herndon's books were much more readable. Although the authors had not written about Lincoln's presidency—the most important period of his life and the reason he was remembered—they brought him alive as a human being. Herndon's goal had been to capture the "real Lincoln" ("*just* as he lived, breathed—ate and laughed"). What he did was to help create the Lincoln of American folklore. In contrast to the staid statesman of the east coast writers, Herndon's Lincoln was a jokester from the frontier—a shrewd, lusty Paul Bunyan with women problems, who rose through sheer political sagacity. It was these two literary traditions, working at first independently, then in concert, that shaped the legend of Lincoln that spread through American culture in the closing years of the nineteenth century.

But in fact Herndon had known Lincoln "far better than all other living men combined," as Lincoln's friend Henry Clay Whitney once wrote. And as Herndon himself had insisted to Ward Hill Lamon, "If you and I had not told the exact truth about Lincoln, he would have been a myth within a hundred years."

Breaking his agreement with Herndon, Jesse Weik (below) insisted that his name be displayed as coauthor in advertisements (left) and on the book's frontispiece.

Over the course of 1886 and 1887 Weik interviewed and corresponded with numerous people who had known Lincoln. But by now, with the smoothing out of the Lincoln legend, eyewitnesses had begun to suppress information. "You will note I have stricken out all allusion to Lincoln's swearing," wrote Leonard Swett to Weik in 1887, having earlier made many references to it. "[T]he reason is that I am satisfied the public does not want to hear them."

"A Window in His Breast"

John Lothrop Motley

1889

In this letter written on May 27, 1865, and published for the first time in 1889, Motley gave his assessment of Lincoln's character.

I cannot trust myself yet to speak of President Lincoln, for I am afraid of possible exaggeration. I had a great reverence for his character—a sentiment which has been steadily growing for the last two years. On the very first interview that I had with him in the summer of 1861, he impressed me as a man of the most extraordinary conscientiousness. He seemed to have a window in his breast. There was something almost childlike in his absence of guile and affectation of any kind. Of course, on the few occasions when I had the privilege of conversing with him, it was impossible for me to pretend to form an estimate as to his intellectual power, but I was struck with his simple wisdom, his straightforward, unsophisticated common sense. What our Republic, what the whole world has to be grateful for, is that God has endowed our chief magistrate at such a momentous period of history with so lofty a moral nature and with so loving and forgiving a disposition.

His mental abilities were large, and they became the more robust as the more weight was imposed upon them, and his faculty of divining the right amid a conflict of dogmas, theories, and of weighing other men's opinions while retaining his own judgment, almost amounted to political genius, but his great characteristic was devotion to duty. I am very glad that you admire that little inaugural address of last March. The children in every American school ought to be made to learn it by heart. "With malice towards none, with charity to all, with firmness in the right as God gives us to see the right, let us strive on to finish the work we are in"—those words should be his epitaph, and who in the long roll of the world's rulers have deserved a nobler one?

1889

A Historian on Lincoln

John Lothrop Motley was one of the greatest historical writers of his era. A friend of Nathaniel Hawthorne, Henry Wadsworth Longfellow, and Oliver Wendell Holmes, in 1861 he had been appointed minister to Austria by Lincoln, whom Motley first met in person shortly before his departure for Vienna. "I am now satisfied that he is a man of very considerable natural sagacity," he wrote to his wife, Mary, on June 23, "and that he has an ingenuous, unsophisticated, frank, and noble character. I believe him to be as true as steel, and as courageous as true. . . . [I] feel that . . . the country will be safe in his hands." Over the next four years Motley wrote often about Lincoln and came to call his administration "an epoch in the world's history" that he believed would "regenerate" the Republic. He was devastated by the news of Lincoln's assassination and wrote a private tribute of him in May. In 1889, twelve years after Motley's death, his daughter published his correspondence. His assessments revealed the uncanny power Lincoln had had to inspire the finest minds of his time.

John Lothrop Motley's letters about Lincoln were not published until more than a decade after Motley's death.

Lincoln in 1863, when Motley
served as his minister to Austria

December 6, 1889

He Never Forgave His Foes

In the closing days of the 1880s came word that Lincoln's old adversary Jefferson Davis had died, going to his grave still passionately committed to the South's "Lost Cause." In the North he was still widely despised as a traitor to the nation—the closest thing in the nineteenth century to Benedict Arnold. But even Southerners had failed to warm to him. As the central figure of their war of independence, he had combined fierce dedication with contentiousness and arrogance and had possessed none of Lincoln's ability to win the affection of his people.

He had gained some sympathy after the war during a two-year imprisonment at Fortress Monroe, where it was learned he was treated harshly—denied the right to read or exercise, his letters censored, his comforts limited, even his sleep constantly interrupted in order to wear him down. By the time of his release his eyesight was almost ruined, and he had lost so much weight he was a shadow of his former self.

Jefferson Davis, near the end of his life, relaxed near the beach at Biloxi, Mississippi.

Davis settled in Tennessee, where he became president of a life insurance company, but for years he struggled with poverty. Finally in 1879 a sympathetic dowager left him her plantation, allowing him to return to his beloved Mississippi. In 1881 he published a two-volume history, *The Rise and Fall of the Confederacy*. It was a densely argued work, predicting that the issue of state sovereignty would one day reassert itself and arguing for the continuing right of secession. It showed nothing but disdain for his former Northern enemies. The book found few readers and was a financial failure.

At his death many Southerners did mourn. The *Atlanta Constitution* called him "The Defender of the Nation's Honor" and noted that his passing represented the end of an era. "He was the last of the mighty leaders of the lost cause," the paper proclaimed. "Cobb, Stephens, the kingly Toombs . . . Hill, Yancey . . . Lee . . . and Jackson . . . all gone!" But in the North many papers noted the passing of a "traitor." And even the *Washington Post*, attempting to be balanced, called him "a Southerner of the intensest sort . . . an upholder of slavery, as of constitutional if not of divine right." Although most veterans of the Civil War were now growing "in a spirit of fraternity," the paper said, Davis had gone to his grave a fiercely partisan man. "There was much in his attitude to admire," the *Post* summed up, "but more to deplore."

Jefferson Davis and Abraham Lincoln Contrasted

December 13, 1889

This passage from an article in the Whitehall Chronicle of Whitehall, New York, was typical of the negative articles in the North about Jefferson Davis.

Mr. Lincoln and the North approached . . . [the crisis], oppressed with the consciousness of the awful responsibility for coming events, and of the far reaching consequences of the dreadful drama about to open. Mr. Davis felt the physical elation of coming conflict and the gratification of accomplished ambition; Mr. Lincoln felt only the greatness and moral grandeur of the eventful moment and the need of Divine aid to be equal to it. The one began in bluster and ended in disaster; the other began in doubt and with a sense of his own weakness, and ended in immortal triumph. Such is the difference between the crafty, ambitious and unprincipled conspirator on the one hand; and the sober, reflecting, almost sorrowful patriot on the other. The former is of the earth, earthly; the latter, consecrated to a lofty purpose is radiant with a celestial spirit.

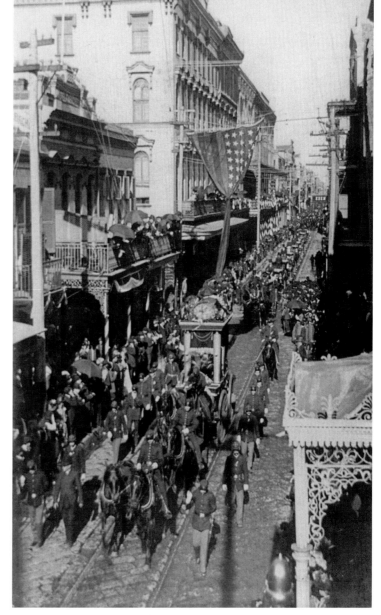

The funeral procession for Jefferson Davis slowly made its way through the French Quarter in New Orleans. As his body lay in state, Northern papers reported on the death of a "traitor" while many Southerners mourned.

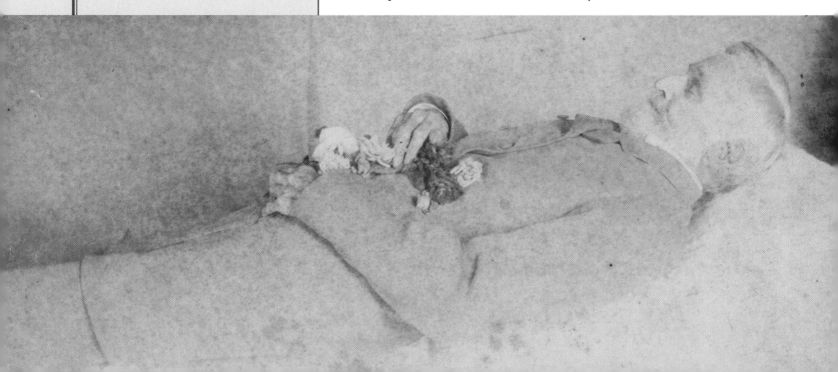

Veneration of Lincoln was strong among African Americans at the turn of the century. A poem from the period said: "Reverence him, though our skins are dark; Reverence him in our churches and parks; Let us teach our children to do the same, And teach them never to forget his name. He was our Moses, to us and our race, And our children should never forget his face."

Part Four

1890–1908

Looking Back

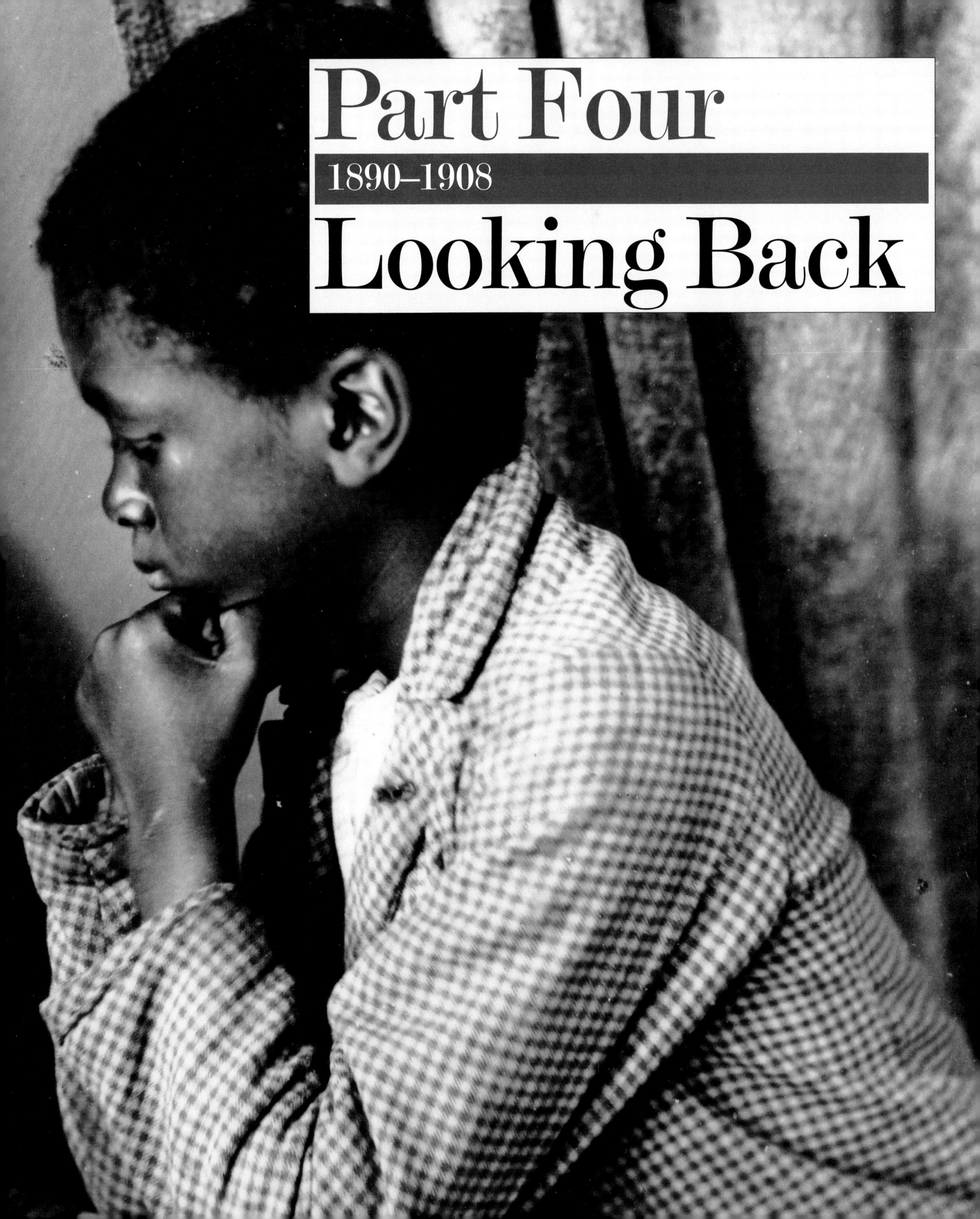

Remembering and Forgetting
1890–1908

There were still people living in the 1890s who remembered Lincoln well—John Hay, Dennis Hanks, Frederick Douglass, Henry Clay Whitney. But increasingly, as old friends and colleagues died, Lincoln's memory came to be dominated by people who never knew him. To this new generation Lincoln became an icon, appealing to groups from a wide variety of backgrounds. And with the outbreak of the Spanish-American War, there was a heightened need to hold on to the nation's heritage, which for many was symbolized by Abraham Lincoln. He was lifted up as a model by conservatives and progressives, by immigrants and native born, by easterners and westerners, and by some southerners too, though there remained diehard anti-Lincoln men and women throughout the South.

During these years Ida Tarbell emerged as a new kind of Lincoln scholar, an investigative journalist whose work opened up fresh terrain in Lincoln appreciation. Frederick Hill Meserve became an impassioned expert on Lincoln photography, collaborating closely with Robert Lincoln. And Presidents McKinley and Roosevelt both became outspoken admirers of their great predecessor. Though new controversies erupted over what Lincoln actually said and did, nothing seemed to slow the burgeoning of his reputation. "During each succeeding decade since the end of that tragic life," wrote the *Review of Reviews* in 1906, "the American people have . . . found their appreciation of his great character and achievements constantly growing." Few noted the irony of the *Plessy v Ferguson* decision in 1896, instituting segregation as the law of the land; or how, as Lincoln loomed ever larger in the national imagination, there was a corresponding worsening of race relations in America. It was as if, in enthusiastically remembering Lincoln, the country was at the same time forgetting a central component of what he stood for.

Members of the Old Guard of Richmond posed together in the uniforms they had worn at Appomattox.

Abraham Lincoln II

Robert Lincoln arrived in London in late May 1899 to take up residence as the new United States minister to Great Britain. For the first time in years he was happy. He held the most prestigious appointment in the Foreign Service and was being hailed as a superb choice for the job. His wife and children were with him, and there was time for family excursions. His daughters, Mamie and Jessie, were considered "belles" of London. And his son, sixteen-year-old Abraham Lincoln II, was his pride and joy.

Born in 1873, a year and a half after the death of Tad, the boy had grown up in Washington, where Robert was serving as secretary of war. Out of respect for his grandfather, who had disliked the nickname "Abe," the boy became known as "Jack." He was a "jolly, sturdy little fellow," one reporter wrote, "who makes friends as easily as his grandfather did, and very much more easily than his father." Granted special access, he often visited the Washington Navy Yard where he loved to board ships and spend time with the sailors on deck. He was an outstanding student, proficient in Latin, Greek, mathematics, and English literature and possessing a fascination for the history of the Civil War. One teacher described him as "the best student in my school." Proud of his famous name, he learned to imitate his grandfather's handwriting and liked to sign his papers "A. Lincoln." "I had good reason for setting no limit in our hopes in him," Robert Lincoln wrote. His plan was to send Jack to Exeter and Harvard and then have him join him at the Chicago law firm of Isham, Lincoln and Beale.

That fall Jack traveled to Versailles, to study French. While there he developed a growth in his left armpit that caused the swelling of his arm and hand. Following surgery, the wound refused to heal and blood poisoning set in. In late November newspapers were reporting that he was dying, and his father traveled to France to be with him. When his condition improved just before Christmas, it was decided to bring the boy back to London. But Jack's problems persisted. He continued to lose weight and developed difficulty breathing. And on the morning of Wednesday, March 5, Abraham Lincoln II died. He was just seventeen.

Robert and his wife Mary were devastated. "Jack was to us all that any father and mother could wish," Robert wrote to John Hay. "I did not realize until he was gone how deeply my thoughts of the future were in him."

Mary and the girls left for the United States, where they would stay for the next six months with her parents. Robert remained in England to carry on his work alone. In late October, after requesting a two-month leave of absence, he sailed for New York along with the body of his son. A private railroad car took them from New York to Springfield, where Abraham Lincoln II was buried inside the Lincoln tomb, alongside his grandparents and his father's three brothers.

Jack Lincoln rode a bicycle and kept a rock collection. He signed his name A. Lincoln, so that it looked just like his famous grandfather's signature. "I never want to call you Abraham," Robert once said to him, "until you are worthy of being called that name."

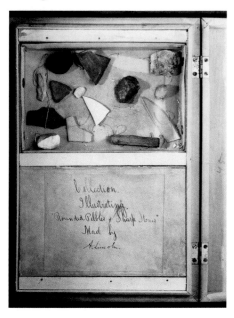

Jack was photographed during his fatal illness at Christmastime 1889. When he died in March, he left Robert with no male heir, and no chance for passing on the Lincoln name. Robert's in-laws, Senator James and Ann Harlan, had already lost three children and any hope for their name to be carried on. In a moment of despair after Jack's death the senator wrote, "And so my coal is quenched—both Mr. Lincoln's and mine."

YOUNG LINCOLN IS DEAD

The Brave Youth Yields at Last to
the Ravages of Disease.

HE FADED AWAY WITHOUT PAIN

Minister Lincoln and Wife Prostrated by
Grief—A Message of Condolence from
the Queen—Interment in America—The
Boy Resembled the Martyred President.

LONDON, March 5.—Young Abraham
Lincoln, son of United States Minister
Robert T. Lincoln, died at 11:15 this
morning.

His condition during the night had been

John G. Nicolay, wrote a contemporary, had a "methodical, silent German way about him."

John Milton Hay, scintillating and literary, was in many ways the opposite of his dour partner. Loving change and independence, and disliking routine, he called it part of his "Illinois nature."

1890

The Authorized Biography

After four years of serialization in *Century Magazine*, in 1890 there finally appeared Nicolay and Hay's full biography: *Abraham Lincoln: A History*. Published in ten large volumes, containing and a million and a half words, it was one of the most complete biographies of any figure in history and 20 percent longer than Gibbon's *Rise and Fall of the Roman Empire*. "We have devoted to it twenty years," wrote the authors. "We have aimed to write a sufficiently full and absolutely honest history." The volumes were dedicated to Robert Todd Lincoln, who, in return for his cooperation, had insisted on the right to make corrections and deletions. In the end Robert had done little meddling. He hadn't needed to: the book was outspokenly laudatory.

Upon its publication, newspaper critics gave it mostly positive reviews. "The volume charms and cultivates in all its thoughts," wrote the *Boston Globe*, after perusing one of the books. The historian George Bancroft, after reading all ten, wrote that it "must be regarded as the most valuable contribution to United States history that has been made for many years." But Bancroft also saw problems with the work. Noting that "few critical and satisfactory lives of statesmen have been written by their secretaries," he pointed to the authors' overly partisan point of view. "A very large part of their work," Bancroft wrote, "is to bring out Lincoln's merits in bolder relief. . . . Hence, in their eyes, all Confederates are scheming rebels without a good impulse or a redeeming quality."

The authors' close acquaintanceship with Lincoln was surely one of their greatest assets, but it was also a liability. If they possessed an extraordinary grasp of historical detail, they also lacked distance and perspective, as if they were too close to their subject matter and unable to see events except through their own and Lincoln's eyes. And given their determination to write not just a biography but "a history," ironically they often lost sight of their central character.

The ten volumes were also excessively long. "If biographies are to be read," commented the otherwise admiring *New York Times*, "they must be of such length as to permit to be read by human beings who know that life is short and who wish occasionally to be otherwise employed." As well researched and written as the books were, few people could be expected to read them, unless they were someone's "sole companion while cast away on a desert island."

William Herndon, who had read Nicolay and Hay's chapters in *Century Magazine*, found them boring, and thought the authors "suppressed many facts." He had heard about Robert Lincoln's involvement—how he had been allowed to censor anything he didn't like, and how Nicolay and Hay had accepted all his corrections. "No wonder that Lincoln had contempt for all history and biography," Herndon wrote indignantly. "Lincoln wanted to know the whole truth & nothing less."

TO THE HONORABLE

ROBERT TODD LINCOLN

THIS WORK IS DEDICATED

IN TOKEN OF

A LIFE-LONG FRIENDSHIP

AND ESTEEM

The authors dedicated their multivolume work to the man who had provided them with exclusive access to Lincoln's papers.

An April 1861 newspaper illustration depicted eager office-seekers crowding the hallways outside Lincoln's office.

Catching Him in the Hallways
Nicolay and Hay

1890

In this passage of their book, not included in the Century *serializations, Nicolay and Hay described the daily surge of people trying to gain access to President Lincoln early in his administration.*

The city was full of strangers; the White House full of applicants from the North. At any hour of the day one might see at the outer door and on the staircase, one line going, one coming. In the anteroom and in the broad corridor adjoining the President's office there was a restless and persistent crowd,—ten, twenty, sometimes fifty, varying with the day and hour,—each one in pursuit of one of the many crumbs of official patronage. They walked the floor; they talked in groups; they scowled at every arrival and blessed every departure; they wrangled with the door-keepers for the right of entrance; they intrigued with them for surreptitious chances; they crowded forward to get even as much as an instant's

In 1864 artist David Hunter Strother sketched Lincoln outdoors as he patiently listened to an office-seeker.

glance through the half-opened door into the Executive chamber. They besieged the Representatives and Senators who had privilege of precedence; they glared with envy at the Cabinet Ministers who, by right and usage, pushed through the throng and walked unquestioned through the doors. At that day the arrangement of the rooms compelled the President to pass through this corridor and the midst of this throng

Senator Henry Wilson of Massachusetts told Lincoln not to meet with the uninvited people who came to see him each day. The President replied, "They don't want much; they get but little, and I must see them."

when he went to his meals at the other end of the Executive Mansion; and thus, once or twice a day, the waiting expectants would be rewarded by the chance of speaking a word, or handing a paper direct to the President himself—a chance which the more bold and persistent were not slow to improve.

November 1890

John Hay's Observant Eye

The publication of their ten-volume history established Nicolay and Hay as the foremost Lincoln authorities in the world. But those who knew the sparkling prose of Hay's earlier work searched in vain for any sign of his poetical hand in the 4,700-page history. Instead they found a workmanlike, impersonal prose in which no one could tell what was written by Nicolay and what by Hay. That was how Nicolay had wanted it, and Hay had to suppress much of his own literary flair.

That spring the editor of *Century Magazine*, Richard Watson Gilder, approached Hay and asked him to write a personal article on Lincoln to be published under his sole byline. It was time for Hay to step out of the shadows and become known as a Lincoln author on his own.

Hay's marriage in 1874 to Clara Stone, the daughter of a multimillionaire Ohio industrialist, gave him the leisure to pursue his writing. Living in a large mansion in Washington, he published poetry and wrote articles on a wide variety of subjects and counted Henry Adams and Theodore Roosevelt among his close friends.

On June 19, 1890, Hay answered Richard Gilder. He had "at last yielded to your furious importunity and have written an article on 'Life at the White House in Lincoln's Time.'" Based on his personal White House diaries, in which little had escaped Hay's observant eye, his article turned out to be the most vivid firsthand account ever written of President Lincoln's daily life during the years of the Civil War.

A quarter century after Lincoln's death, his portrait still hung over John Hay's desk. Hay understood Lincoln like few others. And according to Speaker of the House Galusha Grow, there was "no person in whom the . . . President reposed more confidence."

Life in the White House
John Hay

November 1890

An Abstemious Man

The President rose early, as his sleep was light and capricious. In the summer, when he lived at the Soldiers' Home, he would take his frugal breakfast and ride into town in time to be at his desk at eight o'clock.... He was one of the most abstemious of men; the pleasures of the table had few attractions for him. His breakfast was an egg and a cup of coffee; at luncheon he rarely took more than a biscuit and a glass of milk, a plate of fruit in its season; at dinner he ate sparingly of one or two courses. He drank little or no wine; ... never cared for wine or liquors of any sort, and never used tobacco.

He Enjoyed Public Receptions

The great public receptions, with their vast rushing multitudes pouring past him to shake hands, he rather enjoyed; they were not a disagreeable task to him, and he seemed surprised when people commiserated him upon them. He would shake hands with thousands of people, seemingly unconscious of what he was doing, murmuring some monotonous salutation as they went by, his eye dim, his thoughts far withdrawn; then suddenly he would see some familiar face,—his memory for faces was very good—and his eye would brighten and his whole form grow attentive; he would greet the visitor with a hearty grasp and a ringing word and dismiss him with a cheery laugh that filled the Red Room with infectious good nature.

His Boys Kept the House Lively

During the first year of the administration the house was made lively by the games and pranks of Mr. Lincoln's two younger children, William and Thomas—Robert, the elder was away at Harvard, only coming home for short vacations. The two little boys, aged eight and ten, with their western independence and enterprise, kept the house in an uproar. They drove their tutor wild with their good natured disobedience; they organized a minstrel show in the attic; they made acquaintance with the office seekers and became the hot champions of the distressed. William was, with all his boyish frolic, a child of great promise, capable of close application and study. He had a fancy for drawing up railway time tables, and would conduct an imaginary train from Chicago to New York with perfect precision. He wrote childish verses, which sometimes attained the unmerited honors of print. But this bright, gentle, studious child sickened and died in February 1862. His father was profoundly moved by his death, though he gave no outward sign of his trouble, but kept about his work the same as ever. His bereaved heart seemed afterwards to pour out its fulness on his youngest child. "Tad" was a merry, warm-blooded, kindly little boy, perfectly lawless and full of odd fancies and inventions, the "chartered libertine" of the Executive Mansion.

The Cry of the Orphan

As time wore on and the war held its terrible course, upon no one of all those who lived through it was its effect more apparent than upon the President. He bore the sorrows of the nation in his own heart; he suffered deeply, not only from disappointments, from treachery, from hope deferred, from the open assaults of enemies and from the sincere anger of discontented friends, but also from the world-wide distress and affliction which flowed from the great conflict in which he was engaged and which he could not evade. One of the most tender and compassionate of men, he was forced to give orders which cost thousands of lives; by nature a man of order and thrift, he saw the daily spectacle of unutterable waste and destruction which he could not prevent. The cry of the widow and the orphan was always in his ears; the awful responsibility resting upon him as the protector of an imperilled republic kept him true to his duty, but could not make him unmindful of the intimate details of that vast sum of human misery involved in a civil war.

In April 1861 Willie and Tad Lincoln met with their mother's cousin Lockwood Todd for a photograph at Brady's Gallery.

An engraving titled "Abraham Lincoln's Last Reception" was filled with identifiable faces.

Thomas Nast's drawing of Lincoln and the Little Orphan Boy

The Bloody End of Lincoln's Indian Policy

In late December 1890 newspapers reported a military victory against Indians in the Dakota Territories. Few realized at the time that it was an outright massacre.

The U.S. government's clashes with these tribes began back in 1862 with the federal suppression of the Sioux uprising in Minnesota. With Abraham Lincoln's approval, thirty-eight Sioux men were hanged in the largest mass execution in U.S. history. But in contrast to his generals, who had wanted to hang them all, Lincoln placed limits on the executions, and his exoneration of 264 men was the broadest act of clemency in American history. Though he shared many of Americans' racial prejudices against Indians, he went on to support reforms in the government's Indian policies. But when these reforms floundered, a harried Lincoln approved a new policy of Indian concentration. Then in November 1864 the army attacked Cheyenne Indians at Sand Creek, Colorado, killing more than fifty men and a hundred women and children. Lincoln never spoke out publicly about the massacre. His final written statement on the whole subject of Native Americans was to severely criticize them for their "savage warfare upon the sparse settlements of the frontier."

After the Civil War many of the most famous Union generals went west. William Tecumseh Sherman became commanding general, in charge of what were now called the Indian Wars. And in 1876 General George Custer and all his men were killed at the Battle of Little Bighorn, which led to a period of national outrage and reprisals. Fourteen years later the federal government had its revenge. After the killing of the great Lakota chief Sitting Bull in 1890, the army pursued and finally captured a group of Indians on December 29. The massacre of men, women, and children at Wounded Knee left almost three hundred dead.

On March 27, 1863, Lincoln met with Comanche chiefs Pricked Forehead and Ten Bears in the East Room of the White House. But, weighed down by the war, he did little to defend Indian rights, and in the years ahead many were slaughtered by Civil War soldiers who headed west.

The frozen bodies of dead Lakota Indians were buried in a mass grave at Wounded Knee, South Dakota (left). Nearly three hundred men, women, and children were massacred at Wounded Knee. To the right is one of the few survivors.

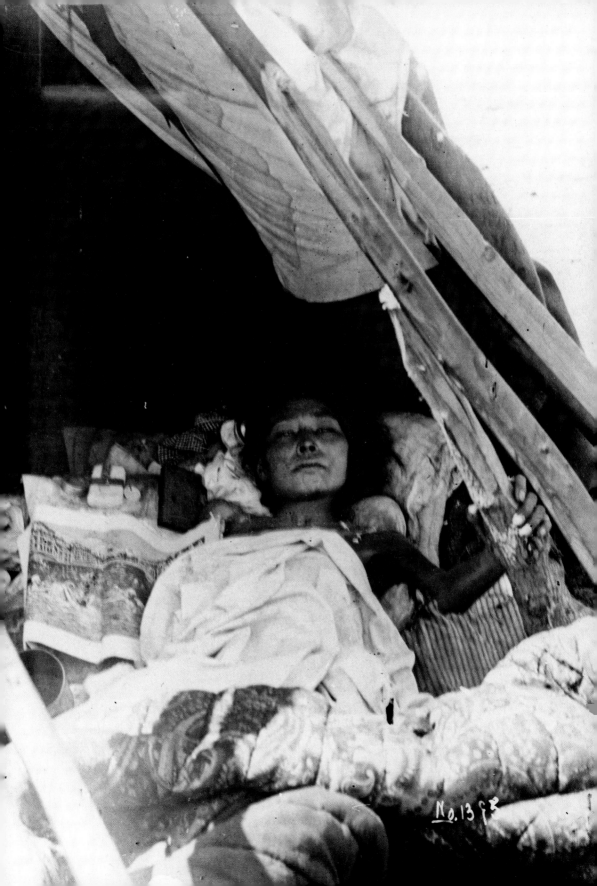

No. 13 93

June 1891
The Lincoln Log Cabin

By the 1890s a new association had been formed in Chicago dedicated to the preservation and promotion of "the old Lincoln Cabin" in Coles County that had belonged to Thomas and Sarah Lincoln. The cabin was by now famous, and sightseers had begun to seek it out. Although it was probably erected in 1837, after Thomas purchased the property, it was publicized that Lincoln had helped build it in 1831 and that he himself had briefly lived there.

In the summer of 1891 the Log Cabin Association sent its secretary and literary editor, Eleanor Gridley, to gather stories for a written account of the cabin's history and to investigate the possibility of buying the building. The property was owned by Sarah Bush's grandson John Hall, who had bought it after Thomas Lincoln's death, and who had helped care for Lincoln's stepmother until her death in 1869. Hall had continued to live in the cabin until 1890, when he moved into a new farmhouse nearby on the property and kept the old building as a family memento.

"Nora" Gridley, who was a cousin of Mary Lincoln, researched the cabin's history with her typist May Coleman.

Eleanor and her party arrived at the farm on June 19. After meeting John Hall, they were walked out to the old cabin. "Weather-beaten, dilapidated, and pitifully forlorn," Gridley wrote, "it stood before us as a reminder of the hardship, toil, and privation" of Lincoln's early life. For Gridley the deserted cabin was a "sacred site"—a shrine harboring the ghost of Abraham Lincoln. Stooping, she walked through the low doorway and entered into the cramped interior. Hall told her how he still remembered Lincoln's visits here in the 1850s and pointed out the spot where he used to sleep. Over the next days Gridley interviewed him at length—"milking me dry," he later said.

On the sixth day she decided to spend a night inside the cabin. They would sleep near the spot where Hall had told them Lincoln always slept. At midnight she and her secretary were startled by a rap on the window and then by a face peering in that looked just like Abraham Lincoln. In the morning they discovered that their night visitor had been a newly arrived custodian.

Gridley remained in Coles County for two weeks, soaking up local lore about Abraham Lincoln and meeting with dozens of people who remembered him. And before she left, she convinced Hall to sell the cabin to the association along with a half acre of land and gardens surrounding the building.

On the final day of her stay Gridley brought in Chicago photographer J. W. Root to photograph the cabin inside and out. It was the last time anyone would ever see the old building on its property. Though the land would be safeguarded as a memorial to Lincoln, the cabin was dismantled and in August moved in its entirety to Chicago. Two years later it appeared at the Chicago World's Fair, then disappeared and was never seen again.

John Hall, sitting on a tree stump with family members (above), had grown up knowing his "Uncle Abe." Below, Eleanor Gridley met with two architects, as one of Sarah Lincoln's great-grandsons peeked out of the cabin window.

A Controversy over Lincoln's Vice President

On July 4, 1891, Hannibal Hamlin, Lincoln's first Vice President, died near his home in Bangor, Maine. He was a well-liked figure in his region, and for years it had been widely believed that he had been cheated out of a second term by the trickery of the Republican Party. Nicolay and Hay had all but said this in their official biography of Lincoln, and Hamlin's family was convinced that Abraham Lincoln had wanted him as his running mate in 1864. But just two days after Hamlin's death, a contentious editorial appeared in the *Philadelphia Times* written by its editor Alexander K. McClure. He said that a change in nominees from Hamlin to Andrew Johnson could not have taken place without Lincoln's favoring the change. McClure then claimed to have special knowledge about the facts. He said he had been summoned to the White House to a secret session and been "gravely urged" by Lincoln to nominate Johnson for Vice President.

When John G. Nicolay read the editorial, he was furious. For one thing, the timing was deeply insulting to Hamlin's family. For another, Nicolay was convinced that McClure was wrong, and he had a memorandum from Lincoln to prove it. In a public letter to Ellen Hamlin he called McClure a liar—saying his reminiscence was "entirely erroneous." Lincoln had remained officially neutral throughout the period, he insisted, and on a personal level had preferred Hamlin.

It was the beginning of a war of words. In his rebuttal McClure attacked Nicolay personally, calling him a "routine clerk"—a "plodding" and "mechanical" underling whom Lincoln would never have consulted on such matters. Even if he possessed a written memorandum from Lincoln, Nicolay was incapable of properly understanding its context. "He was utterly inefficient as the Secretary of the President," McClure attacked, "and only the proverbial kindness of Lincoln saved him from dismissal." He himself, on the other hand, had been one of the President's most trusted advisers, McClure boasted, able to speak with him "at all hours of the day and night."

Trying to ignore the "personal abuse," Nicolay countered that McClure was claiming too much intimacy with Lincoln and too much influence in the proceedings of the convention. Compared to numerous other Pennsylvania delegates, he had played a "minor part." Not even listed as one of the speakers at the convention, he "did not give forth the squeak of the smallest mouse," Nicolay insisted. "Is it probable that Lincoln among all these men would have called you alone to receive his secret instructions?"

And so it continued, back and forth, sinking to deeper and deeper lows. On July 12 McClure wrote venomously, "It would have been better for Lincoln's memory and for the country had such a biographer [as you] been drowned when a pup."

Nicolay's reverence for Lincoln, it must be said, in some ways blinded him to the

Former Vice President Hannibal Hamlin in the last decade of his life. The Republican from Maine had strongly supported Lincoln's policies of emancipation and the use of black troops.

sixteenth President's complex political skills. And in the weeks that followed numerous witnesses stepped forward to reveal how Lincoln had indeed wanted a change in the nominee—how he thought a prominent Union Democrat would better balance the ticket and ensure a Republican victory. And so, despite his personal feelings for Hamlin, Lincoln had been willing to leave him aside if that could assist Republican success. But he hadn't wanted to alienate Hamlin or his supporters in New England, and so he had kept his role quiet, leaking out his wishes in private meetings that he could later deny if necessary.

Nicolay could not fathom how Lincoln could be so duplicitous—how he could write one thing to him while believing another. But in the words of Charles Dana, a close associate of McClure, "Mr. Lincoln was by no means a simple or transparent character: and he was far . . . from the crude, guileless, and mushy philanthropist which some people imagine him to have been. . . . He was not only a great statesman, but a great and shrewd, and all-considering politician also. Nothing could be farther from his character . . . than to blurt out before the public that which prudence required to be kept in private."

In 1860 Currier and Ives depicted Lincoln and his running mate, Hannibal Hamlin of Maine. Hamlin was dropped from the ticket four years later.

"I Learned to Reverence the Man"
A. K. McClure

June 1892

In June 1892 McClure published his long-awaited recollections, Abraham Lincoln and Men of War-Times. *Nicolay and Hay despised the book as well as its author. Hay, who would later call McClure a "professional liar" who "never had two hours' conversation [with Lincoln] in his life," now wrote, in a response to McClure's book, "Every dead-beat politician in the country is coming forward to protest that he was the depository of Lincoln's inmost secrets." Nevertheless McClure's book had memorable sections, such as his description of his first meeting with Lincoln in 1860.*

I went directly from the dépôt to Lincoln's house and rang the bell, which was answered by Lincoln himself opening the door. I doubt whether I wholly concealed my disappointment at meeting him. Tall, gaunt, ungainly, ill clad, with a homeliness of manner that was unique in itself, I confess that my heart sank within me as I remembered that this was the man chosen by a great nation to become its ruler in the gravest period of its history. I remember his dress as if it were but yesterday—snuff-colored and slouchy pantaloons; open black vest, held by a few brass buttons; straight or evening dress-coat, with tightly-fitting sleeves to exaggerate his long, bony arms, and all supplemented by an awkwardness that was uncommon among men of intelligence. Such was the picture I met in the person of Abraham Lincoln. We sat down in his plainly furnished parlor, and were uninterrupted during the nearly four hours that I remained with him, and little by little, as his earnestness, sincerity, and candor were developed in conversation, I forgot all the grotesque qualities which so confounded me when I first greeted him. Before half an hour had passed I learned not only to respect, but, indeed, to reverence the man.

311

October 21, 1892

The Demise of Dennis Hanks

Dennis Hanks's prize possession was the silver watch that Lincoln had given him in 1864. But at age ninety-two, needing money, he agreed to let a granddaughter sell it to Charles F. Gunther, who wanted to place it on exhibit in his Libby Prison War Museum in Chicago. Gunther asked the old man to write an affidavit telling of the watch's history. At the end of it Dennis added "I am a full cousin of Abraham Lincoln, and taught him to read and write."

That same summer of 1891 Hanks was visited by the Log Cabin Association's Eleanor Gridley, as part of her ongoing research into Lincoln's early life. She found the old man in a surly mood, wanting to be paid before he would open up to her. "I think I ought ter hev some credit and lots of money," he said, adding, "if it hadn't been for me ther'd hev been nothin' for folks ter mak such fools of themselves." Dennis was disgusted with what a sacred hero Lincoln had become—how people continued to mourn him after all these years, even still shedding tears for him. "Abe wasn't nobody nor nothin'," Hanks said. "The people made him and he wasn't worth cryin' over." He then told some sour stories about Lincoln's laziness and self-absorption that left Gridley struck by the meanness of his spirit. Later, when she asked John Hall how Hanks could speak so poorly of his cousin, he speculated that it was out of jealousy and envy. But in earlier days, John asserted, it had been different. "Uncle Dennis often bragged up Uncle Abe," he recalled, "and sed he allers knowed he was a natural lawyer, and expected he wus goin' to git to the top of the ladder."

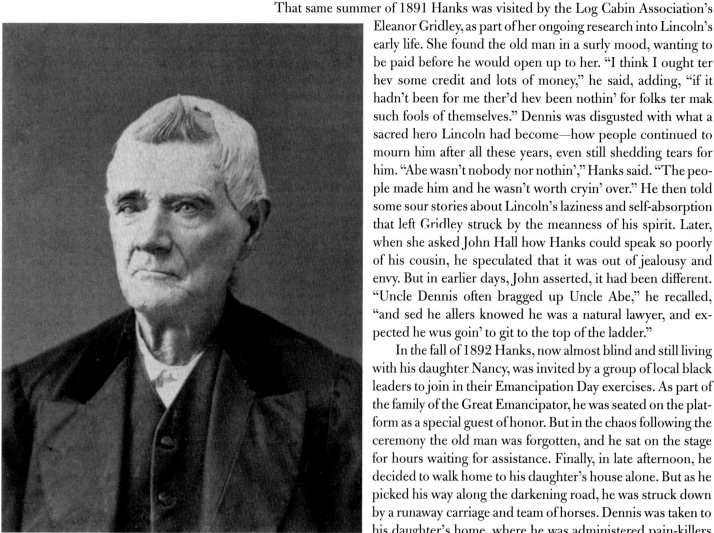

Dennis Hanks liked to brag that it was he who had "learnt Lincoln to read and write." Henry C. Whitney called him "a common liar."

In the fall of 1892 Hanks, now almost blind and still living with his daughter Nancy, was invited by a group of local black leaders to join in their Emancipation Day exercises. As part of the family of the Great Emancipator, he was seated on the platform as a special guest of honor. But in the chaos following the ceremony the old man was forgotten, and he sat on the stage for hours waiting for assistance. Finally, in late afternoon, he decided to walk home to his daughter's house alone. But as he picked his way along the darkening road, he was struck down by a runaway carriage and team of horses. Dennis was taken to his daughter's home, where he was administered pain-killers and put to bed. He never recovered.

Abraham Lincoln had been at the center of Dennis Hanks's long life. "I am dubious about us knowing each other in Heaven," he had once said about Lincoln, "but if I know any one I'll know him. He is over thar somewhere, I know that."

December 1892

On the Circuit with Lincoln

For many Lincoln biographers there was a lucrative financial motivation behind their work. Writing to Ward Hill Lamon in the late 1860s, William Herndon once said, "Ward, there is fame in this; there is money, too, my good friend." And while neither Lamon nor Herndon was financially successful in their Lincoln project, that didn't keep others from trying. One of these was Lincoln's former Illinois colleague Henry Clay Whitney.

Though he had been twenty-two years his junior, Whitney's friendship with Lincoln was well known in Illinois. For seven years in the 1850s they had traveled together on the law circuit, often sharing a bed in the local taverns. Because of his vivid recall of Lincoln stories, early biographers sought Whitney out, and he was especially generous in his letters to William Herndon. Eventually, though, he realized he should be writing about Lincoln himself, and in the fall of 1887 he began planning a lecture tour of the Midwest.

But then his law career took a terrible turn. In the midst of a divorce trial in which he was representing the husband, Whitney was approached by his client's wife and shot twice at close range. Over the next months as he recovered from his wounds, Whitney began writing his Lincoln lectures, planning to "work the business part of it for all it is worth." But when he realized his voice would not be strong enough to speak to large crowds, he turned his texts into published articles, and then fashioned them into a full biography. Whitney's *Life on the Circuit with Lincoln* appeared in 1892—the last biography of Lincoln to be written by someone who had known him well.

As an historical work critics recognized it was flawed. But his depiction of the years 1854 to 1861, when he had known Lincoln firsthand as they traveled the prairies together, was accurate, unique, and compelling. No other writer had described this period of Lincoln's life with so much interesting detail, including vivid accounts from the Lincoln-Douglas debates, and moving stories about Lincoln's final days in Springfield.

Much to his dismay, however, Whitney never made any money off his book. Like Lamon's and Herndon's it was a financial failure. And at the end of his life he said to a friend that he was "sorry he ever invested" in it.

Henry C. Whitney traveled the prairies with Lincoln and in his book vividly depicted their circuit riding days.

"His Preference Was Lincoln"
Henry C. Whitney

December 1892

Whitney's Life on the Circuit *astonished people with the freshness of his memory. "It is like Herndon's book," wrote the* New York Times, *"in being a record supplied by one who knew Lincoln intimately in his early days."*

When I first knew him his attire and physical habits were on a plane with those of an ordinary farmer:—his hat was innocent of a nap:—his boots had no acquaintance with blacking:—his clothes had not been introduced to the whisk broom:—his carpet-bag was well worn and dilapidated;— his umbrella was substantial, but of a faded green, well worn, the knob gone, and the name "A. Lincoln" cut out of white muslin, and sewed in the inside:—and for an outer garment a short circular blue cloak, which he got in Washington in 1849, and kept for ten years. . . .

He probably had as little taste about dress and attire as anybody that ever was born: he simply wore clothes because it was needful and customary: whether they fitted or looked well was entirely above, or beneath, his comprehension. . . .

Of dress, food, and the ordinary comforts and luxuries of this life, he was an incompetent judge. He could not discern between well and ill-cooked and served food. He did not know whether or not clothes fitted. He did not know when music was artistic or in bad taste. He did know, however, if it suited him, and he had a certain taste in that direction, but it was not for anything classical, but something of a style to please the rustic ear. . . .

But although I have heard of cheap fellows, professing that they were wont to address him as "Abe," I never knew of any one who ever did it in my presence. Lincoln disdained ceremony, but he gave no license for being called "Abe." His preference was being called "Lincoln" with no handle at all. I don't recollect of his applying the prefix "Mr." to any one.

February 13, 1893

Lincoln and Lynching

In the 1890s, as lynchings and mob violence began spreading across the South, once again Frederick Douglass rose to do combat. Now in his seventies, he had recently returned from Santo Domingo, where he had served as President Harrison's minister to Haiti. Now he confronted Harrison face to face in the White House on the controversial issue of lynching. But the timid President was unwilling to take action. Deciding to launch his own antilynching campaign, Douglass began to speak out publicly and publish articles on the subject. At no point since the days of his antislavery crusades was he so alive and forceful as he was now. He was incensed at the cruelty of Southern mobs, which, he pointed out, often included women. "Think of an American woman," he wrote in the *North American Review*, "mingling with a howling mob and with her own hand applying the torch to the faggots around the body of a Negro condemned to death without a trial."

He criticized not only the ignorant mobs but the entire system of support that existed throughout the South, including local governments that did nothing to stop lynchers, a Southern press that urged them on, and churches that often took the side of white "Southern honor." And he criticized the North too for its unwillingness to intervene and for having betrayed the great inheritance of the Civil War and period of Reconstruction that followed it.

In the midst of his antilynching campaign Douglass accepted an invitation to address an audience of Republicans in Brooklyn, at a Lincoln birthday celebration on February 13, 1893. He entitled his remarks "Abraham Lincoln: The Great Man of Our Century" and delivered it to three hundred listeners gathered in the dining room of the Union League Club, near a "fine oil painting of the martyred President." It was Douglass's last oration on Lincoln. "I have met no . . . man, at home or abroad, who made upon my mind the impression as possessing a more godlike nature than did Abraham Lincoln. (Cheers and applause.)"

Once again Douglass brought out his old story of first meeting Lincoln—how he had been welcomed into the White house without racial prejudice. He recalled "seeing Mr. Lincoln several times after this interview" and always finding him "the same large hearted man as when I first met him." He told the story of being present for Lincoln's second inaugural—hearing his "remarkable, memorable, and I might say wonderful speech on that occasion." He said he had discerned something almost divine in Lincoln's message, echoing the greatness of his character. "To me he seemed more the saint and prophet . . . than he did the President of a great nation." He spoke with "a voice of deep solemnity, bordering on inconsolable sadness; but a voice as firm as the ever lasting hills. . . . There seemed at the time to be in the man's soul the united souls of all the Hebrew prophets."

At the end of his speech Douglass did something remarkable—he invoked Lincoln's presence into the crisis of the 1890s. If he were still alive today, and "at the

Frederick Douglass came alive with prophetic fire as he attacked the practice of lynching in the 1890s.

The lynching of Henry Smith in Paris, Texas, on February 1, 1893, was just one illustration of vigilante justice in the 1890s. Smith's executioners first tortured him, burning his feet with a red-hot iron.

helm of state," Douglass said, "we should not, as now, hear from the Nation's Capital the weak and helpless . . . confession that . . . there is no power under the United States Constitution to protect the lives and liberties of American citizens in any of our own Southern states from barbarous, inhuman and lawless violence." It was an astonishing finale to his speech. If Republicans wanted to revere Lincoln's memory, Douglass charged, they needed once again to govern in Lincoln's spirit. They needed to put an end to lynching and to reinstate the powers of the Fifteenth Amendment. They needed to stand up and affirm once again the federal government's right, and duty, to enforce civil rights in the states. Newspaper accounts of Douglass's speech recorded numerous breaks of applause as he told his Lincoln stories. But when he ended with this thunderous challenge, his audience sat in stunned silence.

Abraham Lincoln, as Douglass remembered him

Frederick Douglass sometimes pointed out Lincoln's shortcomings, but routinely praised him as African Americans' greatest hero. "We saw him, measured him, and estimated him; not by stray utterances . . . ; not by isolated facts torn from their connection; . . . but by a broad survey, in the light of the stern logic of great events . . . we came to the conclusion that the hour and the man of our redemption had somehow met in the person of Abraham Lincoln."

The Last Time I Saw Him

Frederick Douglass

February 13, 1893

In his last speech on Lincoln, Douglass spoke movingly of his final visit with the sixteenth President, in words that went beyond his earlier published account of the incident.

Having witnessed the inauguration of Mr. Lincoln in the morning, my colored friends urged me to attend the inauguration reception at the executive mansion in the evening. Here, indeed, I found solid ice to break, for no man of my race, color or previous condition, had ever attended such a reception, except as a servant or waiter. I did not look upon the matter lightly, either subjectively or objectively. To me it was a serious thing to break in upon the established usage of the country, and run the risk of being repulsed; but I went to the reception, determined to break the ice, which I [did] in an unexpectedly rough way.

When myself and companion presented ourselves at the door of the White House we were met by two sturdy policemen, who promptly informed us that we could not be allowed to enter, and when we attempted to enter without their consent they pushed us back with some violence. I was, however, determined not to be repulsed and forced myself and lady inside the door, despite the guard. But my trouble was not ended by that advantage. A policeman inside met us and with a show of friendliness, said to us: "Oh, yes; come this way! come this way!" Thinking that he was about to conduct us to the famous East Room, where the reception was proceeding, we followed the lead of our new, red-faced, burly, blue-coated friend; but just when we thought that we were entering, we found ourselves being conducted through an outside window on a plank for the exit of the visitors. (Laughter.) . . .

To a gentleman who was passing at the moment I said "Tell Mr. Lincoln that Frederick Douglass is at the door and is refused admission." I did not walk the plank, and, to the policeman's astonishment, was especially invited into the spacious East Room, and we found ourselves in a bewildering sea of beauty and elegance (applause), such as my poor eyes had never before seen in any one room at home or abroad. High above every other figure in the room, and overlooking the brilliant scene, stood the towering form of Mr. Lincoln, completely hemmed in by the concourse of visitors passing and taking his hand as they passed. The scene was so splendid, so glorious that I almost repented of my audacity in daring to enter.

But as soon as President Lincoln saw me I was relieved of all embarrassment. In a loud voice, so that all could hear, and looking toward me, he said "And here comes my friend, Frederick Douglass!" (Good! Good!) I had some trouble in getting through the crowd of elegantly dressed people to Mr. Lincoln.

When I did succeed, and shook hands with him, he detained me and said, "Douglass I saw you in the crowd today, listening to my inaugural address. How did you like it?" I replied, "Mr. Lincoln, I must not stop to talk now. Thousands are here, wishing to shake your hand." But he said, "You must stop. There is no man in the United States whose opinion I value more than yours. How did you like it?" (Applause.) I said, "Mr. Lincoln, it was a sacred effort." . . . And this was the last time that I heard the voice and saw the face and form of honest Abraham Lincoln.

1893

Colonization

In 1893, just prior to the Supreme Court decision of *Plessy v Ferguson* establishing federally sanctioned segregation, a debate erupted in Washington on the subject of racial colonization. Senator John T. Ingalls went on record as calling black suffrage a "dismal failure" and advocating a serious contemplation of colonizing black Americans to Africa. "Lincoln was not an abolitionist," Ingalls proclaimed. Nor did the Thirteenth Amendment that he helped sponsor ever contemplate black suffrage. The problem came from the Reconstruction amendments, Ingalls said, the hopes of which "have not been realized. . . . The experiment of negro suffrage has been a disaster both to the whites and the blacks." Expressing deep sympathy for black America, and for their increasingly dismal fate, Ingalls reluctantly suggested the old solution of deportation.

Abraham Lincoln had long advocated colonization, a policy going back to leading figures from Thomas Jefferson to Henry Clay. But if many white liberals saw nothing wrong with the policy, for most blacks it represented a total breach of faith. Frederick Douglass once branded Lincoln an "itinerant colonization lecturer" and "a genuine representative of human prejudice." And Isaiah Wears pointed to the injustice of Lincoln's proposals to deport blacks. "To be asked, after so many years of oppression and wrong . . . to pull up stakes" and leave America "is unreasonable and anti-Christian in the extreme."

Wears was responding to Lincoln's meeting with a "Committee of Colored Men" on August 14, 1862, in which he had once again advocated colonization. "Whether it is right or wrong I need not discuss," Lincoln had said, "but . . . I think your race suffer very greatly . . . by living among us while ours suffers from your presence." While Lincoln admitted that the injustice of slavery was largely at fault, he went on to blame the war on the slaves themselves. "[W]ithout the institution of slavery and the Colored race as a basis, the war could not have an existence," he told them. "It is better for us both, therefore, to be separated." (Wears rebutted, "[I]t is not the Negro that is the cause of the war; it is the unwillingness on the part of the American people to do the race simple justice.")

But after 1862 Lincoln had started to change on the issue of race. Following the Emancipation Proclamation and the use of black soldiers in the Union Army, he had gained the respect of the radicals, both black and white. By 1864 he was discarding his colonization views and had begun to imagine an integrated postwar America. In a letter to Governor Michael Hahn of Louisiana he suggested that the new free state include blacks among those gaining the vote—including as a first start "the very intelligent, and especially those who have fought gallantly in our ranks." And in his last public address Lincoln had criticized Louisiana for not taking his advice. "[T]he election is not given to the colored man. I would prefer that it were now conferred on the very intelligent, and those who serve our cause as soldiers." It was this speech, heard by John Wilkes Booth, that led him to decide to murder the President.

In the first years of his presidency Lincoln supported voluntary colonization.

318

Wilson Chinn, a branded slave from Louisiana; also exhibiting instruments of torture used to punish slaves.

PHOTOGRAPHED BY KIMBALL, 477 BROADWAY, N. Y.

Ent'd accord'g to act of Congress in the year 1863, by GEO. H. HANKS, in the Clerk's Office of the U.S for the So. Dist, of N. Y.

Emancipated slave Wilson Chinn was photographed in New York wearing instruments of torture used to punish slaves and make their escape more difficult. On his forehead was the brand "VBM" made by his Louisiana owner Volsey B. Marmillion.

1893

Oldroyd Evicted

Since moving into Lincoln's Springfield house in 1883, Osborn Oldroyd had turned it into a popular tourist attraction. Admiring journalists wrote how he had transformed it into a museum; how at his own expense he had scoured the country, gathering articles that had once belonged to Lincoln. "There is a constant and increasing longing to learn more of him whose death caused humanity to sigh," wrote one reporter. Because of Oldroyd's efforts the younger generation "will have a clearer conception of Lincoln and his home life than the present has of any man of note." By now more than 83,000 visitors had signed Oldroyd's guest book, and groups of schoolchildren regularly made the trip to tour Lincoln's house.

But in his enthusiasm Oldroyd had crossed the line of good taste. According to journalist Parker Temple, he had filled it with "alleged relics, from an old splintered rail to a neck yoke, and proclaimed to the world that they were the handiwork of the martyred President." He had crammed so many Lincoln mementoes into every corner of the ground floor, and into one of the upper parlors as well, that the house had come to resemble a junk shop.

From the start Robert Lincoln did not approve of his tenant's collection and refused to visit the exhibits. He objected to how Oldroyd had turned himself into a spokesman of his family's memory. He was angry that, counter to his published promises, he now charged the public admission to see the home. He was appalled how Oldroyd—who used the backyard as a dumping ground, littering it with empty cans and piles of rubbish—was chipping off small pieces of the house and selling them as souvenirs. And when his tenant stopped sending in his monthly rent, Robert began referring to him as a "dead beat."

By the 1890s Osborn Oldroyd had what one reviewer called "the oldest and probably the largest collection of Lincolniana that has been made." Robert Lincoln had a hand in his eviction from the Springfield home.

In 1887, in an attempt to save the historic house, Robert gave it to the state of Illinois, with the proviso that it be kept in "good repair" and be "forever free" to the public. Though Oldroyd continued on as custodian, Robert wanted him out. In 1892 he officially requested a new custodian and the matter became a political debate. "If the administration should see fit to dispossess the present custodian," wrote one article, "he would be compelled to take his collection with him." In spite of Oldroyd's threats, in 1893 he was forced to vacate. But the savvy entrepreneur had already found a new location. He moved to Washington, D.C., with his entire collection and rented the Petersen House, where Lincoln had died, and set up his relics there.

Oldroyd moved his Lincoln collection to the Petersen House in Washington, D.C., the boardinghouse where Lincoln had died. He renamed it "the Lincoln Memorial House," where he displayed paintings, photographs, Lincoln's law office furniture, the Lincoln family Bible, and the Lincolns' cradle.

The Collapse of Ford's Theatre

Osborn Oldroyd's new museum in Washington was directly across the street from Ford's Theatre, which for twenty-eight years had been in almost constant use. Closed by military police on the night of Lincoln's assassination, the building had remained in government hands until the hanging of the co-conspirators. When it reverted to its owner, John Ford, there was widespread public sentiment that it should never be reopened as a theater. But Ford announced that for financial reasons he was "compelled" to start up "in the earliest practicable moment." On July 9 he advertised a new play, *The Octoroon*. That same day he received a death threat saying that a reopening would "not be tolerated." Ford canceled the production, and signs were soon posted on the building that read "closed by order of the War Department."

John Ford was furious that his business was being attacked and that his motives were being called into question. Contrary to what critics might say, theater was a noble profession, he said, and one that Lincoln himself had deeply appreciated. "The late President was . . . my friend, my patron, my benefactor," he wrote to the *New York Times*. Eventually the government got involved, first renting, then purchasing the building outright. By August 1865 it was being remodeled to be used as a "bureau of rebel archives." Then the surgeon general applied to keep Civil War medical records here, and the War Department decided it should also house a medical museum.

By 1867 the renovation was complete. Three stories had been fitted to house the various collections, with the top floor dedicated to the new Army Medical Museum. Displaying thousands of wounded body parts floating in jars, including three vertebrae from the neck of John Wilkes Booth, it was a grisly reminder of the Civil War.

Ford's Theatre was closed down after Lincoln's assassination, but two years later reopened as the Army Medical Museum. To the right is the main exhibit hall of the museum.

Over the years the popular museum would come to hold other "treasures"—including the entire skeleton of the assassin of James Garfield. But, amid growing concerns that the building was not safe, in the late 1880s the museum was moved out to make room for more War Department records.

In 1893 the rickety building housed not only millions of records, but 420 clerks working on three floors. There were so many people inside that a ventilation system was needed. And to put one in, the army began excavating the cellar.

At 9:40 A.M. on June 9, four hundred workers were already at their desks—packed in, one paper said, "like bees in a hive, without a chance of escape." Suddenly a loud rumbling noise was heard, and then a crashing sound as two floors collapsed and fell to the ground. One hundred clerks were swept down instantly into a tangled mass of bricks and beams. Others huddled on upstairs sections that had not yet fallen. Panic swept through the building and men jumped out of windows. When the dust had cleared, and the rubble had been sifted through, twenty-two were dead and sixty-eight injured in one of the city's most horrifying disasters.

When both interior floors collapsed, twenty-two employees died. The *Los Angeles Times* wrote of the doomed building, "[Had it] borne a curse upon it from that time [of Lincoln's murder] it could not have ended its career in a more fitting manner."

Deconstructing Lincoln

One of the strangest books to come out about Abraham Lincoln was published in 1894. It was written by a convert to Roman Catholicism, the New York lawyer Oliver Prince Buel, whose stepson David was preparing for the Catholic priesthood and may well have contributed to the work. The satirical book was purported to have been written by "Bocardo Bramantip," identified as "the Huxleyan Professor of Dialectics at the University of the Congo." The supposed date of publication was the year 3663—the eighteen hundredth anniversary of Lincoln's Emancipation Proclamation. Entitled *The Abraham Lincoln Myth: An Essay in Higher Criticism,* it was meant to ridicule the radical critics of the nineteenth century currently holding sway in the field of religion. The author of the spoof clearly had knowledge of the field. He was also a racist.

By the year 3663, according to the book, African civilization was dominant across the planet. Now it was time for Africans to deconstruct their myths, including the view that they owed their freedom in America "to a white man—one of the degenerate Caucasian race." Just as the higher critics were questioning whether Jesus of Nazareth had ever lived, these Africans were now asking the same question about Abraham Lincoln, who appeared to them to be a literary invention. "The story of his assassination suggests, in all its details, the hand of a novelist or a playwright," the book said; "the story looks artificial and suspicious on its face. As a myth thrown up by an ignorant former era—the Dark Ages of the period of Aryan supremacy—it now needed to be expunged. The story is the outgrowth of 'hero worship,' so prevalent in the nineteenth century. The Aryan race was given to the love of the wonderful, and to the idolatry of its great men."

Beneath the convoluted exterior of the book lay admiration for Lincoln and an obvious distaste for literary criticism. Just as it was absurd to doubt the existence and meaning of Abraham Lincoln, the book implied, it was equally absurd to doubt the existence of Jesus. It was another example of how Lincoln and Christ were being compared. Even as the author, in his racist manner, tried to mock the idea of mythicizing Lincoln, he was in fact contributing to the still-growing Lincoln myth that he was purporting to explode.

Abraham Lincoln in 1864

Confusion at Gettysburg

This close-up detail of a crowd shot taken by Alexander Gardner at Gettysburg on November 19, 1863, shows a figure on horseback who, though visible only in profile, appears to be Abraham Lincoln.

Boys mingle on the outskirts of the public ceremony on the day of Lincoln's Gettysburg Address. Hidden in the crowds behind them is the unmistakable face of Abraham Lincoln (see larger close-up, page 470).

By the 1890s Lincoln's Gettysburg Address was widely recognized as his masterpiece. Back in 1865 Ralph Waldo Emerson had said that it would "not be easily surpassed by words on any recorded occasion." But it had taken three decades for the address's fame to spread widely. By now there was huge interest in exactly how it was written. An 1887 article attributed to Edward McPherson claimed that Lincoln had written the address on his knee on the train ride to Gettysburg, using "a rough piece of foolscap" and a lead pencil. "It was practically an extemporaneous composition," the author attested; "it was wholly unpremeditated." This triggered a variety of eyewitnesses to step forward to try to shed light on Lincoln's "immortal words." Lincoln's former attorney general James Speed wrote that Lincoln had told him that the speech was already partially written before he left Washington and that he had finished it after arriving in Gettysburg. And Lincoln's host David Wills wrote to say that yes indeed, Lincoln had finished writing his address in an upper room in his house at Gettysburg.

McPherson also claimed that Lincoln had read his remarks on November 19 "in a low voice, which could be heard but a few feet away from the stage." That meant that for the "vast throng who saw him the oration made no impression whatever, because no one heard it." This assertion also elicited strong reactions. One eyewitness who had stood on the outer periphery of the large crowd recalled hearing Lincoln's "clear, distinct voice, perfectly audible where my regiment was stationed, outside of the audience proper."

To try to make sense out of the chaos, John G. Nicolay wrote an article for *Century Magazine* in February 1894. Nicolay had accompanied Lincoln on the journey to Gettysburg and had seen nothing of any writing on board the train, upon a knee or otherwise. Instead, he confirmed that Lincoln had indeed finished the work at the home of Wills, where he had been invited to stay since all the hotels in town were booked. Nicolay had been in the room with Lincoln while he completed the writing on the morning of the nineteenth. As to the question of how the address was received, Nicolay recalled interruptions of applause punctuating the entire speech, just as the Associated Press had reported it. And he said that Lincoln had delivered the speech boldly, hardly looking at his manuscript.

Other witnesses, such as John Russell Young, disagreed, writing that the speech was so short he didn't even have time to take out his pencil to begin taking shorthand. There was no emotion, Young insisted, no great applause or interruptions. The speech, as Ward Lamon had earlier said, was indeed a failure.

The fact that there were so many conflicting stories revealed how fascinated the public was with Lincoln and his famous address. By 1894 it was already widely considered the most enduring of all American orations.

The Complete Works of Abraham Lincoln

John Nicolay followed up his February article in *Century* with a second piece in April entitled "Lincoln's Literary Experiments." His idea was to analyze Lincoln the writer. "It is a constant puzzle to many men of letters," he wrote, "how a person growing up without the advantage of schools and books could have acquired the art which enabled him to write the Gettysburg address and the second inaugural."

Nicolay had witnessed the development of Lincoln's writing talent. He had seen how when a piece of writing was important, Lincoln had sought complete privacy to work on it—in an upstairs room in Springfield; in the Telegraph Office at the War Department; anywhere he could get away for a few hours from the crowds. Somehow in the privacy of his own efforts, Lincoln's remarkable powers of literary expression came forth.

Nicolay's article was meant in part to introduce a new series of volumes he and John Hay were preparing, entitled *The Complete Works of Abraham Lincoln.* The previous year Robert Lincoln had written requesting that they follow up their "great work," the ten-volume biography, "by collecting, editing, and publishing the speeches, letters, state papers and miscellaneous writings of my father." The authors had his full consent and authorization, Robert said, to publish any and all Lincoln writings that were in his possession.

The Century Company, which agreed to publish the books, wanted them to look just like the volumes of the biography—to serve as an appendix to that work. But with more than 1,700 entries to include, the edition would have required five new volumes. To economize, the books were printed on thinner paper with twice as many words per page, so that the entire collection came out in two thick books. It was a remarkable achievement. Every important speech and state paper was here and, in addition, many of Lincoln's letters, with minimal editing or editorial notes.

The public was already familiar with the Lincoln masterpieces—"the best things he said or wrote are household words now," commented the *Chicago Tribune.* But here was a wealth of material utterly fresh for most readers. Reviewers were drawn to Lincoln's early speeches, to his youthful poetry, and to his private letters. Here were evidences of the real man in evolution, a unique window into his development as a national leader. Over the past thirty years there had been many efforts to gather the evidences of Lincoln's life—firsthand testimonies about him, personal relics from his life, photographs, drawings, and other depictions of him. What Nicolay and Hay realized was that the most important relic of all was Lincoln's own writings—the vast corpus of his letters, speeches, and papers.

Nicolay and Hay's collection of Lincoln writings spanned his presidential and pre-presidential years.

"To the People of Sangamo County"

March 9, 1832

Nicolay and Hay's Complete Works *included a transcription of Lincoln's first political letter, published in New Salem just six months after he moved there. As with most of their transcriptions, they altered Lincoln's punctuation, misread "county" as "country", and wrote "Sangamon" instead of "Sangamo."*

Fellow citizens: Having become a candidate for the honorable office of one of your Representatives in the next General Assembly of this State, in accordance with an established custom, and the principles of true Republicanism, it becomes my duty to make known to you,—the people whom I propose to represent,—my sentiments with regard to local affairs. . . .

Every man is said to have his peculiar ambition. Whether it be true or not, I can say, for one, that I have no other so great as that of being truly esteemed of my fellow-men, by rendering myself worthy of their esteem. How far I shall succeed in gratifying this ambition is yet to be developed. I am young, and unknown to many of you. I was born, and have ever remained, in the most humble walks of life. I have no wealthy or popular relations to recommend me. My case is thrown exclusively upon the independent voters of the country; and, if elected, they will have conferred a favor upon me, for which I shall be unremitting in my labors to compensate. But, if the good people in their wisdom shall see fit to keep me in the background, I have been too familiar with disappointments to be very much chagrined.

"My Childhood's Home I See Again"

April 18, 1846

Lincoln's early experiments with poetry included this verse sent to a friend in 1846. "In the fall of 1844," Lincoln wrote, "thinking I might aid some to carry the State of Indiana for Mr. Clay, I went into the neighborhood in that State in which I was raised, where my mother and only sister were buried, and from which I had been absent about fifteen years. That part of the country is, within itself, as unpoetical as any spot of the earth; but still, seeing it and its objects and inhabitants aroused feelings in me which were certainly poetry; though whether my expression of those feelings is poetry is quite another question."

My childhood's home I see again,
And sadden with the view;
And still, as memory crowds my brain,
There's pleasure in it too. . . .

Near twenty years have passed away
Since here I bid farewell
To woods and fields, and scenes of play,
And playmates loved so well.

Where many were, but few remain
Of old familiar things;
But seeing them, to mind again
The lost and absent brings.

The friends I left that parting day,
How changed, as time has sped!
Young childhood grown, strong manhood gray,
And half of all are dead.

I hear the loved survivors tell
How nought from death could save,
Till every sound appears a knell,
And every spot a grave.

I range the fields with pensive tread,
And pace the hollow rooms,
And feel (companion of the dead)
I'm living in the tombs.

An Honest Lawyer

July 1, 1850 [?]

The following fragment of writing containing notes for a law lecture was published by Nicolay and Hay for the first time. The editors estimated the date of composition to be July 1, 1850.

The leading rule for the lawyer, as for the man of every other calling, is diligence. Leave nothing for to-morrow which can be done to-day. Never let your correspondence fall behind. Whatever piece of business you have in hand, before stopping, do all the labor pertaining to it which can then be done. . . .

Discourage litigation. Persuade your neighbors to compromise whenever you can. Point out to them how the nominal winner is often a real loser—in fees, expenses, and waste of time. As a peacemaker the lawyer has a superior opportunity of being a good man. There will still be business enough.

Never stir up litigation. A worse man can scarcely be found than one who does this. Who can be more nearly a fiend than he who habitually overhauls the register of deeds in search of defects in titles, whereon to stir up strife, and put money in his pocket? A moral tone ought to be infused into the profession which should drive such men out of it. . . .

There is a vague popular belief that lawyers are necessarily dishonest. . . . Let no young man choosing the law for a calling for a moment yield to the popular belief—resolve to be honest at all events; and if in your own judgment you cannot be an honest lawyer, resolve to be honest without being a lawyer.

The Death of Frederick Douglass

At his Washington funeral a letter from Elizabeth Cady Stanton proclaimed, "Frederick Douglass is not dead. His great character will long be an object lesson in our Nation's history." Below is Douglass's final service at the Central Presbyterian Church in Rochester, New York.

Frederick Douglass spent most of February 20, 1895, with his friend and fellow warrior Susan B. Anthony. For years he had aligned himself with the women's rights movement. Though frustrated that some of its leaders had failed to support the Fifteenth Amendment, immediately upon its ratification Douglass had called for an amendment enfranchising women. He was a member of the National Woman Suffrage Association and regularly attended its meetings. On this day, now seventy-seven years old, he came to take part in the association's Triennial. When he was introduced at its council meeting that morning, he took a deep bow and then was seated beside Susan Anthony. He remained all day, taking great interest in the proceedings, and that evening at dinner told his wife Helen all about it. As he grew excited in his storytelling and began to mimic one of the day's speakers, he was suddenly struck with severe pain and fell to the floor. A few moments later, when a carriage arrived to take him to a lecture he was scheduled to give, Frederick Douglass died.

Douglass's funeral echoed that of Lincoln thirty years earlier and was the most interracial event since the unveiling of the Freedmen's Memorial. For hour after hour black and white Americans paid homage at the Metropolitan African Methodist Episcopal Church. With many schools closed in his honor, thousands of black children filed past his open casket. Among the honored guests were Chief Justice John Marshall Harlan, Senators John Sherman, George Gage, and Blanche K. Bruce, Congressman John R. Lynch, and Douglass's old friend Susan B. Anthony. The entire faculty of Howard University attended.

Following the Washington funeral, Douglass's body was taken by train to his hometown of Rochester, New York, where it lay in state in the city hall so that thousands more could pay their final respects. Across the country sermons were given in his honor. In Brooklyn he was called "the most picturesque historical figure in modern times." In terms of how far he had traveled in life he exceeded even Lincoln, said the Rev. Louis A. Banks. From slavery to freedom to undisputed leader of his race to major public figure, "the story of his life is the most romantic of all [in] modern times," said Banks. "No man began so low and climbed so high as he." Douglass often compared himself to Lincoln, speaking of "the similarity with which I had fought my way up, we both having started at the lowest round of the ladder." All agreed—he was one of the greatest orators of his age, a fine writer, and a courageous social prophet. It was extraordinary how often he was compared to Abraham Lincoln. It was as if they belonged together in the nation's memory.

In the mid-1890s the progressive religious journal *The Independent* dedicated a special issue to appear on the thirtieth anniversary of Lincoln's death, and to include reminiscences from a broad array of people who had known him. With many of Lincoln's closest associates now dead, it had been a difficult task for editor William Hayes Ward. He obtained articles from William O. Stoddard, Francis Carpenter, William Herndon, and Lucius Chittenden—all figures the public already knew well. But he also reached out to some newcomers—George S. Boutwell, a congressman during Lincoln's presidency who had remained silent all these years; Charles Tinker, a Washington telegrapher in Lincoln's day; Henry W. Knight, a War Department guard; Grace Greenwood, aka Sarah Lippincott, a leading woman journalist; and General Oliver Otis Howard, former head of the Freedmen's Bureau and currently helping to launch Lincoln Memorial University in Tennessee. In all there were forty recollections, all describing, in Hayes's words, "the most picturesque, perhaps the most noble, character in American history."

The collection suffered from the fact that so many eyewitnesses had already died, and that many of its contributors were growing old. Some, now in their seventies, were already drifting away from earlier versions of their recollections. Coming out during the Democratic presidency of Grover Cleveland, there was a strong desire to be bipartisan and inclusive. Colonel B. F. Watson contributed "Abraham Lincoln as Seen by a Life-Long Democrat." And in an era when North-South reunion was an increasingly important part of the national agenda, there was a pronounced effort to recall Lincoln as a sympathizer to Southerners.

There was in general by now a smoothing out of the Lincoln memories and an incorporation of vintage stories that were becoming securely established in the literary canon. These included such stories as Lincoln's concern for a sleeping sentinel, an account that was now cropping up in dozens of firsthand narratives. And there were multiple versions of Lincoln speaking about his own "ugliness." Most prominent in the new collection was a tendency to spiritualize Lincoln, something perhaps not unexpected in a religious journal. James F. Rusling's story of Lincoln praying before the Battle of Gettysburg was greeted enthusiastically in the pietistic 1890s but did not mesh with what was already known about Lincoln. Rusling put the following words into Lincoln's mouth: "I went into my room one day and locked the door, and got down on my knees before Almighty God, and prayed to him mightily for a victory at Gettysburg. . . . And then and there I made a solemn vow to Almighty God that if he would stand by our boys at Gettysburg I would stand by him. And he did, and I will." The words did not fit with Lincoln's theology as revealed in his Second Inaugural Address.

But despite the mixed quality of the reminiscences, there were superb pieces in Ward's collection, including vivid new word-pictures of the sixteenth President. A few months after *The Independent*'s special issue, the collection was published as a book, *Tributes from His Associates*. Reviewers marveled at the number of fresh reminiscences—which would no doubt continue until all who had known Lincoln were dead.

ABRAHAM LINCOLN.*

The Thirtieth Anniversary of his Assassination.

TRIBUTES FROM HIS ASSOCIATES.

Incidents and Stories.

HIS SPEECHES IN NEW YORK AND NEW ENGLAND.

The Tragedy at Ford's Theater.

REMINISCENCES OF SOLDIERS, STATESMEN AND CITIZENS.

The Independent, April 4, 1895

"We Are Elected!"
Henry C. Bowen

1895

Henry Bowen was the founder and owner of The Independent, *the most influential religious journal of the 1860s, then under the editorship of Henry Ward Beecher. On several occasions Bowen met with Lincoln, including for "a long and private conversation" at the time of his inauguration in 1861 in which Lincoln told him the story of how he had received the news of his election.*

In November, on the day of the election, he said he was calm and sure of the result. The first news he received, mostly from New York, was unfavorable, and he felt a little discouraged. Later the dispatches indicated a turn in the tide. . . .

At a late hour he left the Club rooms and went home to talk over matters with his wife. Before going to the Club that evening to get the election news as it came in, he said: "I told my wife to go to bed, as probably I should not be back before midnight. When at about twelve o'clock the news came informing me of my election, I said: 'Boys, I think I will go home now: for there is a little woman there who would like to hear the news.' The Club gave me three rousing cheers, and then I left. On my arrival I went to my bedroom and found my wife sound asleep. I gently touched her shoulder and said 'Mary'; she made no answer. I spoke again, a little louder, saying, 'Mary, Mary! *we are elected!*'"

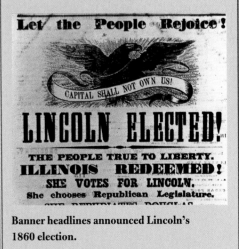

Banner headlines announced Lincoln's 1860 election.

An Unusual Meeting
Grace Greenwood

1895

Grace Greenwood

Grace Greenwood, also known as Sarah Clarke Lippincott, was a writer and reformer whom Abraham Lincoln dubbed "Grace Greenwood the Patriot." For The Independent *she described meeting Lincoln in the White House along with the famous Barnum midgets Mr. and Mrs. Charles Stratton.*

During a visit to Washington, in late war time, I received an informal invitation to a reception *extraordinaire* at the White House. It was to meet Mr. and Mrs. Charles S. Stratton—"General Tom Thumb"—and his wife, Lavinia, then on their bridal tour. . . .

The reception took place in the East room; and when, following the loud announcement, "Mr. and Mrs. Charles Stratton," the guests of honor entered from the corridor, and walked slowly up the long *salon,* to where Mr. and Mrs. Lincoln stood, to welcome them, the scene became interesting, though a little bizarre. The pigmy "General," at that time still rather good-looking, though slightly *blasé,* wore his elegant wedding suit, and his wife, a plump but symmetrical little woman, with a bright, intelligent face, her wedding dress—the regulation white satin, with point lace, orange blossoms and pearls—while a train some two yards long swept out behind her. I well remember the "pigeon-like stateliness" with which they advanced, almost to the feet of the President, and the profound respect with which they looked up, up, to his kindly face. It was pleasant to see their tall host bend, and bend, to take their little hands in his great palm, holding Madame's with especial chariness, as though it were a robin's egg, and he were fearful of breaking

it. Yet he did not *talk* down to them, but made them feel from the first as though he regarded them as real "folks," sensible, and knowing a good deal of the world. He presented them, very courteously and soberly, to Mrs. Lincoln, and in his compliments and congratulations there was not the slightest touch of the exaggeration which a lesser man might have been tempted to make use of, for the quiet amusement of onlookers; in fact, nothing to reveal to that shrewd little pair his keen sense of the incongruity of the scene.

Charles and Lavinia Stratton, known as "Mr. and Mrs. Tom Thumb," before their White House visit

A Guard's Recollections
Henry W. Knight

1895

Henry Knight had been a young soldier in the Civil War, later assigned to guard duty in Washington.

I was assigned to duty at Washington. I was placed in charge of the guard at the War Department, and here it was that I frequently saw Mr. Lincoln. His favorite time for visiting the War Department was between eleven and twelve at night, and when there was no one in the building but the telegraph operator and his two or three

messengers and the guard in charge of the building. We were all quite sure of one thing—the harder it rained or the fiercer the winds blew, the more certainly would he come; for he seemed to love to go out in the elements, and to commune with Nature in her wildest moods.

I seem to see him now, as—his tall, ungainly form wrapped in an old gray shawl, wearing usually a "shockingly bad hat," and carrying a worse umbrella—he came up the steps into the building. Secretary Stanton, who knew Mr. Lincoln's midnight habits, gave a standing order that, although Mr. Lincoln might come from the White House alone (and he seldom came in any other way), he should never be permitted to return alone, but should be escorted by a file of four soldiers and a noncommissioned officer. I was on duty every other night. When Mr. Lincoln was ready to return we

would take up a position near him, and accompany him safely to the White House. I presume I performed this duty fifty times. On the way to the White House, Mr. Lincoln would converse with us on various topics. I remember one night when it was raining very hard that he came over, and about one o'clock he started back. As he saw us at the door, ready to escort him, he addressed us in these words: "Don't come out in this storm with me to-night, boys; I have my umbrella, and can get home safely without you." "But," I replied, "Mr. President, we have positive orders from Mr. Stanton not to allow you to return alone; and you know we dare not disobey his orders." "No," replied Mr. Lincoln, "I suppose not; for if Stanton should learn that you had let me return alone, he would have you court-martialed and shot inside of twenty-four hours."

Gettysburg National Military Park

In the same year as Nicolay's Gettysburg article, General Daniel Sickles, who had lost his leg at the Battle of Gettysburg, raised a bill in Congress to establish a national military park at the site of what many considered the central battle of the Civil War. It called for federal acquisition of eight hundred acres encompassing the battlefields and for the proper marking of the now-famous scenes there. A special feature of the park would be a monument honoring Abraham Lincoln and his Gettysburg Address—his "sudden flash of inspiration," as one paper called it, "struck like a spark from the battlefield of the war." The new park would be a first of its kind in the nation and make Gettysburg "preeminent among the world's battlefields," one paper noted. The idea had broad popular support, and by Lincoln's birthday the following year President Grover Cleveland had approved the act. That spring the local association that had owned the property since 1864 voted to turn over its possession to the federal government.

There was to be no partisanship in the presentations—Union and Confederate soldiers were to be commemorated here. And Gettysburg was to be one of three great battlefields to be protected, along with Shiloh and Chickamauga in Tennessee. That summer a major gathering of Union and Confederate veterans assembled at Gettysburg for a Civil War reunion, before heading south to visit the other two sites. Earlier attempts at such North-South gatherings had failed miserably, until finally in 1887 when representatives of Pickett's Charge and its Union defenders put their quarter-century of anger behind them and had managed a successful gathering here. Now thousands of veterans, in blue and gray, marched in from Washington, D.C., and from all direcions to take part in a grand reunion on the fields of Gettysburg.

Union dead on the fields at Gettysburg

General Daniel Sickles returned to the spot at Gettysburg where he had lost his leg. He led the effort to turn the battle-fields into a national military park.

A "Most Tender Hearted Man"
Frances Todd Wallace

September 2, 1895

Frances Todd Wallace

The death of Elizabeth Edwards in 1888, and of Ann Todd Smith three years later, left only one of Mary Lincoln's sisters still alive. (There was also one brother still living, George Todd, a doctor in South Carolina who had served as a surgeon in the Confederate Army.) Like her sisters, Frances Todd had followed Elizabeth to Springfield. There she had married William Wallace, a man who later was Eddy Lincoln's physician in his final days, and after whom Willie Lincoln was named. The opposite of her caustic older sister Elizabeth, Frances was called the "angel" of the family. Lincoln was extremely fond of her. And unlike others who recalled Mary in unflattering terms, Frances had warm and loving memories of their days together in Springfield. On September 2, 1895, she gave this interview to a reporter.

I don't see why people should say Mr. Lincoln's home life was not happy, for I certainly never saw a thing there that would make me think either of them was unhappy. He was devoted to his home, and Mrs. Lincoln thought everything of him. She almost worshiped him. Why, she need not have married him if she had not wanted to. She could have married Mr. Douglas, I have no doubt. She had gone with Mr. Douglas to several places. They were very well acquainted, and were very good friends.

And Mr. Lincoln was not compelled to marry Mary. He had become quite a promising young man, and we were all proud of him. He could have married any other girl, no doubt, if he had wanted to. But they did not lead an unhappy life at all. Why, she was devoted to him and to her children. And he was certainly all to her that any husband could have been.

Abraham and Tad Lincoln

He was the most tender hearted man I ever knew. I have seen him carry Tad half way to the office, when Tad was a great big boy. And I said to him once: "Why, Mr. Lincoln, put down that great big boy. He's big enough to walk." And he said:

"Oh, don't you think his little feet get too tired?"...

They say that he had an affair with a young woman at Salem, and that he . . . was half distracted with love for his other girl. . . . I don't know anything about that. . . . But I certainly saw him the night he was married, and he was not distracted with

In this composite portrait, Mary Lincoln appears taller than her five-foot-two height.

grief, or anything else. He was cheerful as he ever had been, for all we could see. He acted just as he always had in company. . . .

No one but members of the family were there, or almost none. As I remember it there was Mr. and Mrs. Ninian Edwards, Mr. and Mrs. Ben Edwards, Major Stuart and his wife, Mr. and Mrs. Dresser, Dr. Todd's family, and Mr. Wallace and myself. I don't think there was anyone else there. There couldn't have been more than one or two more.

And then they say that Mrs. Lincoln was an ambitious woman. But she was not an ambitious woman at all. She was devoted to her home. She was one of the best seamstresses I ever knew. She made all her clothes and her children's clothes; and they were better made than most anyone else's. It was before the day of sewing machines, you know, and all her work had to be done by hand. And they always looked well.

Lincoln's Journalist
Noah Brooks

October 1895

Noah Brooks's favorite subject was Abraham Lincoln. Over the decades, drawing on his newspaper articles and notes from the 1860s, he poured forth reminiscences of the sixteenth President. In 1888 he published a biography of Lincoln for young readers that went on to numerous editions. And in 1895 he wrote a series of articles for Century Magazine *that he then combined with his earlier accounts into a book published that autumn,* Washington in Lincoln's Time.

Lincoln's "Tired Spot"

Early in April, 1863, I accompanied the President, Mrs. Lincoln, and their youngest son, "Tad," on a visit to the Army of the Potomac—Hooker then being in command, with headquarters on Falmouth Heights, opposite Fredericksburg.... The infantry reviews were held on several different days. On April 8th was the review of the Fifth Corps, under Meade; the Second, under Couch; the Third, under Sickles, and the Sixth, under Sedgwick. It was reckoned that these four corps numbered some 60,000 men, and it was a splendid sight to witness their grand martial array as they wound over hills and rolling ground, coming from miles away, their arms shining in the distance, and their bayonets bristling like a forest on the horizon as they marched away. The President expressed himself as delighted with the appearance of the soldiery, and he was much impressed by the parade.... It was noticeable that the President merely touched his hat in return salute to the officers, but uncovered to the men in the ranks.... After a few days the weather grew warm and bright ... and the President became more cheerful and even jocular. I remarked this one evening as we sat in Hooker's headquarters, after a long and laborious day of reviewing. Lincoln replied: "It is a great relief to get away from Washington and the politicians. But nothing touches the tired spot."

Noah Brooks at his desk in the 1890s

"What Will the Country Say!"

[On May 6, 1863, following the Union loss at Chancellorsville,] the door opened, and Lincoln came into the room. I shall never forget that picture of despair. He held a telegram in his hand, and as he closed the door and came toward us I mechanically noticed that his face, usually sallow, was ashen in hue. The paper on the wall behind him was of the tint known as "French gray," and even in that moment of sorrow and dread expectation I vaguely took in the thought that the complexion of the anguished President's visage was almost exactly like that of the wall. He gave me the telegram, and in a voice trembling with emotion, said, "Read it—news from the army." The despatch was from General Butterfield, Hooker's chief of staff, addressed to the War Department, and was to the effect that the Army had been withdrawn from the south side of the Rappahannock, and was then "safely encamped" in its former position. The appearance of the President, as I read aloud these fateful words, was piteous. Never as long as I knew him, did he seem to be so broken, so dispirited, and so ghostlike. Clasping his hands behind his back, he walked up and down the room, saying, "My God! My God! What will the country say! What will the country say!"

Lincoln rode with General Joseph Hooker during a review of the army on May 2, 1863. Four days later Hooker's retreat after the Battle of Chancellorsville left Lincoln in despair.

In Search of Lincoln

Thirty years after Lincoln's death, a thirty-seven-year-old writer named Ida M. Tarbell was assigned to work on his biography for *McClure's Magazine*. Her technique was unlike any ever attempted. She approached her subject as an investigative journalist, setting up what she called a "Lincoln Bureau." Tarbell was promised by owner Samuel S. McClure that he would spare no expense in searching out fresh material—unpublished reminiscences, Lincoln documents, and photographs. John G. Nicolay advised Tarbell to drop the "hopeless" assignment, saying there was "nothing of importance" left to be written about Lincoln, and that his own work on the subject was "complete." But Nicolay was mistaken. Tarbell would use the magazine's national exposure to make a public call for new Lincoln material. "The response was immediate and amazing," she wrote. "Hundreds of persons from all parts of the country replied."

In February 1895 Tarbell took to the road for what would become months of intensive field research. Her plan was to retrace the steps of the Lincoln family's migrations, from Kentucky to Indiana to Illinois, stopping to interview people who had known Lincoln and to search local courthouses and newspaper morgues for unpublished evidence of his life. To assist her in Illinois, Tarbell hired a Springfield lawyer named J. McCan Davis. With persistence and patience he combed through back issues of the *Sangamo Journal*, unearthing forgotten speeches of Lincoln's early career; collected dozens of unpublished Lincoln documents and pictures; drew maps to accompany Tarbell's articles; and conducted interviews with important eyewitnesses. He and Tarbell each carried a camera along with them, to capture unusual images to accompany her writing—the supposed log cabin on Nolin Creek where Lincoln was born (rebuilt from the "original logs," it was said, that same year); the old Lincoln homestead in Indiana, where several original buildings still stood; the abandoned site of New Salem, where thirty years earlier Herndon had come for inspiration. They photographed furniture and kitchen equipment once used in New Salem; Ann Rutledge's gravestone in Petersburg, Illinois; and relics of Lincoln's remote relative Daniel Boone. And they began a wide-ranging hunt for Lincoln photographs—reaching out to family members, neighbors, and Lincoln collectors, convincing them to let *McClure's* publish their unique images. They obtained photographs of Lincoln from Noah Brooks, from Harriet Chapman (Sarah Bush Lincoln's granddaughter), from James Speed, and from collectors across Illinois. In Boston, Tarbell met with the sculptor Truman Bartlett, who had been amassing Lincoln photographs for more than twenty years. It was "the most complete and the most intelligently arranged" collection in existence, she wrote, and with great generosity Bartlett placed it at her disposal. Eventually the magazine would garner some fifty Lincoln photographs, more than twice as many as had ever been published before. "The series of portraits will cover a period of twenty years," announced *McClure's*, "and consist of reproductions of every photograph, ambrotype, daguerreotype, or painting of Lincoln known to exist."

Tarbell made her most exciting photographic discovery when she met with Robert Lincoln. Given his exclusive relationship with Nicolay and Hay, he declined to grant her access to his father's papers, but at the urging of a mutual friend he agreed to loan her an extraordinary treasure—a never-before-published daguerreo-

Ida Tarbell brought a journalist's instincts to a field previously dominated by Lincoln insiders. Unlike Nicolay and Hay, who had concentrated on Lincoln's public life, Tarbell focused on "the development of his mind" and "moral qualities." She wrote, "It is Lincoln the man, as seen by his fellows and revealed by his own acts and words, that the author has tried to picture."

Dismayed when John Nicolay refused to help in any way on her Lincoln project, Ida Tarbell later wrote, "Mr. Nicolay's tragedy was in not having found a fresh field. How different it was with his colleague John Hay, whose secretaryship with Lincoln [was] . . . an episode in a diplomatic career of unusual distinction and usefulness!" She occupied her desk at *McClure's* for ten years and traveled by horse and buggy to do her field research.

Tarbell's articles drew large volumes of mail to McClure's *magazine. From Beachmont, Massachusetts, Lincoln's old friend Henry C. Whitney wrote to comment on the daguerreotype procured by Ida Tarbell from Robert Lincoln, the first photograph ever taken of Lincoln.*

My Dear Sir: I am greatly obliged for your early picture of Abraham Lincoln, which I regard as an important contribution to history. It is without doubt authentic and accurate; and dispels the illusion so common (but never shared by me) that Mr. Lincoln was an ugly-looking man. In point of fact, Mr. Lincoln was always a noble-looking—always a highly intellectual looking man—not handsome, but no one of any force ever thought of that. All pictures, as well as the living man, show *manliness* in its highest tension—this as emphatically as the rest. This picture was a surprise and pleasure to me. I doubt not it is its first appearance. It will be hailed with pleasure by friends of Mr. Lincoln. . . . I never saw him with his hair combed before.
Yours,
Henry C. Whitney

type of Lincoln as he looked around 1846. (Up until then the earliest known photograph of Lincoln was an 1857 view by Alexander Hesler.) Tarbell was stunned by what she saw. The thirty-seven-year-old Lincoln looked nothing at all like the vulgar backwoodsman described by Ward Hill Lamon and others. Here was a well-dressed, carefully groomed, ambitious-looking young man whose face appeared intelligent and kind. For Tarbell the photograph was a revelation and became a central clue in her reevaluation of Lincoln's early years. In contrast to Herndon's description of Lincoln's family roots as a "stagnant, putrid pool," Tarbell wrote that his upbringing had been an "ennobling" way for him to have begun life, instilling in him many of the virtues that made him such a unique leader. She wrote that Thomas Lincoln, contrary to what Lamon and Herndon had written, was not a shiftless derelict but a proud, successful frontiersman who had provided for his family. She questioned John Hanks's romantic account of how Lincoln had responded to a slave auction in New Orleans, supposedly saying, "If I get a chance to hit that thing I'll hit it hard." (She pointed out that Hanks hadn't been with Lincoln in New Orleans.) And she correctly rejected Herndon's story of Lincoln failing to appear at his own wedding—an apocryphal account that Herndon had been all too willing to accept. Though she made her own share of historical mistakes, here was a professional journalist with fresh views on a subject that others had said was already exhausted. Unlike Lamon or Herndon or Nicolay or Hay, she had never known Lincoln. But she represented a new generation with its own interests in the subject.

The first of Tarbell's articles appeared in the November 1895 issue of *McClure's*. Previous biographies had been mostly words; Tarbell's was an extraordinary mixture of words and pictures. "From a pictorial standpoint this Life of Lincoln will be unique," read an editorial note. "We shall illustrate the scenes of Lincoln's career on a scale never before attempted." The daguerreotype Tarbell had discovered was featured prominently on the frontispiece, and the Lincoln article became an instant sensation. Joseph Medill of the *Chicago Tribune* wrote, "It is not only full of new things, but is so distinct and clear in local color that an interest attaches to it which is not found in other biographies." It represented "one of the most important and interesting contributions yet made to Lincoln literature." Within ten days after her first article was published, the magazine had 40,000 new buyers. The following month, after her second installment, circulation doubled to 250,000, making *McClure's* the most popular of all American magazines.

THE EARLIEST PORTRAIT OF ABRAHAM LINCOLN.
From a daguerreotype taken when Lincoln was about forty; owned by his son, the Hon. Robert T. Lincoln, through whose courtesy it is here reproduced for the first time.

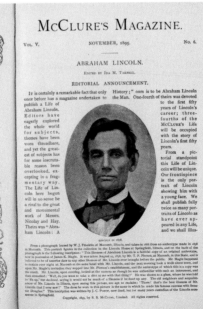

MCCLURE'S MAGAZINE.

VOL. V.   NOVEMBER, 1895.   No. 6.

ABRAHAM LINCOLN.

EDITED BY IDA M. TARBELL.

EDITORIAL ANNOUNCEMENT.

The earliest known photograph of Abraham Lincoln was first published in the November 1895 issue of *McClure's* (on left). Woodrow Wilson, then a Princeton professor, wrote in that he would treasure the "striking and singular" portrait with its "expression of dreaminess [on] the familiar face without its later sadness." (It was shown exactly as it looked, in the reverse style of daguerreotypes, as it also is in the enlargement to the right.)

McClure's reprinted thirty-seven-year-old Lincoln's head and shoulders. The full daguerreotype also revealed his enormous hands.

Recollections of Lamon

After his controversial 1872 biography, Ward Hill Lamon had pushed forward on the promised sequel. Focusing on Lincoln's administration and the Civil War, it turned out to be a task beyond Lamon's capacities. And though he produced at least a fragmentary manuscript, without Chauncey Black he was never able to get it published.

In 1883, after drifting between jobs, Lamon applied to President Chester Arthur for the position of postmaster in Denver, Colorado. But when Robert Lincoln, Arthur's secretary of war, heard that Lamon was a candidate for the position, he recoiled, then decided to intervene. Robert despised Lamon ever since the release of his *Life of Abraham Lincoln*. Although he had never read the book, he knew of its allusions to his father's supposed illegitimacy and religious infidelity, and he considered the book "largely made up of inventions, some of them inspired by malice." Robert went straight to the postmaster general, Timothy Howe, and said that an appointment of Lamon would be "personally offensive" to him. That was all it took to end Lamon's candidacy. When he learned what Robert had done, Lamon wrote to him demanding an explanation, and on May 10, 1883, Robert replied, outlining his reasons. "They are that notwithstanding the especially kind considerations accorded to you by my father . . . you, after his death, published a volume . . . so offensive in its character that . . . I have never until today opened it." Robert went on to detail the offending paragraphs, one by one. Together they represented "an astonishing

Ward Hill Lamon never stopped writing about Abraham Lincoln. In one of his memos he recalled his first meeting with the prairie lawyer, when Lincoln mocked him for his swallowtail coat and ruffled shirt.

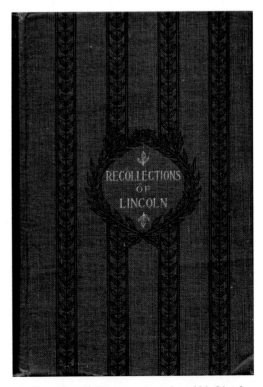

"Call me Lincoln," Lamon remembered his friend saying; "Mr. President is entirely too formal for us."

exhibition of malicious ingratitude on your part towards your dead benefactor."

As an old man, Lamon spent much of the remainder of his life reminiscing about Abraham Lincoln, and over time his unique friendship with Lincoln was gradually recognized. John P. Usher, secretary of the interior under Lincoln, wrote him that "there are few left who were intimately acquainted with Mr. Lincoln. I do not call to mind any one who was so much with him as yourself." In 1890 Lyman Trumbull, Lincoln's friend from Springfield, wrote Lamon that his book was "the only true history of Lincoln's early life that I have ever read." He liked it because it humanized a man who was fast becoming a fixed icon. "Lincoln possessed many noble qualities," Trumbull admitted, "but like other mortals [he] had his weaknesses, & it is folly to picture him as more than a man."

After Lamon's death in 1893 his daughter Dorothy gathered up his papers and materials and was astonished by their contents. Here, among letters and notes and unpublished articles, were the most original of all her father's writings, containing stories he had not included in books. Since he had never written a book of reminiscences, she edited one posthumously.

When *Recollections of Lincoln* came out in late 1895, it received the positive reviews that had previously eluded Ward Hill Lamon. Once again he was remembered as Lincoln's intimate and confidential friend, his law partner on the circuit, and his personal bodyguard—the man Lincoln had chosen for the job because of his physical power and loyalty. As marshal in Washington he had been in charge of the President's safety, working to prevent attacks on Lincoln's life. Only the fact that he had been out of town on April 14, 1865, had prevented him from being present on the night of Lincoln's murder. If his 1872 biography had besmirched his reputation, the 1895 book, published under his name, went a long way to restoring it.

Lamon accompanied Lincoln from Philadelphia (above) to Washington in 1861, to protect the President-elect. Pennsylvania state senator A. K. McClure recalled, "[H]e was literally armed to the teeth. In addition to a pair of heavy revolvers, he had a slung-shot and brass knuckles and a huge knife nestled under his vest."

His "Certificate of Moral Character"
Ward Hill Lamon

1895

Mr. Lincoln had prepared his Inaugural Address with great care, and up to the time of his arrival in Washington he had not shown it to any one. No one had been consulted as to what he should say on that occasion. During the journey the Address was made an object of special care, and was guarded with more than ordinary vigilance. It was carefully stored away in a satchel, which for the most of the time received his personal supervision. At Harrisburg, however, the precious bag was lost sight of. This was a matter which for prudential reasons could not be much talked about, and concerning which no great amount of anxiety could be shown. Mr. Lincoln had about concluded that his Address was lost. It at length dawned upon him that on arriving at Harrisburg he had intrusted the satchel to his son Bob, then a boy in his teens. He at once hunted up the boy and asked him what he had done with the bag. Robert confessed that in the excitement of the reception he thought that he had given it to a waiter of the hotel or to some one, he couldn't tell whom. Lincoln was in despair. Only ten days remained until the inauguration, and no Address; not even a trace of the notes was preserved from which it had been prepared.

I had never seen Mr. Lincoln so much annoyed, so much perplexed, and for the time so angry. He seldom manifested a spirit of anger toward his children, —this was the nearest approach to it I had ever witnessed. He and I started in search of the satchel. We went first to the hotel office, where we were informed that, if an employé of the hotel had taken charge of it, it would be found in the baggage-room. On going there, we found a great pile of all kinds of baggage in promiscuous confusion. Mr. Lincoln's keen eye soon discovered a satchel which he thought his own; taking it in his hand eagerly he tried his key; it fitted the lock, —the bag opened, and to our astonishment it contained nothing but a soiled shirt, several paper collars, a pack of cards, and a bottle of whiskey nearly full. In spite of his perplexity, the ludicrous mistake overcame Mr. Lincoln's gravity, and we both laughed heartily, much to the amusement of the bystanders. Shortly afterward we found among the mass the bag containing the precious document.

I shall never forget Mr. Lincoln's expression and what he said when he first informed me of his supposed loss, and enlisted my services in search of it. He held his head down for a moment, and then whispered: "Lamon, I guess I have lost my certificate of moral character, written by myself."

The Death of Lincoln's Photographer

The last twenty years of Mathew Brady's life were a faint echo of his glory days when he had been Lincoln's photographer and the great chronicler of the Civil War. The loss of his New York studio in the 1870s had been followed by the closure of his Washington gallery in 1881. After this Brady worked for his nephew and former associate Levi Handy. No longer at the center of the photographic world, he entered the worst years of his life. And when his wife, Julia, died in 1887, he descended into depression and alcohol. In 1890 there was a brief renaissance when Brady and Handy opened a studio together in Washington. A new generation began to flock around this living legend from the era of Lincoln. In a long interview published in April 1891, George A. Townsend, still writing for the *New York World*, compared Brady to "a ray of light still traveling toward the vision from some past world or star." At a time when virtually every other Civil War photographer was dead, Brady lived on, as a precious link to the past—a man who had known not only Abraham Lincoln but just about every important person of Lincoln's era. "They all came to me," Brady told Townsend, "and I can see them in my mind's eye, like a procession of ghosts, passing in review." When Townsend asked Brady to recall his first meeting with Lincoln, he said, "When . . . [Lincoln] became President Marshal Lamon said, 'I have not introduced Mr. Brady.' Mr. Lincoln answered in his ready [way], 'Brady and the Cooper Union Institute made me President!' "

Brady told Townsend that his wife and many of his friends had begged him not to risk his fortune on the Civil War project, but that he had felt he simply had to do it. "A spirit in my feet said 'Go,' and I went." It was the highest, most marvelous period in his life—a time when he had "men in all parts of the army, like a rich newspaper." But it had bankrupted him.

Unable to retire in old age, Brady was still making pictures in 1894 despite his failing eyesight. On April 16, the evening of Emancipation Day celebrations in New York City, he was struck by a horse and carriage and knocked unconscious, his leg badly shattered at the ankle. The bones were slow to heal, but by late July he could walk on crutches. In desperate financial straits, he moved from boardinghouse to boardinghouse. It was his fellow veterans from the New York Seventh Regiment who found a place for him in New York's Presbyterian Hospital as his kidneys now also began to fail him. In January he emerged briefly to attend an auction of his last glass negatives, which sold to a single bidder for a dollar per image. It was a sad end to his once magnificent collection, and Mathew Brady sat silently staring at the floor through his blue-tinted glasses. A few days later his kidneys finally gave out and he died. Another link to the era of Abraham Lincoln was gone.

During the 1860s Mathew Brady captured dozens of images of Abraham Lincoln, including this sober portrait of a wartime president. In later life (right) he looked back on the Lincoln years as the pinnacle of his career.

Robert Lincoln Breaks His Silence

Grover Cleveland's election as President in 1892 made Robert Lincoln a lame duck minister to England. In March he submitted his letter of resignation, and by May he was back in the United States. Over the next years he had trouble returning to the practice of law, writing that "the shop has ceased to interest me." And though he was often mentioned as a possible candidate for president, nothing ever came of it. In fact, as he once blurted out, he could imagine "no greater misfortune" than to serve in the White House, and viewed "with utter abhorrence even the mention of my name for that high place." Though only fifty-one years old—the same age his father had been upon election to the presidency—he felt chronically tired. In a letter to John Nicolay he asked, "I wonder if you are getting to feel so miserably old as I do. . . . [T]he whole future seems, miserably, so many days to be passed."

To fill his empty days, Robert drifted into high society, making friends with the likes of Andrew Carnegie and George Pullman. In 1893 he became special counsel to the Pullman Car Company, serving as legal adviser during the controversial workers' strike. By now a wealthy man, he took fishing trips to Ohio, rented cottages on the New England shore, and dreamed of owning a summer mansion of his own. But he wasn't happy. Part of the problem was his longstanding psychological issue over being the son of Abraham Lincoln. Though he had distinguished himself in public service, he continued to labor under an inferiority complex. He once said dejectedly to his friend Nicholas Murray Butler, "No one wanted me for Secretary of

In a rare public appearance, Robert Lincoln addressed crowds in the city where his father had debated Stephen A. Douglas thirty-eight years earlier. "The people have always maintained the morally right against the morally wrong," Robert intoned; "and with the Chief Magistrate of five and thirty years ago, I have an abiding faith that they always will."

War; they wanted Abraham Lincoln's son. No one wanted me for Minister to England; they wanted Abraham Lincoln's son. " For thirty years he had refused to speak publicly about his father, routinely turning down invitations that came often. But in October 1896, for the first and only time, he agreed to speak at a ceremony in Galesburg, Illinois, commemorating the thirty-eighth anniversary of the Lincoln-Douglas debate there.

It was the biggest event at Knox College since the original debate here in 1858. On that day, beset with an "Arctic frost" and a "sour northwest wind," Abraham Lincoln had set forth his vision of the Declaration of Independence, which he insisted applied to black people as well as to white. He had called slavery a "moral, social, and political evil," even if difficult to do away with quickly. And he had said that he personally looked forward, with great hope, "to the time when as a wrong it may come to an end."

In 1896, 25,000 people poured into Galesburg for the anniversary. A speakers' stand, large enough to accommodate five hundred visiting dignitaries, was built on the spot where the original debate had taken place. Many who had been present at the original debate now returned, including Henry R. Sanderson, in whose home Lincoln had stayed, and Thomas Frost, who had officially welcomed him to town.

President John Finley of Knox College introduced the speakers. Alumnus Clark E. Carr, who had been present at the original debate, gave his recollections of that day. The keynote speaker was Chauncey Depew, one of the most sought-after orators of the day. And then it was Robert Lincoln's turn, rising to speak at the same spot where his father had stood four decades earlier. In the crowd was eighteen-year-old Carl Sandburg, a native of Galesburg who was working as a milkman. "I got away from my milk wagon long enough to have a look at Robert Lincoln," he later wrote. "And as I watched him I felt myself wondering what kind of talks he had had with his father in the White House."

The speech was not long, but the very fact that Robert gave it made it a historic occasion. And for Robert himself it was a personal breakthrough. After this his life seemed to take a new, positive turn. He cast away some of his psychological burdens, changed his career from law to business, and embraced himself as a man quite distinct from his father.

Crowds gathered at Knox College in Galesburg, Illinois, to hear Robert Lincoln speak about his father.

The Memory of My Father
Robert Lincoln

October 7, 1896

Mr. President and Ladies and Gentlemen:

On an occasion of this peculiar character it would better suit me to be only a listener, or at most to do no more than to assure you of the grateful emotions which overwhelm me at such a demonstration of the respect and affection in which the memory of my father is held by you. He knew in his life that in this community he had many devoted friends and earnest sympathizers in his great work, but how few examples in all history could he have recalled to lead him to indulge the thought that when the changes of nearly forty years had come—when his work had been completely done —and he himself had been numbered with the dead for more than thirty years, there would come together such a multitude as this, having him and his work for their inspiration!

It is for others, and not for me, to say why you have come, but I will give a brief expression of one thought the memories bring to me.

The question that my father discussed here has long been settled. He called it a contest between Right and Wrong,—a part of the eternal struggle throughout the world. In the contest the odds were great against him, but he battled on, supported by his conscience and by the firm belief that when the fogs were cleared away from such an issue, the people were for the right and against the wrong. . . . And so they are; if he could return to us today, he could not, I believe, find in all our broad land a single man who would not resist the restoration of the evil against which he and others waged the fight that seemed for years almost a hopeless one.

Such an end to the great contest in which he was engaged must give us courage and confidence in meeting the phases of the eternal struggle that beset our times.

William McKinley

McKinley's Lincoln

The Spanish-American War was a turning point in America's history. Lincoln's former assistant John Hay, now William McKinley's secretary of state, called the ten-week conflict of 1898 "a splendid little war" that propelled the nation onto the world stage and helped unite it as never before. With Northerners and Southerners fighting side by side, it fundamentally changed the relationship between the former enemies of the Civil War. And with black soldiers once again contributing to the American cause, it seemed a harbinger of improvements for race relations in America. "We are all prouder to be Americans," Hay wrote following the U.S. victories in Cuba, "and have a broader and truer understanding of the greatness of our country and of the grander destiny that lies before the American people." Under McKinley's leadership, once again the presidency itself seemed more important. In the press McKinley was widely compared with Lincoln and he often claimed him as a guiding influence and inspiration.

In the fall of 1898, after the close of the war, the President made a cross-country tour on behalf of local Republicans. Traveling by special train, he made stops throughout the Midwest testing public opinion about whether or not to hold on to the Philippines. Wherever he went were enthusiastic crowds. One of the largest assembled in Lincoln's hometown of Springfield. Republican Presidents were expected to make pilgrimages to Lincoln's tomb, and McKinley was thrilled to be here in the city of his great forebear. In his October 12 speech he linked the war in Cuba with Lincoln's effort to free the slaves. And in a heartfelt tribute he praised the efforts of black soldiers who had fought on freedom's behalf in places like San Juan Hill.

Camp Lincoln
-1897-

An African American soldier during the presidency of McKinley stands guard at "Camp Lincoln," possibly in Springfield.

Northerners and southerners fought side by side in the
Spanish-American War, helping the cause of national reconciliation.

The Family of Freedom
William McKinley

I am going to meet the people of the state of
Illinois at their State capital. I am glad to be
at the home of the martyred President. His
name is an inspiration, and a holy one, to all
lovers of liberty the world over. He saved
the Union. He liberated a race—a race
which he once said ought to be free because there might come a time when these
black men could help keep the jewel of
liberty within the family of nations. If any
vindication of that act or of that prophecy
were needed, it was found when these brave
black men ascended the hill of San Juan in
Cuba, and charged the enemy at El Caney.
They vindicated their own title to liberty
on that field, and, with our other brave
soldiers, gave the priceless gift of liberty to
another suffering race.

My fellow-citizens, the name of Lincoln
will live forever in immortal story. His fame,
his work, his life, are not only an inspiration
to every American boy and girl, but to all
mankind. And what an encouragement his
life work has been to all of his successors in
the presidential office. If any one of them, at
any time, has felt that his burden was heavy,
he had but to reflect upon the greater burdens of Abraham Lincoln to make his seem
light. My fellow-citizens, I congratulate you
that your great State furnished him to the
country and the world. You guard his sacred ashes here, but the whole country
guards with you his sacred memory.

President McKinley frequently said that
Lincoln would have supported the Spanish-
American War.

Booker T. Washington often said that Abraham Lincoln had found him "as a piece of property and left him as an American citizen." "Father Abraham, we are coming, ten million strong," he now proclaimed. "[T]here is no power that can permanently stop our progress."

Washington brought smiles to the faces of an audience in Lakeland, Florida.

February 14, 1899

Booker T. Washington

In 1895, the year of Frederick Douglass's death, a young Southern leader named Booker T. Washington set forth his "Atlanta Compromise"—a plan for black educational and economic "uplift" in the face of the growing entrenchment of segregation. Unlike Douglass, who had always counseled struggle and resistance, Washington argued it was black people's duty "to face the present and not wail over the past"—and that it was useless to argue about who was "responsible" for slavery. He called blacks to have "love and sympathy" for Southern whites, to forgive the former slaveholders and move on. Critics charged that he was giving up on the struggle for political and social equality. A young black leader in the North named W. E. B. Du Bois wrote that "Mr. Washington represents . . . the old attitude of adjustment and submission. . . . [His] program practically accepts the alleged inferiority of the Negro races." But Booker T. Washington could not be so easily written off. He saw education as the key to furthering black advancement and didn't want stridency to undermine his people's progress. And not only did millions of black Americans follow his example, whites began to refer to him as the most trusted African American leader.

Washington's hero was Abraham Lincoln. He made an effort to read every book written about him, and often called him his "patron saint." And in February 1899 he agreed to speak at a Lincoln Day celebration in Philadelphia. It was scheduled to take place at the Union League Club on the twelfth, but a heavy snow prevented him from arriving. Two days later, before a rapt audience at the large home of Henry C. Davis, Washington spoke of his earliest memories of Abraham Lincoln.

Our Hero and Benefactor
Booker T. Washington

February 14, 1899

Night after night, before the dawn of day, on an old slave plantation in Virginia, I recall the form of my sainted mother, bending over a batch of rags that enveloped my body, on a dirt floor, breathing a fervent prayer to Heaven that "Marsa Lincoln" might succeed, and that one day she and I might be free; and so, on your invitation, I come here to-night to celebrate with you the answer to those prayers. But be it far from me to revive the bitter memories of the past, nor would I narrow the work of Abraham Lincoln to the black race of this country; rather would I call him the Emancipator of America—the liberator of the white man North, of the white man South; the one who, in unshackling the chains of the Negro has turned loose the enslaved forces of nature in the South, and has knit all sections of our country together by the indissoluble bonds of commerce. . . .

But all is not done, and it remains for us, the living, to finish the work that Lincoln left uncompleted. You of the great and prosperous North still owe a serious and uncompleted duty to your less fortunate brothers of the white race South, who suffered and are still suffering the consequence of American slavery. What was the task you asked them to perform? Returning to their destitute homes after years of war, to face blasted hopes, devastation, a shattered industrial system, you ask them to add to their burden that of preparing in education, politics, and economics, in a few short years, for citizenship, four or five millions of former slaves. That the South, staggering under the burden, made blunders, that in some measure there has been disappointment, no one need be surprised.

The four million slaves that Lincoln freed are now nearly ten million freemen. That which was three hundred years in doing can hardly be undone in thirty years. How can you help the South and the Negro in the completion of Lincoln's work? A large majority of the people Lincoln freed are still ignorant, without proper food, or property, or skill, or correct habits—are without the requisites for intelligent and independent citizenship. The mere fiat of law could not make a dependent man independent; it could not make an ignorant man an intelligent voter; it could not make one man respect another man. The results only come by beginning at the bottom and working upward; by recognizing our weakness as well as our strength. . . .

And, may I say, you do well to keep the name of Abraham Lincoln permanently linked with the highest interests of the Negro race. His was the hand, the brain, and the conscience that gave us the first opportunity to make the attempt to be men instead of property. What Lincoln so nobly began, the philanthropy and wealth of this nation, aided by our own efforts, should complete. . . .

The struggle of Abraham Lincoln up from the lowest poverty and ignorance to the highest usefulness gives hope and inspiration to the Negro. . . . Like Lincoln, the Negro knows the meaning of the one-room cabin; he knows the bed of rags and hay; he knows what it is to be minus books and school-house; he has tasted the lowliest poverty, but through them all he is making his way to the top.

A Meeting with the President
Julia Ward Howe

1899

Julia Ward Howe

Despite Noah Brooks's 1898 prediction that the era of Lincoln remembrances was over, vivid new recollections of Lincoln continued to appear in print and would do so for the next two decades. In 1899, eighty-year-old Julia Ward Howe, president of the New England Woman Suffrage Association, published her account of meeting Lincoln in the White House in 1862. "The Battle Hymn of the Republic," written by Howe soon after that visit, reportedly caused Lincoln to cry.

Among my recollections of this period I especially cherish that of an interview with President Abraham Lincoln, arranged for us by our kind friend, Governor Andrew. The President was laboring at this time under a terrible pressure of doubt and anxiety. He received us in one of the drawing rooms of the White House, where we were invited to take seats, in full view of Stuart's portrait of Washington. . . . I remember well the sad expression of Mr. Lincoln's deep blue eyes, the only feature of his face which could be called other than plain. Mrs. Andrew, being of the company, inquired when we could have the pleasure of seeing Mrs. Lincoln, and Mr. Lincoln named to us the day of her reception. He said to Governor Andrew, apropos of I know not what, "I once heerd 'George' Sumner tell a story." The unusual pronunciation fixed in my memory this one unimportant sentence. The talk, indeed, ran mostly on indifferent topics.

When we had taken leave, and were out of hearing, Mr. Clarke said of Mr. Lincoln, "We have seen it in his face; hopeless honesty—that is all!" He said it as if he felt that it was far from enough.

None of us knew then—how could we have known?—how deeply God's wisdom had touched and inspired that devout and patient soul. At the moment few people praised or trusted him. "Why did he not do this, or that, or the other? He a President indeed! Look at this war, dragging on so slowly! Look at our many defeats and rare victories!" Such was the talk that one constantly heard regarding him. The most charitable held that he meant well. Governor Andrew was one of the few whose faith in him never wavered.

James C. Conkling

Conkling had known Lincoln for a quarter of a century when he was asked to publicly read Lincoln's letter to him expressing the President's commitment to black freedom.

March 1, 1899

James C. Conkling's Famous Letter

Early in 1899 came word that Lincoln's old friend James C. Conkling was on his deathbed. Conkling's friendship with Lincoln went back nearly sixty years to when they were bachelors in Springfield and part of a group that met regularly at Joshua Speed's store. He had married Mary Todd's closest friend, Mercy Levering, and later supported Lincoln after his temporary breakup with Mary in 1841, which left him "reduced and emaciated," Conkling recalled, and scarcely possessing "strength enough to speak above a whisper." As Lincoln's political career unfolded, Conkling remained a close friend, assisting in his 1860 campaign and staying in regular contact during the presidential years. Lincoln called him his "fellow townsman" and "a particular friend"—meaning someone he knew well and trusted implicitly. And it was to Conkling that Lincoln sent one of his greatest presidential letters—a masterful defense of the Emancipation Proclamation and the Union Army's use of black soldiers.

In mid-August 1863 Conkling invited Lincoln to travel west and take part in a rally in defense of administration war goals. It was in part to be an answer to an earlier gathering of Democrats who had declared their loss of faith in Lincoln's "offensive prosecution of the war." In response "we intend to make the most imposing demonstration that has ever been held in the Northwest," Conkling wrote. Perhaps a "visit to your old home would not be inappropriate if you can break away from the pressure of public duties."

Lincoln was sorely tempted to make the trip, and for a time, according to his secretaries, "cherished the hope of going to Springfield." "It would be very agreeable to

Executive Mansion,

Washington, August 26, 1863.

Hon. James C. Conkling
My dear Sir:

Your letter inviting me to attend a mass-meeting of unconditional Union men, to be held at the capital of Illinois, on the 3rd day of September, has been received. It would be very agreeable to me, to thus meet my old friends, at my own home; but I can not, just now, be absent from here, so long as a visit there, would require.

The meeting is to be of all those who maintain unconditional devotion to the union; and I am sure my old political friends will thank me for tendering, as I do, the nation's me, to thus meet my old friends," he wrote. But when he decided that he could not leave Washington for so long a period, Lincoln wrote a letter instead, to be read aloud to a crowd anticipated to be more than fifty thousand people. He worked on the letter intermittently for three days, "usually alone in his room," recalled William O. Stoddard, to whom Lincoln read an early draft. He wrote it with the kind of care he had previously used on his inaugural address and on his public letter to Northern industrialist Erastus Corning. On August 26 it was finished. In a cover letter, Lincoln asked Conkling to read it aloud at the rally, remembering above all to "read it very slowly." (Conkling passed the job on to another reader.)

The letter began with a salutation to Conkling and to Lincoln's loyal supporters, then shifted to an address to his opponents—those unhappy with his commitment to freeing slaves. In eloquent terms, Lincoln demonstrated to all doubters that his commitment to emancipation was absolute—that it was a moral and political stance that could not be reversed.

The letter was instantly recognized as a Lincoln classic. "The most consummate rhetorician never used language more . . . to the purpose," reported the *New York Times*, reflecting a widely positive response. Lincoln's public writings, culminating in this one, the paper said, had made him "the most popular man in the Republic." Praised by all the early biographers, by the 1890s it was considered "Lincoln's famous letter"—and the defining moment in James C. Conkling's life. "I have the original letter now on my desk before me," wrote Conkling as an old man in 1895, reminiscing about the heady days of 1863. "The Emancipation Proclamation had been issued and the rebellion was being crushed. The rifle was placed in the hands of the slave, and he became an efficient part of our armies and bravely fought for the preservation of the Union. This was one of the grandest measures of the administration, and Mr. Lincoln naturally felt solicitous for its complete success."

Lincoln's letter to Conkling helped him gain important support for emancipation and the use of black soldiers in the Union Army. Charles Sumner called it a "true and noble letter." "Nothing he ever uttered had a more instantaneous success," commented Nicolay and Hay.

The Promise of Freedom
Abraham Lincoln

August 26, 1863

In his long letter Lincoln addressed not only his friend James Conkling, and the thousands of gathered supporters on Springfield's fairgrounds, but the large number of Americans angry with his emancipation policy who were now pushing for the rescinding of the proclamation.

[T]o be plain, you are dissatisfied with me about the negro. Quite likely there is a difference of opinion between you and myself upon that subject. I certainly wish that all men could be free, while I suppose you do not. . . .

You dislike the emancipation proclamation; and, perhaps, would have it retracted. You say it is unconstitutional—I think differently. I think the constitution invests its commander-in-chief, with the law of war, in time of war. . . .

You say you will not fight to free negroes. Some of them seem willing to fight for you; but, no matter. Fight you, then, exclusively to save the Union. I issued the proclamation on purpose to aid you in saving the Union. Whenever you shall have conquered all resistance to the Union, if I shall urge you to continue fighting, it will be an apt time, then, for you to declare you will not fight to free negroes.

I thought that in your struggle for the Union, to whatever extent the negroes should cease helping the enemy, to that extent it weakened the enemy in his resistance to you. Do you think differently? I thought that whatever negroes can be got to do as soldiers, leaves just so much less for

white soldiers to do, in saving the Union. Does it appear otherwise to you? But negroes, like other people, act upon motives. Why should they do any thing for us, if we will do nothing for them? If they stake their lives for us, they must be prompted by the strongest motive—even the promise of freedom. And the promise being made, must be kept. . . .

Peace does not appear so distant as it did. I hope it will come soon, and come to stay; and so come as to be worth the keeping in all future time. . . . And then, there will be some black men who can remember that, with silent tongue, and clenched teeth, and steady eye, and well-poised bayonet, they have helped mankind on to this great consummation; while, I fear, there will be some white ones, unable to forget that, with malignant heart, and deceitful speech, they have strove to hinder it.

A Lost Autobiography

In 1900 few had heard of a Lincoln campaign biography written forty years earlier by John Locke Scripps. Copies of it had become so rare that not even Scripps's daughter, Grace Dyche, had been able to locate a single complete volume. "The only copy I could find . . . was a mutilated copy . . . owned by my aunt," she wrote. So that her father's book should not be lost to posterity, she was determined to republish it in a new edition in his honor.

John Scripps, who had worked for the *Chicago Press and Tribune*, had covered Lincoln ever since 1856. He had heard him speak at the Bloomington Convention that year and witnessed his extraordinary effect upon the huge crowd. "Never was an audience more completely electrified by human eloquence," he wrote. In June 1860, shortly after Lincoln had received the nomination for the presidency, Scripps visited him in Springfield and told him he had been assigned to write a campaign biography. "Why, Scripps," Lincoln responded, "it is a great piece of folly to attempt to make anything out of me or my early life. It can all be condensed into a single sentence . . . 'The short and simple annals of the poor.' That's my life, and that's all you or any one else can make out if it." Despite Lincoln's "painful" feelings about "the extreme poverty of his early surroundings," Scripps persuaded him to compose a brief autobiography. Lincoln decided to write it in the third person, and to add far more detail than in the one he had written earlier for Jesse Fell.

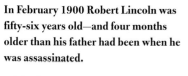

In February 1900 Robert Lincoln was fifty-six years old—and four months older than his father had been when he was assassinated.

With the 3,500-word autobiography in hand, Scripps turned to the writing of the biography. "I never performed a work more conscientiously in my life," he later admitted to William Herndon. "I am also sure that Mr. Lincoln was equally sincere and conscientious in furnishing me with the facts, connected with his own and his family's history." With a print run of a million, the timetable was tight and Lincoln was not given the chance to review the final text, something Scripps profusely apologized for. The biography appeared in July 1860, published jointly by the *New York Tribune* and the *Chicago Press and Tribune*. Since the Wigwam edition and the Howells campaign biography both beat it to press, it became the third life of Lincoln to be published.

For a pamphlet that once numbered a million copies, it was astonishing how rare it had become by 1900. Again and again in her search Scripps's daughter ran into dead ends. Robert Lincoln wrote to say that it didn't exist among his father's papers, and Whitelaw Reid, searching the *New York Tribune* archives, also failed to find it. All copies in Chicago seem to have been lost in the Great Fire. Finally, after contacting John G. Nicolay in Washington, Dyche located a complete and undamaged copy. Nicolay wouldn't part with it, but he had his secretary write out in longhand the sections missing from Dyche's damaged copy.

The republishing of Scripps's Lincoln book in February 1900 caused a stir among reviewers, who immediately recognized the importance of the third-person autobiography that lay at its heart. Lincoln's original manuscript would not be seen by the public for another four decades. It was part of the papers owned by Robert Lincoln, who more than anyone recognized how special it was.

Also in 1900 members of the Lincoln Club of Geneva, Ohio, posed holding Lincoln plaques.

February 1900

Ida Tarbell's Life of Lincoln

The original plan at *McClure's* magazine was for Ida Tarbell to write articles on the young Lincoln, covering the years from his birth until 1858. But public response was so overwhelming that two years into the project the magazine expanded its scope and commissioned a new series focusing on Lincoln's presidency. When Tarbell finished these articles in late 1899, she had covered Lincoln's entire life—in a bold, pictorial fashion that merged a reporter's detective work with vivid writing. Tarbell became so popular that McClure decided her articles should become the basis for a book. And in 1900 a massive work came out under a long title: *The Life of Abraham Lincoln, Drawn from Original Sources and Containing Many Speeches, Letters, and Telegrams hitherto Unpublished.*

In her preface Tarbell thanked hundreds of individuals from across the country who had responded to her pleas and sent in valuable Lincoln materials. And she thanked numerous individuals who had helped her in her work. First and foremost was J. McCan Davis of Springfield, her tireless researcher who had come up with so many important discoveries. Next she thanked the Lincoln collectors who had so generously shared with her—William H. Lambert of Philadelphia; Osborn Oldroyd of Washington, D.C.; Charles F. Gunther of Chicago; and others. And then she acknowledged her obligation to the biographers who had come before her, singling out nine: Nicolay and Hay, William Herndon, William O. Stoddard, John T. Morse, Isaac Arnold, Ward Hill Lamon, Henry C. Whitney, and Josiah Holland.

Tarbell's book was not going to be a "history of Lincoln's times," she wrote, but rather a "picture" of "Lincoln the man . . . as seen by his fellows and revealed by his own acts and words." The biography became the most popular of Lincoln ever published, reprinted in more than eleven editions and drawing a whole new generation of readers to the story of Lincoln. "A perusal of the volumes leaves a very satisfied feeling," wrote the *New York Times* about "Miss Tarbell's new and striking life." "It makes our hearts warm more than ever toward that homely figure." Tarbell's work, the *Times* judged, would rank in importance just behind those of Nicolay and Hay and William Herndon, and far above all the other Lincoln biographies. And for the period of his young adulthood until his admittance to the bar, it traced the story "with more detail than in any other biography." Writing in a later issue of the *Times*, Augustus Buell declared that there were only two "lives" of Lincoln that he cared to keep in his library. "One was Ida Tarbell's; the other that of Nicolay and John Hay. I put Miss Tarbell's first . . . because I like it best. It is the case of a biographer losing her self in her subject." And even the once skeptical Robert Lincoln came to agree, praising Tarbell for her "untiring research," and finding her biography of his father "indispensable."

Ida Tarbell's first book, *The Early Life of Abraham Lincoln*, was announced in *McClure's* magazine.

MCCLURE'S

A NEW AND RICHLY ILLUSTRATED LIFE OF

ABRAHAM LINCOLN

300 Pictures. The Only Early Portrait (hitherto unpublished). Forty Portraits of Lincoln. The Most Important Collection of Lincoln Pictures Ever Published. Much new and valuable material from people now living about Lincoln's youth and public career. Begins in

McCLURE'S FOR NOVEMBER
10 CENTS A COPY

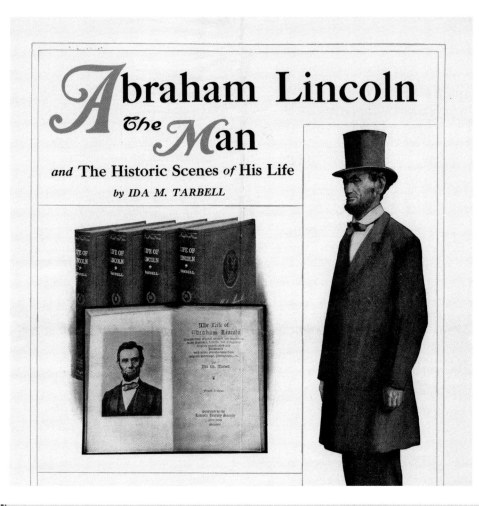

A Hunt for an Idea
Ida Tarbell

1900

In her book Tarbell included unfamiliar reminiscences, including one from Dr. John P. Gulliver, who had met Lincoln on a train in 1860. Tarbell introduced him as "an acquaintance."

[The] ability to explain clearly and to illustrate by simple figures of speech must be counted as the great mental achievement of Lincoln's boyhood. It was a power which he gained by hard labor. Years later he related his experience to an acquaintance who had been surprised by the lucidity and simplicity of his speeches and who had asked where he was educated.

"I never went to school more than six months in my life, . . . but I can say this: that among my earliest recollections I remember how, when a mere child, I used to get irritated when anybody talked to me in a way I could not understand. I do not think I ever got angry at anything else in my life; but that always disturbed my temper; and has ever since. I can remember going to my little bedroom, after hearing the neighbors talk of an evening with my father, and spending no small part of the night walking up and down and trying to make out what was the exact meaning of some of their, to me, dark sayings.

"I could not sleep, although I tried to, when I got on such a hunt for an idea until I had caught it; and when I thought I had got it, I was not satisfied until I had repeated it over and over; until I had put it in language plain enough, as I thought, for any boy I knew to comprehend. This was a kind of passion with me, and it has stuck by me; for I am never easy now, when I am handling a thought, till I have bounded it north, and bounded it south, and bounded it east, and bounded it west."

To the end of her life Tarbell remained fascinated by Lincoln. He came "to mean more to me as a human being than anybody I had studied," she wrote. "I never doubted his motives, and he never bored me."

Lincoln Memorial University

A sign of a new era in North-South relations came with the founding of Lincoln Memorial University in Tennessee. The Cumberland Gap region, with its independent mountain people, had long been opposed to slavery. An impoverished area, formerly a stopping place on the Underground Railroad, its loyalty to the Union had been much admired by Lincoln. He once told General Oliver Otis Howard, later commander of the Army of the Tennessee, that if they came out of the war alive, he wanted both of them to do all they could to aid "these mountain people." Howard never forgot these words.

After the war, Howard served as head of the Freedmen's Bureau, taking charge of the government's program for the emancipated slaves. Few leaders in his day were more committed to African American welfare. And in 1867 he co-founded Howard University in Washington, D.C., going on to become its president. After returning to military service in the 1870s and 1880s, Howard left the army in 1894 and finally returned to his promise made to Lincoln thirty years earlier. He began to look for ways to help the people of Appalachia, whose lives had been so devastated by the Civil War, and who were among the poorest communities in America.

A school dedicated to the discovery and development of belated youth Serves America by liberating worthy manhood and womanhood from the bondage of ignorance

As a sign of healing between North and South, Lincoln Memorial University in Tennessee named its first building Grant-Lee Hall (below).

In 1895 Howard traveled to Tennessee to address the graduating class at Harrow Academy. Seeing the possibility of transforming the school into something much more influential, the following year he returned to help convert it into a college. Before long a group of supporters had purchased an old resort hotel and grounds, and on February 12, 1897—what would have been Lincoln's eighty-eighth birthday—Lincoln Memorial University was chartered.

From the beginning it was a monument to North-South reunion. Its charter called the college "an expression of renewed good will and fraternal feelings between the people of the sections of this country once opposed to each other in civil war." The first building on the new campus was named Grant-Lee Hall.

Reconciliation like this could not have happened in prior decades, but the timing for such an institution was now right. In 1899 Howard became president of the board of trustees, taking over responsibility for fundraising, much of it in the North. "[Give] for the sake of Abraham Lincoln," he said; "for the sake of education; for the sake of . . . humanity." At a large event at Carnegie Hall on Lincoln's birthday in 1901 he was joined on the podium by Mark Twain. The Southern-born author noted the irony of his presence at a Lincoln event, recalling that his father had been a slaveholder and that he himself had fought in the Confederate Army. "But are not the blue and gray one today?" he asked. "The old wounds are healed, and you of the North and we of the South are brothers yet." Then turning to address the subject of Abraham Lincoln, Twain called him "the best man after Washington that this land, or any other land, has yet produced."

Two students at Lincoln Memorial were Livingston Mzimba (left) and Harry Mantenga, both from South Africa.

355

William Dean Howells wrote the first Lincoln campaign biography.

Samuel C. Parks asked Lincoln to correct Howells's book by writing in the margins.

Lincoln's Own Edits

Back in 1860 William Dean Howells was a young writer for the *Ohio State Journal* working on a new campaign biography of Lincoln. Uninterested in making the trip to Springfield to meet the candidate (he later said he thus missed "the greatest chance" of his life), Howells sent a young law student in his place, James Quay Howard. Howard spent the better part of a week in Lincoln's hometown, interviewing Lincoln's friends, reading back issues of the *Sangamo Journal*, and speaking with the candidate himself. Lincoln said he "took pains to facilitate" the young man's work and gave him a copy of the autobiographical material he had recently written for John Scripps. Howard returned to Ohio with copious research notes, and Howells immediately recognized "the wild charm and poetry" of Lincoln's life. To compete with other campaign literature, Howells's book was rushed to press on June 25 and trumpeted as the only "authorized biography." When Lincoln heard this, he was "astounded" and immediately denied it, saying he would never authorize a book "without time and opportunity to carefully examine and consider every word of it." A few weeks later he got a chance to do just that. An old friend who used to ride the circuit with him, Samuel C. Parks, asked Lincoln to read Howells's biography and make corrections in the book. Lincoln agreed.

The result in some ways was a new Lincoln autobiography. What the candidate left uncorrected often bore the stamp of his approval, although, perhaps in haste, he let stand several descriptions that were untrue. What Lincoln amended offered up his own imprimatur and included information that might not otherwise have come to light. Through his edits, and lack thereof, he confirmed stories in Howell that were not found elsewhere—how he had once walked eight miles to borrow a copy of *Kirkham's Grammar*; how he had bought his first copy of *Blackstone's Law* at a Springfield auction (and hadn't found it at the bottom of a junk barrel as tradition had long had it); how he possessed a lifelong love for the stories of Edgar Allan Poe.

Lincoln's edits also gave a window into his personality. He corrected minor details that might have given him political capital—such as that he used to walk the law circuit while other lawyers rode horseback. "No harm, if true," Lincoln noted in the margin, "but, in fact, not true." But sometimes modesty trumped literal truth. Though Lincoln was in reality six foot four, Howells described him as an inch shorter. Lincoln ignored the slight. He let stand, however, Howells's compliment at the end of the work: "The great feature of the man's face is his brilliant and piercing eye, which has never been dimmed by any vice, great or small.... [H]e is now, at fifty, in the prime of life, with rugged health, though bearing, in the lines of his face, the trace of severe and earnest thought."

On May 22, 1901, Samuel Parks wrote an inscription in the book's flyleaf: "This life of Lincoln was corrected by him for me, on request in the Summer of 1860, by notes in his handwriting, in pencil on the margin. It is to be preserved by my children, as a lasting memorial of that great man, and of his friendship for me."

Lincoln the candidate in May 1860

Robert's Curse

Ever since his retirement from government service Robert Lincoln had flourished as a corporate lawyer with growing ties to the Pullman Car Company. Following the death of George Pullman in 1897, he filled in as temporary president of the company, though the new responsibilities gave him "great anxiety," he wrote, and left him little time for the leisure he now yearned for. That same year his daughter Jessie eloped with a college football star, Warren Beckwith. "He is not satisfactory to us to be the husband of our daughter," Robert said brusquely to the press after learning of the secret wedding.

In 1901 Robert Lincoln became president of the Pullman Car Company, a position he would hold for the next ten years. Though he had resisted all attempts to be reenlisted into politics, he had remained a vigorous campaigner for Republican candidates for President, working hard for William McKinley in 1896 and 1900. On September 6, 1901, he planned to meet with President McKinley at the Pan American Exposition in Buffalo, New York. But as he approached the scene, chaos broke out. A young anarchist named Leon Czolgosz, who had been stalking McKinley, stepped forward out of a receiving line wearing a bandage on his right hand. From out of the bandage a blaze emerged as Czolgosz fired two bullets into McKinley's body. Robert was swept up into a new national crisis. Thirty-six years after the murder of his father, and twenty since he was with James Garfield when he was shot, once again Robert was at hand at a presidential assassination.

McKinley lingered on for eight days as the horrified nation staged an around-the-clock vigil. "He is a great man and a good president," wrote Lincoln's old friend Shelby Cullom. "He is nearer to the hearts of the great body of the people than any other since Lincoln." Following national ceremonies McKinley was taken home to Canton, Ohio, where he was buried in a service that was widely compared to that of Lincoln. Robert, who attended, afterward came to see himself as cursed, and for the next twenty years avoided being anywhere near a president.

William McKinley on the day of the shooting

LESLIE'S WEEKLY
McKINLEY EXTRA

New York, September 9, 1901 · PRICE 10 CENTS

LEON F. CZOLGOSZ, THE ASSASSIN.

Leon Czolgosz fired a bullet at President McKinley (right), then wound up behind bars (left). For Robert Lincoln it was all too reminiscent of the assassination of his father.

APRIL 15 1865

SEP. 19 1881

SEP. 14 1901

IT IS GODS WAY

IN MORY

HIS WILL NOT OURS

BE DONE

William McKinley was the third U.S. President to be assassinated. "It is God's way," one shrine pronounced. "His will not ours be done."

September 26, 1901

Lincoln's Final Burial

As William McKinley was buried in Ohio, questions were being raised at Lincoln's tomb in Springfield. Lincoln's resting place had been anything but final. Fourteen years earlier the construction of a new vault had been completed, and on April 14, 1887, the casket had been transferred back into its burial chamber. But when rumors began to circulate that Lincoln's body was not in his coffin, it was determined that another identification was needed. In a secret ceremony, in front of a large group of witnesses, a twelve-inch square was cut in the lead of Lincoln's coffin so that nineteen aging men could peer in and confirm the face of Lincoln. His features, wrote monument custodian John C. Power, "were almost as perfect as they are in the bronze statue on the Monument, and the color was about as dark as the statue." Members of the association present that day said they "readily recognized" their "former friend and fellow citizen." With the identification assured, the coffins of Abraham and Mary Lincoln were set into a bed of concrete in what was meant to be their final burial.

The coffin of Abraham Lincoln was temporarily held at the bottom of this underground vault, resting upon wooden four-by-fours. It was kept here for a year, alongside the coffins of Mary, Willie, Tad, Eddy, and Jack.

But this did not mark the end of the story. Within just a decade the monument was in a "villainous state of disrepair" due to the uneven settling of the building. Large cracks appeared, masonry was crumbling to dust, stalactites were dripping from the ceiling of the corridors, and water was making its way into the burial chamber. It was decided that the monument would have to be demolished and a better-engineered replica erected in its place. The Illinois legislature appropriated $100,000, and in March 1900 the bodies were once again disinterred and transferred into a temporary underground vault. Over the next year the massive new building went up, with a soaring new shaft fourteen feet taller than its predecessor. On April 24, 1901, a crowd of three hundred, including Mary Lincoln's niece Josephine Edwards, gathered to watch as the Lincolns' bodies were moved into the new memorial.

Robert Lincoln, haunted by memories of the attempted heist in 1876, was reported to have disguised himself as a workman and traveled to Springfield to investigate firsthand. After spending an entire day in and around the monument, he complained that the coffins remained in the open, vulnerable to theft, and that no watchmen were assigned to the monument at night. He demanded immediate action be taken to secure the sacred remains of his father—in a place, he said, from which "it would be impossible for ever to move him again."

The temporary vault, which was just twenty-five feet away from the Lincoln Monument, took hours to open. Lincoln's coffin was then lifted by crane out of the underground casing to be moved to its final resting place.

By autumn a permanent plan was in place—to secure the coffins inside a concrete chamber, fifteen feet beneath the floor of the sarcophagus. And finally on September 26, just three weeks after McKinley's funeral, all was ready for the most secret ceremony of them all. Since this was to be Lincoln's final interment, despite vigorous objections from Robert Lincoln, for the seventh time Lincoln's body was to be identified by witnesses. Master plumber Leon P. Hopkins, who had done the same fourteen years earlier, once again made the uncovering, cutting open the green lead plating that covered Lincoln's face and shoulders. Twenty-three hand-chosen witnesses crowded forward to see, including at least one—Clinton Conkling—who remembered Lincoln from life. A hush of silence fell over the room. There he lay, his face still completely recognizable, attested Hopkins, a face that all Americans knew so well. "He looked like a statue of himself," one witness attested. Someone noticed that Lincoln, who had always hated gloves, and pulled them off when his wife, Mary, wasn't looking, had been buried in a pair of fancy French kid gloves. And then Hopkins soldered Lincoln's coffin closed, and it was taken back to the burial chamber, where it was lowered into a steel cage below the floor. Finally Lincoln and Mary were sealed into their concrete tomb and covered by cement.

As 300 witnesses looked on, Willie Lincoln's small casket was carried by four men from the temporary vault to its new home inside the Lincoln Tomb.

Frederick Hill Meserve

In 1897 thirty-one-year-old businessman Frederick Hill Meserve began illustrating his father's Civil War memoirs. William Neal Meserve had shaken hands with Lincoln early in the war, had been wounded at Antietam, and was among the troops that closed off Washington after Lincoln's assassination. Long after the war he used his diary to write a memoir of his experience. "I thought it would be appropriate to illustrate this family keepsake with some Civil War photographs," recalled his son, who had been born the year Lincoln died. And so he headed out to find images of battlefields and soldiers. He began haunting old bookshops and second-hand stores and turning up exciting treasures. "In those days there were still floating around gems," he later recalled, "which are now under lock and key in institutions." In 1900 he attended an auction in New York City and bid, sight unseen, on a package containing an unknown quantity of old photographs. Bidding just a dollar and ten cents, to his astonishment he won. "That night I had my first experience of the sensation of intoxication," he wrote, "—that intoxication . . . that comes from the possession of a rare find." The packet turned out to contain more than a hundred exquisite prints, many of them taken by Mathew Brady. "After that I attended auction after auction," Meserve recalled. "My appetite had been whetted." His interests expanded far beyond his father's memoir and came to take in almost every aspect of the nineteenth century.

In April 1902 Meserve followed a hunch that brought him to a New Jersey warehouse. "I knew that Mathew Brady had died in 1896," he recalled, and "I knew that at the Civil War's end he had been dispossessed, for debts, of his great collection of negatives." He tracked down the name of the recipient of these photographs—Brady's printer, E. and H. T. Anthony, later the Anthony-Scoville company. Meserve found the glass negatives on the second floor of an old warehouse, heaped up in piles, some of them broken. Picking one up, he recognized the presidential face of Abraham Lincoln. Without hesitation he offered a price for the entire lot, and after negotiating it was accepted.

What he had bought were more than fifteen thousand glass negatives—two truckloads' worth—which he moved into his house in New York City. Among the astonishing array of portraits were seven of Lincoln himself. The discovery "illuminated my mind, and gave wings to my feet," Meserve said. "Now commenced the pleasure of study and examination, through months and years, of the contents of the boxes." It was the beginning of a passionate love affair with history that would make Meserve the preeminent collector of American photography and eventually the world authority on the portraiture of Abraham Lincoln.

Frederick Hill Meserve with his daughter Dorothy, who would carry on his Lincoln work

Meserve discovered Brady's glass negative of Lincoln in profile, the image later used on the U.S. penny.

Albert S. Edwards

Young Albert (right) with his brother Charles

The Lincoln Home

After the eviction of Osborn Oldroyd from the Lincoln home in Springfield, it took a while before Robert Lincoln was able to maneuver his choice for curator into the job. Ever since he had donated the homestead to the state of Illinois, it had been presided over by a board consisting of the governor and other key officers. The position of curator became a political appointment that was outside Robert Lincoln's control. But in June 1899 he managed to get his way when his cousin Albert Edwards, son of Mary's sister Elizabeth, was named for the job. He and his wife, Josephine, would now restore the house to its earlier simplicity.

Both caretakers had known Lincoln well. Albert had grown up alongside Robert in Springfield, a frequent guest at his home. Josephine was the daughter of the Lincolns' good friends Henry and Mary Remann. When her father died in 1849, seven-year-old Josie was informally adopted by the Lincoln family. Treating her like the daughter he never had, Lincoln would carry her on his shoulders and come to her rescue in times of trouble.

Albert and Josie were married in 1863 and continued to live in Springfield. During Mary Lincoln's final years in the 1880s her beloved "Joe" was one of her faithful supporters, and her daughter Mary helped to care for her invalid great-aunt. "I would sit with her—she was quite ill," the girl later recalled, "and talk to her by the hour."

In the 1890s, now both in their fifties, Albert and Josephine were an ideal cou-

Albert Edwards became custodian of the Lincoln home and oversaw a major restoration of the sixty-year-old building.

ple to take over the Lincoln home, Oldroyd's treasures now stripped from it. When they moved in, they brought with them their family mementos and Lincoln relics, which over time grew to become a formidable collection.

After years of abuse the house was in terrible condition—its foundations crumbling, rot in the wood frame itself, and the interior in need of thoroughgoing repairs and painting. Under Albert's direction, a major restoration was launched by the state and completed by September 1900. With the rooms painted and repapered, and family furniture brought back into the house, it was finally ready to be reopened to the public.

Visitors began streaming in at a rate of fifteen thousand a year. Open mornings and afternoons, the house was presided over by Josephine and by her now married daughter Mary, described by one visitor as "a young lady of commanding presence, tall and slender, with black eyes and hair." Visitors were taken into the double parlors on the main floor, arranged much as they had been in Lincoln's day, and hung with portraits of Lincoln, Mary, and their children. Here was the horsehair sofa from the Edwards house on which Lincoln and Mary had courted, and on the mantel were the sperm oil lamps that had shone on Mary and Abraham at their wedding. Outside, in the backyard near the shed and the outhouses, stood the old brass cannon that had fired the salute at the time of the election of Mr. Lincoln.

Albert Edwards embraced his new job with enthusiasm, leading tours and becoming a widely admired lecturer. "It seems to me but eminently natural," he said in an interview, "that patriotic Americans should find in Lincoln's home their Mecca. . . . It is one of the most cherished realities of this nation's life."

Josephine Remann Edwards

Lincoln carried young Josie Remann on his shoulders fifty years before she and her husband, Albert Edwards, became custodians of the Lincoln home. To the left is the upstairs room where Lincoln slept, next door to Mary's bedroom, as it looked in 1903.

Failing His Father's Legacy

As president of the Pullman Car Company, Robert Lincoln became increasingly wealthy. He purchased a sprawling mansion in Vermont, which he named Hildene, close by the golf courses that now meant so much to him. Set on hundreds of acres, it pleased him so much he began referring to it as his "ancestral home." He was by now part of America's ruling elite—a man of wealth unlike anything his father had ever known. On his board of directors were William K. Vanderbilt and J. P. Morgan, and among his friends was John D. Rockefeller. But Robert's money could not shield him from controversy or strife. A decade earlier, when he had served as counsel during the Pullman Car strike of 1894, he had been accused of refusing a fair wage to the Pullman porters—black professionals whom the son of Abraham Lincoln had been expected to support. Now that he was president of the company, the issue flared up again in a new form. In 1902 a young black professor named William Edward Burghardt Du Bois filed a lawsuit against the Southern Railway for denying him a sleeping car berth. Since the Southern Railway was part of the Pullman empire, the suit soon came to the attention of Robert Lincoln.

The problem escalated when Booker T. Washington got involved. Working secretly, he encouraged local groups in the South to initiate their own lawsuits and offered to reimburse Du Bois for a portion of his expenses. In January 1903 he wrote a letter to Robert Lincoln protesting the discriminatory treatment "on one of your cars, of a young colored man [Du Bois], a graduate of a college in Iowa, and one of the most intelligent a[n]d refined men I have ever met." Washington suggested a quiet and businesslike reparation, and a change in policy to remove discrimination against blacks. "It does seem to me that a rich and powerful corporation like yours could find some way to extend to some degree, protection to the weak." But Robert did nothing to address the issue.

Over time W. E. B. Du Bois grew fed up with Booker T. Washington's cautious, deferential ways. In an impassioned book published in February titled *The Souls of Black Folk*, Du Bois branded Washington a "compromiser" willing to surrender blacks' civil and political rights. His program of accommodation, Du Bois declared, had helped speed in the new era of segregation, disfranchisement, and abandonment of black welfare.

Booker T. Washington was stung by Du Bois's criticism, but he nevertheless continued

Robert Lincoln became president of the Pullman Car Company. Under the stress of his job his "nerves" got so frayed, he said, he had to take temporary leaves of absence. He came to live for vacations at his Vermont estate, Hildene.

to work with him and pressed hard for a meeting with Robert Lincoln. "Mr. Lincoln is evidently waiting for some development in the South, or trying to hedge," Washington wrote to Du Bois on November 5. In fact Robert had already decided not to meet with any black leaders, saying that such a conference might do "more harm than good." He was in any case fully aware of black opinion on the subject, he said, and didn't need any further information. In a diplomatically worded letter to a colleague, Booker T. Washington wrote that as "individuals none of us I think, would have any trouble . . . being received by Mr. Lincoln, but it is evident for some reason he means to avoid receiving any committee."

Privately Washington was disgusted by Robert Lincoln's behavior. It was in direct contradiction with the well-known policy of George Pullman, who during his life had said that no discrimination would ever be tolerated on his trains. And maybe even more painful, it was a deeply disappointing stance coming from the son of Booker T.'s greatest hero. It also revealed how Lincoln's legacy of racial progress was giving way to an era of worsening race relations.

In February 1904 Washington wrote a final judgment on the issue. "In regard to the sleeping car matter, I think Robert Lincoln, son of Abraham Lincoln, is largely to blame. If Mr. Lincoln would stand up straight there would be little trouble regarding Negroes and the sleeping cars." But Robert never did.

Believing that Robert Lincoln, as president of the Pullman Company, would not refuse a meeting with the nation's leading black leader, in November 1903 Booker T. Washington (left) came up with a plan. He would travel to Chicago with W. E. B. Du Bois (right) and others and meet with Robert Lincoln to discuss segregation on Pullman trains. In a telegram to Washington, Robert requested the names of all the committee members who would be present at such a meeting, then failed to answer Washington's follow-up letter. The meeting never took place.

Theodore Roosevelt's ring contained a strand of Lincoln's hair.

March 4, 1905

The Ring

On the night before Theodore Roosevelt's inauguration in 1905 he received a package from John Hay. In it was a ring stamped with Roosevelt's and Abraham Lincoln's monograms. Inside, in a compartment beneath a glass face, was a lock of Lincoln's hair, given to Hay by the son of Lincoln's attending physician. "Please wear this tomorrow," Hay wrote his friend the President. "You are one of the men who most thoroughly understands and appreciates Lincoln."

Lincoln was Theodore Roosevelt's greatest hero and his principal model for vigorous leadership in the name of the people. Ever since childhood, when he had witnessed Lincoln's New York City funeral, he had worshipped the sixteenth President. He considered Lincoln "a progressive in his own time," a "tempered radical" whose approach was now badly needed in the twentieth century. And with the assassination of William McKinley in 1901, he had gained the opportunity to try to become a President like Lincoln.

Roosevelt inherited McKinley's secretary of state—none other than Lincoln's former secretary John Hay, now in his sixties—who quickly became TR's best friend in Washington. Nearly every Sunday after church the President would stop at the Hay house, and the two men would share stories and interests, with Hay often speaking to Roosevelt about his famous predecessor. In the White House Roosevelt placed a portrait of Lincoln behind his desk and said that in difficult situations he would al-

Roosevelt's Homage

June 4, 1903

Two years before his inauguration Theodore Roosevelt left Washington on a transcontinental tour to shore up support for his foreign policy. Following a keynote speech in Chicago, he headed west, visiting Yellowstone and the Grand Canyon before reaching California. On the trip back his principal destination in Illinois was the city of Springfield.

It is a deep pleasure for me to have the chance of speaking to you today, and, above all, to speak to you here, in Lincoln's home, after having driven out to see Lincoln's tomb. . . . I have met in Illinois many men who knew Lincoln personally, and at every place that I have stopped, I have seen men who fought in the army when Lincoln called the country to arms. All of us now pay our tribute to the greatness that is achieved; all of us now looking back over the past forty years can see the figure of Lincoln—sad, kindly, patient Lincoln—as it looms above his contemporaries, as it will loom ever larger through the centuries to come.

It is a good thing for us by speech to pay homage to the memory of Abraham Lincoln, but it is an infinitely better thing for us in our lives to pay homage to his memory in the only way in which that homage can be effectively paid, by seeing to it that this republic's life, social and political, civic, and industrial is shaped now in accordance with the ideals which Lincoln preached and which all his life long he practiced.

Thousands of veterans showed up in Rockford, Illinois, to hear President Theodore Roosevelt speak. "The more I study the Civil War and the time following it," he later said, "the more I feel . . . the towering greatness of Lincoln."

ways try to do "what Lincoln would have done." He read from Lincoln's speeches and letters and admitted sensing Lincoln's ghost in the mansion. "I see him in the different rooms, and in the halls," he wrote to a friend. "I think of Lincoln . . . all the time."

In 1901, in a move reminiscent of Lincoln's grand gesture to Frederick Douglass, Roosevelt invited Booker T. Washington to the White House to dine with him. The highly publicized act angered Southerners and Democrats but was praised by others who increasingly compared Roosevelt to Lincoln. Two years later the President made a pilgrimage to Lincoln's tomb in Springfield and was struck by the presence there of black soldiers serving as guards. He told the crowd that he found this "eminently fitting." Roosevelt struggled throughout his presidency with "the Southern question"—the need on one hand for national reunion between North and South and on the other to protect the rights of black people. He said he hoped to meet the challenge "in the spirit of Abraham Lincoln," navigating between the twin dangers of Southern "arrogance" and Northern "folly." "The more I study the Civil War and the time following it," he wrote, "the more I feel . . . the towering greatness of Lincoln."

And so at his inauguration in 1905 Roosevelt wore on his left ring finger a lock of Lincoln's hair given to him by John Hay. "I often thereafter told John," TR later wrote, "that when I wore such a ring on such an occasion I bound myself more than ever to treat the Constitution, after the manner of Abraham Lincoln, as a document that put human rights above property rights when the two conflicted."

John Hay's career stretched forty-five years, from his appointment as personal secretary under Abraham Lincoln (below) to his position as secretary of state under Roosevelt (above).

Roosevelt invited Booker T. Washington to dine with him at the White House, the first African American hosted there since Lincoln had welcomed Frederick Douglass. The composite picture at left depicts the historic meeting.

July 1, 1905

The Death of John Hay

By his mid-sixties Secretary of State John Hay was wearing out. All his life he had suffered from headaches and eyestrain, and from attacks of nervous exhaustion. "I am getting old," he had written his brother-in-law in 1902. Now, three years later, serious illness forced him to take a leave of absence from the State Department. Though he agreed to serve for another term, in March, following the inauguration, he sailed for Europe for rest and recuperation. He was already sensing the approaching end. On his return voyage in June he awakened one night from a dream so deeply affected that he recorded it in his diary. "I dreamed last night that I was in Washington," he wrote, "and that I went to the White House to report to the President who turned out to be Mr. Lincoln. He was very kind and considerate, and sympathetic about my illness. . . . I was not in the least surprised at Lincoln's presence in the White House. But the impression of the dream was one of overpowering melancholy."

In one of his last journal entries, written just two weeks before he died at his beloved summer home on Lake Sunapee in New Hampshire, Hay spoke of his continuing passion for life. "I know death is a common lot," he wrote, ". . . and yet—instead of confronting it with dignity and philosophy, I cling instinctively to life and the things of life, as eagerly as if I had not had my chance at happiness and gained nearly all the great prizes." His greatest prize had been his friendship with Abraham Lincoln. "Perhaps in all American public life," wrote historian Brooks Adams, "nothing is more charming than the story of the relations that existed between these two men, the one in the bloom of life, the other hastening toward his tragic end. Lincoln treated Hay with the affection of a father, only with more than a father's freedom. If he waked at night he roused Hay, and they read together; in summer they rode in the afternoon and dined in the evenings at the soldiers' home. In public matters the older man reposed in the younger unlimited confidence."

A youthful-looking John Hay wore a top hat to appear older when Lincoln first hired him.

"I have lived to be old, something I never expected in my youth," wrote Secretary of State John Hay toward the end of his life. "I have had success beyond all the dreams of my boyhood."

In his Reminiscences *Schurz described first meeting Lincoln in 1858 aboard a train bound for Quincy, Illinois, the site of a Lincoln-Douglas debate the next day. Schurz was a young immigrant, and Lincoln was besieged by hundreds of well-wishers, but the candidate found time to talk with him.*

He received me with an off-hand cordiality, like an old acquaintance, having been informed of what I was doing in the campaign, and we sat down together. In a somewhat high-pitched but pleasant voice he began to talk to me, telling me much about the points he and Douglas had made in the debates at different places, and about those he intended to make at Quincy on the morrow.

When, in a tone of perfect ingenuousness, he asked me—a young beginner in politics—what I thought about this and that, I should have felt myself very much honored by his confidence, had he permitted me to regard him as a great man. But he talked in so simple and familiar a strain, and his manner and homely phrase were so absolutely free from any semblance of self-consciousness or pretension to superiority, that I soon felt as if I had known him all my life and we had long been close friends.

Carl Schurz, during the 1860s

1906
Carl Schurz Speaks Up

Journalist, ambassador, Civil War general, and senator, for five decades Carl Schurz was the leader of the German-American community in America. In Lincoln's day, Illinois was a land of immigrants; in 1854 the oldest native of Chicago was said to be a twenty-two-year-old woman. Nearly everyone came from somewhere else, and among the newcomers were representatives from many other countries, and especially from Germany. Without the German vote Lincoln could not be elected President, and from early on he courted it carefully.

Although originally a supporter of William Seward, Schurz switched to Lincoln after the nomination, vowing to "do the work of a hundred men for Abr. Lincoln's election." For German Protestants the antislavery campaign was a moral crusade as well as a political necessity, and Schurz helped fan the fire of pro-Lincoln sentiment. No one was more instrumental than he in delivering to Lincoln the German vote. For this he was rewarded with the ministry to Spain, though he returned to fight in the war and was named a brigadier general under Frémont.

But as the Civil War ground on, Schurz became increasingly frustrated with Lincoln and with the inability of his generals to win battles. And in the fall of 1862 he told him so. The former German revolutionary announced that it was Lincoln's tolerance toward General McClellan that lay behind the war's failure and behind Republican election losses in November. Never shy, he took it upon himself to give the President a stiff lecture. "The defeat of the Administration is the Administration's fault," he wrote, adding that his "open" remarks came because "I am your friend." This arrogance posing as honesty did not sit well with Lincoln, who wrote back a pointed letter. Convinced of his own rectitude, Schurz fired off another missive, which led to an invitation to speak with Lincoln in the White House.

The letters of this exchange were liberally quoted in Nicolay and Hay and reported in newspapers at the turn of the century. That led to a widespread distrust of Schurz, who was labeled a "hot-head" and a perennial "grumbler." In his seventies, Schurz decided to write about the exchange in the pages of a massive new book of reminiscences. Serialized in *McClure's* monthly magazine, the chapters began appearing in early 1906 and did much to renovate Schurz's reputation. It was soon clear that

his memoir was an important history that shed light on the fifty-year span in American life in which he had participated. And among the most memorable moments in the writing was his description of his meeting with Lincoln in 1862.

Schurz had always spoken his mind; he once described Ulysses S. Grant as "dumb as a fish" and said that Lincoln was an "overgrown nature child." But as his *Reminiscences* showed, his admiration for Abraham Lincoln was strong. He wanted to avoid the eulogistic tone of Nicolay and Hay, he said, and in praising Lincoln did not want to conceal his limi-

Schurz toward the end of his life

tations. The very secret of Lincoln's success came from a "weird mixture of qualities and powers in him, of the lofty and the common, the ideal and the uncouth." These qualities gave Lincoln a "singular power over minds and hearts, and fitted him to be the greatest leader in the greatest crisis in our national life." Schurz pointed to his tremendous growth as a man—from inglorious beginnings to the highest reaches of secular power; to his moral vision and courage—by which he was able to preside over the Civil War and the end of slavery; and perhaps most of all, to his awe-inspiring eloquence. Schurz described the Second Inaugural Address as "like a sacred poem," and said that "no American President had ever spoken words like these to the American people." Americans, he wrote, "never had a President who found such words in the depth of his heart."

"I loved him," Schurz wrote of Lincoln.

Lincoln's Letter to Schurz

November 24, 1862

My dear Sir

I have just received, and read, your letter of the 20th. The purport of it is that we lost the late elections, and the administration is failing, because the war is unsuccessful; and that I must not flatter myself that I am not justly to blame for it. I certainly know that if the war fails, the administration fails, and that I will be blamed for it, whether I deserve it or not. And I ought to be blamed, if I could do better. You think I could do better; therefore you blame me already. I think I could not do better; therefore I blame you for blaming me. I understand you now to be willing to accept the help of men, who are not republicans, provided they have "heart in it." Agreed. I want no others. But who is to be the judge of hearts, or of "heart in it"? If I must discard my own judgment, and take yours, I must also take that of others; and by the time I should reject all I should be advised to reject, I should have none left, republicans, or others—not even yourself. For, be assured, my dear sir, there are men who have "heart in it" that think you are performing your part as poorly as you think I am performing mine.

Confrontation in the White House

Carl Schurz

1906

Two or three days after Mr. Lincoln's letter had reached me, a special messenger from him brought me another communication from him, a short note in his own hand asking me to come to see him as soon as my duties would permit; he wished me, if possible, to call early in the morning before the usual crowd of visitors arrived. At once I obtained the necessary leave from my corps commander, and the next morning at seven I reported myself at the White House. I was promptly shown into the little room upstairs which was at that time used for Cabinet meetings—the room with the Jackson portrait above the mantel-piece—and found Mr. Lincoln seated in an arm chair before the open-grate fire, his feet in his gigantic morocco slippers. He greeted me cordially as of old and bade me pull up a chair and sit by his side. Then he brought his large hand with a slap down on my knee and said with a smile: "Now tell me, young man, whether you really think that I am as poor a fellow as you have made me out in your letter!" I must confess, this reception disconcerted me. I looked into his face and felt something like a big lump in my throat. After a while I gathered up my wits and

after a word of sorrow, if I had written anything that could have pained him, I explained to him my impressions of the situation and my reasons for writing to him as I had done. He listened with silent attention and when I stopped, said very seriously: "Well, I know that you are a warm anti-slavery man and a good friend to me. Now let me tell you all about it." Then he unfolded in his peculiar way his view of the then existing state of affairs, his hopes and his apprehensions, his troubles and embarrassments, making many quaint remarks about men and things. I regret I cannot remember all. Then he described how the criticisms coming down upon him from all sides chafed him, and how my letter, although containing some points that were well founded and useful, had touched him as a terse summing up of all the principal criticisms and offered him a good chance at me for a reply. Then, slapping my knee again, he broke out in a loud laugh and exclaimed: "Didn't I give it to you hard in my letter? Didn't I? But it didn't hurt, did it? I did not mean to, and therefore I wanted you to come so quickly." He laughed again and seemed to enjoy the matter heartily. "Well," he added, "I guess we understand one another now, and it's all right." When after a conversation of more than an hour I left him, I asked whether he still wished that I should write to him. "Why, certainly," he answered; "write me whenever the spirit moves you." We parted as better friends than ever.

June 1906

The Log Cabin Returns to Kentucky

The one-room cabin in which Abraham Lincoln was born in 1809 was for most of the nineteenth century ignored and neglected. According to a local account, it had been acquired by a neighboring farmer in 1861, who tore it down and removed it to his own property. In 1894 a New York investor named Alfred W. Dennett purchased the Lincoln farm and made a search for the missing cabin. He discovered it "intact" on the nearby property of John Davenport and moved it to the high hilltop where Thomas Lincoln had first built it in 1806. But then the cabin began an extraordinary new journey. In 1897 Dennett took it on the road, exhibiting it in Nashville, Tennessee, next to the so-called cabin of Jefferson Davis. Later it surfaced again, under questionable new ownership, at the Buffalo Exposition of 1901. "It was torn down, dragged about the country, and shown in settings so vulgar and inappropriate that it was made to seem almost a ridiculous thing," wrote Ida Tarbell. Finally, after the Lincoln farm came under new ownership, the missing logs were traced to the basement of a Long Island mansion and bought by the newly formed Lincoln Farm Association for $1,000. "There is a natural human instinct," wrote Mark Twain about these logs, "that is gratified by the sight of anything hallowed by association with a great man or great deeds." Since the farm was now widely considered a "sacred site," the logs were the sacred relics that had to be returned there. In June 1906 they were transported back to Kentucky on a special railroad car. All along the route the train made scheduled stops to allow Americans to see and touch the relics. The cabin's journey became part of a weeklong "homecoming" celebration in Kentucky, "one of the most elaborate affairs ever held in the South." Although there was little proof that the logs were from the original cabin, there was enough evidence that at least some of them might have been authentic. A board of review endorsed the project, and planning began for a permanent home for the cabin on the Lincoln farm.

The logs of Lincoln's birth cabin were transported from New York to Kentucky.

At the Louisiana Purchase Exposition in 1904 the Lincoln cabin appeared beside Jefferson Davis's birth cabin.
When they were disassembled, it is likely that some logs from the two houses got mixed up.

David Homer Bates

Former President Grover Cleveland received David Bates's book as a Christmas present from its publisher, Richard Watson Gilder. "I am delighted with . . . *Lincoln in the Telegraph Office*," Cleveland wrote back. "I have already read enough of it to be impressed with what it contains of a new closeness to a supremely great and good man. This 'closeness' grows more valuable to me and somehow, more—more—sacredly enshrined in my passionate Americanism, with every year of my life." To the right, an illustration from Bates's book shows Lincoln in the telegraph office working on a draft of the Emancipation Proclamation.

October 1907

Finally Willing to Tell His Story

By the opening decade of the twentieth century there was hope that Robert Lincoln might write his memoirs. Although that never happened, he did write one of the most revealing letters of his life after reading the 1907 memoir of a former telegraph operator named David Homer Bates, who had seen Lincoln on hundreds of occasions in the 1860s.

Throughout the war the White House had no telegraph service; it was housed in the nearby War Department building. Lincoln often walked over, at all hours of the day and night, particularly when the war required his close supervision. The Telegraph Office became his retreat from the fray of the White House, and he began to use it as a quiet place to work on important papers. "He seldom failed to come over late in the evening before retiring," Bates wrote, "and sometimes he would stay all night in the War Department."

It was at the Telegraph Office, at the war's beginning, that Lincoln learned of the death of his friend Elmer Ellsworth. And it was here, at war's end, that he received the dispatch announcing Ulysses S. Grant's capture of Richmond. In between, there were countless visits and vigils, as word from the front arrived requiring action or announcing victories and defeats. Through it all David Homer Bates was there—and in his book he revealed stories never heard before, leading up to Lincoln's last day, when he made his usual visit to the War Department. On that morning he tried to convince Superintendent Thomas T. Eckert to join him and Mary that evening at Ford's Theatre, to take the place of the Grants, who had just canceled. Stanton was furious with Lincoln for planning this visit to the theater and vigorously tried to dissuade him from going. When Lincoln refused to cancel, Stanton ordered Eckert not to accept, telling him he had too much work to do that night. "Very well," Lincoln sighed, "I shall take Major Rathbone."

LINCOLN IN THE TELEGRAPH OFFICE

is a book which not only appeals to popular interest, but is pronounced by Mr. Bates's associates in the War Department Telegraph Office a work of absolute accuracy and of permanent interest and value.

WHAT ROBERT T. LINCOLN SAYS OF IT

MANCHESTER, VERMONT, August 26, 1907.

Dear Mr. Bates:

I have just read in the September *Century* your concluding article, with a personal interest that no one can have but myself. I cannot refrain from telling you how much I have been affected by the feeling you have shown of love and regard for my father. It is very grateful to me. . . .

I must thank you earnestly for the pleasure I have had in your articles. They bring back very vividly the most exciting and interesting days of my life, and the reminiscences of my father make him seem to me to be alive again.

Believe me, sincerely yours,

ROBERT T. LINCOLN.

Robert Lincoln's heartfelt response to David Bates's book was reproduced in advertising by the publisher.

The Secret History of the Emancipation Proclamation
Thomas T. Eckert

1907

In Lincoln in the Telegraph Office *David Homer Bates quoted extensively from Thomas T. Eckert, telegraph superintendent of the War Department. Eckert revealed the previously unknown story of Lincoln's writing of what he believed to be an early draft (now lost) of the Preliminary Emancipation Proclamation.*

As you know, the President came to the office every day and invariably sat at my desk while there. Upon his arrival early one morning in June, 1862, shortly after McClellan's "Seven Days' Fight," he asked me for some paper, as he wanted to write something special. I procured some foolscap and handed it to him. He then sat down and began to write. . . . He would look out of the window a while and then put his pen to paper, but he did not write much at once. He would study between times and when he had made up his mind he would put down a line or two, and then sit quiet for a few minutes. After a time he would resume his writing, only to stop again at intervals to make some remark to me or to one of the cipher operators as a fresh dispatch from the front was handed to him. . . .

On the first day . . . [w]hen ready to leave, he asked me to take charge of what he had written and not allow any one to see it. I told him I would do this with pleasure and would not read it myself. "Well," he said, "I should be glad to know that no one will see it, although there is no objection to your looking at it; but please keep it locked up until I call for it to-morrow." I said his wishes would be strictly complied with.

When he came to the office on the following day he asked for the papers, and I unlocked my desk and handed them to him and he again sat down to write. This he did nearly every day for several weeks, always handing me what he had written when ready to leave the office each day. Sometimes he would not write more than a line or two, and once I observed that he had put question-marks on the margin of what he had written. He would read over each day all the matter he had previously written and revise it, studying carefully each sentence.

On one occasion he took the papers away with him, but he brought them back a day or two later. I became much interested in the matter and was impressed with the idea that he was engaged upon something of great importance, but did not know what it was until he had finished the document and then for the first time he told me that he had been writing an order giving freedom to the slaves in the South, for the purpose of hastening the end of the war. He said he had been able to work at my desk more quietly and command his thoughts better than at the White House, where he was frequently interrupted.

Thomas T. Eckert

377

A Drinking Man?

Lincoln's position on alcohol was a minor issue during his lifetime and a nonissue throughout the rest of the nineteenth century. But in the lead-up to Prohibition in the first decades of the twentieth century, it became a burning concern for millions of Americans. "Wets" routinely cited Lincoln's 1842 Temperance Address, in which he had criticized those who would prohibit alcohol by moral censure. Alcoholism did not arise "from the use of a bad thing," he had said, "but from the abuse of a very good thing." "Dries" on the other hand pointed to Lincoln's personal abstinence and opposition to drunkenness. In that same 1842 address, they pointed out, Lincoln had cursed "the demon of intemperance" and said "the world would be vastly benefited by a total and final banishment from it of all intoxicating drinks."

Lincoln's abstinence from liquor was widely attested. His stepmother, Sarah Bush, once said she thought if anything he was "too temperate" as a young man. Others recalled that his New Salem store sold whiskey by the gallon, but that he himself was always a strict teetotaler. In Springfield Lincoln once told his friend Leonard Swett that he "had never tasted liquor in his life." Only William Herndon—a temperance advocate and on-and-off-again binge drinker—remembered Lincoln as taking an occasional drink, "when he thought it would do him good." His preferred everyday liquid was plain water; "Adam's Ale" was what he called it.

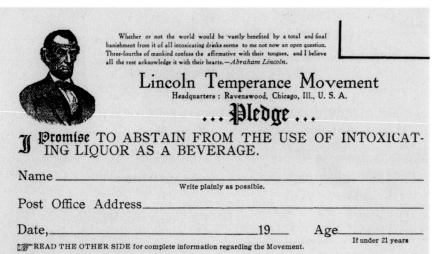

Whether or not the world would be vastly benefited by a total and final banishment from it of all intoxicating drinks seems to me not now an open question. Three-fourths of mankind confess the affirmative with their tongues, and I believe all the rest acknowledge it with their hearts.—*Abraham Lincoln.*

Lincoln Temperance Movement
Headquarters : Ravenswood, Chicago, Ill., U. S. A.
... Pledge ...

I Promise TO ABSTAIN FROM THE USE OF INTOXICATING LIQUOR AS A BEVERAGE.

Name _____
Write plainly as possible.

Post Office Address_____

Date,_____ 19___ Age_____
If under 21 years

☞ READ THE OTHER SIDE for complete information regarding the Movement.

In the lead-up to Prohibition in the first decade of the twentieth century, people on both sides of the issue tried to enlist Lincoln to their cause. Prohibitionists issued a "dry pledge" modeled after one Lincoln had supposedly taken.

Though store records show that Lincoln sometimes bought brandy, he never served alcohol in his home. In 1860, when an official notification committee visited after he had won the presidential nomination, he offered them ice water instead of the customary liquor. Shortly afterward he explained why he treated them so spartanly: "Having kept house sixteen years, and having never held the 'cup' to the lips of my friends then, my judgment was that I should not, in my new position, change my habit in this respect."

But Lincoln was never self-righteous about liquor, or considered his own sobriety a personal accomplishment. "I am entitled to little credit for not drinking because I hate the stuff," he said to William Herndon. "It is unpleasant and always leaves me feeling flabby and undone." Drinking was "a punishment to him, not an indulgence," agreed Ward Hill Lamon. "He seems to have taken liquor only when in social situations it was pressed upon him. He would rather have avoided it." As President, Lincoln rarely drank. According to John Nicolay, he might "sip a little wine" at a state dinner, "but even then in a perfunctory way, in complying with social custom." Once, to a visiting delegation, Lincoln revealed his true feelings on temperance. In September 1863, in the words of John Hay, "an assembly of cold-water men and coldwater women" arrived in Washington to make "a temperance speech" to the President. "They filed into the East Room looking blue and thin ... a few invalid soldiers ... in the dismal procession. They made a long speech at the Tycoon in which they called Intemperance the cause of our [military] defeats. He could not see it, as the rebels drink more and worse whiskey than we do." In his respectful, if humorous response to the delegation, Lincoln went on to point out his own temperance background and said he had been true to the cause ever since he was a young man. And he called intemperance "one of the greatest, if not the very greatest of all evils amongst mankind"—perhaps the strongest statement he ever made on the subject. It was "the mode of cure," he added subtly, about which "there may be differences of opinion."

As the Prohibition debate heated up in the twentieth century, efforts continued to enlist Lincoln to each side's cause. Declaring Lincoln the "apostle of temperance and prohibition," Prohibitionists issued a "dry pledge" modeled after one Lincoln had supposedly taken, and enlisted signatures from a million children across the nation. "Why . . . should any young man handicap himself . . . by the drink habit?" asked a 1907 editorial in the *Boston Globe*. "Why not follow Lincoln's example?" In response, liquor dealers sponsored research into Lincoln's years as a New Salem store owner, unearthing a copy of his saloon license, which was widely publicized.

In 1908, at a meeting at the Young Men's Prohibition Club in Chicago, Alonzo E. Wilson offered a fifty-dollar reward to anyone who could prove that Lincoln ever took a drink. In response, a local saloonkeeper named "Uncle Dan" Coleman came forward and said he had served a large glass of port wine to Lincoln in 1861, and that the President-elect had drunk it down "as if he had liked it." "Everyone knew in those days that Mr. Lincoln took a drink whenever he felt like it," insisted Coleman. But his word alone was not considered proof enough for him to win the prize.

Anti-Prohibition forces uncovered Lincoln's New Salem liquor license and publicized it. "Everyone knew in those days that Mr. Lincoln took a drink when he felt like it," attested a Chicago saloonkeeper named "Uncle Dan" Coleman. In fact Lincoln rarely drank, but he opposed the criminalization of alcohol.

Drinking with Both Hands
Edward Rosewater

Edward Rosewater worked in the War Department Telegraph Office during Lincoln's presidency and wrote this account in the Washington Times, *describing an incident in July 1863.*

We were working day and night at fever heat, and when the news came of the fall of Vicksburg, I remember that we sent a messenger out for a can of beer. . . . We were passing the bucket around when, to our astonishment and alarm, in strode the president, who had come to look over our dispatches at first hand. You can imagine our embarrassment. There was no use of attempting to deny or conceal. We had been caught by the chief executive. He had seen the tell-tale can, and, although this was now practically empty, Lincoln was too shrewd a man not to know that we were all guilty of violating one of the strictest orders of the war department. But he affected at first not to notice. Coming over to my instrument, he asked to see the latest dispatch. He read it slowly, handed it back, and turning to the messenger, who had been hoping for a favorable moment to make his escape with the can, Lincoln asked:

"What have you in that bucket?"

Answering for the startled messenger, I explained what we had been doing.

"Any beer left?" said the president.

I told him that we had drunk it all.

"Here," said Lincoln, pulling a .25-cent piece from his pocket, "go and fill it up again." So saying he turned again to the telegrams.

The messenger arrived with the beer, and Mr. Lincoln looked up and told him to pass it around. . . .

Of course we all insisted that he take the first drink, and with a message still clutched in his right hand, telling how Grant had won the great victory, President Lincoln grasped the bucket with both hands, and, tipping it up, drank heartily.

379

William Donnegan, Lincoln's friend and bootmaker, was one of the victims of the Springfield riots. Below, a crowd of white vigilantes lingered after hanging one of Springfield's black citizens.

Race Riots in Lincoln's Hometown

Black Americans in the early twentieth century had few greater heroes than Abraham Lincoln. But ironically, in his hometown of Springfield, racial tensions were among the worst in the nation. A newspaper article in 1881 described how local hotel owners routinely refused service to black customers, even famous ones like the Fisk Jubilee Singers. By 1908 the atmosphere had become dangerous, with one white businessman blaming the situation on the blacks themselves: "They were getting too bold and impudent. People outside the city cannot realize how offensive this was."

On Friday, August 15, a white woman, Mabel Hallam, accused a local black man, George Robinson, of rape. Outside the jail where he was held, an angry crowd assembled demanding Robinson's release into their hands. When the sheriff refused, they turned their wrath on black Springfield. Beginning in the slums in the eastern part of the city, two thousand men and boys began to throw stones at black bystanders and set fire to black businesses. "Lincoln freed you," rioters were heard to yell out; "we'll show you where you belong." Some black residents grabbed guns and knives to protect their homes and businesses; others fled for safety. When the black owner of a barbershop, Scott Burton, came out and stood at the doorway, the mob shot him dead, then hung him from a nearby tree.

By Saturday, the National Guard took control of the city. As rioters attacked "Camp Lincoln," where many blacks had fled for refuge, they were rebuffed by armed troops. So they began attacking individual homes in town, singling out middle-class black families. On Saturday night they approached the house of an eighty-four-year-old shoemaker named William Donnegan, a longtime resident of Springfield who had once made boots for Abraham Lincoln. His niece, an eyewitness, said that the "hoodlums and desperadoes" who attacked her uncle did so because of his independence and prosperity. "He was even told by some of the

Soldiers picked through the ruins of a burned-out black residence in Springfield.

A crowd assembled outside a building destroyed in the riots.

Another of the victims of the Springfield mob was a local barber named Scott Burton, whose body was hanged from a tree outside a Springfield saloon. As white crowds posed by the tree, much of Springfield lay in ruins.

ringleaders of the mob that he had too much property for a 'nigger.'" Setting fire to Donnegan's shop, the mob drove the old man outside, where they hit him with stones and bricks. Then they slashed his throat. Donnegan was still alive as he was dragged across the street into a school courtyard. There he was hoisted up on a tree and left to die, not far from the city's statue of Abraham Lincoln. "The scenes at Springfield were terrible beyond description," Donnegan's niece related. "The better class of white people have done all they could to protect the peaceable and decent colored people, but they were powerless to cope with that mob. . . . As for my poor uncle, it was just murder."

By Sunday forty black homes had been burned to the ground; hundreds of people were injured; and more than two thousand black residents had been driven from the city, many never to return. "The race rioting in Springfield . . . paralyzes optimism and makes the lover of progress stand aghast," wrote the *Washington Post*. "It happened in the home of Abraham Lincoln, in the very shadow of his statue!" At church the next week, the Rev. Reverdy C. Ransom asked, "What would the emancipator of our race have thought had he witnessed the crime of that horrible mob? Would he not have regarded his life as given in vain to see the people he freed subjected to such treatment?"

Though there were many in town who decried the violence, a majority seemed to approve of the mob actions against the black community. Even the local newspaper, the *Illinois State Journal*, wrote sympathetically about the perpetrators. "[M]any good citizens," it editorialized, "could find no other remedy than that applied by the mob. It was not the fact of the white's hatred toward the negroes, but of the negroes' own misconduct, general inferiority or unfitness for free institutions that was at fault."

There was little motivation for legal justice following the riots, even when in September Mabel Hallam admitted that she had invented her rape accusations in order to hide a love affair from her husband. That same month the confessed murderer of William Donnegan was found not guilty by a jury of his peers. Of the 107 indictments handed down, the only conviction was of a man who had stolen a saber from a guard.

In striking contrast to that summer of riots, Americans celebrated the fiftieth anniversary of the Lincoln-Douglas debates. Festive ceremonies took place in Alton, Illinois, and in the six other cities where the debates had been held.

Part Five

1909–1926

His Unfinished Work

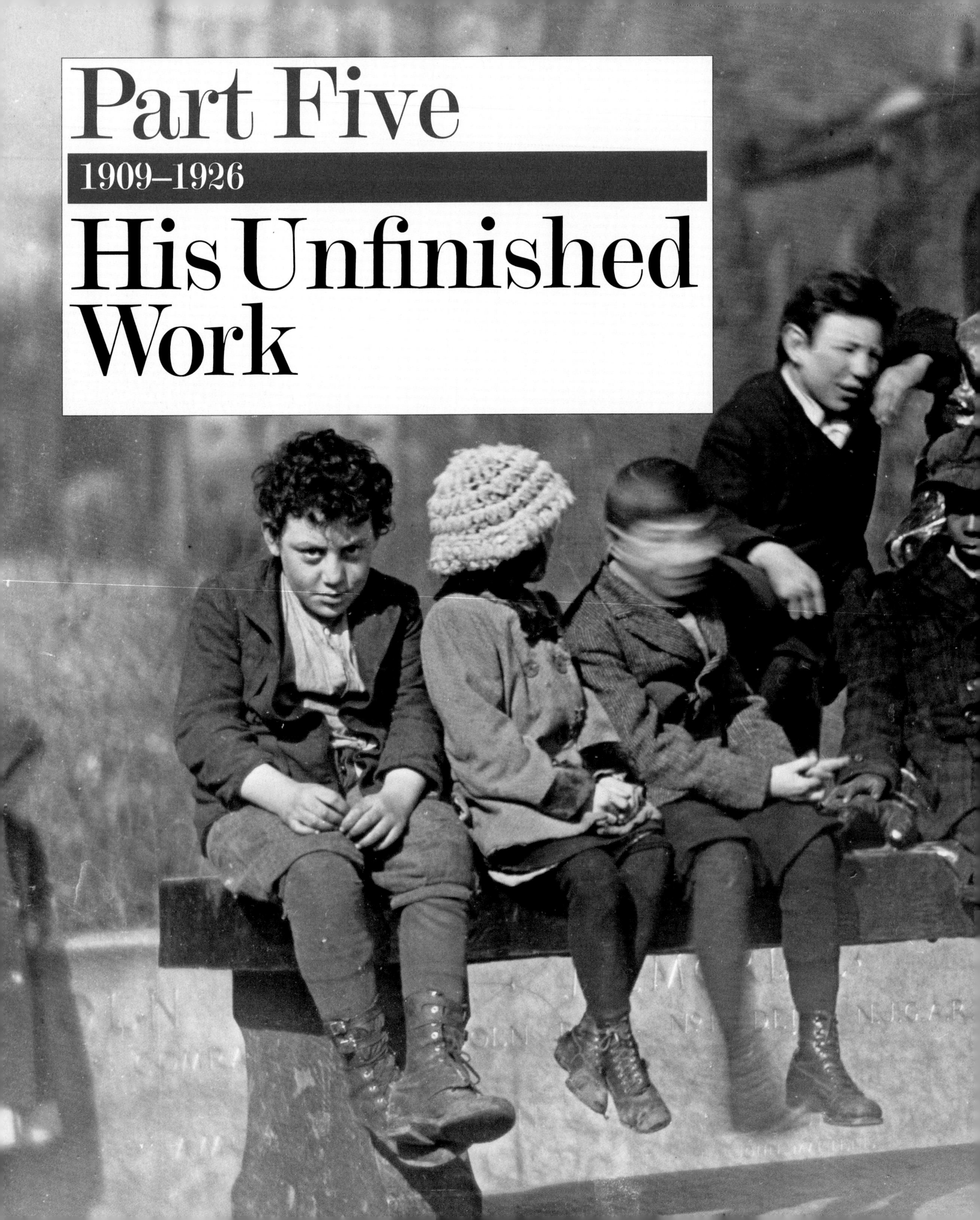

Children gathering around Gutzon Borglum's Lincoln bench in Newark, New Jersey, around 1916

Why We Love Him
1909–1926

In 1909 Lincoln reverence reached its high-water mark, as virtually the entire nation paused to honor his hundredth birthday. Over the next decades he would loom as a universal icon, embodied at the Lincoln Memorial in Washington and at Lincoln shrines across the nation. New immigrants looked to him for what it meant to be American, and Northerners and Southerners finally found a consensus. But the higher he rose in people's estimations, the less specificity he came to have. The quirky westerner with his own way of thinking and speaking was gradually replaced by a silent marble statesman. Though he was now a world figure representing humane and progressive values, he was increasingly vied for by people from all political viewpoints. Everyone seemed to find in him something for them.

As long as Robert Lincoln remained alive, his father's memory was carefully controlled, and the huge collection of Lincoln's papers remained under lock and key. This was the final period of influence for those who had known Lincoln; one by one they dropped away, leaving only those who had encountered him as children. But as Lincoln's era receded into distant history, replaced by an industrial America ever stronger on the world stage, Lincoln the man attained an even more intimate place in people's lives. In the February 1909 edition of *Pearson's Magazine*, James Creelman published an article entitled "Why We Love Lincoln." In an age of "money-worshipping greed," he wrote, "preparations are being made to celebrate the one hundredth anniversary of the birth of Abraham Lincoln, the humblest, simplest, and plainest of our national leaders." While George Washington evoked universal pride in Americans, Jefferson and Madison "intellectual reverence," and Jackson and Grant "grateful consciousness of their strength," the memory of Lincoln even now "stirs the tenderest love of the nation." Why had he of all others risen to such a place in the American heart? Creelman's answer was simple but profound. "In the secret recesses where every man communes with the highest, bravest, and most unselfish elements of his own nature, the average American is an Abraham Lincoln to himself."

The Wanderer finds Liberty in America

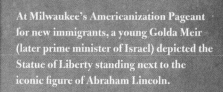

At Milwaukee's Americanization Pageant for new immigrants, a young Golda Meir (later prime minister of Israel) depicted the Statue of Liberty standing next to the iconic figure of Abraham Lincoln.

The Lincoln penny, issued in the Centennial year, was the first U.S. coin to bear the image of a historical figure.

The Centennial was a commercial opportunity for advertisers. The makers of a Waterman Ideal Fountain Pen promised "emancipation from pen troubles."

February 12, 1909

The Abraham Lincoln Centennial

Lincoln's hundredth birthday was a grassroots effort, sprouting up locally across the country, with civic organizations, schools, churches, and the press all taking part. Observances were planned in every state of the nation, as well as in places as far away as Japan. "Probably never before," wrote one commentator, "was the character and career of any man so profoundly shared by so many people at one time."

For years the most esteemed American icon had been George Washington, whose own centennial—of his inauguration—had been celebrated with great fanfare in 1889. But unlike the aristocratic "father of his country," Lincoln was a man of the people, and it was as such that his Centennial honored him. "As a representative of triumphal democracy he stands foremost," wrote the *Chicago Tribune*.

Illinois was at the center of the excitement, and in Chicago forty-nine school buildings were chosen as Lincoln "centers" to host public lectures by distinguished speakers. Businesses of all kinds embraced the occasion. Virtually every American magazine either put Lincoln on its cover or ran a major story about him; newspapers offered Lincoln books and mementos; Centennial postcards were sold as popular keepsakes; and the Waterman Company issued a Lincoln Fountain Pen, which because it needed no dipping promised "the emancipation of millions of slaves to the ink bottle."

In Washington, President Roosevelt approved a Lincoln coin—the first to bear the image of an American president. (Originally it was to have been a half-dollar piece; eventually it became the Lincoln penny.) A new two cent stamp was issued with Lincoln's face on it. And a limited-edition Centennial medallion was commissioned. Talks began about a grand Lincoln monument for the nation's capital, though it would take years before the Lincoln Memorial would become a reality. And discussions were held in Congress about a new "Lincoln Road," to connect the capital city to Gettysburg, Pennsylvania, with a second branch to run westward all the way to San Francisco. Referred to as a "twentieth century Appian Way," it showed how deeply the Centennial was linked to the idea of American progress.

On February 12 there were celebrations everywhere. At the last moment Congress had declared it a national holiday, but most schools and colleges stayed open for the special day, using it for an extended focus on Abraham Lincoln. At Lincoln City, Indiana, a hundred schoolchildren led a procession to the grave of Abraham Lincoln's mother, who had died in 1818 when her son was just nine. At Gettysburg ceremonies were held at the local college and included a solemn reading of the Gettysburg Address. At Howard University in Washington, a painting was unveiled in Lincoln's honor depicting the activities of the Underground Railroad.

In Boston a special issue of the *Globe* presented forty-three accounts by men from across New England who had known Abraham Lincoln. And inside Boston's Symphony Hall, an aging Julia Ward Howe, author of "The Battle Hymn of the Republic," read a new poem about Lincoln's rise from obscurity.

And so it went in city after city, as the nation came together to seek unity through Lincoln. "Never before in the history of the world," wrote the *Review of Reviews*, "has the hundredth anniversary of the birth of any man been celebrated with such a depth of feeling." And the *Chicago Tribune* echoed widespread sentiment: "The nation hasn't felt this deeply since Lincoln's death."

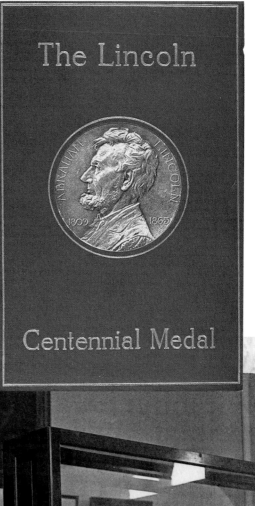

In 1909 Lincoln's image was used on a new two-cent stamp and on a large Centennial medal, issued in gold, silver, or bronze. Below, Illinois teenagers studied Lincoln treasures in a Centennial exhibit at the Chicago Historical Society.

A Man Who Couldn't Look Lincoln in the Eye
Thomas B. Bancroft

February 1909

Bancroft was a Philadelphia businessman who had met Lincoln in the summer of 1862. His account was published in the Centennial issue of McClure's *magazine.*

He sat in his chair loungingly, giving no evidence of his unusual height; a pair of short-shanked gold spectacles sat low down upon his nose, the shanks catching his temples, and he could easily look over them if he so desired. As I came up to the railing in front of him, he was reading a paper that had just been presented to him by a man who sat in the chair opposite him and who seemed, by his restlessness and his unsteady eyes, to be of a nervous disposition, or under great excitement.

Mr. Lincoln, still holding the paper up and without movement of any kind, paused and, raising his eyes, looked for a long time at this man's face and seemed to be looking down into his very soul. Then, resuming his reading for a few moments, he again paused and cast the same piercing look upon his visitor.

Suddenly, without warning, he dropped the paper and stretching out his long arm he pointed his finger directly in the face of his vis-à-vis and said, "What's the matter with you?"

The man stammered and finally replied, "Nothing."

Dozens of magazines put Lincoln on their February cover, including *Hampton's*, *Collier's*, and *National Magazine*.

"Yes, there is," said Lincoln. "You can't look me in the face! You have not looked me in the face since you sat there! Even now you are looking out that window and cannot look me in the eye!"

Then, flinging the paper in the man's lap, he cried, "Take it back! There is something wrong about this! I will have nothing to do with it!" —and the discomfited individual retired. I have often regretted that I was unable to discover the nature of this case.

An Unguarded Sleeper
James Rowan O'Beirne

January 1909

During the winter of 1864-65 James Rowan O'Beirne served as provost marshal of the District of Columbia. Part of his job was to help protect the President. His reminiscence was published in The Scrap Book.

One night I was roused out of bed by the military Governor, Colonel M. N. Wisewell, and told to report at the War Office. The President had gone out to sleep at the Soldiers' Home just outside Washington, as was his custom those warm summer nights, and we had to ride out there to be sure he had his guard. It was a quiet, restful night, and when Colonel Wisewell and I got out there we found all the guards sound asleep, not even on post, but in their temporary tents, and the sergeant of the guard in his headquarters.

Brigadier General James R. O'Beirne

"He's probably told them all to go to bed," remarked the colonel dryly.

After inspection we discovered the room where Mr. Lincoln was sleeping. The shutter was raised freely, and the lintel was about on a level with my chin, so that any one could have easily climbed into the room and captured him. But there he lay, sleeping comfortably and soundly, as the sounds from within testified.

Well, we roused the commanding officer, routed out the guard, and saw that they were placed at proper points near that window and along the avenues. We rode back to Washington about three in the morning. And I remember how we laughed over the idea of Lincoln being captured as a hostage, and the trouble of placing guards over a man who didn't want to have guards over him.

A Reminder of Willie Lincoln
James Grant Wilson

February 1909

James Wilson served under Ulysses S. Grant and later wrote a biography of the general. In the Centennial year he described meeting Lincoln in 1862. It was published in Putnam's Magazine.

General Grant gave me a leave of absence to go to Washington to visit a younger brother who, having been mortally wounded in the battle of Fredericksburg, had been removed to the Georgetown hospital. After seeing my brother I called at the White House, and the President said . . . "[W]hat brings you to Washington?" When informed he remarked, "If you will come in this afternoon at four o'-clock, we will walk over to Georgetown and see the young captain." . . .

When we arrived at the hospital, Mr. Lincoln saw, or thought he saw, a strong resemblance between my brother and his favorite son Willie, who had recently died. This interested him so deeply that the following afternoon Mrs. Lincoln drove out with us, and she too saw the likeness. During the fortnight that my brother survived, the President visited him several times, and Mrs. Lincoln sent the young soldier little delicacies made by herself.

General James G. Wilson

A Centennial Lincoln statue was dedicated in Wisconsin.

391

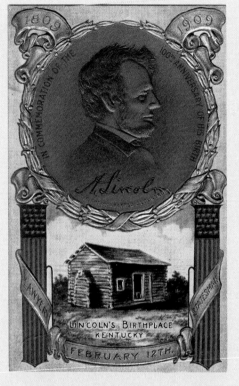

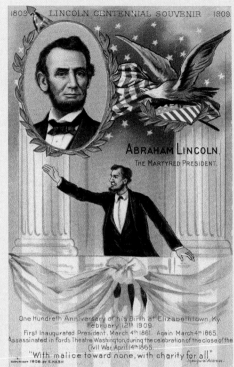

Meeting of President Lincoln and Gen'l Grant.

LINCOLN'S ADDRESS AT GETTYSBURG.

The most popular collectibles during the Centennial year were souvenir postcards, which depicted dozens of scenes from Lincoln's life.

Boys posed for a photograph at Henry Kirke Brown's statue of Lincoln in Union Square, New York.

A Lincoln celebration at Manhattan Public School number 94

New York's Big Party

One thousand different Lincoln events took place in New York City on February 12, in what was called the "largest celebration" ever given to "any human being, living or dead." Veterans showed up at armories across the city for patriotic services that began with the singing of "The Star-Spangled Banner" and usually included a reading of the Gettysburg Address. Events took place at Carnegie Hall, at the City College of New York, and at the Cooper Union, where Lincoln had given his memorable campaign speech in 1860. Here an address was given by the mayor of New York City, George B. McClellan, son of the former general.

At the Republican Club dinner at the Waldorf-Astoria Hotel, guests gathered to hear Booker T. Washington speak about Lincoln. "In the very highest sense he lives in the present more potently than fifty years ago," Washington said. "He . . . lives in the steady, unalterable determination of these millions of black citizens."

At the Brooklyn Academy of Music thousands gathered to hear playwright Percy MacKaye read his "Ode on the Centennial of Abraham Lincoln." Lush and romantic, and written for this occasion, the ode revealed much about the nation's thinking in 1909, and why the Centennial itself was being so widely celebrated. With the distance of time, Lincoln had become a literary, epic character. His humble birth, his rise to power, his mortal struggle with slavery, his martyrdom, all added up to a "homely, native Odyssey." He is "the mystic demi-god of common man," rang out MacKaye, "democracy's own brow—the American ideal." Lincoln's journey had become symbolic of America's own, from its humble beginnings to its growing eminence on the world stage. The most fitting tribute to him was not in stone or bronze, MacKaye said, but in this memorial in time that was uniting the nation, as "one vast communion makes today his temple."

The Republican Club Lincoln dinner at the Waldorf-Astoria

"Why Did You Not Say It Yesterday?"
Booker T. Washington

February 12, 1909

Booker T. Washington came to New York City to address the Republican Club dinner on what would have been Lincoln's 100th birthday. Three days earlier he had written, "Every member of my race ... who leads a law-abiding, sober life is justifying the faith which the sainted Lincoln placed in us.... With equal emphasis I wish to add that no man who hallows the name of Lincoln will inflict injustice upon the Negro."

Booker T. Washington began his New York City address by repeating a story he had told many times, about hearing his slave mother praying for Abraham Lincoln.

I am not fitted by ancestry or training to be your teacher tonight, for, as I have stated, I was born a slave.

My first knowledge of Abraham Lincoln came in this way: I was awakened early one morning before the dawn of day, as I lay wrapped in a bundle of rags on the dirt floor of our slave cabin, by the prayers of my mother, just before leaving for her day's work, as she was kneeling over my body earnestly praying that Abraham Lincoln might succeed, and that one day she and her boy might be free. You give me the opportunity here this evening to celebrate with you and the nation the answer to that prayer....

Lincoln was in the truest sense great because he unfettered himself. He climbed up out of the valley, where his vision was narrowed and weakened by the fog and miasma, onto the mountain top, where in a pure and unclouded atmosphere he could see the truth which enabled him to rate all men at their true worth.... In his rise from the most abject poverty and ignorance to a position of high usefulness and power, he

taught the world one of the greatest of all lessons.... Today, throughout the world, because Lincoln lived, struggled, and triumphed, every boy who is ignorant, is in poverty, is despised or discouraged, holds his head a little higher. His heart beats a little faster, his ambition to do something and to be something is a little stronger, because Lincoln blazed the way....

Lincoln lives today because he had a courage that made him refuse to hate the man at the South or the man at the North when they did not agree with him. He had the courage, as well as the patience and foresight to suffer in silence, to be misunderstood, to be abused, to refuse to revile when reviled. For he knew that, if he was right, the ridicule of today would be the applause of tomorrow. He knew, too, that at some time in the distant future our nation would repent of the folly of cursing its public servants while they live and blessing them only when they die. In this connection I cannot refrain from suggesting the question to the millions of voices raised today in his praise: "Why did you not say it yesterday?" Yesterday, when one word of approval and gratitude would have meant so much to him in strengthening his hand and heart.

February 12, 1909
Chicago Celebrates

Forty-four years earlier the city of Chicago had been draped in black to honor a slain president. Today it was festooned in red, white, and blue, with portraits of Lincoln everywhere. To take part in the festivities, the very women who as young girls had participated in Lincoln's Chicago funeral wearing white dresses were invited back four decades later to once again appear in his honor. Six great public meetings had been scheduled for Lincoln Day, beginning with a morning speech by the president of Princeton University, Woodrow Wilson, and stretching throughout the day. At several meetings, Lincoln's emancipation legacy was highlighted. At an Irish-American gathering at the Seventh Regiment Armory, Canadian speaker J. A. Mac-Donald spoke of Lincoln's service to human liberty. "Lincoln did more for democracy in the United States than save the Union," he sang out. "Union was not enough. There must be freedom as well . . . for all people." The climactic event of the day was at Dexter Pavilion, near the stockyards, where nearly twenty thousand people gathered to take part in the evening's events. "Every nook and cranny was filled," reported the *Chicago Times*, "and men and women stood shoulder to shoulder for three hours while the exercises were in progress." The lead speaker was Unitarian minister Jenkin Lloyd Jones, founder of the Abraham Lincoln Center in Chicago, which offered educational opportunities to underprivileged children and young adults. Jones had prepared a slide show on the life of Lincoln to accompany his lecture on what Lincoln meant to the present day. "He is not dead," roared the white-bearded activist. "Chicago is today under the spell of a living force, of an immortal Lincoln." He lived on, Jenkins proclaimed, in the women's suffrage movement, in the struggles for workers' rights, in campaigns against child abuse, and in liberation movements around the world.

Above, one of the many Abraham Lincoln Centennial ribbons; to the right, Chicago's Board of Trade, decorated for the Lincoln Centennial

Crowds gathered for a Centennial celebration at Augustus Saint-Gaudens's statue in Lincoln Park, Chicago.

The Spirit of Brotherhood
Thomas S. Inborden

February 1909

T. S. Inborden, a graduate of Fisk University, was the principal of the Joseph K. Brick Agricultural, Industrial and Normal School in Enfield, North Carolina.

Whether a State is created and named or a canal dug or a great public highway built, nine-tenths of the Negroes of this country will never know, and it will not appear too unpatriotic to say, they will not care very much for fear that it will afford another opportunity for adverse legislation against them, but *ten-tenths* of the American Negroes will hold in sacred honor and perpetuate to their children forever the name of their emancipator—*Abraham Lincoln.* They may not know Barnard's statuary from the Egyptian Sphinx, but they know that this pioneer from the West, this man who educated himself by the light of the pine torch, who could split more rails than any other man in his community, whose home-spun clothes and rural appearance readily identified him with the common people, attained the highest eminence in the gift of the nation and that he had the courage of his convictions to sign the emancipation proclamation which gave them the liberty of American citizens.

They need no other monument, they ask for no insignia of greatness more enduring than the spirit of brotherhood and justice that inspired the thought of total emancipation for these dependent subjects.

Two boys during the Lincoln Centennial

February 1909
An African American Centennial

In many cities African Americans were excluded from the Centennial events and were obliged to hold their own Lincoln observances in churches and armories. Other than Booker T. Washington, who spoke to the Republicans in New York, there were few black speakers outside of these all-black meetings. And of the thousands of Lincoln speeches in February 1909, very few whites dwelled on the subject of racial injustice. Once again, as in the days of Frederick Douglass, it was primarily the black community that kept alive Lincoln's emancipationist legacy.

In New York City, the American Missionary Society dedicated its February magazine to Lincoln and "the Negro Problem." The society created a special memorial offering for "Lincoln Sunday," February 7, "to complete the work which Abraham Lincoln began." The society had been formed in 1846 for the specific purpose of eliminating slavery, then went on to promote black education and racial equality. In 1866 it founded Fisk University, a college in Tennessee for black men. By 1909 Fisk included among its distinguished alumni W. E. B. Du Bois, who had gone on to earn a doctorate from Harvard University. The *American Missionary*'s February 1909 issue included articles by Fisk faculty members G.W. Henderson and J. W. Work, both accomplished African Americans. And there were powerful articles by William Pickens of Talladega College, and by T. S. Inborden of the Joseph K. Brick Agricultural, Industrial and Normal School in North Carolina. Inborden wrote about the country's Centennial plans: a Lincoln highway, a Lincoln canal, and new Lincoln statues. These were fine projects, he proclaimed, but how much more important it would be, he said, to decisively deal with the issue of racism in America, a subject never truly faced after the death of Lincoln. "If the nation, including particularly the individual states, had but followed the principle of this great emancipator, the principle of exact justice and equality for every citizen before the law, there would have been no problem," he wrote.

The black writers all spoke of Lincoln's lowly origins and of his difficult rise from obscurity. Henderson compared Lincoln to Moses and said, "There is no third name to be placed by their side." Both were "world figures," he explained, "because both identified with the cause of human liberty, which is the conscience of universal humanity." Henderson noted Lincoln's role in the passage of the Thirteenth Amendment and called attention to his extraordinary growth on the issue of race. "He believed his country would be just," Henderson said, then asked, "Will it?" He was worried because so much attention had shifted from matters of race to an overarching concern for North/South reunion. "Let the two sections of the country come together by all means," he wrote, "but not over the grave of the colored man's political rights."

LINCOLN CENTENNIAL!
At St. Paul A. M. E. Church, Friday, Feb. 12 at 8 p. m.

Under auspicies of "ILLINOIS COLORED HISTORICAL SOCIETY"

Free Admission   Everybody Invited

African Americans organized their own celebrations in 1909. Unlike many segregated events, theirs welcomed anyone to attend.

A Kentucky woman sits with pen in hand next to a portrait of Abraham Lincoln. By 1909 many African American homes had a portrait of "The Great Emancipator" on their walls.

The Lincoln Centennial in the South

All across the once-reluctant South, cities and towns participated in the Centennial, with Texas and Arkansas observing Lincoln's birthday for the first time. Southerners' relationship to Lincoln remained complex, with a diversity of viewpoints still vying for attention. Lyon G. Tyler, president of William and Mary College and son of former president John Tyler, represented the old anti-Lincoln tradition, still strong in parts. When he was approached with the idea of building a Centennial memorial to Lincoln in the city of Richmond, Virginia, he angrily rejected the proposal. "To ask the South," he wrote, "to put up a monument to Lincoln, who represents Northern invasion of the homes and firesides of the South, would be as absurd as if I were to ask the North to put up a monument to Jefferson Davis.... I am sure that the South can never be brought to regard Mr. Lincoln in any other political light than that in which Mr. Davis is regarded in the North—as the champion of a section."

The author Thomas Dixon represented a different approach. In his best-selling novel and play *The Clansman*, he portrayed a genial Lincoln under the control of a strident Thaddeus Stevens ("Austin Stoneman") who wanted the slaves to become equal citizens with whites. Dixon's Lincoln replies to him, "We can never attain the ideal Union of our father's dreams, with millions of an alien, inferior race among us, whose assimilation is neither possible nor desirable. The Nation cannot now exist half white and half black." In the same vein, William P. Pickett put finishing touches on his Centennial book, *The Negro Problem: Abraham Lincoln's Solution*. Arguing for the deportation of all blacks to Africa, the Caribbean, or onto western reservations, Pickett justified his opinions by invoking Lincoln. "[H]ave we in our hearts the courage and in our minds the intelligence and resolution to solve the negro problem as Lincoln would have it solved?" Pickett asked.

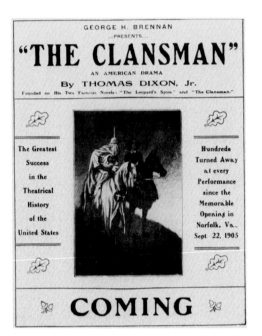

Thomas Dixon's play *The Clansman* opened in Norfolk, Virginia, in 1905 and was hailed as "the greatest success in theatrical history." Below right is the title page of William P. Pickett's *The Negro Problem*. Published in the centennial year, it incorrectly claimed that Lincoln was in favor of the deportation of American blacks.

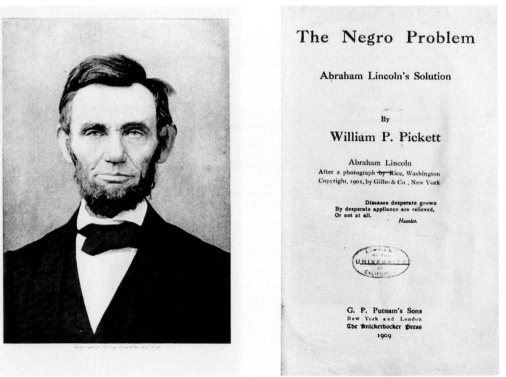

But the Centennial also saw a new openness to Lincoln in younger Southerners eager to become fully part of the nation. For the first time Southern children, long taught to hate Lincoln, were told that he was a great American. Southern orators focused on Lincoln's southern roots and those of his Kentucky wife, Mary Todd. Even in his views on slavery, one historian argued, "he was very close to the large body of non-slaveholding Southerners." And the South was far better off without slavery, it was widely agreed. In some cities elaborate memorial exercises took place on February 12. The largest was held at Atlanta's Methodist Episcopal Church, where the ceremony included Union and Confederate veterans and a reading of Lincoln's Gettysburg Address. Pastor James W. Lee called Lincoln "a true son of the South" and held him up beside Robert E. Lee as a man inspired by God. Lee's centenary had taken place just two years earlier, and he had been called a true American by the northerner Charles Francis Adams. Now in 1909 Woodrow Wilson, addressing a Southern audience, paired Lincoln and Lee as twin symbols of a reinvented America.

IN MEMORIAM.

NO NORTH, NO SOUTH.

Nation Honors Lincoln's Birthday.

The goal of the organizers of the Lincoln Centennial was to unite North and South around the figure of Lincoln. But some Southerners, in particular, resisted celebrating their former enemy. Below, a Confederate veteran marches alongside a carriage carrying members of the United Daughters of the Confederacy.

The Lincoln Bank in Springfield exhibited the desk at which Lincoln had written his First Inaugural Address in the weeks before his journey east to Washington. Below right, there was not a single African American among the thousands of invited guests at Springfield's Centennial dinner.

February 12, 1909
Springfield's Centennial

No city in the nation was more central to the Centennial than was Lincoln's hometown of Springfield, now known as the "Mecca of Lincoln pilgrims." The commemoration here spanned a "Lincoln week," culminating on February 12, that was organized to celebrate Lincoln in all his dimensions. On the morning of the big day, the Grand Army of the Republic honored Lincoln as the Union's savior, planting what was called the "Lincoln Elm," then marching out to Oak Ridge Cemetery where they served as a Lincoln Honor Guard. An exercise at the courthouse paid tribute to Lincoln the lawyer and included the dedication of a bronze tablet to mark the site of his first law office. At the Lincoln home, the Daughters of the American Revolution held a special reception to honor Lincoln as neighbor. At the site of the Lincolns' home parish, he was honored as a spiritual leader; at the high school he was remembered as an opponent of slavery; at the State Historical Library, as a friend to all; and at the newly built Tabernacle, erected for the evangelist Billy Sunday, ten thousand came out to honor Lincoln as Man of the People.

Robert Lincoln had been invited and had agreed to come, as long as he didn't have to speak at any of the ceremonies. He had not been back to Springfield much over the last years, and this would be his final visit to the place of his birth. He arrived with his wife, Mary, in his own private railroad car, bringing with him several of the chief dignitaries of the day. At the Lincoln Tomb, he was seen standing near the sarcophagus "with tear-dimmed eyes in silent meditation," reported the *Illinois State Register*. Next he paid a visit to his old home at Eighth and Jackson Streets, where his cousin Albert Edwards was still serving as custodian. Visitors, lined up to see the house, were asked to wait while Robert went inside. Climbing upstairs to see his boyhood room, he entered and sat quietly alone with his own thoughts.

That evening was the Lincoln banquet, where eight hundred guests met for a

luxurious dinner and to listen to a series of illustrious speakers. James Bryce and Jean Jules Jusserand, the ambassadors from England and France, were special guests of honor. So too was William Jennings Bryan, who proclaimed Abraham Lincoln America's greatest orator. Senator Jonathan Dolliver of Iowa described how he had seen Lincoln's picture hanging in windows all along his route west from Washington. "Lincoln's memory," he said, "has become the chiefest possession of the American people, and the most precious heritage that will be passed on to the generation that has yet to come."

Booker T. Washington had also been invited to speak at the banquet but had already agreed to address the Republicans in New York. He may also have had misgivings about coming to this city where race riots had taken place just six months earlier. "No man who hallows the name of Lincoln will inflict injustice upon the negro," he wrote in his letter of regret. "Every act of injustice, of law-breaking, growing out of the presence of the negro, seeks to pull down the great temple of justice and law and order which he gave his life to make secure."

Not a single black resident was invited to the Springfield banquet, not even to sit in the 1,200-seat spectators' gallery, filled with veterans and members of the DAR. "The dope is out," wrote the *Chicago Tribune*. "The Lincoln day celebration here is to be a lilly white affair from start to finish." Determined to be part of the Lincoln celebration, Springfield blacks organized their own gathering at the nearby African Methodist Episcopal Church. There the Rev. L. H. Magee expressed the widespread feelings of hurt and exclusion. "The colored people are not good enough to mingle their presence with the 'I am better than thou' at the celebration of the one-hundredth anniversary of the great emancipator," he proclaimed. But "we colored people love and revere the meaning of Lincoln for what he has done for us." And then Magee looked ahead into the far distant future—to the bicentennial of Lincoln's birth in the year 2009. And he predicted that Americans by then would have "banished" all prejudice as "a myth . . . relegated to the dark days of 'Salem witchcraft.'"

Among the "distinguished guests" at Lincoln's tomb on February 11 was Robert Todd Lincoln, who seems to have escaped the group picture. It was his last visit to Springfield.

403

Tribute to Abraham Lincoln
The Rev. L. H. Magee

February 12, 1909

Reverend Magee was a well-respected clergyman in Springfield, who summed up the African American response to the Lincoln Centennial.

We colored people love and revere the memory of Lincoln for what he has done for us. He wrote the emancipation proclamation that made us forever free. And he enforced it by the United States army. Yes, we love the name of Abraham Lincoln, for his name is a synonym for the freedom of wife, husband and children, and a chance to live in a free country, fearless of the slave-catcher and his bloodhounds. We would that every colored man, woman and child in these United States could be brought together in one great procession in yonder cemetery where lies the sacred dust of the great emancipator. I would rather be one of that great number of black devotees than toastmaster at a so-called "Lincoln banquet" at twenty-five dollars per.

Lincoln in 1861

Theodore Roosevelt

We have met here to celebrate the hundredth anniversary of the birth of one of the two greatest Americans; of one of the two or three greatest men of the nineteenth century; of one of the greatest men in the world's history. . . .

He grew to know greatness, but never ease. Success came to him, but never happiness, save that which springs from doing well a painful and a vital task. Power was his but not pleasure. The furrows deepened on his brow, but his eyes were undimmed by either hate or fear. His gaunt shoulders were bowed, but his steel sinews never faltered as he bore for a burden the destinies of his people. His great and tender heart shrank from giving pain; and the task allotted him was to pour out like water the life-blood of the young men, and to feel in his every fibre the sorrow of the women. Disaster saddened but never dismayed him.

As the red years of war went by they found him ever doing his duty in the present, ever facing the future with fearless front, high of heart, and dauntless of soul. Unbroken by hatred, unshaken by scorn, he worked and suffered for the people. Triumph was his at the last; and barely had he tasted it before murder found him, and the kindly, patient, fearless eyes were closed forever.

February 12, 1909

The Celebration in Kentucky

For Southerners, the fact that Lincoln had been born in Kentucky was highly significant. They could not be expected to contribute to a national park at Gettysburg, or to the Lincoln Tomb in Springfield with its Unionist themes, or to one of the great Northern emancipation statues. But they could support the commemoration of Lincoln's Southern birthplace, and this quickly became a unifying theme for the Centennial. Located centrally in the nation, Kentucky was neither East nor West, neither of the North nor of the Deep South. It represented the American heartland. The 110-acre farmstead where Lincoln had been born, it was thought, could become a new "national Commons"—a crossroads linking the entire country.

Ever since Thomas Lincoln had been forced to move in 1811, the birthplace farm had gone through a checkered history. Various plans to develop the property had come and gone over the years, with one owner, Alfred Dennett, envisioning a large hotel here. The long-neglected farm had come into responsible hands in 1905, when the new owner, Robert Collier of *Collier's* magazine, established the Lincoln Farm Association, charged with permanently memorializing the site. President Theodore Roosevelt became one of the association's early supporters, and its board soon boasted among its members William Howard Taft, Mark Twain, William Jennings Bryan, Horace Porter, Samuel Gompers, and Ida Tarbell. Though a few wealthy individuals donated large sums to save the property, the vast percentage of contributions came from ordinary Americans, many sending in as little as twenty-five cents. By 1908 tens of thousands had donated a total of $100,000. From the beginning this was a people's effort.

Plans had been laid for a stone "temple" to be erected around the cabin. "The

Members of the Lincoln Farm Association posed by the birth cabin at the time of the dedication. Robert Lincoln shunned the event, feeling that the cabin symbolized "degradation and uncleanliness" and not merely the honest poverty of his father's childhood.

404

little farm in the wilderness which gave America its savior," wrote one newspaper, "will rank with Mount Vernon as the nation's holy shrine." On Centennial Day, February 12, 1909, a brilliantly planned ceremony took place in Hodgenville, Kentucky. Theodore Roosevelt, in the closing days of his presidency, had come to dedicate the birthplace of his greatest hero. Also here to lead the ceremonies were Augustus Willson, the governor of Kentucky; Joseph Folk, the former governor of Missouri and president of the Lincoln Farm Association; General Luke E. Wright, the secretary of war and a former Confederate officer; and General James Grant Wilson representing the Union side. And here also to speak was Isaiah T. Montgomery—a former Mississippi slave once owned by Jefferson Davis, now one of the most successful black entrepreneurs in America. The officiants represented North and South, Republican and Democrat, white and black, young and old.

There were limited accommodations and visitors had been discouraged from coming, but seven thousand persons showed up for the dedication, including African Americans who mingled in with the crowd. The ceremonies took place in a tent beside the cabin, which had been strewn with flowers by Kentucky schoolchildren. The site was on a knoll above the famous Sinking Spring, which had originally attracted Thomas Lincoln to the property and in which Lincoln had played as a young boy. When it came his turn to speak, President Roosevelt hopped onto a chair and was greeted by enthusiastic cheers.

His words stressed not only Lincoln's "greatness" but his "goodness" and his relevance to both Northerners and Southerners. "As the years [roll] by," he said, "and as all of us, wherever we dwell, grow to feel an equal pride in the valor and self-devotion, alike the men who wore the blue and the men who wore the gray, so this whole Nation will grow to feel a peculiar sense of pride in the mightiest of mighty men who mastered the mighty days; the lover of his country and of all mankind; the man whose blood was shed for the union of his people and for the freedom of a race. Abraham Lincoln."

Following the speeches a metal box was opened, and into it was deposited a copy of the Constitution, and the text of each speaker's address. Isaiah Montgomery placed a copy of the Emancipation Proclamation inside the box and made remarks at this point in the ceremony. And then the metal container was placed into a three-thousand-pound cornerstone that had hung from a crane throughout the ceremony, and it was lowered to the ground. President Roosevelt, using a silver trowel, applied the first mortar.

Throughout the dedication ceremony the memorial's cornerstone hung suspended in the air. As soon as President Roosevelt finished his speech, it was lowered to the ground and symbolic objects were placed inside it. Isaiah Montgomery (above) was then given the opportunity to speak.

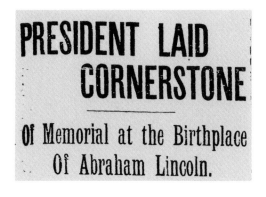

PRESIDENT LAID CORNERSTONE

Of Memorial at the Birthplace Of Abraham Lincoln.

405

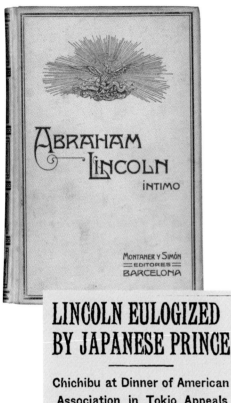

LINCOLN EULOGIZED BY JAPANESE PRINCE

Chichibu at Dinner of American Association in Tokio Appeals for 'People's Diplomacy.'

The Centennial included ceremonies and publications around the world. Count Leo Tolstoy (right, at his estate, Yasnaya Polyana) predicted, "We are still too near his greatness, but after a few centuries more our posterity will find him considerably bigger than we do."

February 1909

A Humanitarian for the World

The Lincoln Centennial made ripples across much of the globe. There were ceremonies in Berlin, Paris, Brazil, and the Philippines, as well as in Rome and in Eastern Europe. In Tokyo a Lincoln society was formed, and major festivities were held in Mexico City and in Honolulu. In England the day coincided with the centennial of the birth of Charles Darwin, and the two great men jockeyed for space in the daily newspapers. Though there was no official Lincoln centennial in London, two thousand people gathered in the Whitefield Tabernacle in a service organized by the city's nonconformists. And in Manchester, a city that had long admired Lincoln, there was a meeting at the mayor's house to honor the hero of the working classes.

But the most memorable international tribute came from Russia, where Count Leo Tolstoy—the world's greatest living writer—was interviewed at his estate. Tolstoy spoke of the extraordinary reach that Lincoln now had, how a tribal chief in the Caucasus, "far away from civilized life in the mountains," had recently asked him to speak to his people about Lincoln. "We want to know something about him," the chief had said. "He spoke with a voice of thunder; he laughed like the sunrise and his deeds were as strong as the rock. . . . Tell us of that man." Tolstoy looked at the chief and at his gathered people, "their faces all aglow, while their eyes were burning," and he realized that Lincoln had become a world hero. The "incident proves how largely the name of Lincoln is worshipped throughout the world," Tolstoy told his interviewer. He went on to call Lincoln "a Christ in miniature" and said of all the national heroes he was the only one he considered a "saint." "Napoleon was a typical Frenchman," he said, "but Lincoln was a humanitarian as broad as the world." Why was he "bigger than all the Presidents together?" Tolstoy asked, "Because he loved his enemies as himself."

Remembering Fido

In a Centennial pamphlet emphasizing Lincoln and temperance, Dr. T. D. Bancroft published a photograph of Abraham Lincoln's dog. Though he misidentified him as "Fritz," the story shed new light on the human side of Lincoln.

As Americans knew well, from Herndon's biography and other sources, Lincoln had long been an animal lover. As a boy he was known for his advocacy on behalf of animals, often chastising other children for playing cruel stunts on turtles and other small creatures. It became a stock theme of Lincoln literature: the young Lincoln rescued birds that had fallen from their nests; once pulled a hog out of the deep mud in which it had become stuck; and refused to kill snakes because "their lives are just as sweet to them as ours are to us." In Springfield he was noted for his kindness to stray cats—Mary Lincoln once called it his "hobby."

Sometime in the 1850s—probably after building an addition to their house—the Lincolns acquired Fido, a yellowish brown mutt. He became a favorite of Willie and Tad, and of their father too. Lincoln would bring the dog with him on his walks to the town market, sometimes giving him a parcel to carry home in his mouth. If his master stopped in town for a shave, Fido would wait outside until he was through. But in 1861 Lincoln decided that Fido could not go with them to Washington, even though the boys begged him to reconsider. Instead he was given to friends, John and Frank Roll, where he found a new and happy home.

Sometime before Lincoln's Springfield funeral, the photographer F. W. Ingmire took portraits of Fido to sell as souvenirs. Popular after the assassination, they became touching keepsakes of the human Lincoln. Tad acquired his own copy of the image, which became a family treasure.

In the late 1860s Fido met a tragic end, as Bancroft now revealed in his 1909 pamphlet. "This dog was assassinated by a drunken, brutish man in Springfield," Bancroft wrote. Years later Frederick Hill Meserve tracked down John Roll in Springfield and had him dictate a full statement about the incident.

Same Fate as His Master
John Linden Roll

The following statement was made by John Linden Roll shortly before his death.

My brother and I were about the same age as Willie and Tad Lincoln. We knowing an uncle (Charles Arnold) living across the street from the Lincoln home, brought us in close contact with the Lincolns. . . . So we became close friends of the Lincoln boys . . . Willie and Tad and their dog Fido. When the Lincolns left for Washington and to . . . the presidency one of the serious questions was what to do with Fido. It was decided inasmuch as the Roll boys were friends of the family we should assume responsibility . . . of his care. We possessed the dog for a number of years when one day the dog, in a playful manner, put his dirty paws upon a drunken man sitting on the street curbing. In his drunken rage [he] thrust a knife into the body of poor old Fido. He was buried by loving hands. So Fido, just a poor yellow dog, met the fate of his illustrious master: ass[ass]ination.

Lincoln's dog Fido

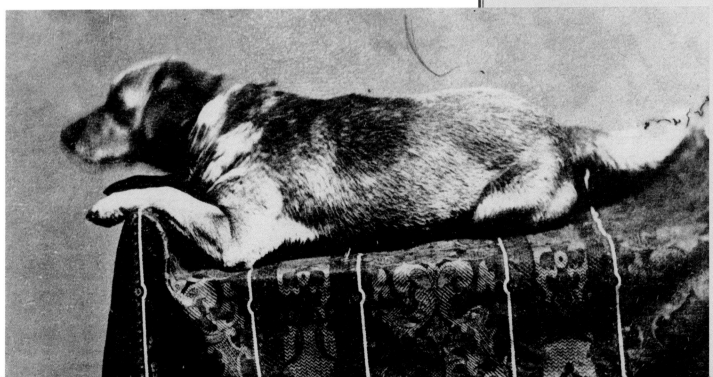

Lincoln's Love Story
Eleanor Atkinson

In the sweet spring weather of 1835, Abraham Lincoln made a memorable journey. It was the beginning of his summer of love on the winding banks of the Sangamon. Only one historian has noted it as a happy interlude in a youth of struggle and unsatisfied longings, but the tender memory of Ann Rutledge, the girl who awaited him at the end of it, must have remained with him to the day of his martyrdom. . . .

It was on such an April morning as this, four years before, that he had first seen Ann Rutledge. She was in the crowd that had come down to the mill to cheer him when he got the flat-boat he was taking to New Orleans safely over New Salem dam. Ann was eighteen then, and she stood out from the villagers gathered on the bank by reason of a certain fineness of beauty and bearing. Her crown of hair was so pale a gold as to be almost flaxen. Besides always being noted as kind and happy, her eyes are described as a dark, violet-blue, with brown brows and lashes. Her colouring was now rose, now pearl, changing like the anemones that blow along the banks of the Sangamon. . . .

When they came to where the sycamore was weaving its old faery weft in the sunset light, she laid the bonnet on the grass, and listened to his stories and comments on the new men and things he had seen, until he made her laugh, almost like the happy girl of old tavern days; for Lincoln was a wizard who could break the spell of bad dreams and revive dead faiths. . . .

In tender retrospect she shared that tragic mystery of his childhood, his mother's early death. And, like all the other women who ever belonged to him, she divined his greatness—had a glimpse of the path of glory already broadening from his feet.

1909
Ann Rutledge Revisited

One of the notable publications of the Centennial year was a small book by Chicago journalist Eleanor Stackhouse Atkinson called *Lincoln's Love Story.* A sentimental romance of Lincoln's early love of Ann Rutledge, it became one of the year's best sellers.

Interest in Rutledge had been building for decades. William Herndon had been the first to push the story of Lincoln's love for her, resting his case on the testimony of numerous of her friends and relations. Hardin Bale, a New Salem neighbor, had spoken to Herndon of Lincoln's passion for Ann and his terrible state following her illness and demise—how he had to be "locked up by his friends . . . so hard did he take her death." From dozens of testimonies it was clear that Ann Rutledge not only had existed but had been loved by the young Lincoln. Herndon promoted the view heavily in his 1889 biography, having now interviewed several cousins as well as the brothers of Rutledge. He quoted Mrs. Hardin Bale who said, "in speaking of her death and her grave Lincoln once said to me, 'My heart lies buried there.'"

In 1895 Ida Tarbell picked up where Herndon left off. In her research she hunted down Ann's cousin, James Rutledge, now eighty-one, and recorded similar stories as he had earlier told to Herndon. She also discovered someone Herndon hadn't known—a sister of Ann's named Jean Berry. "After Ann died," wrote Berry, "I remember that it was common talk how sad Lincoln was; and I remember myself how sad he looked. They told me every time he was in the neighborhood after she died, he would go alone to her grave and sit there in silence for hours." Like Herndon, Tarbell claimed that Lincoln never lost his love for Ann, and she embraced reminis-

PHOTO SAID TO BE THAT OF LINCOLN AND ANN RUTLEDGE

Purported Photograph Showing Lincoln and Ann Rutledge

Bloomington, Ill., Woman Has Faded Daguerreotype Handed Down by Father, Who Knew President.

Special to the Post-Dispatch.

BLOOMINGTON, Ill.—Handed down to his daughter by her father, the late Cyrenius Wakefield, pioneer resident of this city, is a remarkable daguerreotype of what purports to be Abraham Lincoln and his first love, Ann Rutledge. This photograph, faded and time stained, was believed by Wakefield to be genuine and was proudly exhibited as such.

(Daguerreotype is a form of tinplate photography invented in the early Eighteenth century by Daguerre, a Frenchman. The inventor later was made a member of the Legion of honor in 1839 and awarded a pension for life.)

Before the death of the parent, he gave the precious picture to his only daughter, Mrs. Harriet Brady of Bloomington. The elder Wakefield was a close friend of Lincoln and frequently entertained him. Wakefield owned historic Phoenix Hall, where Lincoln delivered a

When a local newspaper claimed that this photograph was an 1835 portrait of Lincoln and Ann Rutledge, it overlooked the fact that photography was not invented until four years after Ann's death.

cences that corroborated this. "In later life," she wrote, "he told a friend who questioned him: 'I really and truly loved the girl and think often of her now.' There was a pause, and then he added: 'And I have loved the name of Rutledge to this day.'"

These reminiscences made Ann a reflection of Lincoln's pioneer mother—beautiful, simple, intelligent, a true commoner. Unlike the aristocratic, well-educated, acid-tongued Mary Todd, she was the embodiment of sweetness and light, the perfect counterpart for the mythic Man of Sorrows Lincoln had become. Her death was seen as the key to his emotional development, supposedly carving out his heart and soul and giving rise to his capacity for tenderness.

By the time of the Centennial it was natural that a romance writer like Eleanor Atkinson should write such a book as *Lincoln's Love Story*. She admitted that "only one historian" had even noted the story, but that didn't stop her from elaborating on it at length—creating a fictionalized version that nevertheless claimed to be authentic history. Atkinson illustrated her book with recently taken photographs: of Bowling Green's house in New Salem, where Lincoln had lived in the 1830s and where he mourned Ann's death; of two trees that still grew from the top of the hill in the old town—a locust and a sycamore intertwined, symbolic of Abe Lincoln and Ann Rutledge; and of Ann's humble grave with its natural stone marker. "Only a field boulder marks the mound today," she wrote, "but the young girls of the city and county, who claim her as their own, are to celebrate Lincoln's centennial year by sending up a shaft of Carrara marble over the grave of Lincoln's lost love." It would make a fitting companion to the Lincoln Tomb, she wrote. If the towering marble tomb at Springfield, twenty miles away, "was Lincoln's crown of glory," here in old New Salem was his "Gethsemane." Forget about that woman buried with him in Springfield, she told her readers—his true love for all eternity lay here.

Outside New Salem were the intertwined "Lincoln trees," a popular landmark in 1909, thought to symbolize Abraham Lincoln and Ann Rutledge.

Ann Rutledge became a cult figure in Petersburg. A large boulder marked the spot where she had been reinterred in 1890.

One of the founding documents of the NAACP was this call issued at the time of the Lincoln Centennial. Written by Oswald Garrison Villard, it was published with fifty-three signers, including Jane Addams, John Dewey, Rabbi Stephen Wise, and W. E. B. Du Bois.

The celebration of the Centennial of the birth of Abraham Lincoln, widespread and grateful as it may be, will fail to justify itself if it takes no note of and makes no recognition of the colored men and women for whom the great Emancipator labored to assure freedom. Besides a day of rejoicing, Lincoln's birthday in 1909 should be one of taking stock of the nation's progress since 1865.

How far has it lived up to the obligations imposed upon it by the Emancipation Proclamation? How far has it gone in assuring to each and every citizen, irrespective of color, the equality of opportunity and equality before the law, which underlie our American institutions and are guaranteed by the Constitution?

If Mr. Lincoln could revisit this country in the flesh, he would be disheartened and discouraged. He would learn that on January 1, 1909, Georgia had rounded out a new confederacy by disfranchising the Negro, after the manner of all the other Southern States. He would learn that the Supreme Court of the United States, supposedly a bulwark of American liberties, had refused every opportunity to pass squarely upon this disfranchisement of millions, by laws avowedly discriminatory and openly enforced in such manner that the white men may vote and that black men be without a vote in their government. . . .

Added to this, the spread of lawless attacks upon the Negro, North, South and West—even in the Springfield made famous by Lincoln—often accompanied by revolting brutalities, sparing neither sex nor age nor youth, could but shock the author of the sentiment that "government of the people, by the people, for the people; should not perish from the earth."

1910

The Birth of the NAACP

Following the race riots in Springfield in 1908, the social reformer William English Walling and his wife, Anna Strunsky, traveled down from Chicago to investigate. In September Walling published a story in *The Independent* entitled "Race War in the North." He described scenes of violence against Springfield blacks that he found particularly ironic in the city of Lincoln. And he issued a challenge to the nation: "Either the spirit of the abolitionists, of Lincoln and of Lovejoy must be revived and we must come to treat the Negro on a plane of absolute political and social equality, or [the opponents of equality] . . . will soon have transferred the race war to the North." Walling called for the banding together of a "powerful group of citizens" to address America's race issue head-on.

Among Walling's readers was a young social worker living in a black tenement in New York City, Mary White Ovington. Impressed by his words, she wrote and arranged for a meeting with him in January, to which New York City official Henry Markowitz was also invited. Here was the genesis of a new movement in America. The small group chose Lincoln's birthday—Centennial Day itself—to announce their new organization, originally named the National Negro Committee. They enlisted the help of Oswald Garrison Villard, president of the *New York Evening Post*, and it was he who drafted a "call" to the nation, linking the committee's work directly to that of Abraham Lincoln. "If Mr. Lincoln would revisit this country in the flesh," Villard wrote, "he would be disheartened and discouraged." Lincoln's memory was invoked to help address the current issue of racism in America—segregation, lynching, and disfranchisement of black people. What was needed was a revival of Lincoln's spirit, Villard wrote—for the country to pick up his "unfinished work" and carry it forward.

On May 30, 1909, the National Negro Committee hosted a conference on the issue of race in America. With hundreds attending, black as well as white, it was an eye-opening exchange that became the basis for future work. Soon it would be renamed the National Association for the Advancement of Colored People—the NAACP. In 1910 William Walling reached out to Atlanta professor W. E. B. Du Bois, asking him to join the board and to serve as editor of the organization's new journal, *The Crisis*. Walling could offer Du Bois little money or job security, he wrote, but he urged him "to take the risk," since "such moments come in the lives of us all, and there are certain risks which ought to be taken." Du Bois accepted the position, which he would hold for the next twenty-five years. The NAACP's mission became entwined with the legacy of Abraham Lincoln, as it made clear in one of its founding statements: "Abraham Lincoln began the emancipation of the Negro American. The National Association for the Advancement of Colored People proposes to complete it."

The pain of her ancestors could be seen in the face of this elementary school girl. The NAACP promised to complete Lincoln's work by continuing to fight for the true meaning of emancipation. Of all the initiatives of the Centennial Year, this may have been the most important.

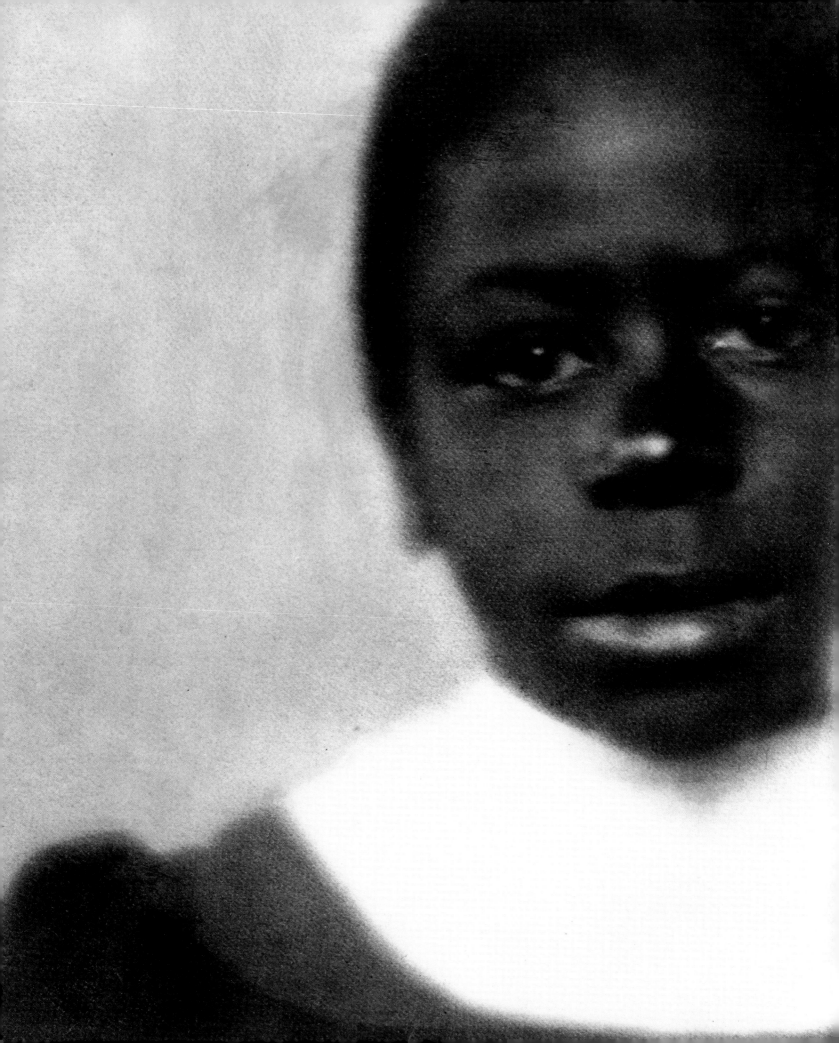

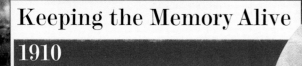

Schools, which for a century had held up George Washington as the national icon, now also began using Lincoln to teach the meaning of America.

JANE ADDAMS.

The Influence of Lincoln
Jane Addams

1910

Social reformer Jane Addams held a lifelong admiration for Abraham Lincoln. In her 1910 memoir, Twenty Years at Hull House, *she devoted a chapter to the "Influence of Lincoln."*

Although I was but four and a half years old when Lincoln died, I distinctly remember the day when I found on our two white gate posts American flags companioned with black. I tumbled down on the harsh gravel walk in my eager rush into the house to inquire what they were "there for." To my amazement I found my father in tears, something that I had never seen before, having assumed, as all children do, that grown-up people never cried. The two flags, my father's tears and his impressive statement that the greatest man in the world

had died, constituted my initiation, my baptism, as it were, into the thrilling and solemn interests of a world lying quite outside the two white gate posts. . . .

My father always spoke of the martyred President as Mr. Lincoln, and I never heard the great name without a thrill. I remember the day—it must have been one of comparative leisure, perhaps a Sunday—when at my request my father took out of his desk a thin packet marked "Mr. Lincoln's Letters," the shortest one of which bore unmistakable traces of that remarkable personality. . . . As my father folded up the bits of paper I fairly held my breath in my desire that he should go on with the reminiscence of this wonderful man, whom he had known in his comparative obscurity, or better still, that he should be moved to tell some of the exciting incidents of the Lincoln-Douglas debates. There were at least two pictures of Lincoln that always hung in my father's room, and one in our old-fashioned upstairs parlor, of Lincoln with little Tad. For one or all of these reasons I always tend to associate Lincoln with the tenderest thoughts of my father.

As a young girl Jane Addams was enamored of Lincoln. She later wrote that he was "the epitome of all that was great and good." Below, the last portrait taken of Lincoln with his son Tad—a picture Jane Addams grew up knowing.

The last Likeness taken of

THE PRESIDENT AND HIS SON THADDEUS.

413

William H. Crook

In his 1911 book Crook told the story of his last exchange with Lincoln.

The only time that President Lincoln failed to say good-night to me . . . was on the evening shortly before he started for Ford's Theater. . . . Mr. Lincoln had told me that afternoon of a dream he had had for three successive nights, concerning his impending assassination. Of course, the constant dread of such a calamity made me somewhat nervous, and I almost begged him to remain in the Executive Mansion that night, and not to go to the theater. But he would not disappoint Mrs. Lincoln and others who were to be present. Then I urged that he allow me to stay on duty and accompany him; but he would not hear of this, either.

"No, Crook," he said, kindly but firmly, "you have had a long, hard day's work already, and must go home to sleep and rest. I cannot afford to have you get all tired out and exhausted."

It was then that he neglected, for the first and only time, to say good-night to me. Instead, he turned, with his kind, grave face, and said: "Good-bye, Crook," and went into his room.

I thought of it at the moment; and a few hours later, when the awful news flashed over Washington that he had been shot, his last words were so burned into my memory that they never have been forgotten, and never can be forgotten.

In 1911 an aging White House employee who had served there continuously since 1865 published his memoirs. William H. Crook, once a Washington policeman, had been assigned to guard duty at the White House in January 1865 and thereby gained entrance to Lincoln's last months of life. Often posted to the overnight watch, he sat in a chair outside Lincoln's bedroom, fearing even to look at a newspaper lest he miss the sign of an approaching assassin. Crook was off duty the night Lincoln was killed.

For thirty-five years after the assassination, he remained silent about his experiences with Abraham Lincoln. Then finally in the early 1900s Crook began telling his tale. "These last years," he wrote in 1906, "when, at a Lincoln birthday celebration or some other memorial gathering, they ask for a few words from the man who used to be Abraham Lincoln's guard, the younger people look at me as if I was some strange spectacle—a man who lived by Lincoln's side. It has made me feel as if the time has come to tell the world the little that I know about him. Soon there will be nothing of him but the things that have been written."

In 1906 Crook sat down with a writer for *Harper's Magazine*, Margarita Spalding Gerry, and told her his story. The article, which appeared in two parts, was entitled "Lincoln as I Knew Him." Newspapers proclaimed him the last man living with whom Lincoln had had daily contact. His articles gave intimate details of life in the White House, including Crook's access one night to Lincoln's bedroom, which he was forced to enter to deliver an important telegram. "The place the president slept in was a noteworthy spot to me," he wrote. "It was handsomely furnished; the bedstead, bureau, and washstand were of heavy mahogany, the bureau and washstand with marble tops; the chairs were of rosewood." Crook described his place of duty outside the President's door, where he could hear Lincoln's "deep breathing" and sometimes "heard him moan in his sleep." It was as if he were "listening at a keyhole," he wrote.

When he was on the day shift, Crook would arrive for duty at eight A.M., always to find Lincoln awake and usually in the library reading. He described the President's stables on the east side of the house near the conservatory and Mrs. Lincoln's garden on the South Lawn, where in the summer she grew strawberries. Crook told how he was drafted into the army in 1865, but then appealed for relief to President Lincoln. "I remember vividly to this day all the circumstances," he narrated. "When I entered Lincoln's presence I found him sitting in one of the easy chairs in the old library, wearing a pair of those old-fashioned carpet slippers and briefly engaged in reading the Bible." Lincoln listened to Crook's story, then wrote out a note to the War Department, saying of Crook and another man, "I cannot spare them . . . please fix." Years later, when he was war secretary, Robert Lincoln located this card and presented it to Crook as a souvenir.

In the Centennial Year, William Crook was in much demand. And with the help of Margarita Gerry he issued a partial autobiography entitled *Through Five Administrations*, detailing his experiences in the White House. In 1911 he brought out a second book, *Memories of the White House: The Home Life of Our Presidents from Lincoln to Roosevelt*. The book was compiled and edited by Henry Edward Rood, another *Harper's Magazine* writer who had suggested it to Crook in 1910. It was a chance for a final telling of his days with Lincoln, and Crook was careful with his words and his memories. He described accompanying Lincoln to Richmond in March 1865 and gave a moment-by-moment account of the President's last week in Washington. And he told stories revealing Lincoln's humanitarian nature—how patient he was with a rugged old veteran who wished to see him one day; how he sat down with the man on a curbside and quietly looked over his papers. "If I could only make people see him as I did," Crook wrote, "—see how simple he was with every one; how he could talk with a child so the child could understand and smile up at him."

During the summer of 1911, the year William Crook's memoirs appeared, an airplane landed on the South Lawn of the White House.

1911

The Diary of Gideon Welles

A few members of Lincoln's cabinet had kept diaries, but none like that of Gideon Welles. William Seward had begun one but then ripped it up when he found himself recording too many accounts of cabinet squabbles. Edward Bates kept a dry account of daily events that rarely rose to interpretive heights. And Salmon Chase made insightful comments in an intermittent diary that in the end was much less comprehensive than Welles's. In 1911 none of these others had yet come to light, and the publication of Welles's three-volume diary was a major event. "They are intensely interesting," commented the *New York Times*, "and, though they appear after nearly half a century of busy waiting . . . they shed new light upon the men and the events of that time." The *Times* would call Welles "one of the world's greatest diarists."

Welles had granted Nicolay and Hay limited access to his journals and had often quoted from them in his own published articles. But after he died in 1878, the bulky manuscript had been left to his son Edgar. Ambivalent about its value, Welles had left it up to him to either publish or destroy it.

Lincoln's secretary of the navy had been a journalist before coming to Washington, and his writing style was vivid, and at times caustic. He despised Edwin Stanton, was highly competitive with William Seward, and found Salmon Chase not at all to his liking. On the pages of his journal he candidly described each of Lincoln's cabinet members and detailed all the cabinet meetings and crises he participated in. For certain key moments, such as Lincoln's discussions of the Emancipation Proclamation, or the cabinet crisis of 1862, his was the most important of all eyewitness accounts.

Critics noted that Welles appeared to have modified some of the entries in a period of revision that took place between 1869 and 1878. And Edgar, who served as the book's editor, also exercised editorial discretions. But all in all, it was an astonishingly faithful work. "The value of these volumes," wrote the *Political Science Quarterly*, "depends chiefly upon two factors: first; the candor and sincerity of the writer, and second; the accuracy and completeness with which his record has been reported in print. In both respects the value of the Diary is unimpeachable." Scholars pointed out that the work contained no new revelations of fact that would change the interpretation of Lincoln's presidency, but that it gave numerous insider details that added richness and nuance. Above all, the diary confirmed Lincoln's constant struggle with his cabinet members. Disliking one another, ambitious, and at times dissentious, these members of Lincoln's inner circle often failed to hold him with the "sincere respect" he deserved, wrote Welles. But over them all, the diarist noted, Lincoln loomed as the "master" of his government.

The diary of Gideon Welles was serialized in the *Atlantic Monthly* starting in November 1909. Two years later it was published in three volumes.

From His Diary
Gideon Welles

1911

Welles wrote often about Lincoln in the pages of his diary.

January 8, 1864

To-day at the Executive Mansion. Only Usher with myself was present, and no business transacted. . . . Conversation was general, with anecdotes as usual. These are usually very appropriate and instructive, conveying much truth in few words, well, if not always elegantly, told. The President's estimate of character is usually very correct, and he frequently divests himself of partiality with a readiness that has surprised me. In the course of conversation to-day, which was desultory, he mentioned that he was selected by the people of Springfield to deliver a eulogy on the death of Mr. Clay, of whom he had been a warm admirer. This, he said, he found to be difficult writing so as to make an address of fifty minutes. In casting about for the material, he had directed his attention to what Mr. Clay had himself done in the line of eulogy and was struck with the fact that, though renowned as an orator and speaker, he had never made any effort of the sort, and the only specimen he could find was embraced in a few lines on the death of Mr. Calhoun.

April 19, 1864

The President did not make his appearance to-day in Cabinet. He was in Baltimore last evening at the opening of the fair, and is reported to have made a speech. He has a fondness for attending these shows only surpassed by Seward. Neither Seward, nor Blair, nor Chase was present with us to-day. Blair was with the President at Baltimore. Being a Marylander, there was propriety in his attendance.

March 4, 1865

The inauguration took place to-day. There was great want of arrangement and completeness in the ceremonies—All was confusion and without order,—a jumble.

The Vice-President elect made a rambling and strange harangue, which was listened to with pain and mortification by all his friends. My impressions were that he was under the influence of stimulants, yet I know not that he drinks. He has been sick and is feeble; perhaps he may have taken medicine, or stimulants, or his brain from sickness may have been overactive in these new responsibilities. Whatever the cause, it was all in very bad taste.

The delivery of the inaugural address, the administering of the oath, and the whole deportment of the President were well done, and the retiring Vice-President appeared to advantage when contrasted with his successor, who has humiliated his friends. Speed, who sat at my left, whispered me that "all this is in wretched bad taste"; and very soon he said, "The man is certainly deranged."

Lincoln, seated next to the Vice President–elect Andrew Johnson, waited to deliver his Second Inaugural Address.

Frederick Hill Meserve in 1911

Robert Todd Lincoln (second from left), as Meserve knew him

The Photographs of Abraham Lincoln

By 1909 Frederick Hill Meserve was well established in his trade. Six years earlier his father had written him from San Francisco, where his itinerant Methodist ministry had taken him. Pleased with the help his son had given him on his memoirs, he was interested in how his avocation was progressing. "You must be doing quite a business in collecting and multiplying, and who knows but you may open a gallery. Do you advertise?"

Meserve had married in 1899 and was settled in New York City with his wife, Edith, and their children, Helen, Dorothy, and Leighton. He was working by day at the textile firm of Deering, Milliken & Co., and spending evening, nights, and weekends on his growing collection. Over the years he had become friends with many of the leading Lincoln collectors, most of whom specialized in rare pamphlets and books. "In their purchase of historical material," Meserve later wrote, "they were sending the photographs to me to buy or to copy, and I, having their want lists, was sending them the records of books and pamphlets offered to me by dealers." Meserve became a photographic sleuth, constantly thinking up new sources. He bought boxloads of photographs from the Century Company that had been used over the decades for their magazines and books. He acquired original pictures as well from *Harper's Magazine*, one of the richest sources of nineteenth-century illustration. He copied War Department daguerreotypes he found in a pile of rubbish after department officials refused to sell the damaged originals. "All my spare time was delightfully spent in study, in writing, and arranging," he wrote. "My wife helped and encouraged me, although at times [was] dismayed by the volume of my acquisitions."

Meserve reached out to thousands of individuals for help. He wrote to Robert Lincoln, beginning a fifteen-year correspondence with him. "I am greatly obliged for your letter of September 11," wrote Robert in 1909 after receiving Meserve's gift of a portrait of his parents. "As you suggest, the composite picture makes my mother relatively too tall, as you can easily see when you remember that my father was himself six feet four inches in height. I do not know my mother's actual height, but I should guess it at about five feet six inches—perhaps not so much. I never saw, or heard of, a photograph of my father and mother taken together. Nor any photograph of my father with any member of his family, except my younger brother Thomas, who was called Tad. . . . It will be a great pleasure to receive from you the new portraits which you mention to add to my collection. Believe me, with kind regards, Robert Lincoln."

By now Meserve was working on his first book, a limited edition printed on thick rag paper with actual photographs glued on the pages. It was entitled *The Photographs of Abraham Lincoln*, and it was the first serious attempt to collect and publish all the known Lincoln photographs in chronological order. Twenty years earlier Ida Tarbell had made an important beginning, pulling together more than fifty widely scattered photographs of Lincoln. And in 1910 Francis Trevelyan Miller published his *Portrait Life of Lincoln*, which included ten unique images from Meserve's col-

One of Meserve's prized discoveries was this Brady portrait of the President-elect in February 1861.

lection. But Meserve knew he had the best overall grasp of the subject and that he possessed more than thirty still-unpublished portraits. He wanted his book to be the first complete gathering.

In March 1910 he wrote to Robert Lincoln asking which was his favorite Lincoln picture. Robert wrote back, "I have always thought the Brady photograph of my father, of which I attach a copy, to be the most satisfactory likeness of him." It was the famous seated Lincoln, later displayed on the five-dollar bill, and Meserve decided to use it as his frontispiece.

Throughout 1910 he labored on the project, gathering and annotating the pictures. He organized them chronologically to his best estimation—from Robert Lincoln's daguerreotype, labeled Meserve Number 1, to Gardner's final "cracked Lincoln," then believed to be the last ever taken and published for the first time as Meserve's "Lincoln 100." Meserve had begun the century with fifty Lincoln portraits, and it had taken him almost a decade to reach one hundred.

Meserve published the book privately for ninety-two subscribers. It came out in the spring of 1911, and Robert Lincoln was one of the first to receive a complimentary copy. "My dear Mr. Meserve," Robert wrote on June 19, "It is a very wonderful collection of the very best photographs of my father, and will, I am sure, be highly prized by all those who have an interest—even though it is not so especially great as my own—in his memory."

In the years ahead Meserve would add to his collection, increasing the number of Lincoln images to 116 and correcting errors in the chronology. He became known as the kindly scholar of Lincoln photography, generously supplying images to authors and magazines, and turned to again and again by Lincoln scholars. One of the hundreds of people who corresponded with him was Clara Barton, who wrote to him in response to his idea for a new book. "I come to thank you, my dear friend," she wrote, "for your esteemed letter—what a delightful volume you will have of our great and good President. We have no other Lincoln and never can have; God grant that there will never come a time when we will so much need him."

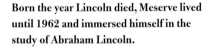

Born the year Lincoln died, Meserve lived until 1962 and immersed himself in the study of Abraham Lincoln.

At right, a page from an early Meserve workbook, showing his numbering system

No. 1   No. 2   No. 3   No. 5

No. 101   No. 6   No. 7   No. 117

No. 112   No. 124   No. 10   No. 11

No. 12   No. 13   No. 17   No. 15

Spurious Lincolns

It was inevitable, as Meserve collected Lincoln photographs, that people would send him "undiscovered" images of Lincoln. Some were authentic, but Meserve also received out-and-out fakes and misidentifications. "I consider that these so-called Lincoln photographs," Meserve wrote, "all of them spurious, which have been sent to me for my opinion on them over a period of many years, by their owners who believed them to be genuine, are fascinating studies of the human face."

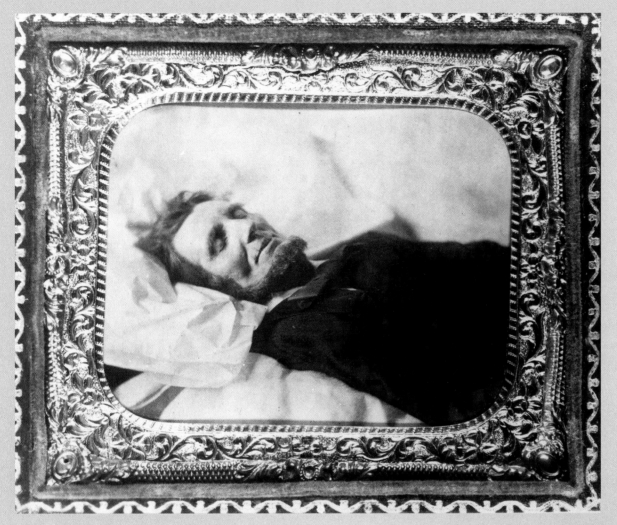

It seemed that almost any
dead man with a beard could
be claimed as Lincoln.

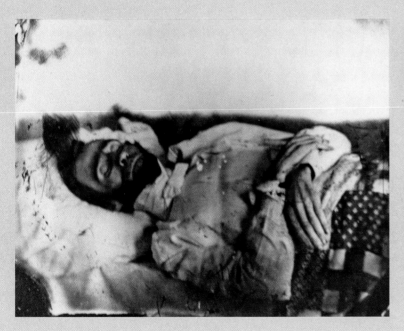

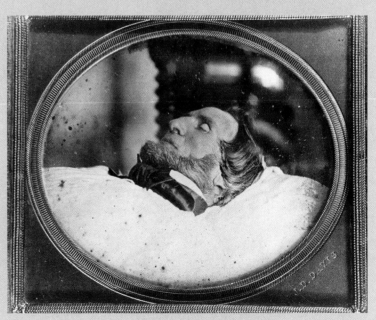

February 1910

[T]he right side of this wonderful face is the key to his life. Here you will find the record of his development, the centuries-old marks of his maturity. All the man grew to seemed engraved on this side. It guards his plan—watches the world, and shows no more of his light than his wisdom deems wise. The left side is immature, plain—and physically not impressive. It is long, drawn, and indecisive; and this brow is anxious, ever slightly elevated and concerned. You will find written on his face literally all the complexity of his great nature—a nature seeing at once the humor and the pathos of each situation as it presents itself to him. You see half smile, half sadness; half anger, half forgiveness; half determination, half pause; a mixture of expression that drew accurately the middle course he would follow—read wrongly by both sides. We see a dual nature struggling with a dual problem, delivering a single result.

1911

Borglum's Lincoln

By the early years of the twentieth century, the Connecticut-based sculptor John Gutzon de la Mothe Borglum had developed a fascination with Abraham Lincoln. In 1908 he agreed to sculpt a giant head of the beardless Lincoln, to be in scale for a figure twenty-eight feet in height. To prepare for the work he immersed himself in Lincoln's writings. "I read all, or nearly all, he had written," Borglum recalled, "his own description of himself, the few immediate records of his coming and going . . . —then returned to the habits of mind which his writings showed."

The finished work was "cut directly into the marble," Borglum wrote, so that there was no cast. To reflect his belief that Lincoln possessed a "dual nature," Borglum carved the left side of the head as if still emerging from the stone, while the right side he fully developed. When it was placed in a Fifth Avenue store window at Christmastime, it attracted wide attention. A passerby was overheard speaking to a companion about it: "I look at that great, lean, troubled face almost every day," he said, "and then I walk down the avenue and look at the faces I meet on the sidewalk. . . . Every face you meet seems trivial or sensual or careless or stupid or earthly in memory of his."

Robert Lincoln was pleased when he saw the sculpture. "I think it is the most extraordinarily good portrait of my father I have ever seen," he wrote Borglum, "and it impressed me deeply as a work of art which speaks for itself in the most wonderful manner." Theodore Roosevelt also admired it and agreed to exhibit the bust inside the White House. In April 1908 it was presented to Congress by Eugene Meyer of New York and placed in the Great Rotunda of the Capitol.

Three years later Borglum landed a coveted new job—a major statue of Lincoln for the city of Newark, New Jersey. Once again the results were astonishing. The finished piece was unlike anything ever seen before—a decidedly unheroic President seated on a bench, careworn and weary, having just received news of the latest battle casualties. There was something exquisitely human and approachable about this Lincoln, and it quickly became the best-loved Lincoln statue in America. The day of its dedication was the grandest in Borglum's life, with 100,000 people coming out for the unveiling.

Borglum's *Seated Lincoln,* in Newark, New Jersey, and, left, the sculptor with his massive bust of Lincoln

Helen Nicolay's Lincoln

In 1912 a new Lincoln book appeared written by the forty-two-year-old daughter of John G. Nicolay. Helen Nicolay had been her father's close assistant. "I sat across the big desk from my father to take dictation in longhand," she later wrote. "His patience with his amateur secretary was unbounded." Slowly but surely she became familiar with Lincoln research. "When Colonel Hay came to dispossess me of my chair," she wrote, "I would retreat to a corner and listen. Devoted to both of them, and immensely proud of the work they were doing, I was yet too young to realize fully the unusual privilege I enjoyed."

Over the next decade and a half Helen Nicolay grew in her knowledge. When her father died in 1901, still at work on a one-volume condensation of his monumental history, it was she who skillfully completed the manuscript. Four years later she brought out her own first book, *The Boy's Life of Abraham Lincoln*. "It is a pity that it should come before the public as a juvenile book," wrote the *Los Angeles Times*. "The book is full of the little touches that make the man real to us. . . . [I]t should take its place not merely as a youth's history of Lincoln, but as a popular biography, read by all."

Helen had inherited from her father the huge desk he had once used in the White House and on which he composed his Lincoln biography. For years she had been intrigued by a bulky envelope inside it labeled "Personal Traits." Here her father had kept his assorted research about Lincoln the man—letters, clippings, personal notes, snatches of interviews. He never used the material in his ten-volume history, and died before he could. "The envelopes, bursting in their load, were put aside," Helen noted—until she was ready to turn the files into a book. With Robert Lincoln's encouragement she began writing. Helen went far beyond her father's notes in her research, turning to Lincoln's writings and to published reminiscences to fill in gaps where the files were silent. This would not be a new Lincoln biography, she wrote, but a human portrait. It would be filled with unfamiliar new stories, and with quoted words of Lincoln that had the smack of authenticity. She worked on the project for years and finally published it in 1912 to rave reviews. The *New York Times* wrote that in her book, *Personal Traits of Abraham Lincoln*, "the personality of the greatest American becomes real and close again to the generation that has not known him, and we must needs love and understand Abraham Lincoln better than, with all our reading, we ever have done before."

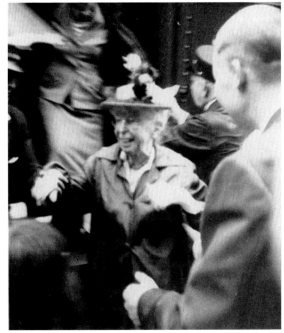

Knowing that Lincoln had stopped here on his way to Gettysburg in 1863, Helen Nicolay stepped from her train at Hanover Junction, Pennsylvania, where she had come to participate in a Civil War dedication.

Helen Nicolay published *The Boy's Life of Abraham Lincoln* (right) and seven years later *Personal Traits of Abraham Lincoln* (left). The latter was based on the extensive unpublished notes of her father.

1913

A Black Festival of Freedom

Four years after the Centennial of Lincoln's birth came the fiftieth anniversary of the Emancipation Proclamation. There couldn't have been more contrast between the two events.

Annual celebrations of Emancipation Day had begun as early as 1864. Widely considered by blacks as their "Freedom Day" (Blanche K. Bruce called it "the natal day of our race"), it went largely unrecognized by the white community. It also tended to drift across the calendar, with different cities and states following different customs. It was celebrated not only on January 1 (the official anniversary) and on September 22 (the date of the Preliminary Proclamation), but also on June 19, the day when news of the proclamation first arrived in Texas, fondly referred to as "Juneteenth." In some areas it was observed in conjunction with an already existing August 1 celebration, the anniversary of black freedom in the British West Indies. And in a precursor of what would become Negro History Week, and later Black History Month, it was often commemorated in mid-February, near the birthdays of Abraham Lincoln and Frederick Douglass. In 1878 a leading newspaper complained about the lack of a fixed date and urged Congress to sponsor a national holiday. But in the waning years of Reconstruction, Congress was uninterested, and the observance remained largely local—and black.

Lincoln continued to be an important focus of these ceremonies, which included singing and dancing and speeches about black progress. Banners bearing his portrait were often raised up outside storefronts, in churches, in parks, and in banquet halls. Though there were those who had begun questioning his relevance to the black community, Lincoln was still the most admired of all white figures. Black Americans could relate to his lowly origins, to his struggle for education, and to his honesty and moral courage. And as the Jim Crow era deepened, he seemed to become even more important. It seemed essential to hold on to the man who had issued the Emancipation Proclamation, widely considered the black Magna Carta. Booker T. Washington commended Lincoln as a model for black self-help.

W. E. B. Du Bois and others put their hope in the approaching fiftieth anniversary of the proclamation, recognizing it as a chance to finally bring Freedom Day into the mainstream.

In 1912 a National Emancipation Commemoration Society was founded, made up of representatives from most of the states. September 22 was chosen as the date for a grand celebration. But the bill sent to Congress to make it official failed; instead Congress passed legislation to fund a Gettysburg reunion for the following summer, to bring together Union and Confederate soldiers. Feeling betrayed, the organizers launched a new effort to make 1913 the "Year of Emancipation."

By now the NAACP had become a rising force in the country. On February 12, appearing

W. E. B. Du Bois (seated, third from left) met in 1913 with fellow organizers of New York's fiftieth anniversary of the Emancipation Proclamation.

426

at Cooper Union on Lincoln's birthday, Du Bois proclaimed that the NAACP had been "called into being on the hundredth anniversary of [Lincoln's birth]" and that it still conceived its mission to be "the completion of the work which the great emancipator began." Its goal was to free American blacks from "the lingering shackles of past slavery" and to provide political and social freedom to the disfranchised and abused.

The year 1913 saw hundreds of celebrations across the country. The largest was in New York City, where Du Bois and others sponsored a National Emancipation Exhibition. Though the federal government refused to fund it, the state of New York contributed $25,000. An exhibit was set up in the Twelfth Regiment Armory, where a grand "Court of Freedom" was erected beside a "Temple of Beauty." Works of art from around the world depicting black life were placed on display, including a rare portrait of an Abyssinian emperor shipped from Paris. The festival's highlight was a grand pageant written by Du Bois called "The Star of Ethiopia." With a cast of 350 and an elaborate musical accompaniment, it depicted five epochs in African and African American history, climaxing in scenes depicting the age of slavery, of struggle, and of emancipation, and culminating in "the gift of freedom" and Abraham Lincoln's role in it. Delegations from the Caribbean made the trip to New York to take part in the festival, including President Oreste of Haiti and President Valdez of Santo Domingo. And yet, except for the opening ceremonies, the ten-day-long event passed with little attention from white America.

Emancipation Day was especially popular in the South, where African Americans celebrated their freedom and remembered Lincoln. Here a large crowd marches through Richmond, Virginia.

The Moses of Her People

In March 1913 came word that the legendary Underground Railroad conductor Harriet Tubman was dying in Auburn, New York. Born Araminta Ross to slave parents in Maryland, she had married John Tubman in 1844 and five years later, calling herself Harriet after her mother, escaped to the North. Throughout the 1850s she was active in the abolitionist movement and helped lead hundreds of Southern slaves to their freedom in Canada. Nicknamed "The Moses of Her People," she settled in Auburn, where Senator William H. Seward became one of her strongest supporters. Tubman was an outspoken critic of Abraham Lincoln, disdaining his views on colonization and, as President, his caution on emancipation. She is said to have written him in 1862 urging him to action. "God won't let Master Lincoln beat the South until he does the right thing," she dictated, according to fellow activist Lydia Maria Child. "Master Lincoln, he's a great man, and I'm a poor Negro but this Negro can tell Master Lincoln how to save money and young men. He can do it by setting the Negroes free."

During the war Tubman worked as a scout for the Union Army, and later as a nurse. While visiting Washington she became friends with Mary Lincoln but never met her famous husband. "I didn't like Lincoln in those days," she later said. "I used to go see Mrs. Lincoln but I never wanted to see him. You see we colored people didn't understand then that he was our friend." Tubman began to admire Lincoln more after 1863 and spoke favorably of him over the years after his death. She spent the last decades of her long life in a house in Auburn that she bought from William Seward. On the adjacent property, with his help, she opened a Home for Indigent and Aged Negroes, and in her final years she moved into it. When she died at ninety-three on March 10, 1913, the citizens of Auburn erected a bronze tablet in her memory at a ceremony at which Booker T. Washington spoke. Newspapers noting her death called her "a friend of Lincoln."

Harriet Tubman (far left) was photographed with slaves she helped lead to freedom before the Civil War. Dignified to the end, she sat for a portrait in her final year of life.

Reunion at Gettysburg

Ever since 1909, a grand reunion had been planned for the fiftieth anniversary of the Battle of Gettysburg. No place in America held such fearsome symbolism. For both Union and Confederate the loss of life had been horrendous, and for many Northerners the fields of battle had then been sanctified by Lincoln's address there. During the half century that followed, a new perspective on the Civil War had emerged, now increasingly seen as a war with noble instincts on each side. "The men on both sides were activated by high, pure purposes," proclaimed Secretary of War Lindley M. Garrison, "and were compelled by their consciences to do what they did."

From the beginning the planners wanted the ceremony to be about national healing. The idea was to gather veterans from both North and South to meet on the fields of combat in order to assert their common citizenship. There were to be no politics here, no disturbing speeches or confrontations, no discussion at all of slavery, or race, or regional antagonisms. In an era of increasing segregation and disfranchisement, there was no will to dredge up the moral issues behind the war, or the unfinished work that Lincoln had alluded to in his Gettysburg Address.

Planning for the big reunion began in earnest in 1912 with state governments offering free transportation to any Civil War veteran who wished to attend. As the four-day July event approached, throngs began to pour into Gettysburg, with more than 53,000 veterans eventually in attendance—almost 45,000 from the North and about 9,000 from the South. With Confederate and U.S. flags flying side by side, men who had survived one another's bullets now reached out to one another in reconciliation.

On July 1 the crowds gathered for an opening ceremony in which a Union and a Confederate veteran symbolically shook hands. "Nowhere in history have men who opposed each other in mighty battle thus come together in peaceful reunion," said Governor John K. Tener of Pennsylvania, speaking in a tent set up for the ceremonies. "It is a spectacle to inspire the world," wrote the *Philadelphia Evening Bulletin*. When a group of former Gettysburg schoolgirls, now in their sixties, sang "Rally 'Round the Flag, Boys," the veterans "wept like boys," wrote the *Chicago Tribune*.

Over the course of the next four days there were innumerable speeches and gatherings, chances to dine together, see old friends, and reminisce about the glory days. General Daniel Sickles was on hand, the only Union corps commander to make it back, receiving visitors near the very spot where he had famously lost his leg. At one point, in a moving sign of no hard feelings, he was lifted onto the shoulders of

Symbolizing the spirit of the Gettysburg reunion, two aging veterans, one Confederate, the other Union, clasp hands.

Fifty years older, survivors of Pickett's Charge reenact their famous run on Cemetery Ridge.

former Confederates and carried out onto the battlefield for photographs. The only violence to break out over the four days took place at a Gettysburg hotel on July 2, when a Union veteran defending the honor of Abraham Lincoln got caught in a brawl.

But reconciliation was the reigning spirit of the reunion. On July 3, the anniversary of Pickett's Charge, in which thousands had died, survivors of the assault re-created the charge, and then shook hands in a moving ceremony on top of the ridge. President Woodrow Wilson addressed the crowds on the final day of the reunion. A Democrat, and the first Southern-born president to be elected since before the Civil War, Wilson felt it his duty to emphasize national healing. "How wholesome and healing this reunion has been!" he said. "We have found one another again as brothers and comrades in arms; enemies no longer, generous friends rather, over battles long past." Wilson made no mention of Lincoln, or of the emancipation of the slaves. It would be an "impertinence," he declared, "to discourse upon . . . [what] the battle . . . signified,"—even though that is precisely what Lincoln had attempted to do at Gettysburg.

Although black veterans were theoretically allowed to participate in the four-day event, it turned out to be an all-white reunion. Blacks served here almost exclusively as laborers. African Americans looked on from afar at the segregated celebration. The *Baltimore Afro-American Ledger* wrote, "We are wondering whether Mr. Lincoln had the slightest idea in his mind that the time would ever come when the people of this country would come to the conclusion that by the 'People' he meant only white people." One week later, as if to emphasize the new era, Wilson issued a new policy segregating the bathrooms of the Treasury Department, opening up a new era of federally enforced segregation.

The Lincoln Monument at the Gettysburg Battlefield

On July 4, 1913, an official group handshake between former Confederates and Federals was photographed for newspapers across the country. "Come let us be comrades," called out President Woodrow Wilson on the final day of the celebration.

A huge tent was erected at Gettysburg to accommodate the anniversary crowds.

At the Gettysburg reunion the only blacks present were relegated to menial duties. These men passed out blankets to white veterans.

A Lincoln for Everyone

By the twentieth century Lincoln's name was being used for a wide range of political purposes. Part of the reason lay in Lincoln's inherent complexity, and in the breadth and subtlety of his views. But his close friends, who in earlier times had often corrected the public record, were no longer around to speak out, and biographers widely differed in their interpretations.

In 1912 a vicious controversy arose between Theodore Roosevelt and Robert Lincoln, representing the two poles of the Republican Party. In April, Robert released a statement in which he condemned Roosevelt for what he considered a deliberate misuse of his father's memory. "My personal feelings are unimportant," Robert wrote, "but I am not only impatient but indignant that President Lincoln's words and plain views should be perverted and misapplied . . . into support of doctrines which I believe he would abhor if living." Robert declared that his father was a "conservative Republican," far removed from what he considered Theodore Roosevelt's radical positions.

Robert's friend the Lincoln collector Judd Steward was also angered by comparisons made between Roosevelt and Lincoln. In a public letter he pointed out what he considered the many differences between the two. He claimed that Roosevelt was pugnacious while Lincoln was forgiving; that he flouted the Constitution while Lincoln had revered it; that he possessed demogogic impulses while Lincoln had warned against them; that he was stirring up class warfare while Lincoln believed in the unity of all working people.

By 1914 the radical author Rose Strunsky pointed out how Lincoln's nineteenth-century individualism was no longer relevant in "this new, volatile, industrial America." Lincoln "suits all sides in the present day problem," she wrote, but in fact "is a stranger to them all." "Except for the inspiration of his ideal of equal economic opportunity," she wrote, "Lincoln can no longer help us."

Robert Lincoln became close to President William Howard Taft, shown here visiting at his home in Vermont.

Twisting His Father's Words
Robert Lincoln

Robert Lincoln disliked how his father's name was invoked by politicians of every kind. "[O]ver the years his name has been a peg on which to hang many things," he said bitterly. Robert's support for the conservative Republican William Howard Taft in 1912 led to his attack on Theodore Roosevelt, who was advocating the popular recall of judicial decisions.

President Lincoln wrote many letters, made many public addresses, and was the author of many documents. I do not know of the existence in any of them of a word of censure, or of complaint of our Government, or of the methods by which it was carried on. He was sincerely and faithfully obedient to our Constitution. . . .

He hated slavery, but his reverence for the Constitution and law was such that he said publicly again and again that if a member of Congress he would faithfully support a fugitive slave law. . . .

He loved the Government under which he lived, and when at Gettysburg he prayed (if I may use the word) that "government of the people, by the people and for the people may not perish from the earth," he meant and could only mean that Government under which he lived, a representative Government of balanced executive, legislative and judicial parts, and not something entirely different—an unchecked democracy.

These often quoted words of President Lincoln are now deliberately altered and argument founded on their altered form.

I may be permitted to say that I do not think the public wishes the Gettysburg Speech to be rewritten and its words changed by any one, however distinguished, for any purpose, least of all in order to support a proposition that President Lincoln could not possibly have had in mind.

The Birth of a Nation

While black Americans kept alive the memory of Lincoln the Emancipator, others labored to transform Lincoln into a white supremacist. Thomas Dixon's novel *The Clansman* had been made into a successful play in the South, where one commentator likened it to "a runaway car loaded with dynamite." Deeply moved by Dixon's work, the Hollywood filmmaker D.W. Griffith obtained production rights to the book. By 1915 he had finished making his screen adaptation, *The Birth of a Nation*. Using cinematic techniques that would revolutionize the film industry, including huge casts, fast editing, close-ups, and dramatic lighting, Griffith produced a landmark moving picture. It was also a racist tirade, filled with scenes of lascivious blacks threatening white Southern women, and members of the Ku Klux Klan coming to their rescue. Abraham Lincoln was portrayed as on the side of the Klan.

Griffith portrayed Lincoln as sympathetic to the white South, in contrast to "negro-loving" Northern radicals like Thaddeus Stevens. A screening in Los Angeles indicated that audience response was going to be tremendous. But it also brought forth protests from the NAACP and calls for the film's suppression. In anticipation of further protests, Griffith approached Woodrow Wilson to screen it at the White House, the first movie ever to be shown there. The screening took place on February 18 and deeply affected President Wilson. He emerged from the three-hour show and remarked, "It is like writing history with lightning. My only regret is that it is all so terribly true." Why wouldn't Wilson approve of it, asked one outraged critic; wasn't he "the man who put into effect the policy of segregation of colored employees of the Government?"

With the help of Wilson's endorsement, the movie opened in New York City in March. Reviewing it, Jane Addams warned that it was "an appeal to race prejudice" and "full of danger." But *The Birth of a Nation* became the most successful movie of its era. "It is the acme of moving picture art," wrote a Boston reviewer in April, "so wonderful and so beautiful, and so full of life that it robs the power of criticism." Slavery assassinated Abraham Lincoln, a black critic declared. Now he was being assassinated again, by Griffith's film.

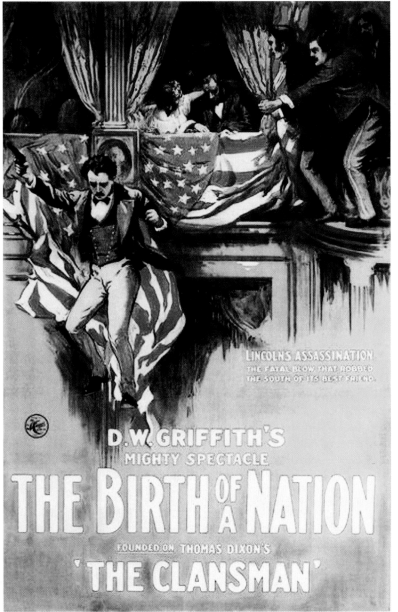

LINCOLN'S ASSASSINATION
THE FATAL BLOW THAT ROBBED
THE SOUTH OF ITS BEST FRIEND.

D.W. GRIFFITH'S
MIGHTY SPECTACLE
THE BIRTH OF A NATION
FOUNDED ON THOMAS DIXON'S
'THE CLANSMAN'

Speaking about the adaptation of his book, Thomas Dixon said "I believe that . . . the white man must and shall be supreme." In the movie poster John Wilkes Booth leaps from the box at Ford's Theatre, having mortally wounded Abraham Lincoln.

The Fiftieth Anniversary of the Assassination

On the fiftieth anniversary of Lincoln's assassination newspapers marked the occasion with a new round of articles. "Every man, woman and child in the United States is thoroughly familiar with the happenings of that eventful night," wrote the *Washington Post*, which chronicled the Lincoln murder and the huge funeral that had followed. The *Boston Daily Globe* launched an ambitious thirty-part series by journalist Winfield M. Thompson, titled "Lincoln and Booth: The Inner Story of the Great Tragedy of Fifty Years Ago." The article detailed Booth's plot, the night of the murder, the assassin's flight and capture, and the trial and execution of the co-conspirators.

Other newspapers sought out still-living eyewitnesses of the murder, now in their seventies or older. J. B. Duff lived in Los Angeles and wrote, "I am probably near the last of those present in Ford's Theater on that fateful night." But in fact there were others, including several members of the production company. Annie F. Wright was an actress and the wife of the stage manager at Ford's Theatre and had sat in the audience with Dr. Taft. She kept mementos of the assassination in her home in Allston, Massachusetts, including a bloodstained lock of Lincoln's hair and a framed program of the play, *Our American Cousin*. And the actress Jeannie Gourlay Struthers was one of three eyewitnesses to see Booth attack the orchestra leader William Withers. Gourlay played Mary Meredith in the production that night. It was her father, Thomas Gourlay, who led Laura Keene to the dying president and who later placed an American flag under Lincoln's head. Jeannie had inherited the flag in 1888 and kept it as a reminder of the terrible evening.

There was also William J. Ferguson, the call boy at the theater who had gone on to a long career on the stage; Mrs. J. H. Evans, who played Sharpe in the production; Harry Hawk, who played Asa Trenchard; and Helen Truman, now Mrs. J. F. Wynkoop, who had played Augusta. Long presumed dead, Helen wrote from California: "Permit me to state that the writer is still alive. . . . I don't want to be killed off so young." Wynkoop disliked the attention brought on by the anniversary. "I have not cared for the notoriety of it," she wrote.

On the fiftieth anniversary year of Lincoln's assassination, Booker T. Washington collapsed and was diagnosed with advanced arteriosclerosis. His death at age fifty-nine saddened the nation. "I mourn his loss," said former president Theodore Roosevelt, "and feel that one of the most useful citizens of our land is gone." And the president of the University of Chicago, Harry Pratt Judson, proclaimed, "As a benefactor of the Negro race in this country, Booker T. Washington can be compared only with Abraham Lincoln."

Abraham Lincoln in bronze, the vision of George Barnard

George Barnard's Controversial Statue

During the ten years before and after the Lincoln Centennial, no fewer than twenty-two Lincoln statues were unveiled to the public. Drawing crowds of thousands, these ceremonies were the height of public theater, often featuring starring roles by presidents and governors. Almost all of the statues were executed in heroic, neo-classical style, depicting the strong, larger-than-life, presidential Lincoln. But in 1917 a decidedly unheroic Lincoln was unveiled in the city of Cincinnati. The eleven-foot-high figure, by George Grey Barnard, had been commissioned in 1910 by Charles P. Taft, the half-brother of President William Howard Taft. Completed in late 1916, it was dedicated the following March, and that might have been the end of the story. Except that Mrs. Taft then offered to provide a copy of the statue as a gift to the city of London. The offer was made and gratefully accepted, with a planned erection in Trafalgar Square next to the looming figure of Lord Nelson. But then the statue became the center of a raging controversy about how Americans wanted to be represented overseas, and how they wished to remember Lincoln.

Barnard's sculpture depicted a beardless Lincoln in his late forties, standing pigeon-toed in ill-fitting clothes with a bewildered look on his face. The sculptor said he aimed to reveal the "plainness" of "the real man," and some admirers called his work imaginative and daring. Ida Tarbell found it the "most interesting" Lincoln tribute she had seen "in any medium," one giving a glimpse into the "profundity" of the man. Theodore Roosevelt adored the homely portrait, saying, "At last we have the Lincoln of the Lincoln-Douglas debates. How long we have been waiting for this."

But for every admirer there were many more critics, chief among them the aging but still influential Robert Lincoln. In a published letter to President Taft he called it "a monstrous figure . . . grotesque as a likeness . . . and defamatory as an effigy." He secretly offered to pay $25,000 if a copy of Saint-Gaudens's heroic *Standing Lincoln* could be sent to London instead. He asked Frederick Hill Meserve to head up a public protest to prevent the erection in Trafalgar Square, and soon Robert was being joined by Henry Cabot Lodge and others in a national argument that raged for months in the newspapers. The *New York Times* called the statue "perverse," saying the Lincoln it depicted was not only "plain but grotesque." The figure "lacked dignity," had no "presence," and appeared like "a long-suffering peasant, crushed by adversity. . . . The huge hands crossed over the stomach suggest that all is not well with his digestion." The "real Lincoln" was entirely absent, claimed the *Times*. "The Barnard statue is the picture of an ugly man alone, and one who is comically ugly."

In June 1917, in an editorial in *Artworld*, the controversy reached the height of invective. Barnard's Lincoln was a "stoop-shouldered, consumptive-chested, chimpanzee-headed, lumpy-footed, giraffe-necked, grimy-fingered clod-hopper, wearing his clothes in a way to disgust a rag-man." From here on the national consensus was fixed. Even critics sympathetic to Barnard, such as those at the *Chicago Tribune*, said his statue "is not Lincoln. It is an idea of Lincoln." And in the war of ideas this one lost. Robert Stanton, son of Lincoln's secretary of war, wrote, "May the statue never go to London but rather be melted down into bullets for our army in France."

In the end, a replica of Saint-Gaudens's *Standing Lincoln* was sent to London (without Robert Lincoln's having to pay for it), and the Barnard statue found another home—in the working-class city of Manchester, England. But though the controversy eventually quieted down, the incident revealed much about America's changing feelings about Lincoln. Earlier generations had loved to laugh at Lincoln's jokes, make fun of his appearance, identify with his humanity. Now, in the midst of World War I, what people wanted was Lincoln the Statesman—one who could help inspire them in a new time of crisis.

ROBERT T. LINCOLN

Robert Lincoln (above) despised Barnard's statue, calling it "a monstrous figure . . . grotesque as a likeness of President Lincoln and defamatory as an effigy." (In the cartoon above, he is depicted reacting to the statue.) Ida Tarbell adored it, calling it "the profoundest thing yet done . . . by anyone in any medium." In later years she wrote, "I have never been able to look at it without tears." (Left, Barnard at work on another piece, a gigantic rendition of Lincoln's head)

A sketch of a ghostly Abraham Lincoln giving guidance to President Woodrow Wilson appeared in newspapers during World War I. Below, Lincoln was used to sell war bonds and was the inspiration for a popular war song in 1918.

1919

Lincoln During World War I

When Woodrow Wilson issued his proclamation of neutrality in 1914, few had thought that the United States would ever enter the Great War in Europe. But in a message seeking America's help, sent on Lincoln's birthday in 1917, British prime minister David Lloyd George declared that the fighting in Europe was fundamentally "the same battle which your countrymen fought under Lincoln's leadership more than fifty years ago." Under German militarism, he declared, freedom itself was being crushed. "Therefore, we believe that the war must be fought out to a finish. In holding this conviction, we have been inspired beyond measure by the example of your great President [Lincoln]." After Wilson finally broke American neutrality, newspapers began to compare him to Lincoln, and cartoons showed the great wartime President watching over his shoulder.

During these war years Americans turned increasingly to Lincoln as a model of courage and wisdom. In 1918 a popular song was sung written by Carol Hirsch entitled "Abraham Lincoln, What Would You Do?" And inspired by Wilson's talk about fighting to preserve democracy, American blacks registered for the army in record numbers. Eventually 367,000 African Americans fought in the war, serving in largely segregated units. For their bravery in battle, the French government decorated twenty-one men of the Eighth Illinois Infantry who helped drive the enemy out of France. But if African Americans thought that the armistice in 1918 would be followed by a new birth of freedom at home, they were to be disappointed. Wilson's racial policies remained intact. And one of the worst periods of race relations in American history began shortly after the soldiers' return.

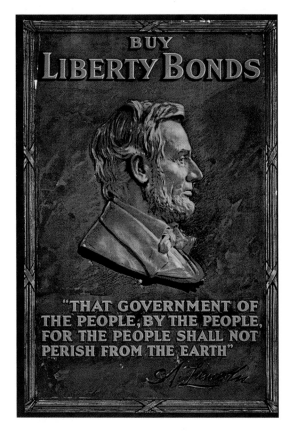

A World War I propaganda scene entitled "True Sons of Freedom" depicted black American soldiers overwhelming German infantry as Lincoln looks on with approval. Below, black soldiers return home after fighting in France.

A Lincoln Memorial

The idea of building a Lincoln memorial in Washington had been debated since the nineteenth century. After the Spanish-American War a congressional commission charged with revitalizing the nation's capital had recommended extending the Mall westward from the Washington Monument to the Potomac River and erecting a memorial to Lincoln there. The proposal had been endorsed by some of the leading figures in American design, including Charles McKim, Frederick Law Olmsted, and Augustus Saint-Gaudens. But it had stalled in Congress as alternative ideas were debated, including a Lincoln memorial highway connecting Washington to Gettysburg, and a major Lincoln monument for downtown Washington. The river site had some powerful critics. Long considered a barren swampland, a place where cattle had been penned back in Lincoln's day, the lonely area, many insisted, was no place for a memorial. Speaker of the House Joseph Cannon, who had known Lincoln in Illinois, swore he would block the choice of "that God damn swamp." But Secretary of State John Hay—widely respected for his knowledge of Lincoln—had supported the Potomac River site before he died, calling it "the place of honor" on the main axis of the Mall. Though it was indeed "lonely" and undeveloped, this was exactly why the Lincoln Memorial belonged here, Hay argued. "His monument should stand alone, remote from the habitations of man . . . isolated, distinguished, and serene."

The 1909 Centennial put Congress in the embarrassing position of still having made no plans to honor Lincoln in the capital city. So in 1911 the Lincoln Memorial Commission was created, with President William Howard Taft serving as ex officio chair-

The cornerstone of the Lincoln Memorial was laid on February 12, 1915, nine months into a six-year-long construction project. To the right, circles of carved marble are swung into place to build the massive columns.

man. The architect Henry Bacon was chosen to design the memorial building, and sculptor Daniel Chester French to create a great statue that would reside inside. Groundbreaking took place in 1914, and construction continued for the next five years, through the entirety of World War I.

From the beginning the commissioners saw the memorial not only as a tribute to Lincoln but also as an important symbol of the reunified nation. With Northerners and Southerners having fought side by side in the Spanish-American War, and now once again in World War I, it was time, they felt, to officially put aside all sectional differences. This meant that the Lincoln honored here must not be the Lincoln who had broken the South militarily, or the Lincoln who had crushed the institution of slavery. Rather the Lincoln here had to be the transcendent figure who had saved the Union, a man who could be honored by both North and South. "By emphasizing his saving the Union you appeal to both sections," wrote Royal Cortissoz, author of the famous inscription that would be placed inside the finished building. "By saying nothing about slavery you avoid rubbing the old sores."

Henry Bacon's building took the form of a Greek temple modeled in part after the Parthenon. The very site of the building emphasized the theme of national union. In its position at the juncture of what would be the new Memorial Bridge, it would be the first building to welcome Southerners to the capital city. Symbols of North-South reunion abounded in the architecture. The building was supported by thirty-six grand columns representing all the states at the time of Lincoln's death, both Northern and Southern. (The names of twelve other states that had come into the Union in the years since were carved into the upper section of the building.) Around the main entablature, between carved names of the thirty-six states, were placed symbolic stone wreaths of interwoven Northern laurel and Southern pine.

The upper foundations of the memorial were put in place in the summer of 1916. Work continued through the years of World War I, until completion in 1920.

The year the Lincoln Memorial was completed, the U.S. Senate passed a resolution to procure an oil painting of Abraham Lincoln to hang in the Capitol. During the Civil War a midwestern artist named Freeman Thorp had served in the Union Army and had seen Abraham Lincoln close up. "[I] studied him very carefully and thoroughly from life just before the inauguration," Thorp recalled, "and later at the White House and at Gettysburg." He made sketches for future reference, wrote down descriptions of Lincoln's face, and memorized "his expression and how he looked when animated." Then in 1879, in his Washington studio on the roof of the Capitol, he finally painted Lincoln in oil. In 1920 the Senate purchased the painting, convinced Thorp had captured Lincoln in a way no other artist could ever do again. "It would be impracticable for any future portrait painter who had not known him in life," the artist agreed, "to put the real Lincoln on canvas."

A Lincoln Forever

Though Henry Bacon's building was largely completed by 1919 there were delays with French's statue. Widely hailed as the successor to Augustus Saint-Gaudens, Daniel Chester French was based out of New York City but spent half the year in western Massachusetts where he had turned a large barn into his main studio. It was here at Chesterwood that the Lincoln statue would be created. To study Lincoln's face, French sought out Lincoln authority Frederick Hill Meserve. Meserve gave him access to his immense collection of photographs, including his glass negatives of Lincoln's face, and French used these to make huge enlargements that he hung in his studio for inspiration. (Later Meserve visited French's studio, where, he said, he "entered his dreams.")

In early 1920 Daniel Chester French and his crew began assembling the massive pieces of his Lincoln statue.

The sculptor had been commissioned to build a twelve-foot-tall statue. In 1920, he and Bacon made the trip to Washington to set up a full-size plaster model in its exact spot in the building. To their dismay they found it to be dwarfed by the space. Just in case, Fench had brought along two "solar prints" of the statue—one eighteen feet high, the other twenty. The twenty-foot-high version fit the space perfectly. This meant Congress would need to approve new monies, which meant further delays.

Finally all was ready to proceed on what would be the largest marble statue ever created. The firm of Piccirilli Brothers performed the carving from French's model, with the sculptor adding the final fine details. Like Bacon, he strove to idealize Lincoln's memory—to lift him above the "sordidness" of politics, race, and war and reveal the "essential nobility" of the man. The finished sculpture depicted the calm strength of Lincoln the statesman. But it would be two more years before the memorial's official opening.

French's workmen were dwarfed beside his looming sculpture. They later carved words on the tablet above Lincoln's head: "In this Temple, as in the hearts of the People for whom he saved the Union, the memory of Abraham Lincoln is enshrined forever."

1920

Attacking the Lincoln Myth

Despite the healing between North and South represented by the Gettysburg Reunion of 1913, some maintained their commitment to the "Lost Cause" and their ongoing hatred of Abraham Lincoln. And no one was a more enthusiastic proponent than Virginia's Lyon Gardiner Tyler, the longtime president of William and Mary College. Tyler was the fourteenth child of John Tyler, born when the former president was already sixty-eight. As a boy during the Civil War he had been taken to the safety of New York City, but he maintained a lifelong commitment to the Confederate cause. Tyler believed that slaves had been well treated in the South and had been in many ways better off than they were under freedom. "[T]he present generation of Southern men see no reason to be ashamed of their ancestors," he wrote in 1917. Beginning his own journal, *Tyler's Quarterly*, he started to publish anti-Lincoln articles. In 1920 he wrote a pamphlet, *Propaganda in History*, which focused primarily on Abraham Lincoln. He castigated Northern hero worship of the sixteenth President, calling the Lincoln myth mere "propagandism." But if the Christlike mythic Lincoln was a blasphemous absurdity, Tyler wrote, the "real" Lincoln was even worse—a coarse-mannered, hypocritical tyrant who had waged brutal war upon the South. Tyler rejected Lincoln's widely hailed humanitarianism, calling him a cruel, indecisive, cynical leader, weak in character, amoral in tactics, and largely under the control of cabinet radicals. And he accused him of having used slavery as an excuse to subjugate the South.

A Confederate Memorial Day celebration took place in 1920. Above, an aging veteran poses in his uniform, fifty-five years after the Civil War.

Still Our Enemy
Lyon Gardiner Tyler

We all know that the North started out with making a hero of John Brown, but abandoned him for the much more desirable character of Mr. Lincoln. His assassination

Lyon Gardiner Tyler

gave propagandists a good starting point, and since then never has propaganda been more active. . . . Everything any way tending to lessen his importance is studiously kept in the background. . . .

It is impossible to associate idealism with coarseness, and Lincoln, judged by every test of historic evidence, was a very coarse man. . . .

The doctrine that there must be no humanity in warfare . . . was . . . voiced by Sherman in his letter to General Grant . . . : ". . . I can make . . . Georgia howl." . . . And Lincoln, in spite of the fine catchy sentiment of his Gettysburg speech, gave his sanction to the same policy. . . .

In prosecuting the war Lincoln appealed to a great idea—the Union—which he declared was his sole idea in prosecuting the war, but the old Union was founded on consent and the Union he had in mind was one of force. His war, therefore, was contrary to the principles of self-government expressed in the Declaration of Independence and to the modern principle of self-determination, now the accepted doctrine of the world. . . .

The truth is, there never was a war more inconsistent in principle than that waged against the Southern States in 1861. . . .

The present Southerners are glad to be free of slavery and are loyal citizens of the Union, but this is far from saying that they approve the violent methods by which slavery was abolished and the Union restored.

Race relations grew worse in the North as riots broke out in 1919.

A policeman and his assistant stone a black man in the Chicago race riots.

Southern veterans march in a 1922 parade in Richmond, Virginia.

In 1918 a road was opened so that tourists could visit the hilltop site of the old town where Lincoln had first lived on his own.

Although work on the Old Rutledge Inn was officially called a "restoration," construction workers were actually building a replica based on historical research.

1921

Lincoln's New Salem

The popularity of the birth site in Kentucky and the homestead in Springfield led to new interest in other places associated with Lincoln's life. Over the next decade the state of Illinois went on a buying spree, acquiring the old capitol building at Vandalia, where Lincoln had served as a legislator, the courthouse at Metamora, where he had practiced law, and the Coles County farm, where his parents had last resided. But the most significant purchase was the six-hundred-acre site of New Salem, where he had lived as a young man, and an elaborate "restoration" of the entire village now got under way.

Lincoln's six-year residency in New Salem had roughly corresponded to the village's lifespan. A grist-mill town built in 1829 on a bluff above the Sangamon River, it served surrounding farmers who came here to have their grain milled and their wood sawed, and who gathered on Saturdays to buy supplies and trade stories. In 1831, twenty-two-year-old Lincoln arrived here by accident when his loaded flatboat headed for New Orleans got stuck on the mill's dam. As its stern took on water, villagers came out to watch the strapping young stranger unload goods as fast as he could, then bore holes in the bow with a borrowed augur, so that when the raft finally righted the water ran out. When the boat lifted and floated over the dam, the industrious young Lincoln was on his way again, with the hole plugged. But he and his employer-partner Denton Offutt had taken an interest in the little village, and not long afterward they both returned and settled here, with Lincoln serving as clerk in a new

LINCOLN LOGS
COMPLETE SET WITH WHEELS

"Lincoln Logs" were invented by the son of architect Frank Lloyd Wright and were very popular in the early 1920s. The boxed sets came with instructions that showed how to build a miniature version of Lincoln's boyhood cabin.

store opened by Offutt at the mill. It was the first time he had lived apart from his parents and the next six years were formative ones.

Here Lincoln "thought of learning the blacksmith trade," but instead opened a store with the even younger William Berry and "did nothing but get deeper and deeper in debt." He served as village postmaster and surveyed land in order to keep "soul and body together." He became known for his prodigious strength, for his storytelling skills, and for his leadership capacity. He was introduced to the writings of Shakespeare and became known as a dreamer who often walked through town with his head in a book. In New Salem Lincoln made his first real friendships; fell in love for the first—and second—time; made political speeches—often on the improvement of rivers; won his first public office—as state legislator; and through it all earned the nickname of "Honest Abe." Carl Sandburg called the town his "nourishing mother," and Lincoln himself knew how much he grew over the course of his time here. In a letter to a friend written just a few years after leaving town, he said his current success as a lawyer in Springfield would "astonish the older citizens of your county, who twelve years ago knew me as a strange, friendless, uneducated, penniless boy, working on a flatboat."

Just as Lincoln's store had "winked out," as he later put it, so did the village of New Salem not long after Lincoln left it. He himself had laid out the town of Petersburg to the north, and after it was named the seat of the new Menard County, New Salem's population moved there after 1839. When they left, the old settlers disassembled and took their houses with them, rebuilding them in the new county seat. By 1840 only ten homes remained of the original two dozen. Five years later only two were left, and by 1847 the place was described as "desolate," the former village now referred to as "Old Salem." It was to a quiet hilltop, mostly in cow pasture and light forest, that William Herndon returned in 1866 to meditate on Lincoln's years there.

"The Mount Vernon of the West"
Thompson Gains Onstot

T. G. Onstot was one of the moving forces behind New Salem's restoration. He predicted great things for the abandoned town where Abraham Lincoln once lived.

A few days ago I was on Salem hill and I stopped in front of the spot where the old hotel stood. Memory carried me back three score years when I saw Abe Lincoln playing marbles and pitching quoits on the very spot where I stood, and where his musical voice and ringing laugh could be heard above all his comrades. It is a wonder the ground at old Salem is not marked so that the visitor to that sacred spot can be better informed as to the locality of the buildings and other historic scenes of the town. I made arrangements with James Bale a few weeks ago in which he was to have old Salem mowed and furnished suitable posts and boards, and I agreed to locate where each building stood, with the owner's name and the business that he followed.

. . . I understand that I am the only person now living that can do it. Salem is destined to become the Mt. Vernon of the West. Every allusion made by speakers at Old Salem Chautauqua that touched upon the history of this spot found a hearty response. While at old Salem Chautauqua a few weeks ago I met Uncle John Roll, who is nearly a hundred years old. He was an old comrade of Lincoln's at an early day. He is still in good health and bids fair to become a centenarian. He assisted Lincoln to build the last flat boat that went down the Sangamon at Sangamontown, and he delights to talk of his early career. They must have been intimate friends for Lincoln gave him his dog when he started for Washington to be inaugurated.

Mr. Roll had a picture of the dog, which he took great delight in showing. . . . It was a great treat to meet a comrade of Lincoln's, who had lived with him, shared his toils and helped him achieve his triumphs.

As he sat on a bluff in the cold wind of a mid-October day, looking out upon the solitary log hut that was all that remained of the village, Herndon remembered the town in its glory days. "In my imagination," he wrote on a pad on his knee, "the little village perched on a hill is astir with the hum of busy men, and the sharp, quick buzz of women. . . . Oh! What a history."

For decades the site remained deserted, with New Salem kept alive only in the memories of the old-timers. Local residents picnicked on the hill for years, and occasionally a stray tourist or journalist would wander up looking for signs of Lincoln's youth. A special attraction was the so-called Lincoln tree—actually three trees growing together as if from a single root from an old cellar hole—an elm, a sycamore, and a locust. Tourists carved their initials in it.

A number of factors conspired to change the fate of this deserted hilltop. The appearance in 1889 of Herndon's biography of Lincoln revived public interest in his early days. The publication of Ida Tarbell's articles a few years later similarly ignited a passion for Lincoln's youth. And in 1897 a local association was formed to help save the property on the hill, and the first attempts were made to reclaim it from forest. When the site came under threat of development in 1906, William Randolph

The reconstructed Berry-Lincoln store in New Salem. Here, Lincoln said, he "did nothing but get deeper and deeper in debt."

Hearst got involved and purchased the tract, donating it as a "sacred trust" to the association. Finally in 1919 the state of Illinois took over the entire site and pledged to create a New Salem State Park there. By 1921 scholars were hard at work on the basic research that would underpin the restoration. The first building to be worked on was the old cooper shop of Isaac Onstot, where Lincoln had once studied Blackstone. Other buildings of the village had to be erected in replica, "constructed after pictures in old county annals and after testimony of Salem residents," a newspaper reported. As the old town began to reappear in the second half of the 1920s, "the semblance of a vanished era is perfect." Though the rebuilt site would not be open to the public until 1933, it was predicted to become one of the most important of all Lincoln shrines. "Here children will come," Governor Horner of Illinois would boldly proclaim, "and gain a clearer insight into the Great Emancipator's soul."

Above, the reconstructed mill at New Salem was located near the dam where Lincoln's barge got stuck in 1831. Below is the second Berry-Lincoln store. Lincoln's six years in New Salem matured him. Here he learned how to think for himself, and for the rest of his life his storytelling was filled with the twang and color of this rural village.

Dedicating the Lincoln Memorial

More than 35,000 gathered for the dedication of the Lincoln Memorial on Memorial Day 1922. Some thought the Hellenic "temple" obscured Lincoln's Americanism, and that French's statue failed to capture his true essence. Neither seemed to bear any relationship, they said, to the homely westerner born in a log cabin who had always been a man of the people. But supporters of the memorial stressed the appropriateness of a classical temple as a shrine for America's "greatest soul." Seated on a thronelike chair within, evoking ancient depictions of Zeus, the gigantic figure gazed eastward toward the Washington Monument, linking the Nation's Father and Savior.

Three American Presidents took part in the dedication ceremonies, as loudspeakers set up on the building's rooftop made the ceremony audible across the entire Mall. The event was broadcast on the new medium of radio, reaching an estimated two million listeners. Representatives of the Union and Confederate armies were here, as were surviving figures from Lincoln's Washington. Robert Lincoln came out of his seclusion and was warmly welcomed as a guest of honor. He had been the memorial's chief advocate, personally rewarding the congressman who shepherded it through the House Committee on Appropriations with a manuscript of one of his father's important speeches. The finished memorial was his "crowning joy," one paper noted.

In keeping with federal policies of segregation, black guests were seated in a "colored section" off to the sides, where it was reported that some were rudely treated by military attendants. The commissioners had included a black speaker in the program and seated him along with the others on the main podium. Not wanting an activist such as W. E. B. Du Bois, who might challenge the mostly white audience, they had chosen Robert Russa Moton, the mild-mannered successor of Booker T. Washington at Tuskegee Institute. One of the leading black businessmen in America, Moton

Robert Lincoln was escorted to his seat at the dedication of the Lincoln Memorial in 1922. It was his first public appearance in many years.

President Warren G. Harding stood with Robert Lincoln at the dedication ceremony. Harding's speech was broadcast to an estimated two million radio listeners. Loudspeakers were placed on the roof of the building (right).

was known to be courteous and respectful of Lincoln. But in what turned out to be the most morally powerful speech of the day, he boldly highlighted the nation's history of slavery and racism and challenged Americans to live up to their calling to be a people of "equal justice and equal opportunity."

The speeches that followed by William Howard Taft, Woodrow Wilson, and Warren G. Harding shifted the discourse to more neutral territory. Chief Justice Taft never once mentioned slavery but repeatedly emphasized the theme of northern and southern reunion. "Here on the banks between the two sections," he said, "it is peculiarly appropriate that [the memorial] should stand. . . . It marks the restoration of brotherly love . . . in the Memorial of the one who is as dear to the hearts of the South as to those of the North." President Harding went even further and seemed to purposely go out of his way to contradict Moton. "The supreme chapter in history is not emancipation," he declared, ". . . [but] maintained union and nationality. . . . How it would comfort [Lincoln's] great soul to know that the States in the Southland joined sincerely in honoring him."

In the days that followed, Moton's speech went almost completely unreported. Even his name was dropped from the record—in most accounts Moton was simply referred to as "a representative of his race." African Americans were outraged. The *Chicago Defender* urged a boycott of the memorial until it was properly dedicated to the true Lincoln of history. And not long afterward, at a large gathering in front of the memorial, Bishop E. D. W. Jones contradicted President Harding's words, saying, "The immortality of the great emancipator lay not in his preservation of the Union, but in his giving freedom to the negroes of America."

The dedication was a turning point in the memorialization of Abraham Lincoln. Far removed from the passionate exercises of 1872 at the Lincoln Tomb, or at the Freedmen's Memorial in 1876, it belonged to a new era in American history in which Lincoln's legacy for black freedom was being deliberately downplayed by the government.

Robert Russa Moton was the only black speaker that day, and gave the most stirring speech of all.

Guests at the dedication packed the grounds in front of the Reflecting Pool, and the crowds of people without invitations stretched all the way back to the Washington Monument.

Southerners Honor His Memory

Lincoln in 1854, the year he reentered politics. For all his ardent opposition to the spread of slavery, Lincoln refused to condemn the South for the institution. Southerners were "just what we would have been in their situation," he said, and "are no more responsible for the origin of slavery than we."

Despite the efforts to reach out to white Southerners, at least some in the South objected vehemently to the new memorial. There were diehards like Lyon G. Tyler and his tireless ally Mildred Lewis Rutherford, president of a Georgia chapter of the United Daughters of the Confederacy and for many years historian-general of the national organization. An outspoken advocate of the South's "Lost Cause," Rutherford was frustrated that the Northern view of the Civil War was now being taught in Southern schools. Believing that the North's adulation of Lincoln was part of the problem, she began to single him out as an icon to smash. In 1922 Rutherford helped prepare a report for the Daughters declaring the Civil War to have been "deliberately and personally conceived" by Abraham Lincoln. Just three weeks after the Lincoln Memorial dedication, the United Confederate Veterans, meeting in Richmond, Virginia, unani-

mously adopted this report. It included a recommendation that Southern schools adopt a textbook written by the Georgia author Huger W. Jackson and published by Rutherford. The textbook would present positive evidence, the report said, that Abraham Lincoln "was personally responsible for forcing the war upon the South."

But following the Richmond convention of 1922 there arose voices of protest across the South. The veterans were written off as a bunch of "old men" who no longer represented the majority of Southerners. "What has come over the old soldiers at this late day," asked the *Birmingham Age-Herald* on July 2, "that they should be guilty of such a foolish and uncalled for attack on Lincoln at a time when Civil War animosities should be dead beyond resurrection?" All across the South came similar messages. Mildred Rutherford was written off as out of step with the times, and a poor historian. "[W]ell-informed Southerners," summed up the *Arkansas Gazette*, "know that Abraham Lincoln . . . was one of the country's greatest and best men. Southerners recognize this and honor his memory."

Lincoln in 1865, the year his life came to an end. In his Second Inaugural Address in March he once again reached out to the South. Both North and South, he said, were guilty of slavery's origins, and both had been punished by "this terrible war."

Most Southerners approved of the Lincoln Memorial. Here, Confederate veterans assemble in 1922.

W. E. B. Du Bois on the speakers' stand in 1920 and, below, at his desk at the New York office of *The Crisis*

W. E. B. Du Bois and Lincoln

Before 1922 most of the people who accused Lincoln of racism were white Southerners. Some, like North Carolina writer Thomas Dixon, or Mississippi's Senator James K. Vardaman, did so in order to embrace Lincoln as one of their own. Vardaman, who once said if he weren't a public figure he would gleefully take part in Southern lynch mobs against black "brutes," was a glowing admirer of Abraham Lincoln. "I have made a very careful study of Mr. Lincoln's ideas," he declared in the Senate, and "my views and his on the race question are substantially identical." In order to depict Lincoln as a white supremacist, Vardaman repeatedly used his words out of context and liked to quote from his Charleston Speech of September 18, 1858. "I am not, nor ever have been in favor of equality of the white and black races," Lincoln had said in his most unfortunate utterance ever on the subject of race. "I as much as any other man am in favor of having the superior position assigned to the white race."

Lincoln shared many of the racial prejudices of his times and made it clear on numerous occasions that he was not in favor of full equality for black people. But if most

of his life he was not an egalitarian, he was far ahead of his Democratic opponents. Where Stephen A. Douglas ranted about white supremacy, Lincoln carefully qualified his racial views and routinely stood up for the humanity of black people. And over the years he grew, eventually developing the beginnings of a vision of a racially integrated postwar America.

For more than fifty years after Lincoln's death black Americans kept alive his emancipationist legacy, honoring him as their liberator and friend. But then in July 1922 a short article appeared in *The Crisis* by the NAACP's W. E. B. Du Bois. Du Bois had grudgingly admired Lincoln's capacity for growth on the race issue, but had long been suspicions of his deeper motives. Hadn't he written Horace Greeley in 1862 saying that freeing the slaves was not his primary concern, but rather saving the Union? "[I]f he could keep the Union from being disrupted," Du Bois had paraphrased, "he would not only allow slavery to exist but would loyally protect it." Now in July Du Bois went even further, writing an editorial on Lincoln that shocked many of his readers. "Abraham Lincoln was a Southern poor white, of illegitimate birth," he wrote, "poorly educated and unusually ugly, awkward, ill-dressed. He liked smutty stories and was a politician down to his toes. Aristocrats—Jeff Davis, Seward and their ilk—despised him, and indeed he had little outwardly that compelled respect. But in that curious human way he was big inside. He had reserves and depths and when habit and convention were torn away there was something left to Lincoln . . . so that at the crisis he was big enough to be inconsistent—cruel, merciful; peace-loving, a fighter; despising Negroes and letting them fight and vote; protecting slavery and freeing slaves. He was a man—a big, inconsistent, brave man."

Du Bois's article triggered a storm of protest and a demand that he publicly recant. Stung by the criticism but convinced he had a message that needed to be heard, Du Bois wrote again in the September issue of *The Crisis*. This time he was more nuanced and respectful, but he held his ground on the issue of Lincoln's racial prejudice. "Do my colored friends really believe the picture would be fairer and finer if we forgot Lincoln's unfortunate speech at Charleston, Illinois, in 1858?" he asked. "Abraham Lincoln said: I will say, then, that I am not, nor ever have been, in favor of bringing about in any way the social and political equality of the white and black races—that I am not, nor ever have been, in favor of making voters or jurors of Negroes, nor of qualifying them to hold office, nor to inter-marry with white people." "We love to think of the Great as flawless," Du Bois declared. "[N]o sooner does a great man die we begin to whitewash him. We seek to forget all that was small and mean and unpleasant and remember the fine and brave and good." It was time to stop the unadulterated hero worship, he insisted, that distorted Lincoln and infantilized the black community. It was time for black people to take charge of their own destiny and not to pin it on a mythical white hero. And it was possible to finally see him as he actually was—flaws and all—and still admire, and even love him.

Lincoln the Imperfect
W. E. B. Du Bois

September 1922

[M]any of my readers were hurt by what I said of Lincoln in the July *Crisis*. I am sorry to hurt them, for some of them were tried friends of me and my cause—particularly one like the veteran, wounded at Chickamauga and a staunch defender of our rights, who thinks my words "unkind and uncalled for."

First and foremost, there comes a question of fact. Was what I said true or false?. . . If my facts were false, my words were wrong—but were my facts false? Beyond this, there is another and deeper question on which most of my critics dwell. They say, What is the use of recalling evil? What good will it do? or as one phrases, "Is this proper food for your people?" I think it is.

Abraham Lincoln was perhaps the greatest figure of the nineteenth century. Certainly of the five masters—Napoleon, Bismarck, Victoria, Browning and Lincoln—Lincoln is to me the most human and lovable. And I love him not because he was perfect but because he was not and yet triumphed. . . . The world is full of folk whose taste was educated in the gutter. The world is full of people born hating and despising their fellows. To these I love to say: See this man. He was one of you and yet he became Abraham Lincoln.

Some may prefer to . . . list him as an original abolitionist and defender of Negroes. But personally I revere him the more because up out of his contradictions and inconsistencies he fought his way to the pinnacle of earth. . . . I care more for Lincoln's great toe than for the whole body of the perfect George Washington, of spotless ancestry, who "never told a lie" and never did anything else interesting. . . .

The scars and foibles and contradictions of the Great do not diminish but enhance the worth and meaning of their upward struggle: it was the bloody sweat that proved the human Christ divine; it was his true history and antecedents that proved Abraham Lincoln a Prince of Men.

The Start of Mount Rushmore

On August 24, 1924, the sculptor Gutzon Borglum received a letter that would profoundly influence the rest of his life. It was an invitation by the head of the South Dakota Historical Society to take on a massive carving project in the Black Hills. For the past nine years he had been under contract to create a colossal tribute to the Old Confederacy on the face of Stone Mountain, Georgia. The carving would be the largest ever attempted, depicting a hundred-foot-tall group of Confederate officers on horseback, riding across the granite face of the mountain. The promoters of the Black Hills project envisioned a similar tribute, only to western heroes—Lewis and Clark, Buffalo Bill Cody, Red Cloud, and other Sioux warriors. Borglum, who had once been a member of the Ku Klux Klan, quickly convinced them that such figures were too "local" in scope and that carved figures of George Washington and Abraham Lincoln would create a monument that would draw visitors from all over the world. On a scouting trip he spotted the perfect spires upon which to carve the faces—a massive outcropping of granite 7,242 feet high known as Harney Peak, on Mount Rushmore.

But at home in Georgia Borglum was being blamed for cost overruns and slow progress, and his well-publicized trip to South Dakota didn't help. On February 25 the Stone Mountain Executive Committee fired him, citing "offensive egotism and delusions of grandeur." He was ordered to turn over all his models and drawings, but in a fit of rage Borglum took an ax to his master sculpture, smashing it to pieces with the help of a black carver named Homer. He then tore up his studio records, gathered up his smaller models, and threw them over the edge of Stone Mountain. When a warrant for his arrest was issued, Borglum fled the state. One week later he announced that he had entered into an agreement to carve the faces of Washington and Lincoln onto Mount Rushmore.

Borglum planned to dedicate the rest of his life to Rushmore. Once again he wanted to attempt the colossal. For years he had been attracted to the towering sculptures of history—the Colossus of Rhodes, the giant Buddhas of China, America's own Statue of Liberty. Colossal scale, Borglum believed, hinted at immortality. "There is something in sheer volume that awes and terrifies," he said, and that "lifts us out of ourselves." He told a reporter he would carve the figures of Washington and Lincoln "on a scale more gigantic than that of the Egyptian Sphinx."

At Stone Mountain, Borglum had pioneered new techniques for massive carving, including the use of a new machine that could project a full-size image of his model onto the nine-hundred-foot-tall cliffs, so that at night it could be outlined in white paint. This time he would work with large-scale models, actually hoisted up the mountainside in front of the spot where the carving was to take place, so that measurements and references to it could be regularly made. Below at base camp a large power plant was set up to run the electric drills.

It would take more than fifteen years to finish the project, which would display the heads of Washington, Jefferson, Lincoln, and Theodore Roosevelt. But from early on Borglum knew that Abraham Lincoln would be the centerpiece. "Who can think of him and not think of the Garden of Gethsemane?" he wrote. "The nation of Washington and Jefferson needed Lincoln. Note how carefully, how ably, and how tenderly he filled that need. He is at once the heart and soul of Mt. Rushmore."

Gutzon Borglum's Model
of Mt. Rushmore Memorial-
Washington, Jefferson,
Roosevelt & Lincoln

-RISE STUDIO-
75

By the time Borglum arrived at Mount Rushmore in 1925, he had decided to carve not only Washington and Lincoln on the mountain, as he first envisioned, but also Thomas Jefferson and Theodore Roosevelt. Before starting to carve, he created a large model.

Robert Lincoln's End

On February 18, 1926, Robert Lincoln accompanied his niece Katherine Helm to the White House for the dedication of her new painting of his mother, to hang in the oval chamber beneath the Blue Room. Robert had commissioned the painting, based on an early photograph, and it represented at least a partial reconciliation with the passionate woman who had been his mother. For forty years he had harbored a deep embarrassment of her—burning hundreds of her letters, and inadvertently in the process probably destroying many of his father's letters to her. To a friend he admitted that her "mental disorder," as he always called it, "nearly wore my life out." But as an old man Robert realized how much he owed to both of his parents. In some ways the joke his father had made upon his birth had come to be true: "I was afraid he might have one of my long legs and one of Mary's short ones, and he'd have a terrible time getting through the world."

Robert finally made his peace with being the son of Abraham Lincoln. He did nothing to add to the published memory of his father. "Unlike so many," wrote one newspaper, "he did not write a book, though it was many times suggested to him." And he was careful never to seize the limelight for himself. Recognizing his many public accomplishments, the *Jersey Journal* suggested that he could have gone much farther in life, "but he did not want to spoil the picture." For Robert there was to be only one great man named Lincoln.

By now Robert had relinquished control over his father's papers. He had once planned to leave them to his son Jack, but when he had died that dream was dashed. Years later, still depressed by the death of his son, he told Ida Tarbell he was considering burning them. After his retirement in 1911 Robert had rarely let the papers out of his sight. Each season when he traveled between his Washington residence and his summer mansion in Vermont, he dragged them along with him in their eight trunks. But eventually he had begun to consider a proper long-term home for them, and on May 26, 1919, following months of negotiations, the Lincoln papers finally passed into the keeping of the Library of Congress. Four years later, in 1923, Robert signed a gift of deed, granting the papers to the library, with one prerequisite—that they be sealed from public view for twenty-one years after his death. Finally he was free of the glorious burden.

On May 11, 1926, Robert and Mary left Washington for what turned out to be their final summer together in Vermont. For two and a half months Robert gloried in his beloved Hildene, taking drives in the country; avoiding the prying and erratic press; occasionally picking up a golf club; and climbing up into his domed observatory to gaze into the night sky. "From it I look nightly into a universe," he wrote a friend, "wherein there is . . . only one body which is at once powerful and erratic . . . the Moon." He called Hildene his escape from "political grief"—a place of consolations that came only when he was out of the public eye. When a few years earlier British prime minister Lloyd George had sought him out in Vermont and asked Robert about his memories of the Civil War, he had said, "I saw my father grow older and sadder as the struggle went on."

Robert too had grown older and sadder. But in rare moments he liked to remi-

LINCOLN'S SON DIES IN HIS SLEEP AT 82

Robert, Last Survivor of the Emancipator's Family, Found Lifeless in Vermont Home.

HIS HEALTH HAD BEEN POOR

He Left Father's Papers to the Nation, but Not to Be Examined for 21 Years.

Newspapers reported Robert Lincoln's death and his lifelong preference to remain private. For sixty-one years following the assassination, he had tried to be careful not to do anything that might diminish his father's legacy. He could have become a major political figure, suggested the *Jersey Journal*, "but he did not want to spoil the picture."

nisce about his father, telling one friend how Lincoln had loved to watch marching troops and often called out to ask where they hailed from. "What is that, boys?" he had once asked, unable to hear a group's answer. "It's a regiment, you damned old fool," came the reply of some nearby workmen. "In a fit of laughter, father closed the door," Robert recalled, "turned to me and said, 'Bob, it does a man good sometimes to hear the truth.' A bit later, somewhat sadly, he added, 'And sometimes I think that's just what I am, a damned old fool.'"

On Sunday, July 25, Robert went to bed as usual. His eighty-third birthday was just one week away, and children and grandchildren had already begun to assemble for the celebration. But in the early hours of Monday morning Abraham Lincoln's last surviving son died in his sleep.

To the end he had been haunted by his father's murder, and by the thought that he might have been able to save his life. How could he forget that evening of April 14, 1865—how he had been exhausted after a day of riding when his father came into his bedroom at the White House. "Robert," he had said, "your mother and I . . . are going to the theatre tonight. . . . Won't you come along?"

In contrast to the millions who had mourned Abraham Lincoln, only a handful showed up for the strictly private ceremony for his son. Robert's coffin was placed in a temporary tomb in Manchester, Vermont. Though it was expected he would be buried in Springfield with his parents, brothers, and son, Robert's widow insisted that he be buried in Arlington Cemetery so that at last he could be out of his father's shadow.

Robert at age sixteen, when his father was still alive

Robert, upon his eighty-second birthday

Gallery

1846–1865

The Photographs of
Abraham Lincoln

Lincoln was photographed more than any other President of his era. It was the beginning of a new kind of media scrutiny and use of imagery, and in this regard, as in others, Lincoln can be considered the first modern President. On several occasions he was photographed in the field; late in his presidency he posed for candid portraits in his office; and in March 1865, in the final photograph of his life, he stood outside for two pictures on the White House balcony.

In the generation after his death, the presidential and pre-presidential photographs of Lincoln became widely scattered and in many cases were either forgotten or purposely sequestered. The first attempt to collect them began in the 1890s when *McClure's* magazine published nearly fifty images. Then in 1911 Frederick Hill Meserve published his groundbreaking work *The Photographs of Abraham Lincoln.* Including dozens of new discoveries, Meserve presented one hundred photographs, each with its own Meserve number. Over the next fifty years this was the scholarly standard, and Meserve continued to add newly discovered images and make revisions until the end of his life. In 1941 the journalist Stefan Lorant brought out *Lincoln: His Life in Photos.* Lorant's numbering system essentially followed Meserve's but omitted images he correctly considered variants.

In the year of Meserve's death, 1963, his friend and longtime student Lloyd Ostendorf, along with coauthor Charles Hamilton, published his own Lincoln numbering system, which he revised over the next thirty-five years. But as the Abraham Lincoln Bicentennial approached, it became clear that a new system was overdue—one that combined the scholarship of all the earlier Lincoln chroniclers and corrected many errors. Research for this new numbering system was started by Meserve's grandson, Philip B. Kunhardt, Jr., who worked on it up until his death in 2006. He and his mother, Dorothy Meserve Kunhardt, had spent much of the twentieth century studying Lincoln's face, and the authors have built upon their work. This list was also developed with the assistance of four leading scholars in the field—James Barber of the National Portrait Gallery; Tom Schwartz of the Abraham Lincoln Presidential Library and Museum; Harold Holzer, cochair of the Abraham Lincoln Bicentennial Commission; and Dan Weinberg, owner of the Abraham Lincoln Book Shop in Chicago.

The system was designed to be flexible, in case new images of Lincoln are discovered in the future. Each number begins with "AL"—for Abraham Lincoln. It includes the year of the photograph, the number of the sitting that year, and whether other images were taken at the same time. (Thus viewers will be able to see clearly which photographs emerged from a single sitting, for example those later used as models for the Lincoln penny and the five-dollar bill.) The list includes, where known, the name of each photographer, the location where each image was taken, and the date, or estimated date, of each photo session. Finally, the descriptions include the original Meserve (M), Lorant (L), and Ostendorf (O) numbers to facilitate cross-referencing with the earlier numbering efforts.

Dorothy Meserve Kunhardt and Philip B. Kunhardt, Jr., review spread designs for their 1965 book, *Twenty Days.* They were the daughter and grandson of Frederick Hill Meserve (opposite), who was born in the year that Lincoln died and spent a lifetime collecting and studying the photographs of Abraham Lincoln.

461

AL.c1846.1
photograph by Nicholas H. Shepherd
Springfield, Illinois
probably 1846
(M-1, O-1, L-1)

AL.1854.1
photograph by J. C. F. Polycarpus Von Schneidau
Chicago, Illinois
probably October 27, 1854
(M-3, O-6, L-5)

AL.1857.1
photograph by Alexander Hesler
Chicago, Illinois
February 28, 1857
(M-6, O-2, L-2)

AL.1857.2
photograph by Amon J. T. Joslin
Danville, Illinois
possibly May 27, 1857
(M-2, O-3, L-10)

AL.1858.1
photograph by Samuel G. Alschuler
Urbana, Illinois
April 25, 1858
(M-5, O-4, L-3)

AL.1858.2
photograph by Abraham B. Byers
Beardstown, Illinois
May 7, 1858
(M-7, O-5, L-4)

AL.1858.3
photograph by Preston Butler
Springfield, Illinois
circa July 18, 1858
(M-17, O-7, L-9)

AL.1858.4
photograph by T. P. Pearson
Macomb, Illinois
August 26, 1858
(M-10, O-8, L-6)

AL.c1858.5
photograph probably by Christopher S. German
Springfield, Illinois
possibly September 26, 1858
(M-9, O-9, L-24)

AL.1858.6
photograph by Calvin Jackson
Pittsfield, Illinois
October 1, 1858
(M-12, O-10, L-7)

AL.1858.7
photograph by William Judkins Thomson
Monmouth, Illinois
October 11, 1858
(M-13, O-11, L-8)

AL.c1858.8
unknown photographer
probably Illinois
circa 1858

AL.c1858.9
photograph possibly by Roderick M. Cole, or Preston Butler
possibly Peoria, Illinois, or Springfield, Illinois
circa 1858
(M-14, O-14, L-13)

AL.c1859.1
unknown photographer
probably Ohio
circa 1859
(M-117, O-13, L-11)

AL.c1859.2
unknown photographer
probably Springfield, Illinois
circa 1859
(M-32, O-15, L-26)

AL.1859.3
photograph by Samuel M. Fassett
Chicago, Illinois
October 4, 1859
(M-8, O-16, L-12)

AL.1860.1
photograph by Mathew B. Brady
New York City
February 27, 1860
(M-20, O-17, L-14)

AL.1860.2
photograph by Edward A. Barnwell
Decatur, Illinois
May 9, 1860
(M-122, O-19, L-16)

AL.1860.3A
photograph probably by Preston Butler
Springfield, Illinois
May 20, 1860
(M-22, O-20, L-19)

AL.1860.3B
photograph probably by Preston Butler
Springfield, Illinois
May 20, 1860
(M-21, O-21, L18)

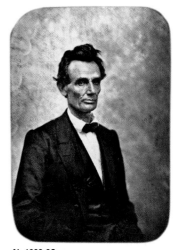

AL.1860.3C
photograph probably by Preston Butler
Springfield, Illinois
May 20, 1860
(M-109, O-22, L-17)

AL.1860.3D
photograph probably by Preston Butler
Springfield, Illinois
May 20, 1860
(O-23)

AL.1860.4
unknown photographer
Springfield, Illinois
circa May 1860
(M-124, O-24)

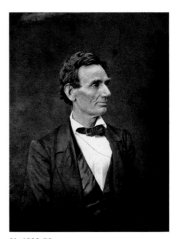

AL.1860.5A
photograph by Alexander Hesler
Springfield, Illinois
June 3, 1860
(M-26, O-26, L-20)

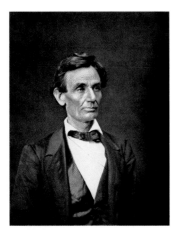

AL.1860.5B
photograph by Alexander Hesler
Springfield, Illinois
June 3, 1860
(M-25, O-27, L-21)

AL.1860.5C
photograph by Alexander Hesler
Springfield, Illinois
June 3, 1860
(M-28, O-28, L-22)

AL.1860.5D
photograph by Alexander Hesler
Springfield, Illinois
June 3, 1860
(M-27, O-29, L-23)

AL.1860.6
photograph by Joseph Hill
Springfield, Illinois
circa June/July 1860
(M-102, O-25, L-25)

AL.1860.7
unknown photographer
possibly Springfield, or Chicago, Illinois
circa spring or summer 1860
(M-110, O-18, L-30)

AL.1860.8
photograph by William Seavy
Springfield, Illinois
circa spring or summer 1860
(M-112, O-30, L-32)

AL.1860.9
unknown photographer
probably Springfield, Illinois
circa spring or summer 1860
(M-111, O-31, L-34)

AL.1860.10
unknown photographer
probably Springfield, Illinois
circa spring or summer 1860
(M-31, O-32, L-28)

AL.1860.11
photograph by William A. Shaw
probably Springfield, Illinois
circa spring or summer 1860
(M-113, O-33, L-29)

AL.1860.12
unknown photographer
probably Springfield, Illinois
circa spring or summer 1860
(M-120, O-35, L-31)

AL.1860.13A
photograph by John Adams Whipple
Springfield, Illinois
summer 1860
(M-23, O-38, L-88)

AL.1860.13B
photograph by John Adams Whipple
Springfield, Illinois
summer 1860
(M-24, O-39, L-89)

465

AL.1860.14
photograph by William A. Shaw
Springfield, Illinois
August 8, 1860
(M-16, O-34, L-87)

AL.1860.15A
photograph by Preston Butler
Springfield, Illinois
August 13, 1860
(M-29, O-36, L-33)

AL.1860.15B
photograph by Preston Butler
Springfield, Illinois
August 13, 1860
(M-30, O-37)

AL.1860.16
photograph by Samuel G. Alschuler
Chicago, Illinois
November 25, 1860
(M-33, O-40, L-35)

AL.1861.1
photograph by Christopher S. German
Springfield, Illinois
probably January 13, 1861
(M-34, O-41, L-36)

AL.1861.2A
photograph by Christopher S. German
Springfield, Illinois
February 9, 1861
(M-35, O-43, L-37)

AL.1861.2B
photograph by Christopher S. German
Springfield, Illinois
February 9, 1861
(M-36, O-44, O-45, L-38)

AL.1861.3A
photograph by Frederick DeBourg Richards
Philadelphia, Pennsylvania
February 22, 1861
(M-103, O-47, L-90)

AL.1861.3B
photograph by Frederick DeBourg Richards
Philadelphia, Pennsylvania
February 22, 1861
(M-37, O-48, L-91)

AL.1861.4A
photograph by Alexander Gardner
Washington, D.C.
probably February 24, 1861
(M-71, O-49, L-40)

AL.1861.4B
photograph by Alexander Gardner
Washington, D.C.
probably February 24, 1861
(M-68, M-118, O-50, L-41)

AL.1861.4C
photograph by Alexander Gardner
Washington, D.C.
probably February 24, 1861
(M-72, O-51, L-42)

AL.1861.4D
photograph by Alexander Gardner
Washington, D.C.
probably February 24, 1861
(M-69, O-52, L-39)

AL.1861.4E
photograph by Alexander Gardner
Washington, D.C.
probably February 24, 1861
(M-70, O-53, L-43)

AL.1861.5
unknown photographer
Washington, D.C.
March 4, 1861
(O-54)

AL.1861.6A
photograph possibly by C. D. Fredericks,
James E. McClee, or W. L. German
Washington, D.C.
circa spring 1861
(O-120, L-44)

AL.1861.6B
photograph possibly by C. D. Fredericks,
James E. McClee, or W. L. German
Washington, D.C.
circa spring 1861
(M-42 O-55)

AL.1861.7A
photograph by unknown operator for
Mathew B. Brady
Washington, D.C.
May 16, 1861
(M-66, O-57, L-46)

AL.1861.7B
photograph by unknown operator for
Mathew B. Brady
Washington, D.C.
May 16, 1861
(M-65, O-58, L-49)

AL.1861.7C
photograph by unknown operator for
Mathew B. Brady
Washington, D.C.
May 16, 1861
(M-67, O-59, L-48)

AL.1861.7D
photograph by unknown operator for
Mathew B. Brady
Washington, D.C.
May 16, 1861
(M-64, O-60, L-47)

AL.1861.7E
photograph by unknown operator for
Mathew B. Brady
Washington, D.C.
May 16, 1861
(M-62, M-63, O-61, L-50)

AL.1861.7F
photograph by unknown operator for
Mathew B. Brady
Washington, D.C.
probably May 16, 1861
(M-38, O-69, L-45)

AL.1861.8
photograph possibly by Edward Bierstadt
Washington, D.C.
circa September 1861
(O-56)

AL.1862.1A
photograph by Alexander Gardner
Antietam, Maryland
October 3, 1862
(M-44, O-62, L-92)

AL.1862.1B
photograph by Alexander Gardner
Antietam, Maryland
October 3, 1862
(M-46, O-63, L-95)

AL.1862.1C
photograph by Alexander Gardner
Antietam, Maryland
October 3, 1862
(M-45, O-64, L-94)

AL.1862.1D
photograph by Alexander Gardner
Antietam, Maryland
October 3, 1862
(M-47, O-65, L-93)

AL.1862.1E
photograph by Alexander Gardner
Antietam, Maryland
October 3, 1862
(M-43, O-66, L-96)

AL.1862.1F
photograph by Alexander Gardner
Antietam, Maryland
October 3, 1862
(M-104, O-67, L-97)

AL.1863.1A
photograph by Alexander Gardner
Washington, D.C.
August 9, 1863
(M-53, O-70, L-55)

AL.1863.1B
photograph by Alexander Gardner
Washington, D.C.
August 9, 1863
(M-51, M-52, M-114, O-71, L-58)

AL.1863.1C
photograph by Alexander Gardner
Washington, D.C.
August 9, 1863
(M-54, O-72, L-57)

AL.1863.1D
photograph by Alexander Gardner
Washington, D.C.
August 9, 1863
(M-49, M-50, O-73, L-56)

AL.1863.1E
photograph by Alexander Gardner
Washington, D.C.
August 9, 1863
(M-55, O-74, L-60)

469

AL.1863.1F
photograph by Alexander Gardner
Washington, D.C.
August 9, 1863
(M-105, O-75, L-59)

AL.1863.1G
photograph by Alexander Gardner
Washington, D.C.
August 9, 1863
(O-121)

AL.1863.2A
photograph by Alexander Gardner
Washington, D.C.
November 8, 1863
(M-56, O-76, L-61)

AL.1863.2B
photograph by Alexander Gardner
Washington, D.C.
November 8, 1863
(M-59, O-77, L-65)

AL.1863.2C
photograph by Alexander Gardner
Washington, D.C.
November 8, 1863
(M-57, M-60, O-78, L-62)

AL.1863.2D
photograph by Alexander Gardner
Washington, D.C.
November 8, 1863
(M-58, O-79, L-63)

AL.1863.2E
photograph by Alexander Gardner
Washington, D.C.
November 8, 1863
(M-61, O-80, L-64)

AL.1863.3
photograph possibly by David Bachrach
Gettysburg, Pennsylvania
November 19, 1863
(M-129, O-81)

AL.c1863.4
photograph by Lewis Emory Walker
Washington, D.C.
circa 1863
(M-88, O-82, L-76)

AL.1864.1A
photograph by Mathew B. Brady
Washington, D.C.
January 8, 1864
(M-73, M-74, O-83, L-51)

AL.1864.1B
photograph by Mathew B. Brady
Washington, D.C.
January 8, 1864
(M-75, M-107, M-115, O-84, L-52)

AL.1864.1C
photograph by Mathew B. Brady
Washington, D.C.
January 8, 1864
(M-78, O-85, L-58)

AL.1864.1D
photograph by Mathew B. Brady
Washington, D.C.
January 8, 1864
(M-76, O-86, L-53)

AL.1864.1E
photograph by Mathew B. Brady
Washington, D.C.
January 8, 1864
(M-77, O-87, L-54)

AL.1864.2A
photograph by Anthony Berger
Washington, D.C.
February 9, 1864
(M-81, M-82, M-83, O-88, L-66)

AL.1864.2B
photograph by Anthony Berger
Washington, D.C.
February 9, 1864
(M-86, O-90, L-67)

AL.1864.2C
photograph by Anthony Berger
Washington, D.C.
February 9, 1864
(M-87, M-108, O-91, L-69)

AL.1864.2D
photograph by Anthony Berger
Washington, D.C.
February 9, 1864
(M-85, O-92, L-68)

AL.1864.2E
photograph by Anthony Berger
Washington, D.C.
February 9, 1864
(M-127, O-93 variant, L-71)

AL.1864.2F
photograph by Anthony Berger
Washington, D.C.
February 9, 1864
(M-119, O-94, L-70)

AL.c1864.3A
photograph by unknown operator
for Wenderoth & Taylor
Washington, D.C.
circa 1864
(M-79, O-95)

AL.c1864.3B
photograph by unknown operator for
Wenderoth & Taylor
Washington, D.C.
circa 1864
(M-80, O-96, L-78)

AL.1864.4A
photograph by Anthony Berger
Washington, D.C.
April 20, 1864
(M-121, O-97, L-72)

AL.1864.4B
photograph by Anthony Berger
Washington, D.C.
April 20, 1864
(O-98)

AL.1864.4C
photograph by Anthony Berger
Washington, D.C.
April 20, 1864
(M-4C, M-133, O-99, L-73)

AL.1864.5A
photograph by Anthony Berger
Washington, D.C.
April 26, 1864
(M-106, O-100, L-74)

AL.1864.5B
photograph by Anthony Berger
Washington, D.C.
April 26, 1864
(M-128, O-101)

AL.1864.5C
photograph by Anthony Berger
Washington, D.C.
April 26, 1864
(M-116, O-102, L-75)

AL.1865.1A
photograph by Alexander Gardner
Washington, D.C.
February 5, 1865
(M-95, O-114, L-82)

AL.1865.1B
photograph by Alexander Gardner
Washington, D.C.
February 5, 1865
(M-99, O-115, L-83)

AL.1865.1C
photograph by Alexander Gardner
Washington, D.C.
February 5, 1865
(M-97, O-116, L-84)

AL.1865.1D
photograph by Alexander Gardner
Washington, D.C.
February 5, 1865
(M-98, O-117, L-85)

AL.1865.1E
photograph by Alexander Gardner
Washington, D.C.
February 5, 1865
(M-100, O-118, L-86)

AL.c1865.2A
photograph by Lewis Emory Walker
Washington, D.C.
circa February 1865
(M-92, O-103, L-80)

AL.c1865.2B
photograph by Lewis Emory Walker
Washington, D.C.
circa February 1865
(M-91, O-104, L-79)

AL.1865.3A
photograph by Alexander Gardner
Washington, D.C.
March 4, 1865
(M-89, O-106, L-99)

AL.1865.3B
photograph by Alexander Gardner
Washington, D.C.
March 4, 1865
(O-122)

473

AL.1865.3C
photograph by Alexander Gardner
Washington, D.C.
March 4, 1865
(M-90, O-108)

AL.1865.3D
photograph by Alexander Gardner
Washington, D.C.
March 4, 1865
(O-109)

AL.1865.4
photograph by William Morris Smith
Washington, D.C.
March 4, 1865
(O-107)

AL.1865.5A
photograph by Henry F. Warren
Washington, D.C.
March 6, 1865
(M-93, O-112, L-81)

AL.1865.5B
photograph by Henry F. Warren
Washington, D.C.
March 6, 1865
(O-113)

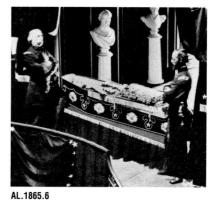

AL.1865.6
photograph by Jeremiah Gurney, Jr.
New York City
April 24, 1865
(M-130, O-119, L-100)

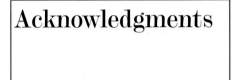

Acknowledgments

The authors would like to thank the many people who have helped make this book possible. It was Esther Newberg who first saw the potential in our idea and reunited us with the publisher of our 1992 volume, *Lincoln*. We thank her for that. At Knopf, Sonny Mehta and Ashbel Green gave us tremendous support, editorial encouragement, and guidance. We also thank Andy Hughes for making every page look so beautiful, and Katherine Hourigan, Sara Sherbill, Lydia Buechler, and all those who have helped us at this extraordinary publishing house. Lisa Montebello, Patricia Johnson, Kim Thornton, Paul Bogaards, Nicholas Latimer, Anne-Lise Spitzer, Christine Gillespie, and James Kimball all had an important hand in the publishing of this book, as did their very hands-on president, Tony Chirico. Janet Biehl was a superb copy editor. Andrew Miller added his support. And the legendary Chip Kidd was the designer of the book's jacket, making the wonderful decision to use Lincoln's hat.

With over 900 illustrations and 180 sidebars, this book was a complicated one to design and we would like to thank our incredible art director, Elton Robinson. This was our third major project working together and, as usual, he was a delight to collaborate with.

We thank the Abraham Lincoln Bicentennial Commission, especially Eileen MacKevich and Harold Holzer. Harold became one of six outstanding scholars to read our complete manuscript and to comment on it in detail, giving us helpful criticism and steady encouragement. Tom Schwartz, Director of the Abraham Lincoln Library in Springfield, Illinois, generously shared his broad knowledge on the subject. Merrill Peterson, a legend in the field of American history and author of *Lincoln in American Memory*, was a vital resource for our effort. So was Barry Schwartz, a sociologist who specializes in the role of memory in the making of historical reputations, who freely gave of his immense knowledge and expertise. And Douglas Wilson, one of the reigning Lincoln authorities, read our book with a penetrating eye. In addition to these, other historians have given help over the course of the project, including Gabor Borritt, Allen Guelzo, David Blight, Jean Harvey Baker, David Hackett Fischer, James McPherson, Wayne Temple, Sidney Milkis, Ron Walters, Joshua

Wolf Shenk, Karal Ann Marling, Harry Jaffa, and Charles Kessler. It was a special pleasure to work with each of them. In addition, four scholars helped us with a new numbering system for the Lincoln photographs—Dan Weinberg, James Barber, Tom Schwartz, and Harold Holzer. To all these we offer our sincere gratitude.

We thank Jill Cowan, our chief picture researcher and longtime associate, whose work has uncovered many unexpected visual treasures as well as fascinating historical information. Over the course of the work Jill received the help of numerous archives, detailed in the Picture Credits. In particular we thank those curators, archivists, and private collectors who got excited about the project and helped us gain access to rare photographs. They include Jennifer Ericson and Roberta Fairburn of the Abraham Lincoln Presidential Library; Gloria Swift of the Ford's Theatre National Historic Site; Curtiss Mann of the Springfield Public Library, and Springfield's City Historian; Jan Grenci of the Library of Congress; Timothy Townsend of the Lincoln Home National Historic Site; Peter Wisbey of Seward House; Cathy Ingram of the Frederick Douglass National Historic Site; Robin Borglum Carter; and Roger Shaffer. We also thank Jill's niece Sarah Cowan, who assisted in important ways during the summer of 2007; and Justin Carretta, Nathaniel Mattison, Samantha Anderson, Jessica Orban, and Emily McCabe, who served as assistants and interns at various points in the process. And we thank Jessie Kunhardt, daughter of one of the authors, who has worked on the project over a series of college vacations and has become yet another family member to become fascinated with Abraham Lincoln. We thank the historian Hampton Carey, who helped organize our in-house library, which became one of the authors' principal research tools. Hampton's thoughtful involvement in an early stage of the project was most appreciated. We also want to thank our longtime colleague Dyllan McGee for her constant help and support. And in addition we offer gratitude to a number of other colleagues who have aided the project in a variety of important ways: Mary Farley, Mike Maron, Amy Rockefeller, Diana Revson, Nancy Steiner, Kathryn Gravdal, Nancy Bond, and Lisa Gerety. Thank you all for your enthusiasm and support.

Over the course of the project we reached out to numerous persons in the field, and made a memorable visit to Springfield in 2006. We would especially like to thank Tim Townsend and Susan Haake of the Abraham Lincoln Home; Dan Stowell, Director of the Abraham Lincoln Papers Project; Daniel Hendrick of New Salem Village; and Wayne Temple of the Illinois State Archives. In addition we express gratitude to Richard Norton Smith, former President of the Abraham

Lincoln Presidential Library and Museum, who from early on has been a friend of this project. And we thank Nicky Stratton and Bryon Andreason, of the Illinois State Tourism Program, who generously allowed us to use their slogan "Looking for Lincoln" as the title for this book.

We thank our incredible support team at Gelfand, Rennert, and Feldman, including Mario Testani, Todd Kamelhar, Stanley Lim, and Brian Dentel, all of whom worked behind the scenes. And we thank Robert Gold, who has helped guide us from the start.

The board members of the Meserve-Kunhardt Foundation have encouraged us to work on this book, and we thank Curt Viebranz, Nina Freedman, Laura Brown, Gene Young, and Dan Tishman for all their support.

We especially want to thank David Herbert Donald, widely acknowledged as the greatest living Lincoln scholar. David not only gave us detailed comments on our book, he also went on to write its Foreword. To him we are immensely grateful. Doris Kearns Goodwin, whose 2006 work, *Team of Rivals*, is one of the finest Lincoln books ever written, wrote our Introduction. Doris not only was an early adviser to the project, she also serves in a key role in the companion PBS series, along with Henry Louis Gates, Jr., whose involvement in the project has been invigorating. Skip has worked with Kunhardt Productions on a series of important films, and we are grateful for everything that he brought to our documentary search for Lincoln.

PBS and CPB realized the potential of a Lincoln project for 2009 and gave us the support that allowed us to move forward on the documentary film, to which this book is the companion volume. We thank them and our partners at Thirteen/WNET for helping us to bring the project to fruition, especially Neal Shapiro, Tammy Robinson, Bill Grant, and Ron Thorpe. Sabin Streeter and Graham Judd did much early work on the series. And we thank Barak Goodman, Muriel Soenens, and John Maggio and their production team for all of their hard work.

Finally we would like to recognize our families, without whom none of this would have been possible. We especially thank Margie and Suzy Kunhardt for their undying support and love, as well as members of the next generation, Jessie, Philip, Harry, Clinton, Abby, Teddy, and George. In addition we would like to thank the siblings of two of the authors who share our interest in the sixteenth President: Jean Kunhardt Herschkowitz, Sandra K. Basile, Sarah Horton, and Michael Kunhardt, and their wonderful families. Most of all we thank Katharine Kunhardt, mother to two of the authors, grandmother of the third. In the end this was a family effort.

Source Notes

Sprinkled throughout this book are 180 boxed selections from primary sources—letters, diary entries, books, and newspaper articles—that shed light on the unfolding of the Lincoln of memory. What follows is a list of where those selections come from. Hundreds of other sources underlie the text of this book. The principal published ones appear in the Select Bibliography.

PART ONE

Page 11

A.M.S. Crawford, Harry Hawk, and James P. Ferguson, in Tanner Papers, Union League Club, Philadelphia

Page 12

Charles A. Leale, letter, July 20, 1867, National Archives; William T. Kent, Affidavit, April 15, 1865, National Archives; Edwin M. Stanton, in *New York Times*, April 15, 1865

Page 16

Maunsell B. Field, in *New York Times*, April 17, 1865

Page 21

Edward Curtis, M.D., letter, quoted online at www.nlm.nih.gov/visibleproofs/galleries/cases/lincoln.html; Anson Henry, letter, April 19, 1865, Abraham Lincoln Presidential Library

Page 23

Buffalo, N.Y. Announcement, April 15, 1865, quoted in *In Memoriam: Abraham Lincoln Assassinated*, pp. 7-8

Page 25

Rev. C. B. Crane, *Sermon on the Occasion of the Death of President Lincoln*, April 16, 1865, pamphlet online at http://beck.library.emory.edu/lincoln/sermon.php?id-crane.001

Page 26

John Wilkes Booth, letter, c.1864, quoted in *Forney's War Press*, April 22, 1865

Page 28

Parke Godwin, address, April 18, 1865, quoted in *In Memoriam: Abraham Lincoln Commemorative Proceedings of the Athenaeum Club*, pp. 17-18

Page 31

"The Mourning of the Slaves," The *New York Times*, April 19, 1865

Page 33

Galveston News, April 28, 1865; Caroline S. Jones, Letter, April 15, 1865, quoted in Carolyn L. Harrell, *When the Bells Tolled for Lincoln*, p. 69

Page 39

John Carroll Power, *Abraham Lincoln: His Life, Public Services, Death, and Great Funeral Cortege*, p. 132

Page 42

Henry Ward Beecher, in John Gilmary Shea, *Lincoln Memorial*, pp.101ff.

Page 44

George Alfred Townsend, in *New York World*, April 28, 1865; also in Townsend, *The Life, Crime and Capture of John Wilkes Booth*

Page 46

George Alfred Townsend, The *New York World*, April 28, 1865; also printed in George Alfred Townsend, *The Life, Crime and Capture of John Wilkes Booth*

Page 49

Noah Brooks, in *Sacramento Daily Union*, May 17, 1865

Page 52

Henry Bromwell, letter, April 30, 1865, Bromwell Papers, Library of Congress; also in Harry E. Pratt, *Concerning Mr. Lincoln*, p. 129

Page 56

Presidential Proclamation, April 14, 1865, in James D. Richardson, *Compilation of Messages and Papers of the Presidents, p.* 8:350

Page 65

Silas T. Cobb, May 16, 1865, in Benn Pitman, *The Assassination of President Lincoln and the Trial of the Conspirators*, p. 84

Page 66

Noah Brooks, in *Sacramento Daily Union*, May 22, 1865

Page 68

Noah Brooks, in *Sacramento Daily Union*, May 23, 1865

Page 70

Mary Lincoln, letter, June 10, 1865, in Justin G. Turner and Linda L. Turner, *Mary Todd Lincoln: Her Life and Letters*, p. 243

Page 74

William Howard Day, July 4, 1865, and Frederick Douglass, July 1, 1865, in *Celebration by the Colored People's Educational Monument Association in Memory of Abraham Lincoln*, pp. 5, 10

Page 76

George Alfred Townsend, iin *New York World*, July 7, 1865; also in Townsend, *The Life, Crime and Capture of John Wilkes Booth*

PART TWO

Page 84

David Davis, address, *Indianapolis Daily State Sentinel*, May 20, 1865, quoted in Rufus Rockwell Wilson, *Intimate Memories of Lincoln*, pp. 68f.; Francis B. Carpenter, in *Chicago Tribune*, April 28, 1865; Thomas Drummond, in *New York Times*, April 30, 1865

Page 85

Charles G. Halpine, in *Chicago Tribune*, May 31, 1865

Page 86

Henry Champion Deming, *Eulogy of Abraham Lincoln*, pp. 40-41; Noah Brooks, in *Harper's Monthly*, July, 1865

Page 89

Mary Lincoln, letter, August 5, 1865, photostat, in authors' collection

Page 91

Dennis Hanks, interview by Herndon, June 13, 1865, in Douglas Wilson and Rodney Davis, *Herndon's Informants*, p. 35

Page 95

Joseph C. Richardson, interview by Herndon, September 14, 1865(?), in Wilson and Davis, *Herndon's Informants,* p. 119; David Turnham, interview by Herndon, September 15, 1865, ibid., p.120; John Romine, interview by Herndon, September 14, 1865, ibid., p. 116

Page 96

James Gourley, interview by Herndon, February 9, 1866(?), in Wilson and Davis, *Herndon's Informants*, p. 451

Page 98

Frances Todd Wallace, interview by Herndon, 1865-66, in Wilson and Davis, *Herndon's Informants,* p. 485; John B. Weber, interview by Herndon, c. November 1, 1866, ibid., p. 388; Henry Enoch Dummer, interview by Herndon, c.1865-66, ibid., p. 442

Page 101

Josiah Holland, *The Life of Abraham Lincoln*, pp. 61, 235, 435, 542

Page 103

Frederick Douglass, manuscript, December 1865, Library of Congress (online at at http://memory.loc.gov/mss/mfd/22/22015/0001d.gif)

Page 106

George Bancroft, *Memorial Address: Life and Character of Abraham Lincoln*

Page 107

David Davis, letter to Herndon, February 22, 1866, in Wilson and Davis, *Herndon's Informants*, p. 218

Page 109

Frederick Douglass, in *Chicago Tribune*, March 1, 1866

Page 110

Benjamin French, *Witness to the Young Republic*, p. 507

Page 112

Lincoln, letter to Mary Owens Vineyard, Letter from A. Lincoln, in *Collected Works*, p. I:45; Elizabeth Todd Edwards, interview by Herndon, 1865-66, in Wilson and Davis, *Herndon's Informants*, p. 443

Page 114

Isaac Arnold, *The History of Abraham Lincoln and the Overthrow of Slavery,* p. 304.

Page 115

Francis B. Carpenter, *Six Months at the White House with Abraham Lincoln*, p. 149

Page 117

William O. Stoddard, in *New York Citizen*, August 25, 1866; Stoddard, *Inside the White House in War Times*, p. 163

Page 118

Chicago Tribune, September 9, 1866

Page 119

Isaac N. Arnold, letter, in *Chicago Tribune*, October 2, 1866

Page 121

David Davis, interview by Herndon, September 20, 1866, in Wilson and Davis, *Herndon's Informants*, p. 348; Joshua F. Speed, letter to Herndon, December 6, 1866, ibid., p. 499; John S. Bliss, letter to Herndon, January 29, 1867, ibid., p. 551

Page 123

John Wilkes Booth, quoted in George S. Bryan, *The Great American Myth*, p. 302

Page 126

William Herndon, "Analysis of the Character of Abraham Lincoln," I,(1940-41); pp. 343-83; (original manuscript in Henry E. Huntington Library)

Page 127

William Herndon, *Abraham Lincoln, Ann Rutledge, New Salem, Pioneering, the Poem*, p. 55ff.; Mary Lincoln, letter, March 4, 1867, in Turner and Turner, *Mary Todd Lincoln: Her Life and Letters*, p. 414

Page 131

Elizabeth Keckley, *Behind the Scenes*, pp. 188ff., 102ff., 120ff.

Page 132

William Florville, letter, December 27, 1863, Abraham Lincoln Papers, Library of Congress

Page 135

Statements by Charles Sumner, Garrett Davis, Joseph Fowler, in *Trial of Andrew Johnson*, pp. 917, 958, 980,1082

Page 141

Abraham Lincoln, letter, April 30, 1864 *Collected Works*, Vol. 7:324; Ulysses S. Grant, letter, May 1, 1864, Abraham Lincoln Papers, Library of Congress, quoted in *Collected Works*, Vol. 7: 324f.

Page 149

Lawrence Gobright, *Recollections of Men and Things at Washington*, p. 328

Page 154

Sarah Orne, letter, September 12, 1869, Houghton Library, Harvard University

Page 155

Mary Lincoln, letter, November 7, 1870, Chicago Historical Society

Page 156

Robert E. Lee, letter, February 25, 1868, in *Recollections and Letters of General Robert E. Lee*, p. 27

Page 161

John Hay, in *New York Tribune*, July 17, 1871

Page 165

Abraham Lincoln, letter, December 20, 1859, in *Collected Works*, p. 3:511ff.

Page 168

Ward H. Lamon, *The Life of Abraham Lincoln*, p. iii.

Page 169

Robert Lincoln, letter, December 4, 1872, in Thomas F. Schwartz, "I never had any doubt of your good intentions," *Journal of Abraham Lincoln Association* 14, no. 1, Winter, 1993

Page 171

Abraham Lincoln, letter, January 12, 1851, in *Collected Works*, p. 2:97

Page 174

Gideon Welles, in *Galaxy* 16 no. 6 (December 1873), p. 804

Page 177

Salmon P. Chase, diary entry, September 22, 1862, in Chase *Inside Lincoln's Cabinet*, p. 149f.

Page 178

James M. Winchell, in *Galaxy,* 16, no. 1 (July 1873), pp. 34, 40

Page 180

Noyes W. Miner, in *Quincy Whig*, March 16, 1872, also in *New York Times*, March 23, 1872

Page 183

August Laugel, in *Boston Daily Globe*, August 19, 1874

Page 186

Ulysses S. Grant, address, October 15, 1874, in John Carroll Power, *Abraham Lincoln: His Life, Public Services, Death, and Great Funeral Cortege*, pp. 334-35

Page 190

William T. Sherman, *Memoirs of General William T. Sherman*, p. 291f.

Page 196

John T. Stuart, interview by Nicolay, June 23, 1875, in Michael Burlingame, ed. *An Oral History of Abraham Lincoln*, p. 77; Jesse K. Dubois, interview by Nicolay, July 4, 1875, ibid., pp. 29f.; Stephen Trigg Logan, interview by Nicolay, July 6, 1875, ibid., pp. 34f.

Page 197

Peter Van Bergen, interview by Nicolay, July 7, 1875, in Burlingame, *Oral History*, p. 33; Joseph Holt, interview by Nicolay, October 29, 1875, ibid., pp. 68f.; Norman B. Judd, interview by Nicolay, February 28, 1876, ibid., p. 44f.

Page 203

Frederick Douglass, in *New York Times*, April 22, 1876

Part Three
Page 211

John Carroll Power, *History of an Attempt to Steal the Body of Abraham Lincoln*, pp. 51f.

Page 215

Albert Rhodes, in *St. Nicholas Magazine*. 4 (November, 1876), p. 9

Page 219

James Garfield, in *New York Times*, September 28, 1881; Alexander Stephens, in *Daily Atlanta Constitution*, February 13, 1878

Page 223

Frederick Douglass, in *New York Times*, May 31, 1878

Page 224

Grace Bedell Billings, letter, October 2, 1878, in Power, *Abraham Lincoln: His Life,* p. 393

Page 225

Grace Bedell, letter, October 15, 1860, in *Lincoln, Collected Works*, p. 4:130; Abraham Lincoln, letter, October 19, 1860, in *Collected Works*, Vol. p. 4:129

Page 226-27

J. B. McClure, *Anecdotes of Abraham Lincoln*, pp. 24, 43, 50, 92, 100, 129, 162

Page 228

Ward Hill Lamon and Murat Halstead, in *Chicago Daily Tribune*, November 14, 1879

Page 231

Joshua Fry Speed, *Reminiscences of Abraham Lincoln and Notes on a Visit to California*, pp. 21f.

Page 240

Leonard Volk, in *Century,* December 1881, pp. 223ff.

Page 245

Adeline Judd, in Osborne Oldroyd, *The Lincoln Memorial, Album-Immortelles*, pp. 520f.; Jane Grey Swisshelm, ibid, pp. 413f.; Alexander H. Stephens, ibid, pp. 241f.

Page 247

James S. Rollins, in e Oldroyd, *Lincoln Memorial: Album*, pp. 491f.

Page 248

Alexander Starbuck, "The Portraits of Lincoln," in *Century* 24 (October 1882), p. 853

Page 251

Abraham Lincoln, letter, August 18, 1863, quoted in D. Mark Katz, *Witness to an Era,* p. 120

Page 258

Robert Todd Lincoln, letter, January 5, 1885, quoted in Burlingame, *Oral History of Lincoln*, pp. 88f.

Page 260

Isaac Newton Arnold, *Life of Abraham Lincoln*, 1901 ed., p. 453f.

Page 261

Charles Chiniquy, *Fifty Years in the Church of Rome*, chapt. 60

Page 265

Ulysses S. Grant, *Personal Memoirs*

Page 267

George B. McClellan, *McClellan's Own Story*, pp. 195f.

Page 269

William Herndon, Letters, October 21, 1885, November 19, 1885, February 18, 1887, in Emanuel Hertz *The Hidden Lincoln*, pp. 95, 104f, 177

Page 271

David R. Locke, in Allen Thorndike Rice, ed., *Reminiscences of Abraham Lincoln*, pp. 440f.; James B. Fry, ibid., pp. 402f.; John B. Alley, ibid., pp. 589f.

Page 272

Donn Piatt, in Rice, *Reminiscences of Lincoln*, pp. 479f.; Absalom Markland, ibid., pp. 325f.; Charles A. Dana, ibid., pp. 375f.

Page 273

Frederick Douglass, in Rice, *Reminiscences of Lincoln*, pp. 191f.

Page 274

Page Eaton, in Fracis F. Brown, *The Everyday Life of Abraham Lincoln*, p. 204

Page 275

Gibson W. Harris, in Brown, *Everyday Life of Lincoln*, pp. 219f.; John W. Nichols, ibid., p. 665f.

Page 279

Elizabeth Edwards, interview by Herndon, July 27, 1887, in Wilson and Davis, *Herndon's Informants*, pp. 622f.; William Jayne, letter, August 17, 1887, ibid., p. 624; James H. Matheny, letter, August 21, 1888, ibid., p. 665

Page 285

Dennis Hanks, quoted in Eleanor Atkinson, *The Boyhood of Lincoln*, pp. 77f.

Page 292

John Lothrop Motley, letter, May 27, 1865, in *The Correspondence of John Lothrop Motley*, pp. 2:202f.

Page 295

Whitehall Chronicle, December 13, 1889, clipping in authors' collection

Part Four
Page 303

John G. Nicolay and John Hay, *Abraham Lincoln: A History*, pp. 4:68f.

Page 305

John Hay, *Century*, 41 (November 1890), pp. 33ff.

Page 311

A.K. McClure, *Abraham Lincoln and the Men of War-Times,* p. 41f.

Page 313

Henry C. Whitney, *Life on the Circuit with Lincoln*, pp. 55, 72f.

Page 316

Frederick Douglass, address, February 13, 1893, in John W. Blassingame and John R. McKivigan, eds., *The Frederick Douglass Papers*, section 1, pp. 5:544f.

Page 327

Abraham Lincoln, March 9, 1832, in John G. Nicolay and John Hay, *Complete Works*, p. 1:2; Lincoln, April 18, 1846, ibid., pp. 1:86f.; Lincoln, July 1, 1850, ibid., pp. 1:162f.

Page 329

Henry C. Bowen, in *Abraham Lincoln: Tributes from His Associates*, pp. 31f.

Page 330

Grace Greenwood, in *Lincoln: Tributes from Associates*, pp. 108, 111f.; Henry W. Knight, ibid., p. 189f.

Page 332

Frances Todd Wallace, interview, September 2, 1895, in *Lincoln's Marriage*, privately printed, 1917, in authors' collection

Page 333

Noah Brooks, *Washington in Lincoln's Time*, pp. 45, 49f., 57f.

Page 336

Henry C. Whitney, in *McClure's Magazine*, 6 (December 1895), p. 110

Page 339

Ward Hill Lamon, *Recollections of Abraham Lincoln*, pp. 37f.

Page 343

Robert Lincoln, address, October 7, 1896, Knox College Archives, Galesburg, Illinois

Page 345

William McKinley, in *Washington Post*, October 16, 1898

Page 347

Booker T. Washington, in Washington, *Papers*, p. 5:32ff.; Julia Ward Howe, *Reminiscences*, p. 271f.

Page 349

Abraham Lincoln, letter, August 26, 1863, in *Collected Works*, Vol. 6, pp. 6:406f.

Page 353

Ida Tarbell, *The Life of Abraham Lincoln*, pp. 1:43f.

Page 355

General Oliver Otis Howard, in *Chicago Tribune*, February 12, 1900

Page 368

Theodore Roosevelt, address, in *Chicago Tribune*, June 5, 1903

Page 372

Carl Schurz, *Reminiscences*, p. 2:91

Page 373

Abraham Lincoln, letter, November 24, 1862, in *Collected Works*, p. 5:509; Carl Schurz, *Reminiscences*, p. 2:395

Page 377

Thomas T. Eckert, in David Homer Bates, *Lincoln in the Telegraph Office*, p. 138

Page 379

Edward Rosewater, in *Washington Times*, c. 1903, clipping in authors' collection

PART FIVE

Page 390

Thomas B. Bancroft, "An Audience with the President," *McClure's*, February 1909

Page 391

James Rowan O'Beirne, in Izola Forrester, "Living Men Who Knew and Talked with Lincoln," *Scrap Book,* January 1909; James Grant Wilson, "Recollections of Lincoln," *Putnam's,* February 1909

Page 395

Booker T. Washington, address, February 12, 1909, in Washington, *Papers*, pp. 10:33ff.

Page 398

Thomas S. Inborden, in *American Missionary*, 63, no. 2, 1909 pp. 36ff.

Page 403

Rev. L. H. Magee, address, February 12, 1909, quoted online at http://haleycourt.com/magee.htm

Page 404

Theodore Roosevelt, in *Chicago Tribune*, February 13, 1909

Page 407

John Linden Roll, undated letter to Dorothy Meserve Kunhardt, authors' collection

Page 408

Eleanor Atkinson, *Lincoln's Love Story,* p. 3ff.

Page 410

"The Call," quoted online at www.naacp.org/about/history/howbegan

Page 413

Jane Addams, *Twenty Years at Hull House*, pp. 234, 31f.

Page 414

William H. Crook, *Memories of the White House*, pp. 39ff.

Page 417

Gideon Welles, *Diary of Gideon Welles,* pp. 1:506f.; p. 2:15; 251f.

Page 424

Gutzon Borglum, "The Beauty of Lincoln," *Everybody's Magazine*, February, 1910

Page 433

Robert Lincoln, in *New York Times*, April 29, 1912

Page 445

Lyon Gardiner Tyler, *Propaganda in History*, pp. 12, 19

Page 448

Thompson Gains Onstot, *Lincoln and Salem*, p. 97

Page 455

W.E.B. DuBois, in *The Crisis*, September 1922

Select Bibliography

Abraham Lincoln: Tributes from His Associates. New York, 1895.

Addams, Jane. *Twenty Years at Hull House.* New York, 1910.

Angle, Paul M. *"Here I Have Lived." A History of Lincoln's Springfield, 1821-1865.* Springfield, Ill. 1935.

——. *A Shelf of Lincoln Books.* New Brunswick, N.J.,1946.

Arnold, Isaac N. *The History of Abraham Lincoln and the Overthrow of Slavery.* Chicago, 1866.

——. *The Life of Abraham Lincoln.* Chicago, 1884.

Atkinson, Eleanor. *The Boyhood of Lincoln.* New York, 1908.

——. *Lincoln's Love Story.* New York, 1909.

Baker, Jean Harvey. *Mary Todd Lincoln: A Biography.* New York, 1987.

Bancroft, George. *Memorial Address: Life and Character of Abraham Lincoln.* Washington, D.C.,1866.

Baringer, William E. *Lincoln Day by Day: A Chronology 1809–1865.* edited by Earl Schenck Miers. Washington, D.C.,1960.

Barnard's Lincoln. Cincinnati, 1917.

Barrett, Joseph H. *The Life of Abraham Lincoln.* Cincinnati, 1864.

Bartlett, David W. *The Life and Public Service of Hon. Abraham Lincoln of Illinois and Hon. Hannibal Hamlin of Maine.* Boston, 1860.

Basler, Ray P. *The Lincoln Legend.* Boston, 1935.

Bates, David Homer. *Lincoln in the Telegraph Office.* New York, 1907.

Beale, Howard K., ed. *The Diary of Edward Bates.* Washington, D.C., 1933.

Beveridge, Albert J. *Abraham Lincoln: 1809–1858.* 2 vols. Boston, 1928.

Blassingame, John W., and John R. McKivigan; eds. *The Frederick Douglass Papers.* New Haven, Conn.; 1979-92, 1999-2004.

Blight, David W. *Race and Reunion.* Cambridge, Mass., 2001.

Booth, Asia Clarke. *The Unlocked Box: A Memoir of John Wilkes Booth.* New York, 1938.

Brady, Kathleen. *Ida Tarbell: Portrait of a Muckraker.* Pittsburgh, 1989.

Brooks, Noah. *Abraham Lincoln.* Centennial ed. New York, 1888.

——. *Washington in Lincoln's Time.* New York, 1896.

——. *Mr. Lincoln's Washington: The Civil War Dispatches of Noah Brooks.* edited by P. J. Staudenraus. New York, 1967.

Brown, Francis F. *The Everyday Life of Abraham Lincoln.* New York, 1886.

Bryan, George S. *The Great American Myth.* New York, 1940.

Buckingham, J.E. *Reminiscences and Souvenirs of the Assassination of Abraham Lincoln.* Washington, D.C.,1894.

Bullard, F. Lauriston. *Lincoln in Marble and Bronze.* New Brunswick, N.J.,1952.

Burlingame, Michael, ed. *An Oral History of Abraham Lincoln.* Carbondale, 1996.

——. ed. *At Lincoln's Side.* Carbondale, Ill., 2000.

——. ed. *With Lincoln in the White House.* Carbondale, Ill., 2000.

Burlingame, Michael, and John R. Turner Ettlinger, eds. *Inside Lincoln's White House.* Carbondale, Ill., 1997.

Carpenter, Francis B. *Six Months at the White House with Abraham Lincoln.* New York, 1866.

Celebration by the Colored People's Educational Monument Association in Memory of Abraham Lincoln, Washington, D.C., 1865

Charnwood, Lord. *Abraham Lincoln.* Garden City, N.Y., 1917.

Chase, Salmon P. *Inside Lincoln's Cabinet.* Edited by David Herbert Donald. New York, 1954.

Chiniquy, Charles. *The Assassination of President Lincoln.* Cleveland, 1886.

——. *Fifty Years in the Church of Rome.* New York, 1886

Chittenden, L. E. *Recollections of President Lincoln and His Administration.* New York, 1891.

Coleman, Charles H. *Abraham Lincoln and Coles County, Illinois.* New Brunswick, N.J., 1955.

Conwell, Russell H. *Magnolia Journey.* University, Ala., 1974.

Crane, C. B. *Sermon on the Occasion of the Death of President Lincoln.* Hartford, Conn., 1865.

Crook, William H. *Memories of the White House.* Boston, 1911.

Current, Richard N. *The Lincoln Nobody Knows.* New York, 1958.

Curtis, William Eleroy. *The True Abraham Lincoln.* Philadelphia, 1903.

Davis, Michael. *The Image of Lincoln in the South.* Knoxville, Tenn.,1971.

Deming, Henry Champion, *Eulogy of Abraham Lincoln.* Hartford, Conn., 1865.

Dennett, Tyler. *John Hay.* New York, 1934.

——. ed. *Lincoln and the Civil War.* New York, 1939.

Dixon, Thomas. *The Clansman.* New York, 1905.

Dodge, Daniel K. *Abraham Lincoln.* Champaign, Ill., 1900.

Donald, David Herbert. *Lincoln's Herndon.* New York, 1948.

——. *Lincoln Reconsidered.* New York, 1959.

——. *Lincoln.* New York, 1995.

——. *"We Are Lincoln Men."* New York, 2003.

Douglass, Frederick. *Life and Times of Frederick Douglass.* Hartford, Conn., 1882.

DuBois, W.E.B. *The Crisis Writings.* Edited by Daniel Walden. Greenwich, Conn., 1972.

Fehrenbacher, Don E. *Prelude to Greatness.* Stanford, Calif., 1962.

——. *Lincoln in Text and Context.* Stanford, Calif., 1987.

Fehrenbacher, Don E., and Virginia Fehrenbacher, eds. *Recollected Works of Abraham Lincoln.* Stanford, 1996.

Foner, Philip S., ed. *W.E.B. DuBois Speaks.* New York, 1970.

——, ed. *The Voice of Black America.* Vol. 1. New York, 1975.

Franklin, John Hope, and Alfred A. Moss, Jr. *From Slavery to Freedom.* 8th ed. New York, 2004.

French, Benjamin Brown. *Witness to the Young Republic.* Edited by Donald B. Cole and John J. McDonough. Hanover, N.H., 1989.

Gobright, Lawrence. *Recollections of Men and Things at Washington.* Philadelphia, 1869.

Goff, John S. *Robert Todd Lincoln.* Oklahoma, 1969.

Good, Timothy S. *We Saw Lincoln Shot.* Mississippi, 1995.

Goodwin, Doris Kearns. *Team of Rivals.* New York, 2005.

Grant, Ulysses S. *Personal Memoirs of Ulysses S. Grant.* (2 vols.) New York, 1885-86.

Gray, William C. *The Life of Abraham Lincoln.* Cincinnati, 1868.

Gridley, Eleanor. *The Story of Abraham Lincoln.* Chicago, 1900.

Guelzo, Allen C. *Abraham Lincoln: Redeemer President.* Grand Rapids, Mich., 1999.

Hanaford, Phebe A. *Abraham Lincoln: His Life and Public Services.* Boston, 1865.

Harrell, Carolyn L. *When the Bells Tolled for Lincoln.* Macon, Ga., 1997.

Hendrick, Burton J. *Lincoln's War Cabinet.* Boston, 1946.

Herndon, William H. *Abraham Lincoln, Miss Ann Rutledge, New Salem, Pioneering, The Poem.* Springfield, Ill., 1910.

Herndon, William H., and Jesse W. Weik. *Herndon's Lincoln.* 3 vols. Chicago, 1889.

Hertz, Emanuel, ed. *The Hidden Lincoln.* New York, 1938.

Hewitt, Robert. *The Lincoln Centennial Medal.* New York, 1908.

History and Improvements of Oak Ridge Cemetery. Springfield, Ill., 1901.

Hobson, J. T. *Footprints of Abraham Lincoln.* Dayton, Ohio, 1909.

Holland, J. G. *The Life of Abraham Lincoln.* Springfield Ill., 1866.

Holzer, Harold, ed. *Lincoln as I Knew Him.* Chapel Hill, N.C., 1999.

——. *Lincoln at Cooper Union.* New York, 2004.

Howe, Julia Ward. *Reminiscences.* Boston, 1899.

Howells, W. D. *Life of Abraham Lincoln.* Bloomington, Ind., 1960.

Huebner, Richard Alden, ed. *Meserve Civil War Record.* Oak Park, Ill., 1987.

In Memoriam: Abraham Lincoln Commemorative Proceedings of the Athenaeum Club. New York, 1865.

In Memoriam: Abraham Lincoln Assassinated. Buffalo, N.Y., 1865

Jayne, William. *Abraham Lincoln.* Chicago, 1908.

Kammen, Michael. *Mystic Chords of Memory.* New York, 1993.

Katz, D. Mark. *Witness to an Era.* New York, 1981

Keckley, Elizabeth. *Behind the Scenes.* Buffalo, N.Y., 1931.

Kincaid, Robert L. *Joshua Fry Speed.* Harrogate, U.K., 1943.

King, William L. *Lincoln's Manager: David Davis.* Cambridge, Mass., 1960.

Kunhardt, Dorothy Meserve, and Philip B. Kunhardt, Jr. *Twenty Days.* New York, 1965.

——. *Mathew Brady and His World.* Alexandria, Va., 1977.

Kunhardt, Philip B. Jr. *A New Birth of Freedom.* Boston, 1983.

Kunhardt, Philip B. Jr., Philip B Kunhardt III, and Peter W. Kunhardt. *Lincoln: An Illustrated Biography.* New York, 1992.

Lamon, Ward H. *The Life of Abraham Lincoln.* Boston, 1872.

——. *Recollections of Abraham Lincoln.* Chicago, 1895.

Lee, Robert E. *Recollections and Letters of General Robert E. Lee.* New York, 1904.

Leland, Charles Godfrey. *Abraham Lincoln and the Abolition of Slavery in the United States.* New York, 1879.

Lewis, Lloyd. *Myths After Lincoln.* New York, 1941.

Lewis, Montgomery S. *Legends That Libel Lincoln.* New York, 1946.

Lincoln, Abraham. *The Collected Works of Abraham Lincoln,* ed. Roy P. Basler. 8 vols. New Brunswick, N.J., 1953.

Lincoln Centennial Addresses. Springfield, Ill., 1909.

Lincoln Fellowship. *Proceedings at the First Annual Meeting and Dinner of the Lincoln Fellowship,* New York, 1908.

Lorant, Stefan. *Lincoln: His Life in Photographs.* New York, 1941.

——. *Lincoln: A Picture Story of His Life.* New York, 1952.

Luzerne, Frank. *Through the Flames and Beyond: Chicago As It Was and As It Is!* New York, 1872.

MacKaye, Percy. *Ode on the Centenary of Abraham Lincoln.* New York, 1909.

McClellan, George B. *McClellan's Own Story.* New York, 1887.

McClure, A. K. *Abraham Lincoln and the Men of War-Times.* Philadelphia, 1892.

McClure, J. B., ed. *Anecdotes of Abraham Lincoln.* Chicago, 1879.

McFeely, William S. *Frederick Douglass.* New York, 1991.

McPherson, James M. *The Negro's Civil War.* New York, 1965.

Mead, Franklin B. *Heroic Statues in Bronze of Abraham Lincoln.* Fort Wayne, Ind., 1932.

Mearns, David C. *The Lincoln Papers.* 2 vols.. Garden City, N.Y., 1948.

Mellon, James, ed. *The Face of Lincoln.* New York, 1979.

Meserve, Frederick Hill, and Carl Sandburg. *The Photographs of Abraham Lincoln.* New York, 1944.

Miller, Francis Trevelyan. *Portrait Life of Lincoln.* Springfield, Mass., 1910.

Mitgang, Herbert, ed. *Lincoln as They Saw Him.* New York, 1956.

Morris, B. F., ed. *The Nation's Tribute to Abraham Lincoln.* Washington, D.C., 1865.

Motley, John Lothrop. *The Correspondence of John Lothrop Motley.* Edited by George William Curtis. 2 vols. New York, 1889.

National Republican Club. *Addresses Delivered at the Lincoln Dinner of the Republican Club of the City of New York in Response to the Toast, Abraham Lincoln.* New York, 1909.

Neely, Mark E., Jr. *The Abraham Lincoln Encyclopedia.* New York, 1982.

Neely, Mark E., Jr., and Harold Holzer. *The Lincoln Family Album.* New York, 1990.

Newton, Joseph Fort. *Lincoln and Herndon.* Cedar Rapids, Iowa, 1910.

Nichols, David A. *Lincoln and the Indians.* Urbana, Ill., 2000.

Nicolay, Helen. *Personal Traits of Abraham Lincoln.* New York, 1912.

——. *Lincoln's Secretary: A Biography of John G. Nicolay.* New York, 1949.

Nicolay, John G. and John Hay. *Abraham Lincoln: A History.* 10 vols. New York, 1890.

——. *Abraham Lincoln: Complete Works.* New York, 1894.

Oakes, James. *The Radical and the Republican.* New York, 2007.

Oakleaf, Joseph B. *The Gettysburg Address.* Moliner Ill., 1908.

Oldroyd, Osborn H., ed. *The Lincoln Memorial, Album-Immortelles.* New York, 1882.

Onstot, Thompson Gains. *Lincoln and Salem: Pioneers of Menard and Mason Counties.* Forest City, Ill., 1902.

Ostendorf, Lloyd. *Lincoln's Photographs: A Complete Album.* Dayton, Ohio, 1998.

Pease, Theodore Calvin, and James G. Randall, eds. *The Diary of Orville Hickman Browning.* Vol. 1. Springfield Ill., 1925.

Peterson, Merrill D. *Lincoln in American Memory.* New York, 1994.

Pitman, Benn. *The Assassination of President Lincoln and the Trial of the Conspirators.* New York, 1865.

Pollard, Edward A. *The Lost Cause.* New York, 1866.

Power, John Carroll. *Abraham Lincoln: His Life, Public Services, Death, and Great Funeral Cortege.* Chicago, 1889.

——. *History of an Attempt to Steal the Body of Abraham Lincoln.* Springfield Ill., 1890.

Pratt, Harry E. *Concerning Mr. Lincoln.* Springfield Ill., 1944.

Quarles, Benjamin. *The Negro in the Civil War*. Boston, 1953.

———. *The Negro in the Making of America*. New York, 1969.

Randall, J. G. *Lincoln and the South*. Baton Rouge, La., 1946.

Randall, Ruth Painter. *Mary Lincoln: A Biography of a Marriage*. Boston, 1953.

———. *Lincoln's Sons*. Boston, 1955.

Rankin, Henry B. *Personal Recollections of Abraham Lincoln*. New York, 1916.

Rice, Allen Thorndike, ed. *Reminiscences of Abraham Lincoln*. 8th ed. New York, 1889.

Saint-Gaudens, Homer. *Augustus Saint-Gaudens*. Cornish, N.H., 1927.

Sandburg, Carl. *Lincoln Collector*. New York, 1950.

Scarborough, William Kauffman, ed. *The Diary of Edmund Ruffin*. Vol. 1. Baton Rouge, La., 1972.

Schurz, Carl. *Abraham Lincoln*. Boston, 1907.

———. *The Reminiscences of Carl Schurz*. New York, 1907–08.

Schwartz, Barry. *Abraham Lincoln and the Forge of National Memory*. Chicago, 2000.

Scripps, John Locke. *Life of Abraham Lincoln*. Bloomington, Ind., 1961.

Segal, Charles M., ed. *Conversations with Lincoln*. New York, 1961.

Shaw, Albert. *Abraham Lincoln: His Path to Presidency*. New York, 1930.

Shea, John Gilmary. *Lincoln Memorial*. New York, 1865.

Sherman, William T. *Memoirs of General William T. Sherman*, New York, 1875.

Speed, Joshua Fry. *Reminiscences of Abraham Lincoln and Notes on a Visit to California*. Louisville, Ky., 1884.

Speer, Bonnie Stahlman. *The Great Abraham Lincoln Hijack*. Norman, Okla., 1997.

Steers, Edward, Jr. *Blood on the Moon*. Lexington Ky., 2001.

Stevens, Walter B. *A Reporter's Lincoln*. Edited by Michael Burlingame. Lincoln, Neb., 1998.

Stoddard, William O. *Lincoln's Third Secretary*. Edited by William O. Stoddard Jr. New York, 1955.

———. *Inside the White House in War Times*. Edited by Michael Burlingame. Lincoln, Neb., 2000.

Strozier, Charles B. *Lincoln's Quest for Union*. Urbana, Ill., 1987.

Tarbell, Ida M. *The Early Life of Abraham Lincoln*. New York, 1896.

———. *The Life of Abraham Lincoln*. 2 vols. New York, 1900.

———. *In the Footsteps of the Lincoln*. New York, 1924.

The Life, Speeches, and Public Services of Abraham Lincoln. "Wigwam Edition." New York, 1860.

The Trial of Andrew Johnson. Washington, D.C., 1968.

The Trial of the Assassins and Conspirators. Philadelphia, 1865.

Thayer, William Roscoe. *The Life of John Hay*. Boston, 1908.

Thomas, Benjamin P. *Lincoln's New Salem*. Springfield, Ill., 1934.

———. *Portrait for Posterity*. New Brunswick, N.J. 1947.

———. *Abraham Lincoln*. New York, 1952.

Thomas, Christopher. *The Lincoln Memorial and American Life*. Princeton, N.J., 2002.

Townsend, George Alfred. *The Life, Crime and Capture of John Wilkes Booth*. New York, 1865.

Townsend, William H. *Lincoln and Liquor*. New York, 1934.

Turner, Justin G., and Linda L. Turner. *Mary Todd Lincoln: Her Life and Letters*. New York, 1928.

Tyler, Lyon Gardiner. *Propaganda in History*. Jamestown, Va., 1920.

Villard, Henry. *Lincoln on the Eve of '61*. New York, 1941.

Warren, Louis A. *Lincoln's Youth*. New York, 1959.

Washington, Booker T. *The Booker T. Washington Papers*. Edited by Louis R. Harlan et al. 14 vols. Urbana, Ill., 1972–1989.

Washington, John E. *They Knew Lincoln*. New York, 1942.

Weik, Jesse W. *The Real Lincoln*. Boston, 1922.

Welles, Gideon. *Diary of Gideon Welles*. 3 vols. Boston, 1911.

Whipple, Wayne. *The Story-Life of Lincoln*. Philadelphia, 1908.

White, Charles T. *Lincoln and Prohibition*. New York, 1921.

Whitney, Henry Clay. *Life on the Circuit with Lincoln*. Caldwell, N.J., 1940.

Wills, Garry. *Lincoln at Gettysburg*. New York, 1992.

Wilson, Douglas L. *Honor's Voice: The Transformation of Abraham Lincoln*. New York, 1998.

———. *Lincoln's Sword: The Presidency and the Power of Words*. New York, 2006.

Wilson, Douglas L. and Rodney O. Davis, eds. *Herndon's Informants*. Urbana, Ill., 1998.

Wilson, Rufus Rockwell. *Lincoln in Portraiture*. New York, 1935.

———. *Lincoln Among His Friends*. Caldwell, N.J., 1942.

———. *Intimate Memories of Lincoln*. Elmira, N.Y., 1945.

Index

Page numbers in *italics* indicate illustrations.

Picture Credits

Whenever there is no credit given below, the picture is from the Meserve-Kunhardt Collection or the Mellon Collection.

3: Library of Congress. 5: Library of Congress. 6: National Museum of American History, Smithsonian Institution. (top). 10: National Archives (bottom). 13: National Museum of American History, Smithsonian Institution. 14: National Portrait Gallery, Smithsonian Institution/Art Resource, NY. (top). 20: Library of Congress (top); Robert N. Dennis Collection of Stereoscopic views, Miriam and Ira D. Wallach Division of Art, Prints and Photographs, The New York Public Library, Astor, Lenox and Tilden Foundations (bottom). 28: Library of Congress (bottom). 29: National Archives (left). 31: Library of Congress (bottom). 35: Courtesy Ford's Theatre National Historic Site (bottom right). 49: Library of Congress (top); Abraham Lincoln Presidential Library & Museum (bottom). 50: Chicago History Museum, IChi-50379; Brady & Co (bottom left); Chicago History Museum, IChi-50381, Brady & Co (bottom middle); Chicago History Museum, IChi-50385, Brady & Co (bottom right). 51: Chicago History Museum, IChi-50375, Brady & Co. 52: Library of Congress (bottom). 57: Library of Congress. 60: From the Abraham Lincoln Collection of the Lincoln Financial Foundation, Fort Wayne, IN #2422. 65: Library of Congress (bottom right). 66: Courtesy of the Illinois State Library/ Illinois Digital Archives (left). 70: Abraham Lincoln Presidential Library & Museum (right). 72: Library of Congress. 74: Reproduced with permission from the Methodist Collections of Drew University (left); Library of Congress. 81: Abraham Lincoln Birthplace National Historic Site. 87: Library of Congress (right). 88: Chicago History Museum, IChi-00727 (bottom). 92: Courtesy Lilly Library, Indiana University, Bloomington, IN (bottom right). 95: Abraham Lincoln Birthplace National Historic Site. 100: Courtesy of the Nantucket Historical Association P14374 (left). 103: Frederick Douglass NHS. 106: Library of Congress. 107: Smithsonian National Postal Museum (right). 109: Library of Congress. 110: Library of Congress (bottom). 112: Abraham Lincoln Presidential Library & Museum (left). 115: Library of Congress (top left). 119: National

Park Service, Andrew Johnson National Historic Park. 120: Library of Congress (right). 122: The Gilder Lehrman Collection, on deposit at the New-York Historical Society, New York, GLC 8763. 125: Abraham Lincoln Presidential Library & Museum. 128: Library of Congress (bottom). 131: Library of Congress (right). 133: Library of Congress (bottom). 146: Library of Congress. 148: Library of Congress. 149: Library of Congress (bottom); White House Historical Association (White House Collection) (top left); White House Historical Association (White House Collection) (top right). 152: Library of Congress (right); National Archives (left). 153: Courtesy of The Maryland Historical Society (top). 154: Library of Congress (bottom). 156: Special Collections, The Leyburn Library, Washington and Lee University (bottom). 157: Virginia Military Institute Archives (top right). 158: Library of Congress (top). 159: Library of Congress. 162: Library of Congress (top). 163: Library of Congress. 173: Collections of Seward House, Auburn, NY (top); Collections of Seward House, Auburn, NY (bottom). 183: Library of Congress. 184: Indiana Historical Society, P0406 (right). 193: Library of Congress (top). 198: National Park Service, Andrew Johnson National Historic Park (top left); © E.O. Hoppe/CORBIS (bottom right); Library of Congress (bottom left). 199: Library of Congress (top middle). 201: William G. Eliot Papers, University Archives, Department of Special Collections, Washington University Libraries (left); William G. Eliot Papers, University Archives, Department of Special Collections, Washington University Libraries (bottom right). 202: Library of Congress (left); Library of Congress (right). 204: Print and Picture Collection, The Free Library of Philadelphia (bottom). 205: Print and Picture Collection, The Free Library of Philadelphia (left); Collection of the Trustees of the Hartley Dodge Memorial, photographed by Jim Del Giudice (right). 209: Courtesy Ford's Theatre National Historic Site. 210: Abraham Lincoln Presidential Library & Museum. 213: Benjamin Franklin Upton, Minnesota Historical Society (bottom). 214: Adrian J. Ebell, Minnesota Historical Society (bottom right). 215: Library of Congress. 219: Library of Congress (top). 222: Image courtesy Maine State Archives. 223: Library of Congress. 224: Chautauqua County Historical Society, Westfield, NY (right). 230: Abraham Lincoln Presidential Library & Museum (left). 231: The Filson Historical Society, Louisville, KY. 232: Russell Sturgis Photograph Collection, University Archives, Department of Special Collections, Washington University Libraries. 235: The Abraham Lincoln Collection of the Lincoln Financial Foundation, Fort Wayne, IN, #3787

(bottom). 237: Courtesy Ford's Theatre National Historic Site (bottom left). 239: Library of Congress (bottom). 248: Courtesy of the Nantucket Historical Association F6704 (left). 252: Burton Historical Collection, Detroit Public Library. 253: Bentley Historical Library, University of Michigan (bottom). 254: Chicago History Museum; IChi-50385; Brady & Co (right). 256: Courtesy Ford's Theatre National Historic Site (top). 257: Lincoln Home National Historic Site (top). 258: National Archives. 265: Print Collection, Miriam and Ira D. Wallach Division of Art, Prints and Photographs, The New York Public Library, Astor, Lenox and Tilden Foundations (middle). 268: De Pauw University Archives and Special Collections (top). 272: Library of Congress (left); Library of Congress (right). 275: Abraham Lincoln Presidential Library & Museum (left). 279: Library of Congress (bottom left). 281: Courtesy of the Saint-Gaudens National Historic Site, Cornish, NH. 282: Library of Congress. 283: Courtesy National Park Service, Museum Management Program and Frederick Douglass NHS. 284: University of Chicago Library. 286: Library of Congress. 288: Chicago History Museum; IChi-10584 (left). 289: Chicago History Museum, IChi-35976 (top); Chicago History Museum, IChi-30993; A. Whiting Watriss (bottom right); Chicago History Museum, IChi-30986; A. Whiting Watriss (bottom left). 291: Abraham Lincoln Presidential Library & Museum (right); Library of Congress (left). 295: The South Carolina Confederate Relic Room and Military Museum, Columbia, SC (bottom); Library of Congress (top). 297: Library of Congress. 299: The Museum of the Confederacy. 300: From the Abraham Lincoln Collection of the Lincoln Financial Foundation, Fort Wayne, IN, #3806 (top). 302: From the Abraham Lincoln Collection of the Lincoln Financial Foundation, Fort Wayne, IN, #2528 (top). 304: Library of Congress. 307: Nebraska State Historical Society. 308: Library of Congress. 309 Library of Congress (top); Library of Congress (bottom). 312: The Gilder Lehrman Collection, on deposit at the New-York Historical Society, New York, GLC05111.01.0635. 314: Ohio Historical Society. 315: Library of Congress. 317: Courtesy National Park Service, Museum Management Program and Frederick Douglass NHS. 320: Courtesy Ford's Theatre National Historic Site. 322: National Museum of Health and Medicine, Armed Forces of Pathology (Woodward 1872B) (right). 323: Courtesy Ford's Theatre National Historic Site (top); Courtesy Ford's Theatre National Historic Site (bottom). 325: Library of Congress (top). 328: Library of Congress (top); The Collection of the Rochester Public Library Local History Division rpf 02337 (bottom). 331: Library of Congress (bottom). 333:

Castine Historical Society (top). **334:** Library of Congress. **335:** The Ida M. Tarbell Collection, Pelletier Library, Allegheny College (top); Library of Congress (bottom). **341:** Library of Congress. **343:** Special Collections and Archives, Knox College Library, Galesburg, Illinois. **344:** Library of Congress (top); Library of Congress (bottom). **345** Library of Congress (left). **346:** Library of Congress (bottom). **348:** Library of Congress (bottom). **351:** The Rail Splitter: A Journal for the Lincoln Collector. **352:** Art & Architecture Collection, Miriam and Ira D. Wallach Division of Art, Prints and Photographs, The New York Public Library, Astor, Lenox and Tilden Foundations. **353:** The Ida M. Tarbell Collection, Pelletier Library, Allegheny College (bottom). **354:** Archives of Lincoln Memorial University, Harrogate, Tennessee (bottom). **355:** Lincoln University of Pennsylvania, Langston Hughes Memorial Library, Archives and Special Collections (left). **356:** Abraham Lincoln Presidential Library & Museum (bottom). **358:** Library of Congress (top); Library of Congress bottom left). **359:** Library of Congress. **367:** Special Collections Department, W.E.B. Du Bois Library, University of Massachusetts Amherst (right). **368:** The Rail Splitter: A Journal for the Lincoln Collector (top). **369:** Library of Congress (top right). **374:** Library of Congress. **375:** Missouri History Museum, St. Louis. **376:** Library of Congress (bottom left); Library of Congress (right). **378:** Brown University Library. **379:** Brown University Library (top). **380:** Abraham Lincoln Presidential Library & Museum (top); Abraham Lincoln Presidential Library & Museum (bottom). **381:** Abraham Lincoln Presidential Library & Museum (bottom); Sangamon Valley Collection, Lincoln Library (top). **382:** Abraham Lincoln Presidential Library & Museum (bottom); Sangamon Valley Collection, Lincoln Library (top). **383:** Special Collections and Archives, Knox College Library, Galesburg, Illinois (top left); Special Collections and Archives, Knox College Library, Galesburg, Illinois (bottom left). **385:** Library of Congress. **387:** Wisconsin Historical Society. **389:** Chicago History Museum, IChi-18778 (bottom); Smithsonian National Postal Museum (top). **391:** University of Wisconsin Digital Collections (right). **394:** Robert N. Dennis Collection of Stereoscopic Views, Miriam and Ira D. Wallach Division of Art, Prints and Photographs, The New York Public Library, Astor, Lenox and Tilden Foundations (top); Milstein Division of United States History, Local History & Genealogy, The New York Public Library, Astor, Lenox and Tilden Foundations (bottom). **395:** Library of Congress (top); Library of Congress (bottom). **396:** Chicago History Museum, DN-0007071, CDN (left); Chicago History Museum,

DN-0007702, CDN (right). **397:** Chicago History Museum, DN-0054035; CDN. **398:** Abraham Lincoln Presidential Library & Museum (right); Library of Congress (left). **399:** Courtesy of The Jean Thomas Collection, Special Collections, University of Louisville. **401:** Valentine Richmond History Center (bottom). **402:** Abraham Lincoln Presidential Library & Museum (bottom). **403:** Abraham Lincoln Presidential Library & Museum (left). **404:** Abraham Lincoln Birthplace National Historic Site (right); Library of Congress (left). **405:** Mississippi Department of Archives and History (top); National Park Service (bottom right). **406:** Library of Congress (bottom); Department of Special Collections, Davidson Library, University of California, Santa Barbara (top). **411:** Library of Congress. **412:** Library of Congress. **413:** Library of Congress (top). **414:** Library of Congress. **415:** Library of Congress (bottom). **424:** Borglum Archives (left); Newark Public Library (right). **425:** Photo by Roger E. Shaffer (top). **426:** Special Collections Department, W.E.B. Du Bois Library, University of Massachusetts, Amherst. **427:** VCU Libraries. **428:** Sophia Smith Collection, Smith College. **429:** Library of Congress. **430:** Library of Congress (top); Record Group 25: 50th Anniversary of the Battle of Gettysburg/ Recreation of Pickett's Charge/ PA State Archives (bottom). **431:** Record Group 25: 50th Anniversary of the Battle of Gettysburg/ The Blue and the Gray at Lincoln Memorial/ PA State Archives (top); Record Group 25: 50th Anniversary of the Battle of Gettysburg/ Phil. Brigade and Pickett's Div./ PA State Archives (bottom). **432:** Library of Congress (top); Record Group 25: 50th Anniversary of the Battle of Gettysburg/ Distributing Blankets/ PA State Archives (bottom). **435:** Library of Congress. **437:** George Grey Barnard working in his Lincoln sculpture in his studio, ca. 1900, Courtesy of the George Grey Barnard papers, 1884-1963, Archives of American Art, Smithsonian Institute (left); Library of Congress (right). **438:** Library of Congress (bottom left); Sam DeVincent Collection of Illustrated American Sheet Music, Archives Center, National Museum of American History, Behring Center, Smithsonian Institution (bottom right). **439:** Library of Congress (top); National Archives (bottom). **440:** Library of Congress (top); National Archives (bottom). **441:** Library of Congress (top). **444:** North Carolina Collection, University of North Carolina at Chapel Hill (top); North Carolina Collection, University of North Carolina at Chapel Hill (bottom). **445:** Chicago Public Library, Special Collections and Preservation Division, F548.9N312, p.12 (right middle); © Bettmann/CORBIS (right top); Valentine Richmond History Center (right bot-

tom); University Archives Photograph Collection, Special Collections Research Center, Swen Library, College of William and Mary (left). **446:** Courtesy of the Illinois State Library/ Illinois Digital Archives (top); Courtesy of the Illinois State Library/ Illinois Digital Archives (bottom). **450:** Library of Congress (top). **451:** Library of Congress (top); Library of Congress (bottom). **453:** Library of Congress (left). **454:** Special Collections Department, W.E.B. Du Bois Library, University of Massachusetts Amherst (top); Special Collections Department, W.E.B. Du Bois Library, University of Massachusetts Amherst (bottom). **457:** Library of Congress. **459:** Archives of Lincoln Memorial University, Harrogate, Tennessee (bottom right).

A Note About the Authors

Philip B. Kunhardt III is a writer-producer with Kunhardt Productions and is currently a Bard Center Fellow. Peter W. Kunhardt is executive producer of Kunhardt Productions. Peter W. Kunhardt, Jr., is assistant director of photography at the Meserve-Kunhardt Foundation. Along with their father, the late Philip B. Kunhardt, Jr., Philip and Peter are coauthors of *Lincoln: An Illustrated Biography*. *Looking for Lincoln* will be a companion volume to a PBS special of the same name to be aired in the winter of 2009. The Kunhardts are based in Westchester County, New York.

A Note on the Type

The text of this book is set in a typeface called Bulmer. This distinguished letter is replica of a type long famous in the history of English printing which was designed and cut by William Martin about 1790 for William Bulmer of the Shakespeare Press. In design, it is all but a modern face, with vertical stress, sharp differentiation between the thick and thin strokes, and nearly flat serifs. The decorative italic shows the influence of Baskerville, as Martin was a pupil of Baskerville's. The display face is Modern No.20.

Printed and bound by R. R. Donnelley, Willard, Ohio

Designed by Elton Robinson

This is the companion volume to the PBS special *Looking for Lincoln*, produced by Kunhardt McGee Productions, Inkwell Films, and Thirteen/WNET, with underwriting from PBS, CPB, and State Farm.